Frommer's®

Turkey

7th Edition

by Lynn A. Levine

with Jamie Ehrlich

WILEY

John Wiley & Sons, Inc.

ABOUT THE AUTHORS

Lynn A. Levine is author of *Frommer's Istanbul* and has contributed to a number of other titles, including *Frommer's Southeast Asia*. Her work has appeared in the *Boston Globe, Ottawa Citizen, Elle, MSNBC/ Newsweek Budget Travel, Travel Holiday,* and the *UN Chronicle.* When not writing about travel, she works as an advocate for mission-driven organizations committed to human rights, humanitarian issues, and the environment. She also runs the website www.talkingturkey.com.

Jamie Ehrlich is a longtime editor at Frommer's Travel Guides. She has edited several guidebooks to Turkey and traveled extensively within the country, from its popular attractions to off-the-beaten-path villages. In addition to editing, she writes for the Frommers.com website and covers hotels in a column called "Frommer's Checks In" for the site's Behind the Guides blog. She's previously lived as an expat in London and Prague and now lives in Brooklyn.

Published by:

JOHN WILEY & SONS, INC.

111 River St.
Hoboken, NJ 07030-5774

ISBN 978-1-118-28756-9 (paper); ISBN 978-1-118-33138-5 (ebk); ISBN 978-1-118-33364-8 (ebk); ISBN 978-1-118-33478-2 (ebk)

Editor: Linda Barth
Production Editor: Eric T. Schroeder
Cartographer: Guy Ruggiero
Photo Editor: Richard Fox
Production by Wiley Indianapolis Composition Services
Front Cover Photo: Sultanahmet Mosque interior, Istanbul ©Tetra Images / Getty Images
Back Cover Photo: Scenic lagoon, Ölüdeniz Beach, Fethiye ©Russell Kord / Alamy Images

For information on our other products and services or to obtain technical support, please contact our Customer Care Department within the U.S. at 877/762-2974, outside the U.S. at 317/572-3993 or fax 317/572-4002.

Wiley also publishes its books in a variety of electronic formats. Some content that appears in print may not be available in electronic formats.

Manufactured in the United States of America

5 4 3 2 1

CONTENTS

5 ÇANAKKALE, GALLIPOLI & THE TROAD 189

6 THE CENTRAL & SOUTHERN AEGEAN COASTS (GREATER IZMIR) 208

7 THE BODRUM PENINSULA 253

8 THE TURQUOISE & MEDITERRANEAN COASTS 282

LIST OF MAPS

ACKNOWLEDGMENTS

From Lynn Levine: Special thanks are in order for a handful of incredibly wonderful and supportive individuals. Thanks to Sırma and the whole Credo Tours crew; to Aydïn, Suha, Süleyman, and Hakan; and to Tuğba, Mustafa, and tiny little Asya, for their professional assistance and personal friendship. Each has been instrumental in supporting me in my work on this guide and in introducing me to the soul of Turkey. Warm thanks also go out to the people and the country of Turkey for exposing me to countless true friendships made during the course of working in Turkey.

From Jamie Ehrlich: Many thanks to Haldun Dinccetin, for his enthusiasm for his homeland and invaluable help; and culinary expert Filiz Hösükoğlu, for introducing me to the world of Gaziantep baklava and for her friendship. Thanks as well to Umit Isin and Taylan Tasbasi for their archaeology expertise and insight into the region. Finally, thanks to Boris, for all our adventures on my first trip to Turkey and being my favorite travel companion.

HOW TO CONTACT US

In researching this book, we discovered many wonderful places—hotels, restaurants, shops, and more. We're sure you'll find others. Please tell us about them, so we can share the information with your fellow travelers in upcoming editions. If you were disappointed with a recommendation, we'd love to know that, too. Please write to:

Frommer's Turkey, 7th Edition
John Wiley & Sons, Inc. • 111 River St. • Hoboken, NJ 07030-5774
frommersfeedback@wiley.com

ADVISORY & DISCLAIMER

FROMMER'S STAR RATINGS, ICONS & ABBREVIATIONS

Every hotel, restaurant, and attraction listing in this guide has been ranked for quality, value, service, amenities, and special features using a **star-rating system.** In country, state, and regional guides, we also rate towns and regions to help you narrow down your choices and budget your time accordingly. Hotels and restaurants are rated on a scale of zero (recommended) to three stars (exceptional). Attractions, shopping, nightlife, towns, and regions are rated according to the following scale: zero stars (recommended), one star (highly recommended), two stars (very highly recommended), and three stars (must-see).

In addition to the star-rating system, we also use **seven feature icons** that point you to the great deals, in-the-know advice, and unique experiences that separate travelers from tourists. Throughout the book, look for:

special finds—those places only insiders know about

fun facts—details that make travelers more informed and their trips more fun

kids—best bets for kids and advice for the whole family

special moments—those experiences that memories are made of

overrated—places or experiences not worth your time or money

insider tips—great ways to save time and money

great values—where to get the best deals

The following abbreviations are used for credit cards:

AE American Express   DISC Discover   V Visa

DC Diners Club   MC MasterCard

TRAVEL RESOURCES AT FROMMERS.COM

Frommer's travel resources don't end with this guide. Frommer's website, **www.frommers. com**, has travel information on more than 4,000 destinations. We update features regularly, giving you access to the most current trip-planning information and the best airfare, lodging, and car-rental bargains. You can also listen to podcasts, connect with other Frommers.com members through our active-reader forums, share your travel photos, read blogs from guidebook editors and fellow travelers, and much more.

THE BEST OF TURKEY

First-time visitors to Turkey (or anywhere, for that matter) often leave home with preconceived notions about what their destination will be like. But Turkey represents many, often contradictory things: It's ancient and modern, Westernized and Oriental, religious and secular, wondrous and ordinary, familiar and exotic. But there is one undeniable common denominator, and that is that Turkey, and the Turkish people, know how to do hospitality. This from a population in which 20% of the people live below the poverty line and yet the native language has no word for "bitter."

Turkey is a unique country: a rich, layered, and magical world full of history, culture, gastronomy, humanity, and commerce—increasingly Europeanized yet (notwithstanding the über-cosmopolitan center that is Istanbul) still somewhat pastoral and innocent. In the heartland, villagers are still pleasantly surprised and proud of the fact that people come to visit from far and wide.

Yet it wasn't until recently that Turkey's tourism industry finally began reaping the rewards appropriate for the custodian of three world empires, countless potent kingdoms, and a dazzling 8,333km (5,178-mile) coastline. This geographic and cultural bridge boasts more Greek ruins than Greece, more Roman archaeological sites than all of Italy, and—in Antalya alone—more resort hotels than all the coast of Spain. Turkey is also a major custodian of sacred sites revered by Christians, Jews, and Muslims alike, and of invaluable artifacts of early Greek civilization, Byzantine majesty, and Ottoman supremacy. Business is now booming, the middle class is spending, and cities are growing and expanding. Turkey's turnaround economy is creating opportunity, advancement, and geopolitical influence not seen there in centuries. Dirt roads are now paved; single-lane asphalt roads have doubled in width; and new (toll) superhighways now serve Istanbul, Ankara, and Izmir. Turkey is also directing an unparalleled amount of funding into the country's cultural sites, exposing "secondary" archaeological sites to the light of day while increasing the visibility and longevity of the A-list sites.

Meanwhile, foreigners are descending on Turkey as if it were going out of business. Istanbul, Antalya, Ankara, and Cappadocia witnessed in 2007 as much as a 20% increase in arrivals from 2006. And the numbers keep trending upward. In 2010, 28,632,204 visitors saw fit to see what all the fuss was about. Contrast that with 8,000,000 visitors that went to Turkey in 2000, the first year this guide was published. Parallel to this new—and renewed—popularity in Turkey as a travel destination is that Europeans, and particularly Brits, are profiting by unprecedented strength in their respective currencies, and where there's demand, there are both higher prices and growth. Hotels that once quoted prices in U.S. dollars now default to the €, and to the British pound sterling on the Mediterranean coast. With prices now rivaling any European destination, Turkey is anything but the bargain it used to be. So is all of this dynamism worth it?

Absolutely. But you'll need to find the right balance. Traveling off-season will give you the strongest bargaining power, and you may have to forego that sunrise balloon ride over Cappadocia. But if you go, I guarantee that you'll soon see why people in the know just can't get enough of Turkey.

The most UNFORGETTABLE TRAVEL EXPERIENCES

o **Taking a Hamam:** Visiting a Turkish bath rose out of the Islamic requirement for cleanliness, and public *hamams* made this obligation easily available to the masses. Going to the *hamam* fell out of favor among middle-class Turks until recently; with growing popularity of spas, a Turkish bath provides a minivacation. For historical and architectural value, you can't beat a local *hamam*. If the royal treatment is your thing, you can try to get an appointment at one of the luxury hotels listed in this guide.

o **Taking a Boat Ride up the Bosphorus:** Nowhere else in the world can you cross to another continent every 15 minutes. Connecting trade routes from the East to the West, it's no surprise that any conqueror who was anybody had his sights set on the Bosphorus. Float in the wake of Jason and the Argonauts and Constantine the Great, and enjoy the breezes, the stately wooden manses, the monumental Ottoman domes, and the fortresses that helped win the battle (p. 124).

o **Sharing Tea with the Locals:** Tea is at the center of Turkish culture; no significant negotiation takes place without some. But more than commerce, tea stops the hands of time in Turkey; it renews the bonds of friends and family. Having tea is inevitable, as is the invitation to share a glass with a total stranger. Accept the invitation: There's more in the glass than just a beverage.

o **Soaking in a Thermal Pool:** Sometimes Turkey seems like one big open-air spa; chemically rich waters bubble up from below while frigid spring water rushes down from above. The **Çeşme Peninsula** seems like one big hot bath, and a whole slew of brand-new luxury facilities are willing to accommodate (see "Highlights of the Çeşme Peninsula," in chapter 6). In the Sacred Pool of Hierapolis at the **Pamukkale Thermal** (p. 278), you swim amid the detritus of ancient civilizations as sulfur bubbles tingle your skin. Bursa's **Çelik Palas Hotel** (p. 183) has a domed pool hot enough to make your knees weak. Down the road at the **Kervansaray Termal Hotel** (p. 183), the pools of running water are enclosed in a 700-year-old original *hamam.*

o **Exploring the Covered Bazaar:** Nobody should pass through Turkey without spending a day at the mother of all exotic bazaars. The atmosphere crackles with the electricity of the hunt—but are you the hunter or the hunted? The excitement is tangible, even if you're on the trail of a simple pair of elf shoes or an evil-eye talisman. It's the disciplined shopper who gets out unscathed. See "Shopping," in chapter 4.

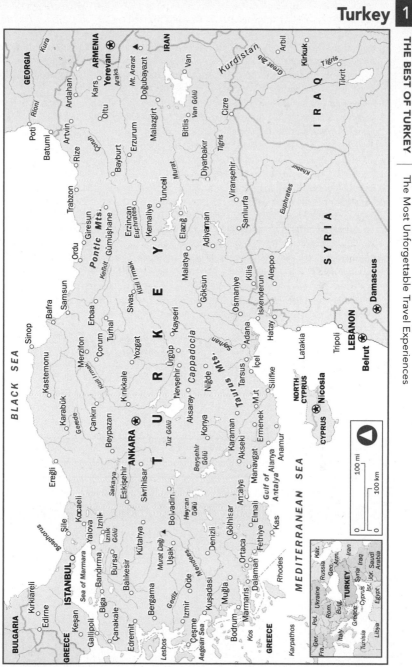

- **Cruising the Turquoise Coast:** Words just don't do this justice. Aboard a wooden gulet (a traditional broad-beamed boat), you drift past majestic mountains, undiscovered ruins, and impossibly azure waters as the sun caresses your skin from sunrise to sunset. In this environment the morning aroma of Nescafé takes on an almost pleasant quality when enjoyed on deck, anchored just offshore a pine-enclosed inlet. By 9am, you're diving off the rail and cursing the day it all has to end. See "All About the Blue Voyage," on p. 54.

- **Paragliding over Ölüdeniz:** There's no better place in the world than the surging summit of Babadağ for this wildly exhilarating and terrifying sport. For 15 brief minutes, you're flying high above the magnificent turquoise waters of Ölüdeniz with the mountains in the foreground. The safety factor? Not to be underestimated, but that nice body of water should break your fall. See "Fethiye & Ölüdeniz," in chapter 8.

- **Ballooning over Cappadocia:** Watch this surreal landscape change character right before your eyes: In a matter of minutes, the sun rises over the cliffs, valleys, and ravines, and colors morph from hazy blue to orange, pink, and finally yellow. The capper? A post-flight champagne breakfast. See "The Active Explorer in Cappadocia," in chapter 9.

- **Spending the (Hopefully Romantic) Night in a Cave:** The ceilings are low, the light is dim, and there are niches in the wall for your alarm clock—this is the troglodyte life as the Cappadocians lived it for thousands of years. Some of these "cave hotels" are rudimentary, others extravagant; but all are cool in summer, warm in winter, and as still as the daybreak. See chapter 9.

THE best FOOD & DRINK EXPERIENCES

- **Noshing Waterside at Eminönü:** For 12 to 14 hours a day, the Tarihi Eminönü Balıkçısı grills fresh fish quayside, wrapped in a roll and presented for a spectacular 3TL by a hearty man in traditional costume. Grab your sandwich and step aside; the condiments are to the right on the railing. See p. 129.

- **Melting Kanlıca Yogurt in Your Mouth:** For more than 100 years, creamy rich yogurt has been a specialty of the tiny Bosphorus front village of Kanlıca, on the upper Asian side. It's a hell of a haul for a cup of yogurt, but oh, what glorious spoonfuls they are. See p. 69.

- **Morning Simit from a Street Vendor:** I grew up on sesame bagels, so call me biased, but these doughy little morning delicacies really do hit the spot. Spread some cheese on one (or slather with butter and jam) and weep.

- **Eating Your Way Through Ortaköy:** This neighborhood is particularly vibrant on a summer evening, with the lights twinkling beneath the Bosphorus Bridge. The streets behind the mosque are a food fair of Turkish fast-food stalls selling such things as stuffed mussels (for the fearless) and potatoes to drown in your preferred toppings. See p. 152.

- **Ottoman Cuisine:** Many restaurants bill themselves as "Ottoman," but few of them can actually boast of having translated the recipes from the kitchens of Topkapı. See p. 39.

- **Lunch at a Lokanta:** These unassuming eateries have some of the best home-style food around. Casseroles and stews such as *moussaka* or *orman kebap* (lamb stew with potatoes and carrots) are the types of labor-intensive dishes the tourist places can't be bothered to prepare. If you have time, indulge your senses at **Çiya**. See p. 139.

- **Sunset Dining on a Village Jetty:** In tiny fishing villages all along the coastline, the setting of the sun is the villagers' cue to transform their narrow fishing piers into open-air dining rooms. And this is your cue to take a seat at one of the candlelit tables beneath the moonlight. See chapters 7 and 8.
- **Snacking at Tea Time on Baklava:** When that afternoon fatigue sets in, pop into a cafe and order a sampling of baklava, *with a scoop of ice cream*. Sounds like overkill; it even sounds a little gross. But trust me, you'll never want to eat it any other way.
- **Sipping Turkish Wine:** Used to be that you'd need some serious ambiance to make up for the inferiority of Turkey's wines. No more. Now you can imbibe in a cave, a Byzantine cistern or atop Ottoman ramparts.
- **Munching on Gözleme:** This cheese, or spinach, or potato (or mixed) crepe is Turkey's answer to fast food. Grab some at a roadside snack bar, or on the beach, or in a public park. It's usually oversized, served in a greasy piece of paper and utterly satisfying.

THE best WAYS TO SEE TURKEY LIKE A LOCAL

- **Toasting the Lights of the Old City at Dusk:** It's a magical sight to watch the lights of the Old City come to life. From a rooftop bar in Beyoğlu or a *nargile* cafe on the Galata Bridge, you can watch the monuments light up one by one. If you're on the ground in Sultanahmet, it's impossible not to enjoy the poetry of the seagulls in flight circling under the spotlights of the Blue Mosque. See chapter 4.
- **Crossing the Galata Bridge on Foot:** Fishermen line the railings above, while dinner (or tea, or backgammon) is served below as the majestic and inspiring silhouettes of the Süleymaniye, Rüstem Paşa, and Yeni Camii loom in the distance. If you wait until after sunset, you get to see the seagulls circling the minarets. See chapter 4.
- **Strolling Along Istanbul's City's Defensive Walls:** Ancient history is juxtaposed against the present-day neighborhoods at Yedikule, Edirnekapı, and Ayvansaray, each reflecting its own interpretation of Turkey's past, present, and future. See chapter 4.
- **Sunday Brunch:** This weekly ritual sees locals queuing for tables at cafes up and down the Bosphorus. Expect to leave in pain, after chowing on morning grub like börek, menemen, fresh cheese, olives, a variety of delectable breads or an omelet. Top it off with a Turkish coffee and you'll be napping at a waterside park bench in no time. See chapter 4.
- **Aboard a Gulet (the Turquoise Coast):** There's nothing like sleeping under the stars in a cove along the shores of the Mediterranean, far from the madding crowd. At the end of the day, the blazing sun gives way to a mild summer night, and you wake up at dawn with your shipmates on the rear deck of the gulet, covered in fresh morning dew. See "All About the Blue Voyage," on p. 54.
- **Sleeping in a Cave: (Cappadocia):** Anatolians have been doing it for millennia. But now many of these troglodyte homes have been transformed into hotels offering comfort fit for Roman kings and Ottoman sultans. Truly, where else could sleeping in a cave be so sweet? See chapter 9.

o **Shopping the Local Market:** Whether you're in the market for plastic slip-on shoes, fresh olives, hand-harvested almonds or a counterfeit sweatshirt, there's nothing like trolling a locality's weekly market to get a sense of what daily life in Turkey is all about.

THE best FAMILY EXPERIENCES

o **Together Time on a Blue Cruise:** Whether it's a day trip or a full week of sailing bliss, there's just you, the deck, the sea, and your offspring, tooling around the Blue Lagoon, or to ancient seaside ports of Side, Halicarnassus, or Knidos. See p. 353, p. 275, and p. 294.

o **Trolling the Grand Bazaar:** If you think only your teenage daughter will be in her glory amidst all of the shiny things, your son will undoubtedly be mesmerized by the sheer scale, the colorful domes, and faux Ottoman swords.

o **Do-it-Yourself, Al Fresco Dining:** Grilling your own kebaps in a garden restaurant in the shadow of a sheep's meadow, or chowing on fresh cooked trout at a mountain trout farm. See p. 313 and p. 309.

o **Scrambling Around the Ruins of Ancient Civilizations:** No city was complete without its amphitheatre, and no holiday to Turkey will be complete until you've scaled the steps of the Great Theater of Ephesus, the theatre at Pergamon or the cloud-borne city of Termessos.

o **Pretending You're the Flintstones:** They certainly didn't have flatscreen satellite TVs, but the troglodytes who lived here never slept as well as you will here, tucked under a feather duvet in a king-size bed in a cave hotel, or burrowing through the narrow warren of underground cities of Cappadocia. See chapter 9.

o **Feasting on the Delights of the Turkish Fast Food:** Even the most finicky child can be sated with a plate of cheesey *pide* or *lahmacun*, two of Turkey's versions of pizza, or a bowl of mantı, Turkey's answer to ravioli. If that doesn't work, many of the street vendors in Istanbul dress in period costume.

o **Splashing Around in a Thermal Pool:** While your offspring are frolicking, you and your better half can submit to the soothing and curative waters in pools in Pamukkale, Ilica or Bursa. See p. 278, p. 224 or p. 183.

THE best SMALL TOWNS

o **Assos:** Both hilltop and waterfront, Assos (known interchangeably by the name of the modern village on-site, Behramkale) is a picturesque slice of the Turkish Aegean that is fast fading into oblivion. The ancient ruins and village life intermingle, while the fishing port below welcomes weary travelers with lovely little quay-front hotels and a fabulously tiny stretch of sand. See "Assos," in chapter 5.

o **Alaçatı:** A hilltop mound of windmills and 800-year-old Selçuk barrelhouses guard the entrance to the tiny Aegean village of Alaçatı. So close to the sea, and yet so far . . . See "Highlights of the Çeşme Peninsula," in chapter 6.

o **Şirince:** Originally a sanctuary for Greeks in the dying days of Ephesus, this dense hillside of preserved houses enclosed within a landscape of grape orchards is the perfect antidote to an overdose of archaeological sites. A bottle of local wine enjoyed amid the atmosphere of a former schoolhouse helps the medicine go down, too. See p. 244.

○ **Gümüşlük:** The chance to walk on water—or nearly so—thanks to the sunken city walls of ancient Myndos—what more could one want? How about an undiscovered enclosed bay, a beach, and waterfront fish shacks. See "Bodrum," in chapter 7.

○ **Palamutbükü:** Boasting the cleanest waters on the Mediterranean, this little strip of paradise is all about the sea. Pick a lounge chair with a view, stroll along the sand while crunching on fresh almonds or snack at one of the family-owned eateries lining the bay. See p. 295.

○ **Karmylassos/Kayaköy:** Haunting panoramas of lives interrupted blanket the hillside of this once-thriving Greek settlement, abandoned during the 1924 population exchange between Turkey and Greece. Rather than reinhabit the houses—now crumbling and roofless—local Turkish residents have settled in the rolling and fertile plains of the surrounding valley. See p. 307.

○ **Kaleköy:** Also known as Simena, this seaside village clings to the side of the rock more efficiently than its sunken neighbors. With only 300 inhabitants living practically on top of one another, the town is too small to even have a street; a haphazard nonsystem of paths weaves around the village houses. There's no such thing as trespassing—it's just blissfully simple. See "Kaş," in chapter 8.

○ **Ayvalı:** The smell of apricots permeates the village as the harvest blankets the roofs of the flat-topped houses. Down in the valley is an almost eerie grouping of cave facades that retain the curvy lines of the smooth cave surfaces. At sunset, the sound of drums in the distance and the image of village women baking the evening meal's bread in ancient rock ovens create an unforgettable vision of rural life. See p. 366.

THE best RUINS & ARCHAEOLOGICAL SITES

○ **Troy:** It's taken archaeologists more than a century to try to undo the damage done by Heinrich Schliemann, the archaeologist and plunderer who discovered the site. There's still a way to go, but the progress made here in the past 10 years alone is remarkable. Troy is quite a sight. See "Troy," in chapter 5.

○ **Pergamum:** Pergamum was once one of the most influential societies in the ancient world. Only traces of its greatness remain—but high atop the hillside, the acropolis still sings the songs of the wind through its broken pillars. The theater is the most extraordinary remnant of this forgotten society, clinging stubbornly to the side of a hill that overlooks a fruitful and expansive plain. See "Bergama & Pergamum," in chapter 6.

○ **St. John's Basilica (Selçuk):** Most of the marble or cut-stone ruins you'll see in Turkey are ankle-high, a shadowy evocation of what once was. That's why the preserved redbrick walls of St. John's Basilica create such a pleasantly unexpected surprise. This holy site retains the soul of its original purpose; pilgrims gather around the presumed saint's tomb in an unabashed atmosphere of goodwill. See p. 243.

○ **Sardis:** Famed for its synagogue (impressively restored and preserved), the Jewish community's place of worship was hardly the main attraction when the city was the capital of ancient Lydia or a splendid outpost of the Roman Empire. The intact shops, remnants of the bath house, and soaring gymnasium walls cover just a small portion of the 290-acre expanse that was Sardis. See p. 218.

- **Ephesus:** Ephesus is among the best-preserved ancient sites in the Mediterranean, rivaled only by Pompeii. Frankly, it's humbling to see how efficiently life functioned before the advent of mechanized whatnots. The partially reconstructed Library of Celsus, the newly excavated portions of the terraced housing, and the strangely evocative Public Latrine are a few highlights of this sprawling, marble-strewn site. See "Selçuk & Ephesus," in chapter 6.

- **Ancient Theatre (Hierapolis):** The acoustics are as great down in the pit as they were 3,000 years ago. The extreme upper tiers overlook the great expanse of ancient Hierapolis—and now, thanks to UNESCO, unobstructed views of Pamukkale's whitening terraces. See "Pamukkale, Hierapolis, & Laodicea," in chapter 7.

- **Aphrodisias:** Blessed by the proximity of nearby quarries of white and blue-gray marble, it's no wonder that this ancient city hid an unprecedented quantity of sculpture. The site itself also preserves an unusually concentrated collection of grand Hellenistic monuments. See "A Side Trip to Aphrodisias," in chapter 7.

- **Lycian Tombs:** Expertly carved into inaccessible vertical cliffs to resemble a classical temple, the Lycian tombs and sarcophagi are mysterious and dramatic, with their Gothic headdresses perched above the ghosts of royalty. The best spots to see them? Dalyan, Kaunos, Myra, and while boating the pristine waters of Kekova Bay. See "Boat Trips to the Sunken City," in chapter 8.

- **Cappadocia Monasteries and Underground Cities:** What do you get when you combine an amazing feat of engineering and artistry in fresco? You get ancient painted chapels—arches, pilasters, and all—carved into rock, and a hideaway for the earliest Christians fleeing from persecution. See chapter 9.

- **Yazılıkaya:** The stony lineup of cone-headed deities at this sacred Hittite shrine is undeniably more impressive in person than in pictures. The true mystery is who was the first to discover Chamber B, a room of enigmatic carved reliefs inconspicuously hidden inside a jagged chasm in the rock? See p. 409.

THE best MUSEUMS, MOSQUES & CHURCHES

- **Blue Mosque (Istanbul):** This landmark mosque assumes a stance of authority over Sultanahmet Park. Just under the dome, hundreds of stained-glass windows sparkle like jewels. The blue of the mosque actually changes to yellow, orange, and red, depending on the time of day and the entrance you choose to use. See p. 91.

- **Hagia Sophia (Istanbul):** When faced with the dome of this masterpiece, it's tempting to mimic the actions of Mehmet the Conqueror almost 600 years ago and drop to your knees in a gesture of utter humility. The sensation is increased by the low level of filtered light that finds its way in, temporarily blinding you to everything except the source of illumination. See p. 88.

- **Topkapı Palace (Istanbul):** Perspective check—this was once somebody's *house*. Actually, it was the home of a whole lot of people—up to 5,000 at a time, all in the service of one man. Six hundred years of Ottoman history, and it's all behind these grand ornamental gates. See p. 97.

- **Istanbul Archaeology Museum (Istanbul):** This is one of those must-see museums that all too many overlook. It's actually the largest museum in the country, chronicling in stone both the life of Istanbul and of Byzantium's emperors. Recovered artifacts date back to 6000 B.C. (as of the time of this writing) and proceed through the centuries. A separate building houses the Museum of the Ancient Orient, exhibiting artifacts obtained during the course of the Ottoman period. See p. 95.

- **St. Savior in Chora (Istanbul):** An empire's devotion to the faith is mirrored in the opulence of the finest preserved collections of **Byzantine mosaics** just about anywhere. See p. 107.

- **Ephesus Museum (Selçuk):** Not all of the treasures of Ephesus were smuggled out of the country to end up in Western museums. There's certainly enough here to keep you busy for a while; the explanations are succinct and the labeling clear. Now you'll finally know the story behind those omnipresent souvenir statues of the little god Beş. See p. 235.

- **Bodrum Underwater Archaeology Museum:** The only one of its kind, the Underwater Archaeology Museum displays the vast findings from the discovery of a pre-14th-century shipwreck, made all the more amazing, because when divers stumbled on it, all they were looking for were a few sponges. See p. 272.

- **Underground Cities of Derinkuyu & Kaymaklı:** In Cappadocia, not everyone got a room with a view—at least not if your life was at stake. These multilevel cave cities, thought to date back to the 2nd century B.C., have supported up to 20,000 people at once in times of danger and religious persecution (though some speculation puts the number closer to 60,000). Clamber through the surprisingly intricate warren of passageways and living quarters where entire villages thrived in safety and darkness for months at a time. But claustrophobes beware—it's very dark and sometimes very snug. See p. 378 and p. 382.

- **Open-Air Museums of Zelve & Göreme:** When you live amid a landscape composed primarily of porous volcanic tufa, it doesn't take long before you realize, "Hey, I could make a great house out of this stuff." In Göreme, you'll see cave churches decorated with stunning medieval frescoes; the ingenious structures at Zelve are more a window into daily living, troglodyte-style. See p. 385 and p. 374.

- **Museum of Anatolian Civilizations (Ankara):** It's rare that a museum has the material to catalog a culture's backbone from beginning to end—but here, it happens. Looking for prehistoric cave paintings of Cappadocia's volcanoes? Got it. How about detailed archives of commerce from 2000 B.C.? Got that, too. See p. 399.

THE best STUFF TO BRING HOME

- **Carpets & Kilims:** No matter how lame your bargaining skills, it's still cheaper than Bloomingdale's—and boy, do they look good unrolled under (or on) your coffee table. Turkey's tribal carpets and *kilims* represent a cultural tradition that goes back for centuries. The symmetrical designs we're most accustomed to are found in rugs from **Kayseri** and Hereke—the latter traditionally boasts the most exquisite silk-on-silk showpieces.

- **Ottoman Books & Rare Prints:** The Ottomans were masters of calligraphy, embellishing the page with dust from sapphires, lapis lazuli, gold, and other gems. Miniatures generally represent scenes from the life of a sultan and his family, with colorful shades to give the page life. One of the most valuable of originals or reproductions is the *tuğra*, the sultan's elaborately ornate and personal seal. The **Sahaflar Çarşısı** in Istanbul is the best place to find these treasures, as are the streets near **Tünel** in Beyoğlu. See "Shopping," in chapter 4.

- **Turkish Delight:** This gummy, marshmallowy treat made of dried nuts, fruits, syrup, and cornstarch is a national favorite. I personally hate the stuff, but to each his own. It's known as *lokum* in Turkish—a word also used to refer to a voluptuous woman. The best *lokum* is available at **Hacı Bekir** in Istanbul (see "Shopping," in chapter 4), but you can find it at the Egyptian Bazaar or in practically every *pastane,* or souvenir shop.

- **Pottery & Ceramics:** These arts thrived under the Ottomans, whose skilled craftsmen perfected the coral red and cobalt blue of the Iznik tile. No one has ever been able to reproduce the intensity of these colors, until now. The only authentic reproductions come out of the **Iznik Foundation**'s workshop and showroom in Iznik (see "Bursa: Gateway to an Empire" in chapter 4), which has a branch in Istanbul (see "Shopping," in chapter 4). Ordinary but equally stunning porcelain designs on white clay come from Kütahya and are sold throughout Turkey.

- **Turkish Textiles:** Check the manufacturer's label on your fine linens, terry-cloth supplies, and cotton T-shirts. I bet you didn't realize it, but Turkey exports a huge amount of textiles, supplying the raw materials for well-known retailers such as OP, Calvin Klein, Walt Disney, and XOXO. **Bursa** and **Pamukkale** are both famous for the quality of their goods; while increasingly, Istanbul entrepreneurs are commissioning plush, organic cotton linens for the bath and tabletop. Bursa is also famous for its silks. See ""Shopping" and "Bursa: Gateway to an Empire," in chapter 4, and "Pamukkale, Hierapolis, & Laodicea," in chapter 7.

- ***Copper:** Turks use copper for everything, probably because it looks so good (particularly the white copper). Tea servers with triangular handles pass you by countless times a day; the wide copper platters that double as tables represent typical Turkish style. Those shiny white bowls you see in a *hamam* are copper, too. For the best prices and selection, head to **Çadırcılar Caddesi,** near the Grand Bazaar (see "Shopping," in chapter 4), or **Bakırcılar Çarşısı,** near the citadel in Ankara (see "Shopping," in chapter 10).

- **Gold & Silver:** The price by weight is the same, but with labor so cheap, you're bound to get a deal. Shopping thoroughfares glitter with the stuff—some of it attractive, some of it hideous. The **Istanbul Handicrafts Center** (see "Shopping," in chapter 4) has an atelier where an artisan crafts his own work. In **Ürgüp** (see "Ürgüp," in chapter 9), many of the pieces have local precious stones. Museum gift shops are also great sources of unique jewelry.

- **Foodstuffs:** The exoticism of the East is in full bloom at Istanbul's **Egyptian Spice Bazaar,** where you can find a dizzying assortment of spices, dried fruits and nutty concoctions. Don't bother with the saffron—you really do need to pay for the good stuff. Although this isn't Tuscany, you won't know it by the quality of the olive oil; head to the local supermarket and stock up on a few bottles. The smoothest and most delicious of the household brands is bottled by Komili. See "Shopping," in chapter 4.

- **Meerschaum Pipes:** Carved from the magnesium silicate found primarily in Eskişehir, these ivory-colored pipes are hollowed out and polished to mimic playful or grotesque images. The pipes are sold in most souvenir shops and make fun, frolicsome showpieces.

THE best BEACHES

Most of Turkey's best beaches have been snatched up by big hotels or full-service entertainment beach clubs—leaving less-than-stellar public alternatives. Thankfully, those big operations keep their beaches clean (the public ones with no services are very often littered) and the prices for their lounges pretty low, and they usually are associated with some of the best patches of sand or pebbles anyway. The bonus: Hotels and beach clubs (even the small ones) have snack bars, watersports, and clean toilets; and for the most part, the beaches have been left in their natural states.

○ **Suada** (Istanbul): Once the private floating playground of the Galatasaray football club, this tiny bobbing Bosphorus island in the center of Istanbul is now a morning, afternoon, and evening getaway for the city's denizens. See "Istanbul After Dark," in chapter 4.

○ **Assos** (Çanakkale and the Troad): It's hard to resist the lure of a beach sitting at the base of a steep outcropping backed by historic buildings, even if the result is a beach the size of a postage stamp. Once the sun goes down and the glow of the moon bounces off the calm waters, you'll think you were floating among the stars. See chapter 5.

○ **Alaçatı Bay** (Çeşme Peninsula): The small beach here opens up to an enormous bay blessed with lofty winds—paradise for windsurfers. The high winds are attributed to the sizable stretch of shallow water and the absence of anything obstructing it. The beach is backed by hills, hills, and more hills, all topped by dry, barren brush. See "Highlights of the Çeşme Peninsula," in chapter 6.

○ **Pırlanta Beach** (Çeşme Peninsula): Pırlanta, which means "diamond" in Turkish, describes the creamy whiteness of this sandy stretch of the peninsula. The beach is long and wide and faces the open Aegean. It's also easily accessible by *dolmuş* (minivan-type public transportation) from Çeşme's town center. See "Highlights of the Çeşme Peninsula," in chapter 6.

○ **Altınkum Beach** (Çeşme Peninsula): The golden-colored sand from which the beach takes its name is located in a relatively hard-to-find spot at the southernmost tip of the peninsula. As luck would have it, this only serves to keep this public park blissfully empty and undervisited. Because this beach faces the open sea, the water is a refreshing few degrees cooler than elsewhere on the peninsula. See "Highlights of the Çeşme Peninsula," in chapter 6.

○ **Ayayorgı Beach** (Çeşme Peninsula): This is not a beach per se, but a few narrow concrete piers jutting out over the water. Nevertheless, Ayayorgı is a charming spot, hidden in an overgrowth of orange and olive groves and open to a small and intimate cove. See "Highlights of the Çeşme Peninsula," in chapter 6.

○ **Göltürkbükü** (Bodrum Peninsula): Still waters embraced by the shoreline of twin villages characterize this part of the peninsula. The jet set may need to find alternative haunts now that the mayor has announced the dismantling of all of the private-access beach clubs. By the time you read this, the magical destination of Türkbükü may have opened up its shoreline to the common man. See "Bodrum," in chapter 7.

○ **Knidos** (Datça): The rough and tumble feel of the beach is very much part of the experience at this ancient harbor, where the tumbled detritus of the ancient city peeks out from above the waterline, and the harbor waves lap up over earthenware shards and marble relics. See chapter 8.

○ **Palamutbükü** (Datça): Friends and acquaintances will ostracize me forever for revealing this little unspoiled corner of the Mediterranean. The sweeping expanse of bay is served by little more than a single, unpretentious little strip of cafes and pensions, fronting the most pristine waters on the Mediterranean. See chapter 8.

○ **Ölüdeniz Beach** (Ölüdeniz): The posters just don't do it justice. On one end is the great expanse of Belceğiz Beach, enclosed by the brittle silhouette of Babadağ and the landing pad for paragliders sporting jet-propulsion packs. And on the beach is the jaw-dropper, the Blue Lagoon made real: still waters in no less than three shades of turquoise. See "Fethiye & Ölüdeniz," in chapter 8.

o **Butterfly Valley** (Fethiye): After reaching the Blue Lagoon—the holy grail of Turkish beaches—it seems odd to want to go elsewhere. But the Fethiye area abounds with stunning scenery. If you can tear yourself away from the main event, take the 30-minute boat ride to Butterfly Valley, a sandy paradise hewn out of a soaring gorge. See "Fethiye & Ölüdeniz," in chapter 8.

o **Iztuzu Beach** (Dalyan): There are strict rules of conduct here: Iztuzu Beach is a national preserve and breeding ground for the *Caretta caretta,* or loggerhead turtle. But at night, after the crowds have gone home, you can watch the lights move out to sea, or listen to the sounds of home life glide over the river from a nearby fishing village. Just don't wander too close to the waterline, and on behalf of the turtles, stay away from the off-limits areas. See "The Dalyan Delta," in chapter 8.

o **Kaputaş Beach** (near Kalkan): Hundreds of years ago, a huge chasm opened up the side of the mountain face. The gorge has dried up, but what's left is Kaputaş Beach, a small, sandy patch 400 steps down from the highway that feels like the middle of nowhere. From here, it's just a short swim to some nearby phosphorescent caves. See "Kalkan," in chapter 9.

o **Patara Beach** (near Kalkan): Eighteen kilometers (11 miles) of beach backed by dunes and marshlands—need I say more? The Mediterranean rises to the challenge in the summer, when it turns a deep shade of blue. See "Kalkan," in chapter 8.

o **Konyaaltı** (Antalya): The newly developed waterfront in center-city Antalya breathes new life into a seaside resort that risked second-rate status. Miles of pebble beaches, waterfront promenades, meandering lawns, cafes, and activities make this one of Turkey's most coveted destinations. Bodrum, look out! See "Antalya," in chapter 8.

THE best ONE-OF-A-KIND PLACES TO STAY

o **Çırağan Palace** (Istanbul): More than just Istanbul's original posh hotel, the Çırağan Palace is a destination in its own right. The grandeur of the lobby—tinted by light coming through the stained glass and imbued with the fragrance of fresh roses—hardly prepares you for what's to come. Expect regal gardens, a delicious Bosphorus-side pool, big fluffy beds, and flawless service. Make sure you splurge for that sea view, or all bets are off. See p. 118.

o **Four Seasons Hotel** (Istanbul): Nothing drives home the magnitude of this Istanbul hotel's history more than watching a former political prisoner incarcerated here when the place was a run-down prison break down and cry in the hallway. Some original tile and marble details were preserved and reused in the renovation, and you might encounter the rough etchings of an inmate's name in one of the columns. But these days, the unqualified opulence and comfort of this grand hotel couldn't be further from its bread-and-water past. The new **Four Seasons the Bosphorus** (also in Istanbul) promises the royal treatment—but without the historic background. See p. 160.

- **Les Ottomans** (Istanbul): You'll find rooms truly fit for royalty here, if you can get a reservation. Every detail, from the chandeliers, to the salon chairs, to the bedding, is a unique creation that screams "one of a kind." This very personalized nature of the hotel foreshadows the high standard of hospitality. See p. 173.
- **Ada Hotel** (Türkbükü, Bodrum Peninsula): If you're looking for quintessential Turkish elegance, the Ada Hotel's got it, and more. Characteristic, stylish, romantic, and utterly memorable, all rolled into a boutique experience on the hillside above the trendy yet serene outpost of Türkbükü. See p. 268.
- **Mehmet Ali Ağa** Konağı Datça): This restored mansion turned living museum offers regular folk like me the chance to *really* experience a home in the same way the Ottoman Paşas did. The museum rooms may actually be too authentic for some, but the more modern, albeit traditionally curated, annex, caters to those with contemporary needs. And everybody gets to experience the lush gardens and atmospheric colonnaded courtyard restaurant. See chapter 8.
- **Hillside Su** (Antalya; ✆ **0242/249-0700**): The over-the-top, snow-blinding white design concept is sleek and razor-sharp in its wit. See p. 348.
- **Aboard a Gulet** (the Turquoise Coast): The blazing August sun gives way to a mild summer night, and you wake up at dawn with your shipmates on the rear deck of the gulet, covered in fresh morning dew. There's nothing like sleeping under the stars in a cove along the shores of the Mediterranean. See "All About the Blue Voyage," on p. 54.
- **A Cappadocian Cave Hotel** (Cappadocia): Truly, where else could sleeping in a cave be so sweet? The secret is out, and every year the hotels entice you with more and more romance. I'm convinced, but I'm preaching to the converted. See chapter 9.

1

THE BEST OF TURKEY

The Best One-of-a-Kind Places to Stay

TURKEY IN DEPTH

2

The history of Turkey reads like the history of ancient and modern civilizations. Virtually every major player, from Greece's Alexander the Great, to Persia's Cyrus, to the long lineup of Roman, Byzantine, and Ottoman emperors and sultans, fought for control of this land and its surrounding waters. The result is a fascinating cultural and historical amalgam, a land with countless archaeological treasures still waiting to be discovered and modern structures to understand. While a visit to the country's historic sites and monuments will undoubtedly awe, your exploration of this cultural crossroads will be made much more rewarding if you know what you're looking at. This section provides a basic introduction into Turkey's experience with ancient Greece, Rome, and the Ottoman Empire, as well as the religious and political influences that made Turkey what it is today.

TURKEY TODAY

Ever since the Justice and Development Party (AKP) was propelled into power in 2002, Turkey has experienced an historic level of economic expansion and stability. With strong sectors in agriculture and textiles, a burgeoning tourism industry that saw 25 million visitors in the first 9 months of 2011 alone, and projected economic growth of 7.5%, Turkey is certainly enjoying its role as the second fastest-growing economy in the world.

Moreover, with the European Union in financial chaos and the Middle East seemingly in perpetual turmoil, Turkey's star as a major international player and influence peddler seems to be rising. Prime Minister Recep Tayyıp Erdoğan has embraced his new role of statesman, speaking out fiercely against its historic ally, Israel, imposing sanctions against Syria, and threatening military strikes in both cases.

Erdoğan, the conservative former mayor of Istanbul and Turkey's controversial Prime Minister for more than a decade, has also been at the helm of his country's rapid-fire economic growth since 2003. But while praised by many, he's also rattled more than his share of Turks: He's been accused of stealthily turning Turkey into an Islamic state and governing as an autocrat. One strategy of maintaining an iron-fisted grip on the body politic seems to have been through cracking the military—either guardian of the secular state or cronies fearful of the democratic process—depending on whom you ask. Together with members of academia, the judiciary, and the media, hundreds of military officers have been jailed, accused of membership in the clandestine "Ergenekon" organization allegedly plotting since 2003 to overthrow the government. In the summer of 2011, the top military brass resigned in protest, a move that for the first time since the founding of the Republic, effectively subordinated the military to governmental control. Critics of the crackdown see this as a consolidation of power by the ruling AKP aimed at eliminating the opposition. In the absence of any institutional resistance to further reforms easing restrictions on religion in public life, the very character of the Turkish state might very well be in question. Erdoğan insists that his intentions are for modernization, economic expansion, E.U. accession, and a strong, peaceful, and democratic Turkish state. Turkish progressives fear that it is a slippery slope down the same path taken by Iran's Revolutionary Guard.

The religious credentials of the ruling party are certainly apparent in reforms aimed at elevating the role of religion in public life, including easing restrictions on teaching the Koran, allowing women to wear headscarves in state buildings (overturned) and proposing a law criminalizing adultery (abandoned). The ruling party has also taken steps toward more anti-democratic levels of censorship. Turkey continues to block the popular video-sharing site YouTube.com, after a volley of insults were traded via the site between Turkish and Greek users. And in August 2011, authorities put "voluntary" Internet filters in place forbidding 138 seemingly arbitrary keywords.

Controversy has followed the AKP from its inception, given its roots in political Islam. Turkey's citizenry is polarized between those who fear "religion creep" and those who applaud the present government's accomplishments as well as the conservative

CYPRUS 101

Cyprus is another one of these divisive territorial issues not entirely dissimilar to the Northern Ireland, Palestinian, or Kashmir conflicts. Situated 65km (40 miles) off the Turkish coast, Cyprus was a part of the Ottoman Empire for centuries, with sizable migrations of Muslim Turks adding to the Orthodox Christian Greek inhabitants of the island. The island became a British colony in 1878. The London Agreement of 1960, negotiated by Britain, Greece, and Turkey, established Cyprus as an independent republic, with a Greek president, a Turkish vice president, and a fair proportion of representatives in the government.

This bicommunal state functioned for only 3 years, as militant Greek Cypriots (backed by Greece) ousted the Turkish Cypriot members, which resulted in a series of brutal attacks on both Greek and Turkish villages. Once again, it is a case of finger-pointing about who threw the first punch. A Greek coup aimed at

annexing the island and aided by local Greek Cypriot forces in 1974 called Turkey to action. Turkey sent in troops and occupied the northern third of the island, which in 1983 proclaimed itself the Turkish Republic of Northern Cyprus. Greek inhabitants of the northern territory fled south.

The United Nations has called for a unified state made up of two politically equal communities, and in 2005, Turkey voted yes for reunification. But the Greek Cypriots voted no. Since then, there have been some confidence-building measures, most notably, in 2008, the opening of the Ledra Street border crossing, which had been walled up since 1963. But with Turkey's stalled attempts at EU accession underlying the conflict, and with Greece scheduled to head the EU Council in 2012, any hopes at reconciliation in the near future seem pretty much comatose.

direction in which the country is moving. Beyond Turkey's borders, the country is held as a model of how democracy and Islam can coexist. The question is, is this fact or fantasy?

LOOKING BACK: TURKEY THROUGH THE AGES

In the Beginning

In the beginning, Noah's Ark landed on Mount Ararat, or so recovered fossilized wood and boatlike support beams might indicate. Actually, the beginning in Turkey was much earlier; archaeological findings in central Anatolia indicate the presence of cave dwellers dating back to the Paleolithic era. The oldest documented tribe in Anatolia was the Hatti, a nameless, faceless civilization that seems to have established small city kingdoms in central Anatolia and ruled there for about 500 years. Cuneiform tablets discovered in the regions to the east of Kayseri provide evidence of a thriving trade between these indigenous settlers and Assyrian merchants, who appear on the scene around 2000 B.C. With the arrival of the Hittites, an ancient tribe of uncertain mixed Indo-European origins, all evidence of the Hatti seems to dissolve.

The Hittites (2000–1100 B.C.)

Who were these Hittites who subdued the indigenous Hatti kingdoms and appropriated their language, customs, and women? No one really knows (thus the hedgy term "Indo-European"). Whoever they were, the Hittites assumed Hatti names—even the term "Hittite" derives from the Hittite expression for "people in the land of the Hatti."

The Hittites built an empire of city-states, and by the mid–13th century B.C., had taken control of a large part of Anatolia. Persistent invasions by Hittite successors to the south and east created border tensions with Egypt, leading to the historic battle of Kadesh (ca. 1300 B.C.) between Hittite Emperor Muwattalis and Egyptian Pharaoh Ramses II. Although historical accounts of the battle are contradictory (both

DATELINE

ca. 14,000 B.C. Cave deposits in Antalya and surface discoveries around Ankara, Konya and Hatay regions suggest earliest cultures.

ca. 1940–1780 B.C. Assyrian merchants from Mesopotamia establish trading colonies in central and eastern Anatolia; Indo-European people arrive, assimilating with existing Assyrian colonies.

ca. 1750 B.C. The Old Hittite Kingdom is established.

ca. 1300 B.C. The battle of Kadesh.

ca. 1284 B.C. Hattusilis III and Ramses II sign peace treaty.

ca. 1200 B.C. "Sea Peoples" arrive and destroy Hittite power in Anatolia; the Trojan War.

ca. 1200–700 B.C. Greek migration to Aegean; establishment of Phrygian, Ionian, Lycian, Lydian, Carian, and Urartu kingdoms.

ca. 546 B.C. Persian King Cyrus the Great conquers Croesus of Lydia.

ca. 499 B.C. Persians drive out the Greeks.

334 B.C. Alexander the Great drives Persians out of Anatolia.

sides claimed victory), for the first time in the history of mankind, a written treaty between the two countries was concluded, between Hattusilis III, Muwattalis's successor, and Ramses II (ca. 1284 B.C.), who eventually married two of Hattusilis's daughters to seal the pact. A copy of the treaty is in the Istanbul Archaeology Museum (p. 95). The Hittite Empire soon fell into decline and was finally destroyed by the invasion of a "Sea People."

The Hellenic Age

The displacement of the Hittites by the **Phrygians** marked the beginning of the end for the Hittite Empire, which subsequently fractured into independent principalities. Of unknown origins but thought to have been the "Sea People" or migrants from Thrace, the Phrygians became the dominant Anatolian power in the 8th and 9th centuries B.C. They prospered up until the reign of **King Midas,** the last Phrygian king—yes, that very one. He succumbed to invasions by the **Cimmerian** nomadic people around 725 B.C. The **Hurrians,** a native Anatolian mountain people, gave way to the **Urartians,** who, up until around 850 B.C., occupied the eastern region around Lake Van; they constructed walled citadels and an elaborate system of escape tunnels for their own defense. The **Lycians,** probably survivors of a nation of sailors or pirates—and possibly one of the "Sea Peoples" who caused the fall of the Hittite Empire—settled along the southwest coast.

At about the same time the Phrygians rose to power, several Hellenistic tribes were fleeing Greece to escape the invading Dorians. One group, the **Ionians,** migrated to the Aegean islands and into the central west coast of Anatolia (although the term Ionia often refers to the entire west coast). Ephesus, Miletus, and Priene are among the settlements formed during this migration, around 850 B.C.. Originally an agricultural civilization, Ionia developed an advanced artistic and literary tradition, taking its influences from other, more advanced groups in Anatolia as well as from contact with Egyptians, Assyrians, and Phoenicians. Miletus became a vibrant center for the exchange of scientific ideas, and here you find a foundation for modern-day mathematics, geometry, astronomy, and philosophy.

133 B.C.	Attalus III dies, leaving Pergamum to Rome; Pergamum becomes the province of Asia with its capital at Ephesus.	476	Rome falls; Constantinople emerges as sole religious and cultural capital of Roman Empire.
40 B.C.	Mark Antony and Cleopatra marry in Antioch.	527	Justinian ascends the throne.
		726	Leo III rejects the idea of icons.
A.D. 47–57	St. Paul establishes first Christian community in Antioch.	1054	Catholic and Greek Orthodox churches split.
313	Edict of Milan establishes official tolerance of Christianity.	1071	Selçuks defeat Byzantine army at Malazgirt.
330	Constantine establishes his capital, renaming it New Rome, then Constantinople.	1204	Crusaders sack Constantinople.
		1243	Mongol invasions destroy Selçuk power.

continues

Around the 7th century B.C., the **Lydians** appeared on the coast, establishing their capital at Sardis and inhabiting the inland district of western Anatolia. The Lydians were the first to coin modern money, mixing gold from the rich Pactolos Valley with silver and thus immortalizing the (apparently very rich) King Croesus. The Lydians also claim to have invented the game of dice.

Under **Croesus,** Lydia conquered and incorporated Ionia into its kingdom, but was conquered in 546 B.C. by **Cyrus the Great of Persia,** who was consolidating Persian power in Asia Minor. Cyrus the Great's successor, **Darius I,** crossed the Bosphorus and incorporated Thrace and Macedonia into the Persian Empire.

The **Carians,** mostly known as mercenaries, settled along the southwestern coast, having been chased off the Aegean islands by invading Greeks. They established, among other cities, Halicarnassus. In the 6th century B.C., Caria was incorporated into the Lydian kingdom, but later it, too, succumbed to Persian domination. But many Ionians, dissatisfied with their status as subjects of Persia, including most of the philosophers and artists, migrated back to either Athens or Italy. Other Ionians regained their freedom by joining the **Delian League,** a federation of Greek city-states formed in 478 B.C. as security against the renewal of Persian aggression.

In the summer of 334 B.C., **Alexander the Great** began his war on the Persian Empire, retaking Thrace, crossing the Dardanelles, and confronting the Persian armies near Troy. He succeeded in annexing all of Anatolia under **Macedonian/Greco** rule. Alexander's untimely death in 323 B.C. was the catalyst for internal conflict among his generals, resulting in generations of clashes over the division of his territories.

During the 3rd and 2nd centuries B.C., several independent Greek states emerged in western Anatolia. The city of **Pergamum** was established and, under Eumenes II, enjoyed its greatest period of prosperity, earning itself a privileged position with Rome.

Rome & the Eastern Provinces

When Attalus III, the last of the ruling Attalid dynasty of Pergamum, died without a successor in 133 B.C., the Romans interpreted his ambiguous bequest in their favor and claimed the city, beginning the **Roman Empire's** mass penetration into Asia

1261 Michael VIII Palaeologus reclaims Constantinople.

1326 Ottoman capital established at Bursa.

1453 Mehmet the Conqueror takes Constantinople.

1481 Reign of Beyazıt II begins.

1492 Columbus discovers the New World.

1512 Reign of Selim I begins.

1517 Selim I captures Cairo and proclaims himself caliph.

1520 Reign of Süleyman begins.

1566 Reign of Selim II begins.

1571 Ottomans defeated at battle of Lepanto.

1574 Reign of Murad III begins.

1622 Osman II assassinated by the Janissaries; Ahmed I restored to throne.

1687 Reign of Süleyman II begins.

1699 The Treaty of Karlowitz sees Ottomans cede territory for the first time.

1711 Defeat of Peter the Great at Prut River.

Minor. The Romans claimed Pergamum and effectively absorbed the independent states of Bithynia, Cappadocia, and Pontus. Except for sporadic conflict—most notably with **Mithridates of Pontus,** who between 88 and 63 B.C. massacred over 80,000 Romans at Ephesus—the Asian Provinces enjoyed a relatively long and prosperous period of peace. It was during the 1st century A.D. that **St. Paul** began his missionary travels through Anatolia.

In A.D. 284, **Emperor Diocletian** divided the empire into two administrative units, both to be ruled by an emperor (an *Augustus*) and a designated heir (or *Caesar*). It was a system destined to collapse into civil war; but the long-term effect was a more theological schism, as Christianity grew and took hold. **Constantine** emerged victorious and established his capital at the Greek town of Byzantium, rebuilding the city to equal, if not surpass, the splendor of Rome. Six years later, in 330, its architectural eminence realized, the city was baptized "New Rome," then renamed Constantinopolis in honor of the emperor.

Constantine publicly espoused the Christian faith in the **Edict of Milan** in 313, which mandated the tolerance of this new, emergent sect within the Roman Empire. Under **Theodosius,** paganism was outlawed and Christianity was made the official religion of the state. By Theodosius's death in 395, the eastern and western provinces had grown apart ideologically, and the Roman Empire was in effect divided in two.

The Age of Byzantium

The reign of Emperor **Justinian** and his Queen **Theodora** (527–565) inaugurated a period of great prosperity in Anatolia. Justinian reconquered the West, and eventually regained North Africa and Italy. His construction of the incomparable Hagia Sophia (Church of Holy Wisdom) established Constantinople as the spiritual center of Christendom. Justinian commissioned new buildings and conducted restorations all across the empire—an undertaking so vast that it thrust the empire into economic crisis after his death. His primary legacy was the **Justinian Code**—his attempt to codify and organize the ancient system of Roman laws—that ultimately became the foundation for many modern Western legal systems.

1774	Reign of Abdülhamid I begins; Treaty of Küçük Kaynarca follows defeat by Catherine the Great.		Abdülhamid is deposed.
1826	Janissaries massacred and corps abolished; Tanzimat Reforms.	ca. 1908–09	Mehmet V installed as lame-duck sultan.
1839	Reign of Abdülmecid begins.	1914	Ottoman Empire enters World War I as ally of Germany.
1854	Crimean War.	1915	Turkish forces repel Anzacs at Battle of Gallipoli.
1861	Reign of Abdülaziz begins.	1918	Reign of Mehmet VI begins; Turks surrender.
1876	Reign of Abdülhamid II begins.	1919	Greek army lands at Smyrna; Atatürk leads resistance against occupiers.
1878	The "Sick Man of Europe" progressively deteriorates.		
1881	Mustafa Kemal born in Salonika.		
1908	Coup d'état led by Young Turks;		

continues

Around the end of the 9th century, a rivalry emerged between the Eastern (Orthodox) and Western (Papacy) provinces over the veneration of icons. The worship of idols was first condemned by **Emperor Leo III** in 726 and then reiterated by successive emperors. In 1054, over this and other theological disagreements, the pope severed any ties that had united Byzantium with the West.

Distracted by religious and bureaucratic disputes, the Byzantines were unprepared for the arrival of nomadic Turkish warriors raiding lands as they swept southwestward from their origins on the Mongolian steppes. Around the 7th or 8th century, they met up with Arab tribes centered around Baghdad, home of the caliphate, and by the 10th century, the bulk of Turks—still nomads and warriors by nature—had accepted Islam as their religion. Some Turks, such as the **Selçuks,** subscribed to the orthodox Sunni form, while others, such as the **Turkomans,** accepted the splinter Shiite sect.

These *gazi* tribes, or "warriors of the faith," marched northwest from Baghdad, conquering lands in the name of Islam and penetrating deep into the heart of Anatolia. An accidental encounter with the Byzantine army resulted in a Selçuk victory in the **Battle of Malazgirt** in 1071, opening the floodgates to a mass Turkish migration into Anatolia.

To stave off the threat of invasion by these Turks, Byzantine Emperor **Alexius Comnenus** turned to the Christians of western Europe for aid. **The first Crusade** saw the recapturing of Jerusalem and the regaining of control of most of Anatolia.

The Selçuk Turks triumphed over the **second Crusade** in 1147 and eventually set up the **Sultanate of Rum,** centered around Konya, where they presided over significant cultural growth and territorial expansion. They also revived the classical Islamic system of education, attracting philosophers, poets, and craftsmen to the court. One of the most influential arrivals was the scholar **Celaleddin Rumi,** who founded the Order of the Mevlevi (or "Whirling") Dervişes. The Selçuks are also credited with the development of a system of way stations, called ***kervansarays*** (caravansaries), designed to meet the needs of merchants traveling on behalf of the state, and established insurance for the loss of tradesmen.

1920 Grand National Assembly created in Ankara with Atatürk at helm.

1922 Greeks driven from Anatolia; sultanate abolished.

1923 The modern Republic of Turkey is established; "Atatürk" is elected president; Capital moves to Ankara.

1924 Caliphate abolished.

1924–38 Atatürk's reforms.

1938 Atatürk dies.

1945 Turkey declares war on Germany.

1946 Turkey becomes charter member of United Nations.

1952 Turkey joins NATO.

1960 Military coup.

1961 Army restores parliamentary government.

1964 Turkey granted associate member status in European Union.

1974 Turkey sends troops to northern Cyprus.

1980 Military coup.

1999 Kurdistan Workers Party (PKK) leader Abdullah Ocalan captured in Kenya, convicted of treason, and sentenced to death. Two major earthquakes

As the Crusades continued, tensions arose because the Crusaders had no specific mandate from the pope, little sympathy toward the Greek Orthodox religion, and no agreement on the nature of their association with the Byzantine Empire. Allied with Venetian merchants who had an eye on the riches of the East, the Crusaders sacked and plundered Constantinople in 1204 in the **fourth Crusade,** creating the Latin Empire of Constantinople and widening the schism between the churches of the East and West. Driven from Constantinople, what was left of the Eastern Empire (Byzantines) established a small base in exile at Nicaea (now Bursa). The flourishing Selçuk Sultanate of Rum saw defeat at the hands of the Mongols in 1243, leaving a vacuum of power.

Michael VIII Palaeologus, ruler of the empire in exile, succeeded in reclaiming the city of Constantinople in 1261. Though their territory was drastically reduced, subsequent Byzantine emperors repeatedly tried to reunite the Orthodox and Catholic churches against the constant onslaught of invading Turks.

Ottoman Beginnings

Numerous independent Turkish principalities occupied the frontiers between the Selçuk Sultanate and the Byzantine Empire. The **Osmanlıs** (or Uthmanlı, better known as the Ottomans) were particularly successful in rousing the surrounding Turkic tribes and under the leadership of the fearless **Osman,** patriarch of the Osman (Uthman, Ottoman, whatever) clan, and his son **Orhan,** the Ottoman expansion began.

The Osmanlıs (hereafter referred to as the Ottomans) entered Bursa in 1326, where they set up their first permanent capital. Heading northwest, they rapidly conquered the Marmara shores, crossed the Dardanelles, and established a second fortified base at Gallipoli in 1354.

Orhan was the first Ottoman leader to assume the title of Sultan (formerly an honorary title that caliphs granted to chiefs of Islamic-influenced territories to emphasize their role as spiritual leaders). For the Ottomans, the title had military and political connotations as well. "Sultan" became the standard designation for those in power who answered to no superior other than Allah.

rock northwestern Turkey in August and November, killing an estimated 20,000 people.

2002 Turkey lifts bans on education and broadcasting in Kurdish.

2002–3 Justice and Development Party (AKP) wins landslide victory at the polls.

2003 Terrorist bombing at Neve Shalom synagogue and HSBC Bank in Istanbul. More than 250 are killed.

2004 Turkey abolishes death penalty.

2005 E.U. accession talks officially begin and are projected to last at least a decade.

2006 Ribbon-cutting on new Baku Tblisi Ceyhan pipeline.

2009 Turkey and Armenia establish diplomatic relations.

2010 The Mavi Marmara incident causes severe deterioration of ties between Turkey and Israel.

2011 AKP elected for third term.

GORDIUS, FROM pauper TO PRINCE

Legend has it that the Phrygian elders, seeking a leader to mediate quarrels and to gain status with their neighbors, consulted a local oracle for advice on how to select a king. The oracle responded that the next person to pass his shrine riding in a cart should be king, and soon enough, a farmer named Gordius rode by in his oxcart on the way to market. Gordius was proclaimed king, and the capital (near present-day Ankara) assumed his name, Gordion.

The expression "Gordion knot," which refers to a highly complex problem, takes its name from Gordius as well. Apparently, Gordius was quite proud of the fittings on his oxcart—particularly of the unusual knot he used to tie the cart's pole to the axle. He challenged all potential passersby to untie it, but the knot remained intact long after his death. When Alexander the Great arrived in Gordion more than 500 years later, he carefully studied the knot and then decisively severed it in two with his sword, before continuing on to more challenging conquests.

Orhan's son **Murat I** enjoyed one military success after another. Carving out a wide buffer circumventing Constantinople, he established a European presence at his new capital of Adrianople (now Edirne), and then directed his armies east into the Turkish emirates as well as west into the Balkans, Albania, and Bulgar territories. Finding himself surrounded, the Byzantine emperor, isolated except for sea access, became a vassal of the Sultan and was left with little recourse other than to aid the Ottomans in their conquests of the East.

Murat I defeated a Serbian coalition at the Battle of Kosovo, though he was killed in that campaign. Murat's son **Beyazıt** continued his father's expansionistic tendencies, striking both west and east and earning himself the nickname of *Yıldırım*, Turkish for "lightning" or "thunderbolt." The Ottoman advance to the west began to alarm the pope, who was unable to galvanize a proper offensive, except for two dismal attempts by the French and Hungarian armies during a lull in the Hundred Years' War. Meanwhile, the Ottomans' continued campaigns into the west left their eastern flanks vulnerable. The Mongols, led by **Tamerlane,** emerged as a major threat in the east, supported by Turkish emirates inflamed by Beyazıt's warring on his Muslim brothers—an act expressly forbidden in the Koran. Beyazıt was eventually imprisoned by Tamerlane, who restored the independent territories. Beyazıt died in prison, leaving behind a 10-year power vacuum in which his sons would fight for control.

Mehmet I was the triumphant son, and he and his son **Murat II** are credited with consolidating the Ottoman territories and absorbing, either by force or by marriage, the Turkish emirates to the east. Nonetheless, they were unable to either penetrate Constantinople's defenses or cut off the city's sea routes.

Mehmet II set a nasty royal precedent by strangling his infant brother in order to solve his own problems of succession. He eventually sanctioned fratricide by law: Whoever got acclaimed first was ruler and all his brothers had to die—ostensibly assuring the ascension of the most capable son.

Mehmet II set his sights immediately on Constantinople, and in 1453, in a brilliant strategy, circumvented the Byzantine defenses of the Golden Horn by carrying his fleet, ship by ship (by means of a brilliantly engineered "movable path"), over land,

Turkey's Ancient Civilizations

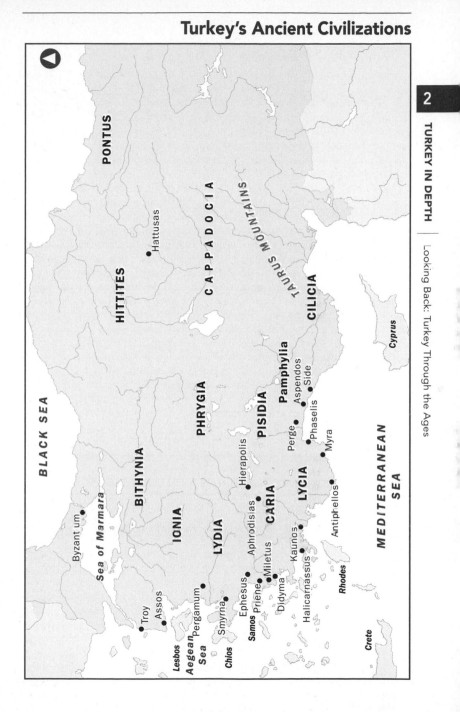

BLACK SEA

PONTUS

HITTITES

• Hattusas

CAPPADOCIA

TAURUS MOUNTAINS

CILICIA

Cyprus

PHRYGIA

BITHYNIA

Pamphylia

Aspendos
• Side

PISIDIA

Perge •
Phaselis •

Myra •

Byzantium •

Sea of Marmara

IONIA

LYDIA

Hierapolis •

Aphrodisias

CARIA

LYCIA

Antiphellos •

MEDITERRANEAN
SEA

Troy •
Assos •

Pergamum •

Smyrna •

Ephesus •
Samos Priene •

Miletus •
Didyma •

Kaunos •

Halicarnassus •

Lesbos

Aegean
Sea

Chios

Crete

Rhodes

behind the Byzantine naval barricade. After centuries of decline and decay, the Byzantine Empire had come to an end.

The Ottoman Empire

With his victory over Constantinople, Mehmet II acquired the title of Fatih, or conqueror, and named his new capital Istanbul, probably after having heard the Greeks say "eis ten polin" (to the city). He immediately began reconstruction, converting churches into mosques and repopulating the city with artisans, merchants, and farmers from all over the empire. Istanbul quickly became an international city with a mixture of cultures as Christians, Greeks, Armenians, and Jews all were welcomed by the sultan. After all, these diverse peoples brought with them a wealth of knowledge—and new tax revenues.

Having removed the final obstacle to the unity of his empire, Mehmet the Conqueror resumed his holy wars, dreaming of a world united under Islam. Soon the empire extended into Europe, with conquests of the Balkans, Greece, Albania, Serbia, and Bosnia. The Turks had suddenly become a major European presence, influencing the balance of power to the west.

Mehmet's son **Beyazıt II** took up his father's sword, pursuing his empire's expansion eastward against the Safavid dynasty in Iran, a Shiite presence that would challenge the Ottomans' legitimacy for centuries. Beyazıt's son **Selim the Fierce** (known as Selim the Grim, in the West, for his cruelty), impatient with his father's lagging military campaigns, assassinated him and slew his brothers, along with any other possible contender for the throne. He conquered and subjugated the heretic Safavids, and then moved on to subjugate the Mamluk sultans of Syria and Egypt. The guardian of the holy cities of Mecca and Medina wasted no time in recognizing Selim as the new spiritual leader of Islam, and he promptly proclaimed himself caliph.

The long reign of Selim's son **Süleyman the Lawgiver** (aka "The Magnificent") was the golden age of the Ottoman Empire, distinguished by military successes, administrative organization, economic prosperity, social order, and cultural greatness.

Ottoman Administrative Structure

The Ottoman ruling class was organized into five Imperial Institutions: the military; the scribes, or "men of the pen"; the *ulema,* Muslim leaders educated in theology and law, assigned the tasks of religious leadership, education, and justice; and the Inner and Outer Palace Services, who took care of the general day-to-day administration of the palace and care of the sultan.

Through territorial conquest, the sultan was provided with a steady supply of the best and most promising boys to serve as slaves and loyal subjects. This "recruitment" was called the *devşirme* (literally, collection). Candidates between the ages of 8 and 15 were selected and sent to Istanbul, where they were converted to Islam and educated in the palace school. The finest of the *devşirme* were chosen for continued education and placement in high palace positions, while the majority of the trainees entered into the elite military corps of Janissaries. By 1700, the Janissaries (*yeniçeri;* literally "new troops") had swelled to over 100,000 from 12,000 during the reign of Mehmet the Conqueror, ultimately becoming more powerful than the government they served and inciting frequent rebellions.

The Turkish aristocracy, composed of Muslims, Turks, Arabs, and Iranians, shared the rank of *askerî,* with the newer *devşirme* class of Christian converts making up the ruling class. Driven by the *gazi* guiding principle of *jihad* (struggle), the Ottomans had transformed themselves from plunderers into conquerors.

THE OTTOMAN sultans

Sultan	Reign
Osman I	1290–1326
Orhan	1326–59
Murat I	1359–89
Beyazıt I Yıldırım (the Thunderbolt)	1389–1402
Mehmet I	1402–21
Murat II	1421–51
Mehmet II (*Fatih*, the Conqueror)	1451–81
Beyazıt II	1481–1512
Selim I Yavuz (the Grim)	1512–20
Süleyman I (*Kanuni*, the Magnificent)	1520–66
Selim II	1566–74
Murat III	1574–95
Mehmet III	1595–1603
Ahmed I	1603–17
Mustafa I	1617–18
Osman II	1618–22
Ahmed I (restored)	1622–23
Murat IV	1623–40
Ibrahim	1640–48
Mehmet IV	1648–87
Süleyman II	1687–91
Ahmed II	1691–95
Mustafa II	1695–1703
Ahmed III	1703–30
Mahmud I	1730–54
Osman III	1754–57
Mustafa III	1757–74
Abdülhamid I	1774–89
Selim III	1789–1807
Mustafa IV	1807–08
Mahmud II	1808–39
Abdülmecid I	1839–61
Abdül Aziz	1861–76
Murat V	1876
Abdülhamid II (the Damned)	1876–1909
Mehmet V	1909–18
Mehmet VI	1918–22
Abdülmecid II (Caliph only)	1922–24

The Ottoman Decline

Several factors, both foreign and domestic, contributed to the progressive deterioration of the Ottoman Empire over the subsequent 2½ centuries. Although Süleyman left an Empire with territories on three continents and the splendor without equal, he also left behind a scheming widow—Roxelana, the Circassian-born concubine he took as his wife and trusted advisor. Roxelana manipulated her husband, his sons, and the court with fatal results. She orchestrated events culminating in the murder of

SÜLEYMAN THE magnificent:
PRAGMATIC STATESMAN

In 1520, Süleyman ascended to the Ottoman Empire throne and immediately launched invasions into Europe. In 1521, he gained control of Belgrade and the Danube. He then turned his attention to Rhodes, the last Crusader stronghold and bastion of the Knights of St. John—the island that stood between him and his Egyptian territories, not to mention Mecca and Medina. Süleyman triumphed after a 145-day siege and mercifully released all the Knights and mercenaries (though he'd come to regret this act later in his career). Eight years later, the Knights were granted Tripoli and the Island of Malta in a charter sealed by Holy Roman Emperor Charles V to thwart movement of Ottoman fleets in the Mediterranean.

Süleyman insinuated himself into the politics of Europe and attempted to destabilize both the Roman Catholic Church and the Roman Empire, believing them to be a threat to Islam. Urged on by Francis I of France, Süleyman defeated the young Hungarian king, Louis II (nephew of Charles V), in 1526, at the battle of Mohács. In 1529, at the request of the appointed king of Hungary, he returned to confront Archduke Ferdinand of Austria. Süleyman drove Ferdinand back to Vienna but was unable to penetrate the city's defenses—a failure that would become a recurrent theme for the Ottomans.

Although Süleyman's reign was characterized by almost constant war, he brought peace to the lands that he conquered. Süleyman was said to have embodied perfectly the characteristics of *adale* (justice), much like his namesake, King Solomon. Conquered lands often fared better once he took over. Looting was forbidden, and the sultan gained respect by placing provisions along the route of a carefully planned military campaign so as not to take anything from the local peasants along the way. Kings were retained as vassals of the sultan, and as long as the tributes (taxes) were sent to Istanbul, life continued as before.

Above all, Süleyman was a pragmatic statesman. In 1536, he signed a treaty with Francis I of France, conceding commercial privileges to the French in exchange for an informal alliance against their common enemy, the Hapsburgs. With these "Capitulations," the French were exempt from Ottoman taxes and were permitted to fall under French jurisdiction. In response to this French-Turkish cooperation, the Hapsburgs urged the Persians to wage war against the sultan. Turning his attentions east, Süleyman wrestled Iraq from Persian control, arriving as far as the Persian Gulf.

The Mediterranean Sea was another source of annoyance; despite Süleyman's conquest of Tripoli in 1551, the Knights of Malta (including many of the Knights released after the sultan's victory over Rhodes) were aggressively cutting off Ottoman sea routes. Süleyman began his siege of Malta in 1565, but the Knights fought back ferociously, the battle dragged on to winter, and Süleyman was forced to stand down.

The Ottoman armor was beginning to show weakness, provoking Süleyman, at age 72, to reassert his empire's superiority by taking Vienna once and for all. But he died in his tent during the campaign on the Danube. According to tradition, his heart is buried in Szigetvár on the spot where he passed away.

Süleyman's favorite sons, Mustafa and Beyazıt, thus clearing the path of ascension for her utterly incompetent son, Selim II, nicknamed Selim the Sot.

The abandonment of the traditional practice of fratricide contributed to the weakening of the system as well. Rather than kill off all potential heirs and risk the endangerment of the line, all sultans, beginning with Mehmet III in 1595, adopted the practice of imprisoning their sons and heirs instead of assassinating them. Isolated from daily life, inexperienced in the ways of the government or military, accustomed to excess, they either went crazy or emerged completely unprepared for the demands of leadership when called to the task.

Meanwhile, with the abandonment of the policy of celibacy in the Janissary Corps, sons of Janissaries—who were born free Muslims—began to enroll. By the mid–17th century, the Janissary Corps had grown to 200,000, squeezing the state for the payroll to support the increase in numbers. The purchasing of office also undermined the merit system, and although the palace school continued to function, the *devşirme* was abandoned. Sultans, beginning with Osman II in 1622, recognized the threat of a too powerful military, and made attempts at reining them in. Eventually, the internal deterioration of the corps was inevitable, as was the weakening of Ottoman military might.

With the government decentralized, corrupt, and morally hollow, the Ottomans were unable to deal effectively with outside threats or absorb the economic pressures of a Europe in Renaissance. Vasco da Gama's circumnavigation of Africa opened up new trade routes to the east; the East India Company of London could therefore sell its goods in Istanbul for less than the Ottomans would pay for direct trade with India. And with new sea trade routes, merchants no longer paid levies for passage through Ottoman territory. Meanwhile, Western industrialization produced cheaper goods that flooded the Ottoman market, thanks to Süleyman's Capitulations (see "Süleyman the Magnificent: Pragmatic Statesman," above). Silver and gold mined in the Americas drove up prices, the cost of living rose, and peasants abandoned their villages, which had disastrous effects on agricultural production.

The gradual decline was arrested later that century with the reign of **Murat IV,** who reignited the *gazi* spirit that would inspire decades of new campaigns toward further expansion.

The Ottomans' second attempt to capture Vienna in 1683 ended in failure, and for the first time in history–with the signing of the Treaty of **Karlowitz** in 1699–the Ottomans relinquished territory.

The 18th century was, for the most part, characterized by wars with Austria and Russia. In the first half of the century, the Ottoman military met with many successes, not the least of which was the defeat of **Peter the Great** at the Prut River in 1711. Nonetheless, two additional clashes with Russia culminated in the **Treaty of Küçük Kaynarca,** which followed a 1774 victory by Catherine the Great. In addition to annexing European territories, the treaty granted the Russians extensive commercial privileges in the Black Sea, a diplomatic presence in Istanbul, and the protection of the Orthodox Christian faith on Turkish soil. The desire for territorial and economic dominance, along with the trafficking of loyalties, would characterize the Russian-Turkish conflict well into the 20th century.

AN OVERVIEW OF islam

The history of Islam dates to the beginning of the 7th century in the city of Mecca, in today's Saudi Arabia. At the time, Mecca contained what was believed to be the first holy shrine built by Adam and Eve. Later, after Abraham was spared the task of sacrificing his only son, he rebuilt a temple on the same spot and dedicated it to the One True God. This shrine, constructed in the shape of a simple cube (hence the word Ka'aba), attracted the devotion of a host of pagan cults and, by the end of the second half of the first millennium, contained over 360 types of statuettes and cult objects. Pilgrims representing a broad range of cults flocked to the city, and the wealthy and influential members of the community were delighted with the revenue that these pilgrimages brought.

Mohammed was born in Mecca around A.D. 570 (or C.E., for "Common Era") and grew up in a monotheistic family tradition. A naturally pious man, Mohammed often headed off into the hills for moments of isolated contemplation and prayer. On one of these occasions, Muslims believe that the angel Gabriel appeared with a message from God, a revelation that is accepted as the first verse of the Koran (Koran means

"The Recitation"). The Koran forms the foundation of the Islamic faith and is believed by Muslims to be the direct word of God.

In a world of inequality, poverty, and misery, Mohammed's preachings of purity of heart, charity, humility, and justice gained a devoted following well beyond the borders of Mecca. The tribesmen of Mecca, perfectly content with the (economic benefits of the) status quo, grew alarmed and hostile at these developments, eventually forcing Mohammed and his followers to leave Mecca in fear for their lives. The town of Yathrib welcomed Mohammed and gave him an honored position as leader, changing its name to Madinat al-Nabi, or "the town of the Prophet." The town was later to become known simply as Medina.

The basic principles of Islam are quite admirable, and every requirement has a practical purpose. The act of prayer sets specific time aside for the recognition of a greater power, and the act of physical prostration is a constant reminder of one's humility and man's equality. Practically speaking, regular prayer develops a sense of peace and tranquillity, of punctuality, obedience, and gratitude. Furthermore, the setting aside of 5 minutes

Reform Attempts

It was obvious to Selim III that reform was needed. Inspired by the American and French revolutions, he created a new corps, the *nizam-i jedid* ("the new order"), on Western models, even adopting European-style uniforms. The Janissaries revolted over what they saw as a loss of power and privilege, and in a conciliatory gesture that cost him the throne, Selim dissolved the *nizam-i jedid* in 1807. In the next few years, the Janissaries executed many of the reformers as well as Selim's successor, Mustafa IV; **Mahmud II** was spared only because he was the sole surviving Ottoman prince. Proceeding with caution, Mahmud's first action was to deal with the anarchy that had taken root in the provinces, but as nationalist uprisings in Serbia, Greece, Algeria, and Romania saw the empire eroding at its borders, it was clear that the Janissaries were of little use in the defense of the empire. This allowed Mahmud to gain enough support to finally have the corps destroyed.

five times a day for introspection and meditation can only have positive effects on one's overall health, especially in the face of the stresses that the modern world has to offer. The month of ritual fasting, or Ramadan (*Ramazan* in Turkish), reinforces principles of discipline and teaches people to appreciate what they have and to understand what it's like to do without. Ramadan also brings families and communities together in a feeling of brotherhood and unity.

Islam is a socially conscious religion that attends not only to inner growth but to external affairs as well. The concept of charity is implicit in Islam, which calls for a specific contribution to be made to those less fortunate (2.5%), unless doing so would cause undue hardship to the giver.

Islam preaches modesty, and in many societies, particularly in Saudi Arabia and Iran, this concept has been taken to extremes, requiring women to wear a black chador in public (or burka in Afghanistan). Arguably, there is absolutely nothing in the Koran or any of the *hadiths* that requires a woman to wear any specific garment. In fact, the requirement of modesty applies to men as well. To force or coerce a women (or anyone) in matters of religion goes against the true spirit of Islam. (Here's a solution: Blindfold the men.)

While the political atmosphere in Turkey represents both liberal and conservative extremes (and everything in between), Atatürk's reforms regarding secularism provided the country with the basis for personal freedoms not available to other Muslim countries where national law is based on an interpretation of *shariah* (the way of Islam).

The universal reaction of Westerners arriving in Turkey is the revelation that Islam is not synonymous with terrorism, and Muslims are just people like you and me living their lives, celebrating their families, and worrying about the bills. While it's true that throughout the history of Islam (and Christianity, and others . . .) religion has been manipulated for political purposes, it's edifying to learn that Islam represents a generosity of spirit, a gentleness of heart, and the practice of good, clean, altruistic living. The Anatolian influences in Turkish culture add some rich traditions and folklore into the mix, the result being that many Turks have found a way to adapt to the contradictions inherent in a changing world.

Finally rid of the Janissaries' influence, Mahmud II, followed by his successor, **Abdülmecid,** was able to embark on significant modernization that would last for 40 years. The period of **Tanzimat** (literally, "reordering") was ushered in, aimed at strengthening the power of the government while encouraging an economic and social structure similar to that of Europe.

Influential during this period was the arrival of telegraph lines into Istanbul in 1855, facilitating a literary renaissance that would develop into an incubator for new (dissident) nationalistic ideas. Supporters of this patriotism were called "New Ottomans," whose objectives of preserving territory and limiting autocratic rule would be attained through the adoption of a constitution. But at the same time, the empire was being bankrupted. The financial crisis had degenerated to such an extent that the Ottoman State became known as "the Sick Man of Europe."

Abdülhamid II succeeded in temporarily reinvigorating the failing empire, but it was too little too late. In 1875, a rebellion in the Balkan territories drove back the Ottoman army to Istanbul, and the Ottomans were forced to sign the disastrous **Treaty of San Stefano** in which much of the Ottomans' European territory was lost. The Ottoman territorial hemorrhaging would later continue: Tunisia would be lost to the French in 1881, Egypt to the British in 1882, and East Rumalia to Bulgaria in 1885.

Abdülhamid II responded by reaffirming his designation as caliph and beginning a policy of reinvigorating Islamic unity. But the tidal wave of nationalism was relentless. Succumbing to external and internal pressures, he reluctantly instituted the first written constitution establishing a parliamentary system modeled on those in the West. For the first time in the history of the empire, absolute Ottoman rule had been relinquished, but as a condition to accepting the document, Abdülhamid insisted on retaining the right as final arbiter on unresolved issues. When the opposition became too outspoken in 1877, he simply neglected to reconvene the parliament and ruled autocratically and in an almost constant state of paranoia for the next 30 years.

In the late 1880s an organized movement called the Committee for Union and Progress (CUP), made up primarily of military officers and rebels in Macedonia, was organized in the name of "Liberty, Justice, Equality, and Fraternity." These **Young Turks,** led by a triumvirate dominated by **Enver Paşa,** orchestrated a successful nonviolent coup d'état in 1908, which was designed to reinstate the constitution. Abdülhamid was deposed, and his brother **Mehmet V** was released from prison as token head of state.

World War I

Although the Turks favored neutrality in the conflict germinating between the Central Powers of Germany and Austria and the allied countries of England, France, and Russia, Enver Paşa, who declared himself war minister in 1914, favored cooperation with the Germans.

In the summer of 1914, Enver Paşa signed a secret peace treaty with the Germans promising naval assistance in the face of Russian aggression in the Black Sea. Two months later, the Ottoman Empire was dragged into a war. With the Arab revolts in the east and the Russians on the northern border, the Turks were surrounded by hostile forces. Atatürk's legendary defense of Gallipoli in 1915 succeeded in saving the Straits, and therefore Istanbul, from invasion. But Turkish forces were no match for Allied tanks, automatic weapons, and airplanes. On October 30, 1918, the Turks, represented by the CUP government, agreed to an armistice with England and France.

The Treaty of Sèvres was signed on August 20, 1920 by the government of **Mehmet VI.** Under the treaty, the Ottomans relinquished all European territories except for a small area around Istanbul. Armenia and Kurdistan gained autonomy, Greece was assigned the administration of the region around Izmir, and French and Italian troops were left to occupy portions of the rest of Anatolia. Control of Turkish finances was taken over by the Allies.

Turkish Statehood

Atatürk—who was already an active nationalist, having taken part in the CUP overthrow of 1909—began organizing various nationalist factions, with the twin goals of recognition of a national movement and the liberation of Anatolia from foreign occupation.

In the fall of 1919, the Greeks got greedy and began moving inland, arriving almost to Ankara. Troops led by **Ismet Paşa** beat the Greeks back to Izmir, and in several decisive victories, Atatürk succeeded in driving the Greek troops completely off the peninsula. This last victory in the war for independence earned Atatürk recognition by foreign governments as the de facto leader of the Turks. The Soviet Union was the first power to sign a treaty with the nationalists in 1920, and France and Britain soon followed suit. Atatürk had succeeded in retaking possession of Istanbul, the Straits, and Thrace, and the Treaty of Sèvres was essentially null and void. In a bold move that was to be the beginning of the Turkish Republic, Atatürk declared the sultanate abolished and sent Ismet Paşa as sole representative of Turkey in the drafting of the **Treaty of Lausanne.** Sultan Mehmet VI was allegedly smuggled to Malta on a British ship where he remained in exile, putting the final nail in the coffin of the "Sick Man of Europe" and ending 6 centuries of an empire. The role of caliph was given to his cousin Abdümecid, heir to a defunct Ottoman Empire.

Mustafa Kemal Atatürk & The Republican Period

At the beginning of the war for liberation, Atatürk saw a country in ruins. His vision for the republic was Westernization, modernization, solidarity, secularization, and equality for all Turks. He formed the Republican People's Party (RPP), which became the exclusive political vehicle for his programs. When Abdümecid indicated a desire to expand his role as caliph into the political sphere, Atatürk, wary of opposition from anti-reformers and traditionalists, abolished the caliphate and banished all members of the house of Osman.

In 1924, the Grand National Assembly drew up a constitution establishing guaranteed civil rights and a legal framework for the government. Formally elected president by the assembly, Atatürk set out virtually unobstructed on a path of brisk modernization.

He closed the religious courts and ordered all religious schools secular. Years earlier on a trip to Europe, Atatürk had borne the brunt of ridicule for his tasseled red felt hat; so in 1925 the fez, symbol of Ottoman oppression, was outlawed. Derviş orders were outlawed (but not completely suppressed). The praying at tombs was prohibited. Honorary titles were abolished. It seemed to the people that Atatürk was determined to sever all ties with the past and with tradition, and the people in the outlying regions rioted. Mindful that a drastic measure such as banning the veil would enrage his critics, he opted for discouragement instead.

The legal code was overhauled, and civil law, previously the dominion of the religious leaders, was secularized. In a move toward equality, polygamy was outlawed and marriage became a civil contract, depriving husbands of the absolute right provided by Islamic law to divorce for any reason. Women were also granted equal rights in matters of custody and inheritance, while education for women on the secondary level was recognized as equal in importance to that of men. By 1934, women's rights had extended to universal suffrage, and Turkey won the distinction of being the first country in the world to have elected a woman to the Supreme Court.

Atatürk's flurry of reforms angered many who wanted a larger role for Islam in the state, and in 1926 a plot to assassinate the president was uncovered. Fifteen conspirators were hanged, including members of the extinct Republican People's Party and a former deputy, while others were either tried and exiled or acquitted. In 1928, a constitutional provision declaring Islam as the state religion was deleted, completing the secularism of the Republic of Turkey.

Atatürk's next task was aimed at both engendering Turkish pride and uniting his polyglot nation under one tongue. By the 1920s, Arabic, Persian, and French words made up 80% of language use, and Atatürk ordered his scholars to the task of constructing a pure Turkish language purged of foreign influences. Arabic script was replaced with Latin characters. Atatürk personally traveled around the country teaching the new alphabet in public squares when necessary. Not even Islam was spared: In 1932, the state made it mandatory for the traditional call to prayer to be broadcast from the loudspeakers in Turkish instead of Arabic.

All this modernization and bureaucratic reorganization only served to underline yet another need for change. Keeping track of all these Mohammeds, Mahmuts, and Mehmets was getting confusing, and it was obvious that a better method of identification would be necessary. Citizens were ordered to select a last name, lest they be assigned one less imaginative. Atatürk (known by his given of Mustafa Kemal at the time) was given the name Atatürk ("father of the Turks") by the Grand National Assembly. Ismet Paşa (the Paşa meaning "general") adopted Inönü, the site of one of his victorious battles, while others selected surnames ranging from the less original Bey ("Mr.") to the creative Kabasakal ("Grey Beard").

In 15 years of presidency, Atatürk transformed a feeble dictatorship into a modern, reasonably democratic, forward-thinking republic. On November 10, 1938, his efforts finally took their toll, when, after years of drinking, he died of cirrhosis of the liver. The League of Nations offered tribute at his death by calling him a "genius international peacemaker." Atatürk's legacy lives on, and even to this day, the time of his death is always observed with a minute of silence.

World War II Through the Cold War

As World War II raged on, Turkey managed to maintain its neutrality at least until February 1945, when a declaration of war on Germany became a prerequisite for admittance into the San Francisco Conference (the precursor to the United Nations, of which Turkey was one of the original 51 members).

Nevertheless, war took its toll on the Turkish economy. Simultaneously, pressure mounted in postwar Turkey over the state's increasingly authoritarian rule. Responding to spreading dissension, then-President Inönü yielded to his critics and authorized multiparty activity. By the election of May 1950, the Democratic Party had attracted enough of the displaced minorities to win a sweeping majority, appealing to private business owners, Islamic reactionaries, and the struggling rural population. In a move to appease their Islamic supporters, the Democratic Party approved the reinstatement of religious instruction as an optional educational program and reversed Atatürk's decree requiring Turkish as the language of the call to prayer.

Despite a brief period of progress in the early 1950s, Turkey's economy took a nosedive. To finance its poorly managed reforms, the government was forced to take out foreign loans, and Turks began seeking employment beyond their borders. Meanwhile, in a move to return to a one-party system, Menderes began undermining his opposition by banning political meetings, invoking censorship, and creating a special Democratic Party to "investigate political activity," a sufficiently vague mandate for random arrests. Although Menderes maintained a high degree of popularity, the military elite and the foreign-educated intelligentsia began to sow the seeds of rebellion. In response, Menderes imposed martial law. Within a week, students were demonstrating in the streets and cadets from the military academy were staging protests. Cemal Gürsel, a commander of the ground forces and one of the leaders of the movement, decided it was time to act, and despite the lack of a clear plan, set the military machine into motion. On May 27, 1960, in a nonviolent coup d'état, the armed forces arrested President Bayar, whose later sentence of death was changed to life in prison. Menderes was hanged on charges of treason, along with hundreds of members of the Democratic Party (DP). The Committee of National Unity, composed of high-level military officials who had participated in the coup, dissolved the Democratic Party government and took over. The people, jubilant of the overthrow, were rewarded with a new constitution; Gürsel was elected president of the Assembly, and former President Inönü, 37 years after his first appointment as prime minister, assumed the position again, along with the task of constructing the Second Republic.

Four political parties offered candidates in the 1961 election, of which only three won seats: the Atatürk-influenced Justice Party (JP), led by Süleyman Demirel; Inönü's social democratic RPP; the right-to-moderate Turkish Workers Party; and the communist Confederation of Progressive Trade Unions. Despite Inönü's popularity, the RPP lost ground, while the JP, plumped up by displaced members of the late DP, made gains. Nevertheless, neither was able to summon a majority and legislation was paralyzed. After a year and a half, the military handed over control of the state to civilian rule but maintained a watchful eye on the government in the ensuing years. In 1965, the JP was successful in acquiring a majority in the Grand National Assembly, sidelining the RPP for the first time since 1961 and providing Demirel with enough votes to end the coalition-style government in favor of a cabinet.

Modern Turkey & the Third Republic

In spite of the new structure, bickering, crossing of party lines, and splinter groups plagued the political machine. Confidence in the system plummeted, as did the value of the Turkish lira, resulting in unemployment, poverty, hunger, and ultimately social repression. The social and economic situation deteriorated so much that in 1971, in what became known as the "coup by memorandum," Demirel was forced by the military to resign.

The 1970s were a reactionary time in Turkey, much as the 1960s were in the United States, with Marxist and Leninist doctrines clogging impressionable minds. It wasn't long before antigovernment organizations turned to violence in order to further their cause. The left-wing Turkish People's Liberation Army resorted to political assassinations, kidnappings, and fantastic bank robberies, while the Grey Wolves, the terrorist arm of the Islamic-minded National Salvation Party, made standing in a bus line a potentially fatal activity. By mid-1979 the death toll attributed to terrorist violence had reached 20 a day. The military again stepped in.

The military coup of 1980, led by army Chief of Staff General Kenan Evren, was greeted with relief by the general population as well as by concerned members of NATO. Two years later, just as they did after previous coups, the military restored civilian government, although they did only offer one candidate for president: Kenan Evren.

The new government found a secure identity in the Motherland Party, led by Turgut Özal, an economist with a proven track record in economic policy. Özal removed Atatürk's policy of etatism and replaced it with a policy of private enterprise with mixed success: Some of Turkey's nouveau riche got accustomed to the excesses of the 1980s, although not always by legitimate means. Upon Özal's death in 1993, Demirel, representing the True Path Party (Doğru Yol Partısı, or DYP) composed of former

THE kurdish QUESTION

Who are the Kurds, these people without a country? History books pinpoint their origins to western Iran, but it's more accurate to say that the Kurds have roots in many different lands. Over time, the Kurds have developed a distinctive culture, and today the Kurdish population spreads over eastern Anatolia, northeastern Iraq, Syria, and western Iran.

In the wake of World War I, Kurdish demands for an independent state were met in the Treaty of Sèvres (1920), but the treaty was nullified by Atatürk's victories over foreign occupation and replaced by the Treaty of Lausanne (1923). This new treaty made no mention of the Kurds, who have been struggling for independence ever since, suffering from repression not only in Turkey, but also in other countries in the region. In the 1980-to-1988 Iran-Iraq War, entire Kurdish villages were annihilated due to Iraq's use of poison gas; as a result the Turkish government allowed 100,000 refugees to flow over the border into Turkey.

In 1978, Abdullah Öcalan formed the Kurdistan Workers' Party (PKK) as an organized separatist movement, accusing the Turkish government of oppression, repression, torture, and censorship. The Turkish government labeled the PKK a terrorist organization with a limited following intent on destabilizing the Turkish

members of the now defunct JP, made yet another political comeback as Turkey's seventh elected president. By 1995, with pro-Islamic sentiment on the rise, the Islamic partisans, having formed the Welfare Party, had gained enough votes in the parliamentary elections to make the coalitions stand up and take notice. With Necmettin Erbakan at the helm, the Welfare Party obtained legitimacy through a coalition with the majority DYP, an alliance that most factions had tried to avoid. Erbakan was appointed to serve alternating years as prime minister with the current prime minister, making him the first Islamic leader in the history of the Turkish Republic.

Erbakan's participation as prime minister was an outright affront to the 1982 constitution's prohibiting of "even partially basing the fundamental, social, economic, political, and legal order of the state on religious tenets." Erbakan was widely criticized, especially by the military, which later forced him to resign. The Welfare Party was accused of being antisecular and was banned in 1998 along with Erbakan, who was prohibited from participating in politics until 2003. The **Justice and Development Party** (Adalet ve Kalkınma Partısı, or **AKP** in Turkish), formed in August 2001, took over where the Welfare Party left off, claiming a new, moderate stance and a willingness to work within the secular system.

TRADITIONAL ART & ARCHITECTURE

First impressions of Turkey reveal a society much more European than one expects, but echoes of a strong, proud, and decidedly Oriental heritage shine through in the traditional arts, culture, music, and folklore. Tourists flock to those "Turkish Nights" shows, expecting to cram in a few hours' worth of "authentic" folklore. But while a belly dancer in a glittery harem hat may seem the epitome of exoticism, this ritual crowd-pleaser is anything but a Turkish invention.

nation and threatening its sovereignty. Turkey considers its Kurdish population Turkish citizens, although in practice, many of the predominantly Kurdish territories, typically in remote regions, are impoverished and lack basic public services.

The PKK took up arms in 1984, and the violence persisted until Öcalan's capture in 1999. Over the course of this 16-year armed conflict, the Turkish government estimates that more than 40,000 people lost their lives, although this estimate is probably a modest one. At the end of Öcalan's trial, the PKK leader was sentenced to death; since that time, Turkey has abolished the death penalty and Öcalan can expect to live out his days in a Turkish prison. Yet in spite of on-again, off-again cease fires, the cycle of assassinations, attacks, and counterattacks has escalated in the southeast, as separatists and soldiers vie for control over the region. The violence extends into Northern Iraq (home of the oil-rich city of Kirkuk and a historically disputed region), as Turkish military orders airstrikes on PKK bases over the Iraqi border. These tensions don't bode well for Iraqi, Turkish, or American foreign policy. For now, it's a wait-and-see situation.

Turkish culture developed by absorbing the artistic traditions of conquered lands, so more than any one defining style, the Turkish arts are characterized by layers and layers of complexity. From the time the Turkish tribes spread through Anatolia in the 11th century until the end of the Ottoman Empire, the Turks had incorporated decorative and architectural styles from the Sassanids (a pre-Islamic Persian dynasty), the Romans, the early Christians, the Byzantines, and Renaissance-era Europeans.

Architecture

The architectural and decorative arts of Turkey are closely linked to the Islamic faith, which gave major importance to mosques, *medreses* (theological schools), and mausoleums. Almost all mosques follow the plan of Mohammed's house, which was composed of an enclosed courtyard surrounded by huts, with a building at one end for prayer and an arcade to provide shade. Whereas in Mohammed's time the call to prayer was sung from the rooftops, minarets were added later for convenience and style.

The main objective reflected in Selçuk architecture was the proliferation of the purist Sunni orthodoxy, which was achieved by concentrating its efforts on the construction of *medreses* and other public works such as mosques and baths. To provide a means of safe passage for trade as well as the means for communication from one end of the empire to another, the Selçuks built a network of fortified caravansaries. Although Rum Selçuk architecture at first reflected the influences of the Iranian Selçuks, over time they developed a distinct style, incorporating features such as pointed arches from the Crusaders and lofty arched spaces from Christian Armenians and Syrians employed under the sultan. They also developed the squinch, a triangular architectural device that allowed the placement of a circular dome atop a square base, laying the groundwork of what was later to become an outstanding feature of Ottoman mosque architecture. The Selçuks also combined traditional arabesque styles with indigenous Anatolian decorative motifs that literally flowered into a unique style of geometric architectural ornamentation.

THE IMPERIAL OTTOMAN mosque

The majority of the mosques in Istanbul, and those highlighted in this book, are Ottoman Imperial structures. As their architecture is about the evolution of prayer space, there is no one floor plan per se, such as the cross plan of a Catholic church. However, you will notice several recurring elements:

○ **avlu:** A monumental courtyard preceding the entryway to the mosque.

○ **hünkar mahfili:** The sultan's loge, located in variable places and only in imperial mosques. This is where the sultan would (privately) attend services.

○ **kürsü:** Generally located to the left of the *mihrab*, this is where the imam sits when reading from the Koran.

○ **mihrab:** The niche indicating the *kıble*, or direction of Mecca.

○ **mimbar** (or **minbar**): The "pulpit" from which the imam delivers his sermon.

○ **minaret:** The more minarets, the more prestigious the building/ builder/namesake. The Blue Mosque, with its six minarets, is the only one in the world to match the number of minarets on the mosque in Mecca.

○ **şadırvan:** An ornamental fountain, usually at the center of the courtyard, for ritual ablutions. In practice, these are decorative, and worshipers use faucets available on the side of the mosque.

○ **şerefe:** The balcony of the minaret from which the *muezzin* calls the faithful to prayer.

Some Imperial and philanthropic mosques were the centerpiece of an entire complex, or *külliye*, serving the community. This complex would include some of the following: hospital, soup kitchen, primary school, public bath, public fountains, tombs/mausoleums, and a market.

A defining feature of Ottoman architecture became the dome, a form that expanded on earlier Turkish architecture but was later haunted by the feat of superior engineering accomplished in the soaring dome of the Hagia Sophia. As the Turks conquered Christian lands and churches were converted into mosques, traditionally Byzantine ideas were crossing cultural barriers and finding their way into the Selçuk and Ottoman vocabulary.

Ottoman architecture reached its zenith in the 16th century under Süleyman the Magnificent, in the expert hands of his master builder, Sinan. In the service of the sultan, Sinan built no fewer than 355 buildings and complexes throughout the empire, including the Süleymaniye, whose grand and cascading series of domes has become not only a defining feature of the Istanbul skyline but also a pinnacle in Ottoman architecture. (Sinan succeeded in surpassing the Hagia Sophia with the Selimiye in Edirne, a destination not covered in this guide.)

Art

Whereas Byzantine art featured elaborate religious interiors and the use of luxury materials such as gold and silver, Islamic *hadith* frowned on the use of luxury items in its mosques, favoring instead unpretentious items such as ceramics, woodcarvings, and inlay. Additionally, because of the Islamic prohibition against religious images of living creatures, Turkish decorative arts were channeled into such alternative features as flowers, geometric forms, and Arabic script.

The Selçuks introduced the use of glazed bricks and tiles in the decoration of their mosques, and by the 16th century, the Ottomans had developed important centers of ceramic production at Iznik and Kütahya. Ottoman tiles incorporated a new style of foliage motif and used turquoises, blues, greens, and whites as the dominant colors. Spectacular uses of tile can be seen all over the country, in mosques, palaces, *hamams* (Turkish baths), and even private homes.

Woodworking and mother-of-pearl or ivory inlay were primarily used in the decoration of the *minbar* (pulpit), but this craft extended to the creation of Koran holders, cradles, royal thrones, and even musical instruments.

Calligraphy is intimately related to the Islamic faith and dates back to the earliest surviving Koran manuscripts. Over the centuries, different styles of calligraphy emerged, with one of the basic requirements being that the text be legible. The Selçuk period brought about a more graceful cursive script, while the earlier Arabic script was more suited to stone carving. The ornamentation of holy manuscripts became an art in itself, as seen in pages that are gilded with gold leaf or sprinkled with gold dust, and in script whose diacritical marks are accented with red ink.

Besides the use of calligraphy in religious manuscripts, under the Ottomans, the application of an imperial seal, or *tuğra* (pronounced *too*-rah), on all official edicts became customary. The earliest example of a *tuğra* can be traced back to Orhan Gazi, on a 1324 endowment deed, with each successive sultan creating his own distinct and personal representation. Today these seals are significant works of art, bearing price tags that stretch into the hundred- or even thousand-dollar ranges.

The art of marbled paper is another traditional Anatolian art that flourished under the Ottomans. Known as *ebru,* the art of marbling calls for natural dyes and materials, and a precise hand to create a collection of spectacular, one-of-a-kind designs.

The art of carpet weaving has a complex heritage that goes back for thousands and thousands of years. Based on the necessity of a nomadic existence, carpets had more practical functions: warmth and cleanliness. As tribes migrated and integrated, designs and symbols crossed over borders as well. Carpet designs parallel those of the other artistic media, with geometric patterns a common feature of the 13th century.

Wool carpets provided warmth for the harsh winters, while *kilims,* also placed on the ground, provided coverings for cushions in a *şark*-style (or Oriental-style) setting that later could be used to transport the contents of the tent. Prayer rugs, identifiable by a deliberate lack of symmetry (the "arrow" will always be lain in the direction of Mecca), continue to be one of the more beautiful categories of traditional Turkish rugs.

Although Turkish carpets became one of the more coveted trappings of status in Europe, appearing in the backgrounds of many a Renaissance artist such as Giovanni Bellini and Ghirlandaio, the more ornate and sophisticated designs preferred by Europeans were the creation of non-Turkic (mostly Armenian) craftsmen. Today, however, even these stunning pieces are part of the traditional Turkish carpet-weaving lexicon.

TURKEY IN POPULAR CULTURE

Books

The definitive modern interpretive work on the history of Turkey is by the renowned Middle East historian Bernard Lewis, in *The Emergence of Modern Turkey.*

Turkey Unveiled: A History of Modern Turkey, by Hugh and Nicole Pope, two journalists working for the *Wall Street Journal* and *Le Monde,* gives us insights into the most divisive issues of Turkey today. A more recent analysis of modern problems and trends in Turkey, written from a Western insider's point of view, is provided by Stephen Kinzer, former Istanbul bureau chief of the *New York Times,* in *Crescent and Star: Turkey Between Two Worlds.*

John Ash approaches the history of the city in *Istanbul: The Imperial City* by casting a lens on the more than 20 pivotal historical events or periods, beginning with the pre-classical era through to the present day.

Another great read on the Byzantine empire is *A Short History of Byzantium,* John Julius Norwich's condensed version of a three-volume epic about one of the most enduring empires on Earth.

Ottoman Centuries: The Rise and Fall of the Turkish Empire, by Lord Kinross, has established itself as the definitive guidebook on Turkey during the Ottoman Empire. In a thoroughly readable prose, Kinross leads you through history while providing the contexts for understanding Turkey today.

Another book by Kinross is *Atatürk, the Rebirth of a Nation* (titled *Atatürk: A Biography of Mustafa Kemal, Father of Modern Turkey* in the U.S. and currently out of print), also respected as *the* handbook on the man who single-handedly reconstructed a nation. Also see Andrew Mango's more recent *Atatürk.*

Constantinople: City of the World's Desire, 1453–1924, by Philip Mansel, provides an accurate and colorful history of the Ottoman Empire while sprinkling the pages with attention-grabbing little morsels of lesser-known trivia.

Coverage of terrorist actions committed by militant Muslims has prejudiced much of the Western world against anything Islamic, causing many tourists to Turkey to be unnecessarily apprehensive. *What Went Wrong,* a balanced and scholarly work by Bernard Lewis, guides readers through the transformation of Islam from a cultural, scientific, and economic powerhouse to a significantly tarnished underdog. Follow this up with *What's Right With Islam,* in which Feisal Abdul Rauf argues how the violence perceived by the West to be at the heart of terrorism has, in fact, nothing to do with religion and everything to do with economics and politics.

Mary Lee Settle's *Turkish Reflections* and Jeremy Seal's *A Fez of the Heart: Travels Around Turkey in Search of a Hat* are two excellent travelogues that have established themselves as de facto reads for anyone interested in pre-boom, traditional Turkey. *Turkish Reflections,* although accused of being outdated, succeeds in providing an accurate portrayal of the Turkish people and vivid images of the physical landscape. In *A Fez of the Heart,* Jeremy Seal succeeds in capturing the sights and smells of his destinations while ostensibly on the hunt for the legacy left by the fez. Seal tosses in bits of history while you're not looking and throws in unexpected episodes of hilarity that will garner you unwanted attention in public places.

For Orhan Pamuk, *Istanbul: Memories and the City* is a (tedious) personal reflection on life growing up in the "melancholy" of an Istanbul in transition. Descriptions of faded apartment buildings, and the tension between tradition and convention are as much a self-portrait as a window into the city at the crossroads of civilization. The book also includes dozens of black-and-white photos of the city, allowing a glimpse of Istanbul before major investments in restoration.

For a modern woman's view of what it's like to work, live, and travel in Turkey, pick up the recently compiled and released *Tales From the Expat Harem: Foreign Women*

Walking through a bazaar or past a restaurant entrance may elicit a *"buyurun"* or *"buyurun efendem,"* both of which are expressions of courtesy. *Buyurun* has no English equivalent; it's used as an invitation to "Please feel free" (to look, to come in), or as a "You're welcome," much like the Italian *prego*. *Efendem* is a highly polite gender-neutral form of address that also means "Pardon?"

in Modern Turkey. It's a compilation of essays, stories, and travelogues by various non-Turkish women.

In fiction, obviously, the most insightful reads will be those books written by native Turks, and in recent years, several Turkish authors have created mesmerizing works of fiction set within a vivid Turkish reality. Orhan Pamuk made quite a splash well before he won himself a Nobel Prize in 2006 for literature. Irfan Orga's *Portrait of a Turkish Family* is a poignant account of a simple Turkish family caught between the Ottoman Empire and Atatürk's Republic. Journalist and leading satirist Aziz Nesin spent much of his life in prison, where he penned a large portion of his highly biographical essays—colorful images of growing up in a traditional Turkish family at the beginning of the 20th century.

Films

The Turks rigorously resent the unfair characterization of Turkish people in the 1978 film *Midnight Express,* a movie that has been accused of encouraging prejudices in Westerners. They point out that the movie was financed by Greek cinema magnate Kirk Kerkorian and filmed using actors of predominantly Greek and Armenian origin—two nations notorious for their bad blood with Turkey. Nevertheless, it's a movie classic, it did win an Oscar, and it *was* set in Istanbul.

Coming soon to a theater near you is Part II of *The Thomas Crown Affair,* with Angelina Jolie and Pierce Brosnan sparring over the disappearance of the illustrious Kaşıkçı (Spoonmaker's Diamond). Called *The Topkapı Affair,* the movie is based on the book *Light of Day* and adapted from Ustinov's 1964 film *Topkapı.*

EATING & DRINKING

As nomads, the Turks were limited by what the land offered and by what could be prepared over a crude open fire, so it's not a stretch to understand how kebaps and *köfte became the centerpieces of Turkish cooking. Turkish food today concentrates on simple combinations, few ingredients, and fresh produce.*

With access to vast cupboards stocked with ingredients from the four corners of the empire, the palace chefs developed a more complex cuisine. The majority of these recipes, recorded in Arabic script, were regrettably lost in the language reforms. Some Ottoman favorites have made it to us nevertheless, like the *hünkar beğendi* (the sultan was pleased), *imam bayaldı* (the priest fainted; Barbara Cartland might have likened it to a woman's "flower"), and *hanım göbeği* (lady's navel), a syrupy dessert with a thumbprint in the middle. These have become staples in many run-of-the-mill restaurants, but true Ottoman cuisine is difficult to come by. Several restaurants in Istanbul have researched the palace archives to restore some of those lost delicacies

You'll Never Count Sheep Again

Bus drivers in Turkey abide by an unwritten rule never to eat *cacık*—a salad of yogurt, cucumber, and garlic, often served as a soup—while on duty. The dish is believed to be a surefire, and natural, cure for insomnia.

to the modern table, providing a rare opportunity to sample the artistry and intricate combinations of exotic flavors in the world's first fusion food. The Turkish kitchen is always stocked with only the freshest vegetables, the most succulent fruits, the creamiest of cheeses and yogurt, and the best cuts of meat. But unless you're a pro, like the chefs to the sultans whose lives depended on pleasing the palate of their leader, it takes a lot of creativity to turn such seemingly simple ingredients into dishes fit for a king.

A typical Turkish meal begins with a selection of cold then hot mezes, or appetizers. These often become a meal in themselves, accompanied by an ample serving of raki (see the "Drinks" section, below), that when taken together, form a recipe for friendship, laughter, and song. The menu of mezes often includes several types of eggplant, called *patlican; ezme,* a fiery hot salad of red peppers; *sigara böregi,* fried cheese "cigars"; and *dolmalar,* anything from peppers to vine leaves stuffed with rice, pine nuts, cumin, and fresh mint.

The dilemma is whether or not to fill up on these delectables or save room for the kebaps, a national dish whose stature rivals that of pasta in Italy. While *izgara* means "grilled," the catchall word *kebap,* simply put, means "roasted," and denotes an entire class of meats cooked using various methods. Typical kebaps include lamb "shish"; spicy *Adana kebap,* a spicy narrow sausage made of ground lamb; *döner kebap,* slices of lamb cooked on a vertical revolving spit; *patlican kebap,* slices of eggplant and lamb grilled on a skewer; and the artery-clogging *Iskender kebap,* layers of *pide,* tomatoes, yogurt, and thinly sliced lamb (shwarma) drenched in melted butter. To confuse things a bit, stews can also be called kebaps.

Turks are equally nationalistic over their *köfte,* Turkey's answer to the hamburger: flat or round little meatballs served with slices of tomato and whole green chili peppers. But even though signs for kebap houses may mar the view, Turkish citizens are anything but carnivores, preferring instead to fill up on grains and vegetables. *Saç kavurma* represents a class of casseroles sautéed or roasted in an earthenware dish that, with the help of an ample amount of velvety Turkish olive oil, brings to life the flavors of ingredients such as potatoes, zucchini, tomatoes, eggplant, and beef chunks. No self-respecting gourmand should leave Turkey without having had a plate of *mantı,* a meat-filled ravioli, dumpling, or *kreplach,* adapted to the local palate by adding a garlic-and-yogurt sauce. *Pide* is yet another interpretation of pizza made up of fluffy oven-baked bread topped with a variety of ingredients and sliced in strips. *Lahmacun* is another version of the pizza, only this time the bread is as thin as a crepe and lightly covered with chopped onions, lamb, and tomatoes. Picking up some "street food" can be a great diversion, especially in the shelter of some roadside shack where the corn and *gözleme*—a freshly made cheese or potato (or whatever) crepe that is the providence of expert rolling-pin-wielding village matrons—are hot off the grill.

On the Aegean, along the Mediterranean or at a fashionable restaurant along the Bosphorus, Turks are also crazy about their fish. Fish restaurants offer an alternative to meat-centric joints, plus a festive, usually outdoor, ambiance that befits a seaside ambiance.

Desserts fall into two categories: baklava and milk-based. Baklava, a type of dessert made of thin layers of pastry dough soaked in syrup, is a sugary sweet bomb best enjoyed around teatime (with ice cream, please), although several varieties are made so light and fluffy that you'll be tempted to top off dinner with a sampling. The milk-based desserts have no eggs or butter and are a guilt-free pick-me-up in the late-afternoon hours, although there's no bad time to treat yourself to some creamy *sütlaç* (rice pudding). The sprinkling of pistachio bits is a liberal addition to these and many a Turkish dessert, while comfort food includes the *irmik helva,* a delicious yet simple family tradition of modestly sweet semolina, pine nuts, milk, and butter (okay, I lied about the guilt-free part).

So what's the deal with Turkish delight? Otherwise known as *lokum,* this sweet candy is made of cornstarch, nuts, syrup, and an endless variety of flavorings to form a skwooshy tidbit whose appeal seems to be more in the gift-giving than on its own merit.

Drinks

Rather than the question, "Would you like something to drink?" Turkish hospitality leaps immediately to the "What?" Tea, called *çay* (chai) in Turkish, is not so much a national drink as it is a ritual. Boil the water incorrectly and you're in for trouble. Let the tea steep without prior rinsing and you've committed an unforgivable transgression. What's amazing is that so many tea drinkers manage to maintain white teeth, and as you'll see, some don't. Tea is served extremely hot and strong in tiny tulip-shaped glasses, accompanied by exactly two sugar cubes. The size of the glass ensures that the tea gets consumed while hot, and before you slurp your final sip, a new glass will arrive. If you find the tea a bit strong, especially on an empty stomach, request that it be *"açik,"* or "opened," so that the ratio of water to steeped tea is increased.

The coffee culture is a little less prevalent (notwithstanding the current siege by Starbucks, Gloria Jean's, and Kahve Dünyası), but no less steeped in tradition. Early clerics believed it to be an intoxicant and consequently had it banned. But the *kahvehane* (coffeehouse) refused to go away, and now the sharing of a cup of Turkish coffee is an excuse to prolong a discussion, plan, negotiate, or just plain relax. Turkish coffee is ground to a fine dust, boiled directly in the correct quantity of water, and served as is. Whether you wait for the grinds to settle or down the cup in one shot is entirely an individual choice, although if you leave the muddy residue at the bottom of the cup, you may be able to coax somebody to read your fortune.

There are two national drinks: raki and *ayran.* Raki is an alcoholic drink distilled from raisins and then redistilled with aniseed. Even when diluted with water, this "lion's milk" still packs a punch, so drink responsibly! Raki is enjoyed everywhere, but is particularly complementary to a meal of mezes.

A Punishment Worse Than the Crime?

In Turkey, tripe soup, called *işkembe çorbası,* or *korkoreç,* is a widely accepted remedy for a hangover.

Ayran is a refreshing beverage made by diluting yogurt with water. Westerners more accustomed to a sweet-tasting yogurt drink may at first be put off by the saltiness of *ayran,* but when mentally prepared, it's impossible to dismiss the advantages and pure enjoyment of this concoction. A few other typical drinks ebb and flow according to the season. **Sahlep** is a creamy cold-weather drink made by combining the starchy powder (called sahlep) derived from ground wild orchid tubers with hot milk, and sweetening with sugar and cinnamon. Unfortunately, the drink's popularity and the endangerment of wild orchids are not unrelated, and not surprisingly, the powder doesn't come cheap. So while you can grab a cup off of a street vendor, the drink will most likely have used cornstarch in place of the sahlep powder. Another winter favorite is **boza,** a thick fermented whip that uses bulgur as its base.

WHEN TO GO

Depending on whether the goal of your trip is beachfront leisure, explorations into antiquity, high-octane pursuits, or coordinating your vacation with the Tulip Festival or music festival performances in the Aspendos Theatre (in which case, see the Calendar of Events, below), the seasonal ebbs and flows of tourism follow some general patterns. If you're hoping to hit the village resorts and historical sites of the Mediterranean or Aegean on your summer vacation, know that half of Europe and Russia have the same idea.

Better to enjoy the "shoulder season" months of April, May, June, September, and October, when families are home, kids are in school, museum sites are less crowded and the Mediterranean sun reflected off the white stone of archaeological sites won't have you wilting. Winter is obviously not everyone's favorite time for travel, but certainly, there will be no lines and everything will be a lot less expensive.

For watersports enthusiasts (rafting, canoeing), the spring melt requires nothing but the most expert or at least courageous. For that matter, Cappadocia is a great destination for rafting in the spring as well as for the autumn colors, while hiking, biking, and camping around the coastal villages are great spring or fall diversions.

Cappadocia takes on an otherworldly wonderland aspect covered with a dusting of snow, but icy conditions may ruin a horseback-riding trek. Similarly, the hilltops of the Gallipoli Peninsula can get very wet and windy, so a pilgrimage to the battlegrounds—if not coinciding with Anzac Day—may be best planned for the summertime.

Times to avoid? I'm on the fence about Ramadan, when dining options become very limited by day and unapproachable by night. But with Ramadan comes a festival atmosphere that permeates the cities and villages. Your choice. Other limitations pertain more to challenges with travel planning than with inconvenience, namely, that it's near impossible to find a hotel room during a major Istanbul festival or a seat on an airplane during one of the religious holidays, or *bayrams*.

Weather

Turkey's Average Daytime Temperature (°F/°C)

	JAN	FEB	MAR	APR	MAY	JUNE	JULY	AUG	SEPT	OCT	NOV	DEC
ANTALYA												
TEMP. (°F)	50	50	55	61	68	76	82	82	77	69	59	52
TEMP. (°C)	10	10	13	16	20	24	28	28	25	21	15	11
IZMIR												
TEMP. (°F)	46	47	52	60	68	76	80	79	73	65	55	49
TEMP. (°C)	8	8	11	16	20	24	27	26	23	18	13	9
ISTANBUL												
TEMP. (°F)	42	42	46	54	62	70	74	74	69	61	52	46
TEMP. (°C)	6	6	8	12	17	21	23	23	21	16	11	8
ANKARA												
TEMP. (°F)	27	32	40	49	56	63	69	69	62	52	41	33
TEMP. (°C)	−3	0	4	9	13	17	21	21	17	11	5	1

Holidays

Most shops, official offices and museums are closed on January 1, April 23 (National Independence & Children's Day), May 19 (Youth & Sports Day), August 30 (Victory Day), and October 28 to 29 (Republic Day). These same establishments also

A restaurant PRIMER

The idiosyncrasies of a foreign culture can create some frustrating experiences, especially when they get in the way of eating. In Turkey, dining out in often boisterous groups has traditionally been the province of men, and a smoke-filled room that reeks of macho may not be the most relaxing prospect for a meal. A woman dining alone will often be whisked away to an upstairs "family salon," called the *aile salonu*, where—what else—families, and yes, even guys, can enjoy a night out in peace and quiet.

Restaurants are everywhere, and although the name *restoran* was a European import used for the best establishments, nowadays practically every type of place goes by that name. Cheap, simple, home-style meals can be had at a family-run place called a *lokanta*, where the food is often prepared in advance (*hazır yemek*) and presented in a steam table. The dining room is generally bare. A *meyhane* is a tavern full of those smokin' Turks I mentioned earlier, but in the major cities, these have become extremely popular places for a fun and

sophisticated night out. Decor in the *meyhane* is usually as stark as in the *lokanta*, but not necessarily. A *birahane* is basically a potentially unruly beer hall.

Now that you've picked the place, it's time to sit down and read the menu, right? Wrong. Not all restaurants automatically provide menus, instead offering whatever's seasonal or the specialty of the house. If you'd feel more comfortable with a menu, don't be shy about asking, and politely say, "*Menüyü var mı?*" Mezes (appetizers) are often brought over on a platter, and the protocol is to simply point at the ones you want. Don't feel pressured into accepting every plate the waiter offers (none of it is free) or into ordering a main dish; Turks often make a meal out of an array of mezes, accompanied by raki. When ordering fish, it's perfectly acceptable (nay, advisable) to have your selection weighed for cost; if the price is higher than you planned to pay, either choose a less expensive fish or ask the waiter if it's possible to buy only half.

generally close on the first day of religious holidays. During the 30 days of Ramadan, many shops and businesses close early, while many restaurants either close down completely or offer limited menus at lunchtime.

Calendar of Events

Listed here is a selection of events wacky, weird, or wonderful enough (or all three) to go out of your way for. It would be impossible to list all of the local or regional festivals—besides, this book doesn't attempt to list all of Turkey's tourist destinations. But once arrived, keep your ear to the ground for colorful happenings such as the traditional *mesir* festival in Manisa, the International Pamukkale Song Competition, the Hittite Festival in Çorum, the Rose Festival in Isparta, the Golden Pistachio Festival in Gaziantep, and the Javelin games in Konya. For more information on these localized festivities, contact the tourism office in the corresponding region.

Islam follows the lunar calendar, which is shorter than the Gregorian calendar by 11 days. The result is that Muslim religious holidays fall on different dates each year. The dates for religious holidays listed here are accurate for 2012 and 2013.

For an exhaustive list of events beyond those listed here, check http://events.frommers. com, where you'll find a searchable, up-to-the-minute roster of what's happening in cities all over the world.

JANUARY

Camel Wrestling Festival, Selçuk. Did you know that as the temperature drops, a camel's aggression level rises? This event, scheduled erratically in January or February, provides a natural, if not inhumane, tension release as much for the poor beasts as for the testosterone-heavy locals nervously betting against the odds. The camels' mouths are bound to prevent biting, and 14 rope bearers stand by in case the scene starts to get out of hand. The last one to remain standing or in the ring wins. Third Sunday in January. (www.selcuk.bel.tr).

MARCH

Ankara International Film Days. Ankara. Having completed 22 years of screenings, the Ankara Film Festival showcases features, shorts and documentary films from around the world (© **0312/468-7745;** www.film festankara.org.tr). Two weeks in mid-March.

Istanbul Shopping Festival. Istanbul. Inaugurated in 2011, this city-wide shopping extravaganza brings together street fairs, concerts, kids' activities, fashion shows, late shopping and most importantly: *discounts* (including tax-free purchases). Countless locations around town. www.istshopfest. com. June 9–29, 2012. See website for 2013 dates.

APRIL

International Istanbul Film Festival, Istanbul. This festival lasts 2 weeks, from the last Saturday of March to mid-April, offering movie buffs the rare opportunity to view Turkish movies with English subtitles. For schedules and tickets log on to www.iksv. org (© **0212/334-0700**). Early April.

Eastern Orthodox Easter Sunday. If Istanbul was the birthplace of Eastern Orthodox Christianity (simply known as Christianity, in the day), then the Greek Patriarchate of Istanbul represents the bull's-eye for observance of the holiest day in Christendom, Eastern style. Mass is celebrated annually, led by Ecumenical Patriarch Bartholomew I, with prayers and candlelight. (© **0212/531-9670;** www.ecupatriarchate.org).

Tulip Festival, Istanbul. The tulip, widely accepted as having been imported from Holland and cultivated by an appreciative Turkish 17th-century society, is celebrated annually in Istanbul.

National Sovereignty and Children's Day, Istanbul and Ankara. This day celebrates the anniversary of the first Grand National Assembly, which met in Ankara in 1920 and was later decreed by Atatürk as Children's Day. The day is marked by parades and processions by schoolchildren. Banks and public offices are closed. April 23.

MAY

Ephesus Festival of Culture and Art, Selçuk and Ephesus. The best part about this local festival is the use of the Great Theatre at Ephesus as a venue for some of the concerts and theatrical presentations. First week of May.

Fatih Festivities, Istanbul. This festival commemorates the conquest of Byzantium in 1453 by Sultan Fatih Mehmet with local celebrations. May 29.

JUNE

Aspendos Opera and Ballet Festival. Live performances in the spectacular (now open-air) Theatre of Aspendos, the best-preserved theater of antiquity. For information, call the Antalya State Opera and Ballet (✆ **0312/231-8515;** www.aspendosfestival. gov.tr). June to mid-September.

Antalya Sand Sculpture Exhibition. Several dozen sand-sculpture artists convene from more than 14 countries to create temporary fantasies in sand. The exhibition takes place at Sandland, located in Lara. For information, log on to www.larasandland. com. Early summer through September.

Kırkpınar Oil Wrestling Tournaments, Edirne (Sarayiçi) and in villages around the country. This revered national sport involves the fittest of Turkish youth and astonishing amounts of olive oil to prevent the opponent from getting a good grip. The event is usually accompanied by a colorful market and fair (www.kirkpinar.com). Late June or early July.

JULY

International Jazz Festival, Istanbul. Performances are held at various locations around the city. For schedules, dates, and tickets, contact the Istanbul Foundation for Culture & the Arts (✆ **0212/334-0700;** www.iksv.org).

AUGUST

Assumption of the Virgin Mary, Ephesus. A special Mass conducted by the archbishop of Izmir celebrates the Assumption at the house of Mary. August 15.

Zafer Bayramı (Victory Day). This national holiday commemorates the decisive victory over the invading Greek armies during the War of Independence in 1922. Parades run through the main streets, and if you go soon, you may still brush elbows with some surviving vets. August 30.

SEPTEMBER

Phaselis Festival, Phaselis. The pine-shaded harbors of ancient Phaselis set the stage for concerts of Turkish jazz, folk, and classical artists in the ancient theater. (www. phaselisfestival.com). Early September.

Şeker Bayramı (or Ramadan Bayramı). This is the 3-day celebration punctuating the end of Ramadan. Presents and sweets are given to the children (şeker means sugar in Turkish), and the Turkish-delight industry makes a killing. August 18 (evening) to August 21, 2012; August 7 (evening) to August 10, 2013.

OCTOBER

Akbank Jazz Festival. This 2-week-long festival brings the blues simultaneously to Istanbul, Ankara, and Izmir. Now in its 17th season, the festival hosts world-renowned performers in the cities' most atmospheric venues (✆ **0212/252-3500;** www.akbank sanat.com). Last 2 weeks in October.

Cumhuriyet Bayramı (Republic Day). This event celebrates the proclamation of the Republic of Turkey in 1923. Parades, public speeches, and fireworks displays are just a few of the organized events, but individual Turkish families do their own celebrating as well. October 29.

NOVEMBER

Anniversary of Atatürk's Death. Turkey comes to a grinding halt at exactly 9:05am, when the population pays its respects to the father and founder of the Republic. Rather than a moment of silence, the streets and waterways echo with the blare of car horns and foghorns. Atatürk-related activities are planned for the day, such as conferences, speeches, and exhibitions, in addition to a memorial concert at the Atatürk Cultural Center. November 10.

Kurban Bayramı. In the Koranic version of an old favorite, it was Abraham's son Ismael, not Isaac, who was spared the knife. Kurban Bayramı celebrates Abraham's willingness to sacrifice his son, with 4 days of feasting and a death sentence to an alarming number of sheep, the likes of which one only sees around Thanksgiving. In fact, the 4-day festival of sacrifice is the culmination of the Hajj (holy pilgrimage), and much of the meat is given to the poor. October 24 to October 28, 2012; October 14 to October 18, 2013.

Contemporary Istanbul Art Festival. The festival, now in its 7th year (in 2012), hosts individual artists, international and Turkey-based galleries, and collectors for 4 days in late November or early December (*(C* **0212/244-7171;** www.contemporary istanbul.com).

DECEMBER

Festival of St. Nicholas, Demre. Santa Claus actually lived on the Mediterranean,

as bishop of Myra in the 4th century. A festival and symposium are held at the Byzantine church that honors old St. Nick. Early December.

Mevlana Festival, Konya. Whirling Dervişes believe that spiritual union with God is achieved through the *sema,* a trance-inducing dancing rite. The mystical ballet is shared with the public during this December festival, providing a window into one of Turkey's most precious cultural treasures. Book your tickets early, either through a travel agent or by contacting the Mevlana Kültür Merkezi (*(C* **0332/352-8111;** www. mkm.gov.tr). The week leading up to December 17.

LAY OF THE LAND

Although Greece gets the credit for having sown the seeds of Western civilization, for the most part it did it (with a good bit of help, too) on what is now Turkish soil. In Turkey, not only do you bear witness to the ancient nomadic civilizations with minor credits in the Old and New Testaments, but you have the opportunity to experience the absurdly rich cultural and historical mosaic laid by the ancient, Greek, Persian, Selçuk, Byzantine, and Ottoman empires. Turkey is also the quintessential destination for sybarites: As an eastern Mediterranean country, it gives you the pearly sands of Iztuzu Beach, the turquoise waters of Lycia, the ski slopes of Uludağ, the thermal springs of Bursa and Çeşme, the gliterrati-ridden bays of Bodrum and a profound connection with history.

Turkey forms a natural bridge between two continents, occupying the westernmost point of Asia while attached to Europe by way of Thrace (the northwesterly region separated from the Asian continent by the Bosphorus Straits, the Sea of Marmara, and the Dardanelles). Turkey is surrounded by four seas: the Black Sea to the north separating Turkey from Russia, the Ukraine, and Romania; the Aegean to the west; the Mediterranean to the south; and the Sea of Marmara. European borders are shared with Bulgaria and Greece, with whom it still has maritime disputes; and in many resort towns along the Turkish coastline, you can skip a stone to the nearest Greek island. To the east and south, Turkey shares borders with Georgia, Armenia, Iran, Iraq, and Syria.

Persistent concerns about the political stability in the eastern and southeastern regions of Turkey, combined with a rudimentary tourist infrastructure, have discouraged all but the most intrepid tourists from venturing to these scenic and historically significant regions. For this reason, this guidebook does not include the regions of the southeast and east. (Editorial and space constraints require the exclusion of the Black Sea Coast as well.) Instead, this guidebook focuses on the bang-for-your-buck absolute musts for a first-time visit to Turkey's western half. Inevitably, the first time won't be your last.

Istanbul & Environs

Many people go to Istanbul expecting an Eastern, exotic, even forbidden city. While it's true that Istanbul is undeniably Asian in the way it operates, most visitors are surprised to find a familiar and infinitely inviting European metropolis. Home to three mighty empires and coveted by others for its strategic hold over access in and out of the Black Sea, Istanbul is truly the original *Jewel in the Crown*. The city itself has one foot in Europe and the other in Asia—the only place in the world where a ferry can transport you to a different continent every 15 minutes. The grandeur of the **Blue Mosque** and the **Hagia Sophia**, the opulence of **Dolmabahçe Palace,** the echo of intrigue behind the walls of **Topkapı,** and the soulful wail of the muezzin's call to prayer from one of the hundreds of graceful minarets all have the power to transport you to another era, an exotic culture, and another way of looking at the world.

But Istanbul, like any complex and important international city, is more than just the sum of its monuments. The outdoor tables of the **Kumkapı** district come to life with singing and dancing, fresh sea bass, and fried calamari, while craftsmanship and commerce vie for business almost everywhere you turn. The lush tea gardens of **Sultanahmet,** the gentrified **coffeehouses** of Galata, the dingy back-alley streets of **Eminönü** teeming with men and women in various layers of modern or Islamic dress, the crush of low-income weekenders lazing along the **Golden Horn,** and the bustle of the jewel-encrusted upper crust in the expensive and exclusive shops of **Nişantaşı**—all are genuine and undisputable facets of this complex city. Two months, let alone 2 days, would never be enough to discover it all.

Surrounded by water and served by multiple ferry and hydrofoil services, Istanbul can easily be a base for 1- or 2-day excursions to Bursa, Gallipoli, and Troy (see below), of even overnight flights to Cappadocia or Ephesus (unfortunately, leaving little time to visit the latter). Closer to home are the beach towns of the Black Sea and the popular getaways of the Princes' Islands.

Around The Sea Of Marmara & The North Aegean Coast

Any army with visions of presiding over Seraglio Point seems to have camped out in this region. Attached to the base of Mount Uludağ sits the city of **Bursa,** whose eminence as the first capital of the Ottoman Empire earned the city a host of **monumental tombs.** Seeing the final resting place of such a density of dead sultans is not the only reason to go there, however. Bursa is important for its Selçuk and early Ottoman architecture, and is famous for its natural **thermal springs;** no visit to the town would be complete without taking a dip in a hot mineral pool or mud bath.

A pilgrimage to the silent cliffs of the **Gallipoli Peninsula** is especially poignant for Australians and New Zealanders, who sent their boys off to one of the bloodiest campaigns of World War I. Here Turkish and Anzac (Australian and New Zealand Army Corps) units dug into trenches, exchanged cigarettes, and fought to the death. The charming fishing and port town of **Çanakkale** is primarily used as a base for excursions to Gallipoli, and fills up beyond capacity with beer-drinking backpackers from Down Under every year on April 25 for the multiple, day-long memorial services commemorating Anzac Day.

Troy is Troy. Everybody says it's disappointing but nobody ever passes it by. That's the dilemma—where else can you get this close to Homer's *Iliad,* to Agamemnon, to Achilles and to Warner Brothers own rendition of the Trojan Horse?

Principal Hellenistic center and later a thriving Roman province, **Pergamum** (also accepted as Pergamon in written documentation), enjoyed an era of prosperity that endured for almost 400 years. Just on the outskirts of modern-day **Bergama,** Pergamum boasts one of Turkey's finest archaeological sites in the **Acropolis,** with its **Temple of Athena,** the remnants of the **great library,** the **Altar of Zeus,** the spectacular hillside **theater,** and the **Agora.** The **Asklepion** was the world's first medical center, using groundbreaking techniques in healing such as bathing, dieting, exercise, and dream therapy. Down the road is the crumbling but impressive **Red Basilica,** originally a temple honoring Serapis (known in Egypt as Osiris), later to become a Byzantine church and one of the seven churches of Asia Minor mentioned by St. John in the Book of Revelation.

The Central & Southern Aegean Coasts

⬚**zmir,** the third largest city in Turkey and the most important port on the Aegean, is typically a stopover on the way in or out of the airport, or as a base for visits to Ephesus and Pamukkale. If you've planned a day in town, take a picturesque seaside walk along the **Kordon** in Alsancak or mill around **Konak Square** to see the ornate architecture of the **clock tower**—the symbol of ⬚zmir.

Only an hour away is the **Çeşme Peninsula,** site of expansive sandy beaches, scenic coves, historic ruins, and the many thermal springs from which it takes its name. The charming little seaside town of **Çeşme** is essentially the last sane stop before getting on the hedonistic highway of the Turquoise and Mediterranean coasts.

Kuşadası is the first in a long line of boisterous beach resort towns and a required stop on the cruise ship circuit because of its convenient proximity to Ephesus. Because there is nothing of significant historical value in Kuşadası, much of the local travel business is geared toward getting you out of town; and, the archaeological ruins of **Didyma, Miletus,** and **Priene** are an easy day trip away. If you do stick around, a few noteworthy beaches in and around town offer an array of watersports options as well as several enchanting tea gardens within the **castle** walls.

No trip to Turkey is complete without a firsthand look at the breathtaking **limestone travertines of Pamukkale,** restored to their original luster through the efforts of UNESCO. Although it is no longer possible to shed your footwear and stroll along the snow-white terraces, the sheer magnitude of this enormous calcium formation is astounding. The Romans seem to have always established cities near curative waters, and the remains of the city of **Hierapolis,** along with its baths, acropolis, and theater, are all located on-site.

The most important Roman center in the Asian Provinces and one of the best preserved antique civilizations in the world, **Ephesus** is the most frequented tourist destination in all of Anatolia. Visitors flock here for the **Library of Celsus,** the **Marble and Arcadian Ways,** and the **Great Theatre,** along with an impossible legacy left to the ancient city through centuries of Greek, Roman, and Byzantine daily life.

The town of **Selçuk** is usually snubbed by visitors to Ephesus, and the few who do stop in usually make a beeline for the archaeological findings in the **Ephesus Museum,** the **House of the Virgin Mary,** and the mysterious remains of the **Temple of Artemesion. St. John's Basilica,** built by Justinian in the 6th century in honor of John, who came to Ephesus in the company of the Virgin Mary, should be included on every faith tour to Turkey; the **Isabey Mosque,** exemplifying Muslim acceptance of the Christian and Jewish prophets, is also worth a visit. A side trip to the former Greek winemaking village of **Şirince** offers another view of typical Turkish life, and the nearby beaches of **Pamucak** are there for anyone going through beach withdrawals.

After 10 years of merciless tourism, the whitewashed hillside and unspoiled bays that make up **Bodrum** are still revered by the Turks as *the* place to vacation. It's the original disembarkation point for the romanticized *Mavi Yolculuk* or **Blue Voyage,** a watery retreat with no distractions but pine cliffs, still expanses of water, and endless days of blissful tranquillity.

Beyond the infamous and cutting-edge nightlife of Bodrum's center, Bodrum offers the ruins of the ancient **Mausoleum,** one of the Seven Wonders of the World (though now a sad shadow of its former self) and the **Underwater Archaeological Museum,** the only museum in the world of its kind and keeper of the oldest known shipwreck, dating to the 14th century B.C. The museum is housed in the **Castle of St. Peter,** a 15th-century fortress built by the Knights of St. John. The castle is perched above the twin bays of Bodrum, presenting breathtaking views from every vantage point. It is also here that the tours for daily and weekly boat excursions pick up momentum.

The Turquoise & Mediterranean Coasts

The Aegean meets the Mediterranean at the tip of the Datça Peninsula, the rugged and mountainous outpost west of Marmaris. The Blue Voyage continues in the craggy inlets and crystalline waters around **Datça, Hisarönü, Türünç, Içmeler,** and **Marmaris,** in short daylong versions or full weeklong *gulet* cruises (the traditional broad-beamed boat), departing from **Netsel Marina,** arguably the best marina in the eastern Mediterranean.

If you've skipped the Blue Voyage, be sure to at least plan a day trip along the **Dalyan River** to see the enigmatic **Lycian rock-cut tombs,** to walk along the protected beaches of **Iztuzu** where the loggerhead turtles lay their eggs, and to mingle with the goats in the ancient city of **Kaunos.**

Not just a turnaround port for cruises back to Marmaris, **Fethiye** and its surroundings make up one of the most enchanting spots on the Mediterranean. A stroll past the marina promenade reveals the ancient city of **Telmessos,** with its limestone **rock tombs,** its **amphitheater,** and the old city, characterized by narrow streets and squares lined with shops, coffeehouses, and restaurants. The surrounding area is also a paradise for nature lovers and athletes alike. An 8km (5-mile) drive through mountainous terrain brings you to **Ölüdeniz Beach,** set below the splendor of **Babadağ,** which provides paragliders with the perfect conditions for a wondrous flight. Down the beach are the pristine waters of the **blue lagoon** from which *Ölüdeniz* (Dead Sea) takes its name. A detour off the road between Ölüdeniz and Fethiye brings you to the abandoned Greek village of **Kayaköy,** a haunting reminder of the population exchange of 1923. The untouched **Butterfly Valley,** accessible only by boat, is a nature lover's dream, where during the months of April and May the bright red Tiger butterfly breaks free of its cocoon. **Saklıkent Gorge** is another wonder of natural design, with torrents of icy water carving an extraordinary path through the rock. The ancient historic sites along this part of the coast, including **Tlos, Xanthos, Letoon,** and **Patara,** which boasts an unbroken 13km (8-mile) sandy beach, are some of the richest and best preserved in the region.

Often mistaken for a fishing village, **Kalkan** is a glossy seaside village nestled at the foot of the Taurus Mountains. Nearby **Kaputaş Beach** is a breathtaking result of a gorge in the making, and the beaches of **Patara** are only 20 minutes away. When all of the tourists left for Kalkan, the charming fishing village of **Kaş** was left much the way it was before the tourists chewed it up and spit it out. The tourist infrastructure has remained, and you will find a quiet town dotted with a few **Lycian tombs,** a 6th-century-B.C. **amphitheater,** and lots of pleasant shopping. Kaş is also the departure point for active excursions like kayaking, mountain biking, diving, and canyoning, as well as the must-do day trip to the sunken city of **Kekova,** which makes stopovers at the ancient village of **Simena,** now a fishing village of some 300 inhabitants. The nearby town of **Demre** lies shoulder to shoulder with the ancient Lycian city of **Myra,** and it was here that the bishop of Myra left his legacy and came to be known as **St. Nicholas.** The ancient site of **Olympos,** with its "fire-breathing" **Chimaera,** lies halfway between Kaş and Antalya, and few take the time to follow the oleander-laden and winding road down from the highway to this waterfront outpost.

Eastward, beyond the rocky coves of Lycia, are the pearly sand beaches of Turkey's Turquoise Coast. **Antalya** is the Mediterranean coast's main port city, as well as Turkey's principal holiday resort. The citadel walls of the **Kaleiçi** district enclose a typically Ottoman residential neighborhood, providing a majestic backdrop to the marina below. Nearby are the ancient ruins of **Termessos,** easily visited as a day excursion from anywhere along the Gulf of Antalya.

Cappadocia & The Interior

Arriving into **Cappadocia** is as much like getting a part as an extra in *Lost in Space* as you can get. The phallic **"fairy chimneys"** were formed by thousands of years of rugged winds and rain, and in fact, the same type of erosion continues today. In **Üchisar, Göreme,** and **Ürgüp,** not only can you ogle the **rock caves** from afar, but you can actually sleep in one. In the valleys of Cappadocia, you can visit some of the hundreds of incredible **frescoed chapels** and **cave churches** from the Iconoclastic and Byzantine eras. The troglodyte cities of **Derinkuyu** and **Kaymaklı** present a sobering image of persecution, where Christians, along with their livestock, hid hundreds of feet below ground, and where a detour down a dark tunnel will teach you just how dark dark can really be.

Beyond the wonder of Cappadocia is the industrial town of **Kayseri,** holding particular interest for scholars of Selçuk art and architecture.

Ankara

The capital of Turkey since 1923 and the administrative center of the country, Ankara is nothing if not clean, modern, and efficient. Lacking in the kind of history that attracts visitors to Istanbul, Ankara merits at least a trip to **The Museum of Anatolian Civilizations,** one of the best museums of its kind, displaying a comprehensive collection of treasures from the beginning of the history of man as we know it. The **Atatürk Mausoleum** is Turkey's equivalent of the Kennedy Memorial, honoring a forward-thinking man without whom modern Turkey would now be a Greek colony. Left over from an earlier era are the **Column of Julian,** the **Temple of Augustus,** and the **Roman Baths.** A visit to the old **citadel** or dinner within the castle walls should be part of any itinerary in Ankara.

Ankara is also an excellent base for excursions to **Hattuşaş,** home to the great Hittite kingdom for more than a thousand years, and the nearby sanctuary of **Yazılıkaya.**

TOURS

Escorted General Interest Tours

Turkey is, essentially, one big open-air museum, and it would be difficult not to have a learning experience while traveling in such a historically rich country. Where better to begin than with **Smithsonian Journeys** (📞 877/338-8687; www.smithsonian journeys.org), billed as "the best in educational travel"? Tours include the "Ancient Worlds of Anatolia," "Legendary Turkey and the Turquoise Coast," an 11-day Black Sea excursion and a new Turkey-focused "Family Adventure," run in partnership with Thomson Family Adventures (📞 800/262-6255 or 617/864-4803; www.family adventures.com). All tours are led by leading scholars in Ancient Greece, and Classical and Byzantine Art.

For their Turkey trips, **Intrepid Travel** (📞 800/970-7299 in the U.S.; www. intrepidtravel.com; 📞 866/360-1151 in Canada; 📞 0800-781-1660 in the U.K.; 📞 1300-018-871 in Australia) manages to effectively combine authentic and active experiences with an optimal cultural overview.

In 1994, archaeologist and professor Peter Sommer (**Peter Sommer Travels;** www.petersommer.com; 📞 0 1600 888 220 in the U.K.) set out from Troy on foot to walk the 2,000-mile path taken by Alexander the Great. His 19-day tour, aptly named "In the Footsteps of Alexander the Great," retraces this trajectory and includes a short gulet cruise through some of the more scenic of the country's turquoise waters. He also runs separate boat trips that take in the Carian coastline or focus on gastronomy, as well as cultural trips in Istanbul, Cappadocia, and Ephesus.

Using a local travel agent can make anybody a bit skittish, but hopefully, a Frommer's recommendation will alleviate any hesitations you might have. Based in Cappadocia, **Argeus Tourism & Travel,** Istiklal Cad. 13 (📞 0384/341-4688; www. argeus.com.tr), specializes in group and private cultural tours anywhere in Turkey, as well as active vacations.

If you're planning a wedding, a honeymoon, or are just in the market for commitment-free romance, contact **Proper Travel's Travel Atelier** site (📞 0384/341-6520; www.travelatelier.com). In the interest of the owner's commitment to supporting environmental and cultural goods, Proper Travel plants two trees any time anyone books a full tour and dedicates the planting to the guests.

You can also rely on the high quality of planning assistance of **Turk Ekspres** (📞 0212/235-9500; www.turkekspres.com.tr), a full-service travel agency with bases in both Istanbul and Izmir. Turk Ekspres is also American Express Travel Services' partner in Turkey.

Based in Bodrum with offices in Izmir and Antalya, **Akustik Travel** (www.akustkc. tc) is another agent with expertise in travel throughout the country.

If it's one-off, painstakingly planned personal tours you're after, **Credo Tours** (📞 0212/254-8175; www.credo.com.tr), is the ticket. Credo's owner specializes in creating theme tours on request.

EXCURSIONS INTO EASTERN TURKEY For a few short years, eastern Turkey enjoyed an extended period of calm, allowing a window of opportunity for the truly intrepid traveler. Regrettably, violence in the form of targeted bombings of military and civilian sites has resumed. Still, if you're willing to throw caution to the wind (and I can make a case for that too), play it somewhat safe and go with a group.

I recommend **Argeus** (see above) and **Ramtur** (📞 **0232/425-2710;** www.
ramtur.com). Another somewhat more affordable outfitter experienced in the east is
Fez Travel (📞 **0212/516-9024;** www.feztravel.com), run by a group of Australians
who made a name for themselves with a hop-on-hop-off circuit of Turkey's hot spots.
Meanwhile, many tour operators based in Göreme, in Cappadocia, run overnight bus
tours to Mount Nemrut.

For more information on escorted general-interest tours, including questions to ask
before booking your trip, see **www.frommers.com/planning.**

Academic Trips & Language Classes

WORKSHOPS IN OTTOMAN ARTS   No visit to the epicenter of Ottoman arts
would be complete without trying your hand at the classic art of *ebru,* or paper marbling, calligraphy, or on a soulful *saz.* Seeking to promote Turkey's rich and vibrant
cultural goods, **Les Arts Turcs,** Incili Çavus Sok. 37, 3rd floor, Sultanahmet/Istan-
bul (📞 **0212/520-7743;** www.lesartsturcs.com), organizes private or group lessons
in all three and then some. Interested in Byzantine mosaic art? Check. Want to learn
how to apply a henna tattoo? Check. Willing to accept a dare to show off your belly
dancing prowess? You can do it all here. Les Arts Turcs also organizes private language
lessons. Some of their group workshops are organized in conjunction with the
Caferağa Medresesi, Caferiye Sokak Soğukkuyu Çıkmazı 1, Sultanahmet/Istanbul
(📞 **0212/528-0089;** www.caferagamedresesi.com), a project of the Turkish Cultural Foundation Service (www.tkhv.org). The restored medrese now serves as a
handicrafts center, offering multiday workshops in *ebru,* calligraphy, illumination,
miniature painting, jewelry, and decorative ornamentation of wood, fabric, or glass,
among others.

LANGUAGE CLASSES   While an increasing number of resources offer language
instruction in Turkish (and other languages) free on the Internet, there's no better
way to learn a language than through immersion. **Tömer** is the language school arm
of Ankara University (www.tomer.ankara.edu.tr), with locations in Istanbul, Ankara,
Bursa, Izmir, Antalya, Denizli, Samsun, and Trabzon. At **Dilmer,** at the language
center's Istanbul Taksim location (www.dilmer.com), you can choose among the
morning, afternoon, evening, or weekend modules, lasting either 4, 8, or 12 weeks.

Adventure & Wellness Trips

ACTIVE VACATIONS   The **Imaginative Traveller** (📞 **800/225-2380;** www.
imaginative-traveller.com), the U.K.'s leading adventure tour company, offers culturally rich, physically active vacations, many with families in mind. Not for the faint of
thigh, **Great Explorations** (📞 **800/242-1825;** www.great-explorations.com),
based in Canada, runs fairly hard-core combo cycling and Blue Cruise tours along the
coast from Bodrum, through Datça, to Dalyan, and along the coast to Kaş, Fethiye,
and Olympos on its way to Antalya. Check their website for details and departure
dates. **The Adventure Finder** (www.adventurefinder.com) is a near encyclopedic
compendium of adventure holidays on one website, directing you to affordable tours
operated by local agents.

In Turkey, **Argeus Tourism & Travel** (see above) is the most qualified local
company for organizing tailor-made hiking, biking and other active tours, with guides
that are both knowledgeable and enthusiastic. Argeus is also responsible for the tour
of turkey biking extravaganza. **Middle Earth Travel,** Gaferli Mahallesi, Cevizler
Sokak, Göreme (📞 **0384/271-2559;** www.middleearthtravel.com), targets the

hardiest of independent adventure travelers, with treks into the Kaçkar Mountains, an 8-day climb up Mount Ararat, a hike from ancient Heraklia to the Stylos monastery (in Muğla near Bodrum), and organized expeditions along the Lycian Way and St. Paul's Trail (see chapter 8).

It's probably just a matter of time before organized tours catch on to the growing number of long-distance, **cultural hiking routes.** Several are already way marked, allowing you to ramble independently along the route Evliya Çelebi took on his pilgrimage to Mecca, along the trails meandering through the remains of the Hittite kingdom, or the road Abraham was said to have taken to get to Jerusalem. For information on these and other routes, go to http://cultureroutesinturkey.com.

If a Mediterranean adventure is more your speed, **Bougainville Travel** (ℂ 0242/836-3737; www.bougainville-turkey.com) organizes sea kayaking, mountain biking, trekking, and canyoning excursions, paragliding adventures, boat tours and diving trips.

In the past few years, Turkey has caught **golfing fever,** and it seems that everybody with a hankering and disposable greens fees wants to get in on the act. Most courses are located in the province of Antalya, taking advantage of the mild Mediterranean winter months. For more information, consult chapter 8.

BOAT TRIPS (AKA THE BLUE VOYAGE) Any of the travel agents in this book (and those not included) can help you arrange a bareboat yacht or gulet, a captained vessel or a cabin charter. Meanwhile, dozens and dozens of yachting specialists and brokers make bareboat and gulet charters their business. Three of the more established marine specialists are **Aegean Yachting** (ℂ 0252/316-1517; www.aegean yacht.com), **Gino Group** (ℂ 0252/412-6486; www.ginogroup.com) and **Bodtur** (ℂ 0232/421-8002; www.bodtur.com), but there are plenty other heavy hitters ready and more than able to compete for your business. In Fethiye, **V-GO Tourism Travel Agency,** Fevzi Çakmak Caddesi (btw. the marina and the Yacht Club; ℂ 0252/612-2113; www.boatcruiseturkey.com), arranges 3-, 4-, and 7-day cruises departing from Fethiye or Olympos. Information (including rates) and pictures of their substantial fleet of broad-beamed gulets, ranging in age and level of luxury, can be viewed on their website. Also, some resort hotels have (access to) their own boats, allowing you a taste of the Blue Voyage without the hassle.

If you're on a limited budget, the cabin charter might be the way to go. (See p. 54.) for the lowdown on cabin charter pitfalls.) Most bareboat brokers also deal in gulet cabin charters, and any travel agent worth his salt will bend over backward to accommodate your cabin charter request.

You can go the extra nautical mile on a Blue Voyage by signing up with a reputable sailing school. **Gökova Yachting,** based in Netsel Marina in Marmaris (ℂ/fax 0252/413-1089; www.gokovasailing.com), is the only licensed international sailing school where students can advance through the five levels of sailing proficiency from beginner to racer. Yacht master Cumhur (Jim) Gökova presides over one of the newest fleets in the Mediterranean and also handles bookings directly. Tuition is 600€ per person per week and covers one proficiency level of instruction.

THERMALS & SPAS Perched atop geologically dynamic soil, Turkey has suffered the fury of earthquakes and volcanic eruptions for millennia. But that same dynamism has also blessed the country with a phenomenal reserve of geothermal resources. Combine these with the centuries-old *hamam* tradition, and place them both squarely in the present where health and wellness have become the new

ALL ABOUT THE BLUE VOYAGE

The *Mavi Yolculuk,* or "Blue Voyage," emerged in the late 1920s, when Cevat Şakir Kabaağaçlı, a dissident political writer whose "punishment" was exile in Bodrum, began cruising visiting friends around the idyllic Gulf of Gökova. Today tooling along the Turkish Mediterranean coastline is one of the highlights of any trip to Turkey, and in some cases, the only way to visit the small fishing villages and islands of the southwestern coast. But to do it right, you should plan in advance and know your options.

The traditional Turkish sea excursion is either by the traditional wooden broad-beamed gulet or sleek yacht cruiser. Hiring a **private yacht** without a crew (known in the lingo as bareboat charter) is a popular choice for those with sailing proficiency and a taste for independence and adventure. Captained yachts are also available as an option. But so are captained and crewed gulets, which typically accommodate 8 to 12 people (or more) and come equipped with many modern conveniences.

In addition to chartering the entire gulet, it is also possible to charter a cabin on an individual basis. This last option, however, is riddled with pitfalls, not the least of which can be safety concerns. Generally, the gulets used for individual cabin charters didn't make the first cut for that season, thanks to torn cushions, faded decks, clogged toilets, smelly cabins, and a boat that should have been sent out to pasture long ago. Many tour operators and yacht agents have responded by acquiring and chartering out their own gulets, so check at the time of booking to make sure you'll be on one of these more recent acquisitions. If your booking agent can't or won't give you specific information about the boat you'll be on, be prepared for the worst, and negotiate a discount in advance if the gulet you were promised gets substituted at the last minute.

The most popular gulet cruises depart from Marmaris and ply the waters to Fethiye and back, stopping at (conditions permitting) Cleopatra's Baths, Dalyan, Kaunos, Istuzu Beach, and Ölüdeniz. See if you can get your agent to book you an excursion out of Marmaris in the opposite direction (to

---

buzzwords, and you've got a recipe for a budding spa industry. Even if Istanbul is your only destination in Turkey, the *embarras de richesses* of deluxe hotel spas will keep your skin smooth, your muscles supple, and your head clear. (For more details, pick up a copy of *Frommer's Istanbul.*)

In the hot-springs-rich peninsula of **Çeşme** (see chapter 6, "The Central & Southern Aegean Coasts [Greater Izmir]"), a luxury thermal spa is now the rule rather than the exception. Two other traditional centers for thermal treatments are **Bursa** and **Pamukkale** (see chapter 6). Where thermal bubbly does not spring up, the deluxe hotels in Istanbul, and along the Aegean and Turquoise coastline provide a worthy consolation. See chapter 5 and chapter 8.

Food & Wine Trips

Only a true foodie can appreciate the rewards of planning a vacation with a special emphasis on the eating habits of a country. In Turkey, where much of the language and expressions refer back to the kitchen, there's no better way to get to the heart of this culture.

Datça), or start in Finike and loiter around Kekova Bay.

Weeklong gulet cruises commonly depart on Sunday mornings (boarding Sat nights) and last 1 week, although it's also possible to arrange minicruises departing from anywhere your heart desires. A typical weeklong Blue Voyage will run you anywhere from 350€ and up per person, with as much as 70% added on for a single supplement. Meals are usually included, but all drinks, even water, are extra (but available and reasonably priced onboard). Boats may come equipped with air-conditioning, but even on a private and comparatively luxurious boat, the generator, and thus the A/C, gets shut down at night.

Although most Turkish boat operators offer their services directly to the public, every travel agent (and his brother) has a friend in the boat business. The problem is wading through all of the brokerage options, especially when the ship's captain lists his boat with multiple agencies. The best way to ensure quality in booking your gulet or yacht cruise is to use one of the reputable local tour brokers that I recommend under "Boat Trips," above. Through long-standing relationships and extensive scrutiny of the boats, these brokers/tour operators can ensure a level of quality, as well as act as your agent in the event of unexpected developments. You will also have the added insurance of dealing with an outfitter working to protect you and your investment. Be an informed buyer and get a detailed description of the boat, keeping in mind that vessels need a complete renovation at least every 5 years. Also, decide whether a hose attachment to the sink faucet is sufficient as a shower or whether you require an enclosed stall. Finally, flush toilets (as opposed to the hand-pump type) are considered a luxury.

But look, the cabin charter is not all bad news. There's really no way to ruin a week of tooling around turquoise waters with a culturally and linguistically diverse passenger list. Hold your nose and just dive in.

The **Istanbul Culinary Institute,** Meşrutiyet Cad. 59, Tepebaşı (℃ **0212/251-2214;** www.istanbulculinary.com), offers professional and amateur programs, as well as short, 1-day crash courses in techniques (cutting, stocks, or sauces), Ottoman cuisine (meat dishes with fruit, for example), or in Turkish basics (rice, böreks, and mantıs). There are also monthly gastronomic walking tours, where groups of at least four people get a course in street food. **Turkish Flavours,** Vali Konak Cad. Uğur Apt. 14/3, Nişantası (℃ **0532/218-0653;** www.turkishflavours.com), takes this culinary concept into private homes in Istanbul, and on the road through private food-focused Istanbul day excursions and tailor-made itineraries into the heart of Anatolia. All tours get to the heart of the Turkish culture through market excursions, house cooking, and even wine tastings.

SUGGESTED TURKEY ITINERARIES

3

T his chapter gives you a rough outline of what you can reasonably see in 1 or 2 weeks in Turkey. Here I make all the tough decisions for you (except for one; you'll need to choose between Ephesus and Cappadocia). If the idea of letting someone else plan your entire trip takes the wind out of your sails (and I can't blame you), you still might peruse this chapter to see my recommendations for exactly how much you can see here in this amount of time.

THE BEST OF TURKEY IN 1 WEEK

Frankly, 1 week isn't enough time to explore very much of anything anywhere, let alone Istanbul, the seat of three former world empires. And that doesn't include the 2 days spent on international travel (assuming you had to cross an ocean to get here). Because all of Turkey's major sights are scattered to the four corners of the country—and getting from one to the next will involve either a flight, a long car or bus ride, or both—a scant 7 days will force you to make some hard choices, and you'll have to hustle at high speed during what traditionally should be "downtime." With 1 week, expect to have barely enough time to cover the basics of Istanbul and one other destination. Because boat captains now regularly offer 3- and 4-day "Blue Cruises," you just may be able to squeeze in one of Turkey's quintessential experiences.

Day 1: Arrive, Off and Running in Istanbul ★★★

Most transatlantic flights arrive in **Istanbul ★★★** in the late morning, so after you check in to your hotel and have a quick nap and a shower, it's time to head out. Spend the first afternoon getting acquainted with the old city of Sultanahmet, beginning with a good orientation point, the **Hippodrome ★** (p. 93). You might duck into a local **tea garden** for a bite to eat (avoid the touristy ones closest to the Hippodrome). Then go directly to the Sultanahmet Mosque, better known as the **Blue Mosque ★★★** (p. 91). Follow this up with a walk through the imposing **Hagia Sophia ★★★** (p. 88). Next stop is the ancient underground **Yerebatan Cistern ★★** (p. 109) across the street at Yerebatan Caddesi. If you haven't yet run out of daylight, scoot over to the **St. Savior in Chora** church ★★★ (p. 107) for some of the finest Byzantine mosaics anywhere—and plan to stay for dinner. (**Asitane** restaurant ★★★ is located in the Kariye Hotel adjacent to the museum; p. 133.)

Day 2: Topkapı Palace ★★★ and the Grand Bazaar ★★★

Begin day 2 fresher and better prepared for an exhausting morning poking around **Topkapı Palace** ★★★ (p. 97), and don't you dare skip out on the **Treasury** ★★★ (p. 99)—although if you're pressed for time or money, you can definitely skip the tour of the **Harem** ★★, which departs at regular intervals. Instead, head back to the first courtyard, where you'll find access to the **Istanbul Archaeology Museum** ★★ (p. 95). Few visitors take the time to visit this impressive collection of ancient and even famous artifacts (for example, the **Treaty of Kadesh,** signed by Pharaoh Ramses and the Hittite King), but I highly recommend this one and add that everyone I've ever sent here has thanked me for the tip. When you finally do exit the palace grounds, turn right immediately outside the main gate, out along the historically preserved **Soğukçeşme Sokağı,** (p. 66) a typical 19th-century Ottoman neighborhood draped in lavender and bougainvillea. Go down the hill and pick up the tram at the nearby Gülhane stop (you'll have to cross the main avenue to get the correct tram), and take it to the Beyazit stop near one of the entrances to the **Grand Bazaar** ★★★ (p. 92). If you ever get out of this shopping labyrinth, there's a sound-and-light show in **Sultanahmet Park** under the Blue Mosque on summer nights at 9pm (the language of the display rotates daily), after which you can grab dinner at one of the numerous rooftop restaurants mentioned in chapter 4.

Day 3: A Day on the Bosphorus, and an Ottoman Band

Set out early in the morning for a daylong cruise up the **Bosphorus** (p. 124), allowing yourself at least an hour to explore the **Egyptian Spice Bazaar** ★★★ (p. 145) and neighboring **Yeni Camii** (p. 117) before you board at the nearby ferry docks. If you're concerned about time, take a half-day guided sightseeing tour, which includes a stop at the Egyptian Bazaar, an informed description of the sights along the Asian and European shores, and a visit to **Rumeli Fortress** (p. 125), which wraps up around lunchtime. If you take the guided tour, spend the remainder of the afternoon walking the length of Istanbul's main artery, on **Istiklal Caddesi** (p. 145) and poking in and around the back streets of **Beyoğlu.** If possible, arrange this afternoon exploration around the 3pm performance of the mighty Ottoman **Mehter Band** ★★★ in the **Military Museum** ★★ up in Harbiye (walking distance from Taksim Square or a short taxi ride; p. 114). If you miss the 3pm English performance, the whole thing repeats in Turkish at 3:30pm. Then, if you allow yourself one unexpected itinerary stop in Istanbul, make it this: From the Military Museum, take a taxi up to the modern and trendy seaside village of **Ortaköy** (just above the Çırağan Palace), where you'll find restaurants, cafes, and sidewalk vendors under the Bosphorus bridge. Reward yourself with a relaxing dinner at one of the many places on the quay, or head back to Beyoğlu for a meal at one of the classic meyhanes (taverns) of the Balıkpazarı (fish bazaar).

For the rest of your week in Turkey, if you haven't decided to blow it all decompressing on Turkey's fabulous Mediterranean, you're faced with the big question: "Ephesus or Cappadocia?" I'm outlining a plan for both:

Plan A
Day 4: The Ancient Site of Ephesus ★★★

Take a domestic flight to Izmir, and using either Selçuk or Kuşadası as your base, spend the day visiting the archaeological site of Ephesus ★★★, the **Ephesus Museum** ★★★, the **Temple of Artemis** ★, St. **John's Basilica** ★★★, and the **House of the Virgin Mary** ★★★. If you have your own car, have dinner up in the village of **Şirince** ★★.

See the "Selçuk & Ephesus" section, beginning on p. 232, for all listings.

Day 5: Pamukkale's Travertine Terraces ★★

You'll need a whole day for a visit to **Pamukkale** ★★, which should include a visit to the **travertines** ★★ and the archaeological site of **Hierapolis** ★★, plus a dip in the effervescent **Sacred Pool** ★★★. If you've got your own wheels, stop along the way at the impressive ruins at **Aphrodisias** ★★ and **Laodicea** ★.

See the "Pamukkale, Hierapolis & Laodicea" section, beginning on p. 276, for all listings.

Day 6: Three Greek Sites

Dedicate the day to exploring the more neighboring ancient sites of **Priene** ★★, **Miletus** ★★, and **Didyma** ★★ (p. 248) on a leisurely drive down to **Bodrum** ★★★.

Day 7: Bodrum and Beyond

On your last day in Turkey, you'll have to decide whether you want to relax on a beach or maintain your holiday in the fast lane. Either way, you should schedule a visit to the **Underwater Archaeology Museum** ★★★, located in the conspicuous and imposing **St. Peter's Castle** ★★★. And although there's not much left of the supposedly wondrous **Mausoleum of Halicarnassus,** you'll have to do some impressive tap-dancing to explain to your friends why you didn't go. (It'll be quick, I promise.) Do both of these things early, to leave plenty of time to drive out to **Gümüşlük** ★★, the as-of-yet unspoiled waterside village and site of submerged ancient ruins. There's a tiny beach there, too, although better beaches are located all along the peninsula, particularly around Yalıkavak and Turgutreis. (If you prefer a beach closer to home, head over to the unpretentious beach at Ortakent, and cap it off with dinner at the Erenler Sofrası.

See the "Bodrum" section, beginning on p. 253, for all listings.
Or you might be tempted by the landscape of Cappadocia:

Plan B
Day 4: Cappadocia's Fairy Chimneys and Monastic Caves ★★★

Take an early domestic flight to **Cappadocia** ★★★. It's about an hour's drive into any of the towns in the region from Kayseri, a little less if your flight lands in Nevşehir. Rent a car and begin your visit in the lesser-visited rock-cut monastery of **Zelve Valley** ★, being careful not to slip during one of the more challenging cave climbs (climbing not obligatory). Depart Zelve, following signs for the **open-air museum of Göreme** ★★★, with its frescoed churches and fairy chimneys. Follow the road into the modern section of the village, and have a bite to eat at the Orient Restaurant. Spend some time in admiring the shops lining the main street, and then head out for a visit to the primitive rock city of **Orta-hisar ★★**. Climb up to the top of the fortress for a splendid panoramic view of the entire region, second only to a sunrise balloon ride, have a glass of wine in the impromptu cave cafe behind the castle, and then head back to your hotel for some old-fashioned Turkish conversation and a glass of tea.

See chapter 9 for all listings.

Day 5: Cappadocia's Underground Cities

Set out early in the morning for the **underground cities ★★★** of Kaymaklı and Derinkuyu, where you will work up an appetite ascending and descending hundreds of underground steps. Drive the short distance to Belisırma, one of the access points for entry into the **Ihlara Valley ★**. Before setting out on your hike, stop at one of the combination restaurant-and-camping sites for a rustic riverside lunch. After lunch, head over to the village of **Güzelyurt ★**, wander through the valley, and poke through the village's own underground city. Finish up with dinner in one of the suggested establishments beginning on p. 361.

See chapter 9 for all listings.

Day 6: Cappadocia: Land of Beautiful Horses

Experience the **valleys of Cappadocia ★★★** firsthand with a horseback-riding tour or a hike through the valleys. Have lunch at the Greek House in **Mustafapaşa** and spend the rest of the day tooling around the village and sur-rounding valley. Try to manage your time so that you're in **Avanos** by evening, leaving plenty of time to shop for ceramics before the 9pm showing of the **Whirling Dervişes** at the 12th-century **Sarıhan** caravansary.

See chapter 9 for all listings.

Day 7: Ankara: Pre- and Post-Republican

Take this day to drive to and visit **Ankara,** from where you can arrange to fly home via Istanbul. Begin your time in Ankara around the ancient **citadel ★**, starting with the remarkable **Museum of Anatolian Civilizations ★★★** (which also has a great gift shop). A few steps up the hill opposite the entrance to the fortress is the restored **Çengelhan,** the 16th-century caravansary now housing the **Rahmi Koç Science Museum.** Spend an hour wandering around the inside of the citadel, then head left outside the entrance you came in through, and work your way through the copper, antiques, and carpet shops on the steeply cobbled streets heading to the daily market on Çıkrıkçılar Caddesi. From the bottom of **Çıkrıkçılar Caddesi,** you will find yourself back in the heart of Ulus. From here, take a taxi to the Atatürk Mausoleum and Museum at **Anıtkabir ★★**. Once finished, have dinner at one of the restaurants off of Tünalı Hilmi, or, if you're staying around the citadel, in one of the traditional Turkish restaurants inside the ramparts.

See chapter 10 for all listings.

THE BEST OF TURKEY IN 2 WEEKS

Follow the suggestions for the 1-week itinerary for the first week. Then assess how much time and energy you want to put into travel and what your travel goals are. Outdoor activities, historic ruins, and extraordinary natural sites converge along **the coast between Antalya and Fethiye** which is where I recommend you spend the remainder of your stay. If you're arriving from "Plan B"

(Cappadocia), you can start your Turquoise Coastal Tour in Antalya (the drive takes about 5½ hr. from Cappadocia; you can also fly via Istanbul) and follow these suggestions, beginning with day 14 and working backward. Or fly into Dalaman, beginning at the top, in Fethiye. In either case, you'll lose a day, unfortunately, either at the airport or on the road.

Day 8: Fly & Drive to Fethiye

Assuming you have any time left over after your travels, spend the day wandering around the old city of **Fethiye,** shopping, eating, and taking a hamam break. Visit the **Roman theater** and the rock-cut **Lycian tombs** ★★ of ancient Telmessos. Have dinner at Meğri Restaurant in the center of the old town, and then have a drink at Türkü Evi, a characteristic Turkish pub.

See the "Fethiye & Ölüdeniz" section, beginning on p. 303, for listings.

Days 9 & 10: Blue Waters and Stunning Scenery

Take a few hours in the National Park area (**Ölüdeniz, or the Blue Lagoon** ★★★), where you can swim in the lagoon that graces the cover of every tourism brochure on Turkey's Mediterranean. From the waterfront of **Belcekız Beach** ★★★, hop on one of the few daily boat shuttles for the half-hour trip to **Butterfly Valley** ★★★, where you can either test out another beach or hike back toward the head of the gorge and the waterfalls. If you abhor crowds (and have a car or scooter), drive up past the ghost village of Kayaköy to the secluded and stunning **Gemiler Beach** ★★★. On the way back, stop off at **Kayaköy** ★★★ for a haunting sunset, and then grill your own wild boar in the garden restaurant of Cin Bal. On day 10, take the **"12-Island Tour"** ★★, a daylong minicruise to watery caves and breathtaking coves where you can swim ashore for a close-up view of abandoned ruins—or, if you've had enough of beautiful blue waters, take this opportunity to visit the 18km (11-mile) gorge of **Saklıkent** ★★.

See the "Fethiye & Ölüdeniz" section, beginning on p. 303, for listings.

Days 11, 12, 13 & 14: The Lovely Lycian Coast

Leave Fethiye early to allow time to explore the ruins of **Xanthos** ★★ and **Patara** ★★ (and perhaps spend a few hours on **Patara Beach** ★★ on your way east). There are a number of points along the coast that are worthy of a stopover; these are generally limited by the location of your hotel. I recommend an overnight in **Kaş** ★★, **Olympos** ★★, or, if you can hold out for a late arrival after a full day of exploration, Antalya ★. Places to stop along the way? There's **Kekova Bay** ★★★ (follow signs for Üçağız), where ancient Lycian tombs tumble into the sea. Take a boat taxi over to the idyllic village of **Kale** ★★ (ancient Simena) for a lunch of fresh fish with your feet dangling in the reeds, and a short walk up to the castle. Olympos is another one of my favorite destinations, located on the outskirts of the small beachfront village of **Çıralı** ★★. It's also a good starting place for a short walk along the **Lycian Way.** An afternoon picnic and stroll through ancient Roman ruins are even more delightful than imaginable at **Phaselis** ★★★, where a pine tree forest meets a particularly lovely trio of harbors. Finish up in Antalya ★★, either with some last-minute shopping in the meandering streets of historic **Kaleiçi,** in the **Antalya Museum** ★★★, at a moonlit performance by the State Opera and Ballet in the ancient Aspendos amphitheater, or curled up on a cushion at one of the choice beach clubs now lining the pebbled waterfront of **Konyaaltı** ★★★.

See chapter 8 for all listings.

ISTANBUL

Rarely will a visit to Turkey exclude the chaotic and glorious wonder that is Istanbul ★★★. Home to a layering of civilization upon civilization, of empire built upon empire, Istanbul is all of the praises one can imagine while being simultaneously the opposite: ancient and modern, western and Oriental, religious and secular, conservative and progressive, wondrous and ordinary, familiar and exotic. But there is one undeniable common denominator among all of these disparate and contradictory traits: Istanbul is growing more and more interesting by the day.

And now to the necessary clichés: As the only city on earth to straddle two continents and literally the city of civilization's desires, Istanbul is an enduring symbol of greatness. It has endured attempted or successful conquests down the historic dateline by Xerxes, Darius, Alexander the Great, the Romans, the Visigoths, the Huns, the Crusaders, the Arab raiders, and the Ottomans.

The parade of civilizations converges on the historic peninsula, also known as Old Stamboul or the Old City. It is the capital of empires and a religious center, the heart of the Greek Orthodox Church and, for centuries, the Islamic faith. Istanbul is the custodian of one of the world's most important cultural heritages and home to some of the world's most opulent displays of art, history, and wealth. A stroll through the neighborhoods that make up the historic peninsula will reveal the foundations of ancient Rome and Byzantium, with gilded mosaics like those in the Hagia Sophia and St. Savior in Chora or the more modest peristyle (open court with porticos) of the Great Palace. The Ottoman dynasty redirected the city's fortunes into the imperial majesty of undulating domes and commanding minarets, and the sumptuous mystique of Topkapı and Dolmabahçe palaces. Fatih Mehmet II was himself astounded at the beauty of the city he had finally conquered, and he as well as subsequent sultans fixated on replicating the symbolic splendor of the Hagia Sophia in what has become a panorama of monumental imperial mosques.

Across the Golden Horn is the modern heart of the city, heir to the future of the country, pulsating with all the electricity of a cutting-edge international metropolis. While the political capital of Ankara sits safely in the heartland, this part of Istanbul is Turkey's center for art, entertainment, music, cuisine, education, and yes, even international diplomacy. Meanwhile on the Asian side of the Bosphorus sprawl residential neighborhoods and commercial centers more reminiscent of Europe than the area's counterpart on the European side. Together, these and Istanbul's far-flung neighborhoods provide a home to 23 million-plus of the 74 million people living in Turkey, many of whom are modest village folk who've migrated to the big city out of economic need. Over pricey brunches, the residents of the more prosperous neighborhoods along the Bosphorus revile the poor wedged into the squalid back streets of Süleymaniye, Çarşamba, and Tarlabaşı, while the religious fundamentalists of the Fatih and Üsküdar neighborhoods stare out through their veils in disapproval.

A few years back, anticipating its reign as Cultural Capital of Europe in 2010, Istanbul undertook an unprecedented frenzy of modernization and renewal. The city's internal transport network has gone from a disjointed conglomerate of disconnected services to a coherent and efficient system in less than a decade. The ambitious Marmaray railway project, spanning the entire province of Istanbul and passing beneath Istanbul's storied waterways, is making steady progress. And you'll be hard-pressed to *avoid* wireless connectivity here.

Meanwhile, excavations are underway at Yenikapı, Sirkeci, and Üsküdar, a result of the work going on related to the transport project. Museums are investing in celebrity-level exhibits showcasing highlights of Turkey's heritage, while forgotten neighborhoods such as Süleymaniye, Balat, Çihangir, and Galata are being reclaimed, restored, and transformed into cutting-edge neighborhoods. It's enough to make a guidebook writer's head spin.

Juxtaposed against the unstoppable machine of progress is groundbreaking evidence of Istanbul's stature throughout the centuries. If you need proof that Istanbul is as momentous as Rome, as captivating as Paris, and—if you know where to go—as exotic as Bangkok, then you've picked up the right book.

As a complex society in transition, and a microcosm of the tug-of-war between East and West, Istanbul, like Turkey, is still a work in progress. Istanbul comprises a long list of polar opposites that creates an exotic, complex, and utterly monumental stew. It's enchanting, it's infuriating, and it's irresistible.

ORIENTATION

Getting There

BY PLANE

For information on arriving into Istanbul from the U.S. the U.K., Canada, Australia, and New Zealand, see "Getting There" in Chapter 12, "Planning Your Trip to Turkey."

Getting into Town from the Airport

The majority of international flights arrive to Istanbul's international airport, Atatürk Hava Limanı. Sabiha Gökçen Airport is primarily a hub for charter airlines as well as for an increasing number of domestic flights.

Most hotels in Istanbul offer free pickup at the Atatürk International Airport for stays of 3 nights or more. Check with your hotel to see if yours is one of them (be sure to confirm whether you will be arriving on an international or domestic flight!!!). Absent this little perk, hotels offer airport transfers for an additional fee of anywhere from 20€ to 65€ to Sultanahmet and 40€ to 110€ to Taksim. Because taxi fares into both the Old City and Taksim are still very affordable, I recommend this door-to-door option first over an official hotel transfer. A taxi into Sultanahmet from Atatürk Airport should cost around 30TL and a ride into Taksim around 36TL, depending on traffic.

From Sabiha Gökçen Airport, located 50km (31 miles) east of Taksim, you can either take a taxi (around 70TL with no traffic) or hop on the Havataş shuttle bus into town (see below).

Istanbul at a Glance

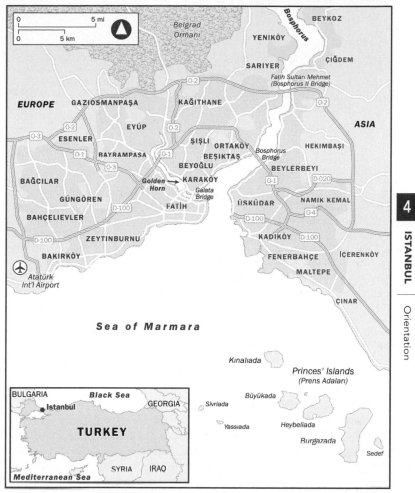

BY BUS Havataş (© 444-2656; www.havatas.com) replaced the old workhorse, Havaş as official shuttle to/from Istanbul's airports in January of 2012. If your destination from Atatürk Airport is around Taksim, Havataş buses depart every 30 minutes between 4am and 1am from just outside the international terminal airport exit and arrive in front of the THY office on Cumhuriyet Caddesi (10TL; trip time 40 min.). You could also take the cheaper, slower, and rarer green municipal **bus no. 97,** but because Havataş is so convenient, the public bus is not an option I recommend. Havataş also runs two shuttles from Sabiha Gökçen Airport, one to Taksim (travel time: 1.5 hr.) and one to Kadiköy (1 hr.), both departing every 30 minutes. The ride costs 12TL and 8TL respectively. Havataş also runs service between the Yenikapı docks and Atatürk Airport (8TL), and between Yanikapı and Taksim (5TL).

Many hotels are now offering free pickup at the airport from both Atatürk International and Sabiha Gökçen airports for multiple-night stays. Technically, this is against city regs (a tip of the hat to taxiists), but it's a great perk, when they show up. (If you get jilted, your hotel will most likely reimburse you for the cost of the taxi). You can play it safe by reserving a seat on the **Airport Shuttle** (www.istanbulairportshuttle. com) running on a regular timetable to both Atatürk and Sabiha Gökçen Airports. The one way fare is 5€ and 10€ respectively.

Havaş, the former holder of the tender providing shuttle service from both airports, may be back in the game as a competitor, so keep your eyes open at the airports (€ **444-0487** or 0212/465-4700; www.havas.net),

BY METRO/TRAMWAY   If you're on a budget and feeling like going the whole nine yards of independent travel, take advantage of the newly completed train connecting Atatürk Airport with the rest of the city (entrance is downstairs next to the international arrivals terminal). If you're headed to a hotel in the Old City, then exit the train at Zeytinburnu, then transfer aboveground to the tramway (stops include Beyazıt, Cağağoğlu, Sultanahmet, Gülhane, Sirkeci, Eminönü). The tramway continues all the way to Kabataş, with stops at Karaköy, Tophane, and Findikli; from the last stop, there's a funicular transporting passengers up one of Istanbul's steeper hills to Taksim Square. If you use the Istanbulkart, the whole trip will cost 1.75TL; otherwise it'll be 1.75TL per single ride *jeton*. The trip will take a little over an hour. Remember though, you'll be hot, tired, hungry, and luggage-laden for this convoluted, albeit convenient, journey.

For more information on taking and paying for public transportation, turn to p. 72.

BY TRAIN

See the chapter 12 for information on arriving into Istanbul by train. Routes can also be searched at www.bahn.de.

   Sirkeci Station (€ **0212/527-0050**) has been serving train passengers arriving (and departing) Istanbul from European cities for well over a century and has served as a model for railway stations throughout central Europe. A tram stop is immediately outside the station entrance, but don't rely on this if you're first arriving, as there is no ticket kiosk at this stop.

Visitor Information

In addition to offices at Atatürk Airport (domestic terminal; € **0212/663-0798**) and Sabiha Gökçen Airport (€ **0216/588-8794**) you may stumble upon an official tourist office (*Turizm Ofisi*) in one of the many tourist hubs around town. The location at the northeast corner of Sultanahmet Meydanı near Divanyolu (€ **0212/518-1802**) is pretty handy, as are the ones in the Hilton Hotel Arcade (€ **0212/233-0592**), in Taksim (Mete Caddesi 6; € **0212/468-4444**), in Beyazıt Meydanı (near the tramway exit outside of the Grand Bazaar; € **0212/522-4902**), in Sirkeci Gar (€ **0212/ 511-5888**) and at the Karaköy Seaport (€ **0212/249-5776**). If you're out and about and encounter trouble (pickpockets, scams, muggings), stop in to the passably

4

Orientation

ISTANBUL

multilingual **Tourism Police** at Yerebatan Cad. 6, in Sultanahmet (☎ **0212/527-4503** or 528-5369).

While wandering around the Old City (the municipality of Fatih), you may also encounter a teen in a blue shirt with huge letters spelling "ASK ME." These eager student volunteer ambassadors are there to help. Just ask! (For general requests and complaints call the Fatih Tourism Line at ☎ **0212/517-0202**).

City Layout

Istanbul is the only city in the world on two continents, split down the middle by the mighty Bosphorus Straits. To the east of the waterway is the **Asian side,** a predominantly residential retreat with little of the chaos of its European counterpart. The modern business district of Taksim and the historic peninsula of the Old City occupy the **European side** of the Bosphorus, separated by the picturesque **Golden Horn** estuary and connected by a number of bridges and by ferry. While the major sightseeing draw is over in the **Old City** (aka the **historic peninsula, Old Istanbul,** and the modern district of Fatih), you should plan to give at least equal time to the modern heart of Istanbul, essential in gaining a balanced picture of the many facets of the city.

HOW TO FIND AN ADDRESS Addresses in Turkey name the major thoroughfare followed by a logical walk-through of the smaller avenues until you get to the actual street address. Of course, in villages, where there are no major thoroughfares, you'll see a lot of the word *mahalle(si),* which means, roughly, neighborhood. For example, if you're trying to find the Hotel Avicenna, located at Mimar Mehmet Ağa Cad., Amiral Tafdil Sok. 31–33, Sultanahmet/Istanbul, isolate the Sultanahmet neighborhood on the map of Istanbul and look for Mimar Mehmet Ağa Caddesi, one of the main arteries. Next, look for a cross street by the name of Amiral Tafdil Sokağı, and you will find the hotel at numbers 31–33. (In this case, the hotel takes up two old Ottoman houses.) In many cases, there is another number after the street address following a slash (/), which specifies the floor on which a place is located—usually in the case of apartments, Internet cafes, offices, and other entities not located on the ground floor. Another handy word is *karşısı,* which means *across from,* as in *Isabey Camii karşısı Serin Sokak, Selçuk* (across from the Isabey Mosque on Serin St., in Selçuk). Where the less orientating *mahalle* is in operation, just ask.

In Istanbul, particularly on the repaved Istiklal Caddesi, there are two types of number plates for addresses: the old blue ones and the new red ones. For example, the address of an establishment may be listed as 51r or 33b.

Free maps are available at any tourist information office (until they run out). Also available for purchase in bookstores are maps with clear and easily identifiable main attractions, but the smaller streets are left nameless, if included at all. None of the maps mentioned above are 100% accurate, but you may not even notice because signs are posted everywhere for museums, hotels, and restaurants, and there will be plenty of people on the street offering to give you a hand. Asking directions is part of the local culture and a great way to get local tips.

Istanbul's Neighborhoods in Brief

Spread over two continents, the sprawling muddle that is Istanbul comprises nearly 100 square miles of history. The city of Istanbul is part of the province of Istanbul—think New York, New York—but seeing as how this is a city guide, we will mainly concern ourselves with the three central districts of **Beyoğlu, Beşiktaş,** and **Fatih,** plus throw in the highlights of the Bosphorus—both the European and Asian sides—because not to do so would be remiss.

The European and Asian sides of the city are bisected by the churning north-south artery that is the Bosphorus Straits. Strategic waterway and stuff of legends, the Bosphorus connects the nations of the Black Sea with the coveted trade routes of the Mediterranean.

The European side of Istanbul is itself separated by the estuary known in English as the Golden Horn and in Turkish as the Haliç. Bordering the south of the Golden Horn are the districts of Eminönü and Fatih, neatly enclosed by what remains of the Byzantine-era defensive walls. These two districts make up the historic peninsula (aka Old Stamboul, Old Istanbul, and Rome of the East). To the north of the Golden Horn are Beyoğlu and Beşiktaş, a hodgepodge of ancient and modern, of historic and progressive.

So as not to confuse readers with a short description of every corner of Istanbul, it's important to know that neighborhoods generally bear the name of a major landmark, such as the mosque that served the quarter, and that neighborhood delineations are anything but clear-cut. Below is a liberal selection of areas ranging from the "must see" to "off the beaten track," but this list is by no means exhaustive.

EUROPEAN SIDE: OLD ISTANBUL

The Historic Peninsula, home to the remnants of Classical, Roman, Byzantine, and Ottoman eras, sits in the modern-day district of **Fatih** (until 2008, this was actually the two districts of Fatih and Eminönü, now merged). The neighborhoods that live within the boundaries of the ancient city walls are oriented around the famed seven hills in a nearly 22 sq. km (8½ sq. miles) area. Eminönü refers to the neighborhood and transportation hub at the base of the Galata Bridge. This transport hub is where you'll find ferries to just about everywhere, a metropolitan bus and *dolmuş* hub, the Egyptian Spice Bazaar, the Yeni Valide Camii (New Queen Mother's Mosque), and Rustem Paşa Mosque, as well as a frenetic warren of passageways and back streets that wind their way uphill through local shops to the Grand Bazaar. Just steps to the east of Eminönü's transport hub is the Sirkeci train station (final stop of the legendary Orient Express), a bustling and utilitarian hub of people with places to go. As expected, it's easy to find comparatively affordable food and lodging around this neighborhood as opposed to the more popular and adjacent neighborhood of Sultanahmet. The easternmost tip of the peninsula known as **Sarayburnu** or Seraglio Point (literally, palace point) is where Topkapı Palace presides over the strategic convergence of the Marmara Sea, the mouth of the Bosphorus, and the Golden Horn. **Soğukçeşme Sokağı** is a cobbled mews of 12 wooden Ottoman houses and a roman cistern, all sandwiched between the outer wall of Topkapı Palace and the imposing backside of the Ayasofya. The buildings were restored in the 1970s by the Turkish Touring Club.

At the heart of the Old City is the neighborhood of **Sultanahmet,** centered around the Hippodrome—ancient racetrack, political arena, and present-day commons. Anchoring the historic center of the city are the Blue Mosque and the Hagia Sophia, two massive and magnificent edifices challenging each other from opposite ends of Sultanahmet Park. Bordering Sultanahmet to the southeast is the as-of-yet still characteristically residential quarter of **Cankurtaran,** named for the train station at Ahırkapi Gate where the commuter rail used to stop and for all intents and purposes, absorbed under the umbrella heading of Sultanahmet.

To the southwest of Sultanahmet along the Marmara Sea and along the ancient Sea Walls is **Kadırga Limanı,** named for the silted ancient port beneath, and now, as real estate around Sultanahmet continues to soar, a former fringe neighborhood undergoing a renaissance.

To the west of Kadırga Limanı is Kumkapı, destination of the daily catch by local fishermen, location of the city's fish market, and home to a dense cluster of touristy fish restaurants.

The Old City is divided by the main avenue of **Divanyolu** (whose name changes to Yeniçeriler Cad. and then Ordu Cad. as it runs westward from the Hagia Sophia to the Land Walls). Paving what was formerly the ceremonial entrance to the Great Palace, Divanyolu begins (or ends, if you were the emperor) at Sultanahmet Park, running westward through the neighborhoods of **Çemberlitaş,** former site of the Forum of Constantine and close to the Nuruosmaniye entrance to the Grand Bazaar; **Beyazıt,** built on the ruins of the Forum of Theodosius and named for the Beyazıt Mosque Complex; and **Laleli.** North and west of Beyazıt is the neighborhood of **Süleymaniye,** named after the mosque complex of the same name, itself bordered to the north and west by **Vefa,** a residential area of old Ottoman homes in various states of restoration or dilapidation.

Back at Divanyolu (now Ordu Cad.), the road splits just as it enters **Aksaray.** The tramway, which follows Divanyolu, continues along the southernmost avenue (Millet Cad., aka Türgüt Özal Cad.), while the northern fork becomes the major thoroughfare of Vatan Caddesi (aka Adnan Menderes Bulv.).

The district of **Fatih** (which before merging with Eminönü was confined to the area of the Old City between Atatürk Bulv. and the Land Walls), takes its name from the Fatih Mosque and complex, built by and for Mehmet the Conqueror immediately after the conquest. It was constructed on the site of the Havariyun, the second-most-revered Byzantine church after the Hagia Sophia, which was the victim of earthquakes and fire. The prominence of the district in both the Byzantine and Ottoman eras can be credited with the great number of monuments that dot this now bustling working-class conglomeration of diverse and authentic (and yes, some fundamentalist) neighborhoods.

From north to south beginning at the Golden Horn are the twin quarters of **Balat** and **Fener,** Ottoman-era enclaves where Armenian, Greek, and Jewish immigrants first settled. This combined quarter is thick with the crumbling remains of monumental Byzantine palaces, synagogues, schools, and mosques and is even the home of the Eastern Orthodox Patriarchate.

Several of the defunct Byzantine defensive gates continue to exert their influence on the surrounding neighborhoods that now bear these names: **Edirnekapı,** which is the gateway to the Church of St. Savior in Chora or Kariye Camii; and **Ayvansaray,** which sits at the base of the Old Galata Bridge near the remains of the Blachernae Palace and sections of the Land Walls. To the west of Adnan Menderes Bulvarı is the neighborhood of **Sulukule,** characterized by mismatched, crumbling, and colorfully painted houses. It's the oldest Roma settlement in the world, but sadly (and not without criticism), "urban transformation" projects are threatening the area's cultural heritage.

Fatih's southeastern-most point is the busy port of **Yenikapı,** departure point for seabuses to Bursa, the Marmara Islands, and the southern shores of the Marmara Sea. Yenikapı is the site of the construction of one of the metro stations for the in-progress Marmaray project, made famous for the extraordinary archaeological discoveries being made there.

Following the southern Marmara Sea shoreline is the **Sahil Yolu** (or the coastal road); this main thoroughfare connects the Old City with the airport and suburbs. The last neighborhood of interest as the road heads out of Fatih is **Yedikule** (literally, seven towers), the fortress constructed by Fatih Mehmet the Conqueror incorporating the earlier Theodosian land and sea walls. Almost no one goes to this neighborhood or museum, which is why you should go. Fewer and fewer places like this can be found in Istanbul these days.

While not within the district boundaries laid out above, I need to mention a few additional neighborhoods in the district of **Eyüp,** which straddles the northern banks of the Golden Horn. West of the estuary and north of Fatih (above Fener and Balat) is the quarter of **Eyüp Sultan,** named for the Prophet Mohammad's warrior companion and standard-bearer, and one of the holiest figures in Islam. Tradition holds that Eyüp Sultan was slain in battle on this hill, and the site, marked by a mosque complex and tomb, is now a point of pilgrimage for Muslims. To the east of the Golden Horn (and still Eyüp) are the industrialized sections of **Sütlüce** and **Hasköy** (to name only two). Although the eastern shores of the Golden Horn are mostly occupied with shipbuilding, some venues stand out, such as the Rahmi Koç Museum and the restored Silahtarağa Power Plant, housing the Santrallstanbul galleries.

EUROPEAN SIDE: BEYOĞLU, BEŞIKTAŞ & THE BOSPHORUS VILLAGES OF EUROPE AND ASIA

If the Old City is the jewel of Empires, then the landmass on the opposite side of the Golden Horn is its crown.

The fairly unwieldy district of **Beyoğlu,** which also straddles the centuries, is subdivided, at least colloquially, into a mosaic of characteristic quarters, with slightly more modern layers of historic, cultural, religious, and political reference than those on the other side of the Golden Horn. Beyoğlu is connected to the Old City by the Galata Bridge (at Eminönü and the opposite port of Karaköy) and via the Atatürk Bridge.

At the base of the Galata Bridge on the shore opposite Eminönü is **Karaköy,** a functionally messy and exhilarating transport hub worth a visit for its local eateries along with a number of significant monumental Ottoman constructions. Recent additions include the Istanbul Modern and collection of waterside warehouses-turned gallery spaces, as well as the leafy tea gardens and waterpipe cafes of **Tophane.** Istanbul's earliest (preclassical) settlements were found in and around **Galata,** today an increasingly fashionable hodgepodge of steeply sloping streets radiating from the Galata Tower. Where Karaköy and Galata merge, you'll find a wealth of architectural monuments left by the European communities that thrived here during the Ottoman period.

At the summit of Galata Hill is **Tünel,** which also refers to the very short and very old one-stop funicular called Tünel. To make matters worse, both the upper and lower entrances of the funicular are called Tünel; thus, to avoid confusion, I refer to the area around the upper entrance as **Upper Tünel** and the lower as **Lower Tünel,** or Karaköy.

Radiating around Upper Tünel (a part of Beyoğlu also referred to specifically as Beyoğlu) are the turn-of-the-century Belle Epoque buildings—including a high density of foreign consulates—of 19th-century **Pera.** Pera recalls a bygone era of wealth, entitlement, and gaiety. Today, strolls along the previous Grand Rue de Pera have evolved into a nightly crush of humanity walking up and down the same artery now known as Istiklal Caddesi.

Lining the slopes southeast of Istiklal Caddesi is the steep-stepped quarter of **Çihangir.** Alternating antique and artistic shops can be found on and around **Çukurcuma.** These combined neighborhoods attract artists, diplomats, expat journalists, and just plain commuters to its streets full of quirky cafes, restaurants, bars, and antique boutiques.

If Beyoğlu is the heart and soul of modern Istanbul, then **Istiklal Caddesi** is its lifeline. This hectic shopping street bisects the district north from Tünel to the modern, pulsating, chaotic nucleus of the city known as **Taksim Square,** Istanbul's equivalent to New York's Times Square. Standing at the center is a statue of Atatürk and the founding fathers of Turkey, representing on one side the War of Independence and on the other the Republic. The Atatürk Cultural Center (Atatürk Kültür Merkezi) serves as a venue for shows, opera, ballet, concerts and a sometime venue for the Biennale; the ugly old building (rather than being torn down, as was considered) is currently undergoing restoration. The area is yet another commuter hub, city commons, business center, and open-air food court. A concentration of full-service, high-rise hotels targeting businesspeople makes the area around Taksim a perfect place for bustle and convenience. The location is also connected to a transportation network that includes the metro, a recently restored cable car/tramway along Istiklal Caddesi, a plethora of municipal buses, and a daunting network of dolmuşes (minibuses).

As the city, even the country's, center, Taksim Square and the neighborhoods on its fringe are thickly dotted with nightclubs, seedy bars, and Internet cafes, attracting the indigents and pilferers of Istanbul. The pregentrified neighborhood of **Tarlabaşı,** located on the opposite side of Tarlabaşı Caddesi, is home to a high density of crumbling architectural gems, but it's also where you'll find Istanbul's subculture of transvestites, criminal indigents, and prostitutes, newly displaced from the now-hip neighborhood of Çukurcuma. Steer clear for now, but watch this space, as the Municipality (and real estate investors) have their sights eagerly set on this neighborhood.

The city gets increasingly more elite the farther north of Taksim you go, with trendy and upscale neighborhoods belonging to the district of **Şişli** then sprawling out to the business districts to the north (and east of the Bosphorus villages). Immediately to the north (and inland) of Taksim Square is the commercial area of **Harbiye,** which sidles up to the fashionable shopping neighborhood of **Nişantaşı** (this is technically in the district of Şişli, but never mind). Boutiques along **Teşvikiye Caddesi** and the smaller side streets are stocked with high-quality merchandise in elegant settings, with major names like Mudo, Emporio Armani, Vakko, and Beyman. Sandwiched between Teşvikiye, Harbiye, and the Bosphorus is **Maçka,** a neighborhood of business and meeting style hotels mostly feeding into the Lutfi Kırdar Convention Center.

Beşiktaş-the-district refers to the Bosphorus-front real estate above Beyoğlu, made popular by a long string of sultans, paşas, and empresses who constructed European-style palaces all along the historic Straits, including the Dolmabahçe, Yıldız, and Çırağan palaces. The better hotels (Les Ottomans, the Four Seasons, W., Radisson Blu) have also of late staked out their claim. Like the demoted (former district absorbed by Fatih) area of Eminönü, **Beşiktaş** is a port neighborhood bustling with shopping, living, and commuting.

To the north is the uptown village with the downtown feel—**Ortaköy,** which sits at the base of the Bosphorus Bridge.

The waterfront northward becomes a picturesque chain of fishing coves transformed into bourgeois residential neighborhoods teeming with cafes and fish restaurants as far north as the Black Sea mouth of the Bosphorus. These include **Ortaköy, Kuruçeşme, Aravutköy, Bebek, Rumeli Hisarı, Emirgan, Istinye, Tarabya, Sarıyer,** and **Rumeli Kavağı.** You can visit these by hopping on a local bus or sightsee from the bow of a Bosphorus ferry.

THE ASIAN SIDE

The Asian side of the Bosphorus is a sprawling collection of quiet and surprisingly Europeanized residential neighborhoods with varying degrees of historical and cultural interest. Next to private vehicles, municipal buses are the primary mode of transportation, making a casual and spontaneous jaunt over to the Asian side a less than efficient prospect. Because of the phenomenal views from the newer hotels (which also provide complimentary boat shuttle service to the European side), Asia might actually be a reasonable place to hang your hat, particularly if it's a wedding veil.

On the northernmost shore is **Anadolu Kavağı,** harboring, literally, the remains of a Genoese castle refortified numerous times under the Ottoman sultans.

The sleepy fishing village of **Kanlıca** is best known for its fabled yogurt, moreso than for its two major landmarks: the Iskender Paşa Mosque, built by Sinan in the 16th century and named after the then Governor of Baghdad, and the Ismail Ağa Coffee House, which now dishes out more yogurt than coffee that made it famous in 1871.

Just to the south is **Anadolu Hisarı,** the fortress built by Beyazıt I as a springboard for his siege on Istanbul. It took another 56 years for his son, Mehmet (the Conqueror), to breach the Byzantine defenses.

The tiny and enchanting village of Çengelköy owes much of its popularity to the thousand-year-old oak trees whose colossal limbs enfold themselves around the waterside cafes and restaurants clustered around the boat landing.

In the 17th century, **Beylerbeyi** was the location of choice for summer palaces for the elite. The crown jewel was naturally Beylerbeyi Sarayı, commanding the banks above the Bosphorus Bridge.

Where much of the Bosphorus villages of Istanbul's Asian side have developed to mirror Istanbul's decidedly European lifestyle, **Üsküdar,** with its numerous Ottoman-era mosques, fountains, *hamams, medreses,* and tombs, maintains a more traditional vibe.

The bustling portside center of **Kadıköy** is a popular choice for day-trippers drawn to the typical cobbled walkways lined with fishmongers, neighborhood *lokantas*, coffee shops, antique shops, and bookstores. On Tuesdays, the neighborhood pulls out all the stops with the very well attended Salı Pazarı ("Tuesday Bazaar").

GETTING AROUND

By Public Transportation

Transportation in Istanbul is like the Internet: It's anonymous, decentralized, and completely indispensable. Thankfully, it's come a long way since its earlier disjointed days and improvements are being advanced at a hearty pace. The system is composed of a network of buses, minibuses, funiculars, ferries, catamarans, subways, trains, trams, and trolley cars, and in spite of the significant and ongoing upgrades to the system, you may have to take one of each to get where you're going.

The full fare for a one-way ride, without a transfer, on the bus, tramway, historic trolley, funicular to Taksim, metro, and most of the commuter ferry crossings costs 1.75TL with the use of a *jeton* or token. Unless you purchase a transit pass (see "Transport Made Easy with a Transit Pass," below), you will have to pay the individual fare again each time you transfer lines or modes of transport. For the purpose of consistency, all prices for transportation are listed here at the pay-per-ride fare.

THE BUS   Metropolitan buses in Istanbul are frequent, comprehensive, economical, and easy—*if you know your way around*. While there is no bus map, the destination of an individual bus line is now clearly marked at the bus stop (usually your typical glass shelter with a metal bench). Plaques at the bus stop provide a list of the stops along the route. The bus's final destination is also indicated above the front windshield, with a selection of major stops listed on the side of the bus next to the entrance (admittedly, not much help if you aren't familiar with the basic layout of the city). You can also do some advance planning via the IETT website (www.iett.gov.tr), which has an interactive map and line-stop assistance. Still, always check with the driver before getting on to make sure the bus is going in the direction you need, and once boarded, frequently ask your neighbor when to get off. Some of the most useful major hubs are at Eminönü, Taksim, and Beşiktaş. Tickets are sold at the major hubs or on the bus—if your bus doesn't have a "cashier" on board, there's an informal system whereby you can pay the driver, who will in turn hand you his own

> **We'll Tell You Where to Go**
>
> Not sure how to get where you're going? The transport arm of the Istanbul municipality operates a great website, **www.iett.gov.tr**, where you can find all the routes for the whole range of transport options.

personal Akbil of Istanbulkart to use (this earns the driver about .10TL per cash-paying customer). Buses run, roughly, from 6 or 6:30am until around 11pm or midnight.

The city also recently instituted the Metrobus to ease travel between the European and Asian sides of the city. The Metrobus travels on a dedicated rail line, connecting Söğütlüçeşme (east of Kadıköy) on the Asian side with Avçilar (west of Atatürk Airport) via the very congested Bosphorus Bridge, cutting what could easily be a 2-hour ordeal in half. It's unlikely that you'll have a use for this service, though.

THE DOLMUŞ *Dolmuşes* are yellow minivans that operate like group taxis with set routes. A relatively informal system, *dolmuşes* run from early morning to early evening daily, including Sundays. A *dolmuş* will leave its terminus (marked with a blue "D") only when it fills up (the word *dolmuş* means "stuffed") and then pick up and drop off passengers along the route. The main *dolmuş* stands are located in Taksim (at Taksim Cad. and Tarlabaşı Cad., near the flower sellers), Sirkeci, and Aksaray, and connect to points all over the city. *Dolmuşes* are often more direct than metropolitan buses and cheaper than taxis, cutting down on time and leaving more money in your pocket. Look for a *dolmuş* with the name of your destination displayed in the window. When boarding, tell the driver your destination and ask how much it will be *(ne kadar?)*. For shorter distances, 3TL to 5TL should cover it. The driver will drop you off at your destination, but if you want to get off sooner, say *inecek var (in-eh-jek*; this is my stop) or *inmek istiyorum, lütfen,* the short version of "I want to get off," with a "please" stuck on the end.

THE TRAMWAY When the tram from Eminönü to Zeytinburnu was built and inaugurated in 1991, the planners had overlooked one very important detail: money collection. Passengers rode for free for 1 year while the system installed booths and printed tickets. The system has grown up quite a bit since then; the city recently extended the tramway from Eminönü all the way to Kabataş (just below Dolmabahçe Palace) and connected it with a new train line that runs from Aksaray north to the *otogar* before heading through Zeytinburnu to the airport. There's also an underground funicular that hoists passengers up the hill from Kabataş to Taksim in just 110 seconds. This collective service cuts trips between Taksim and Sultanahmet down to around 15 minutes (with transfers), while destinations in between (Eminönü, for the Egyptian Spice Bazaar; Çemberlitaş or Beyazıt for the Grand Bazaar; Tophane for the Istanbul Modern) are just a ride away. By the time you read this, the tramway will most likely be extended from Kabataş north along the Bosphorus; the plan is to add stations at Dolmabahçe, Beşiktaş, Şişli, and points north and northwest, all the way to Mahmutbey. Token *(jeton)* booths are located at the entrance to the turnstiles; Istanbulkarts can be purchased/refilled at selected stops, including Eminönü, and Taksim, as well as in any metro station. Hours of operation are from 6am until about midnight.

THE HISTORIC TROLLEY Just when you feel your feet are ready to fall off, you hear the jingle of the lifesaving streetcar, a "Nostalgic Trolley" that plies fresh tracks on newly laid cobblestones along Istiklal Caddesi. As with most public transportation options, you can pay with cash or with the Istanbulkart. The trolley runs daily from 7am to 11pm and makes three intermediary stops at Hüseyn Ağa Camii, at Galatasaray High School/Flower–Fish Market, and in Beyoğlu at Nutru Sokak (in front of the Türkiye Iş Merkezi).

THE FUNICULAR A city of steep hills, Istanbul is easier to tackle thanks to several funiculars. The subway known as Tünel connects the sea-level neighborhood of

TRANSPORT MADE easy WITH A TRANSIT PASS

The entire metropolitan transport system accepts *jetons* (tokens) or one of a number of transit passes currently available. If you rely entirely on the *jetons*, you'll be forced to insert one at every transfer point, whereas use of a transit card gets you discounts for transfers. Currently there are three types of transit cards: the Akbil, the Beşibiryerde and the Istanbulkart, all with a built-in discount of 10% off the full token (or *jeton*) fare, while transfers are .85ks. The Beşibiryerde ("five-in-one") is good for five rides. The newer credit-card-size **Istanbulkart** (designed to replace the Akbil, which is being phased out) operates via radio frequency and is rechargeable at vending/refilling machines located in all metro stations, at major bus and tramway hubs and at the ferry docks. Machines accept both Turkish Lira and major credit cards. The only problem? The machines currently operate in Turkish only (perhaps this will change by the time you read this.

Karaköy near the Galata Bridge with the Tünel neighborhood of Beyoğlu at the southern end of Istiklal Caddesi. Tünel trains run Monday through Saturday from 7am to 9pm and Sunday from 7:30am to 9pm.

A second funicular was completed in 2006, providing a much-needed lift to those down at the docks of Kabataş (near Dolmabahçe Palace) up the very steep hill to Taksim. Combine this with a transfer from the Tramway (from the Old City, for example), and you've made what could be a very long haul by taxi into a 20-minute snap. A third funicular connects the Golden Horn with the revered neighborhood of Eyüp and the Pier Loti Café.

THE METRO/UNDERGROUND   Istanbul's modern underground is growing at a fast clip, currently connecting the new Şişhane stop (located beneath Meşrutiyet Cad., just steps from Tünel), with (as of this writing) the Atatürk Oto Sanayı, passing through Taksim, Osmanbey (walking distance from Nişantaşı), Şişli/Meçidiyeköy (commercial center), Gayrettepe (even more commerce), Levent (guess what, business plus the Kanyon and Metrocity shopping malls), Sanayı and Maşlak, Turkey's equivalent of Wall Street. The metro is open from around 6:30am until midnight.

THE FERRY & SEABUS   With the 2010 privatization of Istanbul's Deniz Otobüsleri (IDO) fast ferry company, the slower, conventional passenger ferries were cut loose to form the separate, still state-owned and newly named **Şehir Hatları**. Şehir Hatları (© **444-1851** or 0212/313-8000; www.sehirhatlari.com.tr) runs Europe-Asia connections between Kadıköy and Beşiktaş, Eminönü, Kabataş and Karaköy; between Karaköy and Haydarpaşa; and between Eminönü and Üsküdar. There's also a scenic and useful Golden Horn line connecting Eyüp to Eminönü, with stops at Sütlüce, Ayvansaray, Hasköy, Fener and Kasıpaşa, plus service to the Princes Islands. Fares for the commuter ferries are 2TL full fare; 1.75TL with the Akbil; for the Princes Islands, the full fare is 4TL; 3TL with the Akbil.

Relatively new on the scene are the **Turyol** passenger ferries (www.turyol.com in Turkish only; © **0212/251-4421**), which branched out to include commuter lines to their tours up the Bosphorus (see below). Turyol's real value is that the company still runs ferries from Eminönü, making travel from the Old City to the Asian side pretty darned convenient. Tickets on one of their many commuter lines is 1.75TL.

SWIFT BOATED THROUGH THE symplegades

According to mythology, Jason and his trusted band of Argonauts had one more hurdle to overcome before claiming the Golden Fleece for their own. At one point in their journey, the Argonauts had been warned by the blind seer, Phineus, that at the mouth of the Symplegades, described as a boiling caldron of black waves, was a sea of clashing rocks threatening to crush all who dared to enter. Indeed, the currents of the Bosphorus are so unforgiving that many a tanker has been grounded on the banks of Istanbul's straits.

According to lore, the first to navigate the treacherous waterway successfully was Jason and his mythical Argonauts

(argo meaning "swift" in Greek) on their quest for the Golden Fleece. But Phineus's prophecy revealed how Jason and his crew could pass the smashing, grinding rocks called the Symplegades alive. Phineus told Jason to simply release a dove into the entrance to the straits and, as the rocks were reopening, to literally row for their lives. The Argonauts did as they were told, and with merely the loss of some dovetail feathers and the stern ornament, they managed to navigate the deathtrap alive. At that moment, the rocks froze in place and the Bosphorus was tamed forever (except for a few grounded oil tankers).

The faster **Istanbul Deniz Otobüsleri** (IDO; national toll-free line © **0212/444-4436;** www.ido.com.tr) seabuses also provide inner-city commuter transport, shuttling passengers between Yenikapı and Kadiköy; Bostanci and Kabataş; Bostanci and the Princes Islands; Kabataş and the Princes Islands; and running service from Pendik to Avcilar (via Kartal, Maltepe, Bostanci, Kabataş and Bakırköy) and up the Bosphorus. There is also a car ferry connecting Sirkeci and Harem. Sample fares are 7TL for a full price token and 4.75TL with the Akbil for the shorter points within Greater Istanbul.

By Car

With traffic getting denser and more aggravating on an hourly basis, having a car in Istanbul is the surest method for going nowhere. In the rare event that traffic moves smoothly, do you really think you know where you're going? Can you read signs in Turkish? Do you know what a "Çevreyolu" is? And once you get there, where are you going to park? If you do decide to disregard better judgment and good counsel (and increasingly efficient traffic-related enforcement), or if you're only planning to pick up the car and drive out, here's some basic information:

The major car-rental companies in Istanbul are **Avis** (www.avis.com), **Sixt** (www.e-sixt.com), **Hertz** (www.hertz.com), **National** (www.nationalcar.com), **Budget** (www.budget.com), and **Alamo** (www.alamo.com). All have desks at Atatürk International Airport, as well as at locations in town. Meanwhile, Hertz has a desk in the international terminal at Sabiha Gökçen Airport, while Avis has one in the domestic terminal. Check your national Avis website (www.avis.co.uk in the UK) for deals; at press time, the price for a manual transmission compact car *in Istanbul* was 85TL per day.

By Taxi

Taxis are plentiful in Istanbul and are more likely to hail you than vice versa. **Avoid taxis that congregate around the main tourist spots** such as Topkapı Palace, Hagia Sophia, and at the cruise ship landing in Karaköy—these are the ones adept at

TAKE A QUICK cruise

Several years ago, an industrious young entrepreneur set a crew of expert craftsmen to replicating a traditional sultan's imperial caïque, fake gild, velvet, and all. The result is a kitschy, and yes, delightfully touristy, front-row seat to the turning of the Ottoman centuries, sea spray and all. **Sultan Kayıkları ★★★ (✆ 0212/ 268-0299;** www.sultankayiklari.com) operates three excursions up the Bosphorus ranging from 1 to 4 hours, the latter allowing stops for quick visits into Küçüksu and Beylerbeyi (a visit to Dolmabahçe, can be front or backloaded to the cruise; admissions ticket included). Tickets for the Bosphorus tours range from 20€ to 50€; there's also a splendid 1-hour tour of the Golden Horn costing 20€. Reservations required; see website contact for departure locations and times.

Şehir Hatları also continues to operate the scenic **Bosphorus Cruise** that has been plying the Bosphorus since 1851. The ferry departs from Eminönü, making stops at Beşiktaş (near Dolmabahçe Palace and the Çırağan Palace) on its crisscross pattern up the channel to Kanlıca, Yeniköy, Sariyer, Rumeli Kavağı and Anadolu Kavağı (15TL one-way or 25TL round-trip; 90 min. each way).

The ferry from Eminönü departs daily, year-round at 10:35am, returning from its final stop at Anadolu Kavağı at 3pm. An additional 1:35pm departure operates from April to early November with a return departure at 5pm. There is also a **Short Circle Cruise,** a 2-hour tour departing daily from Eminönü at 2:30pm, with one stop 15 minutes later in Üsküdar. The shorter version of the original costs 10TL.

On Saturday nights between July 1 to mid-August, Şehir Hatları also operates a **Sunset Bosphorus Cruise** (20TL roundtrip) departing Bostancı and making stops in Moda, Eski Kadıköy, Eminönü, Üsküdar, Beşiktaş, Ortaköy, Çengelköy, Rumeli Kavağı and Anadolu Kavağı. The cruise departs at 6:10pm arriving at Anadolu Kavağı at 8:50; the return departure is at 10pm arriving Bostancı at 12:35am. (Confirm departure times for updates).

Turyol also runs a tour up the historic waterway, offering three tours. Two nonstop circle lines leave from Üsküdar and Kadıköy ports, while the third tour plies the Eminönü-Üsküdar-Eminönü route (I don't recommend the latter for the scenic cruise). The fare, depending on the route, is 10TL or 12TL.

performing a bait-and-switch with large bank notes or taking meandering routes. Better to have your hotel call a cab for you, the agreement being that the hotel will continue giving the taxi stand business only as long as the drivers remain aboveboard (granted, not a fool-proof system). Similarly, when out and about, pop into the nearest hotel and have the receptionist call a taxi for you. The starting rate for a taxi is 2.50TL plus 1.60TL per kilometer; a taxi from Sultanahmet to Taksim will cost between 12TL and 16TL, depending on traffic levels and actual distance.

[FastFACTS] ISTANBUL

American Express
Now that Garanti Bank manages American Express financial services in Turkey,

Amex is now widely accepted. **Türk Ekspres** is the official representative of Amex Travel Related Services

in Turkey, at Cumhuriyet Cad. 47/1, Third Floor, Taksim (✆ **0212/235-9500;** www.turkekspres.com.tr).

For customer assistance with your Amex travelers checks in Turkey call toll free ☎ **0800/4491-4820.** Amex also provides a toll-free number for their Global Assist service (☎ **01-715/ 343-7977).**

Babysitters Most of the larger hotels provide some type of child-care service for a fee, be it an on-site nanny or a babysitter referral.

Climate Istanbul has seen temperatures ranging from 0°F to 104°F (-18°C–40°C), with the more extreme temperatures (plus high humidity) occurring in July and August. Summer lasts roughly from mid-June to mid-September. The city sees a sloshy 27 inches of rain annually, mostly between October and March. In spite of the cold temperatures that sweep in from the Black Sea in winter, large accumulations of snowfall are a rarity, although light dustings do occur.

Consulates The **American Consulate** is located at Üç Şehitler Sokak 2, Istinye (http://istanbul.usconsulate. gov; ☎ **0212/335-9000).** The **British Consulate** is back in its original, pre-terrorist bombing location at Mesrutiyet Cad. 34, Tepebşı (Beyoğlu; www.fco.gov.uk; ☎ **0212/334-6400;** fax 0212/334-6401). The **Australian Consulate** is in the Süzer Plaza at Askerocağı Cad. 15, Elmadağ, Şişli (☎ **0212/243-1333;** www. dfat.gov.au).

Courier Services The post office (PTT) offers an express mail service (*acele posta servisi)*, although you may feel safer with old reliables such as DHL (☎ **0212/ 444-0040),** Federal Express (☎ **0212/444-0606),** TNT (☎ **444-0868)** or UPS (☎ **0212/444-0033).**

Dentist Istanbul seems to have developed its own dental tourism niche. The **Koç American Hospital** in Nişantaşı (☎ **0212/311-2000)** and the **International Hospital** in Yeşilyurt (☎ **0212/468-4444)** can provide emergency dental services in an English-speaking atmosphere. For a selected list of private practitioners, log onto http:// turkey.usembassy.gov/ docistanbul.html.

Emergencies Local emergency numbers are: fire ☎ **110,** police ☎ **155,** and ambulance ☎ **112.** Emergencies may also warrant a call to Medline (☎ **0212/444-1212,** 24 hr. a day), a private company equipped to deal with any medical crisis, including ambulance transfers (cost varies according to distance), lab tests, and home treatment. The **International Hospital** (see "Hospitals," below) also provides ambulance services; call ☎ **0212/468-4444.**

Hospitals For optimal local emergency care, put yourself in the hands of one of the reputed private hospital facilities: the new **Koç American Hospital,** Güzelbahçe Sok., Nişantaşı (☎ **0212/311-2000);** **Metropolitan Florence Nightingale Hospital,** Cemil Aslangüder Sok. 8, Gayrettepe (☎ **0212/288-3400);** the **International Hospital,** Istanbul Cad. 82, Yeşılköy (☎ **0212/468-4444);** the **German Hospital,** Sıraselviler Cad. 119, Taksim (☎ **0212/293-2150);** and the **Balat Jewish Hospital,** Hisarönü Cad. 46–48, Fatih (☎ **0212/491-0000)** are just a few of the establishments with reliable English-speaking staff. Don't forget that payment is required at the time of treatment.

Newspapers & Magazines For local and national information, the *Turkish Daily News* gives a basic rundown of the day's headlines. If you have access to the Internet, log onto the website of Today's Zaman, **www.todays zaman.com,** the bilingual website of the Turkish language national paper. For local listings, the *Guide Istanbul* and *Time Out Istanbul* contain essential listings for tourists. Both are available at newsstands; the former is provided free at some hotels. The website www.mymerhaba.com is a good resource for expats, by expats and locals.

Pharmacies Pharmacists in Turkey are qualified to provide some medical services beyond filling prescriptions, such as administering injections, bandaging minor injuries, and suggesting medication. Local pharmacies (called *eczane)* operate on a rotating schedule so that one is always open for emergencies; each pharmacy posts the schedule in the window, called Nöbetçi.

Restrooms Public restrooms (WC, or *tuvalet*) are located all around town, in addition to those in public buildings such as museums. "Toll money" in Istanbul costs 25kr or 50kr, which occasionally includes a bonus handful of toilet paper. Flushing the toilet paper can sometimes be hazardous to the plumbing; when this is the case, you will usually see a sign above the tank requesting that you dispose of it in the nearby wastebasket.

Taxes See the Fast Facts section of the Planning Chapter.

Websites The Guide Istanbul (**www.theguide istanbul.com**) is now online, providing an insider's guide to the best eating, drinking and events around town.

Wizard Istanbul (www. wizardistanbul.com) is an new online concierge resource with answers to any and all questions about Istanbul. It's a new initiative of the Ministry of Culture and Tourism aimed to put people like me out of a job. **www.byzantium1200.com**

is a research project that has compiled a near-comprehensive illustrated anthology of Byzantine sites in Istanbul as they were in the year 1200–a great companion to wandering around the Old City. Foodies looking for the city's hidden (often hole-in-the-wall) gems are catalogued on Istanbul Eats (**www.istanbuleats.com**), a blog by expat journalists also offering walking tours self-described as "eating binges" through the city's lesser-traveled streets. Also, refer to the Planning Chapter for additional resources.

ISTANBUL ATTRACTIONS

Istanbul is a city that has successfully incorporated a rich past into a promising future—no small feat considering the sheer magnitude of history buried under those cobblestone streets. Three of the greatest empires in Western history each claimed Istanbul as their capital; as a result, the city overflows with extraordinary sites all vying for equal time. Conveniently, all of the top sights are located on or immediately around Sultanahmet Park, but that by no means is an indication that there's nothing worth seeing outside of that neighborhood.

Suggested Istanbul Itineraries

IF YOU HAVE 1 DAY Stick to the Sultanahmet district; begin your tour chronologically at the Hippodrome, and work your way through the centuries with a visit to the Hagia Sophia, the Yerebatan Cistern, and the Blue Mosque. Spend the afternoon exploring the treasures of Topkapı Palace (start from the last courtyard, so you can have lunch at Konyalı right away, and don't blow off the Istanbul Archaeology Museum, although you will want to). If there's any time left, make a beeline to the Grand Bazaar, where you'll have but a few short hours to hone your bargaining

The Museum Pass Istanbul

The 72TL museum pass gets you entrance into the Hagia Sophia, Topkapı Palace (including the harem), St. Savior in Chora, the Istanbul Archaeological Museums, the Museum of Turkish and Islamic Arts and the Mosaic Museum, for a total savings of 26TL. But the savings are potentially higher, as the pass

gets you discounts to a number of other museums and even gift shops. The only catch is that the pass is only good for 72 hours, beginning with activation at the first museum visited. For more information and sales points, log on to www. muze.gov.tr.

If the idea of relying on Istanbul's transportation grid leaves your head spinning and the prospect of mortgaging your home to cover taxi fares leaves you cold, then consider leaving the planning and the driving to the driver of a hop-on, hop-off sightseeing tour. **City Windows Travel** (www.citywindows.com.tr; ✆ **0212/283-1396**) lets you choose among three routes with six to eight hop off options, getting you to "two continents, one bus." Tickets are sold on buses and at kiosks at the Hagia Sophia, Topkapı Palace, the Hippodrome, Sultanahmet Park, and Taksim Square. The price for a ticket is 19.90€ per person for any 24-hour period (29.90€ for 48 hr.; kids under 12 pay discounted rates while those under 4 ride for free). Visit the website or download the free iPhone app to help you navigate their schedule.

prowess. After the Grand Bazaar closes, head over to the nearby Süleymaniye *hamam*, which stays open until midnight. After you've been peeled and pressed, have dinner at Develi or Asitane, or get really ambitious and head up to the Bosphorus, then call it a day well spent. *Note:* The Grand Bazaar is closed on Sundays, while most of the museums listed here are closed on Mondays.

IF YOU HAVE 2 DAYS   Spend the first day following the 1-day itinerary. On day 2, start at St. Savior in Chora museum. Then from there, either (1) head up to Pierre Loti for a rest stop of coffee or tea overlooking the storied Golden Horn, and then wander through the Ottoman cemetery and Eyüp, or (2) stroll through the as-of-yet ungentrified (but not for long) neighborhoods of Fener and Balat, densely dotted with Byzantine churches and buildings, synagogues, and the Greek Patriarchate. In the afternoon, find your way (by bus or taxi) to the streets in and behind the Egyptian Spice Bazaar, then walk across the Galata Bridge, and meander around the streets up to the Galata Tower. If your feet are still hanging on, continue up along Galip Dede Caddesi and the Istiklal Caddesi, stopping to take in the Çiçek Pasajı, the Balıkpazarı, the Avrupa Pasajı, and Fransiz Sokağı. Continue up Istiklal Caddesi to Taksim (or take the nostalgic trolley), and treat yourself to dinner at one of the recommended restaurants in this chapter, or combine dinner with some live Turkish music at one of the authentic "Turkish Houses" on Hasnun Galıp Sokak.

IF YOU HAVE 3 DAYS   Follow the 2-day itinerary for days 1 and 2, and then set out early on day 3 for a daylong cruise up the Bosphorus. If you're concerned about time, take a half-day guided sightseeing tour, which wraps up around lunchtime (they usually include a stop at the Egyptian Spice Bazaar, an informed description of the sights along the Asian and European shores, and a visit to Rumeli Fortress), or hop on the 1½-hour quickie ride up the Bosphorus in the kitschy Sultan's Kayıkları. If you've opted for the do-it-yourself Bosphorus cruise, disembark at Çengelköy on the Asian side, have lunch at the ferry landing (or at Kordon, in the Sumahan Hotel ✆ **0216/321-0473,** or at the adjacent Del Mare ✆ **0216/422-5762**), and then take a ferry back to Kabataş docks. From there, either take the underground funicular up to Taksim and work your way up to the Military Museum in time for the 3pm performance of the Mehter Band (trust me on this one, just GO. If you're running late, there's a repeat of the performance at 3:30 with narration in Turkish, which is beside the point), or grab a cab. After the show, take some time to visit the Military Museum (you'll have to backtrack, as the amphitheater for the Mehter Band showing

Istanbul Attractions

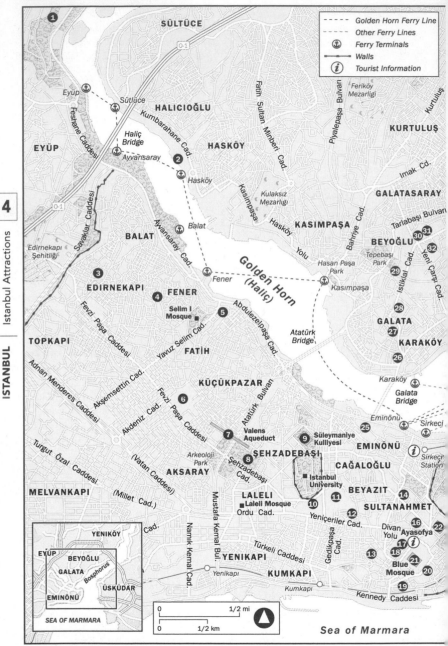

4 | ISTANBUL | Istanbul Attractions

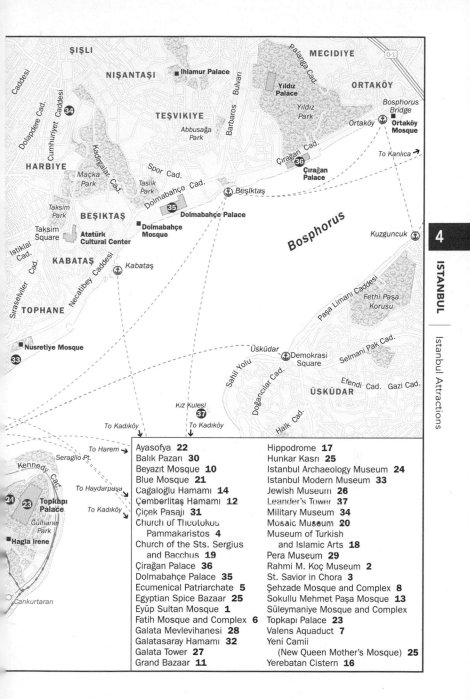

Ayasofya **22**
Balık Pazarı **30**
Beyazıt Mosque **10**
Blue Mosque **21**
Cağaloğlu Hamamı **14**
Çemberlitaş Hamamı **12**
Çiçek Pasajı **31**
Church of Theotokos
   Pammakaristos **4**
Church of the Sts. Sergius
   and Bacchus **19**
Çırağan Palace **36**
Dolmabahçe Palace **35**
Ecumenical Patriarchate **5**
Egyptian Spice Bazaar **25**
Eyüp Sultan Mosque **1**
Fatih Mosque and Complex **6**
Galata Mevlevihanesi **28**
Galatasaray Hamamı **32**
Galata Tower **27**
Grand Bazaar **11**

Hippodrome **17**
Hunkar Kasrı **25**
Istanbul Archaeology Museum **24**
Istanbul Modern Museum **33**
Jewish Museum **26**
Leander's Tower **37**
Military Museum **34**
Mosaic Museum **20**
Museum of Turkish
   and Islamic Arts **18**
Pera Museum **29**
Rahmi M. Koç Museum **2**
St. Savior in Chora **3**
Şehzade Mosque and Complex **8**
Sokullu Mehmet Paşa Mosque **13**
Süleymaniye Mosque and Complex
Topkapı Palace **23**
Valens Aquaduct **7**
Yeni Camii
   (New Queen Mother's Mosque) **25**
Yerebatan Cistern **16**

A visit to the heart of the Ottoman Empire will be richer accompanied by someone who knows his way around. But if you don't have your own tour guide, snap up the Audio Guide available in the museum. It costs an easy 10TL, and comes with a free map.

is located toward the end of the exhibits). From the entrance/exit to the museum, it's but a short walk to the tony neighborhood of Nişantaşı, with a nice selection of excellent restaurants and plenty of shops to keep you occupied.

Istanbul Walks

WALKING TOUR 1: GALATA

START:	**(Upper) Tünel Meydanı**
FINISH:	**(Lower) Tünel Entrance**
TIME:	**90 minutes (about 2km; about 1½ miles)**
BEST TIME:	**Any time in full daylight. To bask in the flurry of humanity, approach this tour during morning or evening rush hour. For those wishing to combine the tour with the performance of the Whirling Dervişes at the Galata Mevlevihanesi, you'll have to start the tour at the end and work your way backward, in order to enjoy this walk in full daylight. Although it's pretty safe, you don't really want to be wandering around here at night.**
WORST TIME:	**Any day that it's raining (streets are slippery). Sunday will see Bankalar Sokağı (Voyvoda Caddesi) completely deserted.**

A stroll through Galata will take you through one of Istanbul's historically most diverse neighborhoods. This hilly section was once the commercial hub of the Ottoman Empire, thanks to communities of enterprising immigrants from Europe and Armenia who had been granted permission to conduct business here in the 13th century. Although this neighborhood suffered decline and neglect throughout the 20th century, today it is enjoying a revitalization, as sidewalk cafes, art galleries, and small shops pull ever more foot traffic up and down these nostalgic streets.

1 Metro Han

Our tour begins at the entrance to the world's third-oldest underground train (construction was completed in 1876; only New York's and London's are older). It's actually an underground funicular connecting "Upper Tünel" to the streets at the base of this steeply sloped hill surrounding "Lower Tünel." Locals just call them both Tünel, and you're left to work out which one they mean. With only one stop, this is the world's shortest line, facilitating the commute for more than a century's worth of daily commuters forced to haul themselves up and down the hill you are about to descend on foot.

Opposite the entrance to Tünel on the other side of the tramway tracks is the entrance to the **Tünel Pasajı,** a neoclassical-style arcade enclosed by three separate buildings. The passageway is one of the more atmospheric spots in Beyoğlu, even if the rare book and antiques dealers have ceded to the trendier (and higher grossing) cafes. With your back to Tünel (funicular), go right onto the continuation of Istiklal Cad., now named:

2 Galip Dede Caddesi

At one time, this street, which goes by its original name of **Yüksek Kaldırım** south of the Galata Tower, wound its way down the slopes of Galata all the way to the Golden Horn. Yüksek Kaldırım, meaning "High Sidewalk," was originally the main bustling thoroughfare of neighborhood Greeks, Armenians, French, Jewish, and Ottoman merchants and a thriving center for publishing and book-sellers. The street is (steeply) sloped rather than stepped as it was a hundred years ago—the characteristic cobblestones have been replaced with modern, evenly surfaced bricks, and hardware vendors are being replaced by smarter shops and boutiques. Yet the essential nostalgia of the street can still be felt through the soul of now-soot-filled buildings standing vigil over a new guard of preoccupied pedestrians. **Librairie de Pera,** one of the oldest booksellers in Istanbul, is located at #22.

A few steps down Galip Dede Cad. on your left is the entrance to the 500-year-old:

3 Galata Mevlevihanesi

This was the first and most important derviş lodge in Istanbul. If you time your walking tour right, you can immerse yourself in the ritual *sema,* performed by dervishes in the extremely atmospheric octagonal wooden *semahane,* modestly embellished with calligraphy and exhibiting musical instruments, manuscripts, and other items related to the Mevlevi Order. For more on the lodge, turn to p. 114.

Continue down Galip Dede Cad. to the junction of Yüksek Kaldırım, and an open plaza.

4 Galata Meydanı

Galıp Dede Caddesi spills out into the mouth of a small open plaza crowned by the medieval **Galata Tower** and encircled by an almost traffic-free street. The plaza is a brick and concrete living room to the neighborhood, where young boys kick around a football, old men contemplate life while seated on a park bench, stray dogs laze, and locals relax at the tea garden down the shaded steps to the left of the tower.

The origins of Galata Tower date back to the 5th or 6th century A.D., but the tower that stands today is a 14th-century reconstruction by the Genoese, built in appreciation of Michael VIII Palaeologus, who granted special permission to allow them to settle the area of Galata. One condition of the agreement was that the Genoese were prohibited from putting up any defensive walls, a ban they unceremoniously ignored. A short set of partial wraparound steps provide access to the elevator to the top of the tower; admission costs 11TL, but frankly, the city is so full of vantage points for stunning views that this one isn't a must-see.

Keeping the Anemon Galata Hotel on your left, follow Büyük Hendek Cad. until you approach, on your left:

5 The Neve Shalom Synagogue

Greater Istanbul is home to a total of 17 synagogues, many of them open to visitors willing to jump through advance notice security hoops, and Neve Shalom is no exception. To visit, you will have to call in advance and fax over a copy of your passport. Built on the former site of a primary school in the late 1930's to accommodate a growing Jewish population of Jews, Neve Shalom's claim to "fame" are three terrorist bombings, on September 6, 1986, March 1, 1992, and November 15, 2003, the latter attack coordinated with attacks on another synagogue, and 5 days later, on the British Consulate and the HSBC Bank. Of the 27 people killed in the attack all but six were congregants. Al Qaeda claimed responsibility soon after the bombings.

Backtrack to the Galata tower and through the plaza and continue straight into the little alley-like Camekan Sok., a characteristic cobbled lane flanked by one or two pre-gentrified bars. Follow Camekan Sok. around to the right and down the sloping street to the next intersection with Bereketzade Camii and Hacı Ali Soks.

6 Beyoğlu Hospital

Founded during the Crimean War by the British Government to care for British seamen, this building was constructed in 1904 and designed by Percy Adams (the architect credited with the design of the Senate House at the University of London). The tower provided a clear sightline to incoming ships, allowing for hospital staff to get advance warning of any major illnesses on board. In 1924, just after the establishment of the Turkish Republic, the British handed the hospital over to the Red Crescent.

You are now following Hacı Ali Sok. around and down yet another one of Galata's treacherous inclines. About 76m (250 ft.), about ¾ of the way down the street and at the top of the brick staircase is a white building with red trim:

7 The Camondo House

As a prominent 19th-century Jewish Galata banker, as well as a banker to the Ottoman government, Avram Camondo, lived in this house. Camondo, who also held Venetian citizenship, was an exceptional philanthropist, and his gifts to Italian charities earned him the title of Count, bestowed upon him by King Victor Emanuel. In his own backyard (that is, in Constantinople), Camondo founded a school in the poorest section of the city. He also established a council to introduce reforms into the administration of the Jewish community, a move that provoked the conservative Jewish establishment to excommunicate him. He eventually died in Paris but was buried in the Camondo family plot in Hasköy (along the Golden Horn). His mansion is now the Galata Residence, a long-stay hotel. (I stayed in the annex above the outdoor staircase and purposely omitted it from this book.) The ruins in front of the building are what's left of the neighborhood *mikva,* the ritual bath serving the Jewish community. The ruins are in a terrible state; it's now a playground and haven for a family of neighborhood cats.

Continue along Felek Sok. with the Camondo House/Galata Residence on your right. Near the end of the street on your left is the:

8 Schneidertempel

When built in 1894 for a working-class and tradesmen community of Ashkenazi Jews, this synagogue was called the Tofre Begadim or Tailor's Synagogue. In 1998, the Ashkenazim Cultural Association converted it into the Schneidertempel Art Center, a gallery for contemporary art exhibits, including Biennial exhibitions. The gallery is open to the public during runs of these art shows.

Turn left and go down the steep Bereketzade Medresesi Sok. (the continuation of Camekan Sok.). The Gaudí-esque staircase at the base of this street is the:

9 Camondo Staircase

Another one of the many structures in the neighborhood built by Avram Camondo, this staircase provided convenient passage for the banker as he made his way from his home to work on Bankalar Sokağı (Bank Street) at the base of the stairs.

Instead of going down the staircase (you'll return later in this tour), go to your right down Kart Çinar Sok. At the intersection with Galata Kulesi Sok. (also known as Kuledibi) is the back of:

10 Bereket Han

You are standing at the back entrance to probably the most historically significant building in all of Galata. Built in 1316 after the Great Fire of 1315, the Bereket Han occupies the site of the Podestà or Palazzo del Comune—essentially the town hall—of the Genoese community. In the 19th century, the building underwent numerous modifications, including removal of a grand marble entry staircase and portions of the building facing the street—to accommodate the Voyvoda Street (Bankalar Sokağı) tramway. Yet some of the building's earliest elements are still visible: The original rear walls and sections of the side walls are part of the 1316 construction. You can see a small Genoese coat of arms above the rear entrance. Inside is another, though it is thought to be a copy of a pre-existing emblem.

In the Genoese building across the street from Bereket Han is the **Galata Derneği,** a cultural center. If it's open, go up the stairs to the loft beneath a hidden treasure—a restored brick vaulted ceiling.

Back on the street, turn right and haul yourself up the steep incline. Just up the street on your left, in a little crook in the sidewalk, is the pink-and-purple doorway and entrance to the:

11 Church of SS. Peter and Paul

Knock on the door and the caretaker will let you in to this Franciscan church. Up the hill a few steps on your right is the Old English Jail, expertly converted from a consular place of incarceration to the clubby Galata House Restaurant.

Retrace your steps and follow the street until it ramps down to Bankalar Sok., today better known as:

12 Voyvoda Caddesi

It's impossible to overstate the centrality of this street in the financial and mercantile activities conducted during the Ottoman Empire. In the waning years of the empire, which was plagued by a hemorrhaging of economic influence, the sultan turned to many a bank on Bankalar Sokağı for credit—provided at crushing rates of interest. More on these banks and the buildings that housed them later.

Continue straight down Perşembe Pazarı Sok., and turn right onto narrow Galata Mahkemesi Sok., where you will soon see the tower of:

13 Arap Camii

This Gothic structure was most likely built as a Dominican church in the first half of the 14th century, incorporating (or including, no one is sure) a chapel dedicated to St. Paul. The church was taken over by a community of Moors who had been expelled from Spain in the 16th century. The building suffered from numerous fires; during the 1913–1919 restoration project, the original flooring was uncovered, revealing a number of Genoese tombstones (now in the Archaeology Museum).

Head back up Perşembe Sok., back to Bankalar Sok., and turn right, where you'll see the beginning of a long parade of stately bank buildings.

14 Voyvoda Caddesi 43–45

These two structures pre-date (and survive) the building boom of the 1890's. Their modest, four-story construction contrasted against the grandeur of the neighboring bank mansions, provide some insight into the early texture of the neighborhood.

Farther on along Voyvoda/Bankalar Sok. is the unmistakably grand:

15 Ottoman Bank

Built in 1890–1892 by architect Alexandre Vallauri, this is actually two buildings in one—twin structures occupied by the Ottoman Bank and later by the Central Bank of the Republic of Turkey. In 1896, a group of nationalist Armenians stormed the building with bombs and a list of grievances against the Ottoman state. The building was recently transformed into SALT Galata, an art space created by Garanti Bank, the successor to the Ottoman Bank upon their merger in 2001. There's as unexpected (and free) exhibit on the lower level chronicling the history of the Ottoman Bank, where you can venture into the various vaults containing crumbling banknotes and legers of financial transactions.

At this point, you see the Camondo Staircase. You can climb it, turn right past the ruined *mikva*, and then right again down the steps back down to Bankalar Sok., or simply continue straight along Bankalar Sok. toward:

16 Karaköy Square

Some impressive architectural jewels, like the Nordstern Han to your right (with Bankalar Sok. at your back) and the neoclassical Ziraat Bank building opposite the square, command this open plaza, attesting to this section of the city as the center of commerce for not only an empire but for the entire Mediterranean. Turn right onto the square and meander passed the *simitçi* (a vendor selling bagel-like sesame rings), the plumbing vendors, and the crush of humanity; then turn right again onto the busy Tersane Caddesi.

Take a right onto the tiny Perçemli Sok., and follow it all the way to the end, where you will find the:

17 Jewish Museum of Turkey (Zulfaris Synagogue)

This museum chronicles 500 years of Turkish Jewry (p. 106). The elegant redbrick town house embellished by marble columns and an ornamental staircase dates to the early 19th century.

Head down to Tersane Cad., and at your right a few steps farther on you will arrive at the entrance to "Lower Tünel". This is the end of the tour, a convenient stop for those heading either back up to Tünel, or, via the tramway, to Taksim or the Old City.

WALKING TOUR 2: ISTANBUL UNDERGROUND

START:	**Yerebatan Sarnıçı (Basilica Cistern), Sultanahmet**
FINISH:	**Istiklal Caddesi, Beyoğlu**
TIME:	**2–4 hours, depending on how much time you spend in the Mosaic Museum and in the Basilica Cistern**
BEST TIME:	**Midafternoon Wednesday, Thursday, or Friday**
WORST TIME:	**Saturday, Sunday, Monday, Tuesday (when at least one of the destinations mentioned in this tour is closed)**

Istanbul sits atop a mind-boggling wealth of significant ancient and Ottoman history. A few of the places featured here have been converted into restaurants, while others are preserved as museums. Some are both, while others are neither. This means that not all the sights on this tour will be open at the same time—museums are open during business hours while restaurants are only open after-hours. A visit to the sites under private ownership will require some warm personal interaction.

1 Yerebatan Sarnıçı

Few would guess that beneath the institutional concrete facade on the corner of Yerebatan Caddesi and Divanyolu lies one of the last remaining, intact monuments to the Byzantine era in Istanbul, the **Yerebatan Cistern** (closed Tues; p. 109). After paying the admission fee, a flight of steps leads down to a humid subterranean underworld of imperial grandeur accentuated by modern spotlights and even a bit of artistry. The cavernous and palatial space glows with the reds and blues of theatrical mood lighting. You might recognize the space from a scene in the James Bond move, *From Russia with Love*, which was filmed here.

Upon exit, with Sultanahmet Park on your left, walk west along Divanyolu toward the Sultanahmet tramway stop. After the tramway stop, turn left onto Işık Sok. Down on your right is the main entrance to:

2 Binbirdirek Sarnıçı (The Philoxenus Cistern)

In contrast to the celebrity of the Yerebatan Cistern, this underground space is generally ignored by the tour groups. Known colloquially as the Cistern of 1,001 Columns, it was built during Constantine's time, but today the dry, cavernous, and vaulted space serves several purposes: In addition to a museum, the cistern also serves as a venue for special events that accommodates exhibits, cultural performances (like the *sema*), and weddings.

If you're visiting between April and December, exit through the rear entrance to your right and turn left onto Klodferer Cad. Turn left onto Dostluk Yurdu Sok., and then cut through the little corner park on your right to Piyer Loti Cad. For visitors at other times of the year, retrace your steps to Divanyolu and turn left. Turn left again down Piyer Loti Cad. The entrance to the next attraction is in the blue Eminönü Municipality Building. Just inside the service entrance, to the right of the main entrance is:

3 The Şerefiye or Theodosius Sarnıç

This cistern is still in a fairly raw state—no mood lighting and mirrors—but at least they've removed the debris that was scattered about the space. A tunnel in the right wall is said to connect this cistern with the neighboring Binbirdirek cistern. This is a great place to practice your Turkish, because if the gate is open, local security and service staff working in the adjacent municipal building hanging outside are eager to let visitors have a look.

Retrace your steps back to Klodferer Cad. and turn right. Klodferer merges onto Üçler Sok., a narrow road with local shops, including a laundry, a grocer, and a neighborhood *pasthane* (mixed in with a creeping arrival of large restaurants and one or two carpet shops geared toward tourists). You will also pass a mosque with a tiny graveyard. Continue straight along the southwestern rim of the **Hippodrome,** veering right down the hill onto Nakılbent Sok. The road curves sharply to the left and opens up onto a raised tea garden on your right and, straight ahead, the:

4 Nakkaş Store & 6th-Century-A.D. Cistern

The sleek operation of Nakkaş is a shopping complex that puts pretty much all of Istanbul's quality commercial ware under one roof. If you can get past the cases of diamond and gold jewelry (carpets, *kilims*, and ceramics are upstairs) without getting sucked into the glamour, ask a salesperson if they wouldn't mind your having a look at their art gallery, essentially a **6th-century-**A.D. **cistern** transformed into a space for exhibitions and concerts.

Turn left out of Nakkaş and stop at the next intersection. Notice on your right the **Spherion,** or retaining wall of the Hippodrome. Turn left. The next street is Küçük Ayasofya Cad.; turn right to see the bright **Eresin Crown Hotel.**

5 Ancient Byzantine-era artifacts

A small section of another ancient cistern was uncovered during the construction of the **Eresin Crown Hotel** (p. 160). To the left of the lobby is a sitting area built on and around the cistern, and above an exposed (preserved) Byzantine mosaic detail. Off the lobby is the Column Bar, where some of the 49 artifacts recovered during construction are on display, including upright columns, capitals, and funerary stelae.

Go up the incline of Küçük Ayasofya Cad. (taking the right fork at the top) and follow the road around to the right past the entrance to the **Arasta Bazaar.** Be careful, as there is little sidewalk to speak of. Just past where the road curves left and in front of the Sultanahmet Sarayı Hotel is the entrance to:

6 The Mosaic Museum

For now, the **Mosaic Museum** (p. 107) is the best (and perhaps the only large-scale) example of the grandiose lost Great Palace. The museum preserves, partially *in situ*, a recovered portion of a peristyle courtyard that was completely tiled in mosaic patterns, in predominantly greens and ochers, of hunting and pastoral scenes. Amazingly, this portion of the "underground" tour was once the top layer of the city. Closed Monday.

The museum exit opens into the middle of the Arasta Bazaar. Continue up (to the left) and exit the bazaar to the right just before the tea garden. Cross Torun Sok. and continue straight along Mimar Mehmet Ağa Caddesi to #39 and:

7 Sedir's Carpet Shop

If you can make your way past the hungry salesman to the basement of this shop, you can find the remains of two significant Byzantine findings. Below, on the floor of the first (upper) level is a **geometric mosaic** depicting patterns found in both religious buildings and in private homes; for this reason the building has not been identified. Speculation is that the mosaic belongs to the Palace of Marina, sister of Theodosius II (5th century). About 5mt/16ft below the level of the mosaic is a barrel vaulted space, and in the south wall, a niche with a **sacred spring**. The presence of a worn depiction of the iconographic Hodegetria (literally: Greek for "She who shows the way", here, the Holy Mother pointing to son as Savior) on the wall of the niche suggests that this was the Monastery of the Panaghia Hodegetria, founded by Saint Pulcheria, daughter of Emperor Arcadius.

Backtrack up Mimar Mehmet Ağa Caddesi and turn right onto Torun/Utangaç Sok. Continue up the steep cobbled incline past the Blue House on your right and the domes of the **Blue Mosque** to your left. Straight ahead (the street changes names to Utangaç Sok.) are some of the more intrusive carpet salesmen in town; ignore them and turn right at the end onto Tevkifhane Sok. past the saffron-colored **Four Seasons Hotel**—converted in the 1970s from a political prison. Opposite, and diagonally to your left on Kutlugün Sok., is the **Asia Minor** carpet shop. Go into the garden courtyard at the back.

8 The Magnaura or Senate House

A cement staircase in the courtyard leads down into the subterranean remains of the Senate House. The salesmen will be more than happy to let you have a look at the gray and dusty stones, and then give you a tour of their carpet collection in the adjacent shop.

This shop is just one of the hundreds of neighborhood structures built atop the ruins of the Great Palace. In fact, excavations and construction are ongoing next door behind the Four Seasons. After the lot behind the hotel was reclassified from an "archaeological park" to an "urban and archaeological site," the hotel obtained permission to build three new wings on the site. The additional wings will be supported by pylons, allowing excavations and eventually visits to continue to the remains of either the former Senate or Magnaura Palace below.

Continue along Kutlugün Sok. along the wall of the Four Seasons (on your left) and some dilapidated painted cement block houses on your right. At the end of the street is a restored Ottoman mansion, now a hotel; turn left here onto Işak Paşa Cad. and head up the hill along the outer wall of Topkapı Palace. Go around to the right of the grand **Sultanahmet Fountain,** past the entrance to **Topkapı Palace,** and enter into the cobbled and picturesque Soğukçeşme Sok. Down on your right, tucked against the palace walls, is:

9 Sarniç

Believe it or not, this 1,600-year-old cistern used to house a mechanic's garage. The auto paraphernalia was removed only 29 years ago, and today the cistern is occupied by Sarniç, an atmospheric restaurant (p. 130). The "wow" quotient goes off the charts when the entryway and staircase down to the dining room/ cistern glows under the light of hundreds of candles. Take a minute to survey this spectacular medieval re-creation. The only "modern" addition is the brick fireplace on the left wall.

Continue along the cobbled Soğukçeşme Sokağı past the rear gardens of the Ayasofya, full of archaeological pieces to the ancient puzzle strewn about the yard. Soğukçeşme Sokağı descends sharply, past the open gardens of the

4

ISTANBUL | Walking Tour 2: Istanbul Underground

Ayasofya Konakları containing a garden conservatory. The sharp descent spills out onto Alemdağ Caddesi, with the entrance to Gülhane Park on your right, enclosed behind the Topkapı Palace walls.

Here is the Gülhane tramway stop; hop on any tram heading toward Eminönü and get off at the third stop, Karaköy, just on the far side of the Galata Bridge. **Note:** If your train ends at Eminönü, just step out and wait for one heading to Kabataş. At Karaköy, exit the tram to the right and go down to the water and seaside promenade at the base of the Galata Bridge. Follow the promenade to the left (away from the bridge), passing seafood restaurants and fishermen along the way. Up on your left you will see a ramshackle but beautiful blue government building and a plaza. Directly behind the blue building is:

10 The Yeraltı Camii (Underground Mosque)

This mosque is a somewhat ominous grid of isolated, individual spaces sectioned off by thick, squat columns supporting a low vaulted ceiling. The scattered prayerful, worshiping in the privacy of their little compartments, may either ignore you or gaze curiously upon you, as few visitors to Istanbul even know to venture here.

The Top Sights

Hagia Sophia (Ayasofya) ★★★ HISTORIC SITE For almost a thousand years, the Hagia Sophia was a triumph of Christianity and the symbol of Byzantium, and until the 16th century, maintained its status as the largest Christian church in the world. The cathedral is so utterly awesome that the Statue of Liberty's torch would barely graze the top. Erected over the ashes of two previous churches using dismantled and toppled columns and marble from some of the greatest temples around the empire, the Hagia Sophia (known in English as St. Sophia, or Church of the Holy Wisdom) was designed to surpass in grandeur, glory, and majesty every other edifice ever constructed as a monument to God. Justinian began construction soon after his suppression of the Nika Revolt (during which the second church was burned to the ground), indicating that combating unemployment was high on the list as well. He chose the two preeminent architects of the day: Anthemius of Tralles (Aydın) and Isidorus of Miletus. After 5 years and 4 months, when the construction of the Hagia Sophia was completed in A.D. 537, the emperor raised his hands to heaven and proclaimed, "Glory to God who has deigned to let me finish so great a work. O Solomon, I have outdone thee!" Enthusiasm for this feat of architecture and engineering was short-lived, because 2 years later, an earthquake caused the dome to collapse. The new dome was slightly smaller in diameter but higher than the original, supported by a series of massive towers to counter the effects of future earthquakes. Glass fittings in the walls were employed to monitor the weight distribution of the dome; the sound of crunching glass was an early warning system indicating that the weight of the dome had shifted. Several more earthquakes caused additional damage to the church, requiring repairs to the dome (among other sections), which was increased in height thanks to the support provided by the addition of flying buttresses (additional buttresses were added at two later dates).

In 1204, led by the Doge of Venice, Enrico Dandolo, the Crusaders successfully breached the defensive walls of Constantinople, occupied the city and distributed the Hagia Sophia's substantial treasures throughout the Holy Roman Empire, a desecration that robbed the church of precious relics and definitively divided the Greek Orthodox and Roman Catholic churches.

After Mehmet II penetrated the city in 1453, his first official stop was to this overwhelming symbol of an empire that he had conquered, and with his head to the ground, he invoked the name of Allah and declared the great house of worship a mosque.

In the years that followed, several adjustments were made to the building including the covering over of the frescoes and mosaics, due to the prohibition of Islam against the representation of figures. (The Iconoclastic movement of the 8th and 9th centuries A.D. had similarly disavowed the use of figural depictions and icons, during which many of the frescoes and mosaics were defaced, destroyed, or cemented over; any figural representations seen today date to after this period.) A single wooden minaret was erected (and later replaced by Mimar Sinan during restorations in the 16th c.), and three additional minarets were added at a later date. The altar was shifted slightly to the right to accommodate a *mihrab* indicating the direction of Mecca, and an ablution fountain, along with a kitchen, was erected in the courtyard.

Hagia Sophia was converted from a mosque into a museum by Atatürk in 1935, after a painstaking restoration led by Thomas Whitmore of the Byzantium Institute of America. Mosaics and icons that were previously defaced or whitewashed were rediscovered and restored.

While this enduring symbol of Byzantium still has the power to instill awe after so many additions and reconstructions (including tombs, schools, and soup kitchens during its tour of duty as a mosque), the exterior's original architecture is marred by large and boxy buttresses; you'll get more of a representation of the intent of Justinian's original from the inside. On your way in, notice the stone cannonballs lining the gravel path of the outer courtyard. These are the actual cannonballs used by Mehmet the Conqueror in his victorious 1453 battle for the city. Also outside the main entrance are the foundations of the original church built by Theodosius.

The main entrance to Hagia Sophia leads to the **exonarthex ★**, a vaulted outer vestibule that was reserved for those not yet baptized. The **inner narthex ★★**, or vestibule, glistens with Justinian's original gold mosaics embellished with floral and geometric patterns. The most central of the nine doors leading into the nave of the church, called the **Imperial Gate ★**, is topped by a **mosaic ★★★** of the Christ Pantocrator holding a book with the inscription "Peace be with you. I am the Light of the World." He is surrounded by roundels portraying the Virgin Mary, the angel Gabriel, and a bearded emperor, believed to represent Leo VI asking for forgiveness for his four marriages.

At 46m (151 ft., 1 in.) high the Statue of Liberty (less the pedestal) could fit under the dome with 10m (32 ft., 11 in.) to spare.

Through the Imperial Gate is a sight that brought emperors and sultans to their knees: a soaring **dome ★★★** that rises 56m (184 ft.) in height (about 15 stories) and spans a width of approximately 31m (102 ft.). Light filters through a crown formed by 40 windows and ribs, glittering with the gold mosaic tiles that cover the entire interior of the dome. At its decorative peak (including the side aisles, semi-domes, inner walls, and upper galleries), Hagia Sophia's interior mosaics covered more than 4 acres of space. Eight **calligraphic discs,** four of which are the largest examples of calligraphy in the Islamic world, ornament the interior and bear the names of Allah and Mohammed (above the apse); the four successive caliphs, Ali, Abu Bakr, Osman, and Omar (at each of the four corners of the dome); and Ali's sons Hassan and Huseyin (in the nave). The main nave, side aisles, apse, and semi-domes are covered with mosaics and frescoes, depicting religious and imperial motifs or floral and geometric designs. At the center of the space is a square of marble flooring called **Coronation Square,** believed to have been the location of the emperor's throne, the place of coronation and therefore, in the minds of the Byzantines (or at least the emperor), the center of the universe.

In the Upper Galleries are some of the best mosaics in the church (restoration just recently completed; thus the additional entrance fee), as well as decorative paintings and of course a closer look at the dome. The **western gallery** (directly opposite the apse) called the **Loge of the Empress,** provided a front-row seat for the Empress and her retinue to the activities below. A green stone at the center of the Loge indicates the location of the best seat in the house—the spot where the Empress's throne was positioned. In the southern gallery is one of the more recent mosaics, the **Deesis ★★★**, dating to around the 14th century. The composition depicting Christ, his mother, and St. John the Baptist pleading for the salvation of mankind is considered to be one of Byzantium's most striking mosaics, in spite of the missing lower two-thirds. (There is another Deesis in the church dating to the 10th century at the latest, in an area of the **southern gallery** not open to the public). Opposite the Deesis is the alleged **tomb of Henrico Dandalo,** the blind Venetian doge whose success in diverting the Fourth Crusade to Constantinople resulted in his capture of the city in 1204. Along the balcony railing near the Deesis is the graffiti of a 9th-century-A.D. Viking—the equivalent to "Halvdan was here." At the far eastern end of the gallery near the apse are two imperial mosaics: one depicting **Empress Zoë ★★** with her third husband, Constantine IX Monomachus (see "Face-Off in the Corner," below), separated by a figure of Christ, and a mosaic portrait of **Emperor John II Comnenus and Empress Eirene, flanked by Mother and Child ★★**. The side panel is a depiction of the Empress and Emperor's son, Prince Alexius (extended onto the panel on the wall to the right).

It's worth it to backtrack over to the north gallery to go on a treasure hunt for the **10th-century mosaic of Emperor Alexander ★**. Depicting the emperor in full medieval regalia, the mosaic was believed to be lost to the earthquake of 1894. But while over time the other mosaics had been plastered over, this one had been camouflaged by paint applied to match the surrounding patterns.

One of the more recent and significant discoveries is a 1.5 sq. m (16 sq. ft.) mosaic panel of a **Six Winged Seraphim ★★**, obscured from the light of day since Swiss architect Gaspare Fossati headed restorations on the basilica in 1847–49. The seraphim is believed to be one of four mosaic angels depicted in each of the four pendentives of the dome as guardians of heaven.

Exit the church through the small **Vestibule of Warriors** in the inner narthex opposite the ramp to the upper gallery. Previously used as an entrance, this is now an exit, so you're forced to turn around to view the mosaic lunette depicting an enthroned **Virgin Mother and Child ★★★**, flanked by Constantine proffering a model of the city and Justinian offering a model (inaccurate) of the Hagia Sophia. (A mirror has been placed above the current exit to alert you to the mosaic behind you.)

Sultanahmet Meydanı 1. www.kultur.gov.tr. ℂ **0212/522-1750.** Admission 20TL. Tues–Sun Apr–Oct 9am–7pm; Nov–Mar 9am–4:30pm. Tram: Sultanahmet.

Blue Mosque (Sultan Ahmet Camii) ★★★ MOSQUE   This grand bubble of masonry, one of the great and defining features of Istanbul's skyline, was constructed between 1609 and 1617 by Sultan Ahmet I, who not only was driven by a desire to leave behind an imperial namesake mosque, but also was determined to build a monument to rival the Hagia Sophia. So great was the Sultan's ambition that he had one unfortunate architect executed before finally choosing Mehmet Ağa, probably a student of Sinan, who came up with a plan commonly accepted as impossible to build. The design is a scheme of successively descending smaller domes that addresses the problem of creating a large covered interior space. The overall effect is one of such great harmony, grace, and power that it's impossible to walk away from this building unaffected.

There are several legends associated with the construction of the **six minarets.** One says that the sultan's desire for gold minarets—*altın* in Turkish—was understood as *altı,* or six. Whatever the reasoning, the construction challenged the preeminence of the mosque in Mecca, which at the time also had six minarets. The ensuing scandal, both in and out of Istanbul, resulted in the sultan's ordering the construction of a seventh minaret at the Ka'aba.

The mosque was completed after just over 6½ years of work and to this day remains one of the finest examples of classical Ottoman architecture. The original complex included a soup kitchen, a *medrese* (Muslim theological school), a primary school, a hospital, and a market. A *türbe,* or mausoleum, stands at the corner of the grounds near the Hippodrome and Sultanahmet Park, and houses the remains of the Sultan Ahmet I, his wife, Kösem, and three of his sons. It also contains some fine examples of calligraphy on cobalt blue Iznik tile.

● Face-Off in the Corner

Empress Zoë had a lot of clout in the early part of the second millennium. First she had this glorious golden mosaic, found at the end of the upper gallery, crafted in her honor, depicting Christ between herself and her first husband. When her husband died in 1034, she ordered the tiles of his face along with the inscription replaced to accommodate her second husband, repeating the procedure for the third.

> ### 💬 Did You Know?
>
> Approximately 21,000 tiles were used to decorate the Blue Mosque.

The main entrance (for worshippers; tourists must enter from a portal on the south side) is off the **Hippodrome,** beneath the symbolic chain that required even the sultan to bow his head when he arrived on horseback. Walk straight through the garden up to the main marbled courtyard of the mosque and you'll see an ablution fountain, no longer in use. The working ablution fountains are located at ground level of the northern facade facing the Hagia Sophia. Visitors should enter from the opposite side (from the Hippodrome entrance, follow the garden path diagonally to your right to the south side of the mosque).

If you plan your visit during the morning hours when the sun is still angled from the east, the first effect once inside will be one of blindness as the light penetrates the stained glass, creating an illusion of false darkness. As your eyes adjust, the swirling blues, greens, reds, and yellows from the tile and stained glass increase the impression of immensity and grandeur. The abundant use of decorative tile represents the pinnacle of **Iznik tile ★★★** craftsmanship, evident in the rich yet subtle blues and greens in traditional Ottoman patterns of lilies, tulips, and carnations. The overall dominance of blue prompted the mosque's early visitors to label it the Blue Mosque, a name that sticks to this day.

Lateral half **domes** resting on enormous elephantine **columns ★★** (actually called elephant foot pillars) enhance the sense of open space, but critics contend that the pillars are too overbearing and cumbersome. The elegant **medallions ★** facing the *mihrab* bear the names of Allah and Mohammed; the ones opposite are decorated with the names of the first four caliphs who ruled the Islamic world.

Sultanahmet. ✆ **0212/458-0776.** Closed to visitors during prayer times. Tram: Sultanahmet.

Grand Bazaar (Kapalı Çarşısı) ★★★ HISTORIC SITE AND MARKET

The mother of all tourist traps, the Grand or Covered Bazaar is a vivid illustration of all that's gone wrong with the free market. The Grand Bazaar is actually the center of a commercial area within and around the covered section of the market that spreads all the way down the hill to Eminönü. The name "Grand Bazaar" refers to a vast collection of over 4,000 shops, 24 *hans* (privately owned inns or marketplaces), 65 streets, 22 gates, 2 *bedestens* (covered markets), restaurants, mosques, fountains, and teahouses within an area of 31 hectares (77 acres). Kapalı Çarşı refers specifically to the indoor and covered portion.

At the heart and soul of the bazaar are two *bedestens* (merchant centers), ordered built by Mehmet the Conqueror for the purpose of gaining revenue for the Hagia Sophia. These were the **İç,** or **Inner Bedesten** (more commonly known as the Old Bedesten), and the **Sandal Bedesten.** These two rectangular structures are typical *bedestens,* meaning that they are solid, significant, and capped by rows of vaults and domes covering a perimeter of cells surrounding an inner courtyard. Ottoman merchants gravitated to this center of commerce; it is estimated that by the end of Mehmet II's rule, the bazaar had already grown to a third of its current size. Artisans tended to congregate in one area, a legacy handed down through names of streets such as Fez Makers Street (Fesçiler Sok.), Street of the Washcloth Makers (Aynacilar Sok.), and Street of Fur Makers (Kürkçüler Sok.).

A number of characteristic *hans* that at one time (and now nominally) operated around a particular craft or trade are situated in and around the covered portion (or Kapalı Çarşı) of the Grand Bazaar. Of particular note inside the Kapalı Çarşı is the **Safran Han** (stuffing/sewing pillows and mattresses). Beyond the covered portion are the 17th-century **Valde Han** (weaving on looms), the **Çuhacılar Hanı** (antique silver and jewelry), and the 15th-century **Kürkçüler Han,** the oldest one still in use (yarns and knitting supplies; the furs are upstairs).

Over the centuries, the shops around the bazaar fell victim to a total of 10 fires and two earthquakes; the current configuration dates to 1894, when the Minister of Public Works under Abdülhamid II reorganized the bazaar following that year's earthquake.

Today, the main drag running from the Nuruosmaniye Gate to the Beyazıt Gate is **Kalpakçilar Caddesi ★**, the glittering main thoroughfare lined on either side with shops of silver and gold, with anything and everything of your heart's desire elsewhere in the market.

For tips on shopping the Grand Bazaar, turn to p. 140.

Beyazıt. www.grandbazaaristanbul.org. Free admission. Best entrances through the Beyazıt Gate (across from the Beyazıt stop on the tram along Divanyolu) and the Nuruosmaniye Gate (from the Çemberlitaş tram stop on Divanyolu; follow Vezirhanı Cad. to the arched entrance to the mosque grounds, which lead to the bazaar). Mon–Sat 9am–7pm. Closed national holidays. Shops close early during Ramadan. Tram: Sultanahmet.

Hippodrome ★ SQUARE   One of Istanbul's most beloved public spaces, today's Hippodrome hardly conveys its centuries-long history of rowdy chariot races, ostentatious royal celebrations, and bloody massacres.

Polo games and horse races were popular sports in the day. The first track was built in A.D. 203 by Septimus Severus out of the ruins of the city he sacked. Modeled on the Circus Maximus in Rome, the Hippodrome was enlarged by Constantine in A.D. 324 through the help of supporting vaults and hefty stone walls on the southern portion of the tract. The lower areas (the **Spherion,** or retaining wall down the hill at the obelisk end of the park) were used as stables and quarters for the gladiators.

Forty rows of seats accommodated up to 100,000 agitated supporters divided into merchant guilds that over time degenerated into political rivalries. These factions were known as the Blues, Greens, Reds, and Whites. The Blues and Greens put aside their disagreements to demonstrate against the emperor in A.D. 532, which resulted in a riot with protesters screaming "Nika!" (Greek for "victory"). In what would become known as the Nika Revolt, much of the imperial palace and the original

---

Cafes and Eateries in the Grand Bazaar

Need a shot of caffeine? **Ethem Tezça-kar** (Halıçılar Cad 61-63; ℂ **0212/513-2133**) has been pouring thick cups of Turkish coffee since 1909. **Café Ist** (Tarakçılar Cad.; ℂ **0212/527-9353**), and **Fes Café** (Halıcılar Cad. 62; ℂ **0212/528-1613**), offer a wide selection of coffees, flavored teas, and fresh-squeezed juices.

Fes also has a bistro just outside the Nuruosmaniye Mosque at **Ali Baba Türbe Sok**. 25/27 (ℂ **0212/526-3070**). A new spot is a husband-and-wife team enterprise. **Julia's Kitchen** (Keseçiler Cad. 110–112; ℂ **0212/512-9677**) serves basic Turkish appetizers, home cooking and even cookies for teatime.

church of Hagia Sophia were destroyed. Justinian eventually regained control of his throne and ordered the massacre of some 30,000 to 40,000 people as punishment. With the arrival of the Fourth Crusade, the Hippodrome fell into disuse, eventually serving as a marble quarry for the Ottomans after their conquest of the city.

At the height of its splendor, the Hippodrome was crowned with a vast collection of trophies, statues, and monuments, either crafted by local artisans or lifted from the far corners of the empire.

At the southern end of the park is the **Magnetic Column ★★**, also known as the Walled Obelisk, the Plaited Column, the Colossus, and the Column of Constantine. This column was erected in the 10th century under Constantine VII Porphyrogenitus and was faced with plaques of gilded bronze and brass plates. At one time this obelisk was used to support a pulley system for raising and lowering awnings to protect the spectators from the sun. In 1204 the bronze and brass plates were removed and smelted by the Crusaders to mint coins.

Farther along is the **Serpentine Column ★★**, a squat spiral standing 25% lower than its original 8m (26 ft.). The column was originally erected outside the Temple of Apollo at Delphi by the 31 Greek city-states to commemorate their victory over the Persians, and later brought to the city by Constantine. Made of melded bronze, the column represents three intertwining serpents and was crowned by three gold serpents' heads supporting a gold bowl, said to have been cast from the shields of the fallen Persian soldiers. The heads were lost until one resurfaced during the restoration of the Hagia Sophia, now in the Archaeology Museum. A second head was discovered and, like many ancient Turkish monuments, slithered its way to the British Museum in London.

The **Obelisk of Tutmosis III ★★★** is easily one of the most astounding feats of engineering in the city. This 13th-century-B.C. solid block of granite weighing over 60 tons was brought to Istanbul by Emperor Theodosius I from its place in front of Egypt's Temple of Luxor at Karnak. The four sides of granite are covered from top to bottom with hieroglyphics celebrating the glory of the pharaoh and the god Horus. The monument was placed in the square in A.D. 390, but *two-thirds* of the original was lost during transport. This portion, standing over 20m (66 ft.) high, was erected in under 30 days, on a Roman base depicting bas-reliefs of Theodosius's family, friends, and triumphs at the races.

At the northern end of the Hippodrome is the **Fountain of Wilhelm II (Alman Çeşmesi) ★★**, crafted in Germany and assembled in Istanbul to commemorate the emperor's visit to the city in 1895. Notice the initials of both the German monarch and Sultan Abdülhamid on the interior of the dome, inlaid with glittering golden mosaics.

The Hippodrome's crowning monument, long a distant memory of its original grandeur atop a disappeared imperial loggia, was a monumental **statue of four bronze horses.** In the Fourth Crusade's looting of the city in 1204, the monument was carried away to grace the facade of the Basilica of St. Marco in Venice. (Today, the ones on the facade are fake; the real ones are being protected from the elements in the Basilica of St. Marco's museum.)

Just to the north of the Hippodrome (on the corner where Divanyolu and Yerebatan Cad. converge) is the **Million (or Milion) Stone,** the point of departure for all roads leading out of the city and essentially ground zero for all measurements to the city from points within the empire. The Milion Stone was modeled after the Milliarium Aureum, erected by Julius Caesar in the Forum in Rome. According to one tradition, the **True Cross** is said to have been brought from Jerusalem to Constantinople and placed by the Milion Stone during the reign of Constantine.

During the month of Ramadan, Ottoman houses full of fast food are set up along the perimeter, while a pink-and-blue fiberglass elephant ride for toddlers wipes away any remaining stains of the Hippodrome's complex past.

At Meydanı (Horse Plaza), Sultanahmet. Always open. Tram: Sultanahmet.

Istanbul Archaeology Museums (Arkeoloji Müzelleri) ★★ MUSEUM

The Istanbul Archaeology Museums are housed in three buildings just inside the first court of Topkapı Palace and includes the Museum of the Ancient Orient (first building on your left) and the Çinili Köşk (opposite the entrance to the main building). These museums, opened officially in 1891, owe their very existence to Osman Hamdi Bey, a 19th-century Turkish painter, archaeologist, curator, and diplomat, who fought for the Antiquities Conservation Act to combat the rampant smuggling of antiquities out of Turkey.

The Istanbul Archaeology Museum houses over one million objects, the most extraordinary of which are the sarcophagi that date back as far as the 4th century B.C. The museum excels, however, in its rich chronological collection of locally found artifacts that shed light on the origins and history of the city.

Near the entrance is a **statue of a lion** representing the only piece saved from the clutches of British archaeologists from the Mausoleum of Halicarnassus. In the halls to the left is a collection of sarcophagi found at Sidon (ancient Syria), representing various architectural styles influenced by outside cultures including Egypt, Phoenicia, and Lycia. The most famous is the **Alexander Sarcophagus ★★★**, covered with astonishingly advanced carvings of battles and the life of Alexander the Great, discovered in 1887 and once believed to have been that of the emperor himself. The discovery that the occupant was in fact Sidonian King Abdalonymos may have initially been disappointing, but it hasn't diminished the impact of this great ancient work of art. Found in the same necropolis at Sidon is the stunningly preserved **Sarcophagus of the Crying Women ★★★**, with 18 intricately carved panels showing figures of women in extreme states of mourning. Don't miss the monumental **Lycian tomb ★★★**, carved in a style befitting a great king and just as impressive in this exhibit as on the hills of Lycia. Farther on is the recently inaugurated **Northern Wing ★★**, which rescues from storage a stunning collection of **monumental sarcophagi ★★★** and partially reconstructed **temple friezes ★★★**.

On the mezzanine level is the exhibit *Istanbul Through the Ages* ★★, a rich and well presented exhibit that won the Council of Europe Museum Award in 1993. To put the exhibit into perspective, the curators have provided maps, plans, and drawings to illustrate the archaeological findings, displayed thematically, which range from prehistoric artifacts found west of Istanbul to 15th-century Byzantine works of art. The recovered **snake's head** ★ from the Serpentine Column in the Hippodrome is on display, as is the 14th-century bell from the Galata Tower. The upper two levels house the Troy exhibit and displays on the evolution of Anatolia over the centuries, as well as sculptures from Cyprus, Syria, and Palestine.

In the **Museum of the Ancient Orient** ★★★ is an exceptionally rich collection of artifacts from the earliest civilizations of Anatolia, Mesopotamia and Egypt, brought to Istanbul while these regions were under Ottoman rule. The tour begins with pre-Islamic divinities and idols taken from the courtyard of the Al-Ula temple, along with artifacts showing ancient Aramaic inscriptions and a small collection of Egyptian antiquities. Although the individual exhibits are modest in size, the recent upgrade rivals Ankara's archaeological museum for organization and presentation.

Uncovered in the region of Mesopotamia and on display is an **obelisk of Adad-Nirari III** inscribed with cuneiform characters. Of particular significance is a series of colored **mosaic panels** ★★ showing animal reliefs of bulls and dragons with serpents' heads from the monumental Gate of Ishtar, built by Nebuchadnezzar, King of Babylonia. A pictorial representation on a **Sumerian devotional basin** of girls carrying pitchers of water whose contents are filling an underground source relates to the ancient Mesopotamian belief that the world was surrounded by water, a belief that has provoked questions over the origins of the biblical Great Flood.

With nothing dating more recent than the 1st century A.D., it's a real challenge to find something in this museum that is not of enormous significance. But two of the highlights are easily the fragments of the 13th-century-B.C. **sphinx** ★ from the Yarkapı Gate at Hattuşaş (sadly underappreciated in its positioning against a passage wall) and one of the three known tablets of the **Treaty of Kadesh** ★★, the oldest recorded peace treaty signed between Ramses II and the Hittites in the 13th century B.C., inscribed in Akkadian, the international language of the era. (The Istanbul Archaeology Museum houses two; the third is in the Staatliche Museum in Berlin.)

Across from the Archaeology Museum is the **Çinili Köşk,** a wonderful pavilion of turquoise ceramic tiles whose facade displays eye-catching blue and white calligraphy. The mansion was originally built by Mehmet the Conqueror as a hunting pavilion, and now more appropriately houses the **Museum of Turkish Ceramics.** The museum contains a modest collection of Anatolian and Selçukian tiles, not the least of which is the 14th-century *mihrab* from the Ibrahim Bey mosque in Karaman in central Anatolia. Other highlights include some fine samples from Iznik and Kütahya, the two most important production centers for pottery, porcelain, and ceramics during the Ottoman period.

Alemdar Cad. Osman Hamdi Bey Yokuşu Sok. 34122, Sultanahmet. Entrance in the first court of Topkapı Palace (second portal on the left, after St. Irene) and uphill at the back of Gülhane Park. www.istanbularkeoloji.gov.tr. (C) **0212/520-7740.** Admission 10TL; includes the Museum of the Ancient Orient and the Çinili Köşk. Archaeology Museum and Çinili Köşk: Tues–Sun Apr–Oct 9am–7pm; Nov–Mar 9am–5pm. Tram: Sultanahmet or Gülhane.

Museum of Turkish and Islamic Arts ★ MUSEUM & HISTORIC HOME

Ibrahim Paşa, swept into slavery by Turkish raids in Greece, became the beloved and trusted boyhood friend of Süleyman the Magnificent. Educated and converted to

Islam and eventually appointed grand vizier, Ibrahim Paşa was the sultan's only companion at mealtime, earning him the favored title of Serasker Sultan (commander in chief). He also earned the sultan's sister's hand in marriage.

The palace was a gift from the sultan and was built by Sinan. From this very special palace on the Hippodrome, the sultan's family and friends had front-row seats for festivities in the square. Roxelana, the sultan's wife, managed to dispose of her rival in one of her infamous intrigues by convincing the sultan that his grand vizier had become too big for his britches.

The palace now houses the changing exhibitions of the Museum of Turkish and Islamic Arts, a fine collection of calligraphy, peace treaties, several examples of the sultan's official seal or *tuğra*, and an insightful ethnographic section depicting the lifestyles of nomads and city-dwelling Ottomans.

At Meydanı Sok. No:46 İbrahim Paşa Sarayı Sultanahmet, in the Ibrahim Paşa Sarayı (on the Hippodrome). www.tiem.gov.tr. © **0212/518-1805.** Admission 10TL. Tues–Sun Apr–Oct 9am–7pm; Nov–Mar 9am–5pm. Tram: Sultanahmet.

Topkapı Palace (Topkapı Sarayı) ★★★ PALACE   Residence of the sultans, administrative seat of the Ottoman Empire for almost 400 years, and the source of legend on life in the harem, Topkapı Palace should be up at the top of the list for anyone interested in the vast and exotic world behind the seraglio walls. It's impossible to rush through the palace, so you should allot at least a half-day and be prepared to encounter a few bottlenecks throughout the enclosed exhibition halls, especially in the Holy Relics Room where the ardent faithful, in their religious fervor, tend to obstruct the display cases. Built by Mehmet the Conqueror over the ruins of Constantine's Imperial Palace, Topkapı Palace occupies one of the seven hills of the city at the tip of the historic peninsula overlooking the sea. Since it is easily the most valuable real estate in the city, it doesn't take a brain surgeon to see why this spot was preferable to the original palace situated on an inland tract where the university stands today. Mehmet II began construction of the palace 9 years after his conquest of the city, where the sultans reigned continually until 1855, when Abdülmecid moved the imperial residence up the Bosphorus to Dolmabahçe Palace.

Entrance to the grounds is through the Bab-ı Hümayün Gate at the end of the Babuhümayun Caddesi (also called the Gate of Augustus, for the square outside the gate that in Byzantine times was a busy crossroads called the Forum of Augustus). Serving as the entrance through which the public would access the grounds, the gate would often display the decapitated heads of uncooperative administrators or rebels as a warning to all who entered. Just outside the gate is the **Ahmet III Fountain ★★**, built by Mehmet Ağa in 1729 atop an ancient source of water as a gift to Sultan Ahmet. A poem by the sultan is inscribed in the stone, inviting passersby to "drink the water and pray from the House of Ahmet."

4

ISTANBUL

Istanbul Attractions

The first courtyard, known as the **Court of the Janissaries,** is a public park of gardens and trees, just as it was in earlier days. Along the center path are the remains of a 5th-century-A.D. Roman cistern. (You can save this for the way out.)

The diagonal path to the left leads to the stunning **Hagia Eirene (St. Irene)** ★★★, the second-largest Byzantine church after Hagia Sophia, and a church that predates the arrival of Constantine's conquest of the city. The first temple on the site was dedicated to the goddess Aphrodite until it became the center of Christian activities between A.D. 272 and 398. During Constantine's pro-Christian reign, the emperor had the church enlarged, and then, following its near destruction in the Nika Revolt (along with that of the Hagia Sophia), Justinian had it reconstructed. Excavation between 1946 and 1950 indicates that a series of buildings existed connecting the church with the Hagia Sophia, and the fact that both churches were completed and rededicated at about the same time indicates that these houses of worship were in some way part of an ecclesiastical complex. The buildings were later demolished to make room for construction of the palace walls. Rumor has it that Mehmet the Conqueror's Italian consort convinced him to store the house porcelain there, where she could then secretly go and pray, but for the record, the Ottomans used the church as an arsenal. Hagia Eirene is closed to the public but is used as a venue for concerts and recitals. The church may be opened on special request (𝄡 **0212/520-6952**).

The ticket booths to the palace are located on the right side of the courtyard. Proceed to the Ortakapı (middle gate), known as the **Gate of Salutation** ★, roughly translated from the Arabic (Turkish version) *Babüsselâm.*

Added by Süleyman the Magnificent in 1524, this gate signaled to all but the sultan to dismount before proceeding into the palace. On either side of the gate are two octagonal towers that essentially served as death row for those who fell out of favor; after a prisoner's execution, the body would be left outside the gate. To the right of the gate (facing), is a marble fountain where the executioner would wash the blood off his hands before reentering the palace.

Begin your visit with the **Palace Kitchens** ★★, a complex composed of a string of lofty chambers topped by a series of chimney-domes, a narrow inner courtyard, and a smaller string of rooms. The largest in the world, the kitchens at one time employed over 1,000 servants working day and night to serve the 5,000 residents of the palace, a number that swelled to 15,000 during Ramadan. At the far end is the original wooden kitchen that survived a 16th-century fire; Sinan, who reconstructed the kitchens, added the massive conical chimneys and enlarged the original space. Suspended from the iron bars in the ceiling were the cauldrons, raised or lowered over the fire pits below according to the desired intensity of the flame. The kitchens are now used to exhibit the palace's rich collection of **porcelain** ★ numbering close to 12,000 pieces, not all of which are displayed. Topkapı houses the third-most-important collection of porcelain in the world, after Beijing and Dresden, while the palace's collection of celadons surpasses that of Beijing because the Chinese destroyed all of theirs during the Cultural Revolution. Besides these 4th- and 5th-century-A.D. celadons are pieces from the Sung and Yuan dynasties (9th–13th c. A.D.), pieces from the Ming Dynasty (14th–17th c.), and porcelain from the Ching Dynasty (16th–20th c.). Many of these treasures found their way to Istanbul as gifts exchanged between the Ottomans, Chinese, and Persians as symbols of solidarity toward the maintenance and protection of the roads. There's also a rich collection of silver, particularly coffee services, candelabras, and mirrors (ornamented on the backside because of the proscription requiring the reflective side to be lain facedown), and a display of Venetian

4

Istanbul Attractions

ISTANBUL

glass and Bohemian crystal. The Ahmet III Fountain outside the main entrance is reproduced here in a stunning mass of silver, but there are examples of collectibles on a less grandiose scale as well.

Following a direct path along the length of the palace grounds, proceed to the **Gate of Felicity (Babüssaade)** ★, also known as the Gate of the White Eunuchs. For 400 years, enthronement ceremonies were held at the entrance to this gate, today used as a backdrop for the annual presentation of Mozart's *Abduction from the Seraglio* during the International Istanbul Music Festival. Decapitated heads found their way above this gate as well. Only the sultan and the grand vizier were allowed past this gate into the third courtyard (while the Valide Sultan used a back gate for entrances and exits), the private quarters of the palace. Immediately inside the Gate of Felicity and acting as a visual barrier to the private quarters beyond is the **Throne Room** ★, a pavilion used by the sultan as an audience chamber to receive (or affront) visiting ambassadors. Notice the interlocking marble used in the construction of the arched doorway; this design technique reinforced the archway and protected it against earthquakes.

Directly to the right is the Seferliler Quarters, now housing the **Palace Clothing Exhibition** or Imperial Wardrobe. Because the sultan's clothing was considered to be holy, a sultan's wardrobe would be wrapped up and preserved in the palace. This opulent display of silk, brocade, and gold-threaded clothing is only a small portion of the whole collection and includes enormously baggy costumes (to give the sultan the visual advantage of size), along with caftans and other garments showing influences from around the empire.

Past the Palace Clothing Exhibition is the Fatih Pavilion, containing a recently restored exhibition of the **Treasury** ★★★, one of the greatest collections of treasures in the world. In 400 years a sultan can amass a great quantity of wealth, supplied through spoils of war, gifts from neighboring kings and queens, and the odd impulse buy. The rooms were off-limits to everyone but the sultan, and in his absence, any visitor was required to be accompanied by at least 40 other men.

Room no. 1 of the Treasury is a collection of Ottoman objects and **ceremonial thrones** ★★★, including one in pure gold, weighing in at 250kg (551 lb.), presented to Murat III in 1585 by the Egyptian governor; an ebony throne crafted for Süleyman the Magnificent; and a jewel-encrusted throne, presented to Mahmut I by Nadir Shah of India.

The eye is immediately drawn to the jewel-studded mother-of-pearl and tortoiseshell throne of Sultan Ahmet I, crafted by the master of inlay, Mehmet Ağa, the same man commissioned by the sultan to build the Blue Mosque. (Rumor has it that during his 1995 visit, Michael Jackson requested permission to sit in one of the thrones; however, his request was denied.) Also of note in room no. 1 is the **sword** belonging to Süleyman the Magnificent, with his name and title inscribed on the blade.

Room no. 2 of the Treasury displays a collection of medals, and non-Ottoman objects and gifts (or plunder) received through the spoils of war. Highlights include figurines crafted in India from seed pearls, and in the same case, a miniature tree of life and a vessel presented as gifts to the tomb of Mohammed.

The focus of room no. 3 is a pair of shoulder-high **candlesticks** ★ crafted of solid gold, caked with several thousand brilliants/diamonds, and weighing over 48kg (106 lb.) each. In a world absent of electricity, candlesticks like these would be placed on either side of the *mihrab* to provide light for the reading of the holy book. This pair was presented to the tomb of Mohammed in Medina and brought back to Istanbul after World War I. The rest of the exhibit in room no. 3, an overwhelming collection of jade, rock crystal, zinc, emeralds, and other precious gems, displays Ottoman objects made by artists and craftsmen for the sultans throughout the centuries.

Room no. 4 is the Treasury's *pièce de résistance,* a breathtaking view into the wealth of the Ottoman Empire. The famous **Topkapı Dagger ★** is here, weighted down by a row of emeralds and diamonds in the hilt and on the cover. This dagger was the protagonist in the 1964 film *Topkapı* (with Peter Ustinov), an amusing film about a plot to rob the Palace Museum. The actual dagger was intended as a gift from Sultan Mahmud I to Nadir Shah to warn him of an impending conspiracy on his life, but was returned by the couriers following a bloody revolution in which the shah was killed.

You'll notice a group of people hovering around a case at the far end of room no. 4, displaying the 86-caret **Spoonmaker's Diamond ★★**, or Kaşıkçı Diamond, the fifth-largest diamond in the world, glittering in a setting of 49 smaller diamonds. The diamond was actually discovered in the 17th century in a city dump by a local peddler who sold it to a jeweler for pennies.

The exhibit finishes with a stunning collection of "lesser" diamonds and gems, plus the **gold and jewel-encrusted chain mail ★★** of Sultan Mustafa III. Also of note is the **ceremonial sword ★**, attributed to either Caliph Osman (7th c. A.D.) or Osman Gazi (13th c.), and used in any sultan's inauguration, usually in front of Eyüp Sultan Mosque.

Another piece of note is the **golden cradle ★★** in which newborn sons were presented to the sultans, as well as an **emerald pendant ★** with 48 strings of pearls originally sent by Sultan Abdülhamid I as a gift to the tomb of the Prophet Mohammed in Mecca. The pendant was returned to Istanbul after Mecca was no longer within the borders of the empire.

Exit the courtyard down the stairs to the right through a long passage. To the right and parallel to the sea is the second terrace, affording one of the best views in the city. Imagine the days of seaside attacks on the palace walls as you watch the maritime traffic go by. During Byzantine times, a chain, composed of links .8m (2⅓ ft.) long, was forged to span the Golden Horn and prevent enemy ships from accessing the waterway.

This fourth courtyard was the realm of the sultan, and a stroll around the gardens will reveal some lovely examples of Ottoman kiosk architecture. Near the center of the upper level of the courtyard is the **Mustafa Paşa Kiosk,** the oldest building in the complex, which served as the physician's quarters and as a wardrobe for the sultan needing to effect swift changes during state functions. From the picture window overlooking the gardens, the sultan was known to observe wrestling matches, and even join in every now and again.

Perched on the upper terrace at the northernmost corner of the palace complex is the **Baghdad Kiosk ★**, magnificently sited to take best advantage of the views of the

---

✎ Topkapı Palace Lunch Break

After touring the Treasury, you've reached the halfway point and a good place to stop for lunch, drinks or to bask in the splendid vistas. The expansive **Konyalı restaurant** (✆ **0212/513-9696;** p. 131) includes indoor and outdoor dining rooms, as well as an outdoor cafeteria-style snack bar.

Golden Horn. The kiosk is decorated with priceless Iznik tiles, both inside and out. In addition to the tiles, the interior space is embellished with stained glass and crowned by a dome decorated with a traditional Ottoman motif in gold leaf. The kiosk served the sultan in colder weather; occupants of the kiosk were warmed by the central brazier. The **Sofa Köşkü** is the only surviving wooden pavilion in the palace. The golden-roofed **Iftariye Pavilion,** or "pavilion for breaking the fast," is the covered balcony on the northern edge of the courtyard, also called the *Mehtaplık,* or "Moon Place."

The **circumcision rooms,** rarely opened to the public, are also located in the fourth courtyard.

Backtrack through the passage and up the steps into the third courtyard. To the right past the Museum Directorate is the **Dormitory of the Pages of the Imperial Treasury,** formerly used to display decorative calligraphy from the Koran as well as jeweled Koran sets. At the far corner of the third courtyard is the **Holy Relic Section ★★★**, the largest collection in the world of this type, containing the personal belongings of the Prophet Mohammed, the caliphs, and even the unexpected **staff of Moses ★**. Also on display is a piece of St. John the Baptist's skull and a section of his forearm, enclosed within a solid gold model. The items on display were brought back to Istanbul by Selim the Grim in 1517, following his conquest of the holy cities of Mecca and Medina, and after declaring himself caliph. Since the Ka'aba was restored annually, pieces of the mosque were regularly kept as ornamentation for mosques. This collection was off-limits to anyone but the most favored members of the sultan's family and was only open to public viewing in 1962. The domed space is ornamented with Iznik tiles and quotations from the Koran along with a priceless set of rain gutters, an intricately carved door, and an old set of keys taken from the Ka'aba. Directly opposite the entrance are the **four sabers** belonging to the first four caliphs, and the first-ever copy of the **Koran ★**, documented on deerskin.

To the right is the **Mohammed Chamber ★★★**, fronted by a booth in which an *imam* (religious guide) has been reciting passages from the Koran continually for the past 500 years. This tradition was started by Mehmet II and sets the stage for the collection of holy relics within. The **golden cloth ★** that once covered the black stone in the central courtyard of the Ka'aba in Mecca now hangs in this exhibit, as a new one is richly prepared each year. Considered a gift falling from the heavens, the stone prompted Abraham to build a temple on the spot, now the Ka'aba, attracting worshippers from all faiths for several hundred years. The display cases here are almost always hidden behind fervent religious visitors communing with the spirit of the prophet through **relics ★★** of his hair, a tooth, his footprints, and even soil from his grave. The **Holy Mantle,** the most sacred item in the collection, is contained in a **gold coffer ★★** and sequestered behind a grilled door.

Turkish and Iranian miniatures as well as portraits of Ottoman sultans are exhibited in the rooms next to the one containing the Holy Relics. While the original collection amounts to a total of 13,000 specimens, this exhibit comes nowhere near this number. The main draw is the collection of portraits (both copies and originals) modeled after those painted by some of the Renaissance's most celebrated artists (Veronese, Bellini). Lacking any record of the physiological characteristics of the first 12 sultans, the Ottomans had the ones painted by the Venetians brought back to Istanbul in 1579.

In the center of the courtyard is the **Ahmet III Library,** constructed in the 16th century of white marble and recently restored and opened to the public. The

To visit the Harem you must purchase a ticket for one of the tours near the Carriage Gate entrance next to the Divan; your tour time will be indicated on your ticket. Tours depart on the half-hour and last about 30 minutes. Buy your ticket to the Harem at the beginning of your visit to the palace because when the

tour buses arrive, the wait on both the ticket and entry lines can be very long. Of the 400 rooms, only around 20 are on the tour, with explanations that are not always audible or, for that matter, intelligible. Nonetheless, the tour is worth taking.

bookcases are inlaid with ivory and contain about 6,000 volumes of Arab and Greek manuscripts. The stained glass is from the early 17th century; the platform divan seating is typically Ottoman, and the carpets are over 500 years old.

Return to the second courtyard, where along the right side you will come upon the **Imperial Armory,** a collection of arms and objects acquired during the various military campaigns. Mehmet the Conqueror's sword is here, as is Süleyman the Magnificent's, but it's the unattributed 2.5m (8¼-ft.) one that really impresses.

Before entering the Harem, take a peek into the **Imperial Council Hall,** or **Divan** ★, constructed during the reign of Süleyman the Magnificent. State affairs were conducted here while the sultan eavesdropped from the grate above, which leads directly to the Harem. From this concealed position, the sultan could interrupt proceedings with a motion to his grand vizier and call for a private conference whenever the need arose. His wife, Roxelana, would often secretly attend these sessions, a privilege that ended in several unfortunate fatalities.

The **Harem** ★★ has three main sections: the outer quarters of the Black Eunuchs charged with guarding the Harem; the inner stone courtyard for the concubines; and the apartments facing the sea reserved for the sultan, his mother, favorite concubines, and future heirs to the throne. The tour begins at the Carriage Gate, where the sultan's mother and wives would be whisked away unseen by outsiders during exits and entrances. Past the first Guard Room is a long courtyard lined with cells that served as the Barracks of the Black Eunuchs. The upper levels were reserved for the younger eunuchs, with the lower cells housing the older ones. Winding through the maze of additions, the tour comes to the quarters of the concubines, unheated and often unsanitary rooms around a claustrophobic stone courtyard. The only way out was to be one of the very lucky few chosen by the mother for the sultan; the others were servants to the sultan, or to the girls higher up on the hierarchy. At its most crowded, the Harem housed over 800 concubines. Even if the sultan rotated every night, the numbers were against those girls, and although some were given to the harems of state officials or grand viziers, many died virgins (but who knows what really went on in there).

In contrast, the **Apartment of the Valide Sultan** ★★, the sultan's mother's room, sandwiched between the girls' quarters and the sultan's, is a domed wonder of mother-of-pearl, ivory, tortoiseshell, gold leaf, porcelain tiles, and frosted glass. The apartment consisted of a bedroom, a dining room, a chamber for prayer, and an office around a courtyard.

The **sultan's private bath** ★, furnished with the usual *hamam* gear but infinitely more lush, has a guarded mesh gate so that the sultan could relax without the fear of being disturbed or assassinated. The sultan's apartments are close by, and the visit continues with the **Imperial Reception Hall** ★★, where celebrations or evenings of entertainment took place while musicians played discreetly from the mezzanine. While the sultan presided from his throne, the women adhered to a strict hierarchy, with the most important women seated at the center of the platform.

One of the few rooms preserving the luster of its creator is the grand domed **Private Chambers of Murat III** ★★, built by Sinan in 1578. The walls are covered with a classic blue Iznik tile with red highlights, a prototype that was never duplicated. A frieze of calligraphy runs the perimeter of the room, and elegant panels of flowers and plums surround a bronze fireplace. The room is also called the Fountain Room because of the marble fountain that was kept running to mask conversations not intended for prying ears.

The **Reading Room** used by Ahmet I is a small but well positioned library that affords distracting views of the convergence of the three waterways: the Golden Horn, the Marmara Sea, and the Bosphorus.

The **Fruit Room** is more of a breakfast nook added by Sultan Ahmet III to his private chambers. One look and it's not hard to figure out how this room got its name. The room is enveloped in fruit and floral overkill, but evidently the sultan's attentions were focused on the Harem pool out the window.

The next stop on the Harem tour is at the twin apartments of the crown prince, better known as **The Cage** ★. In the early years of the empire, a crowned prince was well prepared to fulfill his destiny as a leader, beginning his studies in these rooms and later moving on to actual field experience in one of the provinces. When the practice of fratricide was abandoned, brothers of the sultan were sequestered in these rooms, where they either went crazy or languished in the lap of luxury—or both. The opulence of the stained glass and the tile work and the mother-of-pearl inlaid cabinets belie the chambers' primary function as a jail cell, which supports a recent discovery that the actual cage was located in another part of the Harem. The tour guides continue to perpetuate the myth by billing these two rooms as the bona fide cage.

The Harem tour comes to an end at the **Courtyard of the Favorites** ★★, surrounded by a charming building recalling the medieval residences of Florence. The apartments on the upper floors were reserved for the members of the Harem the sultan liked best, enjoying open space and sea views as far as the Princes' Islands. The circular spot in the center of the courtyard was covered with a tent for shaded outings, and the grooves served as water channels for cooling.

The exit to the second courtyard is through the **Golden Road,** a narrow stone corridor that was the crown prince's first taste of the world beyond the stifling confines of the Harem.

Sultanahmet, entrance at the end of Babuhümayun Cad., behind the Hagia Sophia. www.top kapisarayi.gov.tr. © **0212/512-0480.** Admission to the palace 20TL; Wed–Mon Apr–Oct 9am–7pm; Nov–Mar 9am–5pm. Admission for the Harem 15TL; Wed–Mon Apr–Oct 9am–5pm; Nov–Mar 9am–3:30pm. Closed national holidays and at 1pm on the first day of religious festivals. Tram: Sultanahmet or Gülhane.

Byzantine Sights (or Byzantium Wasn't Built in a Day)

Church of Theotokos Pammakaristos (Joyous Mother of God Church, now the Fethiye Camii) MOSQUE & RELIGIOUS SITE   This church was built in 1292 by John Comnenus, probably related to the royal family, and his wife Anna

Doukaina. Later additions and renovations were made, including the construction of a side chapel in 1315 to house the remains of Michael Glabas, a former general, and his family. In 1456, the Orthodox Patriarchate moved here from the Havariyun (see the Fatih Mosque/Fatih Camii, p. 114) and remained here until 1586. Five years later, Murat III converted the church into a mosque and renamed it in honor of his conquest over Georgia and Azerbaijan. To accommodate a larger inner space for prayer, most of the interior walls were removed.

The interior of the church/mosque contains the best mosaic panels after the Hagia Sophia and St. Savior in Chora. In the dome is a representation of the Pantocrator surrounded by prophets (Moses, Jeremiah, Zephaniah, Micah, Joel, Zechariah, Obadiah, Habakkuk, Jonah, Malachi, Ezekiel, and Isaiah). In the apse Christ Hyperagathos is shown with the Virgin and St. John the Baptist. The Baptism of Christ survives intact to the right of the dome.

From the Kariye Camii, follow Draman Cad. (which becomes Fethiye Cad.), turn left onto Fethiyekapısı Sok. (just before the road bends sharply to the right), Fener. © **0212/528-4500.** Admission 5TL. Thurs–Tues 9:30am–4:30pm. Bus: 90 from Eminönü or 90B from Beyazıt.

4

Ecumenical Patriarchate of Constantinople ★ RELIGIOUS SITE The

Ecumenical Patriarchate of Constantinople is the surviving legacy of a religious empire that dominated the affairs of Christians worldwide for more than 1,100 years. After the fall of Rome in A.D. 476, Constantinople inherited unrivaled leadership of the Christian world under the name "Rome of the East" and "New Rome." The Greeks, Bulgarians, Serbians, Romanians, Albanians, and Georgians who adhered to the Eastern Orthodox creed were referred to as "Romans" (thus the reason why many an Istanbul church include the word "Rum" in its title). While the pope continued to reject the primacy of the Bishop of Constantinople (soon after given the title of Archbishop), the influence of the Patriarch of Constantinople nevertheless grew under the patronage of the emperor. The initial seat of the Patriarchate was pre-Constantine Hagia Eirene, now in the first court of Topkapı Palace. Upon Justinian's completion of the Hagia Sophia, the Church was rooted here for the next 916 years (with a brief respite when the Byzantine Court was forced to flee to Nicaea after the Fourth Crusade in 1204). The Ottoman conquest displaced the Patriarchate to the Havariyun (or Church of the 12 Apostles, now lost under Fatih Camii), before it moved to the Church of the Pammakaristos (Fethiye Camii) in 1456. In 1587, the Eastern Orthodox Church moved to the Church of the Virgin Mary in Vlah Palace, and then to St. Demetrios in Balat. The Patriarchate settled into its current spot in The Church of St. George (Ayios Yeoryios) in 1601. In the 19th century, assertions of national independence and religious autonomy whittled the influence of the Patriarchate, until its reach was constricted to the borders of the Turkish Republic and a mere handful of semi-autonomous communities abroad. Still, the Orthodox community considers the Ecumenical Patriarchate one of the two most prominent Christian institutions in the world, the other being the Holy See in Rome. Today, the Patriarch and Archbishop of Constantinople is *primus inter pares,* or "first among equals," among the 14 autonomous and semi-autonomous Patriarchates-in-communion that make up the Eastern Orthodox Church.

The present church was built in 1720 on a traditional basilica plan. It seems to lack the grandeur one would expect of its station, but the building was constructed under the Ottoman prohibition against non-Muslim use of domes or masonry roofs on their places of worship. Instead, it is topped by a timber roof. The gilded iconostasis provides some insight into the opulence one imagines of Byzantium. The Patriarchal

Throne is believed to date to St. John Chrysostom Patriarchate in the 5th century A.D. His relics and those of St. Gregory the Theologian, which were hijacked after the 1204 Crusader sacking of the city, were brought back from Rome by Patriarch Bartholomew in 2004. In the aisle opposite these relics are the remains of the female saints, St. Euphemia, St. Theophano, and St. Solomone. There are also three invaluable gold mosaic icons including one of the Virgin, as well as the Column of Flagellation. The small complex is composed of the modest Cathedral, the Patriarchate Library, administrative offices, and the Ayios Harambalos spring.

Sadrazam Ali Paşa Cad. 35/3, Fener. www.ec-patr.org. (℃) **0212/531-9670.** Daily 8:30am–6pm. Bus: 36CE, 399B–399D, 44B, 99–99A from Eminönü; 35D from Balat; or 55T from Taksim.

Galata Tower and the Galata Neighborhood ★ MONUMENT & SQUARE
The neighborhood of Galata, located on a steep hump of land north of the Golden Horn and historic peninsula, actually sits on the earliest foundations of the city, dating, as far as present-day archaeologists can tell, to Greek and Roman times. At one time, it was covered in gardens and vineyards; indeed the ancient Greeks called the district "Sykai," meaning "place of fig gardens," and later, the hilly expanse became known as "peran en Skai," or "fig gardens on the other shore." Or just plain Pera. There is also speculation that the name Galata comes from the Italian word for descent (*calata*), an appropriate description of the steep and staired streets that slope down the hill from Beyoğlu to the Golden Horn. The district developed into its present form in the 13th century, when Eastern Roman Emperor Michael VIII Palaeologus granted the Genoese permission to settle here. The district became a magnet for merchants from all over Europe: Italians, Germans, Armenians, Jews, and Austrians, all re-creating their own micro-universe. The Genoese remained neutral during the Ottoman siege, so when Mehmet the Conqueror took over the city, although he installed his own Ottoman administration and assumed control of all commercial affairs, the Sultan granted them, along with the other minority communities, substantial commercial privileges. The ensuing commercial prosperity of the district fed trade throughout the Mediterranean and acted as a magnet for foreigners and ethnic minorities who established the district as centers of business, shipping, and banking. Serving the center of the financial district was a row of stately financial institutions lining both sides of what is now alternately called Bankalar Sokağı (Bank Street) and Voyvoda Caddesi. Bankers wishing to settle near their places of business constructed dignified residences for themselves and their families, and serving the community was a full complement of schools, churches, and synagogues. As Galata prospered, the population burst its boundaries to incorporate the neighborhoods northward (and eventually up to and along the Grand Rue de Pera or Istiklal Cad.). A stroll up and down the steep cobbled streets will reveal schools, private residences, churches, synagogues, and Ottoman-era warehouses. (There are also the ruins of a *mikva*, or Jewish bathhouse, in dire need of restoration opposite the former private mansion of the Camondo banking family, now the Galata Residence.)

The decline of Galata and its subsequent revitalization are both relatively recent phenomena. With the turn-of-the-20th-century flight of the wealthy merchant class to Istanbul's tonier neighborhoods, Galata deteriorated into a magnet for poor rural migrant families and a location no fewer than three thriving brothels. In the 1990s, the nation's trend for historic preservation arrived in Galata with an ambitious architectural revitalization project that created an inviting public square and a couple of charming and characteristic outdoor tea gardens at the base of the Galata Tower. In the past 4 or 5 years, the trend has caught fire, as local real estate gets snapped up

700 YEARS OF TURKISH jews

Jews visiting Turkey inevitably ask for a tour of a local synagogue, and as the default working temple in the heart of Galata, **Neve Shalom** is usually the first and only stop. While interesting to see (particularly after sustaining recurring terrorist attacks), a visit to Neve Shalom is far from the Holy Grail of Jewish sites in Istanbul. It's also not necessarily guaranteed, since a pre-visit request accompanied by a faxed copy of your passport is the *minimum* requirement for entry. (For more information on how to visit Istanbul's synagogues and on the Jewish community in general, got to **www.turkyahudileri.com**, the official site of the Jewish community in Turkey. I'd recommend instead the **Jewish Museum of Turkey,** located in the restored 19th-century Zulfaris Synagogue. The museum represents the vision of the Quincentennial Foundation (named for the 500-year anniversary of the Jewish expulsion from Spain) and showcases the peaceful coexistence of Jews and Turks in Turkey. The foundation's vision came to fruition in 2001 with this anthology of Jewish presence in Turkey beginning with the Ottoman conquest of Bursa, through Sultan Beyazit's invitation to those expelled from Spain, to the present day. The museum/synagogue is located at Karaköy Meydanı, Perçemli Sokak (facing the lower entrance to the Tünel funicular, Perçemli Sok. is the first alley to your right; the museum is at the end of the street on your right; ✆ **0212/292-6333;** www.muze500.com), and is open Monday through Thursday 10am to 4pm, and Friday and Sunday from 10am to 2pm. (Closed for religious holidays). There is no admission fee, but donations are encouraged.

by artists, expat journalists, and private developers and turned into galleries, cafes, hotels, and private homes. At last look, the plaza surrounding the tower and the storied Galip Dede Caddesi had been repaved and a restoration project was under way at the north corner opposite the tower. But the streets leading down to the Golden Horn, while hosting the odd new tea shop or guesthouse, maintain the grit that has settled on the district since its heyday.

The origins of **Galata Tower** date back to the 5th or 6th century A.D., but the tower that stands today is a 14th-century reconstruction by the Genoese, built in appreciation of Michael VIII Palaeologus, who granted special permission to allow them to settle the area of Galata. One condition of the agreement was that the Genoese were prohibited from putting up any defensive walls, a ban that they unceremoniously ignored.

The Galata Tower has been used as a jail, a dormitory, a site for rappelling competitions, and a launching pad in the 17th century when Hezarfen Ahmet Çelebi attached wings to his arms and glided all the way to Üsküdar. The tower rises 135m (443 ft.) above sea level and stands 60m (197 ft.) high, with walls that are more than 3.5m (11 ft.) thick. From the summit of the tower, you can see the Golden Horn, the Bosphorus, and the Marmara Sea, that is, if you don't mind the 11TL elevator ride and the mass of people clamoring for the best viewing spot. The tower is used as a restaurant and nightclub for a traditional **Turkish folkloric** show, at 80€ a pop (they'll take 70€ if you pay in cash), but frankly, I'd pass on both the show and the view, and take advantage of the city's plentiful panoramas elsewhere.

Arranged around a mushrooming fountain with choice seating tucked into the arches of the Sphendome, the **Havusbaşı Çay Bahcesi,** or Pond Head Tea Garden (Nakilbent Sok.; © **0212/638-8819**), couldn't get more atmospheric. Nestle in for fresh squeezed fruit juice, tea, or light fare well into the evening hours, courtesy of Buhara 93 across the street. In the summer, there's live music or a derviş show nightly.

Şişhane. www.galatatower.net. © **0212/293-8180.** Historic gate daily 9am–1am (no access during the folklore show). Elevator to the top of Galata Tower free with reservation to Turkish show. Other times 11TL. Mon–Sat 8:30am–1am. Tram: Karaköy; bus: 28 from Upper and Lower Tünel, 28T from Beşiktaş.

Küçük Ayasofya Camii (Church of the Saints Sergius and Bacchus) ★ 👔

MOSQUE & RELIGIOUS SITE   Started in A.D. 527 by Justinian in the first year of his reign, this former church represents an important stage in the process of Byzantine architecture, particularly in the support of the dome atop an octagonal base. The church took its name from two martyred Roman soldiers later elevated to the status of patron saints; the edifice later assumed the name of "Little Ayasofya" due to its resemblance to the Hagia Sophia in Sultanahmet Park, which was started in A.D. 532. The church was converted into a mosque in the 16th century by the chief eunuch under Beyazıt II, who is buried in the garden. We know from the ancient historian Procopius that the interior of the church was covered in marble and mosaics; however, none of this remains. Opposite the entrance to the mosque is a *medrese* that encloses an uncharacteristically serene and leafy garden. An on-site eatery as well as teahouses share the arcade with a number of bookshops and calligraphy boutiques, and genuine finds offering samples at some of the most competitive prices in the city.

Lower end of Küçük Ayasofya Cad. No phone. Tram: Sultanahmet.

Mosaic Museum ★ RUINS

In 1933, excavators discovered a mosaic pavement below what is now the Arasta Bazaar, identified as a section of Peristyle Courtyard (open court with porticos) of Constantine's Great Palace. As a decorative work of the palace, it is safe to assume (as scholars have) that the creation of the mosaic flooring employed the most gifted craftsmen of the era, collected from around the empire. Because of the exceptional nature of the mosaics, there are no comparable existing Byzantine-era mosaics from which to date these. The current assumption is that they were crafted during either the reign of Constantine or of Justinian.

Archaeologists estimate that the size of the courtyard was 1,872 sq. m (20,150 sq. ft.), requiring a total of 80 million *tesserae* of lime, glass, and terra cotta. Typical of Roman mosaics, the subjects depicted on the panels are representative of an earlier, pre-Christian artistic era absent of religious motifs, showing instead hunting scenes and scenes from mythology.

Entrance at Torun Sok., across from the entrance to the Sultanahmet Sarayı Hotel; accessible through Arasta Bazaar to the southeast of the Blue Mosque. © **0212/518-1205.** Admission 8TL. Tues–Sun Apr–Oct 9am–6:30pm; Nov–Mar 9am–4:30pm. Tram: Sultanahmet.

St. Savior in Chora (Kariye Müzesi; formerly the Kariye Camii) ★★★

RELIGIOUS SITE   Much of what remained in the coffers of the Byzantine Empire

SULTANAHMET'S STREETS PAVED WITH GOLD: THE GREAT palace

The Great Palace complex was the primary residence and administrative center of Byzantine (and Roman) emperors from A.D. 330, when it was begun by Constantine, to 1081, when the Comnenus Dynasty moved to Blachernae. In 1204, the palace became the home of the Latin Crusaders-in-Residence, but through their neglect, the palace slowly fell into decline. It was eventually picked over for parts for use in new construction projects. Tradition has it that when Mehmet the Conqueror took the city (by which time the Byzantine dynasty had returned and installed itself into Blachernae and the Great Palace), the sultan's reaction to the state of the palace was to quote a phrase of the Persian poet, Ferdowsi: "the spider spins his web in the Palace of the Caesars . . ."

Constantine's earliest construction was based on Diocletian's palace on the Dalmatian Coast and covered an area of 10 hectares (almost 25 acres) from the Hippodrome to the Marmara Sea. At its peak, the palace was composed of a complex that included state buildings, throne rooms, gardens, libraries, thermal baths, and fountains (among which were the 5th century A.D. Chalke monumental gate and the Magnaura or Senate building). The Bucoleon (built by Theophilius in A.D. 842) and Justinian's Hormisdas (6th century A.D.; located to the West of the Bucoleon) were later additions. A few places around the neighborhood provide a peak at these remains. A section of the loggia from the Bucoleon that survived the construction of the commuter train can be seen on the southern edge of the peninsula outside the remains of the sea walls, to the east of Aksakal Caddesi. A mosaic floor of one of the peristyle courtyards of the Great Palace is now the **Mosaic Museum** (p. 107). Some remains were uncovered in the construction of the Eresin Crown hotel in Sultanahmet, while the Four Seasons project (they're adding a rear annex building) sits right atop the Magnaura.

was invested in the embellishment of this church, one of the finest preserved galleries of Byzantine mosaics as well as a detailed account of early Christian history. The original church was built in the 4th century A.D. as part of a monastery complex outside the city walls (*chora zonton* means "in the country" in Greek), but the present structure dates to the 11th century. The interior restoration and decoration were the result of the patronage of Theodore Metochites, Grand Logothete of the Treasury during the reign of Andronicus II Paleologos, and date to the first quarter of the 14th century. His benevolence is depicted in a dedicatory panel in the inner narthex over the door to the nave, which shows Metochites presenting the Chora to Jesus.

When the church was converted into a mosque in the 16th century, the mosaics were plastered over. A 19th-century architect uncovered the mosaics but was ordered by the government to re-cover those in the section of the prayer hall. American archaeologists Whittemore and Underwood finally uncovered these masterpieces during World War II, and although the Chora became a museum in 1947, it is still often referred to as the Kariye Camii.

In total, there are about 50 mosaic panels, but because some of them are only partially discernible, there seems to be disagreement on the exact count. Beginning in the exonarthex, the subjects of the mosaic panels fall into one of four themes, presented more or less in chronological order after the New Testament. Broadly, the themes relate to the cycle of the life of Christ and his miracles, stories of the life of Mary, scenes from the infancy of Christ, and stories of Christ's ministry. The panels not included in these themes are the devotional panels in the exonarthex and the narthex, and the three panels in the nave: *The Dormition of the Virgin, Christ,* and the *Virgin Hodegetria.*

The **Paracclesion** (burial section) is decorated with a series of masterful frescoes completed sometime after the mosaics and were presumably executed by the same artist. The frescoes reflect the purpose of the burial chamber with scenes of Heaven and Hell, the Resurrection and the Life, and a stirring **Last Judgment** with a scroll representing infinity above a River of Fire, and a detail of Jesus saving Adam's and Eve's souls from the devil.

Camii Sok., Kariye Meydanı, Edirnekapı. kariye.muze.gov.tr. (C) **0212/631-9241.** Admission 15TL. Thurs–Tues Apr–Oct 9am–7pm; Nov–Mar 9am–4:30pm. Tram: Direction Zeytinburnu, exit at Topkapı station then change to light rail (direction Habibler) exiting at Edirnekapı. Bus: 90B from Beyazıt or 90 from Eminönü direct to the museum, or 91 from Eminönü to Edirnekapı. Bring a map to get you from the stops to the church.

Sphendome ARCHITECTURE   The ancient retaining wall of the closed end of the Hippodrome joins the Obelisks and Spina as the only remaining relics of the early Byzantine period. Today, this enduring infrastructure supports the buildings of Marmara Technical University. The structure is best viewed from below (access down the hill along Şifa Hamamı Sok. to Nakilbent Sok.); notice the 2m-high (6½-ft.) niches that used to contain statues (now evocative seating for an outdoor tea garden and restaurant). The high arched section served as the stables.

Southeastern end of the Hippodrome. Tram: Sultanahmet.

Valens Aqueduct (Bozdoğan Kemeri) ARCHITECTURE   Now nothing more than a scenic overpass for cars traveling down Atatürk Bulvarı, the Valens Aqueduct or "Arcade of the Gray Falcon" was started by Constantine and completed in the 4th century A.D. by Valens. Justinian II had the second tier added; even Mehmet the Conqueror and Sinan had a hand in its restoration and enlargement. The aqueduct connects the third and fourth hills of Istanbul and had an original length of about .8km (½ mile). Water was transported under various rulers to the Byzantine palaces, city cisterns, and then to Topkapı Palace, and the aqueduct served in supplying water to the city for a total of 1,500 years.

Bridging Atatürk Bulv., btw. Aksaray and the Golden Horn. Bus: 36A, 36CV, 36D, 36V, 37C, 37Y, 38B, 39D, 39Y, 77A, or 86V.

Yerebatan Cistern (Yerebatan Sarnıcı) ★★ HISTORIC SITE   Classical music echoing off the still water and the seductive lighting make your descent into the "Sunken Palace" seem like a scene out of *Phantom of the Opera.* The only thing missing is a rowboat, which was an actual means of transportation before the boardwalk was installed in what is now essentially a great underground fishpond and stunning historical artifact. The cistern was first constructed by Constantine and enlarged to its present form by Justinian after the Nika Revolt using 336 marble columns recycled from the Hellenistic ruins in and around the Bosphorus. The water supply, routed from reservoirs around the Black Sea and transported via the Aqueduct of Valens, served as a backup for periods of drought or siege. It was left largely untouched by the Ottomans, who preferred running, not stagnant, water, and eventually used the source to water the Topkapı Gardens. The cistern was later left to collect

STEAM heat: TAKING THE HAMAM

In characteristic socially conscious fashion, the Selçuks were the ones to adopt the Roman and Byzantine tradition of public bathing and treat it like a public work. Lacking running water at home, society embraced the *hamam*, which evolved into not only a place to cleanse body and soul, but a social phenomenon as well. Even the accoutrements of the *hamam* took on symbols of status: wooden clogs inlaid with mother-of-pearl, towels embroidered with gold thread, and so on. Men gathered to talk about politics, sports, and women, while the ladies kept an eagle eye out for suitable wives for their sons.

The utility of the *hamam* evolved and fell out of daily use, probably because the neighborhood ones have a reputation for being dirty, and the historic ones come with a hefty admission charge. As of late though, views of the *hamam* have undergone a complete renaissance, not least of all owing to the arrival of überdeluxe *hamam* spas such as the ones in the Four Seasons the Bosphorus, the Çırağan Palace and Hotel Les Ottomans.

Istanbul's luxury *hamam* scene is a far cry from the perfunctory treatment received at one of the historically touristy *hamams*. What to expect? The main entrance of a Turkish bath opens up to a **camekan,** a central courtyard lined with changing cubicles surrounding an ornamental marble fountain. Visitors are presented with the traditional *pestamal*, a checkered cloth worn like a sarong (up higher for women). Valuables are secured in a private locker, provided for each customer, although it's a good idea to leave the best of it at home.

The experience begins past the cooling section (and often the toilets), into the steam room, or **hararet.** For centuries, architects worked to perfect the design of the *hararet*: a domed, octagonal (or square) room, revetted in marble, often with marvelous oculi to provide entry for sunlight, and with intricate basins at various intervals and a heated marble platform, known as the **naval stone** or *göbektaşı*, in the center. Often the *hamam* is covered with elaborately crafted and ornately designed tiles.

silt and mud until it was cleaned by the Municipality and opened to the public in 1987. The water is clean and aerated thanks to a supply of overgrown goldfish that are replaced every 4 years or so.

Follow the wooden catwalk and notice the "column of tears," a pillar etched with symbols resembling tears. (An identical pattern is visible on the columns scattered along the tramway near the Üniversite stop, where the old Byzantine palace was once located.) At the far end of the walkway are two **Medusa heads,** one inverted and the other on its side; according to mythology, placing her this way caused her to turn herself into stone. Another superstition is that turning her upside down neutralizes her powers. Possibly, the stones were just the right size as pedestals.

Yerebatan Cad. (diagonal from Hagia Sophia), Sultanahmet. www.yerebatan.com. ⓒ **0212/522-1259.** Admission 10TL. Daily 9am–5:30pm. Tram: Sultanahmet.

Historic Hamams (Turkish Baths)

The number of *hamams* in Istanbul mushroomed in the 18th century when the realization hit that they were big business. Mahmut I had the Cağaloğlu Hamamı built to finance the construction of his library near the Hagia Sophia, but new constructions were limited later that century because the *hamams* were using up the city's resources of water and wood. Only about 20 *hamams* have survived.

The *hamam* ritual begins with you supine on the heated naval stone. Many first-time visitors have questions about how much clothing to take off; in segregated *hamams*, it's customary and acceptable to strip (this is a bath, after all) or to wear a bikini bottom. (While generally, the gender of *hamam* attendants in hotels and major tourist centers match that of the client's, it is not uncommon for a neighborhood *hamam* to staff only men. Call ahead if you have any concerns.) Step one is the scrubbing using an abrasive mitt *(kese)* aimed at removing the outer layer of dead skin and other organic detritus. The actual bath is next; the substantial and slippery soap bubbles create the perfect canvas for the accompanying massage. This is primarily where you will notice the difference between a private *hamam* (where you are the only "client") and one of the more commercial ones. In the commercial ones (listed above, all of which I have nevertheless frequented repeatedly), don't be surprised if your massage feels more like a cursory pummeling.

After all, how many clients complain? (Not me.) The private hotel *hamans* have more of a long-term stake and therefore provide high-quality service. The difference is like night and day.

The final act of the ritual is the rinsing (you may even get a relaxing facial massage), followed by a definitive tap on the shoulder followed by "You like?"—an indication that your session is over. At this point, you are most likely dehydrated and sleepy, which is when the purpose of that **cold room** with the lounge chairs becomes evident. Refreshments are available and the price list is usually displayed nearby. (Refreshments are usually included in the price of a hotel *hamam*.) In the commercial *hamams*, you can go back into the *hararet* as often as you like, whereas in a hotel *hamam*, a session lasts 45 minutes to an hour.

Whether you opt for the 30TL version or the 90€ hotel service, definitely sign up for "the works" at least once in your life, and you'll forever comprehend why it was indeed good to be the sultan.

The most visited *hamams* today are the palatial **Çemberlitaş Hamamı,** Vezirhan Cad. 8 (off Divanyolu at the Column of Constantine; ℂ **0212/522-7974;** www.cemberlitashamami.com.tr; daily 6am–midnight with separate sections; MasterCard and Visa accepted), which was based on a design by Sinan, and the 18th-century **Cağaloğlu Hamamı,** Yerebatan Cad. at Ankara Cad. (ℂ **0212/522-2424;** www.cagalogl24u.com.tr, daily 8am–10pm for men, 8am–8pm for women), which allegedly saw the bare bottoms of Franz Liszt, Edward VIII, Kaiser Wilhelm, and Florence Nightingale, and even had a part as an extra in *Indiana Jones and the Temple of Doom.* A skin scrubbing and massage costs 99TL, or you can opt out of the massage for 59TL (or just sweat on the slab for 39TL).

In Beyoğlu, the **Tarıhı Galatasaray Hamamı,** Sütterazı Sok. 24 (from Istiklal Cad. in front of the Galatasaray High School, it's the second street to the left of the gate; ℂ **0212/249-4242** for the men's side; ℂ **0212/249-4342,** women's side; www.galatasarayhamami.com; daily 7am–10pm for men, 8am–8pm for women), was built by Beyazıt II in 1481 as part of the Galata Sarayı school complex. It's the least touristy of the historic *hamams* mentioned here (does John Travolta's recent visit support or belie this? Hmmm), and indeed, sometimes locals working in the area will pop in for a quickie. All of these historic hamams have begun adding spa-like treatments, but because these establishments don't really rely on repeat clientele, the level of service tends to be consistent only in that you won't ever confuse it with the Four Seasons. Still, it's hard to mess up a facial clay mask, and everybody should experience the full-service hamam at least once in his or her life. Expect to pay around 45TL–70TL depending on whether you plan on engaging an attendant or going for the self-serve option.

A better value is the recently restored **Süleymaniye Hamamı ★**, Mimar Sinan Cad. 20 (*©* **0212/519-5569;** www.suleymaniyehamami.com; daily 10am–midnight), part of the Süleymaniye mosque complex and another architectural and social welfare wonder of Sinan and Süleyman the Magnificent. The price of admission includes the massage and *kese* (35€ per person), and if available, a pickup from your hotel. One caveat: Only couples and families are admitted; no single men or women allowed. Or if you really want to experience the city of years ago, take your chances over at the crumbling and awesome **Kadırga Hamamı** (Kadırga Liman Cad 127; *©* **0212/518-1948**) where you can get the traditional service by a non-English speaking local for 40TL and the self-serve for 20TL. It's open 6am to midnight.

Probably the most spectacular *hamam* is the Ayasofya Hamamı, occupying the Ayasofya **Hürrem Sultan Hamamı ★★** (*©* **0212/517-3535;** www.ayasofya hamami.com) in Sultanahmet Park. Built by Sinan in 1557 on a symmetrical plan that provided two separate sections of identical domed halls, the *hamam* was decommissioned when it was found that the elongated layout resulted in too much heat loss. For the past decade or so, it had been used as a carpet exhibition center for the state-owned Dösim group of shops. Then, in the spirit of restoring Istanbul in advance of the city's reign as European Capital of Culture (2010), the bath was restored to its original function as a public, if not exclusive, bath. There is a selection of treatments, from basic to the Elixir of Life royal treatment, 70€ to 160€, which includes your own traditional bath set.

If you're looking for luxury and personal attention, more in the lines of a modern day spa treatment, you'll want to visit a *hamam* at a hotel instead. My personal favorites are **Les Ottomans** (p. 173), **Four Seasons Bosphorus** (p. 173) and the **Çırağan Palace** (p. 118). (**Note:** For any *hamam* treatment, a 10% tip is customary). Expect to pay around 100€ or so for the basic service.

Ottoman Mosques, Tombs & Monuments

Beyazıt Mosque (Beyazıt Camii) MOSQUE   Beyazıt II, son of the Conqueror, is remembered kindly by history as one of the more benevolent of sovereigns, and indeed, in Turkey, he has been elevated to a saint. The mosque and complex bearing his name is the oldest surviving imperial mosque in the city (its predecessor, the Fatih Camii, succumbed to an earthquake and was reconstructed in 1766). The complex was built between 1501 and 1506 using materials taken from Theodosius's Forum of Tauri, on which it is built. Again, the architect of Beyazıt Camii looked to the Hagia Sophia, employing a central dome buttressed by semi-domes and a long nave with double arcades, although the mosque is half the size of the church. The Beyazıt Mosque also borrows elements from the Fatih Mosque, imitating the system of buttressing and the use of great columns alongside the dome. Thanks to Sultan Beyazıt II's patronage, the Ottomans found a style of their own, which served as a bridge to later classical Ottoman architecture. The sultan, who died in 1512, is buried in a simple tomb, decorated in mother-of-pearl and stained glass, at the back of the gardens.

Yeniçeriler Cad., across from the Beyazıt tram stop. No phone. Tram: Beyazıt; bus: 36A, 36CV, 36D, 36V, 37C, 37Y, 38B, 39B, 39Y, 77A, or 86V.

If you've made it all the way to Eyüp to visit the mosque, take a short detour to **Pierre Loti,** Gümüşsuyu Balmumcu Sok. 1 (📞 **0212/581-2696**), a cafe of legend and a spectacular spot for serene views of the Golden Horn. The legend goes that French naval officer Julien Viaud fell in love with Aziyade, a married Turkish woman, during his first visit to Istanbul around 1876. The young woman would sneak out of her husband's harem when he was away for the chance to spend a few fleeting moments in the arms of her lover at his house in the hills of Eyüp. After an absence from Turkey of 10 years, Viaud returned to find Aziyade had died soon after his departure. Viaud gained fame during his lifetime, and his stories are romantic accounts much like the one of legend. This cafe, on the hill of Eyüp, was a favorite of his, and for reasons unknown, became known as Pierre Loti Kahvesi. Eyüp's historic cemetery is on the hill next to the cafe. The cafe is open daily 8am to midnight; no food or alcohol is served here; avoid weekends, when nary an empty table will be your reward for the ride up. A cable car from the shore of the Golden Horn makes the trip straight up to the cafe at the top of the hill a little bit easier than walking up, although you may want to walk down through the old Ottoman cemetery.

Eyüp Sultan Mosque (Eyüp Sultan Camii) RELIGIOUS SITE The holiest site in Istanbul as well as one of the most sacred places in the Islamic world, the Eyüp Sultan Mosque was erected by Mehmet the Conqueror over the tomb of Halid bin Zeyd Ebu Eyyûb (known as Eyüp Sultan), the standard-bearer for the Prophet Mohammed as well as the last survivor of his inner circle of trusted companions. It is popularly accepted that while serving as commander of the Arab forces during the siege of A.D. 668 to 669, Eyüp was killed and buried on the outskirts of the city. One of the conditions of peace after the Arab siege was that the tomb of Eyüp be preserved.

The burial site was "discovered" during Mehmet the Conqueror's siege on the city, although the tomb is mentioned in written accounts as early as the 12th century.

A little village of tombs mushroomed on the spot by those seeking Eyüp Sultan's intervention in the hereafter, and it's still considered a privilege to be buried in the nearby cemeteries. The Girding of the Sword ceremony was traditionally held here. In this Ottoman enthronement rite, Osman Gazi's sword was passed on, maintaining continuity within the dynasty as well as creating a connection with the Turk's early ideal of Holy War.

Eyüp is a popular spot animated by the small bazaar nearby, crowds relaxing by the spray of the fountains, and little boys in blue-and-white satin celebrating their impending circumcisions. Unfortunately, it's a natural magnet for beggars as well. The baroque mosque replaces the original that was destroyed in the earthquake of 1766, but the real attraction here is the ***türbe,*** a sacred burial site that draws masses of pilgrims waiting in line to stand in the presence of the contents of the solid silver sarcophagus or meditate in prayer. Dress appropriately if you're planning to go in: no shorts, and heads covered for women. The line moves quickly in spite of the bottleneck inside the tomb; take a few moments to sense the power of the site. If you go on a Sunday, you'll see families parading around their little boys dressed like sultans (a pre-circumcision tradition).

Eyüp. Meydanı, off of Camii Kebir Cad. and north of the Golden Horn Bridge. No phone. Bus: 37C, 39, 39B, 39Ç, 39D, 39O, 39Y, or 48A; cable car from the Golden Horn.

Fatih Mosque and Complex (Fatih Camii ve Külliyesi) MOSQUE Fatih Sultan Mehmet II had his namesake built on the ruins of the Havariyun, or the Church of Holy Apostles, which served as the seat of Christianity after the conquest, from 1453 to 1456. At that time, the church was second only to the Hagia Sophia in importance and therefore served as the burial place of every emperor from Constantine I to Constantius VIII (from A.D. 337–1028!). Alexius III Angelius looted the graves to fill his imperial coffers; the graves were again looted during the Fourth Crusade. In addition to the commanding mosque, the eight *medreses* (schools) founded by the sultan are the only surviving sections of a complex that included a caravansaray, a hospital, several *hamams*, kitchens, and a market, which combined to form a university that instructed up to 1,000 students at any given time. Wanting a monument more spectacular than that of Hagia Sophia, the sultan cut off the hands of the architect, Atık Sinan (not Süleyman's Sinan), when the Fatih Mosque failed to surpass the height of the church, despite its position atop the fourth of the seven hills of Istanbul. The tombs of Fatih Mehmet II and his wife (mother of Beyazıt II) are located outside of the *mihrab* wall.

Enter on Fevzipaşa Cad., Fatih. No phone. Bus: 28, 31E, 32, 336E, 336I, 36A, 36CV, 36D, 36KE, 36V, 37C, 37E, 37Y, 38B, 38E, 39B, 39Y, 86V, 87, 90, or 91O.

Galata Mevlevihanesi RELIGIOUS SITE This derviş lodge, now a museum, was once one of the most important derviş lodges in Istanbul. The lodge was built on the hunting farm of Iskender Paşa, governor of the province under Sultan Beyazit II, in 1491, but while it is the oldest surviving *tekke* in the city, the buildings on-site date to the period after the 1776 fire. The *tekke* is composed of a *semahane* (ritual hall), derviş cells, library, *sebil* (fountain), kitchen, *türbe*, and cemetery.

The octagonal wooden *semahane*, built in the baroque style of the 18th century, is used as a museum for the display of musical instruments, manuscripts, and other items related to the culture of the sect. One of the more notable residents of the cemetery is Kumbaracı Ahmet Paşa, né Claude Alexandre Bonneval (later Count) in France under the reign of Louis IV. His military career, while distinguished, was punctuated by repeated upheaval; eventually, he offered his services to the Sultan, after which he changed his name to Ahmed and converted to Islam. He swiftly rose in the ranks to Paşa and served the sultan until he died in Istanbul in 1747.

Galip Dede Cad. 15, Tünel. www.galatamevlevi.org. **℗ 0212/245-2121.** Nostalgic tram; Tünel from Karaköy. Closed for restoration.

A Sweet Shop near Galata

Wandering around the spice bazaar, you can really work up an appetite. Across the Galata Bridge at the Karaköy seaport is the humble (and famous) Güllüoğlu (℃ 0212/244-4567) sweet shop, where you'll find the best *börek*— a cheese- or meat-filled pastry that's feathery and delicious. They also keep their glass cases full of baklava.

Hünkar Kasrı ★★ HISTORIC HOME   Adjacent to (and attached to) the Yeni Valide Camii (below) is the Imperial Pavillion, until recently in a desperate state of neglect and closed to the public. But having ridden the wave of restorations preceding Istanbul as European Cultural Capital 2010, the Hünkar Kasrı, has been restored to its original decorative glory. The interior is a dizzying canvas of Ottoman workmanship: 17th-century cobalt and crimson Iznik tile (there are more than 10,000 of them), stained glass, colored calligraphy on carved wood (a technique known as Edirnekâri), mother-of-pearl inlay and gold leaf. The pavilion belongs to the cluster of imperial buildings associated with the Yeni Valide Camii that include the Egyptian Spice Bazaar, a *medrese, hamam,* mausoleum and garden, and was used by the imperial family as a resting place before or after prayers and on holy days. For convenience, the pavilion was connected to the Yeni Valide Camii by way of a long corridor spanning the street-level passageway that connects the square in front of the Yeni Camii with Bankacılar Sokak, allowing the Sultan to directly, and privately, enter and exit the mosque. Entrance to the building is via a stone ramp accessed from Bankacılar Sokak called the Tahtırevan Yolu or Palanquin Way, indicating the high station of those who entered.

Bankacılar Sok. 1, Sirkeci. Contact tourism office (℃ **0212/511-5888** in Sirkeci; ℃ 0212/518-1802 in Sultanahmet) for hours and admission.

Şehzade Külliyesi (Crowned Prince Mosque Complex) ★ MOSQUE   What was at the time considered a masterpiece of Ottoman architecture is now merely a footnote to Sinan's subsequent great works. In fact, Sinan was still an apprentice when he was ordered by Süleyman the Magnificent to build a monument to the memory of his beloved first-born son and intended heir, Şehzade (Prince) Mehmet, who died of smallpox in 1543 at the premature age of 21. The plan of the mosque is an important milestone in the evolution of his works, as it is a simple system of four semi-domes supported by four pillars that has been both criticized for being harsh and praised as harmonic. The use of four elephantine pillars is repeated in the Blue Mosque. The layout of the complex, consisting of the mosque, a *medrese,* a refectory, a double guesthouse, a caravansaray, and some tombs, follows no special plan, and indeed the primary school and public kitchens have been cut off from the rest of the complex by the main avenue. The prince's tomb is an octagonal masterpiece of arabesques, rare tiles, and stained glass housing a unique sarcophagus of wood lattice inlaid with ivory. The smaller octagonal tomb adjacent to that of the prince is that of Rüstem Paşa. For many years the Şehzade remained the largest building in Istanbul, but even before the mosque was completed, Süleyman had already ordered the construction of another, grander mosque as a monument to his reign.

Şehzadebası Cad., Vefa. No phone. Tram: Laleli; bus: 36A, 36CV, 36D, 36V, 37C, 37Y, 38B, 39B, 39Y, 77A, or 86V.

Sokullu Mehmet Paşa Camii MOSQUE   This mosque is considered to be one of the "minor" works of Sinan, architect to the Sultans. But there are several reasons why this mosque is anything but minor. First, it represents a transition in the process of Sinan's experimentation with space: the return to a hexagonal formula (from one where the dome is supported on an octagonal base), resulting in a softening of the transitions from one feature to another and thus of greater spatial homogeneity. Second, it's one of the rare instances where the interior of a mosque is revetted in decorative tile. The Iznik tile motifs featured on the squinches supporting the dome, on the frieze below the galleries, and on the *qibla* (wall panel facing Mecca), depict chrysanthemums, carnations, and cornflowers. The calligraphic tiles proclaim the 99 Attributes of God. Third, and unique in Turkey, are the placement of three tiny black stones said to be from the Ka'aba in Mecca embedded above the main portal, the *mihrab*, and the *mimbar*.

Şehit Çeşmesi Sok., Sultanahmet. No phone. Tram: Sultanahmet or Çemberlitaş.

Süleymaniye Mosque and Complex (Süleymaniye Camii ve Külliyesi) ★★

MOSQUE   Perched on one of the seven hills of Istanbul and dominating the skyline, this complex is considered to be Sinan's masterpiece as it is here where Sinan achieves his goal of outdoing the dome of the Hagia Sophia. Indeed, Sinan returned to the Byzantine basilica model for the construction of the mosque.

Critics have contended that this was an unsuccessful attempt to surpass the engineering feats of the church, but more than likely this was a conscious move on the part of the sultan to create continuity and a symbolic connection with the city's past. As the Hagia Sophia was analogous to the Temple of Solomon in Jerusalem, so was the Süleymaniye, as the name Süleyman is the Islamic version of Solomon. After the project was completed, Sinan recounts in his "biography of the Construction," how the sultan humbly handed the keys over to him and asked him to be the one to unlock the doors, acknowledging that the masterpiece was as much the architect's as his own.

The dome reaches a height of 49m (161 ft.) spanning a diameter of 27m (89 ft.; compared to the Hagia Sophia's 56m/184-ft.-high dome and 34m/112-ft. diameter). The mosque was completed in 7 years (1550–57) and it is said that after the foundation was laid, Sinan stopped work completely for 3 years to ensure that the foundation had settled to his satisfaction.

The complex includes five schools, one *imaret* (kitchens and mess hall, now a restaurant for groups), a caravansaray with stables, a hospital, *hamams,* and a cemetery. The construction of the mosque and complex mobilized the entire city, employing as many as 3,000 workers at any given time, and the 165 ledgers recording the expenses incurred in the building of the mosque are still around to prove it. The great sultan is buried in an elaborate tomb on the grounds, as is his wife Hürrem Sultan (Roxelana). In the courtyard outside the entry to the cemetery and tombs are a pair of slanted marble benches used as a stand for the sarcophagi before burial.

Süleyman carried the tradition of symbolism to his grave with a system of layered domes copied from the Dome of the Rock in Jerusalem. In the garden house next to the complex is the **tomb of Sinan ★**; the garden house is where he spent the last years of his life. The tomb was designed by the master architect himself and is inspiring in its modesty and simplicity.

Vefa. From the Grand Bazaar, cross the University park and follow the domes. © **0212/522-0298.** Tram: Beyazıt.

Yeni Valide Camii or Yeni Camii (The New Queen Mother's Mosque)
MOSQUE   Begun by Valide Safiye, mother of Mehmet III, in 1597, the foundations of this mosque were laid at the water's edge in a neighborhood slum whose inhabitants had to be paid to move out. Designed by the architect Da'ud Ağa, a pupil of Sinan, the Yeni Camii has become a defining feature of Istanbul's skyline.

The building of the mosque dragged on for over 40 years due to water seepage, funding problems, embezzlement, and the death of the sultan, which temporarily shut down operations completely. The mosque was completed by another queen mother, Valide Sultan Turhan Hattice, mother of Mehmet IV, who is buried in the valide sultan's tomb, or *türbe,* in the courtyard.

The mosque is part of a complex that included, at one time, a hospital, primary school, and public bath. The **Mısır Çarşısı** or **Egyptian Spice Market,** was actually constructed as part of the complex. In the open space formed by the inner "L" of the Spice Market and the northeastern-facing side of the mosque are stalls selling garden and pet supplies, a busy and shaded tea garden, and some street vendors. At the far (northwestern) end of the mosque on the opposite corner is the *türbe,* housing, in addition to the Valide Sultan, the remains of sultans Mehmet IV, Mustafa II, Ahmet III, and Mahmut I.

Opposite the *türbe* is the house of the mosque's astronomer, or *muvakkithane,* from where the position of the sun would be monitored to establish the times of the five daily prayers. Just behind the *muvakkithane* is a ramp leading up to the entrance of the royal loge, or private prayer room. The loge is best viewed from inside the mosque; enjoying a view of the sea, it was richly decorated by tiles, a dome, a vaulted antechamber, and a private toilet.

Egyptian Spice Bazaar, Eminönü. No phone. Tram: Eminönü.

Palaces of the Sultans

While the power and prestige of a new and modern Europe were increasing, the Ottoman Empire was on its last leg. To create an image of prosperity and modernization, Sultan Abdülmecid had the Dolmabahçe Palace constructed, and abandoned Topkapı Palace along with what he considered to be the symbol of an old order. With the official, and Europeanized, residence of the Ottoman Empire now on the northern shores of the Bosphorus, it wasn't long before members of the court and government officials began to build mansions in the area. More palaces sprang up, and the official shifting of power from south of the Golden Horn to the waterfront of Beşiktaş was complete. If the royal palaces fail to convince you of the Ottoman Empire's extravagance during its final economic decline, they will surely convince you of its opulence.

Beylerbeyi Palace (Beylerbeyi Sarayı) PALACE   Beylerbeyi, built under Sultan Abdülaziz by another member of the talented Balyan family of architects in the European style of Dolmabahçe, was the second palace to be built on the Bosphorus and served as a summer residence and guest quarters for visiting bey (dignitaries) during their visits to the city. The shah of Iran and the king of Montenegro were guests here as well as the French Empress Eugénie, who admired the palace so much that she had the design of the windows copied on the Tuilleries Palace in Paris. It's a bit dusty, and not as grand as Dolmabahçe, but worth a visit if you're on the Asian side and looking for a diversion.

Beylerbeyi, which replaced Abdülmecid's previous palace, was completed in 1865 on a less extravagant scale than the one on the European shores, employing only 5,000 men to build it. Although less grand and weathered by time, Beylerbeyi has some features worthy of a visit, not least of all the terraced garden of magnolias at the base of the Bosphorus Bridge. The monumental staircase to this marble palace is fronted by a pool and fountain which served as much to cool the air as to look pretty, and the floors are covered with reed mats from Egypt that act as insulation against dampness. The grounds contain sumptuous pavilions and kiosks, including the Stable Pavilion, where the imperial stud was kept.

Ironically, Abdülhamid II spent the last 6 years of his life admiring Dolmabahçe from the other side of the Bosphorus, having been deposed and kept under house arrest here until his death in 1918.

Take a ferry to Üsküdar and then a bus to Çayırbaşı. www.millisaraylar.gov.tr. *©* **0216/321-9320.** Entrance/tour 20TL. Tues, Wed, Fri–Sun 8:30am–4:30pm. Ferry: from Eminönü, ferry to Çengelköy or Üsküdar, and then bus 14M, 15, 15B, 15C, 15ÇK, 15F, 15H, 15KÇ, 15M, 15N, 15P, 15R, 15S, 15ŞN, 15U, or 15Y.

Çırağan Palace PALACE   From the first wooden summer mansion built on the spot in the 16th century to the grand waterfront palace that stands today, the Çırağan Palace was torn down and rebuilt no less than five times. Now a palace of sumptuous suites that make up part of the adjacent **Hotel Kempinski Istanbul** (p. 172), the palace takes its name from the hundreds of torches that lined these former royal gardens during the festivals of the Tulip Period in the latter part of the 18th century.

The foundations were laid in 1855, when Sultan Abdülaziz ordered the construction of a grand palace to be built as a monument to his reign. The architect, Nigogos Balyan, ventured as far as Spain and North Africa to find models in the Arab style called for by the sultan. The fickle Abdülaziz moved out after only a few months, condemning the palace as too damp to live in.

Murad V (who in 1876 deposed his uncle Abdülaziz), Abdülhamid II, and Mehmed V were all born in the palace. Murad V spent the final 27 years of his life imprisoned here, while his brother (who deposed him shortly after Murad V bumped his uncle) kept a watchful eye on him from the Yıldız Palace next door.

After Murad V's death, the Parliament took over the building but convened here for only 2 months because of a fire in the central heating vents that spread and reduced the palace to a stone shell in under 5 hours. (Some of the original doors were given as gifts by Abdülaziz to Kaiser Wilhelm and can now be seen in the Berlin Museum.) In 1946, the Parliament handed the property over to the Municipality, which for the next 40 years used it as a town dump as well as a soccer field. In 1986, the Kempinski Hotel Group saved the shell from yet another demise, using the palace as a showcase of suites for its luxury hotel next door. Since its opening, the Çırağan has laundered the pillowcases of princes, kings, presidents, and rock stars, carrying on at least a modern version of a royal legacy of the original.

In 2007, the hotel focused its energies on rescuing the palace from its faded glory and restoring it to its once and future grandeur. The space is friendlier too: nonguests of the hotel are encouraged to pay a visit to this living museum by way of the ground floor art gallery (bonus: for visits to the gallery, parking is free), by enjoying one of the bi-monthly chamber orchestra recitals or dining at their Ottoman restaurant, Tuğra (p. 138). The grounds are spread along 390m (1,280 ft.) of coastline and can only be visited as part of a stop-off at the main hotel, preferably from the seaside garden terrace, which provides ample views of the Palace Sea Gate, the Palace Garden Gate, and the main building itself.

Çırağan Cad., Beşiktaş. www.ciraganpalacesuites.com. © **0212/258-3377.** Free admission. Hotel common areas open 24 hr.; the bar and restaurant have individual hours. Bus: 22, 22RE, 25E, 30D, 40, 40T, 42, 57UL, DT1, DT2, or U1.

Dolmabahçe Palace (Dolmabahçe Sarayı) ★ PALACE At a time of economic reform when the empire was still known as "The Sick Man of Europe," Sultan Abdülmecid II sank millions into the construction of a new, European-inspired palace to rival the most opulent palaces of France. The project was symbolic: in replacing Topkapı as the seat of the crumbling empire with one inspired by a European model, the Sultan was looking Westward and in the process attempting to project a façade of prosperity and progress. The result is a sumptuous creation extending for almost .8km (½ mile) on the shores of the Bosphorus and consisting of 285 rooms, four grand salons, six galleries, five main staircases, six *hamams* (of which the main one is pure alabaster), and 68 toilets. Fourteen tons of gold and 6 tons of silver were used to build the palace. The extensive use of glass, especially in the Camlı Köşk conservatory, provides a gallery of virtually every known application of glass technology of the day. The palace is a glittering collection of Baccarat, Bohemian, and English crystal as well as Venetian glass, which was used in the construction of walls, roofs, banisters, and even a crystal piano. The chandelier in the Throne Room is the largest one in Europe at 4.5 tons, a bulk that created an engineering challenge during installation but that has withstood repeated earthquake tests. The extravagant collection of objets d'art represents just a small percentage of items presented to the occupants of the palace over the years, and much of the collection is stored in the basement awaiting restoration.

Outside is the ornate Clock Tower, easily admired while sipping tea in the on-site cafe. (There are also two cafes inside the palace).

Tours to the palace and harem accommodate 1,500 visitors per day per section, a stream of gaping onlookers shod in blue plastic hospital booties distributed at the entry to the palace to ensure the longevity of the sumptuous carpets. Tours leave every 15 minutes and last 1 hour for the Selâmlik and around 45 minutes for the Harem. If you're short on time, choose the Selâmlik. Because it is mandatory to join one of the tours, advance reservations are required for visits to the palace and all sections (available via phone or website).

Dolmabahçe Cad., Beşiktaş. www.dolmabahce.gov.tr. © **0212/236-9000.** Admission and guided tour to the Selâmlik (Sultan's Quarters) 30TL and Harem 20TL, or both for 40TL. Clock Tower Museum 20TL. (Additional charge for introduction of camera or camcorder 20TL each.) Tues–Wed and Fri–Sun 8:30am–4pm (last tour leaves at 3pm). Tram: Kabataş; funicular: Kabataş; bus: 22, 22E, 22RF, 25F, 26, 26A, 26B, 27SE, 28, 28T, 29C, 29D, 30D, 325YK1, 41E, 43R, 46K, 52, 58A, 58N, 58S, 58UL, 62, 63, or 70KE.

One If by Land; Two If by Sea: Constantinople's Defensive Walls

Even before the arrival of the great Roman emperors, the city on the hill (then called Megara) was a target for attack. Persian King Darius I took the city in 512 B.C.; then in 478 B.C., the Athenians squeezed out the Persians. Alexander the Great reinforced the city's Hellenistic bend, until in 146 B.C. the city came under Roman domination. For the next 350 years, the city basked in the glow of Pax Romana, notwithstanding Septimus Severus' massacre and destruction of the city when, having proclaimed himself emperor, he was met with resistance by the citizens loyal to his opponent, Pescennius Niger. When Severus rebuilt the city, he expanded the original boundaries to those enclosed by a defensive wall running roughly north-to-south from the Galata Bridge around the Hippodrome to the Marmara Sea. Constantine's walls again enlarged the city, forming a cincture that expanded the city out into the middle of today's Fatih district. Nothing of either the Severus or Constantine walls survive.

Marmara Sea Walls RUINS   While not as impressive a feat as the Theodosian defenses, the Sea Walls, originally built by order of Constantine and extended by Theodosius, are worth a mention. Sadly, there's very little left of the original section along the southern coastal road, because in 1870, railway engineers simply knocked it down to make way for the commuter train. So walls that endured 1,500 years of sieges, earthquakes, and even tsunamis fell to the onward march of urban "improvement."

The crumbling (albeit highly photogenic) decay of the sea walls greets you as you enter the Old City along the coastal road from the airport. The walls are predominantly to your left, leaving you to imagine the waves of the Marmara Sea lapping up over the road you're driving in on. Portions of the wall prop up houses constructed on the hill, and if you know what you're looking for, you can spot a handful of crumbling palatial arches remaining from the grand Bucoleon Palace. The wall was punctuated by eight gates designed to allow ships entry into the inner harbors. The Porta de Condoskali, or the Shallow Harbor Gate, now provides land access to the appropriately named neighborhood of **Kumkapı** (Sand Gate), now a lively area of fish restaurants recalling (barely) the fishermen's harbor that it once was. The **Ahırkapı,** or stable gate, served as the imperial port, but fell into disuse with the construction of the Bucoleon Palace to the west.

The best approach is either from the comfort of a car or on foot to one of the two gates mentioned above. It's also possible to walk along the walls all the way from Sirkeci around Sarayburnu to the southern face of Sultanahmet, but in spite of the views of the Marmara Sea, the traffic flow is too heavy and exhaust fumes too thick to make this a comfortable choice. A good compromise is to exit on foot either Aksakal Cad. (east of the Küçük Ayasofya Camii) or Ahırkapı and reenter the city via the other. You won't want to try this in the height of summer, as the sun's rays are just too strong.

The Theodosian Walls ★★ RUINS   By the time Theodosius II arrived on the throne in A.D. 408, the city of Constantinople was bursting at the seams. As Septimus Severus and Constantine had done before him, Theodosius set about fortifying and enlarging the city, and the alternately towering and crumbling red brick and limestone monoliths you see running north from Yedikule (you'll see it at as you arrive into the city) all the way to Ayvansaray and the Golden Horn are what remain of Theodosius's Land Walls. Twenty-five years after their construction between A.D. 412 and 422, the walls all but collapsed in an earthquake, and with the Huns advancing from the east, the politically polarized factions of the city set aside their grievances and in a period of 2 months, not only fortified the wall, but built another, exterior wall plus a moat. (Constantinople nevertheless wound up paying Atilla the Hun protection money for 10 years after his attack.) Extensions to the wall, which under Theodosius ended at Blachernae, were added later by subsequent emperors. This latter section, from Ayvansaray down to the Golden Horn, was the weak link in the chain, and not surprisingly, the point at which Mehmet the Conqueror's army breached the city.

All together, the system of land defenses represents an impressive period in military architecture. The original, Theodosian wall consisted of a main (inner) wall 5m (16 ft.) thick and 11 to 14m (36–46 ft.) high, punctuated by 96 towers from 18 to 20m (59–66 ft.) in height. The refortification added an outer, crenelated wall reinforced with 92 towers placed at intervals of 50 to 70 or so meters (164–230 ft.), set in alternating position with the towers of the inner wall. Between the inner and outer wall was an inner terrace embankment (called a *peribolos*). Another wider embankment separated the outer wall from the moat, creating a vulnerable open space for those (un)lucky enough to get that far. The moat was the first line of defense, presenting invading armies with a formidable obstacle 20m (66 ft.) wide and 10m (33 ft.) deep. All told (including the additional sections north of Blachernae), the total length of the land walls is 6,670m (4 miles). Entrance and exit into and out of the city was via monumental gates constructed of stone, marble, and even, in the case of the Golden Gate at Yedikule, of gold. One of the most important gates of both the Byzantine and Ottoman periods was **Edirnekapı,** or the gate leading to Edirne. Edirnekapı, which is part of the original Theodosian wall, provided access to the main thoroughfare into the city center. Byzantine emperors used this gate when leaving for and returning from their campaigns abroad, and Fatih Mehmet (aka "the Conqueror") made his victorious entrance here. Later Ottoman sultans, after the official inauguration ceremonies at Eyüp, followed in Mehmet's footsteps and also entered via this gate.

Because of the derelict state of much of the structure and because there are no lights at night, the best approach to visiting the land walls is either to walk along them beginning at Edirnekapı or view them up close and personal at Yedikule, where you can scramble to the top of the ramparts and get a good overview of the entire system heading north (see "Yedikule," below).

Yedikule (Seven Towers Fortress) ★ ☺ CASTLE About a quarter of a mile inland from the Marmara Sea along the land walls is the Golden Gate entrance to the Byzantine city, a triumphal arch built by Theodosius. The arch predates the construction of the famed Theodosian walls and was used as a ceremonial entrance and exit to the city still for the most part confined to the boundaries set by Constantine's earlier defensive walls. From here, the main road, or Mese, led directly through the center of the city, to the Milion Stone and Hagia Sophia. Theodosius later incorporated the gate into the construction of his defensive walls. Nearly a thousand years (and several earthquakes later) in 1457, Mehmet the Conqueror took advantage of the two towers flanking the Golden Gate, added an additional five towers and enclosed them within a new defensive fortress. But the fort was never called to battle and served instead as the imperial treasury and a political prison for the likes of Mahmut Paşa, the Conqueror's Grand Vizier, and the deposed Mamluk caliph. Some unsavory incidents happened here too: When Sultan Osman II tried to reform the Janissaries in 1622, he was thrown in prison and then killed, and his head was tossed into what is now known as the "bloody well" in the center of the garden. Inside the Zindan Kulesi (Inscription Tower), some of the scrapings etched into the stone by the prisoners are still visible. The wooden scaffolding is what remains of the prisoners' cells. Steep and narrow stone stairways provide access to the top of the battlements, where you can breathe deeply the salty sea air and contemplate some of the finest views of the city. The stairway on the eastern curtain wall (to the right of the entrance) has one lone banister; ascend and descend with care.

İmrahor Mah., Kule Meydanı 4, Yedikule/Fatih. **℃ 0212/584-4012.** Admission 5TL. Thurs–Tues 9:30am–4:30pm. Bus: 80 or 81 from Eminönü; 80T from Taksim.

Exploring Modern-Day Istanbul

Istanbul pulsates with the energy of opportunity, prosperity, and optimism. Tourism is at an all-time high, foreign investment keeps rolling in, and the rich are getting richer. This is readily seen in Taksim, Beyoğlu, Çukurcuma, Galata, and Tünel, where you can stroll past freshly restored turn-of-the-19th-century ambassadorial palaces and barracks, converted 16th-century waterhouses, and crisp, minimalist museums, all while shopping for an expensive pair of Levi's. Below is a short list of what to look out for.

Balıkpazarı (Galatasaray Fish Market) SQUARE   This fish market is a colorful cluster of much more than just fishmongers. Having just undergone a period of restoration (which in my opinion whitewashed some of the charm out), it also contains *dükkan* (small grocers), souvenir sellers, restaurants, tempting *tantuni* joints (fast-food sellers of fried spiced beef), and other must-try street food vendors. I'm a bit anxious that eventually it will homogenize into just another outdoor shopping mall, but let's just cross our fingers and not get ahead of ourselves.

Running perpendicular to Şahne Tiyatro Sokağı are three very picturesque alleys as well as an unobtrusive Armenian Church. The **Üc Horon Ermeni Kilisesi** (also called the Surp Yerrortuyan, both meaning Holy Trinity; Balıkpazarı 24Ab/6r) is a working church and the largest Armenian Church in Istanbul. It dates to 1838.

To the right of Şahne Tiyatro Sokağı is **Nevişade Street,** a narrow cobbled mews overflowing with traditional *meyhanes*. One can barely squeeze by on a summer's eve, which makes it half the fun. Try to nab a seat on the upper balconies (or roof terraces) if you can; these are often closed from October through April. From Şahne Tiyatro Sokağı branch off the quieter Duduodalar Street and the **Avrupa Pasajı.** The Avrupa, or European Passage, used to be reveted in mirrors designed to enhance the light emitted by the then-gas lamps, and thus was formerly called the Aynalı Pasajı or Mirrored Arcade. Here is a pleasing mixture of high-end antiques sellers, Anatolian textile boutiques, and down-market souvenir shops.

Istiklal Cad., opposite the Galatasaray Lisesi (near Meşrutiyet Cad.). No phone. Daily dawn to dusk. Restaurants open until late. Nostalgic tram; Tünel from Karaköy.

Çiçek Pasajı (Flower Passage) ARCHITECTURE   An icon of Beyoğlu's past and present, the Çiçek Pasajı occupies a stunning rococo arcade, the original of which dates to 1876. It was constructed as a bazaar and apartment building shortly after the 1870 Beyoğlu fire, when it soon became known as the Cité de Pera. After World War I, Russian aristocrats settled in alongside the cluster of florists and thus the building acquired its present name. This is also where the tradition of tables spilling out onto the street got started. The entire affair collapsed in 1978 due to neglect but was reconstructed a decade later. Today the soaring space teems with *meyhanes* and beer halls, staffed by a collection of eager, competing, and vociferous waitstaff. The arcade follows an "L" shape with the long portion running parallel to the adjacent Şahne Sokağı, better known by the name of the merchandise sold here: fish (see "Balıkpazarı," above).

Istiklal Cad., opposite the Galatasaray Lisesi (near Meşrutiyet Cad.). No phone. Daily dawn to dusk. Restaurants open until late. Nostalgic tram; Tünel from Karaköy.

Istanbul Museum of Modern Art ★ MUSEUM   In a city of ancient empires, in a country whose political and economic supremacy is but a distant memory, Turkey, and in particular Istanbul, is carving itself a new niche. Only this time, it's looking forward, not back. The Istanbul Modern, opened in December 2004, occupies a crisp, utilitarian, and highly functional 7,990 sq. m (86,000 sq. ft.) in a former Customs warehouse just outside the cruise ship docks. The collection of paintings, portraits, sculptures, and photographs in the permanent collection tell us, in some sense, what was going on in the minds of the Turks in the 20th century. Some pieces simply make you tilt your head in wonder. The museum also serves as a sort of cultural center, with video programs, films, and a multimedia research library.

Meclis-I Mebusan Cad., Liman İşletmeleri Sahası, Antrepo 4, Karaköy. www.istanbulmodern.org. © **0212/334-7300.** Admission 14TL; free for children under 12. Tues–Sun 10am–6pm (Thurs until 8pm). Tram: Tophane.

Military Museum ★ ⚔ MUSEUM   Feared, respected, and loathed for 500 years, the Ottoman warrior was the brick on which the Ottoman dynasty was built. Indeed, it was the rising influence of industry and economics over combat and conquest that contributed to the ultimate downfall of the empire. Because war plays a pivotal role in the history and culture of Turkey, no visit to Turkey would be complete without a stopover at the Military Museum. Most people breeze through without a sideways glance, hurriedly following the arrows that direct visitors to the **Mehter Concert ★★★**. This startlingly powerful musical performance re-creates the traditional military band of the Janissaries, the elite Ottoman corps abolished when their power became too great. The musical arrangement is an unexpectedly organized cacophony of sounds that, preceding the approaching army, also served to instill terror in the opposing army.

The exhibit, housed in the former military academy where Atatürk received his education (the building was converted into a museum in 1993), contains a chronological and functional assemblage of artifacts of warfare from the Ottoman era through World War II. The exhibit is anything but dull, showcasing chain mail and bronze armor for both cavalry and horses, leather and metalwork costumes, handsewn leather and arrow bags, swords engraved with fruit and flower motifs or Islamic inscriptions, and even a petroleum-driven rifle. Not to be missed is the hall of tents, an unanticipated display of *in situ* elaborately embroidered and silk encampment tents used on war expeditions.

Askeri Müse ve Kültür Sitesi Komutanlığı, Harbiye (about .8km/½ mile north of Taksim along Cumhuriyet Cad.). www.tsk.tr/muze_internet/askeri_muze.htm. © **0212/233-2720.** Admission 4TL. Wed–Sun 9am–5pm. Closed Jan. 1 and the first day of Ramadan and Kurban Bayramı. *Mehter* concert 3pm (English) and 3:30pm (Turkish). Metro: Osmanbey; bus: 43, 46, 48, 54, 66, 69A, 70, 74 et al.

Pera Museum MUSEUM   Located on five floors in the heart of Old Pera, the Pera Museum houses a small but solid collection of Kütahya ceramics, Ottoman weights and measures, and Ottoman portraiture from the 18th to the 20th centuries rarely seen outside of Turkey. The portraits alone are worth the price of admission, and a quick lap around the museum can be accomplished in an hour, if you really try hard. The museum also mounts some of the city's more prestigious exhibitions and screens independent film, including as host of the International Documentary Film Festival.

Meşrutiyet Cad. 65, Tepebaşı, Beyoğlu. www.peramuzesi.org.tr. © **0212/334-9900.** Admission 10TL. Tues–Sat 10am–7pm; Sun noon–6pm. Closed Jan 1 and first day of Şeker Bayramı and Kurban Bayramı. Nostalgic tram; Tünel from Karaköy; bus: 325YK2, 32T, 35C, 54E, 54HŞ, 54HT, 61B, 69A, 71T, 72T, 74, 74A, 76T, 77MT, 80T, 83, 87, 93T, 96T, E50, E51, or E52.

Tünel Pasajı   This highly evocative arcade is formed by the convergence of three separate buildings. The style is neoclassical, but the dates of construction are unknown. The antiques shops and ateliers occupying the spaces are slowly but surely giving way to modish cafes and restaurants (House Café is on the far corner), but some might say that this enhances the spaces utility.

Tünel, opposite the upper entrance to the Tünel Funicular. Nostalgic Tram; Tünel from Karaköy.

Sights Along the Bosphorus

For over 2,500 years, kings and commanders have confronted the challenge of the Bosphorus, building rudimentary bridges out of boats and floating jetties to increase the size of their empires. Mandrokles of Samos crossed on huge connecting floats in 512 B.C. Persian Emperor Xerxes built a temporary bridge, as did Heraclius I of Byzantium, who crossed a chain of pontoons on horseback. Now that several bridges connect the shores of Europe and Asia, staying on the water has become more fashionable than actually crossing it. The shores are dotted with *yalıs*, or classic waterfront mansions, built as early as the 18th century: yellow, pink, and blue wooden palaces perched along the waterfront. The surrounding neighborhoods (best visited by land) retain much of their characteristic village feel, in stark contrast to the restored homes inhabited by the likes of ex-Prime Minister Tansu Çillar.

Cruising up the straits is a bit easier these days than when Jason and the Argonauts sailed through in search of the Golden Fleece. A number of local tour companies organize daylong or half-day boat cruises up the Bosphorus on private boats, often with a stop at the Rumeli Fortress and visits to Beylerbeyi Sarayı. Unless you've gotten a guarantee that the tour will *not* wind up on one of the public ferries, skip the tour and hop on one of the less-pristine (but serviceable) city ferries and go the route yourself.

Leander's Tower (the Maiden's Tower or Kız Kulesi) ICON   Rising from a rock at the mouth of the Bosphorus is the Kız Kulesi, built by Ibrahim Paşa in 1719 over the remains of a fortress built by Mehmet the Conqueror and of the earliest original building constructed on the rock by Byzantine Emperor Manuel Comnenus I. The romance of the tower finds its root in an ancient myth along the lines of Romeo and Juliet: boy (Leander) falls in love with girl (the Aphrodite Priestess Hero); boy drowns while swimming to meet girl; girl finds lover's corpse; girl commits suicide. The story originated around the Dardanelles, but was too juicy not to attach to this solitary tower. Legend also has it that the tower was connected to the mainland by way of an underwater tunnel, and that there used to be a wall between the tower and the shore—a rumor not altogether implausible considering that, according to a 19th-century historian, the remains of a wall could be seen in calm water. Since as early as the 1600s, the tower has been used as a prison and a quarantine hospital. The tower is currently in service as a (mediocre, overpriced) panoramic restaurant and tea lounge.

Slightly offshore south of Üsküdar, on the Asian side. www.kizkulesi.com.tr. ✆ **0216/342-4747.** Free shuttle boat with dinner reservation. Daytime shuttle 3.50€ to/from Kabataş (furthest dock to the north) hourly from 9am–6:45pm (return every hour on the :45 from 9:45–6:45pm) or from Salacak 2.50€ (shuttles run continuously between 9am and 6:45pm).

Naval Museum (Deniz Müzesi) ☺ MUSEUM   Kids of all ages will be enchanted by this collection of original and model warships, navigational devices, and other tools particular to a naval culture. Keep an eye out for the VIP cabin of the Ertuğrul, used by Atatürk between 1925 and 1937, and a section of the iron chain used in the failed defense of the city, pre-Ottoman conquest. Barbarosa's standard is displayed in a case on the upper floor of the main building, embroidered with a trifecta of religious symbols (the Trinity, the Star of David, and the names of the first four Caliphs) to emphasize the Ottoman reign (or protection) over all three. A copy of Pirit Reis's map of North America, drawn in the first half of the 15th century, is also here, while the original is housed in Topkapı Palace. In the outbuilding at the back of the museum courtyard is a gallery housing a staggering collection of imperial caïques where you'll find original, and highly ornamental, wooden Sultans' caïques, including the *pièce de résistance:* a 40m (131-ft.) long, 5.7m (19-ft.) wide-beamed boat inlaid with nacre, tortoiseshell, and ivory (so much for animal welfare)—the only original two-masted galley still in existence.

Hayrettin Iskelesi Sok. (at the Beşiktaş ferry landing), Beşiktaş. ✆ **0212/327-4345.** Wed–Sun 9am–5pm. Admission 4TL. IDO ferry: from Kadıköy or Üsküdar; bus: 22, 22RE, 25E, 25T, 27E, 28, 28O, 28T, 30A, 30D, 30M, 40, 40B, 40T, 43R, 559C, 57UL, 58N, 58UL, 62, 110, or 112.

Rumeli Fortress (Rumeli Hisarı) CASTLE This citadel was built by Mehmet the Conqueror across from the Anatolia Fortress (Anadolu Hisarı) in preparation for what was to be the seventh and final Ottoman siege of the fortified Byzantine city. Constructed in only 4 months, the fortress served to cut off Black Sea traffic in and out of the city, together with the Anadolu Hisarı built by his great-grandfather across the Bosphorus on the Asian shores. The Ottoman army eventually penetrated the city by carrying the Turkish galleons over land by way of a sled and pulley system, and dropping them into the Golden Horn and behind the city's defenses.

Tarabya Yeniköy Cad. north of Sarıyer (some ferries make the stop at Rumeli Kavağı; otherwise, get off at Sarıyer and take a *dolmuş* the rest of the way). www.kultur.gov.tr. ✆ **0212/263-5305.** 3TL. Tues–Sun 9am–5pm. Bus: 25E or 40.

ISTANBUL'S CONTEMPORARY ART SCENE

Istanbul's **Biennale** (p. 154) may have put the city on the art-world map in 1987, but the city's fast-paced Europeanization and naturally creative and innovative vigor has captured international attention otherwise. If your trip to Istanbul fails to coincide with the installation of this biennial citywide celebration of art, not to worry, as these days, plenty of creative juices flow during in-between years, displayed in unique and sometimes historic environments and as part of noteworthy private collections.

For additional information on current installations, log on to www.mymerhaba.com or pick up a copy of *Time Out Istanbul,* the English edition. If you'll be traveling during the Biennale, the Istanbul Foundation for Culture and Art (www.iksv.org) is the official site for the event. And while strolling around town, keep your eyes open for banners advertising exhibitions (The word "*sanat*" for art, or "*galerie*" should help).

SALT Galata ★★   New on the scene is this arts foundation supported by Garanti Bank who plans to make the space an important source for innovation and ultimately the premier cultural institution of Turkey. Now, SALT hosts exhibitions, film screenings, and lectures; serves as a research library; and is keeper of the Ottoman Bank archives. Activities will be split between its location on Istiklal Caddesi and its digs in the historic Ottoman Bank. Actually, banks were the earliest sponsors of the arts, so a gallery in or adjacent to Akbank or Yapı Kredi is certainly worth a look-see. Istiklal Cad. 136, Beyoğlu. www.saltonline.org. ℂ **0212/377-4200.** Bankalar Caddesi 11, Karaköy. ℂ **0212/334-2200.**

Santralistanbul and the Museum of Energy ★★   The recently restored and repurposed Ottoman era Silahtarağa electric power plant takes up 12 hectares (30 acres) of space on the Bilgi University campus on the northern shore of the Golden Horn. There are concert halls, a public library (in two of the former boiler rooms), an amphitheater, and living space for visiting artists. The industrial space, which also houses, appropriately, the **Museum of Energy ★ ☺**, gives children of all ages an addictive and interactive experience into the history of power. During the daytime, an outsized pavilion offers museum-goers a welcome respite from a thirsty afternoon of art. A free shuttle departs from in front of the Atatürk Cultural Center in Taksim every 20 minutes from 11am to 3pm and 7 to 9pm; call for pickup from 8 to 11am and 3 to 7pm. Eski Silahtarağa Elektrik Santralı, Kazım Karabekir Cad. 2, Eyüp. www.santralistanbul.org. ℂ **0212/311-7878.** Admission to current exhibitions 15TL; free admission to the Museum of Energy. Tues–Fri 10am–6pm and Sat–Sun 10am–8pm.

Galerist ★   Turkey's leading artists are showcased in this, one of Istanbul's and Turkey's more influential artistic spaces. One of Galerist's objectives is to expose the international artistic community to Turkish contemporary art through exhibitions abroad. Istiklal Cad., Mısır Apt. 163/4, Beyoğlu. www.galerist.com.tr. ℂ **0212/244-8230.** Free admission. Mon–Fri 10am–6pm and Sat noon–6pm.

Galeri Nev   Since its founding in Ankara in 1984, Galeri Nev expanded to a second space in Istanbul and has mounted more than 300 exhibitions. The founding partners, architects by trade, concentrated the earliest exhibitions on Turkey's first modernists. The gallery has also hosted exhibitions of European modernists such as Bonnard, Dali, and Picasso. Nev has a private collection of original prints, more than a hundred limited edition reproductions, and 93 volumes of art books and catalogs. stiklal Caddesi 163/18, 4th and 5th floor. www.galerinevistanbul.com. I ℂ **0212/252-1525** and Maçka Cad. 33, Maçka; ℂ **0212/231-6763.** Free admission. Tues–Sat 11am–6:30pm.

Gallery Apel   With all of this contemporary rebound to the antiquity of Istanbul, Gallery Apel offers some refreshing middle ground by featuring works created using traditional materials like felt, ceramic, wood, and glass. Exhibitions are constantly changing and feature modern sculptures, prints, and even full-size architectural mock-ups. Hayriye Cad. 5A, Galatasaray. www.galleryapel.com. ℂ **0212/292-7236.** Free admission. Tues–Sat, 11:30am–6:30pm.

Istanbul's Contemporary Art Scene

ISTANBUL

The Gallery at Çirağan Palace Hotel There's certainly something to be said for viewing contemporary art in the palatially historic ground floor of the Palace Section of the Çirağan Palace Hotel. The gallery (entrance through parking lot) features a different contemporary artist every 6 weeks. Entry is free and access to the gallery is 'round the clock. If you plan to go on the last Saturday of the month, the hotel also hosts a **chamber orchestra** in one of the rooms.

Çirağan Caddesi 32, Beşiktaş. www.kempinski-istanbul.com. © **0212/326-4646.** 11am–1pm. Reservations required. Free admission.

Milk You'll find something a bit more offbeat at Milk, which showcases artists influenced by street art, graffiti, and even cartoons. The exhibitions are even more fun when you exit into the design store, where you'll find funky and fantastic souvenirs, T-shirts, and prints.

Şahkulu Mah. Balkon Çıkmazı 8/A Galata, Beyoğlu. www.whatismilk.com. © **0212/251-5797.** Tues–Sat 1–7pm.

Proje4L/ Elgiz Çağdaş Sanat Müzesi Also leading the charge to elevate the profile of progressive art in Turkey is the not-for-profit Proje4L. In addition to housing the private collections of its founders Sevda and Can Elgiz—representing a range of media by both local and international artists—the museum organizes lectures and seminars and welcomes guest artists.

Beybi Giz Plaza, Meydan Sokak, Maslak; metro to Levent. www.proje4L.org. © **0212/281-5150.** Free admission. Wed–Fri 10am–5pm; Sat 10am–4pm; Tues by appointment.

Especially for Kids

Even though Turks are notorious pushovers for their children, even the most privileged and well educated children will get bored trudging around the recesses of ancient Byzantium day after day. Istanbul does have a series of kid-related cultural events, though, including the **Rahmi M. Koç Museum** (Hasköy Cad. 5; www.rmk-museum.org.tr; © **0212/369-6600**), a hands-on series of exhibitions a la the Smithsonian showcasing the history of human ingenuity in the areas of transportation, industry, and communications. The transparent washing machines, carburetors, decommissioned submarine bridge, trains, and aircraft will definitely push the buttons of any preteen boy (and then some) and are definitely worth a visit. The addition of the planetarium lets the viewer "live the experience of the cosmos in a virtual environment." (Advance reservation required.) Admission is 12.50TL for adults plus an additional 7TL for entry to the submarine exhibit (children under 8 not allowed) and 3TL for the planetarium. The museum is open Tuesday to Friday, 10am to 5pm; Saturday and Sunday, 10am to 7pm.

The **Museum of Energy at Santralistanbul** ★ (Eski Silahtarağa Elektrik Santralı, Silahtar Mah., Kazım Karabekir Cad. 1, Silahtar; © **0212/444-0428;** www.santralistanbul.org; free admission to the Museum of Energy; admission to current exhibitions 14TL) is a real educational hoot. The museum is housed in the old Ottoman Silahtarağa electric plant, and kids can climb up the steel stairs to the control room, get a close-up look at some seriously huge turbines, and pedal an exercise bike rigged to generate power to a radio and a hairdryer. The museum has 21 other cool interactive hands-on displays that show you how power is generated.

Kids will probably be excited to scale the ramparts of the fortresses at **Rumeli Hisarı** (p. 125) or **Yedikule** (p. 121). Traipsing around ancient stones and up the steps of imposing towers should wear kids out enough to get them to sit still through dinner.

Miniaturk (Imrahor Cad. Sütlüce on the eastern banks of the Golden Horn opposite Eyüp; ☎ 0212/222-2882; www.miniaturk.com.tr), which opened in 2003, is an open-air minimuseum sprouting models of Turkey's most-loved monuments reconstructed here at ⅟₂₅ of their actual size. The park is open from 9am to 5pm in winter, later in summer. Admission is 10TL.

It may be a bit off the beaten track and the admission fees might put you over your vacation budget, but if your offspring overhears that **Turkuazoo** (Forum Istanbul 3, Kocatepe Mah. Paşa Cad.; ☎ 0212/640-2015 or 0212/640-2740; www.turkuazoo. com), the largest aquarium in Europe, is just down the road and has an underwater safari that takes visitors through a simulation of the bottom of the ocean floor, you may not have the option of saying no. Individual adult admission is 28TL, children 2 to 16 pay 21TL. Family (two parents and two children) tickets cost 84TL.

If a day trip to the Princes' Islands was not on your to-do list, you may want to add **Büyükada** (preferably in warmer weather; the islands become dreary ghost towns in the fall and winter; see p. 186) so that your progeny can hoist themselves onto one of the horse-drawn carriages waiting for them at the other end of the ferry. As a pedestrian island, these carriages are the main mode of transport. You can also take a donkey ride up to the Aya Yorgi Church and views of the Marmara Sea that even teenagers can appreciate.

Spectator Sports

To say that **soccer** is a popular national sport in Turkey is to miss the point entirely. Soccer is closer to a religious experience; club rivalries are waged with an intensity comparable to the holy wars.

The three main soccer clubs in Istanbul are **Fenerbahçe, Beşiktaş,** and **Galatasaray.** Main matches are played nights at 7pm from late August to May. (A few late summer matches are played at 8pm.) Home matches are played every other week at **Inönü Stadium,** above Dolmabahçe Palace, for Beşiktaş; at **Alisami Yen,** in Mecidiyeköy, for Galatasaray; and at **Fenerbahçe Stadium,** near Kadıköy on the Asian side, for Fenerbahçe. Tickets run from as little as 10TL and are available at the stadium the day of a match, or through **Biletix** (www.biletix.com).

WHERE TO EAT

Turkish food has long been at the forefront of international cuisine thanks to its use of the freshest produce, the incorporation of flavors from the far reaches of the Ottoman Empire, and Imperial Chefs' fear of displeasing the sultan. Today, Istanbul retains its culinary crown with celebrity chefs from the U.K., the U.S., Sweden, Japan, and, of course, Turkey. The progressive kitchens led by these chefs are located north of the Golden Horn, but even without a visit to one of these cover-story kitchens, and apart from a few exceptions, the better meals will be had up in the neighborhoods of Beyoğlu, Beşiktaş, and along

---

📎 **Summer Dining Alfresco**

Restaurant dining rooms resemble ghost-town eateries in the summer, but if you just continue up the steps, you'll see why. Istanbul is a city of rooftop terraces and waterfront dining, and a summer meal is almost exclusively enjoyed high above the city or at a table along the Bosphorus.

the Bosphorus, and will be shared alongside Istanbullus. The vibrant, semi-touristy clusters of *meyhanes* along Nevişade Sok. (in the Balıkpazarı), under the beaux-arts stained glass domes of the Çiçek Pasajı, or at a streetside table along the festive streets of Kumkapı (in the Old City) are good options if atmosphere trumps the meal (which should be satisfactory, if not expensive).

In the Old City, expect a preponderance of high-priced (comparative to counterparts in Beyoğlu) kebap houses and restaurants with less than inspirational menus that try to please every palate. In this neighborhood, I tend to stick to the honest home cooking at the various innocuous *lokantas* (dives with steam tables, particularly along Pierloti Caddesi, between the Hippodrome and Cağaloğlu and in the working streets around the Grand Bazaar), or frequent the few reliable establishments listed here. Because we can't list every place, two good sources for dining are Istanbul Eats (**www.istanbuleats.com**), a blog run by expat journalists and Zagat Survery's "Europe's Best Restaurants" (**www.zagat.com**).

Sirkeci & Eminönü

MODERATE

Hamdi Et Lokantası KEBAPS Hamdi's southeastern kebaps will never come close to Develi Restaurant (p. 133), but this is a good alternative to the overpriced mediocrity of Pandeli Lokantası only steps from the entrance to the Egyptian Spice Market. The popular terrace views of Galata Tower and the Golden Horn add to the convenience of the location, and you can move to the cozy *şark* (Oriental-style seating area) for your after-dinner cup of coffee or tea. Specialties of the house include the *erikli kebap,* minced meat from a suckling lamb in which all of the fat has been cooked out, and the showcase *testi kebap,* a stew of diced meat, tomatoes, shallots, garlic, and green pepper cooked in a terra-cotta pot over an open fire and served tableside by breaking the pot (minimum 10 people, advance orders required). Hamdi caters to vegetarians with the vegetable kebap, spiced with parsley and garlic; don't pass up the *yuvarlama,* a flavorful yogurt soup with tiny rice balls served only at dinnertime.

Tahmis Cad., Kalçin Sok. 17 (set back behind the bus depot), Eminönü. www.hamdi.com.tr. ⓒ **0212/528-0390.** Reservations suggested (required for dinner). Dress smart. Appetizers and main courses 6TL–32TL. AE, MC, V. Daily 11am–midnight. Closed 1st and last 3 days of Ramadan.

Orient Express Cafe 🍴 ✦ TURKISH/OTTOMAN Located next to track no. 1 of Sirkeci station, the Orient Express Cafe—a real find—is proof that you don't have to pay an arm and a leg for white tablecloths, good food, and nostalgia. The elegant niches with their large stained-glass window insets and the handsome clapboard ceiling take you back at least a century, although the decorator would have done well to scrap the enormous *Shining Time Station* oil painting on the wall.

The limited but satisfying menu relies heavily on lamb, with a tender lamb shoulder as the chef's pride. If you're craving eggplant, order the *beğendili kebap,* cubes of flavorful beef atop a bed of eggplant purée (or was that ambrosia?). The crème caramel was a formidable substitute to an empty coffer of rice pudding, and the black-tie service was flawless.

Sirkeci Train Station, Sirkeci. ⓒ **0212/522-2280.** Appetizers and main courses 7TL–35TL. MC, V. Daily noon–11pm.

Pandeli Lokantası ♨ TURKISH Pandeli is one of those neighborhood traditions that lives on more for its location and longevity than for anything particularly outstanding about the food. Indeed, the servers can be surly to tourists. Pandeli was opened in 1901 by a Greek of Turkish descent and has become a local institution ever since its arrival on the upper level of the Egyptian Spice Bazaar. If you nab a table in the main room facing the ancient blue Iznik tiles and windows overlooking the bazaar, you can imagine yourself back in time while watching the human traffic come and go.

Mısır Çarşısı 1, Eminönü (immediately inside the entrance to the Egyptian Bazaar). www.pandeli. com.tr. © **0212/527-3909.** Appetizers and main courses 9TL–28TL. MC, V. Mon–Sat 11am–4pm.

INEXPENSIVE

Paşazade 🏛 OTTOMAN   Few besides those in-the-know are aware of the Ottoman delights available at this enchanting and understated eatery in the heart of Sirkeci. So I'll just cut to the chase by offering a sampling off the menu, to enjoy while overlooking Ebusuud Sokak or against a wall of faux Ottoman architecture. *Terkib-i Ceşidiye*—stewed lamb marinated with apple, apricot, and honey, cooked with almond, walnut, and fresh herbs. *Mahmudiye*—stewed chicken with apple, apricot, quince, currant, and raisin. Sultan's Favorite Seafood Stew—calamari and jumbo shrimps stewed with artichoke, quince, honey, and cinnamon served on eggplant purée. The appetizers are equally, well, appetizing, and there are a solid handful of vegetarian options.

İbn-i Kemal Street 5/A Sirkeci. www.pasazade.com. © **0212/513-3750.** Appetizers and main courses: 6TL–26TL. MC, V. Daily noon–11:30pm.

In & Around Sultanahmet

VERY EXPENSIVE

Balıkçı Sabahattin ★★★ FISH   One of the few consistently good, high-quality restaurants in a neighborhood of amateurs, Balıkçı Sabahattin is still cranking out top-quality treasures from the sea for eager fans. Meals are served alfresco on the cobbled streets in summer. When the air turns crisp, diners fill the many rooms of this restored 1927 house. Don't pass up the tahini ice cream, and what you can't finish you can feed to one of the hungry kittens milling about.

Seyit Hasan Koyu Sok. 1, Cankurtaran, Sultanahmet (behind Armada Hotel). www.balikci sabahattin.com. © **0212/458-1824.** Appetizers and main courses 9TL–45TL (and up, for fish by weight). AE, MC, V. Daily noon–3pm and 7–10:30pm.

Sarnıç ♨ FRENCH/TURKISH   The setting for this restaurant, an old Roman cistern tucked away behind the Hagia Sophia, is nothing less than dramatic. The flickering light of 500 candles bounces off the iron grillwork, the lofty brick domes, and the stone pillars, while the crackling of the fire in the massive stone chimney (an inauthentic but effective addition) supplies more romance than a girl can handle. Only a few years ago, before the Turkish Touring and Automobile Association bought and restored it, the cistern served as a greasy, old auto repair shop. The food is hit or miss and quite expensive. Consider yourselves forearmed and forewarned.

Soğukçeşme Sok., Sultanahmet. www.sarnicrestaurant.com. © **0212/512-4291.** Reservations required. Dress smart. Appetizers and main courses 14TL–47TL. AE, MC, V. Daily 6pm–midnight; lunch available for groups only.

Seasons Restaurant ★★★ MEDITERRANEAN   Rated no. 1 in Zagat's *Best of Europe* since the book first came out, the Four Seasons' restaurant continues to be a favorite, not only for expats and foreign visitors, but for locals as well. The menus for breakfast, lunch, and dinner are each adapted to seasonal offerings approximately every 3 months and the Sunday brunch is a very popular local affair.

In the Four Seasons Hotel (p. 160), Tevkifhane Sok. 1, Sultanahmet. www.fourseasons.com. **℡ 0212/638-8200.** Reservations required. Dress smart. Appetizers and main courses 18TL–45TL. AE, DC, MC, V. Sun 7–11:30am and noon–3pm; Mon–Sat 6:30–11am and noon–2:30pm; daily 7–11pm.

EXPENSIVE

Konyalı Topkapı Sarayı Lokantası ★ TURKISH/OTTOMAN   Diners at Topkapı are treated to a stunningly situated stopover on a short walk through history. Don't confuse the casual cafeteria with the formal restaurant, the latter being where all the culinary action is. Konyalı has been serving celebrity royalty for more than 100 years, and it's got the black-and-white photographs to prove it. Some of the specialties of the house are their *börek,* the slow-cooked *tandır* lamb, and orange baklava. Konyalı also has a second location at the Kanyon shopping center in Levent (**℡ 0212/353-0450;** open daily noon–1am).

Topkapı Palace, Sultanahmet. www.konyalilokantasi.com. **℡ 0212/513-9696.** A la carte main courses 9TL–32TL; does not include entrance fee to the palace. AE, MC, V. Wed–Mon 8:30am–4:30pm.

MODERATE

Khorasanı Ocakbaşı ★ SOUTHEAST ANATOLIAN   This smart standout in a sea of mediocrity brings not only good food, but good recipes from the Gaziantep and Antakya regions of Southeast Anatolia to the neighborhood. The hooded BBQ (that's the *ocakbaşı*), dominates the entryway, a precursor to such perfumes as the hazelnut *lahmacun,* thyme salad, and spicy kebaps emanating from the kitchen. Twin rows of white cloth-clad tables line the narrow brick-walled space, and the slick bar area at the back lends the entire space a metropolitan feel. For those wishing for a more front-row experience, there are three seats at the BBQ, and plenty of outdoor cafe seating.

Divanyolu Cad. Ticarethane Sok 39/41. Sultanahmet. www.khorasanirestaurant.com. **℡ 0212/519-5959.** Appetisers and main courses 8TL–36TL. AE, MC, V. Daily 11:30am–midnight.

Sultanahmet Fish House ★ AEGEAN   After taking over the management of the Sultanahmet Fish House, Yaşar, Özlem, and Ercan, three veterans in hospitality, turned this obscure fish house into a quality kitchen for above-average Aegean and Mediterranean specialties. The two cozy dining areas are split among the building's two stories, warmed by the subtle and colorful lighting from dozens of hand-made lanterns. There's a full bar to accompany the menu, a parade of typical Aegean mezes along with the catch of the day. My eyes and belly were pleasantly surprised by the fish balls, calamari salad, and lentil *köfte* not usually found on menus, while the salt-baked fish, their specialty and my first foray into this preparation, was succulent.

Prof. Ismail Gürkan Cad. 14 (continuation of Yerebatan Cad.), Sultanahmet. www.sultanahmetfish-house.com. **℡ 0212/527-4441.** Reservations suggested. Appetizers and main courses 7TL–26TL and up for fish. AE, MC, V. Daily 11am–11pm; closing time earlier in winter.

INEXPENSIVE

Buhara 93 LOKANTA   For some pretty good, cheap, basic Turkish fare, Buhara is an old reliable. I tend to stick to the *ev yemekleri* (home cooking)—the stewed dishes displayed in the window. Make your choice then head on up to the restaurant's roof-top terrace. Note that the menu narrows to serve only kebaps during Ramadan.

Nakilbent Sok. 15A, Sultanahmet. www.buhara93restaurant.com. **℡ 0212/518-1511.** Menu items 9TL–17TL. MC, V. Daily 9am–10pm.

Cennet ☺ 🍴 TURKISH   One of the first places in town to serve up touristy kitsch with your meal, Cennet, now in its new digs on Divanyolu, encourages silly behavior such as posing for a photo op in one of the available Grand Vizier robes or puffy turbans. The wait staff dresses in the costumes of earlier centuries and the food is adequate enough, but the real reasons to stop here are the traditional Turkish decor, the low seating, and the round, aproned women sitting cross-legged in the middle of the floor rolling out dough for *gözleme* (cheese, potato, or vegetable-filled crepes). Other village-like menu items include Turkish ravioli, omelets, and a small selection of meat dishes.

Divanyolu Cad. 31/A, Çemberlitaş. © **0212/518-8111.** Main courses 5TL–16TL. MC, V. Daily 8am–midnight.

Fatih Belediyesi Sosyal Tesisleri 🏠 TURKISH   The security guards sporadically stationed at the gated entrance aren't exactly an inviting presence, but this is indeed one of the neighborhood's finds. It's actually a combined tea garden and restaurant, placed strategically on an outdoor terrace that makes up part of the ancient Byzantine fortress wall. There's a small clapboard building situated at the back of the grounds, containing a dining room serving traditional Turkish meals that spills out onto the breezy ramparts in summertime. Because it's owned by the Municipality—presumably the reason for the guards—this destination is bone dry (no alcohol).

Ahırkapı Iskele Sok. 1, Cankurtaran (near the Armada Hotel, under the train tracks at the Dede Efendi entrance to the neighborhood from the sea road). www.cankurtarantesisleri.com. © **0212/458-5415.** Appetizers and main courses 4TL–18TL. MC, V. Daily 11am–midnight.

The Pudding Shop 🍴 KEBAPS/TURKISH   In its heyday, the Pudding Shop was an obligatory stop on the "hippie trail," a starting point for restless vagabonds from the West on their way through the exotic East. With its anti-establishment clientele, it wasn't long before it gained the reputation of ground zero for drug dealings and other unsavory business propositions—in Oliver Stone's *Midnight Express*, Billy Hayes gives up his cab-driver supplier here. Today, the Pudding Shop and its fare fade into history alongside the other fast-food restaurants on Divanyolu Caddesi, with fluorescent backlit menu displays and stacks of expat publications. Turkish and Ottoman staples are served cafeteria style; just point at what looks good.

Divanyolu Cad. 6 (across from the tram), Sultanahmet. www.puddingshop.com. © **0212/522-2970.** Appetizers and main courses 4TL–15TL. AE, MC, V. Daily 7am–11pm.

Sultanahmet Köfteçısı ★★ ☺ 🍴 TURKISH   This little, quality dive on the main drag has been around longer than Turkey has been a republic, and after one bite it's easy to see why. It's hard to imagine a simple meatball as delectable as the ones made here, but if you're not in the mood, there's not much in the way of an alternative. They also serve lamb şiş for 9TL but here, it's beside the point. Side dishes are limited to white beans or a shepherd's salad (tomato, cucumber, onions, and chili). Top the meal off with the *irmik helvası*, a modestly sweet semolina comfort food beloved by Turks.

Divanyolu Cad. 12, Sultanahmet. www.sultanahmetkoftesi.com. © **0212/520-0566.** *Köfte* 15TL. No credit cards. Daily 10:30am–10:30pm.

Tamara ★ 🍴 TURKISH   This four-story plus penthouse eatery features the same, unusually broad selection of kebaps, *pides*, and salads. But even with these choices, my advice is to order one of the stewlike regional dishes (ask for the *ana yemekleri*). One such delight is *keldoş*—a delicious concoction of lentils and beef à la Van from

Eastern Turkey. Or the *orman* (forest) *kebap*—a stew of lamb, chickpeas, potatoes, and carrots.

Küçük Ayasofya Cad. 14, Sultanahmet. www.tamararestaurant.com. © **0212/518-4666.** Appetizers and main courses 5TL–16TL. AE, MC, V. Daily 9am–11pm.

The Old City: Near the Land Walls

Asitane ★★★ 🍴 OTTOMAN   Clearly, it was good to be the sultan, if he indeed ate at all like you do when you visit Asitane. From records of meals at Topkapı Palace (sans quantities) and delving into the memoirs of foreign diplomats of the time, the chef of Asitane has succeeded in re-creating 200 palace recipes plus about 200 original Ottoman-style recipes. The *etli elma dolması* (apple stuffed with lean diced lamb, rice, currants, pistachio, and rosemary) still makes my mouth water—the only regrettable thing is that I'll probably never eat it again, because the menu changes each season. There's a menu in honor of Fatih Sultan Mehmet (the Conqueror) May through June, while vegetarian main-course selections are on the menu year-round.

In the Kariye Oteli, Kariye Camii Sok. 18 (adjacent to St. Savior in Chora), Edirnekapı. www.asitanerestaurant.com. © **0212/534-8414.** Reservations recommended. Dress smart. Appetizers and main courses 11TL–38TL. AE, DISC, MC, V. Daily 11am–midnight.

Develi Restaurant ★★★ SOUTHEASTERN TURKISH   Develi's success may have translated into a blossoming of sister locations, including in Istanbul (and a preponderance of English-speaking expat clientele), but no matter how good the others may be, this Develi maintains a level of consistency and fabulousness worthy of more than a simple star rating will allow. For their regional specialties, they follow outstanding recipes from the Gaziantep region of southeastern Turkey—this translates roughly as blisteringly spicy. Adventurous eaters should order the fiery *çiğ köfte,* beefy meatballs combined with every spice in the book, served raw in a soothing lettuce leaf. Other notable menu items include the *muhamara,* a delectable purée of bread, nuts, and chickpeas; the *fındık lahmacun,* a thin-crust pizza made Turkish-style with chopped lamb; or the lamb sausage and pistachio kebap. Leave room for the *künefe,* a warm slab of baklava dough oozing cheese, dipped in syrup, and covered with crushed pistachio nuts.

Balıkpazarı (Samatya Fish Bazaar), Gümüşyüzük Sok. 7, Samatya. www.develikebap.com. © **0212/529-0833.** (also at Tepecik Yolu 22, Etiler © **0212/263-2571** and Hasırcılar Cad. 89, Eminönü © **0212/512-1261**). Reservations required. Dress smart. Appetizers and main courses 7TL–38TL. AE, MC, V. Mon–Sat noon–midnight; Sun 9am–2pm.

Taksim Square to Tünel
VERY EXPENSIVE

Mikla ★★★ MEDITERRANEAN   Located on the top two floors of the new Marmara Pera hotel (p. 171), Mikla is the newest hit of the Istanbul Yiyecek Icecek A.S. ("eat drink") ventures. The Swedish-born chef, Mehmet Gürs, is somewhat of an Istanbul celebrity by now; he settled in Istanbul in the 1990s and has made all of the kitchens he's touched turn to gold. Reservations are hard to come by and the wait for a table is long; the management makes it easy with the upstairs bar views of the lights of the Old City. Raw grouper makes an outstanding appetizer, followed by the whole roast beef tenderloin for two. Try to leave space for the memorable pistachio and tahini ice cream.

Mesrutiyet Cad. 167–185, Tepebaşı. www.miklarestaurant.com. © **0212/293-5656.** Appetizers and main courses 17TL–75TL. AE, MC, V. Daily noon–3:30pm and 6–11:30pm.

Topaz ★★ MEDITERRANEAN/OTTOMAN   This spot has been frequented by A-listers for its fab views of the Bosphorus, the bridge, and the domes of the Bezmi Alem Valide Sultan Mosque, but it was only recently that the food lived up to the panoramas. This intersection of quality occurred with the opening of Topaz, a stylish and modern restaurant/bar pleasing palates with a mix of modern Mediterranean and Sultan-pleasing traditional Ottoman fare.

In addition to the a la carte menu, there are two delectable multicourse prix-fixe menus, both a good value with or without the optional inclusion of the pre-selected wines accompanying each course (selected from the 207-label wine cellar). If you've grown bored of the Ottoman cuisine during your visit, Topaz is sure to reawaken the joy of eating traditional Turkish.

İnönü Cad. 50, Gümüssuyu. www.topazistanbul.com. ℂ **0212/249-1001.** Reservations required. Dress smart. Main courses 34TL–75TL; degustation menus 65TL (without wine)–90TL (with wine). AE, MC, V. Daily noon–3pm and 7pm–2am.

EXPENSIVE

Hacı Abdullah ★ TURKISH   Politicians, businessmen, families, and out-of-towners have been coming to Istanbul's first licensed restaurant for well over a century. The recipes reflect the best of traditional Turkish cuisine, serving substantial stews, whole artichokes baked with vegetables in olive oil, and their signature dish, lamb shank with eggplant. Lining the walls are enormous glass jars filled with fruit compotes made on the premises and incorporated into the chef's proud desserts, such as quince marinated in syrup or the sweetbread custard topped with figs, apricot, pistachio, and coconut. For those wishing to celebrate with a glass of wine, unfortunately, Hacı Abdullah serves no alcohol.

Ağa Camii Atıf Yılmaz Cad. 9/A (Eski Sakizağacı Cad.) Beyoğlu. www.haciabdullah.com.tr. ℂ **0212/293-8561.** Reservations suggested. Appetizers and main courses 9TL–34TL. AE, MC, V. Daily noon–10:30pm; later on Fri–Sun.

House Café BISTRO   In 2002, a little cafe opened in a house in Nişantaşı. But the creative (and enormous) soups, sandwiches, and salads gained a following until House Café burst at the seams. There are now three locations (the other two are in Teşvikiye and Ortaköy) along with a solid and successful Istanbul brand. I barely made a dent in my lentil salad with purslane and goat cheese in truffle oil, although I may have had I not sunk my fork into my companion's huge and unexpectedly authentic Italian (not the Turkish kind) pizza. A handful of tiny tables line the cobbled alley, while indoors is a well styled, cozy space.

Asmali Mescit 9/1, Tünel. ℂ **0212/245-9515** (also locations at Atiye Sok., Iskeçe Apt. 10/1, Teşvikiye. www.thehousecafe.com.tr. ℂ **0212/259-2377;** Salhane Sok. 1, Ortaköy. ℂ **0212/227-2699**). Appetizers and main courses 18TL–30TL. AE, MC, V. Mon–Thurs 9am–11pm; Fri–Sat 9am–11:30pm; Sun 9am–10:30pm. Bar open Sun until midnight; Mon–Thurs until 1am; Fri–Sat until 2am.

MODERATE

Boncuk ★★ 🍴 TURKISH/ARMENIAN   This small rustic *meyhane* is the one restaurant on this saturated stretch of Nevişade Sokak that is consistently full. Boncuk serves delicacies such as fried brains (mmm . . .) and stuffed spleen, but thankfully there's a variety of more recognizable hot and cold mezes like *kızır*, flavorful and spicy bulgur balls, *topik*, an Armenian specialty made of chickpea paste around a nucleus of onions and currants, and *uskumru dolması*, or stuffed mackerel. Because availability is seasonal, try not to be too disappointed when the waiter informs you that your choice of fish is not on the menu that day.

Nevizade Sok. 19, Beyoğlu (in the Balık Pazarı). © **0212/243-1219.** Appetizers and main courses 6TL–24TL and up for fish. Prix fixe menu 60TL includes reasonable number of alcoholic drinks (add 10TL for limitless booze). No credit cards. Daily noon–midnight.

Demeti ★ 🍴 TURKISH   It's not only the views that draw to this charming little eatery tucked down a residential block of Çihangir. The food is really good. And it should be, as Demeti is run by the same talented team that brings us Bahçe in the resort town of Kaş (see chapter 8). There's no actual menu and very few selections. And oh, by the way, no one speaks English here (yet). You can be sure of really fresh, seasonal items like leek salad, and rare traditional specialties such as fish *köfte* and *pastırma* (garlic spiced deli meat like pastrami, but not). The dining room is at the rear of the building where a glass wall opens up to watery views of the ports of Harem and Kadıköy on the Asian side. There's also a small outside terrace with three tiny tables for two.

Şimşirci Sok. 6/1 (corner of Susam Sok.), Çihangir. http://demeti.com.tr. © **0212/244-0628.** Reservations suggested. Appetizers and main courses 4TL–25TL. MC, V. Daily noon–midnight.

Gedikli ★ 🍴 MEYHANE   The lively chatter coming from packed outdoor tables confirms that Gedikli is indeed the latest word among locals for good food, good fun, and good prices. The *meyhane* specializes in fresh fish, grilled, steamed, or fried. Fish is preceded by mezes that pass the discerning muster of local palates. The restaurant is the centerpiece of Sofyalı Sokak, where Istanbul's middle class heads in droves on warm summer's eves. If a whole fish looks daunting, try the *hamsi* (anchovy) stew.

Sofyalı Sok. 22. © **0212/245-9622.** Reservations suggested. Appetizers and main courses 6TL–22TL; 15TL–45TL and up for combination plates up to 4 people). MC, V. Daily 2pm–1am.

Hacı Baba Restaurant OTTOMAN   A Taksim institution since 1921, Hacı Baba serves Ottoman recipes on the second floor of what used to be the living quarters for the priests of Aya Triada next door. For the most nostalgic experience, try to nab a seat in the frescoed dining room overlooking Istiklal Caddesi. The mezes and a variety of ready-to-grill kebaps are displayed at the entrance, but you can also request to see the baked goods in the kitchen to get an idea of what it is you're actually up against. Perhaps the enormous lamb tenderloins with rice spiced with liver and raisins, or crepes stuffed with lamb and cheese?

Istiklal Cad. 39, Beyoğlu (across from the French Embassy). www.hacibabarest.com. © **212/245-4377.** Main courses 8TL–37TL. AE, MC, V. Noon–midnight.

Enstitü at Istanbul Culinary Institute ★★ 🍴 MODERN TURKISH   While still in training, chefs, who apprentice at some of the city's finer restaurants, create the seasonal menu for the on-site restaurant. All of the fresh produce comes from the director's farm in Saros, and the olive oil arrives direct from a neighboring olive grove on the Gallipoli Peninsula. Menu offerings obviously change on a daily basis (the menu is updated daily on the website), but to give you an idea of what to expect, my experience was with the basil and wheat berry soup, a delicious baked mackerel in white wine sauce, and zucchini fritters, accompanied by a basket of just-out-of-the-oven baked items. To boot, four or five better types of Turkish wines are put on the menu each week, allowing diners to sample some of the country's better wines by the glass.

Meşrutiyet Cad. 59, Tepebaşı. www.istanbulculinary.com. © **0212/251-2214.** Reservations suggested. Appetizers and main courses 8TL–26TL. MC, V. Mon–Fri 7:30am–5pm.

9 Ece Aksoy ★ TURKISH   Ece Aksoy has been running her own restaurant since 1987, when she opened a humble bar in a local theater. She then moved to three ambitious (and successful) locations along the Bosphorus, before downscaling to her current, compact and cozy home in Tepebaşı. Aksoy prepares a daily stream of home-made dishes based on what she thought looked good at the market, whipping up incredible Turkish flavors in the miniscule kitchen at the back of the restaurant. Seating is limited, so book ahead and try to score one of the two long and high pub tables that take up the restaurant's front room.

Oteller Sok. 9B, Tepebaşı, Beyoglu. www.dokuzeceaksoy.com. ☎ **0212/245-7628.** Reservations suggested. Main courses 18TL–40TL. AE, MC, V. Mon–Sat noon–2am; Sun 5pm–2am.

Refik ★★ REGIONAL TURKISH This little restaurant has been an institution in the neighborhood since its inception in 1954, remaining in its own unassuming—unimpressive even—time warp, all while Sofyalı Sokak has become the destination of hip and bohemian nightlife. Its success lies equally with the unfailing quality of the ingredients and the pride that goes into the preparation. The earliest shifts arrive at 6am to start preparing for a menu distinct to the Black Sea region, and therefore heavy on dishes with fish and black cabbage. The *hamsibuğulama* (fish steamed in season) and the *arnavut ciğeri* (sautéed Albanian liver and onions) are house specialties, as is the *kara lahana dolması* (stuffed cabbage).

Sofyalı Sok. 7-10–12, Tünel. www.refikrestaurant.com. ☎ **0212/243-2834.** Reservations required. Appetizers and main courses 9TL–28TL; fish by weight. AE, DC, MC, V. Daily noon–10:30pm.

Yakup 2 ★ 🏛TURKISH The regular clientele keeps coming back to this Istanbul *meyhane* for the consistently good traditional Turkish mezes, kebaps, and fair prices. Actually, they come for the hot mezes and wash 'em down with lots of rakı. In the best tradition of Turkish tavernas, the decor is nothing to speak of, and the best you can say about the expansive outdoor terrace is that it's outside.

Asmalı Mescit Mah. 35–37, Tepebaşı. www.yakuprestaurant.com. ☎ **0212/249-2925.** Appetizers and main courses 8TL–28TL; fish by weight. MC, V. Daily noon–2:30pm and 6:30pm–1am.

INEXPENSIVE

Köfteçi Hüseyin ★ 🎁 KEBABS From a tiny pushcart to a storefront near Taksim Square, Köfteçi Hüseyin is considered among the *köfte* cognoscenti as the place to eat Turkish meatballs. And Turks do take their meatballs seriously. The secret here is really no secret at all: more meat and less filler. It's also cooked medium rare. The result is a ball that's charred on the outside and plump and juicy on the inside. If you're going to do it right, order the staple accompaniment of *piyaz*, a vinegary salad of white beans and onions.

Kurabiye Sok. Akgün Isı Hanı 11, Taksim. ☎ **0212/243-7637.** *Köfte* 10TL. AE, MC, V. Daily noon–4pm.

Parsifal 🏛 VEGETARIAN The formerly derelict and now reclaimed Kurabiye Street is now home to an increasing number of tiny restaurants. This one, however, is a standout. The menu is entirely vegetarian—the type of vegetarian that keeps you coming back for more. Some of the creative dishes are broccoli *ograten*, chard lasagna, black-eyed bean salad with walnut, and stuffed artichoke *dolma*.

Kurabiye Sok. 9A (the parallel street to Istiklal), Taksim. www.parsifalde.com. ☎ **0212/245-2588.** Lunch menu main courses 10TL; dinner menu 20% higher. MC, V. Daily noon–11pm.

Saray Muhallebiçileri 🎁 PATISSERIE/KEBAPS People have been flocking to Saray Muhallebiçileri since its establishment in 1949, and a look in the window will tell you why. The colorful array of desserts lures you off the street and into this patisserie, although with such a huge choice and fair prices, it'll be difficult to not order one of everything. Rice-pudding addicts should definitely not pass up this opportunity, although the chocolate pudding is irresistible as well. This is also a good place to try the *tavukgögsü*, a sweet, gummy pudding made with chicken that would be less difficult to avoid in another less-tempting establishment. There are now a number of franchises all over the city; the one in Eminönü has a cafeteria, prepared foods, and the expected wide array of sweets.

Istiklal Cad. 173, Beyoğlu. www.saraymuhallebicisi.com. © **0212/292-3434.** Appetizers and main courses 8TL–16TL. AE, MC, V. Daily 6am–2am.

Galata & Karaköy

Kivahan ★ ✔ REGIONAL ANATOLIAN If you're looking for something easy, authentic, informal, and interesting to eat in Galata, Kivahan is a no-brainer, although it's no replacement for Çiya (p. 139). There are traditional dishes from the various regions of Anatolia not usually seen on menus: grape leaves stuffed with fava or cheese (instead of pilaf) or bulgur balls flavored with pomegranate, cumin, and mint from Adana. With the atypical items on offer, the only way to choose is the point-and-shoot style of ordering so prevalent at Turkish *lokantas*. They'll even mix up a plate for the indecisive palate, the problem being that you'll want more of each.

Galata Kulesi Meydanı 4, Beyoğlu. www.galatakivahan.com. © **0212/292-0037.** Appetizers and main courses 5TL–20TL. MC, V. Daily 11:30am–midnight.

Lokanta Maya ★★ 🏠 NEW TURKISH Chef Didem Hanım earned her chops at New York's venerable Le Cirque, then once back in Istanbul, landed a spot at Nu Teras, before embarking on her own at this hip, new, and noteworthy bistro. The delectable and ever-changing menu offers innovative embellishments on the traditional. Helluomi cheese gets grilled and garnished with a flavorful tomato salad, sea bass is caramelized and topped with sautéed orange. It's the perfect spot for lunch, a romantic dinner, or a casual late-night bite.

Kemankeş Cad. 35A, Karaköy. www.lokantamaya.com. © **0212/252-6884.** Menu 9TL–29TL. MC, V. Mon noon–5pm; Tues–Sat noon–11pm.

Nişantaşı

Hünkar ★★ ✔ OTTOMAN This Istanbul institution was founded in the neighborhood of Fatih in 1950. The Fatih location has since closed, but the restaurant's loyal following ensured its survival in Nişantaşı, with a second branch in Etiler. Istanbullus wax lyrical over the traditional Turkish and Ottoman cooking served here. Hünkar is famous for its *beğendili kebap* and roast lamb. Their warm *irmik helvası* (semolina dessert) is the model for all others. The Nişantaşı location fills up with local professionals at lunchtime; the homey Etiler location has an outdoor trellised sidewalk cafe.

Mim Kemal Öke Cad. 21/1, Nişantaşı. www.hunkarrestaurant.com. © **0212/225-4665.** Reservations suggested. Appetizers and main courses 8TL–32TL. AE, MC, V. Daily 11am–11:30pm.

Köşebaşı Ocakbaşı ★★★ ✔ SOUTHERN ANATOLIAN Yet another restaurant with the best kebaps in town? Yeah, sure. But Köşebaşı was unexpectedly as advertised, boosting my very low blood sugar with the usual offering of apps and kebaps, but with that added something special. Seriously, who'd have thought that a simple plate of arugula, watercress, green mint, and onions in a sour pomegranate sauce could be so transcendent? Lamb (by way of the *terbiyeli şiş*) is treated to perfection here: marinated and tenderized in olive oil and milk for a minimum of 6 hours.

In summer, Köşebaşı sets out a shingle at Reina (the night club on the Bosphorus), but don't bother, because it's not as good as the Nişantaşı branch.

Bronz Sok. 5, Maçka. www.kosebasi.com.tr. © **0212/230-3869.** Reservations recommended. Main courses 5TL–21TL. MC, V. Daily noon–11pm.

Along the Bosphorus
THE EUROPEAN SIDE

Banyan Seaside ★★ ASIAN FUSION   This top-floor hot spot takes full advantage of its position overlooking Ortaköy and the Bosphorus, with an amazing outdoor terrace that in the crisper months is heated by an open firepit and heat lamps. It also capitalizes on a hip menu that fuses Mediterranean staples with Asian accents. There's seafood with ginger sauce, octopus carpaccio with wasabi aioli, and sake-marinated chargrilled filet mignon in a ginger teriyaki sauce. The noodle bar caters to lighter appetites, and you can choose from 20 different types of tea. Banyan has a second location in Nişantaşı at Abdi Ipekci Cad. 40/3 (© **0212/219-6011**).

Muallim Naci Cad., Salhane Sok. 3 (near the ferry landing), Ortaköy. www.banyanrestaurant.com. © **0212/259-9060.** Reservations required. Appetizers and main courses 12TL–46TL. AE, MC, V. Daily 5pm–midnight.

Sıdıka ★★ 🍴 CREATIVE TURKISH   The buzz surrounding this tiny success story is almost as loud as the chatter resulting from the bistro's packed dining room. Barely 10 tables strong, Sıdıka, run by an ex-economist turned masterful and modest chef, has put the excitement back into Turkish cuisine. You may be hard pressed eliminating items from the imaginative menu, but since the prices are so reasonable, you may want to fill up the table with a selection and share. There's a *levrek marine* (sea bass marinated in mustard vinaigrette with peppercorns), *telde karides* (shrimp in flaky pastry with tomatoes), *enginar dolması* (stuffed artichoke with dill) and Aegean greens, along with some of the most delectable sweets I can remember melting in my mouth.

S(cd)air Nedim Cad. 38, Akaretler/Bes(cd)iktas(cd) (behind the W Hotel). www.sidika.com.tr. © **0212/259-7232.** Appetizers and main courses 3TL–20TL. MC, V. Mon–Sat 5pm–midnight.

Tuğra ★★★ OTTOMAN   This place has created a legend for itself with its innovative synthesis of foods from the entire Ottoman Empire against an imperial backdrop of regal colors and traditional floral motifs. Dishes include a delicious mackerel and red mullet *dolma* and a marinated lamb loin grilled with yogurt, tomato, and spicy butter sauce. It's possible to drop upwards of 200TL per person on dinner and a few gin and tonics, but if you don't drink and you order a la carte, you can at least expect an exceptional dining experience without the heart failure.

Çırağan Palace Hotel Kempinski Istanbul (p. 172), Çırağan Cad. 84, Beşiktaş. www.kempinski-istanbul.com. © **0212/326-4646,** ext. 7890**.** Reservations required. Dress smart. Appetizers and main courses 18TL–55TL. AE, DC, MC, V. Daily 7pm–midnight.

Vogue ★★ INTERNATIONAL/SUSHI   Who would expect that a restaurant located in an office building would create the buzz that has surrounded Vogue for years? The success of this restaurant owes to a high-quality international menu that relies heavily on Mediterranean and international cuisine, plus an amazing and ample sushi bar that predates Istanbullus's growing craze for Japanese food. Floor-to-ceiling windows provide panoramic views as far as Maiden's Tower (and including the monuments of the Historic Peninsula), while in summer, an outdoor terrace gets graceful sea breezes.

Spor Cad., BJK Plaza, A Block, 13th Floor, Akaretler, Beşiktaş. www.istanbuldoors.com. © **0212/227-4404.** Appetizers and main courses 16TL–70TL. AE, MC, V. Daily noon–2am.

THE ASIAN SIDE

Çiya Sofrası ★★★ ⭐ TURKISH This modest eatery, whose kitchen is headed by Musa Dagdeviren, formerly of the California branch of the Culinary Institute of America, has become an international phenomenon. It's located up a busy market street not far from the Kadıköy ferry stop (on the Asian side; take the ferry to Kadıköy from Eminönü) and serves delectable and rarely seen regional Anatolian creations worthy of a brief excursion from the European side. The chef was listed in *Saveur's* favorite 100 in the 2006 edition, while the restaurant has been featured in the *New York Times, New Yorker,* and Zagat Survey's *Europe's Best Restaurants.* Çiya has three storefronts including an annex serving only kebaps. At the *lokanta,* you'll have to point at and write down your selections, and hand your cheat sheet to your waiter once seated.

Güneşli Bahçesi Sok. 43–44, Kadıköy (from the Kadıköy/Eminönü dock, cross the busy street and head up toward the Balıkpazarı). www.ciya.com.tr. 🕿 **0216/330-3190.** Appetizers and main courses 4TL–28TL. DC, MC, V. Daily 11am–10pm.

Del Mare FISH There isn't much about this waterfront restaurant that isn't spectacular. The old stone building was part of a string of factories that lined the shorefront at the turn of the century; inside is an expansive dining room that spills out onto a canopied outdoor terrace overlooking the Bosphorus waterway. Local fishing boats cruise beneath the twinkling lights of the Bosphorus Bridge—probably some of the same local fishermen that hauled in today's catch. Del Mare is known for its salt fish and grilled calamari, though the *ahtapot patlican* (eggplant purée and octopus) was an unexpected hit. The chef will prepare the fish or meat of your choice whatever way you want it.

Kuleli Cad. 53/4, Çengelköy. www.del-mare.com. 🕿 **0216/422-5762.** Reservations suggested. The restaurant shuttle will pick you up from Kuruçeşme. Fish by weight (expect around 50€–70€ per person). AE, MC, V. Daily noon–11pm.

SHOPPING
Istanbul's Best Shopping

Local markets offer a window into the vibrancy and color of the neighborhood, and provide a priceless experience in interaction with the locals. Istanbul has more than its fair share of outdoor markets, selling the usual assortment of fresh produce, household staples, sweatshirts, and maybe the odd antique. A walk through one of these provides yet another opportunity to witness another facet of this complex culture. The major markets (open from 9am–sundown) include the daunting **Çarşamba Pazarı** ("Wednesday" market), held in and around the Fatih Mosque, and the **Beşiktaş Cumartesi Pazarı** (Saturday Bazaar), Nüzhetiye Caddesi opposite the lovely Ihlamur Pavilion. There is also a **flea market** between Sahaflar and the Grand Bazaar, and down at Eminönü every Sunday, and a daily **antiques market** in Horhor (Horhor Cad. Kırk Tulumba, Aksaray). With feng shui taking hold of the consciousness of Istanbul's upper crust, it's no surprise to see organic produce close behind. The **Ekolojik Pazarı,** an organic market in Feriköy (in the car park on Bomonti Cad., Lala Şahin Sok.; take the metro from Taksim to Osmanbey), fills the niche. It's open every Saturday from 8am to 5pm. And giving a boost to the embryonic art and design scene in Çihangir, the local municipality has organized the new **Pazart,** an open-air design fair showcasing art, crafts, and artisanal foods against a beguiling backdrop of domes, minarets, and sea. The market is located in Roma Bahcesi, aka Sanatkarlar Parkı, open on the first and third Sunday of every month from 3 to 8pm, 1 to 7pm in winter.

What Should I Buy?

The first thing that comes to mind when plotting a plan of attack for acquisitions in Istanbul is a rug, be it a *kilim* or **tribal carpet.** Carpets, *kilims,* and a whole slew of related items that have lost their nomadic utility comprise an indescribably complex industry, but it is unlikely that you will get very far before being seduced by the irresistible excess of enticing keepsakes.

Most people are unaware that Turkey manufactures some of the best **leather items** in Europe, comparable in quality to those sold in Florence, Italy (and in some stores in Florence, the merchandise *is* Turkish). Because leather items are individually produced in-house, quality and fit may vary, but the advantage of this is that you can have a jacket, skirt, or trousers made to order, change the design of a collar, or exchange an unsightly zipper for buttons at prices far less than what you'd pay back home.

The entire length of Kalpakçılar Caddesi in the Grand Bazaar glitters with precious metals from the Nuruosmaniye Gate to the Beyazıt Gate. But Turkish-bought **gold and silver** are no longer the bargains they used to be, as the cost of precious metals—particularly gold—continues to skyrocket. However, cheap labor in China and India might still keep Turkish jewelers from pricing themselves out of the market, so all hope is not lost.

Some of the world's best **meerschaum** comes from Turkey. This heat-resistant sea foam becomes soft when wet, allowing it to be carved into playful pipes that would make a collector out of the most die-hard nonsmoker. An afternoon in a historic *hamam* will expose you to some of the most beautiful traditional **white copper** objects, available as kitchen and bathing utensils, although keep in mind that you can't cook with this toxic stuff unless the inside has been coated with tin.

As far as **antiques** go, shopkeepers seem to be practiced in manufacturing bogus certificates of origin that will facilitate your trip through Customs, but beware: The certificate may not be the only counterfeit item in the shop. Collectors should keep in mind that it is prohibited by Turkish law to export anything dated prior to the 20th century without the proper authorization from a museum directorate.

Less traditional items can easily fill a suitcase, and with clever Turkish entrepreneurs coming up with new merchandise on a regular basis, you won't get bored on your second or third visit. **Pillowcases, embroidered tablecloths, ornamental tea services,** real **Turkish towels** and **brass coffee grinders** are just some of the goodies that never seem to get old.

That old measure by which you should offer the seller half of his initial price is old hat. They've caught on to our shopping savvy, and in fact they don't care. Plenty of stupendously wealthy Russians and groups of cruise ship passengers with weighty wallets provide easy targets. Still I've heard that a good rule of thumb is to offer about 25% less than you're willing to pay. In my experience, you must hold off your counteroffer for as long as you can get away with it. This method will meet with counteroffers and varying responses, and after a few times you might succeed in talking the price down. If the shopkeeper stonewalls, remember there's another one selling the same stuff next door. You'll get the hang of it.

Here's another bargaining tool: Narrow down your choice to two pieces. Snub your first choice and put it down (with plans to come back to it later). Negotiate on your second choice—undoubtedly one of the finer samples in the shop, and therefore one of the pricier items on sale. Once you've established that it's out of your price range, turn to your first choice with a disappointed "and what about that one?"

Shopping A to Z
ANTIQUES & COLLECTIBLES

Objects dating to the Ottoman make up a popular category for roving antiquers. As a rule, all items displayed can be legally purchased and exported to your home country (unless the piece is unique, in which case you need documentation from a museum director to buy it). Objects dated prior to the Ottoman period are considered fruit from the poisonous tree. Where carpets are concerned, the cutoff is 100 years—you'll need a certificate from the shopkeeper stating the age, origin, and authenticity of the carpet. (This is standard practice anyway.) So if you're serious, your first stop should be the neighborhood along Çukurcuma in the extremely hilly neighborhood below Beyoğlu and Taksim.

Horhor Bit Pazarı　One of the lesser-known and blissfully lesser touristed markets is where you'll find dusty Turkish memorabilia from the 20th century. Merchandise runs the gamut from tableware, lamps, and furniture, and on to oversize architectural remnants, spread out among the more than 200 shops on six floors. Horhor Cad., Kırk Tulumba, Aksaray. Tram. Aksaray.

Khaftan Art and Antiques　The sophistication of Khaftan is immediately apparent. With your big toe barely over the threshold, your eyes and ears are seduced by a relentless assault of good taste. The boutique artfully displays a high-quality mixture of fine Ottoman art both miniature and life-sized, old and new, including 17th-century Ottoman textiles, early 19th-century ceramics, collectable maps and prints, ethnic jewelry and calligraphy. Nakilbent Sok. 32, Sultanahmet. www.khaftan.com. © 0212/458-5425. Tram: Sultanahmet.

Museum Store　As one of 55 museum stores currently operated by Bilkent University, the Topkapı store is a souvenir emporium selling everything from magnets to museum-quality reproductions of the Topkapı Dagger (only 6,000TL for the latter). The quality of items is almost certainly better than what you'll find in quotidian souvenir shops and probably less expensive than what you'll pay the shopkeeper at the Grand Bazaar. Located in Topkapı Palace, the Hagia Sophia, the Mosaic Museum, St. Savior in

Chora, and the Museum of Turkish and Islamic Arts, as well as at other museums around the country. www.bkg.com.tr. Main office ℂ **0212/451-6250.**

Ottomania Located in Beyoğlu just outside the Tünel atrium, Ottomania specializes in high-quality old maps and engravings. Sofyalı Sok. 30–32 (exit Tünel, and walk straight through atrium), Tünel. ℂ **0212/243-2157.**

Sofa Art and Antiques Just steps from the Grand Bazaar, Sofa is a fixture on the wide pedestrian outdoor mall that Nuruosmaniye Caddesi has become. The shop is artfully stocked with an eclectic mix of high-quality framed calligraphic works, illuminations, and miniatures, as well as religious icons, copper, silver, and ceramics. There are also plenty of smaller items (albeit just as unaffordable, at least to a writer's wallet) to finger while browsing your way around the store. Nuruosmaniye Cad. 85 Cağaloğlu. www.kashifsofa.com. ℂ **0212/520-2850.** Tram: Çemberlitaş.

BOOKS

Galeri Kayseri Anything you ever wanted to know about Istanbul or Turkey is somewhere inside this shop, or their branch across the street. Galeri Kayseri also carries a daunting collection of English-language Turkey-centric fiction, cookbooks, guide books (regrettably not this one), and art tomes. Divanyolu 58 and across the street at no. 11, Sultanahmet. www.galerikayseri.com. ℂ **0212/516-3366.** Tram: Sultanahmet.

Homer Kitabevi Down the street from the Galatasaray High School is this absolute superlative of a bookstore, stocking a rich selection of books on Turkish issues, including politics, history, architecture, photography, travel, and religion. If you can't find it here, it's either sold out or it doesn't exist. Yeni Çarşı Cad. 12/A, Galatasaray. www.homerbooks.com. ℂ **0212/249-5902.** Nostalgic tramway to Galatasaray.

Istanbul Kitapçısı Owned and operated by the Istanbul Municipality, this bookstore stocks cassettes, videos, travel books, maps, and coffee-table books in a variety of languages. They also have a selection of prints and posters. Istiklal Cad. 379, Beyoğlu. www.istanbulkitapcisi.com. ℂ **0212/292-7692.** Nostalgic tramway to Galatasaray or Odakule.

Librairie de Pera The last bookseller left on the Grand Rue de Pera (long since renamed) that in its heyday was famed for its booksellers, Librairie de Pera is the little engine that could. The current owner, Ugur Güraca, presides over a multilingual collection of more than 40,000 rare books, some bound with goat skin, as well as prints, photographs, and etchings. Galip Dede Cad. 8 (opposite the Galatasaray Mevlevihanesi), Tünel/Beyoğlu. www.librairiedepera.com. ℂ **0212/243-7447.** Funicular or nostalgic tramway to Tünel.

Robinson Crusoe Just before you head down to the coast for that weeklong Mediterranean vacation, stop off here to find something to read. Robinson Crusoe stocks a limited selection of English-language fiction, travel guides, and books on Istanbul and Turkey. There's also a miniscule used section. Istiklal Cad. 389, Beyoğlu. www.rob389.com. ℂ **0212/293-6968.** Funicular or nostalgic tramway to Tünel.

Sahaflar Çarşısı The Book Bazaar is a wonder of the printed page. Vendors carry books on Turkish subjects ranging from art to architecture to music, both old and new. Also, some of the finest examples of Ottoman art and calligraphy can be found in this book-lover's mecca. Sahaflar Çarşısı, Grand Bazaar (enter from Çadırcılar Cad.). Tram: Beyazıt or Çemberlitaş.

CARPETS

When in Istanbul, my days are filled with powwows with carpet dealers proud to show me the thank-you letters received from Washington, D.C., insiders, foreign

deconstructing THE TURKISH CARPET

Turkish tribal rugs are divided into **kilims,** which are flat, woven rugs, and **carpets,** which are hand-knotted using a double or Gordian Knot, a technique unique to Anatolia that results in a denser, more durable product than the single-knotted carpets found abroad. *Kilims* are probably more recognizable, as they are inexpensive and sold abroad.

There are four types of carpets produced currently in Turkey. **Wool-on-wool** carpets represent the oldest tradition in tribal rugs and are representative of a wide range of Anatolian regions. The earliest examples display geometric designs using natural dyes that were reliant on local resources like plants, flowers, twigs, and even insects, so that the colors of the carpets reflected the color of an individual region. Blues and reds are typical of designs originating around Bergama, which derive from the indigo root and local insects. Reds seem to be dominant in carpets made in Cappadocia. The oranges and beiges of the Üşaks are also becoming more popular among consumers.

Today the business of carpet weaving has been transformed into a mass industry. Weavers have for the most part switched over to chemical-based dyes, although the trend toward organic dyes is experiencing a rebirth.

The second type of carpet is the highly prized **silk-on-silk** samples, which developed in response to the Ottoman Palace's increasing desire for quality and splendor. Silk was a precious commodity imported from China that few could afford. In the 19th century, the sultan established a royal carpet-weaving center at **Hereke** that catered exclusively to the palace. Today silk-on-silk rugs continue to outclass all others, using silk from Bursa woven into reproductions of traditional designs. (**FYI:** Silk threads cannot hold natural dyes.) Silk rugs are also produced in **Kayseri,** but these have yet to attain the high standards set by the Herekes.

A more recent development in carpet production has been the **wool-on-cotton,** which, because of the lower density of the weft, accommodates a higher ratio of knots per inch, and therefore more detail in the design. Carpets of this type come from **Kayseri, Konya (Lakık),** and **Hereke. Cotton-on-cotton** is an even newer invention, duplicating the resolution and sheen of a silk rug without the expense.

Sales tactics include an emphasis on Anatolian carpet and *kilim* weaving as a high art. This certainly applies to rare and older pieces, which command hefty sums. But modern samples—albeit handmade copies of traditional designs—are created from computerized diagrams. Finally, unless you're an expert, you should avoid buying antique rugs, which cost significantly more, and will present some challenges with Customs. The bottom line is that only antiques experts are equipped for a proper appraisal.

dignitaries, and vacationing journalists. I could easily list a handful of stores where I go regularly for a cup of tea, but that wouldn't be fair to the shop owners that I have yet to meet. And just because I gave my business card to someone as a courtesy in passing doesn't mean that I endorse his (and in the rarest of cases, her) shop. In fact, just because I mention a shop in a previous edition of *Frommer's Turkey* doesn't necessarily mean I endorse them now. But if you take away only one piece of information from this page, it should be that profit margins on carpets can be huge, and that the breadth of that margin is really up to you. And because carpet-selling is such a major money-maker in Turkey (in fact, so is selling ceramics and jewelry), everybody you encounter on the street has only one thing on his or her mind: sales. Toward this end, random locals will approach you on tourist-heavy streets offering information, access, or even romance (see "Important Tips for Single Women Travelers" in chapter 12). Accept the attention (or not) with a grain of salt, just be forewarned and forearmed. So where DO you find an honorable carpet seller? What's honorable? Accepting a smaller profit margin? Why should they if you're perfectly willing to pay? Ensuring that you're not sold a fake? Actually, the challenge for the potential buyer is not so much about avoiding fakes and scams, it's about not getting scalped. This doesn't diminish the value of the carpets, nor does it mean that all carpet sellers are dishonest. In fact, Istanbul is full of carpet salesmen whose singular goal is to sell the finest-quality, most beautiful specimens for the absolute highest price they can get. This is, after all, a business. And it's *your* business to be an educated consumer.

My dilemma is that as soon as I recommend a carpet seller, you will automatically be at a disadvantage, because 1) you and many others will move heaven and earth to buy at this location, thus tipping the scales of demand in favor of the seller, and 2) the seller will therefore lose the incentive to compete. The result? You lose. So what's a shopper to do? Recognize that buying a carpet is an extremely labor- and time-intensive activity, and rest assured that these salesmen will find you. Your best, and only defense, is to go armed with the best information you can get, and to recognize in advance that no matter what you do, you're going to pay more than you should.

CERAMICS

Istanbul Handicrafts Center The streetfront shop to the workshops in this restored 17th-century Ottoman *medrese* (see "Crafts" below) has a choice collection of precious ceramic and porcelain reproductions from Kütahya and Iznik. Kabasakal Cad., Istanbul Sanatları Çarşısı, next to the Yeşil Ev/Green House Hotel. ℭ **0212/517-6780.**

Iznik Foundation Having revived the Ottoman-era craft of Iznik tilemaking, the Iznik Foundation is now selling its wares. The trick was identifying the chemical process for achieving the vibrant blues and green pigmentation of the originals. One of the criteria was that the ceramic "canvas" had to be composed of up to 80% quartz. This shop sells hand-painted tiles, platters, urns, and other household decorative items and tableware. Öksüz Çocuk Sok. 7, Kuruçeşme/Beşiktaş. www.iznik.com. ℭ **0212/287-3243.** Bus: 22, 22RE, 25E, 40, 40T, and 42T.

COPPER

Çadırcılar Caddesi If you simply have to have a set of those white copper *hamam* bowls or a copper platter for a table *à la Turque,* root around the slightly disheveled stalls near the book bazaar. That is, if you aren't going to Ankara, where copper is king. Çadırcılar Cad. (past the entrance to the Book Bazaar, near the Grand Bazaar), Grand Bazaar. Tram: Beyazıt or Çemberlitaş.

Zaer-iş Every piece of copper in this tiny shop is hand-worked, from the decorative serverware to the copper trays to the folksy trinkets. Prices here are (currently) about one-third of what you'll pay elsewhere. Mimar Sinan Cad. Şafak Han 40/E, Süleymaniye. ℭ **0212/520-2507.** Tram: Beyazıt.

COVERED BAZAARS & STREET MARKETS

Arasta Bazaar Less overwhelming in scope than the Grand Bazaar is the picturesque shopping arcade attached to the southern edge of the Blue Mosque. It's a total tourist trap, but there are a few high-quality gems mixed in with the stacks of cheap ceramics and evil eyes made in China. Open daily from 9am to 7pm (closes earlier in winter and during Ramadan). Sultanahmet. Entrance on Topçu Cad. (across from the Blue House hotel) and on Küçük Ayasofya Çad. Tram: Sultanahmet.

Egyptian Spice Bazaar (Mısır Carsışı) ★★   At the center of the commercial hub of Eminönü, the Spice Bazaar is an indoor emporium of comestibles, rare (and mostly counterfeit products), colorful elf slippers, and polyester scarves, among other interesting, if not dazzling things. Purveyors will be hawking saffron (don't bother, the stuff sold as Turkish saffron is dried safflower), Turkish delight (if you must, buy it elsewhere) and a caldron's worth of item promising superhuman sexual prowess (no comment). Stick to the fresh and dried fruits and nuts, whole spices (like cinnamon bark, whole peppercorns), teas, any irresistible souvenirs, and remember that the stuff worth eating is in humble shopfronts located just outside the cover of the bazaar. The real action is to the right of the entrance inside the bustling narrow aisle of vending stalls displaying countless varieties of olives, cheeses, fruits, and vegetables. The chaotic streets behind the bazaar deal in general necessities, from housewares, to long johns, to pots and pans, a daunting variety of fresh cheeses and olives, and the odd kitchen gadget normally seen on late-night TV. Sometimes you really never know what you need until you stumble upon it. Open Monday to Saturday 8:30am to 6:30pm. Eminönü, opposite Galata Bridge. No phone. Tram: Eminönü; Buses too numerous to list.

The Grand Bazaar (Kapalıçarşı)   Perhaps it was the renown of the Grand Bazaar (aka the Kapalıçarşısı or Covered Market) that put Istanbul on the map of the world's great shopping destinations. It's certainly one of the world's major tourist traps. It's also a feast of color and texture, of glitter and glitz. It's also not to be missed. So take a deep breath, leave your valuables (and any cash you'd rather not spend) back in the hotel safe, and dive in. Open Monday through Saturday from 8:30am to 7pm (closes earlier during Ramadan). See also p. 92 for more suggestions on touring the historic shops in the Grand Bazaar. Beyazit, Eminönü. No phone. www.kapalicarsi.org.tr. Best entrances through the Beyazit Gate (across from the Beyazit stop on the tramway along Divanyolu) and the Nuruosmaniye Gate (from the Çemberlitaş tramway stop on Divanyolu, follow Vezirhanı Cad. to the arched entrance to the mosque grounds, which leads to the bazaar). Tram: Beyazit or Çemberlitaş.

Istiklal Caddesi   A bustling promenade of cafes, clothing stores, blaring record shops, and bookstores, Istiklal Caddesi from Tünel to Taksim Square may be starting to resemble an open-air mall, but it's still an essential activity for all who visit Istanbul. As the likes of Nike, Polo, Benetton, Desa, Quiksilver and other international retailers crank up the cost of real estate, the numerous galleries or (*pasajı*) found hidden in plain sight all along the street become that much more interesting. Keep a lookout for the grungy **Aznavur Pasajı** (No. 212), the lovely **Avrupa Pasajı** (see the Balıkpazarı below), the Çiçek Pasajı (see below), the posh **Pasaj Markiz** (No. 360/109) and the **Rumeli Han** (No. 88). Istiklal Cad., Beyoğlu. Bus, metro, Nostalgic tramway or tram/funicular to Taksim; Funicular to Tünel.

Ortaköy   The **arts-and-crafts fair** on Sundays (open year-round) in Ortaköy is Istanbul's equivalent of "downtown." Here you'll find a mixture of street-smart jewelry, tie-dyed textiles, and revolutionary Turkish ideas. The street food here is lots of fun. Around the Ortaköy boat landing, along the Bosphorus. Bus: 22, 22RE, 25E, 40, 40T and 42T.

CRAFTS

Caferağa Medresesi   Like the Cedid Mehmet Efendi Medresesi housing the Istanbul Handicrafts Center, this recently restored Ottoman-era seminary is now too the home of a handicrafts center. But the managers of the Caferağa setup have taken the concept to the next level: They run a whole slew of visitor's workshops set in around an on-site picturesque garden cafe. Just outside the *medrese* (access is down a few steps off of Caferiye Sok.) is the art gallery annex, where works created by affiliated artists (watercolors, calligraphy, *ebru*, abstract art, and jewelry) are up for sale. Caferiye Sok. Soğukkuyu Çıkmazı 5, Sultanahmet. www.tkhv.org. ☏ **0212/528-0089.** Tram: Sultanahmet or Gülhane.

Istanbul Handicrafts Center (Istanbul Sanatları Çarşısı) In another one of its commendable preservationist projects, the Touring and Automobile Club of Turkey has provided an outlet for the revival of Turkish and Ottoman crafts. Each room off the central courtyard of this restored 17th-century *medrese* serves as an atelier for a different craft. Here you can watch the creation of handmade treasures, including hand-painted silks, folk art dolls and puppets, gilded calligraphy and miniatures, fine porcelain reproductions, and modern examples of the art of *ebru,* or marbled paper. The center is open year-round, although you may have to knock on some doors to get a personal shopping tour during the off season. Better yet, their fixed pricing takes the guesswork out of buying. Kabasakal Cad. (the side street next to the Derviş Tea Garden and across from the Blue Mosque), Sultanahmet. www.turing.org.tr.☏ **0212/517-6780.** Tram: Sultanahmet.

DEPARTMENT STORES & CHAINS

So you've packed for warmer weather and the winds from the Caucasus have arrived a bit early. Head for these chains, located along Istiklal Caddesi, though you'll find them in major shopping malls and downtowns throughout the country. If you've got champagne taste, you may want to keep your eyes open for some of Turkey's higher-end fashion franchises such as **Sarar, Ipekyol,** and **Abdullah Kiğılı.** Stores for the proletariat (in addition to the majors like Nike, Diesel, Benetton, etc.) include **Koton**, **Mavi Jeans**, **Collezione**, **Colin's** and **LC Waikiki.**

Beyman Beyman is Turkey's answer to Ralph Lauren, without the horsy patch. There's absolutely nothing cheesy about this store, which carries casual chic for men and women as well as housewares worthy of a museum. The Beymen Mega Store in Akmerkez (see "Malls & Shopping Centers," below) is more along the lines of an upscale department store, where you can find cosmetics, stationery, and even furniture. www.beymen.com.tr. Abdi Ipekçi Cad. 23/1, Nişantaşı.☏ **0212/343-4800.** Akmerkez AVM, Etilerl.☏ **0212/316-6900.** stinye Park AVM, Istinye.☏ **0212/335-6700.** See website for additional locations.

Vakko For the best designer men's and women's wear, check out Vakko, Turkey's answer to Barney's New York and worth a look if only for its dazzling scarves rivaling anything Hermes does. There are a number of locations, including at the airport, in Kanyon Shopping Center, on Bağdat Caddesi, and its new flagship store in the Galleria Shopping Center. The V2K line is a hipper version of its parent, with locations in Nişantaşı and at Kanyon mall. www.vakko.com.tr. Abdi Ipekçi Cad. 33, Nişantaşı, ☏ **0212/248-5011.** Akmerkez AVM. Nispetiye Cad., Etiler.☏ **0212/282-0695.** Istinye Park AVM. ☏ **0212/345-5832.** Galleria AVM, Sahilyolu, Ataköy. ☏ **0212/559-5444.** Kanyon AVM, Meçediyeköy Mah., Büyükdere, Levent. ☏ **0212/353-1080.** Bağdat Cad, 422, Suadiye. ☏ **0216/463-2606.**

FOOD

Galatasaray Fish Market (Balıkpazarı) True, the Balıkpazarı is a great big tourist trap, but as a jumble of over 25 fish and fresh-produce vendors, as well as a

Something Smells Fishy

Beware of anything labeled caviar. Turkey is notorious for its illegal trade in smuggled caviar, as well as for representing this lower-quality replacement fish roe as high-quality caviar using counterfeit labels copied from reputable brands.

handful of traditional *meyhanes* and the odd seller of dashboard ornaments, it's also an undeniable hoot. Be sure to weave your way through the narrow **Avrupa Pasajı** in the Balıkpazarı, a narrow gallery of artsy shops selling souvenirs from antique samovars to tiny harem outfits for 2-year-olds (plus merchandise like brass pepper mills at prices lower than in the Egyptian Spice Market). Istiklal Cad., opposite Galatasaray High School (near intersection of Meşrutiyet Cad.), Galatasaray, Beyoğlu. Nostalgic tramway: Galatasaray.

Hacı Bekir For the most extensive variety of Turkish delight, stop in to this legendary sweet shop with locations in Beyoğlu and Eminönü. Istiklal Cad. 129, Taksim, Beyoğlu. ℭ **0212/244-2804.** Hamidiye Cad. 81–83, Eminönü. www.hacibekir.com.tr. ℭ **0212/522-0666.** Tram: Eminönü.

Kurukahveci Mehmet Coffee addicts should head to this corner behind the spice bazaar. A producer of the infamous precious brew of thick, Turkish coffee, Kurukahveci Mehmet is also the best-known retail outlet. Products also include espresso beans and cocoa. Tahmis Sok. 66, Eminönü, Fatih. www.mehmetefendi.com. ℭ **0212/511-4262.** Tram: Eminönü.

La Cave What better symbol that Turkey's wines have arrived than a boutique storefront? La Cave stocks a teasing collection of Turkey's showcase wines, at prices much lower than what you'll find at the airport. You'll also find wines and spirits from all over the world, but remember that the higher the alcohol content, the higher you'll pay in Turkish tax (a common Woodbridge Cabernet was selling for 65TL—ouch). Sıraselviler Cad., 109/A, Çihangir, Beyoğlu. www.lacavesarap.com. ℭ **0212/243-2405.** Bus, metro, nostalgic tramway, and tram/funicular to Taksim.

Namlı Gurme Gida Ferry passengers heading home and local workers and artisans crowd the cash register of Namlı, a specialty food purveyor stocking quality items such as olive oils, cheeses, *helva*, dried fruits, honey, and nuts, many of which are packaged and ready to go. Namlı is renowned for their *pastırma* and deli meats, as well as Kars cheese. They even carry items an extended visitor might not want to be without: HP sauce or Casa Fiesta salsa. The covered outdoor cafe is packed with lunchtime folk or commuters waiting for their ferries to board. It's open Monday to Saturday, 6:30am to 10:30pm. Rıhtım Cad. 1/1 (under the car park), Karaköy. www.namligida.com.tr. ℭ **0212/293-6880.** Tram: Karaköy.

HOME

Beymen Home One could easily spend thousands of Turkish Lira in this shop. Beymen is a candy store of contemporary home items a la Ralph Lauren or Calvin Klein. Here you'll find sleekly designed tableware, Ottoman-style copper serving platters, and sumptuously simple furniture. The Akmerkez location also sells Hiref designs (see below). Abdi Ipekçi Cad. 23/1, Nişantaşı. www.beymen.com.tr. ℭ **0212/373-4800.**

Design Zone Designer Özlem Tuna displays her delicious designs as well as the handiwork of other notable Istanbul artisans in this little shop off of Nuruosmaniye Caddesi. The motifs are familiar to the Turkish eye, featuring icons like the tulip or the evil eye in innovative ways. Expect to find things like coffee/tea services, and all

Olive Oil: Anatolia's Black Gold

Turkey's **olive oil** really doesn't get the kind of respect it deserves—an absence of effective marketing has deprived the rest of the world of one of the country's most treasured resources. But that is changing, by the looks of the gourmet shop in the airport's duty-free area. If you've been bewitched by the flaxen temptress at the bottom of your meze bowl, pick up a bottle at any local convenience-type store. The grocery store chains carry some basic brands like Komili, as well as some more premium brands like Amphora, Tariş, and Olivos.

manner of eye-catching and bejeweled bowls. Alibaba Türbe Sok. Feyzullah Işhanı 21/4, Nuruosmaniye. www.ozlemtuna.com. ☎ **0212/527-9285.**

Hiref   With the vision of "design your culture," Hiref takes the traditional and fuses contemporary design sensibilities. The result? Simply stunning spiral glass "Beykoz" vases, covered silver platters, copper tureens, marble candleholders, each with its own motif reminiscent of a Cappadocia cave, a high sufi-style felt fez, a tulip, or the pleasingly ubiquitous Turkish crescent and star. Istinye Park AVM, 4th floor. ☎ **0212/345-6038.** Kanyon AVM, Floor B2. ☎ **0212/353-5450.**

The Home Store   A veritable emporium of Turkish-made, stylish wear for both the home and for those who live in it, the Home Store deserves a reserved corner in your luggage. Come to think of it, bring a spare bag. www.homestore.com.tr. Istiklal Cad. 189/1, Beyoğlu, ☎ **0212/293-4456.** Akmerkez Shopping Center, Nispetiye Cad., Etiler. ☎ **0212/282-0253.** See website for additional locations.

Mudo   A sort of cross between Pottery Barn and Next, Mudo carries stylish housewares and very wearable clothing for men and women. A Mudo outlet is now located in the Egyptian Spice Bazaar. www.mudo.com.tr. Teşvikiye Cad. 149, Nişantaşı. ☎ **0212/291-7261.** Also on Istiklal Cad., and in the Akmerkez Shopping Center, Nispetiye Cad., Etiler. For store locations call ☎ 444-MUDO (6836).

Paşabahçe   The nationwide chain (with 17 outlets in Istanbul alone) has recently begun making a name overseas for its elegant ceramics, hand-cut glass, and typically Ottoman tableware. The more precious pieces are trimmed in silver or gold plate. The store also stocks everyday tableware, but that's not the stuff you're going to carry home. Istiklal Cad. 314, Beyoğlu. www.pasabahcemagazalari.com. ☎ **0212/244-0544.** Nostalgic tramway to Galatasaray. See website for additional locations.

JEWELRY

Eller Art Gallery   Providing a more down-to-earth showcase for wearable art is this workshop (at the back) and gallery on a side street of Beyoğlu. These very Turkish designs are the work of Nurhan Acun, a 1957 graduate of the State Academy of Fine Arts. His pieces are inspired by jewelry and other artifacts normally seen under protective glass at Ankara's Museum of Anatolian Civilizations, and in fact, have been commissioned by the very museums that have served as his muse. Istiklal Cad., Postacılar Sok. 12, Beyoğlu. www.ellerartgallery.wordpress.com. ☎ **0212/249-2364.** Nostalgic tramway to Odakule.

Evihan   Handmade artistic pieces made using Turkish tiles and hand-blown glass beads are the main feature at this crafty boutique located in the trendy neighborhood of Çukurcuma. Altıpatlar Sok. 4A, Çukurcuma./Beyoğlu. www.evihan.com. ✆ **0212/244-0034.** Funicular or Nostalgic tramway to Tünel.

Urart Ateliers   Urart is an upscale workshop complex of designers, artists, and craftspeople dedicated to re-creating the rich traditions of Anatolian civilizations in gold and silver. Urart's precious (and costly) creations are available to the public in the label's exclusive boutique in Nişantaşı. Some of their pieces are also available in the small gift shop in Topkapı Palace, in the last courtyard, and in hotels around town. www.urart.com.tr. Abdi Ipekçi Cad. 18/1, Nişantaşı. ✆ **0212/246-7194.** Also in the Çirağan Palace and the Vakko in Suadiye.

TEXTILES

Abdulla Natural Products   Thou shall not covet these incredibly thick and plush towels. With two locations in and around the Grand Bazaar, Abdulla stocks goods like deliciously textured bath sheets, herbal olive-oil soaps, and all of the accouterments for a home-style *hamam* (silk pestamal, hand mitt, and so on). www.abdulla. com. Halıcılar Cad. 62, Grand Bazaar. ✆ **0212/527-3684.** Ali Baba Turbe Sok. 25/27, Nuruosmaniye. ✆ **0212/526-3070.** Tram: Beyazit or Çemberlitaş.

Derviş   New ethnic fabrics created based on the traditional villages around Anatolia fill the shelves of this stall in the Grand Bazaar. Samples include a silk-on-silk embroidered man's shawl—the type worn by an Ottoman *zeybek* (parallel image of a Mafioso type); a raw silk waffle-texture bedsheet, a small collection of raw cotton *peştemels*, and handwoven linen towels. www.dervis.com. Keseçiler Cad. 33–35, and Halıcılar Cad. 5, Grand Bazaar (near the Iç Bedesten). ✆ **0212/514-4525** and 0212/528-7883. Tram: Beyazit or Çemberlitaş.

Eğin Tekstil   This miniscule shop has been in the family for so long that Dr. Süleyman (a real medical doctor) proudly displays the *firman,* or order of Sultan

---

Malls & Shopping Centers

You'd really have to have a lot of time on your hands in Istanbul to wind up at a mall, but sometimes the lure of fluorescent lighting and the chill of overtaxed air-conditioning is just too much to resist. The **Akmerkez Mall,** in Etiler, was the pioneer of Istanbul's shopping malls and was actually voted the best shopping mall in Europe several years back Now the ever-growing pool of über-deluxe competition is stiff, so much so that Trump will be adding his brand of excess to the mix. There's also **Istinye Park,** an urban re-creation of a village catering to those accustomed to the stratospheres of commerce; **Astoria** boasts not only commerce but luxury wellness with its on-site Anantara Spa, Luxury Fitness facility, and adjunct Kempinski Residences. Certainly more convenient is the center-city, Bloomingdale's-esque **City's,** an indoor emporium of top brands (Gian Franco Ferre, Roberto Cavalli, D&G, Jean Paul Gaultier) in the tony neighborhood of Nişantaşı. The outdoor **Kanyon** is only a couple of years old, a Guggenheim-esque swirl of tasteful Turkish franchises and one-of-a-kinders in the smart neighborhood of Levent, opposite yet another shopping mecca, **Metrocity.** Other shopping malls include **Capitol Shopping Mall** in Üsküdar, **Carousel Shopping Mall** in Bakırköy, and **Galleria Shopping Mall** near the airport. **Olivium** is a mostly outlet mall located halfway between the airport and Sultanahmet, where you can find various middle-of-the-range name brands at discounted prices.

CAVEAT EMPTOR! CARPET-BUYING tips

"Where are you from?" seems an innocuous enough question from a carpet dealer, but answer it, and you're on your way to being scalped. Questions like "Where are you staying?" actually tell the salesperson about your economic status, as do "What do you do?" *(How much money do you earn?)*, "Where do you live?" *(Hey what a coincidence! My cousin lives near you!)*, "How much time will you be staying here?" *(How much time do you have before you have to make your final decision?)*, "What are you looking for?" *(Do you even have any idea about carpets?)*, and "How long have you been here?" *(How much have you already learned about our sleazy ways?)*.

First rule of thumb: Lie about where you're staying. Take note of the name of the humblest pension near to your actual hotel, and file it away for future use. Also, they know that Americans are among the biggest spenders of any other nationality visiting Turkey (particularly those disgorging from the cruise ships) and easily one of those with the least bargaining prowess. This is where fluency in a foreign language may come in handy. Above all, do your homework

and know what you like before you arrive so you don't waste precious bargaining time overpaying for the "best sample in the shop."

Visitors traveling in groups with a guide will inevitably wind up in the guide's friend's shop, possibly even in one with a girl knotting rugs for show. And any sales pitch worth its salt will begin with a mini course on Turkish carpets (some of which is actually true). Over tea, of course. Although these are interesting from an educational and cultural point of view, just remember: The carpet you buy is only as expensive as the amount you are willing to pay. Oh, and your tour guide, your tour company, and, hell, the bus driver, are each going to earn a hefty commission off of your sale. (Actually, the same commission system applies to almost everything you buy.)

Yes, buying a carpet in Turkey can be a very daunting task. But this is not meant to diminish your admiration of the pieces, only to arm you for the negotiations, which ultimately will get you an exceptional souvenir of a wonderful country and its wonderful crafts.

Abdülhamid II—the equivalent to a license to operate. But that's not even his claim to fame: When a team with the film *Troy* was looking for period textiles, particularly woolens, they came here. Yağlıkçılar Cad. 1 (at the Örücüler Kapısı entrance), Grand Bazaar. © **0212/528-2618**. Tram: Beyazit or Çemberlitaş.

Ethnicon   You can't read an architectural magazine these days without bumping into merchandise made here. Ethnicon puts a contemporary twist on a tribal art tradition by collecting bags, curtains, and other utilitarian objects made from sturdy wool textiles (even burlap) from around the southeast of Turkey, and then has the remnants arranged into a "quilted carpet" by a professional designer. The concept is very popular among local architects; you'll see Ethnicon products adorning places like the Sumahan Hotel, Conran's, and Restoration Hardware. Kapalıcarsı Takkeciler Sok. 58–60, Grand Bazaar. www.ethnicon.com. © **0212/527-6841**. Tram: Beyazit or Çemberlitaş.

Jennifer's Hamam   A few years back, Jennifer Gaudet opened a likeable little coffee house and art gallery opposite the Blue Mosque. Having moved on to her next project, this Canadian expat entrepreneur is once again weaving her own web of success—this time with a curated line of organic, even heritage textiles. Her early research found that traditional weaving was a dying art, and she sought out and singlehandedly revived the art of weaving on old style shuttle looms. Ten families now produce for her tablecloths, runners, sheets, and striped *peştemels* using (partially or entirely) organic cotton, linen, bamboo, and silk. Prices range between 10TL and 115TL. Two locations in the Arasta Bazaar (Nos. 43 and 135). www.jennifershamam.com. ©**0212/ 518-0648**. Tram: Sultanahmet.

LEATHER GOODS

Derimod Locally crafted leather shoes, bags, and jackets for both men and women are sold under this Turkish national brand. Merchandise is made of fine-quality hides and crafted into traditional forms. Akmerkez Shopping Center, Nispetiye Cad., Etiler. www.derimod.com.tr. © **0212/282-0668.** And in shopping malls around town.

Kıyıcı Genuine Fake Bags Just because these are not the originals doesn't mean they're of inferior quality or you're not going to need a full wallet to walk out of here with a little morsel. GFB carries Prada (with bargaining that begins at $250), Louis Vuitton, and other big-name knockoffs. Kürkçüler Han 9, Grand Bazaar. From Beyazıt gate, go to the right). © **0212/526-5181.** Tram: Beyazıt or Çemberlitaş.

Prens Leather You won't get much of a bargain at this high-profile boutique, but you will get quality and reliability. The store stocks a limited collection of its own designs, but they'll gladly piece together a custom jacket. Vezirhan Cad. 64A, Çemberlitaş (near the Nuruosmaniye Gate entrance to the Grand Bazaar). www.prensleather.com. ©**0212/522- 0570.** Tram: Beyazıt or Çemberlitaş.

ISTANBUL AFTER DARK

A typical evening on the town will involve large amounts of food accompanied by even greater amounts of *rakı*, that aniseed-flavored spirit known as "lion's milk"—traditionally consumed in a *meyhane,* a tavern or pub where patrons gather to eat and drink. Where *meyhanes* were once the realm of men only, today they are a hybrid of the lively taverna and sophisticated restaurant, the most popular ones found primarily in the back streets of Beyoğlu. On summer evenings, the main dining room moves to the rooftops (if it's not already there), where guests are treated to the twinkling lights of a timeless city.

The *şaraphane* or wine bar and the counterpart to the *birhane,* or beer hall, is a more recent nightlife trend in Istanbul thanks to the ever-improving quality of Turkey's wines.

Live music is a staple of Turkish nightlife, and Istanbul's cafes, clubs, and Turkish Houses *(Türkü Evleri)* all provide inroads to the niche of your choice, be it jazz, pop, funk, rock, techno, or traditional Turkish folk music. Bars, cafes, and nightclubs in Istanbul are generally not categorized according to the type of music they play, choosing to book instead groups with different styles from night to night. A good rule is, the earlier the hour, the softer the music. Rock and pop resound onto Istiklal Caddesi, where bars, cafes, and clubs, a few of them seedy, are too numerous to cover. Another good rule is to avoid spots with neon lights and security guards and anything with the word "nightclub" or "club" in the name, as these have the reputation of being the seedy places where bad things happen to good visitors.

Türkü Evleri are cozy little cafe/restaurants that book Turkish folk musicians performing typical Anatolian ballads to the accompaniment of the *saz* and drums. Clustered around Büyükparmakkapı Sokak in Beyoğlu, the cafes also serve basic Anatolian fare in a cozy setting, usually a narrow room with banquettes lining the two walls with just enough of an open aisle in the center for dancing as the hours wane.

Meanwhile, no denizen of the night will be able to look him/herself in the mirror without having stood at the velvet ropes of one of Istanbul's **mega-clubs on the Bosphorus.** While different years find these multiplexes with ever-evolving names, the themes and even the locations stay the same and invariably involve multiple candlelit restaurants, numerous bars, a dance floor, strobe lights, and fresh breezes off the Bosphorus, only inches away.

Clubs that book popular musical acts may sell tickets or impose a cover charge where normally there is none, but unless the headliner is very popular, tickets to most performing arts events and concerts can be purchased at the location the day of the performance. For tickets to the city's main events, contact Biletix (a Ticketmaster company; ℂ **0216/556-9800;** www.biletix.com).

Hotel lounges or **rooftop bars** provide a mesmerizing alternative to wall-to-wall smoke-filled cafes. All over the city, splendidly romantic views present themselves from almost every rooftop, or you can succumb to the dubious appeal of one of the several **Turkish Night shows** around town.

The neighborhood of **Ortaköy** is particularly vibrant on summer evenings, when streets lined with outdoor vendors selling crafts, jewelry, and the like create a festival atmosphere. Hip waterside restaurants and coffeehouses are open until late, or you can graze through the stalls of food and gorge yourself on stuffed mussels. Just north of Ortaköy, in Kuruçeşme, is a procession of high style, see and be seen clubs and entertainment complexes taking advantage of Bosphorus breezes and views to really write home about. The pageantry doesn't come cheap; addition to the hefty cover charge (around 50–60TL on weekends), expect to pay 15TL for a beer, and double that for a cocktail.

Gay Istanbul

Although homosexuality can be traced back to Ottoman times, a stigma is still attached to it: Indeed, the worst insult used among Turks (especially at soccer games)

Scenario #1: You're wandering around Taksim and pop into a bar for a quick beer or two. Before you know it, you're surrounded by lovely women and even doted on by the owner. But 2 hours and two beers later, the check arrives: $500. I wish that were a typo. Refuse to pay, and the big boys come out of the woodwork; you may even find your life and limb threatened. It's startling how many times this scenario plays out in seemingly innocuous-looking "establishments" around Taksim. One way to counter, I suppose, is to dispute the charge with your credit card carrier once the bill comes in. But the best way to handle the situation is to avoid it altogether. Stay away from anything with neon and the word "nightclub" or "club" in the sign. But sadly, there is no absolute guarantee. When in doubt, follow the advice of this guidebook, or stick to the hotel bars.

Scenario #2: You're taking an innocent evening stroll through the back streets of Sultanahmet. Suddenly, you are accosted by four young boys who identify themselves as police. Having done nothing wrong and always mindful that you are in a foreign country, you cooperate. They manhandle you (perhaps looking for ID, or even drugs) and then send you packing with a shove. It all happens so fast, except that now your wallet is empty. Unfortunately, with the migration of organized crime, nowhere is safe anymore. Don't walk anywhere alone, and avoid badly lit streets after dark.

Scenario #3: You're out and about or at a bar and you've managed to connect with some very friendly and cool locals. Next thing you know it's the next morning, and you're *sans* wallet, camera, or whatever, stranded and groggy in some sleazy hotel. You can avoid this by walling yourself off in a protective bubble, or you can never, ever let your drink sit unsupervised by you or someone you trust.

is *ibne,* a term referring to the receiving partner in a same-sex act. So while practically speaking, homosexuality in Turkey is legal between consenting partners above the age of 18, the growing LGBT community endures a whole host of societal discrimination. For more specific information on gay- and lesbian-friendly venues, log onto **www. istanbulgay.com**.

The Performing Arts

In addition to State opera, ballet, theater and philharmonic performances, concerts, and recitals are staged regularly in various venues around town, including in the gloriously ancient Aya Irini (Hagia Irene) in Topkapı Palace and the Cemal Reşit Rey Concert Hall (© 0212/232-9830; www.crrks.org). Iş Bank also maintains a prestigious cultural center, including a number of galleries and an 800-seat concert hall in the Iş towers in Levent (© 0212/316-1083; www.issanat.com). For a comprehensive schedule of performances, check out the government's website at **www.kultur. gov.tr** or log onto the venues' websites for upcoming events. **Biletix (www.biletix. com)**, the Turkish arm of Ticketmaster, is also a good starting point for upcoming concerts. The Mymerhaba expat website (**www.mymerhaba.com**) is also a great resource for real-time performances and events in Istanbul.

The annual **International Istanbul Festival** (© 0212/334-0700; www.iksv.org) is organized into four separate arts festivals averaging over 50 events yearly. The festival kicks off with the Film Festival in April, including two national and international

4

ISTANBUL

Istanbul After Dark

Istanbul has been celebrating a **Biennale** since 1987, but it wasn't until 2005, perhaps because of the anchorage of the new Istanbul Modern Museum, that the Biennale hit a home run. Artists were clustered around the revived neighborhood of Galata in venues that included an old apartment block, a tobacco depot, a Customs warehouse, and an office building. Previous exhibitions were housed in the Imperial Mint, in the Kız Kulesi (Maiden's Tower), in Santralistanbul (a former electric generating plant; p. 126), in the Customs "antrepo" warehouse buildings in Kayaköy, on the Bosphorus Bridge, and in Çemberlitaş Hamamı.

competitions. Past festivals saw the screening of over 175 films in a variety of venues in Beyoğlu and Kadıköy. The theater section of the festival brings companies from all over Europe and takes place in May, with one or two offerings in English. At the end of October or in early November, selected international artists come together for the Biennale, but the big to-do takes place in June/July with the International Istanbul Music Festival, representing the worlds of opera, jazz, classical music, and ballet in evocative settings like the St. Irene, and featuring world-renowned performers like Wynton Marsalis or the traditional performance of *Der Entführung aus dem Serail* (Abduction from the Seraglio) appropriately staged in Topkapı Palace.

The Classics

Atatürk Cultural Center (AKM)   Built originally as an opera house, Atatürk Cultural Center (AKM) houses the Istanbul State Opera and Ballet, the Istanbul Philharmonic Orchestra, and the State Theatre Company. During the summer months, AKM hosts the Istanbul Arts Festival, but because of high demand, tickets may be hard to come by. While renovation and modernization of the cultural center continue, performances will take place at alternative locations. For now, the Istanbul State Opera and Ballet is temporarily housed in the restored Süreyya Paşa building in Kadıköy, a lovely setting in an albeit moderately inconvenient location. Taksim Sq., Taksim. ℂ **0212/251-5600.** Bus, metro, nostalgic tramway, or tram/funicular to Taksim.

Süreyya Opera House   The building was designed by parliamentarian Süreyya Ilmen between 1924 and 1927 as an opera house, however no operas were ever staged here, as the incomplete building lacked a stage. Now the Kadıköy Municipality Süreyya Opera House hosts three performances a week of the Istanbul State Opera and Ballet. There is a box office on-site, but tickets can also be purchased at the Atatürk Cultural Center. Showtimes are generally 8pm weekdays, 4pm on Saturdays, and 11am on Sundays. Tickets cost from 10TL for the nosebleed section to 30TL for orchestra seats. Bahariye Cad. 29, Kadıköy. www.sureyyaoperasi.org. ℂ **0216/346-1531.** Ferry to Kadıköy, then taxi to the concert hall.

The Music Scene
TURKISH FOLKLORE
Hodjapasha Dance Show & Sema Show   Part of the attraction of these two separate shows is the setting: the 550-year-old Hodjapasha Hamam, built during the Sultanate of Fatih Sultan Mehmet. A swirl of **Whirling Dervişes** perform 5 nights

per week, warming up the audience on Saturdays and Sundays for the **Hodjapasha Live Music and Dance Show** ★ (staged 4 nights weekly) to follow. Tickets are 20€ and 25€ respectively. Ankara Cad., Hocapaşa Hamam Sok. 3B, Sirkeci. www.hodjapasha.com. Ⓒ **0212/511-4626**. Tram: Sirkeci.

Istanbul Dance Ensemble A project of Istanbul Live Productions, a cultural initiative aimed at reviving and celebrating Turkey's dance traditions, presents two distinct performances weekly. The Spirit of Anatolia is an energized conglomeration of dances and rhythms, embellished with vibrantly colored costumes, representing regional traditions from all over the country. The show takes place every Tuesday and Friday at the Firat Cultural Center (FKM), Divanyolu/Yeniçeriler Cad. (opposite the Column of Constantine). A separate 800 Years of Love Sufi Ceremony of Whirling Dervişes showcases another uniquely Turkish art form every Saturday, Sunday, and Wednesday at the nearby Press Museum. Showtime is 7:30pm for both and tickets cost 35€. Yeniçeriler Cad., Darülsafaka Pasajı 74 (office) or Yeniçeriler Cad. 84 (Press Museum), Çemberlitaş. www.istanbuldanceensemble.com. Ⓒ **0212/458-6215**. Tram: Çemberlitaş.

Sound and Light Show The floodlit domes and minarets of the Blue Mosque are the backdrop to a nightly (in summer) sound-and-light spectacle at the entrance to the Blue Mosque in Sultanahmet Park. The show has a charming spontaneous feel and accommodates visitors from round the globe by presenting shows on a schedule of rotating languages. And, best of all, it's free. For information, see the Tourist Information Office in Sultanahmet Park. Sultanahmet Meydanı. Ⓒ **0212/518-1802**.

TRADITIONAL ANATOLIAN AFTER HOURS

Türku Evi 📗 Backgammon, hookah pipes, and popular local singers performing the traditional yearning nomadic melodies fill these "Turkish Houses." I confess that this listing does not refer to just one spot but instead covers the numerous cozy bars populating Hasnun Galıp Street in Beyoğlu that feature live performers singing traditional Anatolian folk songs. This is really the experience you've come all this way for. Generally, basic dinner items are served. The small space fills up with locals, who, having eaten, get up and dance in the narrow aisle between the musicians and the *kilim*-covered tables and banquettes. Istiklal Cad., Hasnun Galıp Sok. (perpendicular to Büyükparmakkapı Sok.) 18A, Beyoğlu. Bus, metro, or nostalgic tramway to Taksim; tram/funicular via Kabataş to Taksim.

Zarifi ★★ Owned by descendants of Greek residents of Pera, Zarifi puts a new twist on the classic *meyhane* by infusing the melting pot of former Pera into the music and the menu. Did I say menu? You'll need to ask for it, as normally the food would just arrive. Here, you can choose from items on the Balkan, Pera, or Specials menu or opt for one of the two prix fixes. In the summer, Zarifi spreads her wings at the Supper Club at the New Yorker in Kuruçeşme. Compared to the *meyhanes* in the restaurant listings (p. 128), Zarifi has a bit more polish and popularity among Istanbul's yuppie crowd. Expect to drop around 100TL for the food and show. Reservations are required. Çukurlu Çeşme Sok. 13, Beyoğlu. (from Istiklal Cad. turn onto Büyükparmakapı Sok., then turn left onto Tel Sok., then right onto Çukurlu Çeşme Sok. www.zarifi.com.tr. Ⓒ **0212/293-5480**. Bus, metro, or nostalgic tramway to Taksim; tram/funicular via Kabataş to Taksim.

The Local Bar & Club Scene

SULTANAHMET & THE OLD CITY

Çorlulu Alipaşa Medrese Not far from the Grand Bazaar is the outdoor living-room-cum-tea-gardens hidden in the courtyard of the old Çorlulu Alipaşa Medrese.

The tree-filled garden is a perfect way to unwind, with a glass of apple tea and the essence of strawberry in your water pipe while you admire the display of carpets and souvenirs decorating the gardens of the bordering shops. The entrance to the tea gardens is on Yeniçeriler Caddesi near where the road changes names from Divanyolu Caddesi. Çorlulu Alipaşa Medrese, Çarşıkapı, Yeniçeriler Cad. No phone. Tram: Çemberlitaş.

Galata Bridge More central and ridiculously scenic is the cluster of bars, cafes, and fish restaurants newly occupying the upper and lower levels of the Galata Bridge. While there's nothing remarkable about the restaurants per se, a couple of the venues have leapfrogged over the dining experience straight to drinks and backgammon. The east-facing and always packed **Dersaadet Şark Kahvesi** (℗ **0212/292-7002**) is the hot ticket, as it faces the minarets of the Old City. Galata Bridge, btw. Eminönü and Karaköy. Bus or tram to Eminönü or Karaköy.

Meşale Çay Bahçesi Just at the entrance to the Arasta Bazaar is an outdoor collection of benches and tables perfectly placed for a balmy summer's eve or a midday tea break in the shadow of the Blue Mosque. In summer, a lone whirling derviş "performs" nightly at 8 and 10pm. Btw. Nakılbend and Turün Soks., at the entrance to the Arasta Bazaar. ℗ **0212/518-9562.** Tram: Sultanahmet.

Palatium Café 🖸 The atmosphere could barely get any better curled up on some cushions in a courtyard atop the ancient ruins of the Magnaura Palace. Here you can snack on a selection of mezes or cheeses, or sink your fork into a steaming clay pot cooked the traditional way. Not hungry? Relax and share a smoke on a *narghile* (15TL). Kutlugun Sok. 31 (near the entrance to the Four Seasons Hotel). ℗ 0212/516-5132.

Yeni Marmara 🖬 Inconspicuously located on a little-trod street of Sultanahmet, this sleepy little teahouse and nargile (waterpipe) cafe is one of the neighborhood's best-kept secrets. Locals relax on the back terrace jutting out above the old city walls to enjoy a game of backgammon and views of the Marmara Islands. Walls and floors are covered in old rugs, and the whole space has an appealing worn vibe. Open daily 9am to 1am. Küçük Ayasofya Cad., Çayıroğlu Sok. 46, Sultanahmet. ℗ **0212/516-9013.** No cover. Tram: Sultanahmet.

The Local Bar & Club Scene
TAKSIM, TÜNEL & BEYOĞLU

Cezayir The most popular locale among the new restaurants and cafes around the restored buildings of Francız Sokağı occupies an early-20th-century schoolhouse. There's a large garden shaded by enormous plane trees, and the food is creative without veering too far off the Turkish culinary map. Choose from an a la carte menu or from a selection of prix-fixe menus, including a "cocktail menu" for those not in the mood for a full meal. Hayriye Cad. 12 (follow Yeni Çarşı Cad. from Galatasaray High School and turn left on Hayriye Cad.). www.cezayir-istanbul.com. ℗ **0212/245-9980.** Reservations suggested. Nostalgic tramway to Galatasaray.

Enginar As with much of the history of Galata, no one knows for sure what the first building on this site was, but turn the clock back 100 years and envision this bar/bistro as an Italian bank, then later as a coffeehouse for the neighborhood Jewish community, and most recently as an Akbank. (Although the renovations introduced "new" stones, the foundations may date back 400 years.) With its attractive lighting and rustic warehouse-like interior space, Enginar is a comfortable and quiet place for a drink in a very cool neighborhood. Enginar hosts live music a few times a week.

Şah Kapısı Sok. 4/A, Galata (straight down Istiklal Cad. to the Galata Tower, the cafe is on your right). © **0212/251-7321**. Funicular to Upper or Lower Tünel, then walk.

Leb-i-Derya ★★ This candlelit rooftop is another one of Istanbul's exceptional panoramic locations and not surprisingly a popular magnet for the sophisticated night owls of Istanbul. The dinner menu offers some tantalizing options (slow-baked leerfish with tomatoes, capers, and olives; artichoke heart and portobello salad with roasted red peppers and black-eyed peas). In addition to the fab views, the bar is famous for its extensive cocktail menu, including things like Caipirovska and Balalaika, two drinks I've never even heard of. In 2006 Leb-i-Derya began also serving on the sixth floor of the Richmond Hotel, but I prefer the Kumbaracı location. Kumbaracı Yokusu, Kumbaracı Han 115/7, Tünel. www.lebiderya.com. © **0212/243-9555**.

NuPera NuPera is actually the name of a renovated 19th-century building in the neighborhood of Pera, now an utterly reborn neighborhood chock-full of cafes and restaurants. The building contains an entertainment complex of sorts, with two restaurants, Moreish and NuPera, on the ground floor. The latter serves a bit of everything: tapas, homemade pastas, and Turkish comfort food, moving up to the rooftop (and renamed NuTeras) for the cool summer breezes and sweeping views of a twinkling city and the Golden Horn as soon as weather permits. Moreish is new and still in the experimental stages, under the watchful hands of new chef and part owner Esra Muslu. On the weekends, NuPera becomes a club, turning each separate space into a unique venue offering different types of music in each. Meşrutiyet Cad. 67, Tepebaşı. www.nupera.com.tr. © **0212/245-6070**. Funicular to Upper Tünel or bus to Tepebaşı.

Otto Istanbul Otto has rapidly made a name for itself with three locations each offering a different slant on nightlife. Through the large street-side windows at the Otto Sofyalı bar, it's all see and be seen, where black-clad guests crowd the artsy environment for live music or just plain old bar-watching entertainment. Around the corner on Şehbender Sokak is Otto Tünel, a more local-friendly bar/eatery serving a relaxed menu of better-than-bar food accompanied by a long list of creative cocktails. On the campus of Santral Istanbul is Otto's sometime venue for music concerts and events. www.ottoistanbul.com. Otto Sofyalı, Sofyalı Sok. 22A–22/1, Tünel. © **0212/252-6588**. Küçük Otto, Şehbender Sok. 5/1, Tünel. © **0212/292-7015**. Otto Santral, Santrallstanbul, Kazım Karabekir Cad. 1, Eyüp. © **0212/427-1889**.

Şarabı This Istiklal wine bar looks like any other storefront cafe, but just a few steps down to the cellar—where those in-the-know head—is a late-19th-century underground aqueduct that is said to run from the British Embassy all the way to Tophane. The wine bar stocks more than 100 labels, including some of the better Turkish vintages. Try the Sarafin Cabernet, or the Karma Cabernet/Özküküzü blend. Istiklal Cad. 80b, Beyoğlu next to the Çiçek Pasajı. © **0212/244-4609**. Nostalgic tramway to Galatasaray.

360 Istanbul ★★ 360 Istanbul takes advantage of the belfry of St. Antoine and panoramic views of the Golden Horn; on a cool summer's eve, there's really no better place to be. The decor is an unexpectedly pleasing amalgam of brick, steel, glass, and velvet; tables, alfresco banquettes, and a lounge area ensure that everybody gets something he or she wants. The Thai and Turkish menu is rather beside the point, although there are plenty of appetizers and finger foods to hold you over for the real meal. Go early for the best outdoor seating, or arrive late and mill about the wraparound terrace. Reservations are suggested for dinner. Mısır Apartment Building, Istiklal Cad. 311, Beyoğlu. www.360istanbul.com. © **0212/251-1042**. Nostalgic tramway to Odakule.

Viktor Levi Şarap Evi   A veritable institution in Beyoğlu, Viktor Levi is one of Istanbul's oldest wine houses. The *fer forgé* is the first indication of the 19th-century origins of the wine bar; it's a great spot to head to if you're looking to "go where the natives go" (if there is only one such place). Impress your date by ordering a bottle of the Viktor Levi special house wine. Hamalbaşi Cad. 12, Beyoğlu. www.viktorlevi.com. ✆ **0212/249-6085.** Nostalgic tramway to Galatasaray or bus to Tepebaşı.

Live Music & Night Clubs

Babylon   This club was the first among what is now a crowded category of venues for music concerts attended by hip and cosmopolitan Turks in black. Frequent live concerts feature every type of modern genre and then some: from urban folk, to world, to punk, to classic rock, to R&B, to 10 types of jazz, previous acts saw jazz performers Charlie Hunter, Leon Parker, and Harriet Tubman, but more often than not, the musicians are lesser-known imports playing an eclectic (even weird) fusion of music. Tickets are 10TL for SRO up to 70TL for a table; DJ nights are free. Şehbender Sok. 3, Beyoğlu (from Istiklal Cad. near Tünel, turn onto Asmalımecit Sok. and left onto Şehbender). www.babylon.com.tr. ✆ **0212/292-7368**.

Garajistanbul   This spot is a cutting edge (avant-garde!) multi-media art center focused on showcasing the latest in theater, dance, music, and literature arts. **Garajistanbul,** itself a not-for-profit traveling company, features exhibitions and festivals in addition to the regular calendar of events. Yeni Çarşı Caddesi, Kaymakam Reşat Bey Sok. 11a, Galatasaray. www.garajistanbul.com. ✆ **0212/244-4499.** Tickets 9TL–30TL. Nostalgic Tramway to Galatasaray or walk from Taksim or Tünel.

Ghetto   One of Istanbul's newer nightlife venues, Ghetto strives not only to fill your ears with salsa, reggae bossa nova or whatever the act that day brings in, they've got an art gallery and a meyhane—both making the best use of the Beaux Arts Mario Cantoni building backdrop. The three-story lounge and entertainment complex is topped by a slick and smoky rooftop terrace. Tickets are on sale from 11am to 4pm Monday through Saturday and on the day of performance after 8pm and through Biletix (✆ **0216/556-9800;** www.biletix.com). Kamer Hatun Caddesi, 10 (1 block over from Meşrutiyet Caddesi and opposite the British Consulate), Galatasaray. www.ghettoist.com. ✆ **0212/251-7501**. Cover 20TL, 25TL, or 30TL for live music, otherwise free.

Istanbul Jazz Center   With a waterfront terrace for chill-out summer's eves, the Jazz Center, housed within the stylin' Radisson Blu Hotel in Ortaköy wouldn't even need to host good musicians. But that they do, starting with the Mike Stern Band, who was the center's opening night act in 2005. Since then, the "JC" has skyrocketed to the top of the list of Istanbul's international jazz venues. Other jazz greats who've passed through JC's include Branford Marsalis and Ernie Watts. Shows take place Tuesday through Saturday; reservations can be made directly via the website. Çirağan Caddesi, Salhane Sok. 10, Ortaköy in the Radisson Blu hotel. www.istanbuljazz.com. ✆ **0212/327-5050**. Cover for a table cost 25TL (not including the 50TL per person food minimum) and an SRO spot at the bar costs 20TL *per set*. The cover doubles for a full, two-set night. Tues free for ladies. Bus to Ortaköy.

Nardis Jazz Club 🍴   This joint is so small, so intimate, and so New Orleans that you may have to pinch yourself to see if you are indeed in Istanbul. Reservations are essential for seating next to the tiny stage, although an additional handful of tables are up on the mezzanine. Live acts cover the full range of jazz interpretations, from classical to modern, to fusion to popular. Kuledibi Sok. 14, Galata. www.nardisjazz.com.

$\textcircled{C}$ **0212/244-6327.** Ticket prices hover around 30TL. Mon–Thurs 9:30pm–12:30am; Fri–Sat 10:30pm–1:30am. Funicular: Upper or Lower Tünel then walk to club.

ALONG THE BOSPHORUS

Anjelique ★★ This is a sister operation to the majorly successful Vogue, Anna, A'jia, and Da Mario (not all listed here). The formula seems unable to fail. Anjelique takes up the top three floors above Da Mario. Jazz and soul are played during dining hours, complementing a sensual decor backlit by the nighttime glow of the sea and sky. Dinner is served on the top two floors, while the lower floor is dedicated to the dynamic lounge. Open May through October. Muallim Naci Cad., Salhane Sok. 10, Ortaköy. www.istanbuldoors.com. $\textcircled{C}$ **0212/327-2844.** Bus to Ortaköy.

Blackk ★★ Short of being on (Suada) or next to (Reina) the water, the views from Blackk are hard to beat. Inside it's all damask walls, sultry lighting and well, black everything. The clientele hovers a notch above upscale—expect to see international fashion designers and high-profile politicians. The venue has a restaurant (expect around 100TL per person for dinner) and a club, and there's live music on occasional nights. Muallim Naci Cad. 71, Ortaköy. www.blackk.net. $\textcircled{C}$ **0212/236-7256.**

Reina Istanbul's nightlife succumbs to the lure of the Bosphorus in the summer months (generally Apr until the end of Oct), moving alfresco and up to the seafront venues of Ortaköy and Kuruçeşme. The Grande Dame with the most longevity is a sprawling waterfront full-of-attitude megaclub attracting the young and the restless. The cover charge increases exponentially every year (currently at 50TL on weekends, which includes one drink). There are a few noteworthy restaurants with locations on-site (including the Zagat-rated Şamdan). Names tend to change seasonally, but the locations and general theme stays the same. The most popularly frequented venues as of 2011 are listed here. Muallim Naci Cad. 44, Ortaköy. www.reina.com.tr. $\textcircled{C}$ **0212/259-5919.**

Sortie This is the traditional rival to Reina, yet another awesome candle-lit entertainment complex right on the Bosphorus. The vibe is more of a cocktail lounge, in spite of the massive square footage. There are seven restaurants on-site, including Sortie's own. The kicker? You can party in the rain thanks to the state-of-the-art, remote-controlled shelter. Muallim Naci Cad. 141, Ortaköy. www.sortie.com.tr. $\textcircled{C}$ **0212/327-8585.**

Suada ★★ It's a floating platform opposite the Bosphorus village of Kuruçeşme that years ago was privately owned by the football/soccer team Galatasaray. Now a beach club by day, overworked Istanbullus descend on Suada to laze about and swim in the island's pool. The sound gets turned up at night when the "island" nightclub gets cranking. There's a DJ at the bar and 7 restaurants surrounded by the thousands of twinkling lights from both the European and Asian shores of the Bosphorus. The food is top-notch, but seriously, who cares? (Restaurants are Suada Club Kebap, 360, Giritli Idilika, Mezzaluna, Fish Balık and Frederic's Steakhouse). There's a complimentary boat shuttle from Kuruçeşme. Daytime entrance fee (for use of the Olympic-size pool, towel provided) is 60TL weekdays, 80TL Saturday and Sunday. Galatasaray Asası, Kuruçeşme. www.suada.com.tr. $\textcircled{C}$ **0212/263-7300.** Bus to Kuruçesme then take the courtesy boat over.

WHERE TO STAY

For someone new to the sprawling mass that is Istanbul, one of the first questions to ask is "where's a good place to set up base camp?" I used to unreservedly direct my readers to the historic bull's-eye that is **Sultanahmet,** where old dilapidated homes converted into "Special Category" hotels created the perfect gateway to an authentic past. But three very important developments in the past few years have caused me to change my mind.

First, because of unrelenting demand, hotels formerly charging $20 for a basic room now charge 100€ and up, for absolutely no added value. Let me put this into perspective: The luxury five-star Marmara Istanbul (p. 170) has advance-purchase Internet rates from 145€ *with a Bosphorus view* (127€ for a Golden Horn view).

Second, given the enormous profit margins that a hotel can bring in, it seems as if everyone has gotten in on the act—transforming what was a market of family-run houses into a sea of mass-produced, soulless "boutique hotels." Finally, and most disappointingly, the hassling by carpet salesmen and their ilk has reached new levels; one time several hotel guests I encountered opted for the safety of the hotel lobby rather than brave the irritating and stressful storm of harassment by salesmen flooding the streets of the tourist areas. It is therefore with a heavy heart that I recommend this neighborhood only with the admonition to stay vigilant and prepare to drink a lot of tea.

The good alternative is to base yourself in the heart of Istanbul in **Beyoğlu**, where hotels are managed by people schooled in hotel management (and not carpet sales), and the food and nightlife are better anyway. Plus, with the new, efficient transport system connecting Taksim and Sultanahmet, you can spend the day wandering around the Old City, and in under 20 minutes, be back in time for a decent meal.

In any case, make sure you get the hotel's rate quote in writing, to avoid any misunderstandings relating to currency exchange. Prices quoted here for airport transfers (mostly free for bookings of 3 nights or more) refer to pickup only from the Atatürk International Airport. Transfers from Sabiha Gökçen are slightly more, if offered at all. Parents with kids will be pleased to learn that children 6 and under, and in some cases 12 and under, stay free, and often cots will be provided. While this is almost universal, it is wise to double-check when you book.

The Old City
VERY EXPENSIVE
Eresin Crown Hotel ★★   While excavating the foundation to build the Eresin, workers uncovered Byzantine floor mosaics, marble columns, and a cistern, artifacts later identified as belonging to the women's quarters of Justinian's Great Palace. Altogether, the hotel recovered, registered, and now exhibits 49 historically significant museum pieces dating to the Hellenistic and Byzantine times, giving this hotel a "boutique museum" quality. Rooms in this quality hotel are well appointed, with bonus touches like window seats, plaster friezes, and Jacuzzis. Its enormous rooftop terrace has one of the most magnificent panoramic views of Old City in Sultanahmet.

Küçük Ayasofya Cad. 40, 34400 Sultanahmet. www.eresinsultanahmet.com.tr. ℭ **0212/638-4428.** Fax 0212/638-0933. 59 units. 209€–305€ double; 330€–700€ suite. See website for rates as low as 93€. AE, MC, V. Valet parking. **Amenities:** 2 restaurants; 2 bars; airport transfer (65€); concierge; free Wi-Fi. *In room:* A/C, satellite and cable TV, minibar.

Four Seasons Hotel ★★★   This Turkish neoclassical building located in the heart of Sultanahmet was originally a dilapidated prison for political dissidents. Much of the original marble and tile were retained and recycled into the hotel's present-day, five-star interior design. Rooms have plush furniture purchased from local vendors; the architect even stayed true to tradition by applying paint as they did in the Ottoman palaces—with a spatula. The opulent and luxurious bathrooms, all with separate toilet cabin, present a formidable amount of competition for time spent sightseeing,

The Old City Hotels & Restaurants

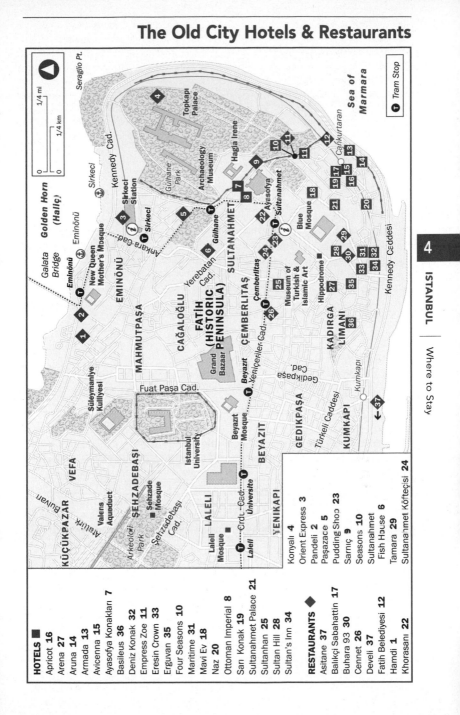

HOTELS ■
Apricot **16**
Arena **27**
Aruna **14**
Armada **13**
Avicenna **15**
Ayasofya Konakları **7**
Basileus **36**
Deniz Konak **32**
Empress Zoe **11**
Eresin Crown **33**
Erguvan **35**
Four Seasons **10**
Maritime **31**
Mavi Ev **18**
Naz **20**
Ottoman Imperial **8**
Sarı Konak **19**
Sultanahmet Palace **21**
Sultanhan **25**
Sultan Hill **28**
Sultan's Inn **34**

RESTAURANTS ◆
Asitane **37**
Balıkçi Sabahattin **17**
Buhara 93 **30**
Cennet **26**
Develi **37**
Fatih Belediyesi **12**
Hamdi **1**
Khorasanı **22**
Konyalı **4**
Orient Express **3**
Pandeli **2**
Paşazace **5**
Pudding Shop **23**
Sarnıç **9**
Seasons **10**
Sultanahmet Fish House **6**
Tamara **29**
Sultanahmet Köftecisi **24**

and the king-size beds are amazingly comfy. Plus, almost all of the rooms have views of something fabulous. Bonus: Guests may use the considerable amenities of the Four Seasons the Bosphorus (p. 173) and it is even possible to divide your stay among the two—the staff will pack up your room and lay it out in the new space precisely where you left it.

Tevkifhane Sok. 1, 34110 Sultanahmet. www.fourseasons.com. © **800/332-3442** in the U.S., or 0212/381-4000. Fax 0212/381-4100. 65 units. 340€–1,160€ double and suites; B&B rates are higher; all rates lower Nov–Mar. AE, DC, MC, V. Free valet and limited on-street parking. **Amenities:** Restaurant (p. 130); 2 bars; airport transfers (65€); concierge; health club and spa; room service; smoke-free rooms. *In room:* A/C, satellite TV, CD player, fax (on request), hair dryer, minibar, free Wi-Fi.

Sultanhan Hotel ★★ Muted echoes of guests' comings and goings bounce off the marble walls of the lobby of this higher-end hotel located a stone's throw from the Grand Bazaar and Çemberlitaş tramway. The rooms are larger than what you might find at one of the many neighborhood "boutique hotels" ensuring that the enormous (55-inch) cable TVs don't overwhelm the space. Some of the fancier rooms have sculpted entry archways and bathtubs (rather than showers), and the concierge can furnish you with a laptop to make use of the free in-room wireless. The hotel also has one of the most spectacular rooftop views in all of the historic peninsula, offering a completely unobstructed panorama of *both* the Blue Mosque and the Hagia Sophia.

Piyer Loti Cad. 15, 34122 Çemberlitaş. www.sultanhanhotel.com. © **0212/516-3232.** Fax 0212/516-5995. 40 units. 250€ double. MC, V. **Amenities:** Rooftop restaurant; bar; concierge; elevator; *hamam* (20€–80€); room service; sauna; smoke-free rooms. *In room:* A/C, cable TV, hair dryer, minibar, free Wi-Fi.

EXPENSIVE

Mavi Ev (Blue House) ★ If the Blue House weren't actually painted blue, one would think the name came from the fact that the hotel is practically attached at the hip to the Blue Mosque. This hotel is a fine example of modern Turkish elegance, with its tile floors, carpets, stained glass, and understated details. Most of the rooms have stall showers, while suites have Jacuzzis. The rooftop restaurant (and bar; summers only) is especially noteworthy, if not for the food, then for the backdoor viewing of the sound-and-light displays above the Blue Mosque. The entire effect is enchanting, and you couldn't get a better view of the domes if you were standing right on top of them.

Dalbastı Sok. 14, 34400 Sultanahmet. www.bluehouse.com.tr. © **0212/638-9010.** Fax 0212/638-9017. 26 units (25 with shower). 180€ double, 250€ suite Apr–June and Sept–Oct; 130€ double, 250€ suite July–Aug. Double rates as low as 90€ in winter. MC, V. Public parking across the street. **Amenities:** Restaurant; bar; elevator; room service. *In room:* A/C, cable TV, hair dryer, minibar, free Wi-Fi.

Sultanahmet Palace Hotel ★ 📷 You either love this one or hate it. That's because in all of the rooms, each small bathroom doubles as a marble-clad mini-*hamam* (no tubs; shower heads are provided for convenience). Sadly, a glitch in the heating system prevents the *hamams* from producing any heat). Most of the rooms on the third (top) floor are disappointingly small, so when reserving, try to nab a second-floor (first-floor) room or one of the two top-floor rooms (nos. 309 and 310) decked out with modern bathrooms and Jacuzzis. (Large-size visitors and creatures of habit used to enclosed showers or bathtubs might want to think twice before booking this hotel.) The hotel was designed in the style of a garden villa, with Byzantine-style hand-carved moldings above Roman terra-cotta flooring, a grand marble central staircase, courtyards, and terrace fountains, and breathtaking views in summer of the Marmara Sea from the breakfast terrace.

Torun Sok. 19, 34400 Sultanahmet. www.sultanahmetpalace.com. ℭ **0212/458-0460.** Fax 0212/518-6224. 36 units. 150€ double; 210€–260€ suite. AE, MC, V. Free parking. **Amenities:** Restaurant; bar; free airport transfer with 2-night minimum stay; elevator; room service. *In room:* A/C, satellite TV, hair dryer, minibar, free Wi-Fi.

MODERATE

Arena Hotel This three-story hotel located in an unpolished corner of Sultanahmet just steps behind the Hippodrome occupies a restored Ottoman house that has remained in the same family for more than 80 years. The owner has retained traditional touches such as family heirloom furnishings and "grandmother Gül's caftan" in the lobby's salon. Rooms feature charming Ottoman-style decor, wood floors, and classic Turkish rugs, but the rickety stall showers (reminiscent of two-star pensions I've stayed at in Rome) indicate that the bathrooms need updating. There are two suites, each with a balcony, the only two tubs in the house, and flatscreen TVs. Better yet, the basement level has a little *hamam* (reservations required).

Küçük Ayasofya Cad., Şehit Mehmet Paşa Yokuşu Üçler Hamam Sok. 13–15, 34400 Sultanahmet. www.arenahotel.com. ℭ **0212/458-0364.** Fax 0212/458-0366. 27 units. 109€ double; 129€–159€ suite Mar–June. Rates higher July–Aug and lower other months. Special Internet promotions according to availability. AE, DC, DISC, MC, V. Limited street parking. **Amenities:** Restaurant; bar; *hamam* (10€); room service. *In room:* A/C, satellite TV, hair dryer, minibar, free Wi-Fi.

Aruna Hotel ★ Many editions ago, I was forced to delete the Hotel Kybele (www.kybelehotel.com) because the hotel was forever fully booked. The Hotel Aruna, a second venture of the same (co-)owner, Alparslan, puts an end to the problem. The Aruna, a new building in the as-of-yet ungentrified streets of Ahırkapı, was constructed to fit in with the neighborhood's other traditional wooden Ottoman houses. The three floors reveal decor that is modern yet elegant with a Turkish flourish. Some rooms have a Jacuzzi, while others come equipped with a modern take on the traditional Turkish *hamam* (there's a marble basin in the shower).

Cankurtaran Mah., Ahırkapı Sok. 74, 34122 Istanbul. www.arunahotel.com. ℭ **0212/458-5488.** Fax 0212/458-5413. 16 units. 80€–100€ double; 110€–120€ suite. Free self-parking. **Amenities:** Restaurant; bar; airport transfer (30€); room service. *In room:* A/C, TV, minibar, free Wi-Fi.

Ayasofya Konakları ★ ▣ In the 1980s, the state-run Turkish Touring and Automobile Club set off a craze for historic preservation when it restored a handful of clapboard Ottoman mansions on the historic, cobblestoned Soğukçeşme Street. Back then, the collection of pension-style rooms saw a veritable stampede of illustrious visitors including Bernardo Bertolucci and Roman Polanski, and in 2000, Sofia, the Queen of Spain. The rooms are best described as being at the high end of shabby chic, and many (but not all) now benefit from a number of additional comforts (including air-conditioning and TV). Book early enough, and you'll score a street-side room with a view of the Hagia Sophia. The *konakları*, or collection of houses, also enjoys one of the city's most characteristic settings, sandwiched between the imperial outer wall of Topkapı Palace and the Hagia Sophia. The area also encompasses open-air garden and terrace cafes, and an expansive garden that surrounds a wonderful orangerie.

Soğukçeşme Sok., 34400 Sultanahmet. www.ayasofyakonaklari.com. ℭ **0212/513-3660.** Fax 0212/514-0213. 64 units. 140€ street-side double; 120€ double in rear; 340€–500€ suite. MC, V. Free self-parking. **Amenities:** Restaurant; 2 bars; airport transfer (40€); room service. *In room:* A/C.

Basileus 🏠 🍴   You'll feel like a member of the clan at this friendly, family-run hotel, getting travel tips and dining suggestions from the presiding brother/cousin with no other motive then making your visit the most authentic. Despite the hotels basic simplicity, and even if you don't book a "superior" room, freshly renovated baths, nicely sized rooms (some with French-style balconettes) and marble tiled hallways make you feel like you got an upgrade. Its neighborhood of Kadırga Limanı is rapidly up and coming, and it's a straight shot to all the major sights and a 10-minutes' walk to the tramway (all uphill).

Küçük Ayasofya Mah. Kadırga Liman Cad. Şehit Mehmet Paşa Sok. 1, 34122 Istanbul. www.basileus hotel.com. ℂ **0212/517-7878.** 20 units. 90€–115€ double. Check for low season rate of 85€ double. Free airport transfer (Atatürk Airport) with 3+ nights otherwise 20€. Free parking. **Amenities:** Concierge, free Internet, room service (limited hours). In room: AC, satellite TV, minibar.

Erguvan Hotel ★

A front-row seat to the Spherion (the ancient retaining wall of the Hippodrome), a stellar location down the steeply sloping cobbled street behind the Hippodrome, and helpful staff are the main draws of the Erguvan. As with most hotels in Sultanahmet, the rooftop-level breakfast room opens up to amazing views over the Old City. Half of the rooms have bathtubs, which is a rarity on this side of town, and every window in the place is double-glazed, whether it needs it or not. The manager made a point of mentioning that the building was reconstructed in compliance with Istanbul's new earthquake code; I'm not sure whether that fact made me feel better or not. Pay an additional 15€ and you'll get a sea-view room.

Aksakal Cad. 3, 34400 Sultanahmet. www.erguvanhotel.com. ℂ **0212/458-2784.** Fax 0212/458-2788. 22 units. 85€ double; 100€ sea-view double Mar–Dec. Rates lower in winter. MC, V. Free self- parking. **Amenities:** Rooftop restaurant and bar (summer only); free airport pickup for 3-day minimum stay; room service. In room: A/C, cable TV, hair dryer, minibar, free Wi-Fi.

Hotel Armada

Located on the outer edges of Sultanahmet in Cankurtaran near the Ahırkapı Gate, the Hotel Armada is a true four-star hotel with extras like an expansive lobby cafe, meeting rooms, a penthouse atrium restaurant, and one of the best rooftop terraces anywhere in the neighborhood. Superior and deluxe rooms are the result of a 2009 upgrade, featuring antique carpets on parquet floors and newly renovated marble baths with rain showers. Standard rooms are small but more than functional, with a negligible amount of wear and tear around the edges. The charming fringe neighborhood retains a bit of a village character, but those who decide to stay here should realize that it's an uphill 5- to 10-minute or so walk to all major sights. Weekend guests may want to request a room away from the evening entertainment to insulate themselves from the late-night echoes through the marble staircases.

Ahırkapı Sok. (just behind the Cankurtaran train station), 34400 Sultanahmet. www.armadahotel. com.tr. ℂ **0212/455-4455.** Fax 0212/455-4499. 108 units. 100€ double; 158€ superior; 288€ suite. Rates do not include VAT. AE, DC, MC, V. Free self-parking. **Amenities:** 2 restaurants; 2 bars; airport transfer (40€); concierge; elevator; room service; smoke-free rooms. In room: A/C, satellite TV, hair dryer, minibar, free Wi-Fi.

Hotel Empress Zoe ★★ 📷

Empress Zoe overlooks (and indeed, is attached to) the crumbling remnants of the oldest *hamam* in the city. Access to the majority of rooms is via a narrow circular iron staircase—good to know if traveling light wasn't on this trip's agenda. If you do hurt your back on the way up, you'll be pleased to find extremely comfortable beds and loads of character when you make it to your room. Rooms all have showers, and only the larger suites have (cable) TV. The hotel combines five separate houses, and rooms range from charming doubles with Byzantine- or Anatolian-style murals, to a variety of garden and penthouse suites. Because of the configuration, secluded courtyards and panoramic terraces unexpectedly appear around almost every corner. The rooftop bar is warmly draped in deeply colored Turkish *kilims* and blankets, and there's a fireplace for those crisp winter evenings.

Akbıyık Cad., 4/1, 34400 Sultanahmet. www.emzoe.com. © **0212/518-2504.** Fax 0212/518-5699. 26 units. 120€–140€ double; 130€–245€ suite. MC, V. Free self-parking. **Amenities:** 3 bars; airport transfer (25€); smoke-free rooms; free Wi-Fi. *In room:* A/C, hair dryer.

Hotel Maritime   Its sparkling and ornate Ottoman façade overlooking a quiet side street just steps from the Arasta Bazaar and Blue Mosque, who wouldn't be drawn inside? And yet, this freshly renovated gem manages to buck the trend of soaring neighborhood hotel rates, while providing guests with typically Turkish and modernized accommodations. Doubles may be a bit small (the hotel is a new renovation after all), but everything about the rooms screams fresh, clean and hospitable. The service is eager and friendly, and the only way to outshine the rooftop (terrace bar and restaurant open in warmish weather only) is to serve an abundant, Turkish breakfast feast overlooking the minarets and Marmara on it.

Küçük Ayasofya Çayıroğlu Sok. 9, Sultanahmet, 34122 Istanbul. www.hotelmaritime.net. © **0212/516-5000.** Fax 0212/516-4000. 16 units. 75€–95€ double. See website for special offers. MC, V. Free self-parking. **Amenities:** 3 bars; airport transfer (25€); free Internet; smoke-free rooms. *In room:* A/C, hair dryer, free Wi-Fi.

Ottoman Imperial ★★   If it's a central location you're looking for, you can't do much better than this without compromising on quality. Located opposite the Hagia Sophia, the building came to being as a dormitory for students of the adjacent Caferağa Medresi, was converted to a hospital and then in 1972, slapped together as a hostel. The conversion of the building to the Ottoman Imperial does it proud, allowing the hotel to join the list of true, Ottoman-influenced hotels. Room size varies, from compact "Superior Vezir and Sultan" standard rooms, to the more comfortable suites, to well, imperial (the "Premium Vezir" rooms and junior Suites). Or go for broke and book the supremely sublime Sultan's suite—with the bathtub adjacent to the bed and the domes of the Hagia Sophia on the other side. The bathrooms, outfitted with albeit new European sit-in bathtubs, are a bit tight. Behind the hotel is an unexpected garden patio restaurant that sits above the undulating domes of the *medresi*.

Caferiye Sok. 6/1, 34400 Sultanahmet. www.ottomanhotelimperial.com. © **0212/513-6150.** Fax 0212/512-7628. 50 units. 150€–240€ double; 320€–360€ suite. AE, DC, MC, V. Valet parking. **Amenities:** Restaurant; bar; free one-way airport transfer for 3-day minimum stay; concierge; elevator; room service; smoke-free rooms. *In room:* A/C, satellite TV, hair dryer, minibar, free Wi-Fi.

Sarı Konak ★★ 🛏   It's easy to see why visitors choose to stay in this small family-run establishment. Bahattin and his son Umit roll out the red carpet for everyone. The rooms are charming and very homey, and some even have little cushioned window seats. The main difference between the room types is the size, but even the smallest standard double is larger than standard at the Ottoman Imperial or the Sultanahmet Palace. The rooftop terrace, even without the choice views of the Blue Mosque and the Marmara Sea, is spectacular, partially shaded under a timber roof and with inviting cushions to relax on. Downstairs, breakfast is served to the soothing trickle of the garden fountain against the backdrop of an ancient Byzantine wall. The building next door was recently renovated into a multiroom, apartment-style annex (these are the suites), offering the opportunity for a real "local" experience.

Mimar Mehmet Ağa Cad. 42–46, 34400 Sultanahmet. www.sarikonak.com. © **0212/638-6258.** Fax 0212/517-8635. 17 units. 109€–159€ double; 179€–259€ suite Mar–Nov. Rates lower off-season. AE, MC, V. Free self-parking. **Amenities:** Bar; elevator; room service; smoke-free rooms. *In room:* A/C, TV, free Wi-Fi.

INEXPENSIVE

Apricot Hotel ★ 🛏   Because of a contract glitch, the Apricot was forced to move from its original location to an even more charming building on a parallel street. Although there are fewer rooms, they are prettier, larger, and better appointed. Indeed, the Apricot's owner, Hakan, has created the perfect example of why inexpensive doesn't have to mean cheap. The building provides an exclusive, stylish, and homey atmosphere at competitive (and fixed) prices with amenities such as Jacuzzis (in two rooms), *hamams* (two other rooms), and balconies (three rooms). With only six rooms, you'd better call now.

Amiral Tafdil Sok. 18, 34400 Sultanahmet. www.apricothotel.com. © **0212/638-1658.** Fax 0212/458-3574. 6 units. 69€–89€ Mar 15–Nov 15; 49€–59€ Nov–Mar. Rates higher Easter, Formula 1 and Festivals. MC, V (add 5% to the room rate for credit card payment). No traveler's checks. Free self-parking. **Amenities:** Airport transfer (25€, or free for 3-night minimum stay). *In room:* A/C, cable TV, minibar, free Wi-Fi.

Avicenna Hotel ★★   Perched on one of the high points of Sultanahmet overlooking the as-of-yet unreclaimed section of Cankurtaran with the Marmara Sea in the distance, the three-story, 19th-century Avicenna (no elevator) makes it hard to believe that this isn't the Mediterranean portion of your vacation. Preservationists restored three forgotten wooden Ottoman buildings, now connected by a covered wooden trellised walkway above a tranquil garden. Stained-glass dormer windows are part of the view from within the rooftop bar, decorated with outstanding Iznik tile replicas inset into original decorative wall molding. The 100-plus-year-old home now features 21st-century comforts. The entire hotel underwent a complete overhaul in 2008, sprucing up once-worn rooms with shiny parquet floors and sleek, modern bathrooms. Book a suite and you'll get a room with a balcony, Marmara Sea breezes at no extra charge.

Amiral Tafdil Sok. 31–33, 34400 Sultanahmet/Istanbul. www.avicennahotel.com. © **0212/517-0550.** Fax 0212/516-6555. 48 units. 79€ double. AE, MC, V. Free parking. **Amenities:** Restaurant; bar; babysitting; room service. *In room:* A/C, satellite TV, hair dryer, minibar, free Wi-Fi.

Naz Wooden House   For anyone interested in sleeping in a room all wrapped up in the history of Byzantium, this is the place. The hotel is built directly into the ancient city walls, so chances are you'll be ducking under a Roman archway or sleeping under an expansive brick vault. Spaces are commensurately small and showers are of the closed sliding stall variety, but it's all very charming and historic. When Naz is booked up (there are only seven rooms, after all), the management encourages you to stay at one of their sister properties, the **Deniz Konak** (© **0212/518-9595;** www.deniz konakhotel.com) or the **Sultan's Inn** (© **0212/638-2562;** www.sultansinn.com).

Akbıyık Degirmeni Sok. 7, 34400 Sultanahmet. www.nazwoodenhouseinn.com. © **0212/516-7130.** Fax 0212/518-5453. 7 units. 70€ double. MC, V. Free self-parking. **Amenities:** Rooftop bar; airport transfer (20€). *In room:* A/C, cable TV, minibar.

Sultan Hill   In 2006, this building was little more than a conglomerate of desiccated beams retaining, but for the grace of God, the shape of a house. Today, this brand-spanking-new replacement of the 18th-century Ottoman house previously on the site is a small but gracious bed-and-breakfast located so centrally that you'll practically trip over the Blue Mosque, the Hippodrome, and the Küçük Ayasofya on your way out the hotel's door. Rooms, all of which have showers, are a bit tight but are set up to be as comfortable as possible. The ground-floor breakfast room opens out onto a courtyard with an inviting traditional Turkish lounging corner. The hotel also makes best use of the requisite rooftop terrace.

Tavukhane Sok. 19, 34400 Sultanahmet. www.hotelsultanhill.com. ℂ **0212/518-3293.** Fax 0212/518-3295. 17 units. 60€–85€ double; 120€–140€ triple and family room. MC, V. Free self-parking. **Amenities:** Rooftop bar; airport transfer (25€); room service. *In room:* A/C, cable TV, hair dryer, minibar, free Wi-Fi.

Beyoğlu and North of Taksim
VERY EXPENSIVE
Park Hyatt Maçka Palas ★★★
Housed in a former government building where a Turkish poet later lived, the Park Hyatt was transformed into a 90-room Italian Art Deco palace by New York-based GKV Architects. The lobby is minimalist and very light, and oversize rooms include vintage photos by Turkish photographer Ara Güler. Spa rooms cater to the world-weary traveler, and include a *hamam* and a tub with color-therapy lights. Ask for a room on a lower level, or you may be kept up by noise from the bar on the eighth floor.

Bronz Sok. 4, 34367 Teşvikiye. www.istanbul.park.hyatt.com. ℂ **0212/315-1234.** Fax 0212/315-1235. 90 units. From 280€ double; 255€–3,000€ suite. Rates do not include breakfast or taxes. AE, MC, V. Valet parking. **Amenities:** Restaurant; bar; airport transfers (90€); babysitting; children's center or programs; concierge; elevator; executive or concierge-level rooms; health club and spa; pool; room service; sauna; smoke-free rooms. *In room:* A/C, satellite TV/DVD, hair dryer, minibar, MP3 docking station, free Wi-Fi.

Pera Palace Hotel ★★
In its heyday, the Pera Palace represented the Francophilia that had taken hold over the Ottoman Empire. It was built in 1892 as lodging befitting the exclusive passengers of the Orient Express, and the renovated, updated guest accommodations reflect this fact with rooms designed to channel their inner Agatha Christie (who wrote *Murder on the Orient Express* in room no. 411), Greta Garbo, or Pier Loti. (The revered and restored Atatürk room no. 101 remains a museum open to guests daily 10–11am and 3–4pm.) Wrought iron balustrades, Murano glass chandeliers and architectural elements recall a more gilded era, while the crown jewel of the property is the Kubbeli Saloon, a grand communal space whose stained-glass domes were previously hidden by the original roof. The Orient Bar has also been revamped to create a seductive space befitting of a place of such historical intrigue, while the Agatha Restaurant's creative international cuisine has already won kudos. Note that an annex of 10 residential suites located in the building across the street will open in 2012.

Meşrutiyet Cad. 52, 80050 Tepebaşı, Istanbul. www.perapalace.com. ℂ **0212/377-4000.** Fax 0212/377-4077. 115 units. 275€–300€ double; 350€–2,500€ suite. Rates fluctuate according to occupancy. AE, MC, V. Free self-parking. **Amenities:** 2 restaurants; bar; airport transfer (via Mercedes or BMW 110€ plus tax); babysitting; concierge; elevator; exercise room and spa; indoor pool; room service; smoke-free rooms. *In room:* A/C, TV, hair dryer, minibar, MP3 docking station, free Wi-Fi.

EXPENSIVE
Divan Istanbul ★★
First among the Koç Group's hotel empire, the Divan, which was constructed in 1956, was the first five-star property to grace Taksim Square. Fifty years later, after other, more modern hotels sprang up, the Divan had declined into a

A mystery WORTHY OF AGATHA CHRISTIE HERSELF

There has been much ado over **Agatha Christie's "mysterious" 11-day disappearance,** especially when it stands to substantiate the factual basis of a movie script *and* boost the profits of a historic hotel. The 1979 Warner Bros. movie *Agatha*, which makes reference to 11 missing days in the life of the author, was met with criticism by those who accused the movie studio of having fabricated the author's disappearance. In response, the movie studio hired a medium to get to the bottom of those 11 days. In a spiritual session, the medium, Tamara Rand, was "advised" by the late author that the answer to the mystery could be found in room no. 411 of the Pera Palace Hotel, where as a repeat guest between 1926 and 1932, Christie penned *Murder on the Orient Express.* In a much-hyped event, representatives of the film company and a group of reporters assembled in room no. 411 while a remote connection was established with Ms.

Rand, who led them to a rusty old key hidden beneath the floorboards. Presumably, the key was to the author's diary and would reveal the answers to those 11 days. The key never left the premises, because the hotel and studio executives were unable to reach an agreement on compensation. (The hotel's chairman asked for $2 million plus 15% of the film's profits "for restoration of the hotel" in exchange for the key.) Rumors persisted about Christie's whereabouts, eventually putting her in a nearby hotel in the arms of Dashiell Hammett. That the author makes no mention of these 11 days in her autobiography has over the years only fueled the fire. In spite of the uproar caused by the recovery of her abandoned car and several cryptic notes she sent before her "disappearance," the truth may be less racy. It seems that she simply checked into a health spa in Yorkshire on December 4, 1926, under the surname of her husband's lover.

dreary five-story concrete block that was an eyesore to clients and owners alike. It was completely demolished in 2008 to make room for this gorgeous, new Thierry Despont-designed reinterpretation of classical Turkish architecture Brass finial posts and lamps created by Despont's longtime collaborator, Robert DuGrenier, infuse guest rooms with characteristic Ottoman elegance with modernized touches, while pillow menus, ergonomically designed desks and rain showers offer deluxe comfort. The hotel has two restaurants, a pub, the requisite Divan patisserie, a spa, an Olympic-sized swimming pool and large, spacious meeting and conference rooms.

Asker Ocağı Cad,, 1, 34367 Şişli/Istanbul. www.divan.com.tr. ℭ **0212/315-5500.** Fax. 0212/315-1515. 191 units. 180€–220€ double; 250€ –320€ suite. See website for special rates and packages. AE, MC, V. Free valet parking. **Amenities:** 3 restaurants; 2 bars; airport transfer (40€); babysitting; concierge; elevator; fitness room; *hamam*; Olympic-sized indoor pool; room service; spa. *In room:* A/C, satellite TV w/pay movies, hair dryer, minibar, MP3 docking station; free Wi-Fi.

Edition ★★★   With the opening of the much-anticipated Edition hotel in Istanbul in 2010, Ian Schrager and Marriott are betting the farm on an expanding empire of exclusive, fashionable, and über luxurious hotels that will include properties in London, Miami, New York, Bangkok, and naturally, Abu Dhabi. The Edition, billed as a "seven star" hotel, boasts all of the restaurant, spa, and service bells and whistles, using a level of understatement only Ian Schrager could pull off. Think Frette linens, featherbeds, silk carpets, and Bang & Olufsen flatscreen TVs. And the amenities are

Beyoğlu Hotels & Restaurants

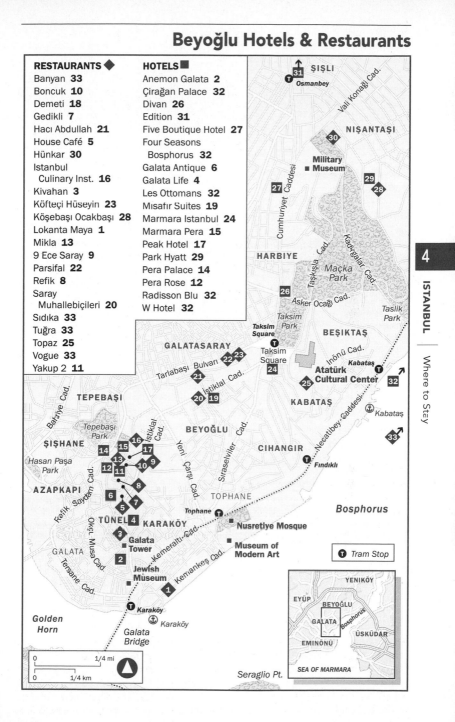

RESTAURANTS ◆

Banyan **33**
Boncuk **10**
Demeti **18**
Gedikli **7**
Hacı Abdullah **21**
House Café **5**
Hünkar **30**
Istanbul
  Culinary Inst. **16**
Kivahan **3**
Köfteçi Hüseyin **23**
Köşebaşı Ocakbaşı **28**
Lokanta Maya **1**
Mikla **13**
9 Ece Saray **9**
Parsifal **22**
Refik **8**
Saray
  Muhallebiçileri **20**
Sıdıka **33**
Tuğra **33**
Topaz **25**
Vogue **33**
Yakup 2 **11**

HOTELS ■

Anemon Galata **2**
Çirağan Palace **32**
Divan **26**
Edition **31**
Five Boutique Hotel **27**
Four Seasons
  Bosphorus **32**
Galata Antique **6**
Galata Life **4**
Les Ottomans **32**
Mısafır Suites **19**
Marmara Istanbul **24**
Marmara Pera **15**
Peak Hotel **17**
Park Hyatt **29**
Pera Palace **14**
Pera Rose **12**
Radisson Blu **32**
W Hotel **32**

4

ISTANBUL | Where to Stay

ŞİŞLI
Osmanbey
Vali Konağı Cad.
NIŞANTAŞI
Military
■ Museum
Cumhuriyet Caddesi
Kadırgalar Cad.
HARBIYE
Taşkışla Cad.
Maçka
Park
Asker Ocağı Cad.
Taslik
Park
Taksim
Taksim Park
Square
BEŞİKTAŞ
Taksim
Square
İnönü Cad.
Kabataş
Atatürk
Cultural Center
GALATASARAY
Tarlabaşı Bulvarı
İstiklal Cad.
KABATAŞ
Kabataş
TEPEBAŞI
Bahriye Cad.
Tepebaşı
Park
İstiklal Cad.
BEYOĞLU
Yeni Çarşı Cad.
Sıraselviler Cad.
CIHANGIR
Necatibey Caddesi
ŞİŞHANE
Hasan Paşa
Park
Refik Saydam Cad.
AZAPKAPI
Okçu Musa Cad.
TÜNEL
KARAKÖY
Kemeraltı Cad.
TOPHANE
Tophane
Nusretiye Mosque
Fındıklı
Bosphorus
Galata
Tower
Jewish
Museum
Museum of
Modern Art
Kemankeş Cad.
GALATA
Tersane Cad.
Karaköy
Golden
Horn
Karaköy
Galata
Bridge
Seraglio Pt.

● Tram Stop

YENİKÖY
EYÜP
BEYOĞLU
GALATA
Bosphorus
EMİNÖNÜ
ÜSKÜDAR
SEA OF MARMARA

0   1/4 mi
0   1/4 km

spread equally throughout, including in the base "superior room" with its not-so-inconsiderable 420 square feet of comfort. The hotel seems designed to encourage lounging, while the ESPA spa and Cipriani Restaurant aim for the stars. It may not be walking distance to anything, but if you're on a business account or don't mind hopping on the metro, this experience might just fit the bill.

Büyükdere Cad. 136, 34330 Levent, Istanbul. www.editionhotels.com. ☎ **0212/317-7700.** Fax 0212/317-7710. 78 units. 282€–575€ double. AE, MC. V. Free parking; valet parking 15€ per hr. **Amenities:** 4 restaurants; 2 bars; airport transfer (135€); concierge; elevator; *hamam;* indoor pool; room service; spa. *In room:* A/C, satellite TV/DVD w/pay movies, hair dryer, minibar, MP3 docking station, free Wi-Fi.

The Marmara Istanbul ★★★ The Marmara is an excellent choice for those traveling for business or pleasure, particularly for its towering location above central and bustling Taksim Square. In fact, the hotel got so popular that they opened a second one, the Marmara Pera, down the street (p. 171) and then another (and so on). The Marmara Istanbul has everything necessary for an exclusive visit to Istanbul, including spacious bathrooms and spectacular views. The recently renovated Club Floor specifically pampers business travelers with 24-hour floor supervision, complimentary breakfast, and in-room fax and coffee service.

Taksim Sq., 34437 Taksim. www.themarmarahotels.com. ☎ **0212/251-4696.** Fax 0212/244-0509. 458 units. 127€–210€ double; 239€ Club Rooms; 400€ and up suites. Rates fluctuate according to demand and are exclusive of tax and breakfast. Special weekend packages available. AE, MC, V. Ticketed parking lot. **Amenities:** 3 restaurants; 3 bars; airport transfer (90€); elevator; executive-level rooms; health club and spa; outdoor pool; room service; smoke-free rooms. *In room:* A/C, satellite TV, DVD player (suites only), hair dryer, minibar, free Wi-Fi.

Mısafir Suites ★★★ 📷 Dutch-born Joost and his partners waited 4 years for the drug addicts and squatters to vacate the derelict building they purchased before razing it and starting from scratch. The facade, however, is original, while the inside is embellished with new basalt floors, marble bathrooms, and artistic textiles. Rooms are enormous (as are the bathrooms, which are stocked with complimentary L'Occitane products), with king-size beds, twin sofas flanking oversize circular ottomans, and long, conveniently placed upholstered benches. It's all very smart, very well planned out, and very, very delightful. The restaurant Sekiz has a hip vibe and top-notch creative cuisine. Airport pickup is included in the price.

Gazeteci Erol Dernek Sok. 1, 34430 Beyoğlu (from the Ağa Mosque on Istiklal, turn down Sadir Alışık Sok.). www.misafirsuites.com. ☎ **0212/249-8930.** Fax 0212/249-8940. 7 units. 160€ and up suites. See website for promotions. AE, MC, V. Free self-parking. **Amenities:** Restaurant; bar; airport transfer (40€); concierge; elevator; room service. *In room:* A/C, satellite TV/DVD, CD player, hair dryer, minibar, free Wi-Fi.

MODERATE

Anemon Galata ★ The restoration of this 19th-century neighborhood gem was at the forefront of the revival of Galata. The building enjoys a front-row seat to the neighborhood plaza at the base of the commanding Galata Tower. The hotel itself offers sophisticated old-world style and in-room architectural features such as original crown moldings and ceiling frescoes. Wall-to-wall carpeting (which I barely tolerate) and staid decor in the rooms do the building less than full justice, but the upside of all that sound-sucking upholstery is that you certainly won't hear the neighbors. For the best views, pick a room on the third floor or above.

Büyükhendek Cad. 11, 80020, Galata/Istanbul. www.anemonhotels.com. ☎ **0212/293-2343.** Fax 0212/292-2340. 27 units. 100€–150€ double; 173€ suite. AE, MC, V. Valet parking. **Amenities:** Rooftop restaurant; bar; concierge; elevator; room service. *In room:* A/C, satellite TV, hair dryer, minibar, free Wi-Fi.

Five Boutique Hotel ★ 👜 Everything's organic in this progressive hotel, from the mattresses, to the curtains, to the cleaning products, down to the 100% certified produce served at breakfast. Even the wall paint is anti-carcinogenic and the wallpaper is recyclable. Five is discreetly located down a cluttered side street in Harbiye, diagonally opposite the Military Museum and a healthy (10 min. or less) walking distance to Nişantaşı and Taksim. All of the rooms are slightly different, with some equipped with bathtubs, rather than showers, and only a few with a balcony. The elevator only goes to the fourth floor, so guests staying in one of the two fifth-floor penthouse suites are required to walk up that last flight of steps.

Cumhuriyet Cad. Prof. Celal Öker Sok. 5, Harbiye. www.fiveboutiquehotel.com. © **0212/296-5553.** 19 units. 105€–160€ double. MC, V. Valet parking. **Amenities:** Organic cafe; airport transfer (30€); elevator; exercise room; smoke-free rooms. *In room:* A/C, minibar, free Wi-Fi.

The Marmara Pera ★ 🥄 The sister property of the Marmara Istanbul hit the ground running in 2005. It occupies a tower flanked by the Pera Palace Hotel and sits in the heart of the more vibrant section of Beyoğlu. And in spite of its 200 rooms, the hotel actually feels like a boutique property, as spaces are kept to manageable scale and the decor is understatedly trendy. The architect even saved the original tile paving where possible. Splurge the extra 50€ or so for a sea-view room; it'll be worth it. There's a patisserie, bar, and restaurant on the ground floor, plus the independently owned contemporary-style Mikla restaurant (p. 133) on the top floors commanding the best views.

Meşrutiyet Cad., Derviş Sok. 1, 34430 Tepebaşı. © **0212/251-4646.** Fax 0212/249-8033. 200 units. 94€–132€ double; 236€ suite. Sample rates fluctuate according to demand. Breakfast and tax not included. AE, MC, V. Free self-parking. **Amenities:** 2 restaurants; bar; airport transfer (55€); concierge; elevator; health club and spa; outdoor rooftop pool. *In room:* A/C, satellite TV, DVD player (suites only), hair dryer, minibar, free Wi-Fi.

INEXPENSIVE

Galata Antique Hotel 🥄 Located just down the street from the British Embassy and a few steps away from the entrance to Tünel and Istiklal Caddesi, the Galata Antique provides a friendly and convenient home base for any stay in Istanbul. You can absorb the 19th-century ambiance while riding up to your room in the caged elevator or sipping tea in the salon, or up in your temporary digs recently renovated to best stay true to French architect Vallaury's intent while providing the crisp comfort rooted in the 21st century. The entrance to the hotel sits in the middle of a steep incline navigated by a flight of exterior steps, so the Galata Antique may not be appropriate for everyone. Breakfast on the top-floor terrace is also a great way to start the morning.

Meşrutiyet Cad., 119, 34430 Beyoğlu. www.galataantiquehotel.com. © **0212/245-5944.** Fax 0212/245-5947. 27 units. 78€–128€ double. MC, V. Free self-parking. **Amenities:** Bar; airport transfer (25€); concierge; elevator; room service. *In room:* A/C, satellite TV, hair dryer, minibar, free Wi-Fi.

Galata Life 🥄 An oasis on the newly bustling street that is Galipdede, Galata Life is a good option for single travelers, casual companions or couples looking for a truly local and bohemian introduction into the city. That rooms are simple, clean, sharp and affordable is the bonus.

Galipdede Cad. 75, 34420 Galata, Istanbul. www.galatalife.com. © **0212/245-2315.** 5 units. 24€–32€ per person. MC, V. No parking. **Amenities:** Restaurant, concierge. *In room:* AC, free Wi-Fi.

The Peak Hotel ★ ⭐ Almost a half a century after opening its doors, the formerly dreary Peak Hotel (formerly the Yenişehir Palace), just completed massive renovations on a full complement of rooms and common areas. Rooms are now fresh—with new carpeting and furniture and an overhaul of the bedclothes (ranging from sleek whites and beiges to Ottoman-style frilly)—and bathrooms are bright and modern. The hotel is ridiculously central: In a 5-minute walk you can be in Galata, Istiklal Caddesi, or Tünel, from which you can hook up with the transport system to Taksim Square or the historic center. The location also implies that guests have business needs, and indeed the hotel has meeting rooms and even a cigar/wine bar facing the trendy Asmalimescit area.

Meşrutiyet Cad., Oteller Sok. 1–3, 34430 Tepebaşı. www.thepeakhotel.com.tr. ⓒ **0212/252-7160.** Fax 0212/249-7507. 171 units. 79€–120€ double; 125€ suite. See website for special offers. MC, V. Free self-parking. **Amenities:** Restaurant; bar; airport transfer (35€); babysitting; concierge; elevator; room service; smoke-free rooms. *In room:* A/C, satellite TV, hair dryer, minibar, free Wi-Fi.

Pera Rose ⭐ When the reception quoted me a rate 30% below the listed rack rate in the fall of 2007, I started to smell a value. The Pera Rose is another renovated and restored business hotel on what used to be a dead end of Meşrutiyet Caddesi (most just passed by on the way to the Pera Palace or the Marmara Pera, both on nearby corners). I actually like this hotel more than the neighboring Peak Hotel, primarily because of the old-world feel and smaller scale. All rooms are outfitted with scrumptious orthopedic mattresses. And as befitting a freshly renovated hotel, bathrooms are brightly tiled. Suites have Jacuzzis, and there are two pretty exciting duplexes.

Meşrutiyet Cad. 87, 34430 Tepebaşı. ⓒ **0212/243-1500.** Fax 0212/243-1501. 52 units. 119€ double; 170€ suite. See website for special rates. MC, V. Free self-parking. **Amenities:** 2 restaurants; bar; concierge; elevator; exercise room; *hamam;* massage; room service; sauna; smoke-free rooms. *In room:* A/C, satellite TV, hair dryer, minibar, free Wi-Fi.

Along the Bosphorus
VERY EXPENSIVE
Çırağan Palace Hotel Kempinski Istanbul ★★★ Residence of the last Ottoman sultans, the hotel that you see today is actually two buildings: the faithfully restored stone-and-marble sultan's palace (housing the VIP suites) and the modern five-star deluxe hotel, both standing majestically on the shores of the Bosphorus and presiding over a magnificent collection of sculpted lawns, marble gates, a waterside swimming pool, and even a putting green. The guest list reads like a who's who of international royalty, all lining up for a Bosphorus-view room (not all get one). It's definitely worth the trouble to upgrade to a standard room with Bosphorus view (why bother for a Park View, really?). The suites in the modern wing add living space, upgraded decor, and views, but it's in the newly renovated palace section where things truly get interesting. These are salons that recall a statelier time: Sumptuous textiles swath elegant antiques, while high ceilings and gilded architectural features remind you that this was indeed once a working palace.

Çırağan Cad. 84, 80700 Beşiktaş. www.kempinski.com/istanbul. ⓒ **800/426-3135** in the U.S., 800/363-0366 in Canada, 0800/868-588 in the U.K., 1800/623-578 in Australia, 0800/446-368 in New Zealand, 0212/326-4646 in Istanbul. Fax 0212/259-6686. 313 units. 505€ double park view; 670€–1,350€ double sea view; 1,375€ and up (way up) suites. Breakfast and tax not included. See website for promotional rates. AE, DC, MC, V. Valet parking. **Amenities:** 3 restaurants (Tuğra on p. 138); 4 bars; airport transfer (125€); babysitting; concierge; concierge-level rooms; elevator; golf putting green; health club and spa; indoor and outdoor pools; room service; smoke-free rooms. *In room:* A/C, satellite TV w/pay movies, high-speed Internet, hair dryer, minibar.

Fit for a Sultan

The Sultan's Suite in the Çırağan Palace has gold bathroom fixtures and goes for 30,000€ a night—one of the most expensive rooms in Europe.

Four Seasons Bosphorus ★★★ 📷 The new Four Seasons property kept hopeful clientele in suspense for more than 4 years before opening in late 2008 with great fanfare. The hotel complex is composed of the restored and stately central property, the Ottoman Atik Paşa mansion, flanked by two regrettably practical modern blocks. (If the Çırağan can get away with it, then why not the Four Seasons?) Apart from that tiny criticism, the hotel is a practically flawless center of hospitality and service. East-facing rooms in the Paşa's mansion benefit from spectacular, head-on views of the Bosphorus. The (heated) outdoor pool sits seamlessly adjacent to the seafront, and a private dock provides convenient access, via the hotel's speedboat service (or one's private yacht) to key points around the city (or to nowhere, whichever is one's pleasure). Parents get to wrap their little ones up in child-sized bathrobes at night and pamper them with free milk and cookies. There's a cinema, banquet rooms, a business center, and a waterside setting to die for. Oh, and one of the amenities they provide is free packing service.

Çırağan Cad. 28, 34349 Beşiktaş. www.fourseasons.com/bosphorus. ✆ **800/332-3442** in the U.S., or operator in Turkey 0212/381-4000. Fax 0212/381-4010. 166 units. 370€ and up doubles and suites. Rates exclude taxes. AE, MC, V. Valet and self-parking. **Amenities:** 2 restaurants; 3 bars; airport transfer (100€); babysitting; concierge; elevator; health club and spa; indoor and outdoor pools; room service; smoke-free rooms; tennis (at the Swissôtel property). *In room:* A/C, satellite TV/VCR, CD/DVD player, fax, hair dryer, minibar, Wi-Fi (5€ per hr.); free in business center).

Les Ottomans ★★★ 📷 This lavish hotel is the talk of the town and only the most overused (but apt) superlatives will describe it. My apologies in advance. Let's start by saying that the powerhouse behind the hotel villa, Ahu Aysal, spared no expense (upwards of $60 million) in the reconstruction of the former Muhzinzade Mehmet Paşa, a wooden mansion that stood on this site (the exterior is an exact replica). The result is a sumptuous, 10-room (plus one; Ahu lives on the top floor) . . . palace? Abode? Shangri-la? In creating the hotel, Ms. Aysal employed the renowned Turkish interior designer Zeynep Fadillioğlu, as well as the feng shui expert Yap Cheng Hai, to ensure the hotel conformed to principles of harmony. Feeling a bit underworthy upon my visit, I found that the hotel is opulent without being ostentatious; it's just what you'd imagine of a modern royal palace: gilded calligraphic friezes (antique), ivory inlay, magnificent silk fabrics, and of course, let's not forget the plasma TVs (some suites have as many as three). And I haven't even gotten to the Caudalie spa, butler service, or cinema.

Muallim Naci Cad. 68, 34345 Kuruçeşme. www.lesottomans.com. ✆ **0212/359-1500.** Fax 0212/359-1540. 10 units. 800€–3,500€ suite single or double. Rates include breakfast and use of minibar but exclude taxes. AE, MC, V. Pets allowed. **Amenities:** 2 restaurants; bar; airport transfer (100€, 130€, or 160€ depending on the Mercedes or BMW model you choose to ride in, plus tax); concierge; exercise room; *hamam;* outdoor pool; room service; spa. *In room:* A/C, satellite TV/VCR, CD player, fax, hair dryer, laptop, minibar, free Wi-Fi.

W Istanbul ★★ A block of abandoned row houses built in 1875 by Sultan Abdülaziz has given rise to a stylish Starwood-branded W Hotel targeting the young, hip, and yes, even club-going set. Now, doormen give the hotel that "velvet rope" feel, and low light, neon-backlit hallways mimic the backstage of a rock concert. Studios and duplex rooms, some with their own balcony, private gardens, or outdoor cabana, all come with the ridiculously comfortable "W Signature Beds," stylish decor and clever (sensual even) lighting to set whatever mood you like. And setting the bar higher for concierges everywhere is the W's "Whatever, Whenever" service, "transforming your dreams into reality . . . as long as it's legal."

Süleyman Seba Cad. 27, 34357 Beşiktaş. www.wistanbul.com.tr.℃ **0212/381-2121.** Fax 0212/381-2199. 130 units. 225€–305€ double; 350€ and up suite. Taxes not included. AE, MC, V. Free valet parking. Pets allowed. **Amenities:** Restaurant; bar; airport transfer (from 115€); babysitting; concierge; elevator; exercise room and spa; room service; smoke-free rooms. *In room:* A/C, satellite TV, hair dryer, minibar, MP3 docking station, Wi-Fi (5€ per hr. or 16€ per day).

EXPENSIVE

Radisson Blu ★   In January 2006, this piece of waterfront real estate adjacent to the artsy neighborhood of Ortaköy became one of the newer additions to the European Bosphorus. The target audience is business travelers, Turkish weekenders, and anyone else in the market for good design, seamless comfort, and a boutique experience. The hotel features a grassy "beach" and a spa offering a variety of treatments. There's a parking garage adjacent to the hotel, which is next door to the charming Ortaköy quay and just steps away from some of the best nightlife the city has to offer.

Çırağan Cad. 46, 34349 Ortaköy. www.radissonblu.com/hotel-istanbul. ℃ **0212/260-5757** or 0212/310-1500. (From the U.S. and Australia ℃ 800/333-3333; from the U.K. and New Zealand ℃ 800/3333-3333.) Fax 0212/260-6555. 120 units. 180€–335€ double; 450€ and up suite. AE, MC, V. Valet parking. Pets allowed. **Amenities:** Restaurant; 3 bars; airport transfer by boat (contact hotel for rate); concierge; *hamam;* health club and spa; indoor pool; room service; smoke-free rooms. *In room:* A/C, satellite TV, hair dryer, minibar, free Wi-Fi.

On the Asian Side

Sumahan ★★★ 📷   From an *ispirito fabrikası* for the production of soma (grain alcohol, today more benignly called ethanol) to an idyllic retreat, the Sumahan (note the apt name) is a prime example of functional architectural preservation. Mark and Nedret Butler met while studying architecture in America. When the Turkish State began proceedings to expropriate the land (owned by Nedret's family) in the 1970s, the Butlers, by then settled into their lives in Minneapolis, entered into a 30-year bureaucratic saga that ended in them relocating back to Istanbul. The rest is a story fit for *Architectural Digest,* with significant input from the Butler's interior designer daughter, Yaşa. Apart from the understated luxury, highlights include duplexes, bathrooms swathed in the same Marmara marble found in Topkapı and Dolmabahçe, and a studied forethought to even the placement of the soaps. The hotel provides three complimentary shuttles per day to the Kabataş docks. Commuter boats from the Çengelköy docks to Eminönü two times daily are a mere 200m (656 ft.) away.

Kuleli Cad. 51, 34684 Çengelköy. www.sumahan.com. ℃ **0216/422-8000.** 20 units. 325€–615€ double and suites. AE, MC, V. Valet parking. **Amenities:** 2 restaurants; bar; babysitting; elevator; exercise room; *hamam;* massage; room service. *In room:* A/C, satellite TV, CD/DVD player, hair dryer, minibar, free Wi-Fi.

Near the Airport

Airport Hotel   Located on the grounds of Istanbul's Atatürk Airport, this is a surefire way to make sure you don't miss your flight. It's also a godsend on long layovers between international flights, because you never have to exit Customs to check in. Not surprisingly, the hotel attracts lots of business travelers—the business center and executive meeting rooms make sure of that—but even the most sun-kissed vagabond will enjoy breakfast views of the runway. Rooms are pleasingly bright, airy, and unusually spacious, and offer high-tech amenities like TVs that show flight details and Wi-Fi. The hotel also offers rooms at hourly rates (for naps on long layovers and such) and a well-appointed fitness room for those crack-of-dawn workouts.

Atatürk Havalimanı Dış Hatlar Terminali, Yeşilköy. www.airporthotelistanbul.com. ✆ **0212/465-4030.** Fax 0212/465-4730. 85 units. 102€–200€ double. Hourly rates available. AE, MC, V. Free self-parking. **Amenities:** Restaurant; bar; free elevator; exercise room (fee); room service; smoke-free rooms. *In room:* A/C, satellite TV, hair dryer, minibar, free Wi-Fi.

Sheraton Istanbul and Four Points by Sheraton   If you have to stay near the airport, this is your best choice. The Sheraton Istanbul is at the Ataköy Marina, on the waterfront halfway between the airport (8km/5 miles) and the city center (10km/6¼ miles) and conveniently located pretty much at the Galleria Shopping Mall. Proving that the Sheraton knows pleasing design and comprehensive service, there isn't a (fee-based) amenity that they don't offer, from shoe-shine, to an on-site drugstore, to the on-staff photographer. They do offer limited free shuttles into town. If you manage to score a package, it's probably worth it to book a room on the Club floor, where you get normally fee-based amenities such as bottled water, Wi-Fi, access to the fitness room, snacks, and complimentary breakfast, as well as a lounge and use of the fax, printer, and copier, for free.

Ataköy. www.starwoodhotels.com. ✆ **888/625-5144** in the U.S. and Canada. 285 units. 109€–235€ double. Breakfast and tax extra. AE, MC, V. Free self-parking. **Amenities:** 3 restaurants; 3 bars; free airport transfer; babysitting; concierge; elevator; executive-level rooms; health club; Jacuzzi; indoor (heated) and outdoor pools; room service; sauna; smoke-free rooms; tennis courts. *In room:* A/C, satellite TV, hair dryer, minibar, Wi-Fi.

SIDE TRIPS FROM ISTANBUL

Bursa: Gateway to an Empire

243km (151 miles) south of Istanbul; 270km (168 miles) east of Çanakkale; 380km (236 miles) west of Ankara; 322km (200 miles) northeast of Izmir

Bursa established itself as an important center as far back as pre-Roman times, attracting emperors and rulers for its rich, fertile soil and healing thermal waters. The arrival of the Ottomans in 1326 ensured the city's prosperity as a cultural and economic center that now represents one of the richest legacies of early Ottoman art and architecture. As the first capital of the Ottoman Empire, Bursa became the beneficiary of the finest mosques, theological schools (*medreses*), humanitarian centers (*imarets*), and social services (*hans, hamams,* and public fountains). The density of arched portals, undulating domes, artfully tiled minarets, and magnificently carved *minbars* (pulpits) could easily provide the coursework for extensive study of the Ottomans, and without a doubt, fill multiple daylong walking tours.

Today Bursa is a thriving industrial and agricultural center, reputed for its fine silk and cotton textiles, and the center of Turkey's automobile industry. The nearby ski resorts at Mount Uludağ provide city dwellers with an easy weekend getaway, while others just make a special trip here to stock up on cotton towels. But many just flock here for the same reasons the Romans, Byzantines, and Ottomans did: the indulgence afforded by the density of rich, hot, mineral springs bubbling up all over the region.

If you plan on just a quick architectural and historical pilgrimage, you could reasonably make Bursa a day trip from Istanbul. An overnight excursion is more realistic if you want to make it a short spa getaway and leave time to wander through the exquisite *hans* (privately owned inns or marketplaces) of the early Ottoman era.

A LOOK AT THE PAST

It was common practice for a conquering king to attach his name to the cities that he founded, so the consensus is that King Prussia of Bithynia established a kingdom on the remains of a preexisting civilization here. Prusia (say it 10 times fast and it starts to sound like Bursa) of Olympus, distinguishing it from King Prusia's other conquests, was later leagued with Rome, a colonization that is attributed to the time of Eumenes II, leader of Pergamum. Bursa thrived, thanks to Rome's influence and the introduction of Christianity by the apostle Andrew. In the 6th century Emperor Justinian constructed baths and a lavish palace in the area, taking full advantage of the region's economic and thermal resources. From 1080 to 1326, Bursa bore the brunt of more than its fair share of invasions, with Selçuks, Turks, raiding Arabs, Byzantines, and Crusaders all trying to get a hold on this prosperous center. One of the Turkic tribes broke the chain when the Osmanlı tribe of Turks, led by Osman and later his son Orhan, entered Bursa in 1326 after a 10-year-long siege. Orhan established Bursa as the first permanent Ottoman capital, building a mosque and *medrese* on the site of a Byzantine monastery in what is now the Hisar District. The city expanded and thrived under sultans Murat I, Yıldırım Beyazıt, Mehmet I, and Murad II. Bursa's importance began to wane when the Ottoman capital was transferred to Adrionople (present-day Edirne).

ESSENTIALS
Getting There

BY FERRY   From Istanbul's Yenikapı docks there are two ferry options for excursions to Bursa. The first is IDO's daily service to the Güzelyalı port (IDO calls this service the Yenikapı/Bursa service; *©* **0212/444-4436**; www.ido.com.tr), currently departing five times a day, at 7:30am, 5:30pm, and 8:30pm (car ferry) and 1:20pm and 6:50pm (passengers only). The ferry takes 80 minutes and costs 28TL per person. From Güzelyalı, take the local city bus (TL1.80) to the *Organize Sanayı* metro stop. From there, hop on the metro (TL1.35) to the *Sehreküstü* stop. From there, it's a 10-minute or so walk to the center of town (ask the locals to point you to the Ulu Camii). Better yet, take a taxi to your final destination. From Güzelyalı to Heykel a taxi costs around 60TL. Total time (including ferry, bus, and metro) from Istanbul to Bursa is about 2½ hours.

The other option is the 70-minute ferry ride (14TL passengers) to Yalova, north of Bursa. Ferries depart out of Istanbul's Yenikapı docks. From the Yalova ferry landing, hop on one of the many buses to Bursa lined up outside the gates; the ride to Bursa's *otogar* (55km/34 miles) takes about 50 minutes and costs around 10TL. Bursa's *otogar* is located more than 10km (6¼ miles) out of town, so it will be necessary to either get on a municipal bus (no. 38 to Heykel or no. 96 to Çekirge) or take a taxi into town. The bus takes between 30 and 50 minutes, depending on traffic, and costs 2TL.

Both the ferry to Yalova and to Güzelyalı accept cars, so if you're not overly excited about the hoops you have to jump through to get there, you can shuttle yourself from the ferry docks straight into Bursa. IDO charges 110TL and 80TL, respectively, for cars plus 25TL and 14TL for each *additional* passenger in the vehicle.

BY BUS   If you prefer to do the entire journey by land, **Nilüfer Turizm** (*©* **0224/444-0099**; www.nilufer.com.tr), based in Bursa, provides the most comprehensive bus service into Bursa. The 3.5-hour trip from Istanbul costs 24TL. **Metro** (*©* **0212/444-3455**) runs buses almost hourly from Istanbul for the same price, as does

Kamil Koç (✆ **444-0562**). All intercity bus service heads directly to the *otogar,* about 20 minutes outside of town. If you're headed to Çekirge, hop on local bus no. 96; to get to the city center/Ulu Camii, take bus no. 38. Important: If Bursa is just one of many stops on your chosen bus company's itinerary, you may get left on the road rather than at the station proper. Confirm your drop-off point when purchasing your ticket to ensure you're transported into the Bursa *otogar,* not just *near* it.

Visitor Information

The **Tourist Information office,** Ulucami Parkı Orhangazi Alt Geçidi 1, Heykel; (✆ **0224/220-1848**) is hidden underneath Atatürk Caddesi in the center of town. There's another tourism office representing the province of Bursa located in Tophane at Osmangazi Cad. 18 (✆ 0224/220-9926). For information on festivals and events, log onto the website of the **Bursa Kültür Sanat ve Turizm Vakfi** (Culture, Art and Tourism Foundation; **www.bkstv.org.tr**). The Bursa municipality also runs a helpful website with background info on Bursa, in English (**www.bursa.bel.tr**).

All of the major bus companies have ticket offices around Heykel; tickets can also be purchased through any local travel agent or at the *otogar.*

Orientation

The concentration of early Selçuk-inspired architecture is clustered in the commercial center of Bursa, in the area better known to the locals as **Heykel,** after the equestrian statue of Atatürk commanding the plaza just a few blocks to the east (*heykel* means "statue" in Turkish). Again, using the Tourist Information office for orientation, to the west/right is **Tophane Park** and the **Hisar District,** where the conquering Ottoman armies set up their capital in the 15th century. The road leads into the posher **Çekirge** section, where ambassadors and statesmen flock for the hotels and thermal hot springs. The winter ski resort of Uludağ is located about 36km (22 miles) to the south of Bursa and reachable via a funicular from the center of town.

Getting Around

In all likelihood, you will spend most of your time between the Heykel and Çekirge neighborhoods. While covering small distances on foot in either neighborhood is possible, the two are just too far apart to think about walking between them. Instead, take advantage of the newish Bursaray, Bursa's two-line metro and growing. The

---

📎 Turkish Towels & Such

If you're in the market for a few fluffy towels or one of those luscious Turkish bathrobes that sell for an arm and a leg in Bloomingdale's, the price for a selection at Bursa's **Covered Bazaar** (see "What to See & Do," below) can't be beat. The subtlest prints and plushest linens and towels are found at **Özdilek,** with branches in both the bazaar (exit the underground passage opposite the PTT and walk 1 block in) and a shopping center at Yenı Yalova Yolu 4, on the highway from the *otogar* (✆ **0224/219-6000**). Silk fabrics, such as scarves, blouses, and tablecloths, are available in shops on the upper level of **Koza Han,** the historic *bedesten* (covered market) next to Orhan Camii. For modern merchandise in a slick mall setting, the new glass pyramid-topped **Zafer Plaza** houses franchises such as Quiksilver, Vakko, Demirel, Mavi Jeans, and Polo Garage.

station stops that will be the most helpful are Şehreküstü (10 minutes to the city center) and Kültürpark (closest to the Çelik Palas Hotel), although there will be a (long) couple of blocks walk to/from either stop. The fare for short distances is 1.10TL. A taxi taking the same route will cost under 15TL.

WHAT TO SEE & DO

Bursa is so jam-packed with historic structures that it would be impossible to list them all here. In addition to the major sites named below, be sure to wander through the marketplace, spread out among open-air and covered streets. *Hans* are traditionally double-storied arcaded buildings with a central courtyard, usually occupied by an ornate fountain or pool or raised *mescit* (a small mosque). The *hans* are still used for trade and make lovely shaded retreats to take a coffee outdoors and poke amid the local merchandise. The **Fidan Han** dates to the 15th century and has a central pool topped by a *mescit*. The **Pirinç Han** (closed) was constructed by Beyazıt II to earn the revenue necessary to cover the expenses of his mosque and soup kitchen in Istanbul. The **Ipek Han** is the largest *han* in Bursa and contains an octagonal *mescit* in the center of the courtyard. The revenue from this *han* was used to pay for the construction of the Yeşil Mosque. The courtyard of **Emir Han** has a graceful marble pool with exterior faucets to allow for ablutions.

Archaeology Museum (Arkeoloji Müzesi) MUSEUM Constructed with the charm of any 1972 institutional project, this museum is worth the 30 minutes it will take to get through, especially if you're strolling through Çekirge or into Kültür Park. The fact that the attendant trails you to turn the lights on and off is a bit unnerving (the museum doesn't see that many tourists), obliging you to react with an appropriate level of enthusiasm. The museum houses regional artifacts dating back to the 3rd century B.C., with crude pottery and tools from as far back as the Neolithic period. Particularly impressive is the collection of ceramic and glass objects from the Classical era, much of which has remained surprisingly intact. The extensive collection of coins displayed on the mezzanine is significant because notable figures had a habit of emblazoning their portraits on the face of the piece, providing a rare window of accessibility to the ancients.

Kültür Park. © **0224/234-4918.** Admission 5TL. Tues–Sun 8am–noon and 1–5pm.

Bursa Museum of Turkish and Islamic Arts (Türk Islam Eserleri Müzesi/ Yeşil Medrese) ★ HISTORIC SITE Housed in the former *medrese* of the Green Mosque, built in 1419 by Çelebi Sultan Mehmet along with the other buildings in the Yeşil complex, this museum is worth a look, particularly because they've gone to the trouble of providing English translations. The exhibits are intimately displayed in small rooms around a central courtyard. There's a space devoted to derviş cult objects, a *hamam* room displaying silver clogs and silk embroidered bath accessories, and a model of a traditional Turkish coffeehouse, complete with barber's chair. The collection also includes Selçuk ceramics, inlaid wood pieces, and objects in iron, copper, bronze, and wood. A visit takes under 30 minutes.

Yeşil Cad., on the left just before the Green Mosque. © **0224/327-7679.** Free admission. Tues–Sun 9am–7pm (until 5pm in winter).

Covered Bazaar (Bedesten) HISTORIC SITE & MARKET The covered bazaar that stands on the site is a modern version of the original that was built by Yıldırım Beyazıt in the 14th century and leveled in the earthquake of 1855. There's no glitz—or tourists—here, evidenced by the distressing concentration of satin embroidered towels and bedspreads. Keep your eyes open for good-quality baby clothes and knockoff sportswear, and if you're looking to stuff a throw pillow, this is the place to do it, as stalls displaying fluffy unspun cotton of varying composition and quality abound.

Enter through Koza Hanı, or follow Çarşı Cad. from Ulu Camii. Daily 8:30am–7pm.

The Great Mosque (Ulu Camii) ★★ MOSQUE When the building was erected in 1396, architects were just beginning to dabble in the problem of covering large spaces with small domes, and the result is the first example of a monumental Ottoman multidomed mosque. The 20 domes, supported on 12 stout pillars, are better admired from within, where the final result comes together in the mosque's five naves and four bays. Upon entering the mosque, eyes naturally are drawn first to the three-tiered ablution fountain beneath a large light well. Although this has its practical purposes, the result is an embracing sensation of serenity, and many worshippers remain on the raised platforms surrounding the fountain for long moments of meditation.

The date of completion (80211—11 is for *hicret,* the day Mohammed left Mecca for Medina) is inscribed on the pulpit door, but several waves of renovations were necessary after the invasion of Tamerlane, with major restorations completed after the earthquake of 1855. Over the years, other, minor housekeeping projects were undertaken, including the application of a thick layer of synthetic varnish on the wooden *minbar* (pulpit) and on the *mahfel* (balcony used by the muezzin) that became darkened by tar over the years. Then in 1983, someone thought it would be a good idea to slap a layer of oil-based paint onto the mosque walls and all of the decorative carvings on the *minbar* and *mahfel.* Then a few years ago, a local expert in historic architectural ornamentation noticed some red specks peeking out from behind a carving, spurring a project completed in 2009 that has successfully restored the mosque's original decorative aspects.

The wooden *minbar* is a masterwork of carved geometric and floral reliefs, as are the banister work and other wood details. On the *mahfel,* a poem, along with rich ornamentation, can now be seen on the stairwell. Decorative etchings on leather were uncovered after the paint was removed from the side of the *mahfel,* leaving leaf, cloud, and floral motifs. To preserve these precious original ornaments, restorers applied a glassy layer to prevent any further "improvements."

Bursa center. Free admission. Daily dawn–dusk.

Green Mosque (Yeşil Camii) ★ MOSQUE Commanding a hillside terrace above the city, Yeşil Camii takes its name from the green and blue tiles in the interior. Intent on leaving his mark on Bursa, Mehmet I ordered the construction of this mosque, built entirely of hewn stone and marble, as a monument to the victorious ending of his 10-year struggle for the throne. Although an architect's inscription over the portal gives the completion date as 1419, the final decorations were ordered in 1424 on the orders of Murad II, and the two minarets were added in the 19th century.

One of the first mosques to employ an inverted T floor plan, the building signals the dawn of a new Turkish architectural tradition. The "Turkish pleat," an ingenious geometric corner detail allowing for the placement of a circular dome atop a square base, is a design device original to Turkey, while the use of multicolored ceramic tile, an influence that arrived with Tamerlane, is intricate enough to make your head spin. The high porcelain *mihrab* (a niche oriented toward Mecca) is a masterpiece of

Ottoman ceramic art, difficult to miss at an understated 10m (33 ft.) high. In the center of the *mihrab* in Arabic script is the word "Allah," mounted on the wall at a later date.

The sumptuous gold mosaics and tile of the Imperial loge were probably an overstated attempt at one-upping the loggia that served the Byzantine emperors; it is flanked on either side by the servants' quarters and the harem, and a closer look is at the discretion of the caretaker.

East of Heykel at the end of Yeşil Cad. No phone. Free admission. Daily dawn–dusk.

Green Tomb (Yeşil Türbesi) ★★ MONUMENT/MEMORIAL   This Selçuk-influenced tomb, representing one of the noblest of its era, has become the symbol of Bursa. If you're looking for a blue building, look no further, as the tiles of this hexagonal structure are actually turquoise, topped by a lead dome resting on a plaster rim. The construction of the tomb was ordered by the tenant himself, Sultan Mehmet I, and was completed around 1421. The color glazing of the interior tile work is an outstanding example of the art, from the window pediments adorned with verses of the Koran and *hadiths* (narrations of the life of Mohammad) in Arabic script, to the tile inscriptions on the sarcophagi. It's also worth noting the workmanship of the colors of the panels on the *mihrab*, which change color according to your perspective.

East of Heykel at the end of Yeşil Cad. Free admission. Daily 8am–noon and 1–5pm.

Koza Hanı ★★ ARCHITECTURE   Meaning "Cocoon Inn," this caravansaray was built in 1490 by Beyazıt II to raise funds for his mosque in Istanbul. Built on two levels, the inn provided a place for the merchants to trade the last of their goods, as this was the final stop on the Silk Road from China. In the middle of the courtyard is a small *şadırvan* (ablution fountain) ★ for the small *mescit* (prayer room) poised above; in the summer the verdant space becomes a peaceful tea garden. The monumental portal decorated with turquoise tiles and carvings leads into the covered bazaar. Today the Koza Hanı continues its legacy of trading in silk with shops and boutiques stocked with scarves and fabrics at exorbitant (and extremely negotiable) prices.

Bursa Center. Free admission. Daily 8:30am–sunset.

Muradiye Mosque Complex (Muradiye Külliye) ★★ MOSQUE   Constructed by Murat II between 1424 and 1426, this complex includes a mosque, a *medrese,* a soup kitchen, a bath, and a royal cemetery found within an overgrown garden of roses, magnolias, and cypress trees. Although the entrance to the grounds is open, many of the tombs and even the mosque are locked up, but the idle yet earnest ticket-window attendant will catch up with you for a private tour of the grounds, proudly locking and unlocking the royal tombs.

The Murat Paşa Mosque is a typical example of early Ottoman architecture, although the *mihrab* and *minbar* are 18th-century baroque. Reverently displayed inside on the upper-left-hand wall is an original piece from the Ka'aba in Mecca.

To the right, beginning toward the rear of the grounds, is no ordinary cemetery. The 12 stately tombs serve as the final resting places of not only some of the first sultans, but a sobering number of members of the royal family as well, including Hüma Hatun (mother of Mehmet the Conqueror), Shehzade Ahmed (son of Beyazıt II and crown prince), Sultan Murat II, Mustafa (son of Süleyman the Magnificent), and Gülşah Hatun (wife of Mehmet the Conqueror). Because succession rights relied not on heredity but on survival of the fittest, it was standard, even expected, practice for the victorious leader to cover his back by strangling his brothers with a wire cord.

When Sultan Orhan arrived in Bursa, he immediately set out to build his mosque. He appointed a man named **Hacıvad** as supervisor, who in turn hired a local blacksmith named **Karagöz** to oversee the installation of the iron supports. Hacıvad and Karagöz used to pass the time with clever quips and witty conversation that kept the laborers in stitches. The two eventually had the workmen doubled over in hysterics, to the point that work on the mosque came to a complete halt.

When the sultan found out about the construction delays, he had Hacıvad and Karagöz hanged (or decapitated, depending on which interpretation of the oral history you hear). The decapitated version is favored, because illustrators have had a grand time depicting the two hapless jokers approaching the sultan's throne to protest with their heads under their arms. Whichever demise, the outcome is the same: Orhan finds someone to relate the dialogues, until the sultan, too, is keeling over with laughter. Realizing his error, the sultan orders a local leather worker to create lifelike figures of the two, so that they can continue their legacy of comedy. This puppetlike shadow play gained momentum and grew into a popular cultural tradition, boasting as many as 200 characters in one presentation.

As you drive from the center of town toward Çekirge, ask your driver to point out the **Karagöz Hacıvad Memorial,** a small but colorful representation of the two folk heroes.

The most recognizable casualty of this practice was the son of Süleyman the Magnificent: Şehzade (Prince) Mustafa, who as object of a plot spun by Roxelana for the succession of her own son was unjustly murdered at the hands of his father. Ironically, the tomb was built by Selim II, Roxelana's son and successor to the throne.

The recently restored opulence of the tomb and its outstanding porcelain tiling is indicative of why the technique for reproducing the superior Iznik tiles is impossible. In contrast, the mausoleum of Murad I, son of Orhan and third Ottoman sultan, is elegant in its simplicity. The tomb has a domed central courtyard surrounded by the traditional ambulatory. Upon the request of the sultan, an oculus was designed in the dome to allow the rains to wash over the open tomb, symbolizing his sameness with the plain folk.

After reigning for just 18 days and living the rest of his life in exile, Cem Sultan, the youngest son of Mehmed II, was brought back to Bursa to receive a royal burial in the tomb that had actually been built for Şehzade Mustafa.

The 15th-century *medrese,* now operating as a clinic, was designed around a central courtyard accessible through vaulted arches at the entrance. No one will bother you if you want to take a quick peek, but the main use for this clinic is as a tuberculosis dispensary, so it might be better to do your admiring from the outside.

The Tarihi II Murat Hamamı next to the mosque is still in operation, with separate days designated for men and women.

Çekirge (from the town center, take *dolmuş* marked MURADIYE). Free admission. Tues–Sun 8:30am–noon and 1–5pm.

Orhan Gazi Mosque (Orhan Camii) ★★ MOSQUE Constructed between
1339 and 1340 by Orhan Gazi, this is one of the most important early Ottoman constructions in Bursa. Pointed arches on the veranda show the beginnings of a

particularly Ottoman detail, while the exterior brickwork recalls its Selçuk origins. The mosque was damaged in 1413 by Karamanoğlu Mehmet Bey and repaired in 1417 by Çelebi Sultan Mehmet. Note the star-shaped decorations representing the course of the sun, and the marble embellishments on the eastern and western facades.

The surrounding complex is one of the first in the Ottoman tradition, consisting of a mosque, *medrese*, soup kitchen, bath, and inn. The cats apparently stay there free of charge, and the whole courtyard and mosque interior have a homey feel.

Bursa town center, across from the municipal building. Free admission. Daily dawn–dusk.

Tombs of Osman and Orhan ★ MONUMENT/MEMORIAL   This lovely park attracts local tourists as much for its tea gardens and stunning views as for the **tombs** of the two founders of the Ottoman Empire. The location in the *Hisar* (fortress), the oldest section of the city, which passed from Roman to Byzantine and finally to Ottoman hands, is a fitting one for the final resting places of Osman Gazi and Orhan Gazi.

According to Osman Gazi's wish to be "laid to rest beneath the silver dome of Bursa," his tomb was constructed on the chapel of St. Elie, the Byzantine monastery formerly on the site. The sarcophagus, surrounded by an ornate brass balustrade, is decorated with mother-of-pearl inlay. At one time, the building also contained the tomb of Orhan, but after it was partially destroyed by fire and then leveled by the 1855 earthquake, Sultan Abdülaziz had Orhan's tomb rebuilt separately. The Orhan tomb, slightly less ornate than his father's tomb, was constructed on the foundation of an 11th-century Byzantine church, from which some mosaics in the floor have survived.

Hisar District (inside the entrance to Tophane Park along Arka Sok., just west of the post office). No phone. Free admission. Daily dawn–dusk.

Uluumay Ottoman Folk Costumes and Jewelry Museum (Uluumay Osmanlı Halk Kıyafetleri ve Takıları Müzesi) ★ MUSEUM   The restored architectural gem that is the Sair Ahmet Paşa Medresesi rivals the museum within. Located in the Muradiye Complex, this assemblage of folk art was collected from around the Ottoman Empire, including the Caucuses, the Balkans, and the home territory of Anatolia. There's an ample ethnographic exhibition that features over 400 pieces of Ottoman-era jewelry, plus household items, saddlebags, silk scarves, and silver watch fobs. To name a few.

2 Murat Paşa Cad, in the Sair Ahmet Paşa Medresesi, opposite the Muradiye Camisi, Muradiye. www.uluumay.com. ℂ **0224/222-7575.** Admission 5TL. Tues–Sun 9am–6pm.

Yıldırım Beyazıt Mosque (Yıldırım Beyazıt Camii) MOSQUE   The two prominent domes, set one behind the other, represent an attempt at a design feature reminiscent of the St. Irene of Constantinople and the St. John's Basilica at Ephesus. Awkwardly juxtaposed above the three remaining domes, the larger two create a prayer hall that was to become a theme in the architecture of Ottoman mosques.

The mosque forms a part of the *külliye,* or complex, comprising a *medrese,* a *hamam,* a hospital, and the tomb of the Sultan Beyazıt I, built by his son Süleyman the Magnificent in 1406.

Northeast of the town center in the Yıldırım District. Free admission. Daily dawn–dusk.

WHERE TO EAT
Çiçek Izgara TURKISH/KÖFTE   A Bursa institution since 1963, Çiçek Izgara was borne of a sort of ode to the meatball, until 2005 recited by its creator, Hasan Erdihan Hınçalan. Today, the family continues with Hasan Bey's labor, showcasing

Turkish cuisine by way of the grill. The menu is geared to grilled meats and various shapes of *köfte*, from the *pastırmalı* patties, to the *kuzu şiş* to the staple *izgara köfte*. They also offer a plentiful salad bar, allowing you to taste test your way through the mezes. The restaurant sits right in the center of town, combining three floors of white linen tablecloths and impeccable service right in the historic heart of Bursa.

Belediye Cad. 15, Osmangazi (just after Orhan Camii on the left, 2nd floor). www.cicekizgara.com. ✆ **0224/221-1288.** Kebaps and *köfte* 9TL–19TL. MC, V. Daily 11am–3:30pm and 5–9pm.

Kebapçı Iskender ISKENDER KEBAP This is ground zero for what has ultimately infiltrated into the daily cultural life of not only Turks, but worldwide. It was in 1867 that grandpa Iskender decided to try a new way of roasting lamb: sticking it on a vertical rotating spit (*döner* means revolving), placing strips of it over a bed of pita with tomatoes and yogurt, and pouring an alarming quantity of butter over the top. Thus, the Iskender Kebap was born. The flavorful meats are spiced with aromatic thyme from Uludağ and butter from local dairy farms. Kebapçı Iskender has 7 locations around Bursa, plus two in Istanbul (and one in Balıkeşir).

Ünlü Cad. 7, Heykel, Bursa. www.kebapciiskender.com.tr. ✆ **0224/221-4615.** Iskender kebap 8TL. MC, V. 11:30am–9pm daily.

Uludağ Kebapçısı ★★ KEBAPS The best food is often found in unremarkable, even divelike places. Although Grandpa Iskender, the inventor of the *döner kebap*, has the historical corner on this much-loved recipe, this place has perfected it. Branched out from two contiguous narrow storefronts near the old bus terminal to a second, more generously spaced restaurant in the Bursa City Area Shopping Center, the Uludağ Kebapçısı is arguably the best place in the world to eat the Iskender *döner kebap*. You can order it with decadent slices of steak (*bonfile*), surprisingly delicious kidney (*böbrek*), or what the owner called "back" (*kantıfile*)—but don't complain to me if your cholesterol levels shoot through the roof: Uludağ goes through 18kg (40 lb.) of butter per day.

Garaj Karşısı Uluyol Şirin Sok. 12 (at the former bus terminal). ✆ **0224/251-4551.** Bursa City Area Shopping Center. ✆ **0224/255-5556.** www.uludagkebapcisi.biz. Single portion kebaps 15TL–20TL. MC, V. Daily 11am–6pm (the shopping center location is open until 10pm).

WHERE TO STAY

Çelik Palas Hotel ★★ Built in the 1930s under instructions by Atatürk, the Çelik Palas holds the title as Turkey's first five-star hotel. But it was a long road in getting there. After years of neglect, the hotel began to show its dubious pedigree in the '90s and early 2000s. It took a series of halfhearted renovations to occur before the current owner put its money where its mouth is. This grand old hotel is new once again, gleaming with a modernized take on a pleasing, art deco style, making the hotel once again the destination hotel of Bursa. Ask for a high floor to enjoy the city or mountain views, and then head straight to the domed, **marble thermal pool,** the crowned jewel of the hotel's deluxe wellness facility (see "Water, Water Everywhere: Turkey's Mineral Springs," below).

Çekirge Cad. 79, 16070 Çekirge. www.celikpalasotel.com. ✆ **0224/233-3800.** Fax 0224/236-1910. 141 units. 120€–140€ double; 175€–400€ suite. AE, MC, V. Free parking. **Amenities:** Restaurants; bar; concierge; *hamam;* indoor and outdoor pools; room service; smoke-free rooms; spa with historic thermal bath. *In room:* A/C, satellite TV, hair dryer, minibar, free Wi-Fi.

Kervansaray Termal Hotel For years, what was once the preferred hotel in Bursa, has rested on its laurels. After all, it was large, inviting, and best of all, has a

WATER, WATER EVERYWHERE: TURKEY'S MINERAL springs

A geologic oddity-cum-spa-treat with which Turkey is uncommonly blessed is the mineral spring. Thermal baths flow freely throughout the countryside and, depending on the properties and temperature of the water, are reputed to address such varied ailments as obesity, digestive problems, rheumatism, and urological disorders. Soaking in the springs and covering yourself with mineral-rich mud are some of the country's lesser-known pleasures. You can experience the thermal springs enclosed in pamper-me surroundings or in humble out-of-the-way sites.

In Bursa, history and pampering go hand in hand, and no historical pilgrimage to this city would be complete without a long soak in a mineral-rich thermal pool. The **Kervansaray Termal Hotel's 700-year-old thermal bath** ★★ (p. 183) takes advantage of the **Eski Kaplıca** thermal spring, an ancient source used as far back as Roman times. The bath was built in grand Ottoman style by Sultan Murat I in 1389, and a soak here (7am–11pm) is made all the more satisfying with its multiple domes and old stonemasonry. The price of admission to the thermal baths is 20TL for women and 28TL for men. Add 15TL each for massage and *kese*.

The more luxurious **Çelik Palas Hotel thermal pool** ★★ (p. 183) rests beneath a single multiple-sky-lit dome, a crowned jewel of pure, marble-clad indulgence. The thermal is ensconced within the hotel's spa, offering a seamless wellness experience enjoyed by guests and non-guests alike.

No one knows who originally occupied the **Yeni Kaplıca hamam** ★★, Yeni Kaplıca Cad. 6, Çekirge (✆ **0224/236-6968**), built in 1555 and reconstructed for Süleyman the Magnificent by Grand Vizier Rüstem Paşa. The *hamam* (or at least, the men's side) still displays its original opulence, allowing wide-eyed tourists to feel like Julius Caesar for a day.

Separated from the Yeni Kaplıca building by a tea garden is the less-impressive **Kaynarca (**Yeni Kaplıca Cad. 8 (✆ **0224/ 236-6955)** essentially a mud pit with locker rooms.

Kara Mustafa Paşa Thermal Bath, Mudanya Cad. 10 (✆ **0224/236-6956**), was left over from the Byzantine era and was actually the first building on the site. There are two sections, including one where you can ooze yourself into a grave-like tile ditch full of scorching hot mud (avoid wearing a white bathing suit for this). There are also the regular bath facilities and cubicles for changing and resting. Kara Mustafa also has rudimentary hotel accommodations. Granted, it's all rather gritty, but thoroughly worth the experience.

700-year old *hamam* as an adjunct to the property. As a result, the Kervansaray became the default host to group tours. They did complete some renovations in 2008, but it appears that they didn't get to all of the rooms (most of which have a balcony with a valley, mountain, or garden view). The health club's cleverly designed swimming pool is divided by a retractable window, providing for both indoor and outdoor swimming, and the water is supplied by nearby mineral springs. As a hotel catering to groups, not surprisingly it's also got meeting and banquet facilities, a shopping arcade, and salon.

Çekirge Meydanı, 16080 Çekirge. www.kervansarayhotels.com. ✆ **0224/233-9300.** Fax 0224/233-9324. 211 units. 150€ double; 250€ and up suite; rates lower June–Dec, higher for religious festivals.

AE, MC, V. Free parking. **Amenities:** 5 restaurants; 2 bars; historic thermal bath w/separate sections for men and women; concierge; health club; outdoor pool; room service. *In room:* A/C, satellite TV, hair dryer, minibar, free Wi-Fi.

Kitap Evi ★★ 📠   Once a sanctuary for the written word, this restored Ottoman wooden house is now a refuge of serenity providing the world weary with comfort, in modern and typical, Turkish style. The building sits atop the crumbling remains of Bursa's ancient fortress. Each of the 11 rooms tempts a different sense, offering space, light, and Ottoman character. Most of the rooms overlook the garden, while the lucky few get to look out over the architectural jewels of the city. Five o'clock tea is served daily in the garden shaded of the magnolia and linden trees, or adjacent to a fireplace in cooler weather.

Kavaklı Mah. Bur Üstü 21, 16040 Bursa (next to the Sultanat Kapı). www.kitapevi.com.tr. © **0224/ 225-4160.** Fax 0224/220-8650. 11 units. 120€–150€ double; 190€–220€ suite. AE, MC, V. Free parking. **Amenities:** Restaurant; bar; *hamam;* massage.

Iznik & Nicaea: A Pilgrimage & Some Plates

To Turks, the sleepy lakeside resort of Iznik provides a respite from the sweltering summer sun; to Christendom, Iznik sits atop modern-day **Nicaea,** the former seat of the Eastern Roman Empire and the site of the first and second Ecumenical councils. It's also synonymous with Ottoman ceramic art, which reached its pinnacle in the 15th and 16th centuries during the reign of Süleyman the Magnificent. While you're here, you should take the time to have lunch at one of the lakeside restaurants.

GETTING THERE & GETTING AROUND *Dolmuşes* regularly depart from Yalova from the main road that passes in front of the ferryboat landing (cross the street and hop on one headed south) as well as from Bursa. Once in Iznik, buses deposit passengers on the main road in front of the church. Drivers should take the car ferry from Istanbul to Yalova. From Yalova, follow the road to Bursa taking the first turnoff at Orhangazi to Iznik and follow the road along the north side of the lake.

Iznik retains the grid plan established in its Hellenistic era. Monuments are well signposted, but without a car, you'll be pounding the pavement for the better part of a day.

WHAT TO SEE & DO

Ancient Nicaea RELIGIOUS SITE   The ancient city of Nicaea and modern-day Iznik are enclosed along the eastern edge of Lake Iznik by about 5km (3 miles) of **ancient city walls ★,** made accessible through several ancient gates of which the **Istanbul Kapısı ★** is the best preserved. In the center of town are the well preserved remains of the **Church of Hagia Sophia ★★** the 11th-century church that served as the Patriarchate during the period of Byzantine exile following the Fourth Crusade. Excavations conducted in 1935, however, revealed traces of an older structure dating to the 6th century A.D. and attributed to Justinian. The church, which served as a mosque after the Ottoman conquest in 1330–1331, remained a roofless artifact until recent work to restore the roof and dome were complete. The building is now up and running again as a mosque. Inside, parts of the original mosaic flooring and a partially exposed fresco of the Pantocrator in the niche of the left aisle are still visible.

Near the southwest corner of the church (across the street) are partially uncovered outdoor tile-production workshops from as early as the 15th century. Many of the **brick and mud kilns** are still intact.

The **Yeşil Camii** dates to the late 14th century and displays a minaret covered with tiles in a colorful zigzag pattern. Unfortunately, these are not originals, as the actual tiles were destroyed. Across the street is the **Nilüfer Hatun Imareti,** built by Murat I and named after his mother, wife of Orhan Gazi and a Greek princess in her own right. Originally used as a charitable foundation and soup kitchen, the well restored *imaret* (soup kitchen) now contains the **Iznik Museum** (admission 3TL), harboring a small collection of Roman and Byzantine artifacts and remnants from nearby burial mounds. There's also a small collection of Iznik tiles, as well as several ethnological items.

Thirty years of excavations have barely made a dent in the uncovering of the **Roman Theatre,** built by Pliny the Younger between 111 and 113 during his time as governor of Bithynia. Rather than building the theater into the side of a hill, the theater was constructed using vaults.

Tourist Information Office: Kılıçarslan Cad. Iznik, Bursa. Iznik Tourism Information Office. ✆**0224/757-1933.**

The Iznik Foundation FACTORY TOUR Tiles, richly decorated with floral designs and colors recalling precious gems, served as architectural decoration in the palace, mosques, tombs, and other buildings with a predominantly religious function. (The sultan was also the caliph, extending religious function to the palace.) For this reason, Iznik ceramics represent one of the most important examples of Islamic art. Sadly, with the decline of the economic and political power of the Ottoman Empire, artisans and ateliers became less and less in demand, and ultimately the techniques used to make the ceramics were lost.

Thanks to the Iznik Foundation, this great artistic tradition is enjoying a steady revival. The foundation, which consists of an educational facility, a research laboratory, and a commercial center, has invested an enormous amount of energy in researching the technologies necessary for achieving success in each complex step of production. One of the first challenges is the acquisition of the raw materials, as authentic Iznik pieces contain a high ratio of quartz, a semiprecious stone. The remaining obstacles are technical, involving the proper ratio of quartz, the chemical composition of each pigment, and the correct application of heat (each pigment must be fired at a different temperature). Ottoman artisans labored their entire lives to perfect just one aspect of the product, with one person expert in the creation of coral red, another in cobalt blue, and yet another in maintaining accurate and consistent heat to a wood-fired kiln made of brick. The foundation's finished products are faithful copies of the originals that sell at prices competitive with the inferior products sold in Avanos, a town in the interior of Anatolia. The price of a plate or tile at the foundation can reach the stratosphere, but remember, these are made of quartz, while the fakes are made of clay. The foundation office is open to visitors. They also have a main office in Istanbul at Cengiz Topel Cad. Tuğcular Sok. 1/A, Etiler (✆ **0212/287-3243**).

Sahil Yolu Vakıf Sok. 13, Iznik. www.iznik.com. ✆**0224/757-6025.** Fax 0224/757-5737. Free admission.

The Princes' Islands

The Princes' Islands are a slice of seaside heaven far from the chaos and scorching sun of the city yet only a hop, skip, and a jump from Istanbul. For some reason, ancients and Ottomans banished their prisoners to the most idyllic spots; the islands were originally used as a place of exile for members of the royalty and clergy during the age of Byzantium. They were later taken over by the more clever residents of the city as summer homes. The atmosphere is one of pure repose thanks to the prohibition against vehicles; the only form of transportation on Büyükada (besides your own steam) is the characteristic and enchanting horse-drawn phaeton. In summer, the islands' populations swell with weekenders eager to stake out a lounge chair on one of the islands' many marvelous beaches. And thanks to the introduction of seabuses that shorten the ferry trip by an hour, the islands are only a half-hour away, making them an accessible retreat from city life.

GETTING THERE Conventional **City Lines/Sehir Hatları** ferries (℃ 444-1851; www.sehirhatlari.com) depart from Kabataş making stops at Kadıköy on the Asian side before puddle-jumping the islands of Kınalıada, Burgazada, Heybeliada, and finally Büyükada. The ride all the way to Büyükada takes about 90 minutes and costs 4TL each way (3TL with the Akbil). **IDO** fast ferries (℃ 444-4436; www.ido.com.tr) depart for the islands from the Kabataş docks adjacent to Dolmabahçe Palace and from Bostancı on the Asian side. The ride from Kabataş to Büyükada takes an hour (one departure in winter and two in spring and summer) and costs a mere 8TL (6.50TL with the Akbil) each way, a pittance considering that seats are reserved compared to the body shuffle inevitable on the more crowded slow boat. Be sure to confirm all departure times in advance, as schedules may change).

EXPLORING THE PRINCES' ISLANDS Thanks to the absence of motorized vehicles, the islands have managed to retain their old-world charm. Horse-drawn carriages serve as local taxis, and bicycles share the meandering roads with domestic donkeys. As expected, Istanbullus inundate the islands in summer, looking to enjoy the architecture of the many Victorian-style clapboard mansions and a relaxing day at the beach.

Big Island, or Büyükada, is the largest of the five islands and the one most inundated during high season. There are several good beaches, diving facilities, pine forests, churches dating from the 16th through the 19th centuries, lovely neoclassical seaside residences, and the old orphanage, originally built in 1898 as a hotel. The crown of the island is the hilltop monastery of Ayayorgi (St. George), a 202m (663-ft.) elevation from which you can almost see all the way back to Istanbul. To get to the monastery, take a carriage to Luna Park and take the 30-minute uphill path to Ayayorgi Peak (via donkey from the bustle of the open square at the base of the hill, if you wish, about 15TL) where you can sip their homemade wine while enjoying the panorama at the monastery's simple restaurant on the hill. One of the highlights of any visit to Büyükada is to tour the island from the back of a phaeton, serenaded by the clip clopping of your horse on the cobbled streets (50TL). To better appreciate what the islands have to offer, organize your excursion for a weekday, when the ferries are not packed like sardine cans and you can still get a glimpse of the sand beneath the blankets of the other sun worshippers. In the fall a stroll along deserted cobblestone lanes met by the occasional donkey cart or a friendly pack of stray dogs transports you back in time.

Kınalıada was the site of a major human rights infraction—the Byzantines gouged out the eyes of and exiled Romanos Diogenes IV here for his defeat by the Selçuks in the Battle of Manzikert. The monastery built for the unfortunate general is still standing. The island was raided many times by pirates and later inhabited mainly by Armenians, but because of a harsh climate, it has attracted fewer people than the other islands. Electricity first came to the island in 1946, and it wasn't until the 1980s that the island received a water supply from the municipality. Kınalıada is also the only one of the Princes' Islands without the services of the 19th-century phaetons.

Burgazada is the second of the Princes' Islands, originally settled as a Greek fishing village. In the 1950s the island attracted the wealthy Jews of Istanbul, who restored existing mansions or built their own. The island is also the home of a famous Turkish writer, Sait Faik, whose home has been turned into a museum. There are two swim clubs near the ferry landing, but if it's beaches you're after, you'll be better off on one of the other islands.

Heybeliada is the island closest to Büyükada and similar in that the natural beauty attracts boatloads of weekenders in the summer. The waterside promenade ensures a steady stream of visitors looking to avoid the crowds on Büyükada, but aside from a few eateries, you'll have to make this a day trip or book a room on Büyükada anyway.

WHERE TO EAT   Restaurants specializing in fish line the wharf to the left of the ferry landing, for breezy and atmospheric waterside dining. **Milano Restaurant,** Gülistan Cad. 8, Büyükada (℗ **0216/382-6352**) has been here for more than 35 years and is the most famous restaurant on the island. Better yet, gobble up some working man's fare at **SofrAda** (Isa Çelebi Sok. 10; ℗ **0216/382-7639**), located down the same street as the Marine Hotel.

WHERE TO STAY   Fantasy becomes reality on Büyükada, the biggest of the islands but not so built up that you want to avoid it. That's why the listings here are all on the "Big Island." The **Splendid Palace Hotel,** 23 Nisan Cad. (turn right at the Büyükada Princess Hotel and drop your jaw at the white domed mansion on your left; ℗ **0216/382-6950;** fax 0216/382-6775; www.splendidhotel.net), is a palatial clapboard house with views of the Marmara with peaceful gardens, a private swimming pool, two restaurants, and an on-site patisserie. It's closed November through March. The **Büyükada Princess Hotel,** Iskele Meydanı 2 (straight up the street from the ferry landing on the right; ℗ **0216/382-1628;** fax 0216/382-1949; www.worldof princess.com), is a more modest but gracious seaside lodge and is open year-round. There's a small pool overlooking the Marmara Sea for use in the summer months. If you want to have a more homey experience, head to the **Naya Istanbul,** Yilmaz Türk Cad. 96, Aya Nikola Mevkii (℗ **0216/382-4598;** www.nayaistanbul.com; rooms from 60€ per night double).

ÇANAKKALE, GALLIPOLI & THE TROAD

The Troad is the ancient name for the region that included Troy plus nearly 100 other ancient cities (most still deprived of the light of day). Among the most important of these are Assos, Alexandria Troas, Dardanos, and Chryse, spread out amidst olive groves, fertile plains, undulating mountains, and crystal seas. The city of **Çanakkale** presides over a region that for centuries—even millennia—was forced to defend a legacy of geographical advantage. The region became victim to the ambitions of empires, as emperors and armies swept through to stake their claims.

The lands of Turkey's Northern Aegean provided the first taste of Asia to those successful in crossing the Bosphorus or breaching the Dardanelle Straits, and the last obstacle to any attempted conquest of Istanbul, as an army's advancement into the Marmara region left the great city surrounded and isolated. Throughout history, each of these civilizations left its own personal mark, from Xerxes through Alexander the Great to Fatih Mehmet the Conqueror. The layers of culture superimposed over the pastoral countryside make for an enriching visit to any of the destinations outlined in this chapter. Plus, the Hellespont boasts some of the Aegean's most scenic beaches.

This region of the country (Troy notwithstanding), while popular among the city slickers of Istanbul, remains blissfully ignored by the tourist hoards, leaving you and me to still (for now) experience the Turkey of yesteryear—before its era of Europeanization. But in spite of the area's treasures, potential visitors see to ask one question: Should I go to Troy? If you're crunched for time, there are certainly more fabulous archaeological sites you could see. On the other hand, it's possible to make any of the destinations in this chapter an overnight or weekend trip, and literally hundreds of tour companies in Istanbul advertise affordable day or overnight excursions with guides.

ÇANAKKALE

15km (9⅓ miles) north of Troy; 325km (202 miles) southwest of Istanbul; 331km (206 miles) north of Izmir; 303km (188 miles) west of Bursa

This charming little port city in the Dardanelles is also the gateway to the battlefields of Gallipoli and the ill-fated city of Troy. When not touring, there's much to enjoy in this corner of the northern Aegean, with easy access to a handful of resort islands.

A visit to the area begins in and around the small fishing port and holiday resort of Çanakkale. There are a handful of satisfactory bed-and-breakfast-style hotels in the city center, conveniently located near transport and tour companies offering guided tours to Troy and Gallipoli (p. 194).

There's not much else to do in town except visit the Naval Museum and Çimenlik Castle, take a ferry over to Kilitbahir Castle on the opposite side of the Dardanelles, or stroll up and down the promenade while waiting for your day tour to Troy. Extremely minor highlights are the Clock Tower; a gift to the town from the Italian Consulate; the model of the Trojan horse used in the film *Troy,* starring Brad Pitt; and the adjacent small model of the archeological site of Troy. Çanakkale also has its own archaeological museum, but the best of the area artifacts are, sadly, elsewhere.

In the summer months, visitors can take advantage of the lovely seaside villages surrounding Çanakkale for relaxation, diving, swimming, or simply sitting in the shade of the pine trees surrounded by olive groves and Mediterranean flora.

Essentials
GETTING THERE
BY PLANE   Turkish Airlines (ⓒ 444-0849 or 0286/214-0458 at the airport; www. thy.com) makes the 45-minute flight from Istanbul three times a week on Mondays, Wednesdays, and Fridays in summer only. It is now also possible to fly direct from Ankara on **Bora Jet** (www.borajet.com.tr; ⓒ 444-2672), year round.

The airport is located 3km (1¾ miles) outside of the center of town. There are taxis at the airport, as well as bus C8 which heads directly to the ferry docks/clock tower in the center of town (walking distance to the Anzac and Karavansary hotels, recommended in "Where to Stay"). From here you can either arrange a tour or transport to the battlefields. The main number for the airport is ⓒ **0286/213-1021.**

BY BUS   The major bus companies serving Çanakkale are **Çanakkale Truva** (ⓒ 444-0017 or ⓒ 0286/217-7778 at the *otogar;* www.truvaturizm.com), **Metro** (ⓒ 444-3455), and **Kamıl Koç** (ⓒ 444-0562 or ⓒ 0286/213-7500). The ride from Istanbul takes about 5 to 6 hours (after a short ferry ride across the Dardanelles) with drop-offs at the Çanakkale ferry dock, located in the bull's-eye of town. All other buses stop at the *otogar,* about 4km (2 miles) east of the town center. (The one exception is the minibus to Troy, which continues to depart from the same location under the bridge in the city center). All of the national bus companies offer a free shuttle from the *otogar* to the ferry docks." Taxis are also plentiful, and cost around 25TL to 30TL one way.

BY CAR   From Istanbul, take the E6 highway (toll road) toward Edirne. Exit at Kinali, and follow the road through Tekirdağ, Malkara, and Kesan. Follow the road through Gelibolu to the turnoff at Gelibolu for the hourly and daily car ferry to Lapseki (20TL per car), where you will take the coastal road south 30km (19 miles) to Çanakkale. Or, instead of taking the turnoff to Gelibolu, continue through to Ecebat, with hourly car ferry service between 7am and midnight (then every other hr.) direct to Çanakkale (23TL per car). For updated schedules and fares, log on to the website of the ferry company **Gestaş Deniz Ulaşim** (ⓒ 444-0752 or ⓒ **0286/814-1033** in Eceabat; www.gestasdenizulasim.com.tr).

VISITOR INFORMATION

The **tourist information office** (✆ 0286/217-1187) is on the main square across from the ferry docks. For emergency traveler's check situations, thank the PTT (post office) for providing a kiosk next to the ferry ticket office.

ORIENTATION

The city of Çanakkale is divided by the somewhat commercialized Demircioğlu Caddesi, which leads directly to Cumhuriyet Meydanı and the ferry docks. The clock tower, 1 block in and slightly to the west of this junction, is a good meeting point for groups.

GETTING AROUND

ON FOOT Çanakkale revolves around the port and extends, roughly, from the Naval Museum to the south and just north of the Trojan Horse—gifted to the city of Çanakkale in 2004 by the production staff of the epic movie starring Brad Pitt. Behind the wooden horse is a model of the seven layers of Troy.

BY TAXI Taxis for travel within the small city limits are metered; however, taxi rates are fixed according to the destination for travel beyond Çanakkale. If the rates seem blown out of proportion to you, try to negotiate a better rate with your driver.

What to See & Do

Archaeological Museum (Arkeoloji Müzesi) MUSEUM I'm not one to admire tchotchkes (there are more than 30,000 of them), so if you're on bone-carved hairpins and carved stele overload, skip this museum. The collection does contain an impressive exhibit of surprisingly detailed terra-cotta statuettes and well-preserved glass perfume bottles salvaged from the ruins of 200 area sites, as well as a trifling fraction of the artifacts Heinrich Schliemann dug up at Troy, along the coast.

Barbaros Mah. 100 Yıl Cad. (Located about 1.5km/1 mile out of the town center, on the road to Troy). ✆ **0286/217-6565.** Admission 5TL. Tues–Sun 8am–5pm.

Naval Museum (Deniz Müzesi), Military Museum (Askeri Müzesi), and Çimenlik Castle (Çimenlik Kalesi) CASTLE The Army Museum houses various types of war paraphernalia such as uniforms, medals, and weapons, but unless you're a war geek, the most interesting part of the exhibit is just inside the main entrance. There's a model of the Gallipoli Campaign, above which are various plaques in English with attention-grabbing anecdotes and quotes of the various battleground memorials. One recounts the story of how on August 10, 1915, Atatürk received a direct hit to the heart, but a pocket watch that he was carrying shielded him from the bullet and certain death. Other sources say it was shrapnel from the doomed 57th Regiment battle, while still others say the whole story is a load of crap. According to the debatable inscription in this museum, the shattered watch is now part of Army Commander General Limon von Sander's family collection.

Next to the Naval Museum is a replica of the 365-ton *Nusrat,* the minelayer that gets the credit for saving the day against invading British warships during the sea offensive. After the war, the underappreciated *Nusrat* was used as a lowly freight carrier and finally capsized in April 1990.

Çimenlik Castle, along with the **Kilitbahir Castle** on the opposite banks of the straits (admission 3TL), was constructed by Mehmet II (the Conqueror) in the 15th century as a strategic prelude to his assault on Constantinople. The castle grounds are full of old cannons from the battles, and if you venture into one of those dark passages, you can get a glimpse of the Turkish positions, as well as the sections of the roof that were destroyed by incoming artillery.

Çimenlik Park. www.denizmuzeleri.tsk.tr/cdmk. © **0286/213-1730.** Admission to museums 3TL. Museums Tues–Wed and Fri–Sun 9am–noon and 1:30–5pm. Park daily 9am–noon and 1:30–5pm.

Where to Eat

Most of the hotels located outside of the city center come with half-board (breakfast and dinner). At the lower end, any *lokanta* is a good bet. While you're in town, don't pass up a taste of the creamy sweet **peynerli helvasi,** a local dessert specialty of cheese and semolina.

Gülen Pide & Kebap TURKISH   This restaurant is a bit fancier than the basic *lokantas* around town, with a menu that covers a predictable but reliable variety of grilled and stewed meats. They've also got *lahmacun*, Turkey's version of thin-crust pizza with chopped lamb and onions for 2.5TL a piece. It's the only proper establishment where you can have an informal sit-down meal without breaking the bank.

Cumhuriyet Meydanı 31, 2 blocks east of the ferry docks. © **0286/212-8800.** Kebabs 6.50TL–13TL. MC, V. Daily noon–midnight.

Yalova Restaurant TURKISH   From a seaside shack to an institution in Çanakkale, the Yalova is reputed to have the best fish in town. The mezes and nonfish selections are also top-notch. Take advantage of dining under a beautiful sunset from the rooftop terrace of this historic fish house.

On the quay south of the main square, entrance on Gümrük Sok. 7. www.yalovarestaurant.com. © **0286/217-1045.** Prix fixe menu 20TL–30TL; 25TL–40TL for fish. AE, MC, V. Daily 1pm–midnight.

Where to Stay
CITY CENTER
Anzac Hotel ✦   This hotel—not to be confused with the backpacker haven Anzac House—sits literally in the shadow of the Italianate Clock Tower. Rooms were renovated in 2004 and offer more quality than you'd expect from a budget option. Think orthopedic mattresses, LCD TVs, and sea views from a handful of the rooms. The hospitality is tireless; if you prefer historic digs, stay over at the hotel's second hotel, the Kervansaray (see below) or their newest addition to the Anzac Hotel chain, the **Grand Anzac** (© **0286/216-0016;** www.grandanzachotel.com), a glistening, full-service hotel in a renovated building with all the creature comforts a visitor could desire (doubles 45€ –50€).

Saat Kulesi Meydanı 8, 17001 Çanakkale (across from the Clock Tower). www.anzachotel.com. © **0286/217-7777.** Fax 0286/217-2018. 27 units. 35€–45€ double. Rates higher the week of Anzac Day and national holidays. MC, V. Free parking. **Amenities:** Restaurant; bar; concierge; room service. *In room:* A/C, satellite TV, minibar, free Wi-Fi.

Kervansaray   It was about time for Çanakkale to get a charming hotel, and this is it. Located just steps from everything, the Kervansaray—or at least the street-side building—was originally the stately mansion of an esteemed Ottoman judge. Now restored, rooms boast high ceilings, decorative moldings, and modern character. There's a large enclosed garden separating the house from the newer addition at back, and what these rooms lack in historic character they make up for in comfort and dependability. Bathrooms in these back rooms offer comfy European sit-in tub showers, while the "main house" has rooms with showers only.

Kemalpaşa Mah. Fetvane Sok. 13, 17001 Çanakkale (down the street from the Anzac Hotel). www. otelkervansaray.com. ✆ **0286/217-8192.** Fax 0286/217-2018. 19 units. 50€–55€ double. Rates higher the week of Anzac Day and national holidays. MC, V. Free parking. **Amenities:** Garden cafe; laundry service; room service. *In room:* A/C, satellite TV, hair dryer, minibar, free Wi-Fi.

KEPEZ & GÜZELYALI (OUTSIDE ÇANAKKALE)

Ida Kale   Located about halfway between town (15km/9⅓ miles) and Troy (20km/12 miles), the Ida Kale is a good beachfront option with easy accessibility to all of the major sites. It's owned and operated by a national tile company, a fact that plays out in the decor—bathrooms are wall-to-wall tile, as are the floors. Rooms are spacious, as are the bathrooms with large tubs.

Mola Cad. Güzelyalı, Çanakkale. www.kaleresort.com. ✆ **0286/232-8332.** Fax 0286/232-8832. 84 units. 65€–100€ double (includes breakfast and dinner). MC, V. **Amenities:** 2 restaurants; bar; beach; exercise room; outdoor pool; room service; tennis. *In room:* A/C, satellite TV, hair dryer, minibar, free Wi-Fi.

Tusan Hotel ★   The Tusan is surrounded by pine forest and perched on a cliff overlooking the Çanakkale Straits. Each of the rooms has a balcony or patio with both sea and forest views. All rooms were renovated in 2002. During your downtime, there are billiards, a fitness room, and an assortment of private beachside terraces accessible via a footpath. The hotel serves lunch and dinner, and all meals can be taken on either the indoor or outdoor terrace. For those without a car, *dolmuşes* pass by the main road approximately every 15 minutes. Otherwise, the only nuisances will be the nighttime chirping of the crickets, and possible soreness from the on-site kayaking, windsurfing, or diving.

Güzelyalı, 17001 Çanakkale (about 9.5km/6 miles out of Çanakkale on the road to Izmir). www. tusanhotel.com. ✆ **0286/232-8746.** Fax 0286/232-8226. 64 units. 75€ double. MC, V. Free on-site parking. **Amenities:** 2 restaurants; bar; beach; concierge; exercise room; room service. *In room:* A/C, cable TV, hair dryer, minibar.

THE GALLIPOLI BATTLEFIELDS (GELIBOLU) ★★★

15km (9⅓ miles) north of Çanakkale; 310km (193 miles) southwest of Istanbul

For millennia, the Dardanelles have been a strategic point of contention—from King Xerxes of Persia, who in the 5th century B.C. created a bridge of boats to transport his troops to Greece; to Alexander the Great, who swept into Asia from the West in 334 B.C. Mehmet the Conqueror knew the tactical value of the straits as well and had two fortresses built as part of his plan to subdue Constantinople.

In modern times, Çanakkale was once again forced onto the front lines with an Allied campaign to take the Dardanelles during WWI. The battlefields of the **Gallipoli Peninsula** theater became a tragic site for all involved, with almost 200,000 fallen in 8 months. Yet at 86,000 deaths, in spite of taking the heaviest losses, the Turks, led by a gutsy lieutenant colonel named Mustafa Kemal (better known as Atatürk), ferociously repelled the assault on their homeland, and a new nation was born.

The name Gallipoli means different things to different nations. For the Australian and New Zealand Army Corps (or Anzacs), who suffered the largest numbers of Allied casualties, Gallipoli is a national icon. For Turks, Gallipoli represents above all

5

ÇANAKKALE, GALLIPOLI & THE TROAD

The Gallipoli Battlefields

A visit to Gallipoli can either be approached as an overnight excursion from Istanbul (usually centered around Çanakkale and attached to a visit to Troy) or independently. Tours depart Istanbul at 6:30am and arrive at the battlefields around lunchtime. It's a long day arriving back in Istanbul after midnight, which is why most people opt in for the overnight in Çanakkale for the next morning's tour of Troy, with buses arriving back in Istanbul around 6pm. The day trip (Gallipoli only) costs 89€ per person, while the full overnight tour (both Gallipoli and Troy) costs from 119€. If you want to make your own arrangements (bus, car, hotel, dining) and only want a tour of the sites, tours to both sites run daily even in winter. If you're game for a crushing, crowded, and memorably solemn experience, join the hoards of Aussies and Kiwis headed to Gallipoli on April 25 to commemorate the tragic landing of the Australian and New Zealand Army Corps (ANZAC) at Gallipoli during WWI. The main agencies specializing in Gallipoli and Troy tours (including from Istanbul) are **Hassle Free Travel Agency,** located in Çanakkale at Cumhuriyet Cad. 61 ((𝒞 **0286/213-5969**) and on Akbıyık Cad. 41/2, **Sultanahmet,** in Istanbul ((𝒞 **0212/458-9500;** www. anzachouse.com), **TJ's Tours** ((𝒞 **0286/ 814-3121;** www.anzacgallipolitours.com) with whom you can independently schedule both the Gallipoli and the Troy tour in 1 day, and **Fez Travel** (www.fez travel.com; in Istanbul: Akbıyık Cad. 17, Sultanahmet, (𝒞 **0212/520-0434;** in Eceabat: Ismetpaşa Mah. Zubeyde Hanım Meydanı 20, (𝒞 **0286/814-1872**), running good quality budget options.

victory by Turkish forces, many of whom were simple farmers, in defending their homeland. But the battlefields of the Gallipoli Peninsula are a solemn reminder to visitors of all nationalities of the brutality of war: jagged cliffs, pockmarked hills, and sprawling valleys where a handful of the scorched earth will most certainly bring up a piece of shrapnel. It was on these fateful shores in 1915 that Australian and New Zealand landing boats went afoul of their intended landing point, unknowingly forced northward where instead of a beach, the troops encountered impossibly vertical cliffs and enemy fire. In spite of the odds, the Anzac troops managed to grab a toehold on the heights, bravely holding out for 249 days until the massacre of the last soldier. The peninsula is now a national park home to 31 war cemeteries and a number of important monuments. The peninsula is accessible by car or bus from Istanbul, and by ferry from the nearby town of Çanakkale on the Asian side of the Dardanelles.

Each year on April 25 the anniversary of the Anzacs' landing is commemorated on the battlefields. The day marks a series of memorial services at a number of the grave sites. Passenger cars are not permitted entry on this day.

For a self-guided tour of Gallipoli, you'll need a car, as the various battlefields, cemeteries, and memorials are spread out over an area of nearly 332 sq. km (128 sq. miles). It's also possible to sign up for guided tours (see info below) or hire a taxi (about 130TL in high season for a half-day unguided tour of the Anzac battlefields).

Essentials
GETTING THERE
By Car   It is inadvisable (and next to impossible) to rely on the ferry/*dolmuş* from Çanakkale to tour the battlefields, an expanse of approximately 73 sq. km (28 sq.

The Gallipoli Peninsula

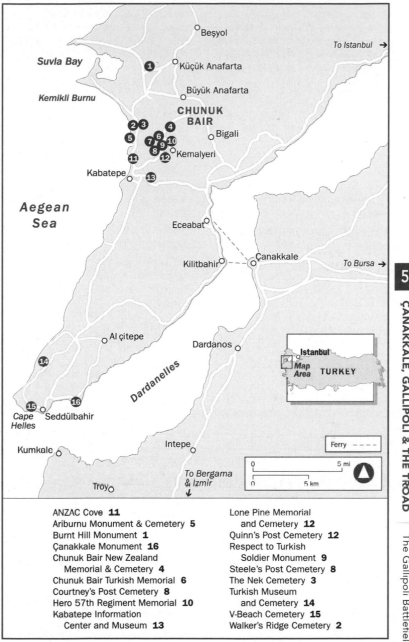

ANZAC Cove **11**
Ariburnu Monument & Cemetery **5**
Burnt Hill Monument **1**
Çanakkale Monument **16**
Chunuk Bair New Zealand
   Memorial & Cemetery **4**
Chunuk Bair Turkish Memorial **6**
Courtney's Post Cemetery **8**
Hero 57th Regiment Memorial **10**
Kabatepe Information
   Center and Museum **13**

Lone Pine Memorial
   and Cemetery **12**
Quinn's Post Cemetery **12**
Respect to Turkish
   Soldier Monument **9**
Steele's Post Cemetery **8**
The Nek Cemetery **3**
Turkish Museum
   and Cemetery **14**
V-Beach Cemetery **15**
Walker's Ridge Cemetery **2**

miles). To drive to the battlefields from Istanbul, take the E6 highway (toll road) toward Edirne and exit at Kınalı. Follow signs for Tekirdağ, passing through Malkara to Kesan, where you will follow signs for Çanakkale. You can either cross the Dardanelles at Gelibolu, (take the Gelibolu exit and follow signs for the hourly/daily car ferry to Lapseki, then from Lapseki follow the coastal road south about 30km/19 miles to Çanakkale) or continue on the road to Eceabat for the car ferry into Çanakkale's centrally located jetty opposite the clock tower. The Eceabat ferry runs between 7am and midnight, then every other hour. (Both ferries cost 23TL; 20 min.).

VISITOR INFORMATION

Visitors to the park should stop at one of the two information centers at the start of their visit. The **Kabatepe Tanıtma Merkezi ve Müzesi** (✆ **0286/814-1297**) is 24km (15 miles) northwest of Eceabat, on a cliff overlooking Anzac Cove and the village of Kabatepe. This location—above Brighton Beach where the Anzac troops were supposed to land—is where you should begin your visit. The information center and memorial grounds claim the plateau that was the objective of the failed operation. The commanding hilltop was heavily fortified with Turkish artillery, but today remains eerily silent, with a few notable monuments and spectacular views of the cliffs.

There's also a visitor center at Çamburnu (**Gelibolu Tarihi Milli Parkı Ana Tanıtma Merkezi;** ✆ **0286/814-1960**), located about 1km (⅔ mile) south of Eceabat. Both have small **museums** (admission 3TL; daily 9am–1pm and 2–6pm) housing examples of the battlefield's detritus along with uniforms and old photographs. Your time is better spent outside. Visits to the battlefields are free.

For a virtual panoramic tour, log on to www.kulturturizm.gov.tr or www.canakkale.gov.tr. The latter has a website completely dedicated to the Gallipoli Campaign.

Exploring the Battlefields

In the power struggle that emerged during World War I, the Russians, who up until then were forced to sail through the icy waters of the Baltic Sea, aligned themselves with the British, hoping to gain a year-round, ice-free passage via the Dardanelles and into Europe's burgeoning commercial arena. For the Allies, control of Istanbul and the straits meant exposing the flanks of Germany and Austria-Hungary, cutting off their oil supply, and forcing Turkey out of the war (and maybe getting a little caviar from the deal as well).

The fact that Vice Admiral John de Robeck's head-on attack of the Dardanelles failed was as much due to Imperial British overconfidence as to Turkish good fortune. Assuming the enemy would crumble at the sight of the great Royal Navy, the admiral sent in a fleet of 16 ships, most of which were just shy of retirement and manned with inexperienced crews. On March 18, 1915, the battleship *Queen Elizabeth* led the fleet into battle. Four of the ships were damaged or sunk by Turkish mines. After 8 futile hours, shortly before the Turkish army would have run out of ammunition, the British Navy called it a day; however, they did not give up battle for the strait.

The resulting offensive lasted 249 days. The line of attack was simple: Secure the heights, destroy the Turkish defenses, and sail on up to Istanbul. If the current hadn't swept the Anzacs' landing boats a mile off course or if someone other than Mustafa Kemal had received the orders, then Turkey would probably be part of Greece right now and y'all would be reading another book. But tides were swift, communications were faulty, decisions were hasty, and watches were unsynchronized.

The death toll was numbing: Roughly 86,000 Turkish forces and more than 160,000 Allied soldiers perished in the campaign. A staggeringly high number of Allied casualties were Anzac men—unfathomable losses for two countries with such small populations. Indeed, it's all but acknowledged that during the campaign, the Brits offered up the Anzac troops as cannon fodder; consequently, a trip to Gallipoli has become a grim pilgrimage of sorts for countless Australian and New Zealand tourists.

The entire peninsula is a national park. Turkish and Allied soldiers are buried side by side in 31 war cemeteries; several important monuments are grouped around two main areas. It's certainly possible to get to the highlights alone, but there's more to be gained by taking a tour. Tour groups are generally small and the information provided by the guides is informative and passionate; however, the real advantage of taking the tour is seeing the battlefields through the eyes of your Australian and Kiwi acquaintances.

For the locations of the monuments and cemeteries mentioned in this section, consult our map of the Gallipoli Peninsula (p. 195).

Arı Burnu Monument & Cemetery (Arı Burnu Anı ve Mezarlığı)   Shortly after 4am on the morning of April 25, 1915, after a long and cramped night in the boats, the Australian and New Zealand Army Corps landed—16,000 men in all—in the dark, expecting to set foot on level ground. The steep cliff that confronted them instead must have come as a horrific surprise; nevertheless, they hauled themselves up and grabbed at anything stable enough to hold them. Not expecting anyone stupid enough to stage a landing at such an unforgiving spot, the Turks were ill prepared to defend the cliff, allowing large numbers of confused Anzacs to gain higher ground. There was no defense at all in the hills, and by 8am, 8,000 heroic men had scrambled ashore, with three soldiers arriving halfway up the hill to strategic Chunuk Bair, 1.6km (a mile) away from the landing site.

The Arı Burnu cemetery is located at the northern end of Anzac Cove. On Anzac Day, a dawn memorial service is held here.

At the northern end of Anzac Cove.

Burnt Hill & Monument (Yusufçuktepe Anıtı)   Also known as Scimitar Hill, Hill 70, and Green Knoll, this ridge was one of the objectives of the Sulva Bay landings in August 1915. Skirmishes went on for 3 days, during which time control over the hill went back and forth. The final day of the attack was a fiasco for the British troops, who suffered the largest number of casualties—5,300—of the entire Gallipoli Campaign.

Cape Helles Landings & Seddülbahir   The Allied landing campaign was launched on two fronts: the beach at Kabatepe (which the Anzac boats overshot) and the village and medieval fortress of Seddülbahir at the toe of the peninsula. The

Seddülbahir landings were carried out on five beaches simultaneously by British troops, but lacking the element of surprise and without even one cellphone among them, the advances were modest at best and fatal at worst.

After a violent bombardment of the village, and assuming that the beach (V Beach) was deserted, the 29th Division approached the shore. The Trojan horse–style landing was to have taken place using the cargo hold of the collier *The River Clyde,* which, once beached, would empty itself of soldiers. Like a scene out of *Saving Private Ryan,* the operation turned into a literal bloodbath, when the Turks, waiting in ambush, opened fire on the unprepared and vulnerable British army.

The landings on the other four beaches were more successful, and the troops dug in waiting for further orders. At Y Beach, a small cove with access to the cliff tops 60m (197 ft.) up, 2,000 men, a number equal to all of the Turkish forces on the tip of the peninsula that day, landed unopposed and unaware of the carnage taking place less than 6.5km (4 miles) away. The Turks finally attacked in the night, and these troops were authorized to withdraw.

Chunuk Bair Memorials (Conkbayırı)   Atatürk's arrival on the scene marks a turning point not only in the Gallipoli Campaign but also in the history of Turkey as a nascent republic. Atatürk immediately recognized the importance of the high ground of Chunuk Bair as the key to the straits.

When Atatürk and his reconnaissance team reached Chunuk Bair, Turkish soldiers were fleeing oncoming Australians, who had gained the high ground during the fateful morning of August 25. Explaining that they had run out of bullets, the soldiers were ordered by Atatürk to lie in the grass, bayonets at the ready. Fearing an ambush, the Anzac soldiers took cover, providing the Turks with the precious time needed for reinforcements to arrive. Relentless New Zealand units briefly gained the summit, but due to a lack of reinforcements, the troops were either slain or forced back to a lower position.

The fateful hill, visited by thousands of pensive visitors each year, is where the main New Zealand memorial shares the crest with a statue of Atatürk as a promising young officer. The Chunuk Bair cemetery is located here, and on Anzac Day, the New Zealand service is held immediately following the Dawn Service at Arı Burnu Cemetery. Nearby are the five enormous tablets of the Turkish Conkbayırı Memorial, symbolizing an outstretched hand to the heavens, and inscribed with a narration (in Turkish) of the events from the defender's point of view.

The Hero 57th Regiment Memorial (57 Piyade Alayı Şehitliği)   With Anzac troops attacking Chunuk Bair, and in order to gain time for reinforcements to arrive, Atatürk gave the order to his best regiment, "I'm not ordering you to attack; I'm ordering you to die. In the time which passes until we die, other troops and commanders can take our places." Stories of the 57th Regiment's courageous sacrifice, when almost 100,000 men died, are part of Turkey's proud lore, but nobody dares to touch upon the possibility that Atatürk's ambition got the better of him that day.

Oddly enough, the memorial grounds and cemetery are a fairly new addition to the national park, and it's the one place where you will run into large groups of Turks and not *one* trying to sell you any memorabilia. The lawns provide a perfect rest stop for contemplating the puzzle of war, and the ablution fountain is a welcome site for washing the grit of the trenches off of your feet.

Lone Pine (Kanlı Sırt)   The largest mass grave on the peninsula and the main memorial to the missing Australians of the campaign, Lone Pine is the final resting

The **Respect to Turkish Soldier Monument (Mehmetçik Anıtı)** commemorates what some say is an apocryphal story told in the battle's aftermath. At one point during the fighting, gunfire downed an Australian soldier in the middle of an open field, and none of his compatriots had the courage to retrieve him. A Turkish soldier got up out of his trench, and both sides froze as the Turk picked up the wounded Australian and carried him over to the enemy side. He then returned to his own trench unharmed.

place of both Turks and Anzac troops, with a heavy number of gravestones reading "Believed to be buried in these trenches." About 2,200 Australians and over 4,000 Turks perished in the 3-day battle that earned Australian soldiers seven Victoria Crosses, the Australian badge of bravery and honor.

The tremendous losses at Lone Pine are even more sobering when you think that this was simply a diversionary tactic away from the main objectives of Suvla Bay and Chunuk Bair to the north. Today the hill is the site of a single pine tree rising above the scrub (the original, destroyed in a brush fire during the battle, gave seed to this one), inspiring the soldiers to name the hill after a then-current popular American hit, "On the Trail of the Lonesome Pine." Australians enter this cemetery with their heads held high, because Lone Pine embodies the spirit, character, and courage of their sons.

The Nek   Imagine the closing scene of the movie *Gallipoli,* with reinforcement after teenage reinforcement charging fearlessly into certain death. This real-life suicide mission was ordered by British commanders on August 7, 1915, to divert Turkish troops away from Sulva Bay, where a landing attempt was being made. A break in a nearby British naval bombardment had given the Turkish army the opportunity they needed to reoccupy their trenches, so when the Australian Lighthorse divisions were ordered to attack, they were summarily slaughtered.

A visit to the manicured cemetery and clean front line reveals nothing of the hardship, disease, and rotting corpses that plagued the ridge, but the wind does.

Turkish Memorial, Museum, and Cemetery (Şehitler Abidesi, Türk Şehitliği ve Müzesi)   Let's not forget that a quarter of a million Turks lost their lives defending their country from invading forces. (This is the unofficial number; the official count stands at 86,000.) This somber memorial, atop a promontory at the southern tip of the peninsula, is a fitting place to pay your final respects.

Walker's Ridge, Quinn's Post, Courtney's Post, and Steele's Post   These positions above Anzac Cove were gained in the first days of fighting. With the cliff to their backs and under constant heavy fire, the soldiers dug crude rifle pits, later deepening and connecting them into a network of trenches.

The confrontation in those first few days was ferocious, and the enemy lines were in some places only a few yards apart. The area between the enemy lines known as "no man's land" is now a modern road, and it is possible to spot overgrown trenches on your way to the cemeteries.

The Turks like to tell stories about the friendship that grew between two sides during the 8-month stalemate. If the Turks had cigarettes, the Anzacs provided the matches; when Anzac supplies failed to arrive, the Turks tossed tomatoes into the

5

ÇANAKKALE, GALLIPOLI & THE TROAD

The Gallipoli Battlefields

ditches. Despite the legends, the truth remains that a great respect between the Anzacs and the Turks grew out of a mutual sense of honor.

TROY ★★

30km (19 miles) south of Çanakkale

Like the conglomerate of nearly 100 ancient cities that make up the province of Çanakkale, this is the land where the lines between history and mythology are blurred. King Priam, Helen, Agamemnon, and Odysseus were lead characters at **Troy ★★★**, made timeless by Homer in his *Iliad* and *Odyssey*. The *Iliad* and *Odyssey* have made Troy one of the most recognizable mythological events in the world, and few can resist the chance to tread among its remains.

Until 1871, when Heinrich Schliemann decided to go dig for buried treasure, finding Troy was about as likely as finding Atlantis. There was (and to a certain extent, still is) no concrete evidence that the civilization of Homer's *Iliad* existed. One of the arguments is that the poet's epic account of the Trojan War is an amalgam of battle stories based on geopolitics of the day, with a little Aaron Spelling thrown in for flavor.

Then Schliemann, a self-taught archaeologist with an ancient-Greece obsession and an even stronger lust for buried treasure, descended upon the nearby village of Hisarlık and started poking around. His shoddy excavation resulted in significant damage to the site, and when the dust settled after his looting, there was some dispute over what it was that he actually "found" there (see "Exploring the Site," below). But there's no disputing that he began the significant excavation and reconstruction process that continues to this day.

The fact that nine civilizations were built one on top of the other is no surprise, given the strategic location. Two thousand years ago, Troy was a port city at the mouth of the Dardanelles, and it would have been surprising if a war *hadn't* been fought here. While it's anyone's guess just how heroic the goings-on were on these ancient shores, the possibility of stepping into a legend is an exciting proposition—as is climbing into the belly of a wooden horse that Walt Disney would be proud of.

Essentials

GETTING THERE FROM ÇANAKKALE

BY BUS *Dolmuşes* depart from under the bridge in Çanakkale. The ride takes approximately 35 minutes and costs 5TL. In summer, there are 10 departures per day; fewer in winter.

BY CAR From Çanakkale, follow the signs south to Troy. You can't miss it.

VISITOR INFORMATION

There is a **visitor information office** (℡ **0286/283-0536**) at the entrance to the archaeological site (next to the Trojan Horse) where you can get an overview of the site as well as peruse reading materials written entirely in Turkish. At the time of this writing, the paint was drying on a world-class museum warehousing the findings from recent excavations of the site.

A TROY PRIMER

Stories about the young Schliemann paint a picture of a child prodigy on a quest from an early age. It seems more likely that his main goal in life was to strike it rich; having achieved that in the California gold rush, he then set his sights on immortality.

At about 44 years old, after years of study of ancient and modern Greek and the classic epic work of Homer, Schliemann proclaimed himself an archaeologist and began digging at Pınarbaşı, which was believed at the time to be the site of Troy. Meanwhile, Frank Calvert had discovered the ruins of a palace or temple on the hill at Hisarlık, and the two agreed that this was a more likely area for the lost city.

Schliemann began bulldozing his way through the hill in 1870 and found little besides obsidian knife blades and clay tiles—which in Turkey, you can pretty much find while bending over and tying your shoe. When he finally discovered something significant—a relief of the sun god Apollo—he immediately attributed it to the ruins of Zeus's throne (and smuggled it out of the country and into his garden). It started to get interesting in August 1872 with the discovery of some gold earrings and a skeleton, and 9 months later his crew uncovered two gates guarding a stone foundation of a large building. To Schliemann, this was obviously the Scaean Gate, and the building was the palace of Priam, the last king of Troy.

Sometime later, Schliemann literally struck gold, shrewdly giving the crew the day off while he and his wife dug alone. That day's findings were monumental: a treasure of goblets; spearheads; knives; and jewelry in copper, silver, and gold, including an incredible 8,750 gold rings and buttons. Eventually Schliemann smuggled the whole lot (except for a few items now in the Archaeology Museum in Çanakkale) out of the country, initially stashing a major part of the treasure with various friends around Greece, where neither Turkish nor Greek authorities could claim ownership. He also donated a portion of the treasure to a Berlin museum, but the artifacts were stolen by the Soviets during World War II and transported to Russia. Schliemann halted and resumed excavation two more times through 1890 but never came near to the findings of that first stash.

So the question remains: Was Schliemann a lying megalomaniac with delusions of grandeur? One biographer points to the evidence. While Schliemann reported that the site of the treasure was located in Priam's Palace, the site of the find was actually outside the city wall. The truly incriminating evidence is in the photographs he took of Priam's treasure; several of the items "found" in 1873 appear in photos taken in 1872 of earlier finds.

Maybe he was just nuts; there's evidence supporting that, too. Schliemann eventually retired in Athens, renamed all of his servants after characters in Greek mythology, and required them to deliver all messages to him in ancient Greek, a language he had taught himself. The inscription on the tomb he had built for himself seems to be his final word on the subject: "For the hero Schliemann."

EXPLORING THE SITE

More than a hundred years of research have revealed that the city was reconstructed at least nine times. The first settlement, referred to as Troy I, dates back to around 3000 B.C.; it lasted 5 centuries and was destroyed by fire. Schliemann's groundbreaking discovery of King Priam's treasure was found on Level II, but later research established that this civilization would have existed more than 1,000 years *before* the Troy of Homer. It is unclear what caused the destruction of the successive three civilizations, but findings from the site indicate that by Troy VI, a new culture had migrated, probably from Mycenae, expanding on the area of preceding settlements. The year 1184 B.C. is traditionally accepted as the year in which classic Troy fell, allowing archaeologists to establish that the Troy of Homer most likely took place during the existence of Troy VII-A, which was analogously destroyed by fire around 1200 B.C. Abandoned for more than 400 years, the site went through repeated cycles of invasion and reconstruction until the 1st century A.D, when the city was rebuilt, apparently under the orders of Julius Caesar, and given the name Ilium Novum (hence the *Iliad* in Homer's title). The prestige of the city during the Roman period is reflected in its illustrious guests: Augustus Caesar, Hadrian, Marcus Aurelius, and Caracalla all slept here.

Archaeologists estimate that Troy is actually 10 times larger than the roughly 165-sq.-m (1,776-sq.-ft.) mound of ruins. The more significant discoveries to date are the Troy VI fortification walls, a *megaron* (aristocratic dwelling), the Temple of Athena and sacrificial altar, the Schliemann Trench (where it all started), a Roman theater, and a *bouleterion* (senate building).

Tevfikiye Köyü. © **0286/283-0061.** Admission 15TL. Daily 8am–7pm (Nov–Mar 8am–5pm).

Passing through Alexander Troas

Approximately 45km (28 miles) along the road southwest from Çanakkale along the coastal road toward Gülpınar, the road passes over the mountains through a handful of tiny and timeless villages (trash and all). Just past the turnoff for Dalyanköy, no sooner do you ascend the hill than the silhouettes of stones—not the ones that occur naturally—begin to emerge. The site was buried and forgotten except for its utility: **Alexander Troas** (admission free; daily 8am–5pm) represents another one of those historically monumental sites looted as a building quarry. Many of the columns were removed and taken to Istanbul to use in the construction of the Yeni Valide Camii.

In the 3rd century B.C., seven of the neighboring cities were incorporated into Alexander Troas in what became at that time one of the largest cities in Anatolia, stretching as far as Troy to the north, Gülpınar in the south, and east to Evciler. So great was Alexander Troas's position, geographically, politically, and economically, that both Julius Caesar and Constantine are said to have considered the city as the capital of their respective empires. The scattered remains of this isolated site are also frequently included on biblical tours, as there are indications that St. Paul visited three times (for more information, see Acts in the Bible).

The first indication that you've arrived at the site is the sight of a neat stack of stones in the form of a tower. (There's a small spot for cars adjacent to this monument.) The tower is actually part of a cornerstone section of the famously photographed intact cradle arch. The arch and "tower" are both parts of the **Herodes Atticus bath,** built in A.D. 135. With its 100m-long (328-ft.) facade, it is the largest Roman-era bath in Anatolia. Prior to the 16th century, when the site was believed to be that of Troy, the structure was called the Palace of Priam, until later, when it was thought to be a temple. Because the site is still in the very early stages of excavation, a visit will find you wading through low Mediterranean brush and past olive trees and oaks—probably accompanied only by the whispering of the wind. Some of the other structures you will stumble upon are sections of the 8km (5 miles) of city walls, interspersed by the remains of what was once a total of 44 intermittent towers. The

foundations of a temple are visible in the clearing, where they've found a bust of Dionysius, **a theater,** and **an aqueduct** attributed to Emperor Trajan. After exploring the fields, continue down the road to the picturesque village of Dalyanköy, with its sandy beach and unpretentious waterside restaurants. This is the site of the ancient city's harbor, now a silted lagoon, artificially enclosed to protect ships from the high winds.

BOZCAADA ★★

55km (34 miles) off the west coast of Geyikli Harbor; 50km (31 miles) southwest of Çanakkale

Off the northwestern coast of the Çanakkale peninsula are two idyllic island getaways, Gökçeada and Bozcaada, second only in popularity to the Princes' Islands in the province of Istanbul. The smaller of the two islands, **Bozcaada ★★**, has the bigger role in mythology. Located opposite Troy, it was from the shelter of Bozcaada (also known as Tenedos, after Poseidon's grandson, Tenes) that Homer tells us the Greek fleet hid while staging the Trojan Horse offensive. What you'll find here today are the predictable remnants of the earlier Greeks, Venetians, and Ottomans, sparsely dotting a pastoral landscape that includes pristine stretches of beach and thermal springs. The absence of any villages, apart from the wharf, combined with the revival of a centuries-old legacy of viniculture, are what make this island so much like the original paradise. It doesn't hurt that guests get to hole up in restored Greek stone mansions set amidst the rolling landscape of vineyards (the island economy also relies, nominally, upon red poppies, used in jams and sherbet), dotted by graceful modern windmills. The island packs in visitors to the gills for the annual grape harvest festival on July 26 and 27, when the island population swells from 2,500 to 15,000.

Meanwhile, Gökçeada (aka Imroz), or the "Island of the God of the Seas," while also appealing in its own right, requires an additional, even heroic, effort to access (1 hr., 45 min. by boat only 2–3 times per week). Assuming our estimable readers have limited time, such a stopover will absorb much of the time required to visit the other stellar destinations we write about in this book! Therefore, regrettably, we don't cover Gökçeada here.

Essentials
GETTING THERE
Ferries making the 35-minute trip depart from the Yükyeri docks west of the Geyikli town center, about 40km (25 miles) south of Çanakkale (ferries run on limited days and less frequently from Oct through mid May). Tickets for passengers cost 5TL; cars cost 45TL. There's also a passenger seabus service direct to Bozcaada from Çanakkale departing on Wednesdays and Saturdays at 9am, returning at 6pm the same day. The trip takes 1 hour and costs 10TL. For updated information contact the Geyikli port offices ☎ **444-0752** or 0286/632-0383 or log on to www.gestas denizulasim.com.tr for current timetables.

WHAT TO SEE & DO
Eat, drink, and be pastorally merry. That's the point of *bellissima* Bozcaada. There are four main wineries on the island; you can either go directly to the factory/farms or to a little **wine-tasting tour ★★★** at a number of establishments on the wharf (they make it easy here). **Talay** is a family-owned vintner established on the island in 1948 (Lale Sok. 5; ☎ **0286/697-8080;** www.talay.com.tr). **Ataol Farms** (also a guesthouse

and restaurant) is located in Tekirbahçe (© **0286/697-0384;** www.ataolciftligi.com). **Çamlıbağ/Yunatcilar** (Eminiyet Sok. 24; © **0286/697-8055;** www.camlibag.com. tr) has been pressing grapes since 1925. **Corvus** is a more ambitious vintner, with vineyards not only on Bozcaada, and sales points all over Turkey (© **0286/697-8181;** www.corvus.com.tr, Tuzburnu Mevkii).

There are other reasons besides wine tasting to come to this island. Visitors flock to the most famous beach, **Ayazma Cove,** known for the cold spring that lies beneath. **Sulubahçe** and **Habbeli** are two other picture-postcard coves. Minibuses depart regularly for service to these beaches from the town center. In season (meaning July–Aug), the lounge chairs shaded by faded straw-hat umbrellas fill up by 9am, so ideally, it's best to set aside 2 days in early summer or September/October. If you're heading here off season, keep in mind that the high winds for which Turkey's largest wind farm was erected gust over the seven rolling hills of Bozcaada, making the island ripe for windsurfing. (Log on to **www.bozcaadarehberi.com** for more information on island activities and attractions).

It'll be impossible to miss the **Medieval Castle,** reconstructed by Mehmet the Conqueror in the 15th century (remember the strategic location of the island). The castle foundations were probably laid by the Phoenicians; it was later inhabited by the Venetians and Genoese. The construction of the **Church of the Virgin Mary** (Meryem Ana Kilisesi) may also date to the Venetians but the current church only dates to 1867–69. Admission is 2TL.

There's also some exceptional diving around the island, including a kilometer-long (⅔-mile) reef that extends down to a depth of about 20m (66 ft.). You might even get a glimpse of the Mediterranean sea lions from **Mermer Burnu.** Special permission from the authorities is required for diving off Bozcaada; for information, contact Aganta Turizm at Belediye Dükk 7 (© **0286/697-0569**).

WHERE TO STAY & EAT

In addition to the two bed-and-breakfasts listed here, I recommend the pastorally located lodgings at the **Ataol Farms** in Tekirbahçe, (© **0286/697-0384;** www. ataolciftligi.com; see below).

Otel Mauna   When traveling outside of the main touristy areas, I never underestimate the value of floor-to-ceiling bathroom tile. Or an enclosed cabin shower. This hotel has both, plus charm to boot. The Mauna is a sweet old stone house on a side street in the center of town, with a rooftop terrace bar with views to the castle and sea beyond—great for an evening aperitif.

Cumhuriyet Mah. 20 Eylül Cad., 17680 Bozcaada. www.otelmauna.com. © **0286/697-0333.** Fax 0286/697-0273. 8 units. 100€ double. MC, V. Free parking. Closed Nov–Mar. **Amenities:** Bar. *In room:* A/C, TV w/pay-per-view, hair dryer, minibar, no phone, free Wi-Fi.

Kaikias 📷   With a spot front and center of the water and the castle, the architect-brothers Beyildi clearly made a winning investment. They've restored this old Greek building, retaining original features like cross barrel arches, patches of decorative frieze, and some original brickwork. They've also added breezy touches like a sailcloth ceiling to keep the relentless sun from beating down on the lobby—essentially a recently enclosed court connecting the two row houses. The dark wood of the original wide plank flooring provides a rich feel to rooms, which range from simple whitewashed rooms kept interesting with gilded mirrors and the odd leather armchair (standard) to regal spaces with canopied four-poster beds (suite). Bathrooms also vary, from sleek and modern to marble-clad with a *hamam* basin. Best to ask ahead if you have a preference.

Kale Arkası, Bozcaada. www.kaikias.com. ©️ **0286/697-0250.** Fax 0286/697-8857. 20 units. 240TL–270TL double Aug–Sept; 160TL–180TL Oct–July MC, V. Free parking. Closed Nov–Mar. **Amenities:** Bar/cafe; beach. *In room:* A/C, free Wi-Fi.

ASSOS ★

420km (261 miles) to Istanbul; 90km (56 miles) south of Çanakkale; 65km (40 miles) south of Troy; 160km (99 miles) north of Bergama; 250km (155 miles) north of Izmir

Several years ago, Jacque Avizou (of Les Maisons de Cappadoce, in Cappadocia) confided in me about a "little paradise" that he described as Turkey's "best-kept secret." He told me it was located far enough off the primary road system to ensure that it remained off the tourist radar, a tiny settlement of Anatolian families living atop the lofty ruins of an ancient commercial and religious center. I was intrigued and set out to plan an entire week's itinerary around the little Aegean village of Behramkale, also known by the name of the ancient city it stands on, **Assos.**

Physically, the village of Assos/Behramkale (which I will from now on call Assos for brevity's sake) occupies the site of a conical volcanic rock on the south-facing shores of the Bay of Edremit. The Acropolis, surrounded by a 3km-long (1¾-mile) defensive wall, is crowned by the **Temple of Athena,** placed artfully, advantageously, and tactically high above the expansive Valley of the Satnioeis and the bay. The **agora, gymnasium,** and **theater,** all still in continuing stages of excavation, are terraced down the steep slopes of the rocky landscape, making a visit to the far-flung sections of the city not just a little bit of a workout. At the base of the city (reachable via a steeply cobbled roadway) is a tiny port made up of a single breakwater and a handful of stone warehouses converted into guest accommodations and waterfront restaurants. The moonlight reflecting off of the tranquil waters of the Aegean is even more romantic when you consider that this same setting served as inspiration for Aristotle during his 3-year sabbatical at Assos. Frankly, Assos has already been discovered, but is thankfully nowhere near overrun. The day that happens, though, it'll be a tight squeeze, because thanks to kryptonite-like volcanic rock upon which the village is built there's not much room—at least at the wharf—for this little village to grow.

Essentials
GETTING THERE FROM ÇANAKKALE
BY MINIBUS The public transport route (on one of Ayvaçık *dolmuşes;* ©️ **0286/217-2141**) from Çanakkale to Assos is a bit convoluted, but here goes: Take a minibus from the Çanakkale *otogar* to Ayvaçık (1 hr.; 12TL), and then change in Ayvaçık to the *dolmuş* to Assos (1½ hr.; 10TL). The latter drops you off at the crossroads near the village entrance and the ancient site (but 238m/781 ft. above the wharf). *Dolmuşes* run hourly on the hour from approximately 7am to 8pm, sometimes not at all in winter.

If you're coming directly from Istanbul or Izmir, take a **Çanakkale Truva** bus (©️ **444-0017;** www.truvaturizm.com) or **Kamıl Koç** (©️ **444-0562**) to Avaçık or Kücükküyü. From both locations you'll have to take one of the hourly minibuses departing for Assos (the minibus from Kücükküyü only runs in summer).

BY CAR From Çanakkale, follow the signs south to Ayvaçık, and then follow the (well-marked) scenic road to Assos/Behramkale.

The longer, alternative route (and the one I took) follows the road south of Çanakkale through **Ezine** (where you should stop for cheese!). You can make this a day of sightseeing beginning with a stop at Troy. On the road south of Troy, take the turnoff for Pınarbaşı, following the road through Mahmudiye, Ovacık, and Geyikli. After Geyikli, if you follow the road toward Dalyan you will encounter the roadside ruins of **Alexander Troas,** an enormous (and as of yet still unexcavated and/or looted) candidate for the capital city of the Roman Empire. Dalyan port is an idyllic and untouched corner of Çanakkale and a great spot to stop for a drink or a bite to eat; on your way keep your eyes open for the **Kestanbol thermal waters,** a natural and artesian hot spring bubbling up to 154°F (68°C).

South of Dalyan (from the road you turned off of) through Kösedere leads to the ancient temple of **Apollon Smyntheon at Chryse** (in the village of Gülpınar). From Gülpınar, depending on your level of stamina, you can either take the turnoff to the Ottoman castle of **Babakale** (another paradise on earth, if you ask me), constructed under Sultanahmed III to protect the villagers from frequent pirate attacks, or continue along the peninsular road to Assos/Behramkale.

The entrance to the village and the ancient acropolis, and a number of pensions and hotels, are clustered together near the turnoff from the main road. The sea-level wharf and additional hotels are accessed by continuing along this same secondary cobbled road (past the entrance to the village/site) as it winds its steeply sloping way along the city's fortification walls.

VISITOR INFORMATION

You should have your information in hand before you arrive at Assos as there is no tourism information office. The Çanakkale Culture and Tourism Office maintains a good guide of Assos archaeological site (www.canakkalekutup.gov.tr), while the **Anzac Hotel** in Çanakkale (www.anzachotel.com) website is packed with information and maps to aid your way through the maze of secondary roads, olive groves, and plane trees.

WHAT TO SEE & DO

The city of **Assos** ★ was established by migrants from the town of Methymna on the island of Lesbos. Over the centuries, the city was ruled as part of Lydia, by the Persians, as a member of the Athenian League in the 5th century B.C., and incorporated into the kingdom of Pergamon.

One of the rulers during the pre-Pergamon era was the freed slave and student of Plato, Hermias. From 348 to 345 B.C., Hermias's schoolmate and friend, **Aristotle,** joined him at Assos to philosophize and lecture; tradition has it that it was here that Aristotle further developed Plato's thinking on government as expounded in *The Republic.*

The ancient site comprises an **acropolis, gymnasium, theater, *bouleuterion*,** and **necropolis,** all for the most part bound by a 3.2km-long (2-mile) defensive wall, and according to leading Turkish archaeologists, the most complete fortification in the Greek world. **The Temple of Athena** was the first and only archaic temple built in Anatolia of the Doric style.

The rubble (much of the good stuff was carried off to the Boston Museum, the Louvre, and the Istanbul Archaeology Museum) is spread out over a wide and arid area littered with stones, sarcophagi, and goat droppings, so unless you're a master orienteer, your visit will be confined to the upper reaches of the acropolis, near the site entrance. Still, the cliff-top setting of the ancient city, which produces an awe-inspiring sunset image from the temple remains over the bay, makes this pile of rocks one of the better secondary sites on the Aegean.

Behramkale Köyü. (Entrance to the site is about 150m/492 ft. up a steep cobbled pedestrian-only road accessed from the center of the village.) © **0286/721-7218**. Admission 5TL. Daily 8am–7pm (until 5pm Nov–Mar).

WHERE TO STAY & EAT

There are a number of pensions (some called motels) and lovely inns up on the hill high above the wharf in the village of Behramkale. From the rooftops or gardens you can see the horizon over the Aegean. Try the **Eski Köprü Evi/Old Bridge House** (Eski Köprü Basi Mevkii 357, Behramkale; © **0286/721-7100;** www.oldbridge house.com.tr) or the **Biber Evi** (© **0286/721-7410;** www.biberevi.com), two smart options. The **Timur Pension** (Behramkale Köyü; © **0286/721-7449;** www.assos. de/timur-pansiyon) is a good budget option, with four spare rooms and a newly added "Hunters Lodge." Whether you stay up at the top of the steep hill in the ruins or down by the waterfront, there is a *dolmuş* that plies the route between the two every hour for 1TL.

Kervansaray   In its heyday, the Kervansaray was one of the many customs depots located on what was a thriving commercial waterfront. In 1997, the stone structure was transformed into an inn, with additions like a sauna, an indoor/outdoor swimming pool, and a juice bar. The hotel is arranged around an atrium, echoing the structure of a historic caravansaray. A room facing the sea will get you a tiny balcony just wide enough to seat a couple with their feet rested atop the stone balcony wall. Some of the rooms are carpeted and some have wood floors, and there's a cozy corner unit arranged around a small stone chimney. It's all very charming and comfortable, without the polish that increasingly makes accommodations in Turkey indistinguishable.

Behramkale Village Iskele (at the port), Assos/Behramkale. www.assoskervansaray.com. © **0286/721-7093.** Fax 0286/721-7200. 44 units. 120€ double; 210€ family room/suite. Rates include breakfast and dinner. MC, V. Free parking. **Amenities:** Restaurant; bar; beach; indoor and outdoor pool; room service; sauna. *In room:* A/C, satellite TV, hair dryer, minibar, free Wi-Fi.

6

THE CENTRAL & SOUTHERN AEGEAN COASTS (GREATER IZMIR)

F or hundreds of years, the stellar ruins at Ephesus have provided voyagers all the impetus they needed to justify a trip to this stretch of picturesque coastlands. Villagers and entrepreneurs of yore were not the first to recognize the commercial value of these scenic hills and crystal waters. Historically, the central and southern Aegean coasts were crossroads for ancient trade routes. Civilization evolved out of the convergence of Eastern and Western cultures; Hellenistic settlers who fled the Dorian invasions emphasized economic expansion and forged ties with people from Egypt, Nubia, Canaan, Mesopotamia, and the Black Sea region. Welcome to the original melting pot.

At one time, the region boasted some of the most illustrious addresses in the world. The Ionian cities of Ephesus, Bergama, Miletus, and Priene served as cultural incubators in the development of Western thought, home to such philosophers and scholars as Thales Anaximenes, Anaximendros, and Heraclites. Other famous ancient Greek guests to the Anatolian coastline of the Aegean were Aristides, Strabo, Pliny, and Homer. Later (according to tradition) Mary, under the care of St. John, settled in Ephesus, permanently altering the way an entire civilization perceived Christianity while contributing to the evolution of the religion itself.

The presence of the sea becomes more insistent south of Izmir, characterized by a coastline backed by olive groves, rocky crags, and pine woods. But in recent years rampant development has been the rule and many of the region's fishing villages and farming towns have been transformed by the irresistible lure of the euro, pound sterling, and yen. The open-air museum of Ephesus, for example, is a human parking lot in August, and Bodrum in high season (mid-June through Aug) brings competition for sand, surf, and sustenance to new heights. The information in this section strives to strike a balance between lesser-traveled areas while acknowledging the fact that no one is coming to this part of Turkey to do a drive-by of Ephesus.

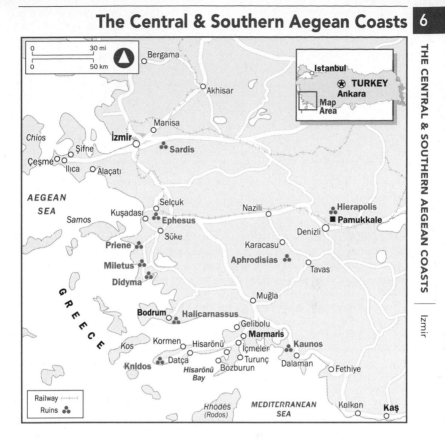

The destinations mentioned in this chapter are all within 3 hours of one another, and buses run regularly between cities. For shorter excursions, the local *dolmuşes* (minivan-type public transportation) are reliable, though they usually call it quits in the early evening. Driving is easy and the new highways provide choice for quick excursions or the scenic route. Time can be split easily between beach activities and visiting the ancient sights. This is the place to take as much time as necessary to decompress from the worries of everyday life.

IZMIR

560km (348 miles) south of Istanbul; 70km (43 miles) north of Selçuk; 90km (56 miles) north of Kuşadası; 325km (202 miles) south of Çanakkale; 279km (173 miles) north of Marmaris

Izmir has come a long way since the late 1800s when the Ottoman elite christened the port city *Kokaryalı* (Smelly Waterfront). Today the city has earned the nobler designation of *Güzelyalı* (Beautiful Waterfront), and with the completion of a multi-million-dollar redevelopment plan that includes a green waterside park, the **Kordon** promenade and the restored customs house (or **Konak Pier**) originally built by **Gustave Eiffel,** the name is more than appropriate.

A flourishing center of commerce in the 15th century, the city opened its arms to waves of immigrant Jews fleeing from the Spanish Inquisition as well as Greeks and Armenians. French and other European merchants, known as the Levantines, set up customs houses here, and each enclave left its own cultural imprint on the city. Sadly, little was left after the fire ignited at the tail end of the War of Independence destroyed all traces of the cultural melting pot that was once Smyrna—and there's that perilous but dormant fault line to contend with. Eighty-two years after the reconstruction began, Izmir has been reinvented as a prosperous, cosmopolitan, commercial city, more livable than Istanbul, less sterile than Ankara, and filled with wide boulevards and swaying palm trees. But with the azure waters of the Aegean and the extraordinary remains of Ephesus competing for tourist attention, Izmir sadly falls short. Despite this, I actually love the place. There's plenty to do here for anyone who chooses to take an extended stay, but for travelers with limited time, I don't recommend it.

Essentials
GETTING THERE
BY PLANE   As the primary entry point for visits to the popular destinations of Çeşme, Ephesus, and Kuşadası, as well as a major hub for international business travelers, Izmir's very modern Adnan Menderes Airport (www.adnanmenderesairport. com) —voted the most environmentally-friendly airport in Europe in 2010—has effortlessly kept pace. In addition to **Turkish Airlines** (see below for contact information), several airlines are now operating direct flights to Izmir from abroad. Pegasus (© 0 845 0848 980 in the UK; www.flypgs.com) flies year round from London's Stansted Airport while **SunExpress** (© 0232/444-0797; www.sunexpress.com.tr) flies twice weekly from Stansted in summer only. **Thomas Cook** (www.thomascook airlines.co.uk) and **Thomson Airways** (www.thomson.co.uk) fly direct from London Gatwick. Easyjet (www.easyjet.com) flies from London Heathrow on Tuesdays and Saturdays. Izmir is now a major hub for direct domestic flights. Turkish Airlines flies direct from Adana, Ankara, Antalya, Diyarbakır, Erzurum, Istanbul, Kayseri, Trabzon, and Van.

If you're departing from Istanbul's Atatürk Airport, you can also choose from **Atlasjet** (© 0216/444-3387; www.atlasjet.com.) **Onur Air** (© 444-6687 or © 0232/ 274-1939 at the airport; www.onurair.com.tr), or **Pegasus Airlines** (© 0850/250-2737; www.flypgs.com). The route from Istanbul's Sabiha Gökçen Airport is served by Pegasus, SunExpress, and Turkish Airlines budget operation, **AnadoluJet** (© 444-2538; www.anadolujet.com), which also flies direct from its hub in Ankara. SunExpress connects Izmir directly to Adana, Antalya, Kayseri and Diyarbakır; Pegasus flies direct from Ankara and Adana.

FROM THE AIRPORT   The **Havaş** shuttle (national toll-free © 444-0487 or local 0232/274-2276) runs daily service from the airport into the center of Izmir with a drop-off point in front of the Swissôtel Grand Efes Hotel on Gaziosmanpaşa Bulvarı. Bus departure times are coordinated with domestic airlines' flight arrivals; expect the ride into the city center to take about an hour. The fare is 10TL (midnight–6am the fare increases 25%). Shuttles from the city center to the airport depart from the same spot in front of the Alsancak Efes daily and hourly from 3:30am to 11:30pm.

If you're feeling a little more ambitious, hop on the new suburban rail located outside the domestic terminal and ride the rails into Izmir's Alsancak station. From there, it's a quick 2km or so to Cumhuriyet Meydanı, around which all of the hotels

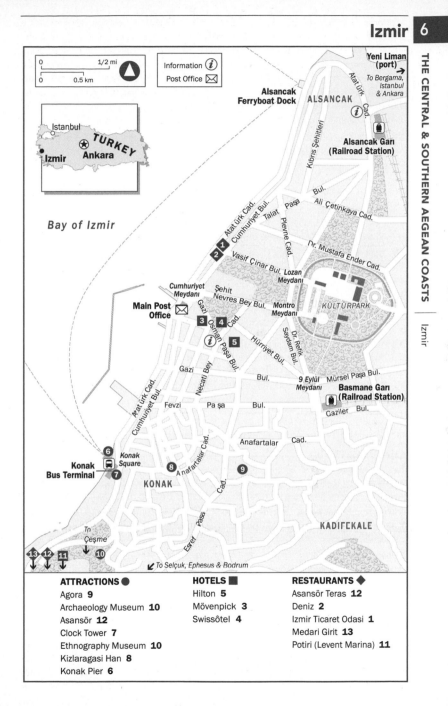

0   1/2 mi
0   0.5 km

Information ⓘ
Post Office ✉

Istanbul
TURKEY
Izmir   ✪ Ankara

Bay of Izmir

Yeni Liman
(port)
To Bergama,
Istanbul
& Ankara

Alsancak
Ferryboat Dock   ALSANCAK
ⓘ

Alsancak Garı
(Railroad Station)

Atatürk Cad.
Kıbrıs Şehitleri
Bul.
Ali Çetinkaya Cad.
Atatürk Cad.
Cumhuriyet Bul.
Talat   Paşa
Plevne Cad.
Dr. Mustafa Ender Cad.
Vasıf Çınar Bul.   Lozan
Meydanı

Cumhuriyet
Meydanı   Şehit
Nevres Bey Bul.   Montro
Meydanı   KÜLTÜRPARK

Main Post
Office   ✉
Gazi   Cad.
Osman Paşa Bul.
Hürriyet Bul.
Dr. Refik
Saydam Bul.

ⓘ

Gazi
Necati Bey
Bul.
9 Eylül   Mürsel Paşa Bul.
Meydanı   Basmane Garı
(Railroad Station)
Gaziler   Bul.

Atatürk Cad.
Cumhuriyet Bul.
Fevzi   Pa şa   Bul.

Anafartalar   Cad.

Konak
Bus Terminal   Konak
Square
KONAK
Anafartalar Cad.

KADİFEKALE

Tn
Çeşme
13 12 11   10
To Selçuk, Ephesus & Bodrum

ATTRACTIONS ●	HOTELS ■	RESTAURANTS ◆
Agora **9**	Hilton **5**	Asansör Teras **12**
Archaeology Museum **10**	Mövenpick **3**	Deniz **2**
Asansör **12**	Swissôtel **4**	Izmir Ticaret Odasi **1**
Clock Tower **7**		Medari Girit **13**
Ethnography Museum **10**		Potiri (Levent Marina) **11**
Kizlaragasi Han **8**		
Konak Pier **6**		

recommended below are located. The train ride costs 4TL and is payable with the Kentkart (valid also on ferries and buses).

Metropolitan **Bus no. 202** runs every hour on the hour daily (no buses at 2am and 4am) from the airport, stopping at all three terminals, to Çumhuriyet Meydanı (in front of the Swissôtel Grand Efes). If you're going to the *otogar* or to Bornova, take **Bus no. 200,** which departs the airport daily and hourly at 20 minutes after the hour. Taxis are also plentiful at the airport. A taxi to the city center will cost around 100TL. Base meter rates go up between midnight and 6am.

BY BUS   Bus service is frequent and comprehensive in and out of Izmir. Service from Istanbul takes around 9½ hours; from Ankara, 9 hours; from Kuşadası, 1½ hours; from Bergama, 2½ hours; and from Bursa, about 5½ hours. As with anywhere else in Turkey, prices vary from one bus company to the next by as much as $10, so shop around before buying your ticket. See chapter 12 for company contact info.

Long-distance buses arrive into Izmir's enormous and modern main *otogar* (bus station), located about 8km (5 miles) outside of town. As part of your fare, the bus companies also provide transfer minibuses into the city center.

BY TRAIN   Turkish State Railways (www.tcdd.gov.tr) operates two trains from Ankara: The **Karesi Ekspresi** leaves at 5:50pm for the 15-hour trip while the **Mavi Tren** departs at 7:50 and takes slightly more than 13 hours. A seat costs 30TL and 32TL, respectively. Trains arrive into Izmir's **Alsancak Garı** (☎ **0232/464-7795**) before arriving at the end of the line at Basmane Garı (*Note*: Train departure schedules may change so confirm your itinerary well in advance.

BY FERRY   Those combining a visit to Turkey with a romp through the Greek islands may hop on a ferry in Chios for service to Çeşme, an hour-long bus ride from Izmir's *otogar*. Ferries run daily from July through September 15 with fewer runs off-season. For information, contact **Ertürk** (www.erturk.com.tr), the agent located in Çeşme.

VISITOR INFORMATION

The tourist information offices are located at Akdeniz Mah. 1344 Sok. 2 Pasaport (☎ **0232/483-6216**); and the Adnan Menderes Airport (☎ **0232/274-2214**).

ORIENTATION

Konak, named for the Ottoman government mansion (Hükümet Konagı) located nearby, is the area roughly containing Izmir's central district and center city, which embraces the Gulf of Izmir. A number of neighborhoods and zones are contained within Konak, including **Konak Square,** with its bustling seafront park, the little **Konak Camii,** and the **Clock Tower (Saat Kulesi),** the symbol of Izmir.

Just behind the tourist information booth at Konak Meydanı (the main square) is **Anafartalar Caddesi;** judging by the magnetic stream of people pouring in, this must be the entrance to the shopping district, also known as Kemeraltı. Winding through the oldest section of town are the narrow back streets of Izmir, where an unexpected 17th-century mosque, several synagogues, and a *bedesten* (privately owned marketplace serving as Izmir's Kapalı Çarşı) cohabit an area long overtaken by stores selling inexpensive gold chains.

To the north along the waterfront is **Konak Pier,** constructed as the Customs Building by Gustave Eiffel between 1875 and 1890 and reopened as a glossy shopping, dining and entertainment complex. About a 15-minute walk farther up is Cumhuriyet Meydanı, punctuated by an equestrian statue of Atatürk, and the grassy waterfront park and promenade of **Kordon.** This neighborhood around Cumhuriyet

Izmir is one of an increasing number of cities to adopt an electronic payment system by way of a magnetic-stripped "city card." Like other prepay fare cards, the Kentkart offers discounts for use, so instead of paying the full fare of 3TL for a token (jeton), that ride on the bus, metro, or ferry will cost you only 1.75TL. But because the Kentkart requires an initial deposit of 3TL, buying one really only makes sense if you're planning on staying in town for the long haul. Alternatively, you can purchase a three-ride electronic ticket for 6.50TL or a five-ride ticket for 10.40TL. Kentkarts are available at bus ticket offices and in select shops; just look for the Kentkart logo for sales points.

Meydanı is home to a cluster of four- and five-star hotels, car-rental offices, and travel agencies. It's also part of the residential neighborhood of **Alsancak,** which boasts some restored homes, and another Atatürk Museum. **Pasaport** refers to the **historic quay** halfway between Konak Pier and Cumhuriyet Meydanı. At the northernmost tip are the harbor and ferry terminal. South of Konak Square is the neighborhood of **Karataş,** today called **Asansör** for the 19th-century elevator that provides access to the cliff-top residential area. Once a thriving Jewish community, this is where you will find the Asansör and the restored houses of **Dario Moreno Sokak.** The neighborhood is just south of Konak and easily reachable by bus.

GETTING AROUND

Much of what might hold a non-local's interest is located in convenient little clusters at various points around the city. Most of your sightseeing and shopping can be done on foot in and around Konak, which includes the museums and main-square attractions, as well as the bazaar, also known as **Kemeraltı.** From Konak, Alsancak is reachable on foot along the scenic waterfront or via ferry service. If you're staying in one of the major hotels around Cumhuriyet Meydanı, you're about dead center between Konak and Alsancak. The fare per ride on buses, the metro and ferries is 1.75TL. Tokens (*jetons*) or the magnetic Kentkart (see below) is available at all stations.

BY BUS There are municipal buses running regularly from the major bus hub at Konak (just in front of the Atatürk Cultural Center and on the street below the Archaeological Museum) south along the waterfront. The system serves all of Greater Izmir, so it's unlikely you'll be needing it much. You can get routes by logging on to the municipality's website, **www.izmir.bel.tr/en/otobus.asp.**

BY METRO At the risk of plowing through millennia of archaeological remains, Izmir has completed the first phase of an ever-expanding **metro.** The one line currently in service runs between Bornova, a residential suburb to the northeast of town, and Üçyol just south of Konak. In-between are stops at Konak, Çankaya, Basmane, and a couple more destinations not mentioned in this guide. The metro runs frequently between 6am and midnight Monday through Friday; service is sparser on weekends.

BY FERRY Public **ferries** crisscross Izmir's bay between the city's eight recently refurbished ferry stations. The most useful routes are between Konak and the busy residential shopping area of Karşıyaka, between Pasaport (at Cumhuriyet Meydanı) and Karşıyaka, and between Pasaport and Alsancak. There's also service between

Konak and Pasaport, easing weary foot traffic along the shoreline. Purchase your *jeton* at the ticket window prior to boarding.

[Fast FACTS] IZMIR

Airport and Airlines Information For airport information, call the general info line (Domestic Terminal ℂ 0232/274-2626; International Terminal ℂ 0232/ 455-0000). Flight information: **Turkish Airlines,** ℂ 0232/484-1220; **Atlas-jet,** ℂ 0850/222-0000; **AnadoluJet,** ℂ 444-2538; **Onur Air,** ℂ 444-6687; **Pegasus Airlines,** ℂ 0850/ 250-2737. The number for the Havaş shuttle bus at the airport is ℂ 0232/274-2276.

Ambulance and Emergency Care In a medical emergency, dial ℂ 112 for an ambulance or faster yet, grab a taxi to one of the private hospitals in the center of town: **Sağlık Hastanesi** (1399 Sok. 25, Alsancak; ℂ 0232/463-7700), the **Altınordu Hastanesi** (Ali Çetinkaya Bulv. 79, Alsancak; ℂ 0232/464-2400), or the **Özel Şifa**

Hastanesi (Fevzipaşa Bulv. 172/2, Basmane; ℂ 0232/ 446-0880).

Car Rentals **Avis** (International terminal ℂ 0535/ 574-0010; Domestic ℂ 0232/274-1790) is located in the city center at Şair Eşref Bulv. 18D, Alsancak, in the Altay İş Merkezi (ℂ 0232/441-4417). **Hertz** is at Kultar Mah. 1377, Sok. 8/F, Alsancak (ℂ 0232/464-3440), and at the airport (International arrivals: ℂ 0232/274-3610; Domestic terminal: ℂ 0232/274-2248). **National Car Rental** has an office both downtown in Alsancak at Şehit Nevres Bey Bulv. 11A (ℂ 0232/422-2499) and in both the domestic and international arrival halls (ℂ 0232/274-6265). Also at the airport is **Europecar** (in domestic arrivals; ℂ 0232/ 274-6420).

Consulates Citizens of the **United Kingdom** have

consular representation at 1442 Sokak 49, PK 300, Alsancak (ℂ 0232/463-5151). The **United States** Consular Agency (1387 Sok. 1/8, Alsancak) provides routine services by appointment only on Mondays and Tuesdays (for appointments call Mon–Tues 9:30–11:30am; ℂ 0232/464-8755) and is closed Wednesday to Friday as well as Turkish and American holidays. (In an emergency, call the Ankara number: ℂ 0312/455-5555. *Note:* The State Department does not publish this address.)

Transport The general number for the **Izmir City Bus Terminal** (the *otogar*) is ℂ 0232/472-1010. Dial ℂ 0232/464-7795 to reach the **Alsancak Railway Station.** For the **Basmane Train Station,** dial ℂ 0232/ 484-8638.

What to See & Do

The Agora RUINS Constructed during the rule of Alexander the Great, the Agora is today mostly in ruins, destroyed by an earthquake in A.D. 178, Faustina, wife of Marcus Aurelius, had the Agora rebuilt. Later, Byzantines and Ottomans both used the space above it as a cemetery, leaving the ancient remains undisturbed and as a result one of the best-preserved Ionian agoras. The open-air museum—impressive at about 120m×78m (394 ft.×256 ft.)—contains the remains of three of the four main gates, some recognizable stalls, and a three-sided perimeter of porticos. Excavations of a monumental gated entrance to the Agora uncovered a treasure of statues of Greek gods and goddesses, along with more mundane figures of people and animals. More recent excavations of the Roman basilica have brought to light graffiti and drawings (in the basement), plus inscriptions of the people who provided aid after the earthquake.

Namazgah Mah. 816 Soka 29, Çankaya (East of Gaziosmanpaşa Bulv. or south of Anafartalar Cad.). ℂ **0232/483-4696.** Admission 3TL. Daily 8am–7pm (closes at 5pm in winter).

Archaeology Museum (Arkeoloji Müzesi) ★ MUSEUM   This place exhibits an impressive collection of ancient and Roman artifacts recovered from area excavations, including Bergama, Iassos, Bayraklı (Izmir's original settlement), and Izmir's Agora. A service path leads you to the gate of the museum grounds, which are full of wondrously oversize amphorae dating to the Hellenistic period, and columns and capitals arranged around the gardens as impromptu seating. The lobby contains a helpful map of Turkey indicating which regions belonged to which kingdoms—a must for understanding the historical evolution of the country and for appreciating the artifacts presented in this and other exhibits. Upstairs is a chronological exhibit of pottery, ceramics, and glass, as well as funerary objects and the reconstruction of a 3rd-millennium-B.C. tomb. Larger stone and marble statues take up the lower floor, including statues of Poseidon, Demeter, and Artemis taken from the altar of Zeus in the Agora, and a river god that ornamented a fountain at Ephesus.

South of Konak Sq. in Bahri Baba Park (main entrance up the hill from Konak Sq.). ℂ **0232/484-8324.** Admission 8TL. Tues–Sun 9am–6pm (closes at 5pm in winter).

Asansör & Dario Morena Sokak ★★ 🖼 LANDMARK & HISTORIC SITE   The Asansör quarter (alternatively known as Karataş) takes its name from the passenger elevator installed to provide access between the cliff-top neighborhoods and the sea-level streets below. Before the completion of the tower-enclosed elevator (*asansör* is the Turkish equivalent of the French word for a lift), itself constructed of bricks imported from Marseilles, residents were faced with 155 steps of pure heart attack. The base of the elevator lies at the end of historic Dario Moreno Sokak (named after a singer from the 1960s), a cobbled mews lined with restored Izmir houses. The view from the top, 50m (164 ft.) up, is as good as anything on the Amalfi Coast, and can be made more enjoyable over a tulip-shaped glass of tea or a meal at the Teras Restaurant Café (see "Where to Eat" on p. 216).

Dario Moreno Sok. Karataş, south of Konak Sq. No phone.

Clock Tower (Saat Kulesi)   LANDMARK   Commanding Konak Square, this elaborately decorated clock tower has become the symbol of Izmir. Designed in a late Ottoman Moorish style, the Clock Tower was presented to the city by Sultan Abdülhamid in 1901 and stands over 24m (79 ft.) high.

Konak Sq.

Kızlarağası Han Bazaar ★ HISTORIC SITE   This Ottoman *bedesten* has been a successful draw since its restoration, not just because few can resist a town bazaar, but also because the prices are amazingly competitive for the stocks of sumac carpets, water pipes, camel bone, and jewelry. Better yet, some of the best coffee in Turkey is served here in the shaded center courtyard.

Kemeraltı, off Anafartalar Cad. (Start asking for directions once you get close.) Daily 9am–7pm.

Konak Pier ENTERTAINMENT COMPLEX   The neighborhood of Konak was another lucky beneficiary of the redevelopment of Izmir's waterfront. Along with the neighborhood's wide-open plazas, there's this restored Customs House built by Gustave Eiffel. They've turned it into a shopping mall, replete with cinema, high-end shops, cafes, and waterside restaurants.

Atatürk Bulv. 19, Konak. ℂ **0232/489-1004.**

Where to Eat

Ever since the completion of the waterside promenade, the **Kordon** has become Izmir's de facto center for restaurants and breezy cafes. This is a great place to go for a stroll and meal. For the ambitious, a bit further out in Ückuyular (at the Levent Marina next to the ferry docks) is the pseudo sea-legged **Potiri Meyhane** (**©** **0232/ 259-0090**; www.leventmarina.com.tr), a Greek-style meyhane sitting atop a manmade bulkhead jutting out into the gulf. (When the metro to Ückuyular is complete, we suggest you run, not walk, to get here). Some more convenient suggestions (both on the Kordon and elsewhere) are listed below.

Asansör ★★ TURKISH   Taking full advantage of its cliff-top location above Dario Moreno Sokak and new management (the municipality of Izmir) Asansör Restaurant is no longer all about the views, which are, incidentally, spectacular. Whereas previously a dining experience here was at best mediocre, now the kitchen is living up to the full potential of the best spot on the Gulf of Izmir. The menu is a parade of the usual suspects (mezes, kebaps, steaks, fish), spread among three spaces, the Teras Café (summers only), Sedir Bar and Restaurant, and Ceneviz Meyhanesi, and live Turkish *fasıl* plays every night. Even better, for the best seat in town, dinner won't (necessarily) break the bank.

Şehit Nihat Bey Cad. 79 (best entry from Dario Moreno Sok. in the Asansör/Karataş neighborhood south of Kordon). www.grandplaza.com.tr.**©** **0232/261-2616.** Reservations suggested. Main courses 12TL–31TL. MC, V. Daily 7pm–midnight. Terrace cafe daily 9am–midnight.

Deniz Restaurant ★★ AEGEAN/FISH   With a reputation that precedes it (and follows it), Deniz easily earns the honors for Izmir's best restaurant, drawing a steady stream of local celebrities that as tourists, we won't recognize. Their specialty is an adaptation of a meaty favorite: *balık kavurma,* a preparation of the flakiest Mediterranean catch in a traditional earthenware pan. The fried ice cream is an unexpected delight, and the restaurant's nonsmoking room and unpretentious surroundings make the meal all the more enjoyable.

Atatürk Cad. 188/B (under Izmir Palas Oteli). www.denizrestaurant.com.tr.**©** **0232/464-4499.** Reservations required. Appetizers 8TL–21TL; fish by weight. DC, MC, V. Daily 11:30am–midnight.

Izmir Ticaret Odası Lokali ★ 🍴 KEBAPS   This unpretentious restaurant is a popular spot among local businessmen for lunch and the perfect, unassuming, and easy spot for dinner you've been asking around for, with (if you're lucky enough to arrive when one is vacant) tables lining great windows overlooking the Kordon. There are no surprises on the menu, except for the *süt kuzu kokoreç*—a soup of sheep's intestine (tripe, essentially), a traditional remedy for hangovers. Maybe try the grills or *pides* (flatbreads) instead.

Vasıf Çınar Bulv. 1 (on the 2nd floor opposite Deniz Restaurant).**©** **0232/421-4249.** Main courses 9TL–34TL. MC, V. Mon–Fri noon–midnight.

Medari Girit ★ AEGEAN   After many years in the restaurant business in Istanbul, Bamze and Medari Doğangır decided it was time for a change of scenery and a slower, calmer pace. Their dream crystallized in 2007 with the opening of this tiny and stylish *meyhane* in one of Izmir's most popular, and certainly characteristic, neighborhoods. If you've tried to get a reservation at Asansör but failed, Medari's place is just a few steps away. If you can forgo the admittedly spectacular views, you may just want to make a beeline here first, where the food, ambience, and authenticity of a lively Turkish evening spent over good food and music (Greek music Thurs–Sat) are guaranteed.

Mithatpaşa Cad. 462A, Konak (a few steps beyond Dario Moreno Sok.). © **0232/446-4886.** www. medarigirit.com. Reservations required. Main courses (fish) priced by weight. MC, V. Daily 7pm–midnight.

Izmir After Dark

The redevelopment of Izmir's waterfront truly infuses new life into this city on the sea. The grassy **Kordon waterfront park,** which runs from Cumhuriyet Meydanı to the ferryboat docks of **Alsancak** and beyond, is rimmed by, at last count, 14 establishments, including restaurants, pubs, and Italian cafes, all with terrace seating, and facing the open park and promenade. According to the locals, they're "all good, all the same, all expensive."

Alsancak, a neighborhood of cobbled streets and typical wooden houses with *cumbas,* or balconies, supported by ornate brackets, is also renowned for its nightlife. Head into 1448 Sokak, where cafe tables spill out onto the street and where a beer costs 3.50TL.

The highly regarded **Izmir State Opera and Ballet** (which also covers the **Izmir State Symphony Orchestra** (© 0232/489-0474; www.dobgm.gov.tr) performs from September to May; check with your travel agent or the official website for calendar and ticket information. Tickets for performances cost from 15TL to 75TL.

Where to Stay

Izmir Hilton ★   The Izmir Hilton needs no listing; the Hiltons are all excellent and they're all the same. This one opened in 1992 to provide a world-class, five-star facility in a town full of wannabes. Now, however, with the arrival of the Swissôtel Grand Efes down the street, along with a whole host of reasonably priced four- and five-star options, the competition is stiff. The staff is professional and dignified; the common areas sparkle; the rooms are plush, and user-friendly; and there isn't a thing the management hasn't thought of to make your stay seamless. And in typical American-management style, there is a price tag on every extra little thing you do.

Gaziosmanpaşa Bulv. 7, 35210 Alsancak, Izmir. www.hilton.com. © **800/445-8667** in the U.S., or 0232/497-6060. Fax 0232/497-6000. 380 units. From 250TL double; 300TL and up suite. AE, DC, MC, V. Parking garage free for guests. **Amenities:** 3 restaurants; 2 bars; babysitting; concierge; executive-level rooms; *hamam;* health club and spa; indoor pool; room service; wet and dry saunas; smoke-free rooms; tennis. *In room:* A/C, satellite TV, hair dryer, minibar, Wi-Fi (26TL per day).

Mövenpick ★   The Swiss-based Mövenpick Group, with locations all over the world, has jumped into the fray of direct competition with its compatriot, the Swissôtel Grand Efes across the street. Replacing the now-defunct Hotel Mercure, the Mövenpick is a well-respected hospitality franchise catering to business travelers on a budget, with decor and amenities pretty close to what you'll find in the Grand Efes. And with only 185 rooms (ranging from superior rooms to king suites), it's also more manageable. The facade of glass will also ensure that you get the best shot at a room with a view of the Gulf of Izmir. And the health club (also with views) complete with regular step, yoga, and Pilates classes will ensure that you don't overdo it (too much) in the hotel restaurant.

Gaziosmanpaşa Bulv. 138, 35210, Izmir. www.moevenpick-hotels.com. © **0232/484-1414.** Fax 0232/484-8070. 185 units. 95€–170€ double; 156€ and up suite. Breakfast and tax not included. Lower rates reflect advance booking. AE, DC, MC, V. Free valet parking. **Amenities:** 2 restaurants;

2 bars; babysitting; concierge; executive-level rooms; *hamam;* health club and spa; indoor pool; room service; smoke-free rooms, free Wi-Fi. *In room:* A/C, satellite TV w/movies, hair dryer, minibar.

Swissôtel Grand Efes ★★★   After 4 transitional years, and with the Swissôtel now at the helm, the Grand Efes can once again hold its head up as Izmir's premier five-star property. A member of The Leading Hotels of the World, the rebuilt and refurbished Grand Efes, convention center, and facilities are geared to a primarily business clientele. There's a state-of-the-art conference center and high-tech room amenities that feature high-speed Internet (wireless and ISDN). Suites have cordless phones, CD players, and the essential espresso machine. The modern decor is business-sleek and stylish, using tasteful woodsy tones, natural fabrics, and black accents for that designer feel. There's plenty of attention paid to relaxation, with an enormous outdoor swimming pool, a lovely palm garden, and the very soothing Amrita Spa.

Gaziosmanpaşa Bulv. 1, 35210 Izmir. www.izmir.swissotel.com. ☏ **0232/414-0000.** Toll free in the U.S./Canada ☏ 800/637-9477; in the U.K. ☏ 0800/6379-4471; in Australia ☏ 800/121043). Fax 0232/414-1010. 402 units. 96€–240€ double; 246€ and up suite. AE, DC, MC, V. Free valet parking. **Amenities:** 4 restaurants; 4 bars; babysitting; concierge; executive-level rooms; *hamam;* health club and spa; indoor and outdoor pools; room service; smoke-free rooms. *In room:* A/C, satellite TV w/movies, hair dryer, minibar, free Wi-Fi.

A Side Trip to Sardis

Not too many years back, a reader wrote to express his disappointment that **Sardis ★★** was absent in the guide. So I set about to find out whether Sardis was indeed all that. Let's just start by saying that even if you have absolutely no context of the ancient city in advance of a visit, you will be wowed.

Sardis was the commercial and religious capital of the ancient kingdom of Lydia, made most famous (or infamous) for the 4th-century-B.C. ruler with the Midas touch: Croesus, who reportedly went about town with his pockets stuffed with gold pieces recovered from the nearby Pactolus River. Hmmm. Announce that there's gold in them thar hills and don't be surprised when the raiding empires arrive. Persian ruler Cyrus wrested control of Lydia from Croesus, and under Persian rule, Lydia rose to become the most powerful kingdom in all of Asia Minor. The kingdom fell to Alexander the Great in 334 B.C., and then was apportioned to the Kingdom of Pergamon after Alexander's death. The city continued to prosper through the Byzantine era (when it was a central diocese and recipient of a solid fifth of the letters to the **Seven Churches of the Revelation**), until the 14th century when it was conquered by the Ottoman Turks.

So my question is: Where are the riches? For the most part, they are all gone, stripped away by looters long ago (but short of digging a very deep hole—I looked). Actually, early in the 20th century, excavations being carried out by Princeton University uncovered a pot of gold and silver coinage, so apparently either we're late or we need bigger shovels. Excavations cosponsored by Harvard and Cornell universities have been ongoing since 1959 and have focused on unearthing the Lydian period, a tall order given that ancient Lydia sits 2m (6½ ft.) below the Roman roadways, which themselves are buried beneath meters of earth sequestered under village residences, chicken coops, and fields of wheat, barley, cotton, and corn. The monumental marble Roman avenue, partially (minusculely, as most of it is buried beneath the asphalt road) excavated on the south side of the site, spanned a width of 19m (62 ft.), more than double the width of the current highway.

In the past 100 or so years of excavations, more than 11,000 artifacts have been uncovered, the more recent and notable of which (found in the Temple of Artemis) was a *1.2m-tall* (4-ft.) marble head of what is presumed to represent either Marcus Aurelius or his son, Commodus.

The open-air museum comprises the section of the city that served as the **Gymnasium and Bathhouse ★★**, a 2-hectare (5-acre) complex that includes the **Palestra, Caldarium,** and **Frigidarium,** as well as the largest **synagogue** of the ancient world, a classically appointed space of geometrical tile mosaics occupying the southeastern corner of the Palestra (gifted to the Jewish community in recognition of its value; synagogues were normally sited on the periphery of the cities). The east-facing **monumental facade ★★★** of the Palestra is believed to be a 3rd-century-A.D. construction of Roman emperors and brothers, Geta and Caracalla.

The **colonnaded arcade ★★** that flanks the exterior of the Palestra is lined by an extended string of Byzantine-era shops, whose second stories have long disappeared, leaving stone staircases to nowhere. Several of the shops are identifiable by inscriptions on the doorway or on the odd marble basin.

Exiting from the museum and heading to the right across the main village road to the next perpendicular on the left is a road leading to the **Temple of Artemis ★★**. On your way to the temple the road passes an enclosed excavation that revealed (thanks to the gold dust found in the cracks of pottery found here) the Lydian mint, or the **gold refinery** where Lydia's renowned coinage was created. A bit farther along the Roman road are the ruins of a 13th-century basilica. The basilica is the only known example in Anatolia with five cupolas.

The temple of Artemis is the fourth-largest Ionic temple of the ancient world, dug out of millennia of landslides and earthquakes. The temple dates to the Hellenistic era inaugurated with Alexander's conquest. The oldest portion of the temple was constructed during this period around a **preexisting altar** of red sandstone also dedicated to Artemis, and perhaps additionally, to Cybele. In 175 to150 B.C., Zeus was added to the pantheon of the temple.

72km (45 miles) east of Izmir (follow the road through Türgütlü and then Ahmetli; the ancient site of Sardis is located in the village of Sart). Admission 5TL. Daily 9am–7pm summer; 8am–5pm winter.

BERGAMA & PERGAMUM ★★

About 250km (155 miles) south of Çanakkale; 103km (64 miles) north of Izmir

The bustling city of Bergama boasts the main attractions of the Acropolis and Asklepion of **Pergamum ★★★**, rightfully listed among the top 100 historical sites on the Mediterranean and home to one of the **seven churches of the Apocalypse.** But flanked by an industrial wasteland to the north and a forgettable series of seaside footnotes to the holiday resorts closer to Izmir, Bergama has long been a stop, look, and leave destination for bus tours and the rare intrepid traveler. Still, while the appeal of Bergama—a typical Anatolian city with layers of historic roots, including a maze of narrow, Ottoman-era lanes winding their way around lovely (if still a bit dilapidated) stone and wooden houses, notable mosques and bare-bones *lokantas*—should be hearty enough to attract people, the 2½ hour's drive from Izmir together with combined admissions fees of 45TL (for the Acropolis, Asklepion, Red Basilica, and the Archaeological Museum), set the bar pretty high. Ultimately, if you're in/around Izmir, or venturing into the province of Çanakkale, you should make the trip. Otherwise, perhaps you should save it for your next trip to Turkey.

Essentials

GETTING THERE

Your best bet for getting into Bergama is on a **Metro Turizm** bus (✆ **444-3455** or 0232/667-2131 at the *otogar;* www.metroturizm.com.tr), which provides long-distance service to Bergama center with a change to a smaller minibus at the *otogar*. From Istanbul, the fare is 60TL (53TL if you buy your ticket online). All other buses (except Truva, which dumps you on the highway opposite the *otogar*) go to the new bus station located approximately 7km (4⅓ miles) outside of town. From there, either hop on the free *dolmuş* shuttle into town (the regular *dolmuş* costs 1.50TL) or take a *metered* taxi.

VISITOR INFORMATION

The **tourist information office** is located at Izmir Cad. 54, to the right of the government building (✆ **0232/633-1862**), and is open weekdays 8:30am to 12:30pm and 2 to 5:30pm.

ORIENTATION

The town of Bergama has developed on and around the ancient city of Pergamum. The heart of the modern city lies around the town's central park and municipal building while the center of Eski, or Old Bergama, with its fruit market and carpet shops, is situated around the adjoining neighborhood of the Red Basilica, with its necklace of dusty souvenir shops and carpet sellers. The road past the Red Basilica winds up and around for about 5km (3 miles) until it arrives at the Acropolis, while the Asklepion is located closer to town behind the military camp. Frequently overlooked are the original old Greek houses of Eski Bergama, whose steep inclined streets intertwine in the neighborhood above the Red Basilica.

GETTING AROUND

A new funicular now transports visitors up the hill to the top of the Akropolis, circumventing what had become a major source of income for local taxi drivers. A round-trip ticket costs 8TL. If you're looking for an uphill hike, there's a way to access the Acropolis on foot, (cross the Tabak Bridge and follow the path up and to the right toward the lower Agora.)

A Look at The Past

The ancient city of Pergamum (also written as Pergamon) dates back to the 12th century B.C. but saw its first notable era of prosperity under Lydian King Croesus in the 6th century B.C. Pergamum briefly fell under Persian control but was wrestled back into Hellenistic hands in 334 B.C. by Alexander the Great. While Alexander was out conquering other lands, Anatolia was left in the hands of his general, Lysimachus, who had entrusted his war chest to the hands of Philataerus, commander of Pergamum. On Lysimachus's death, Philataerus founded a ruling dynasty with the late general's riches and was succeeded by his nephew, Eumenis I. Eumenis II is credited with bringing the empire to its height, ushering in a period of economic, cultural, and artistic expansion in the 2nd century B.C. When Attalus III, the last of the ruling Attalid dynasty, died, his ambiguous testament was interpreted by Rome as carte blanche for the Romans to come take over. Under the Romans, Pergamum reclaimed a measure of its former greatness, but the town was all but forgotten once the Ottomans took control.

What to See & Do

The Acropolis ★★ RUINS   Dominating the summit of a hill almost 300m (984 ft.) high, the Acropolis provides a humbling view of the surrounding plains, aqueducts, and reservoir below. The remains of this once-great empire are no less impressive, despite the fact that most artifacts are now on exhibit at the Pergamum Museum in Berlin. Here it's still possible to ramble around the Upper and Lower cities, amid the palaces, public and private buildings, and temples too large to cart away. Although only the foundation remains, the **Temple of Athena** was probably constructed, using the Acropolis of Athens as a model, in the 3rd century B.C., in the earliest days of the Pergamene kingdom. Today you can see the architrave, along with fragments of columns, in the Berlin Museum.

Eumenis II's construction of the **great library** rivaled the one at Alexandria, provoking the Egyptians into an embargo of papyrus. Lacking such a basic essential, the people of Pergamum were forced to come up with an alternative, and parchment was invented. Ironically, when Pergamum came under Roman rule, Marc Antony gifted the entire 200,000-volume collection to Cleopatra, shipping the contents of the rival library back to Alexandria, where, tragically, the entire collection was destroyed in a fire. A 3m (9¾-ft.) statue of the goddess Athena, discovered in the area of the reading room, is now housed in the Berlin Museum.

Near the temple of Athena are the remnants of the **Palaces of the Pergamene Kings.** The smaller, northern building is believed to have been that of Attalus while the larger palace most likely belonged to Eumenes II. Mosaics discovered in the internal courtyards of the palaces are now in the Berlin Museum.

With the Romanization of Pergamum, many of the Hellenic foundations were simply adapted to suit the arriving Roman emperors and administrators. The **Temple of Trajan ★★** is one example, and because of removal or looting, the temple remains dated to Hellenistic times.

The remarkable **theater ★★★**, built into the hillside and split into three sections of tiers, was composed of 80 extraordinary levels that seated up to 10,000 people. The panorama is awe-inspiring—a fact not overlooked by Eumenes II, who had a 240m-long (787-ft.) *stoa* (covered arcade) constructed along the upper terrace of the theater. At the northern end of the terrace promenade was the **Temple of Dionysus,** which, along with the altar, is in a fairly good state of preservation. The **Temple of Dionysus** was restored by Caracalla after a fire gutted the interior.

The largest building on the Acropolis is the **Altar of Zeus,** built during the reign of Eumenes II. Fragments of the altar were recycled in the construction of the Byzantine fortification walls, but rediscovered by Carl Humann in 1871 and later reconstructed in the Berlin Museum. The reliefs (also in Berlin) depicted the mythological battle between the giants and the gods—an analogy to the Pergamene victory of the Galatians.

The **Agora** and **Agora Temple** lie to the south of the Altar of Zeus. As you head down the hill to the south, you arrive at the **Lower City,** where, up until a brush fire cleared out the overgrowth, not much more than crumbling foundations remained. Ambitious types and those heading down to town on foot should keep an eye out for what's left of the **Sanctuaries of Hera** and of **Demeter,** the **Temple of Asklepios,** several **gymnasiums,** a **House attributed to Attalos,** and a **Lower Agora.**

Hilltop; adjacent to the Garrison at Kurtuluş Mah. Akropol Yolu No. 2. © **0232/631-0778.** Admission 20TL. Nov–Mar daily 8am–5pm; Apr–Oct daily 8am–7pm.

Archaeology Museum (Arkeoloji Müzesi) ★ MUSEUM The collection of statues, objects, and gravestones housed in this museum represents a fraction of the Acropolis and Asklepion ruins that the Germans didn't carry off. In spite of this, a visit here is a worthy complement to the site visits, and the curators have even been kind enough to create a faithful replica of Zeus's Altar, saving you from a trip to Berlin. Some other notable objects amid the artifacts include a statue of Hadrian taken from the Asklepion library; a 2nd-century-A.D. stone horse from the altar of Zeus; and the oldest statue in the museum, a 4th-century-B.C. *kuros*, an early example of the sculpted human form. The ethnographic wing exhibits a collection of objects, costumes, and textiles from the surrounding region.

Zafer Mah. Cumhuriyet Cad. 6 (on left across from the BP gas station). ⓒ **0232/631-2883.** Admission 5TL. Tues–Sun 8:30am–5:30pm.

The Asklepion ★★ RUINS This famed ancient medical center, built in honor of Asklepios, the god of healing, was also the world's first psychiatric hospital. Many of the treatments employed at Pergamum, enhanced by a sacred source of water that was later discovered as having radioactive properties, have been used for centuries, and are once again finding modern application. The treatments included psychotherapy, massage, herbal remedies, mud and bathing treatments, interpretation of dreams, and the drinking of water. The Asklepion gained in prominence under the Romans in the 2nd century A.D., but a sacred site existed prior to this as early as the 4th century B.C.

Oddly enough, everybody who was anybody was dying to get in; patients included Hadrian, Marcus Aurelius, and Caracalla. Therapy included mud baths, music concerts, and doses of water from the sacred fountain. Hours of therapy probed the meaning of the previous night's dreams, as patients believed dreams recounted a visit by the god Asklepios, who held the key to curing the illness. Galen, the influential physician and philosopher who was born in Pergamum in A.D. 129, trained and then later became an attendant to the gladiators here.

Access is via the **Sacred Way ★★**, which at 807m (2,648 ft.) long and colonnaded originally connected the Asklepion with the Acropolis. The Sacred Way becomes the stately Via Tecta near the entrance to the site and leads to a courtyard and fallen Propylaeum, or Monumental Gate. Don't miss the focus of the first courtyard, an **altar** inscribed with the emblem of modern medicine, the serpent. To the right of the courtyard is the Emperor's Room, which was also used as a library. The circular domed **Temple of Asklepios,** with a diameter of 23m (75 ft.), recalls the Pantheon in Rome, which was completed only 20 years earlier. Reachable through an underground tunnel is what is traditionally called the **Temple of Telesphorus ★**, which served as both the treatment rooms and the sleeping chambers, an indication that sleep was integral in the actual healing process. At various spots in the center of the complex are a total of three pools and fountains, used for bathing, drinking, and various other forms of treatment. The semicircular **Roman Theatre ★** flanks the colonnaded promenade on the northwest corner of the site.

Zafer Mahallesi Prof. Dr. Frieldhelm Korte Caddesi No. 1. ⓒ **0232/631-2886.** Admission 15TL. Nov–Mar daily 8am–5:30pm; Apr–Oct daily 8:30am–7pm.

Red Basilica (Kızıl Avlu) ★★ HISTORIC SITE This is one impressive pile of red brick. Built during the reign of Hadrian, this temple dedicated to the Egyptian god Serapis (the model for the Greek god Isis) was later to become one of the seven churches of the Apocalypse. The temple was destroyed in the Arab raids of A.D. 716

to 717, and then was significantly altered by the Byzantines to serve as a basilica. The enormous building straddles the ancient Selinus River (today the Bergama Cayı), whose two subterranean galleries provide a canal. True to the ideal that holy ground is always holy ground, a small mosque resides in one of the towers. (The second tower has been recently restored and exhibits works recovered during the ongoing excavations.) Rounding out the trifecta of great religions making use of this site, there are a number of stone tablets engraved in Hebrew, indicating the presence of a vibrant Jewish community here as well.

Outskirts of town, at the base of the hill to the Old City and the road up to the Acropolis. ℰ **0232/631-2885.** Admission 5TL. Winter daily 8:30am–5:30pm; summer daily 8:30am–6:30pm.

Where to Eat

There are a number of restaurants with courtyard gardens targeting groups and a few tiny *pide* joints and *lokantas* lining the road between the Red Basilica and the Archaeology Museum (some take a detour past the Selçuk Minaret). Try **Paksoy** (Istiklal Meydanı 39; ℰ **0232/633-1722**) and sink your teeth into their cholesterol-heavy *kıymalı yumurtalı* (meat and egg) *pide*, or sit down for a meal at **Meydan Restaurant** (Istiklal Meydanı 4; ℰ **0232/633-1793**), an eating institution in Bergama.

Berto Sosyal Tesisleri TURKISH   Run by the Bergama Chamber of Commerce, this "social establishment" is filling the dining void with this lovely restaurant near the Ulu Mosque (sure, the town has other restaurants, but they ebb and flow with the tourist tide, as does the freshness of the dishes served). The restored building dates to 1850 and the outdoor terrace and ground-level cafe take advantage of the manicured landscaping. The menu sticks to the expected salads, meatballs, and grills.

Ulucami Mah. Büyük Alan Mevkii. ℰ **0232/632-9641.** Appetizers and main courses 6TL–12TL. MC, V. Daily noon–10pm. Closed for Ramadan.

Where to Stay

Hera Hotel 🏨   For years, Bergama remained a wasteland for anybody looking for more than just a less-than-satisfactory place to stay. Until June 2011, that is. Charm abounds at the Hera, named after the goddess' symbol, the pomegranate, owing to the pomegranate tree that overtakes the courtyard of what are two restored 200-year-old Greek stone houses. The hotel gleams with wood floors and ceilings, traditional Turkish decor and a cozy wine cellar. Breakfast (or any drink, any time of day, for that matter) is served on the rooftop terrace, with a panoramic view of the Red Basilica and the Acropolis that simply enchants. If you're all about the views, you may want to book the Zeus room, large enough to look out both on the city and on the Acropolis, or the Hera room, which overlooks the Red Basilica.

Talatpaşa Mah. Tabak Köprü Cad. 21, 35700 Bergama. www.hotelhera.com. ℰ **0232/631-0634.** Fax 0232/631-0635. 10 units. 95€–115€ double. MC, V. **Amenities:** Restaurant; bar; room service. *In room:* A/C, satellite TV, hair dryer, free Wi-Fi.

HIGHLIGHTS OF THE ÇEŞME PENINSULA ★

81km (50 miles) west of Izmir

Given the density of cultural riches on the tried-and-true paths of the Anatolian "mainland," few foreigners venture out to Çeşme, Izmir's sun-kissed western peninsula.

Perhaps now with the new superhighway, driving those scant 81km (50 miles) won't seem so insurmountable. Add another half hour's drive and you're at Ephesus, and that's why you came to these parts anyway, right?

Çeşme, named after the many springs found in the area during the 18th and 19th centuries, is a world-class Aegean resort, blessed with picturesque beaches and thermal spas both numbering well into the double digits. When the jet set discovered the haunts of the Bodrum Peninsula, typical Turks on holiday migrated north to the crystalline beaches of Çeşme, which responded to the influx with a nightlife scene that rivals (or replaces) that of Istanbul off-season.

Despite Çeşme's newfound popularity, it still manages to remain relatively untarnished, offering a perfect balance between sybaritic and simple pleasures, such as the appreciation of unspoiled stretches of fertile fields of aniseed, mastic trees, and olive groves. And each corner has its own character. **Alaçatı town,** with its density of historical restored Greek houses, wins hands down for charm, and thanks to all of the restaurants, cafes, boutiques, and bougainvillea, you may not even want a car to drive out. Windsurfers and watersports enthusiasts prefer the wind-swept **Alaçatı Bay,** gifting athletes with high winds, shallow waters, and deep blue expanses. **Ilica Beach** has long attracted visitors seeking out the healing thermal waters of the **Şifne Springs** and has one of the more scenic expanses of sand. The arrival of a number of first-class hotels with spas, and a vibrant resort center, makes Ilica a worthy stopover. The enclosed harbor of **Dalyan** is a quiet and serene fishing port, where you can shut out the world until dinnertime, when you'll show up at one of the postcardperfect restaurants in the marina very, very hungry. There are a few pensions here and one boutique hotel. And in **Çeşme** proper, you'll get the widest choice of food, shopping, and history and easy access to car rentals, ferry excursions, or day trips.

Orientation

The Çeşme Peninsula stretches out into the Aegean to the west of Izmir. At the extreme western tip passing through is the small resort town of Çeşme, about an hour's drive out of Izmir. About 10km (6¼ miles) before arriving in Çeşme on the highway is the turnoff for **Alaçatı the old town and bay.** Along the northeast coastal road is the beach and thermal resort of **Ilica,** the thermals of **Şifne,** and, farther northeast along the coast, the ruins of **Erythrai** and the picturesque fishing village of **Ildırı.** (Villages farther north such as **Foca** and **Karaburun**—easily 2 hours to the north—require more time than I recommend for a short visit to Çeşme.)

South of Çeşme and the *limanı* (harbor) are some of the finest beaches in the area, namely **Pırlanta** and **Altınkum.**

From the Izmir highway exit road down to the waterfront, a right turn onto the harbor road leads into the heart of Çeşme, where a cluster of travel agents and restaurants, as well as the tourist information office, are located. Dominating the main square is the **Genovese Castle,** which, together with the **Selçuk caravansaray,** is a striking sight from the sea. Perpendicular to the main square is the pedestrian **Inkılap Caddesi,** Çeşme's main shopping street, which heads inland from the waterfront. The road from the harbor to Tekke Beach at the northern end of Çeşme town, sends traffic in a one-way direction. At Tekke Beach, drivers can either circle back up and around town or follow signs for **Ayayorgı Beach** or the small port village of **Dalyan.**

Essentials

GETTING THERE

BY CAR   The E881 Izmir-Çeşme toll expressway runs the length of the peninsula and connects Çeşme with Izmir and the region beyond. You can also take the somewhat (but not terribly) scenic D300 into town.

BY BUS   Buses from Izmir leave from the main *otogar* outside of town, heading westward through Izmir before getting on the highway. Therefore, if you're staying around Konak, it makes more sense to get the bus near Fahrettin Altay Meydanı; ask your taxi driver to go to this secondary bus stop (once the Izmir Metro expansion reaches this far, you'll be able to hop on a train to Fahrettin Altay Meydanı). Alternatively, you can take the no. 7 city bus that runs along the coastal road from Cumhuriyet Meydanı through Üçkuyular. Bus connections from other cities in the region must be made at the main *otogar*. If you're arriving directly from Izmir's Adnan Menderes Airport, your best bet is to avoid Izmir center entirely and take a taxi to the bus station in Üçkuyular, from where you can grab a bus into Çeşme. Bus companies serving Çeşme include **Çeşme Seyahat** (*€* **0232/712-6499**), **Kamıl Koç** (*€* **0232/712-9832**), **Metro** (*€* **444-3455** or 0232/712-0033), **Pamukkale** (*€* **444-3535** or 0232/712-9954), **Ulusoy** (*€* **444-1888** or 0232/712-1313), and **Varan** (*€* **0232/712-0493**). The number for the *otogar* in Çeşme is *€* **0232/712-6499**.

Buses arriving into Çeşme arrive into town by way of the harbor road, stopping at the top of Inkılap Caddesi before arriving at the new *otogar* at the junction of the *çevreyolu* and the Izmir-Çeşme highway extension, just uphill from the main harbor. There is a taxi stand at both the main town square and at the *otogar*. (**Note:** all buses into Çeşme make stops in Alaçatı.)

BY FERRY   The Turkish-based **Ertürk Lines** (www.erturk.com.tr; *€* **0232/712-6768**; travel agency located opposite the marina) operates year-round service between Chios and Çeşme, departing at 5 or 6pm (plus 9:30am on Sat). Passage costs 10€ for a one-way trip and or same-day round-trip (non-same-day returns are 20€).

VISITOR INFORMATION

The staff at the tourist information office (*€* **0232/712-6653**), located on the waterfront across from the castle, is ready, willing, and able to provide thorough and useful information on a wide range of subjects. If I had any influence with the local municipality, I'd give these people a raise. Closed Sundays. For advance planning, surf over to www.cesme.gen.tr.

 Mastic: The Truth About Gum

The resin-producing mastic tree that grows all over the Çeşme Peninsula (and the Eastern Mediterranean) has been used for centuries in many ways: to heal stomach ulcers, to clean and polish teeth, as a sunscreen and a sunburn soother, and more. In Çeşme, mastic is used in jams, to make pudding, or as a flavoring for raki (an alcoholic drink), while in the United States, the same ingredient is used chiefly as a varnish or adhesive substance. Mastic pudding, along with other cleverly bottled marmalades, is available at **Rumeli Pastanesi**, Inkılap Cad. 46, Çeşme (*€* **0232/712-6759**; www.rumelipastanesi.com).

GETTING AROUND

With a car at your disposal, the peninsula will more readily show its special appeal, and several rental agencies can be found at the beginning and end of Inkılap Caddesi. For advance reservations (which are rarely necessary), call **Blue Rent a Car** (16 Eylül Mah. Gümrük Sok. 11; © **0232/712-0939;** www.cesmebluerentacar.com); Ismet, the manager, speaks fantastic English and plays entirely by the book.

A number of local car rental companies or travel agencies rent out scooters for around 20€ to 25€ per day—but know that technically, only drivers with an "A" class Turkish license can rent one. Still, many establishments ignore this rule at their and your peril; in the event of an accident, your home insurance may not cover losses.

Dolmuş service to points beyond operates from downtown Çeşme (in front of the municipal building at the end of Inkılap Cad., near waterfront, or from the *otogar*) to nearby beaches and sights. Fares vary only slightly and hover around 3TL to 4TL.

There's a taxi stand (© **0232/712-6690**) next to the castle in downtown Çeşme, but the rates are outrageous, and *dolmuşes* are fast, reliable, and cheap.

What to See & Do

Genovese Castle CASTLE   Built in the 14th century by the Genovese to protect wine shipments, this fortress was expanded and reconstructed by the Ottoman Sultan Beyazıt II in the beginning of the 16th century. It was destroyed during the wars with Venice in the 17th century, restored again in the 18th, and continued to serve as a defense system until 1833. The fortress is now the **Çeşme Archaeological Museum** housing artifacts recovered during excavations of Erythrai. The mosque that was built within the castle walls is now used as the museum's administration building.

Opposite the ferry landing. © **0232/712-6609.** Admission 3TL. Daily 8:30am–12:30pm and 1:30–5:30pm.

The Village of Ildırı and the Ancient Ruins of Erythrai ★ ⬛ RUINS

Located about a half-hour's drive (17km/11 miles) on the coastal road north from Ilica is **Ildırı,** which enjoys the shelter of a small bay protected by a series of offshore islands. Not surprisingly, the locals, who number only about 350, make their livings on fishing boats as well as in artichoke and olive fields (and until 15 years ago, in tobacco fields, too). A number of fish restaurants line the small dock as well as the road leading to the village. On the road at the edge of town are a couple of covered shacks called restaurants—the characteristic covered, stone terraces overlook the artichoke and olive fields toward the sea. Stop here for some *gözleme* (a crepe filled with cheese, spinach, or both) and an *ayran* (a buttermilk-like salty yogurt drink), or for some fish only recently pulled out of the water.

On the edge of Ildırı is the ancient Greek city of **Erythrai ★**, whose remains are still mostly hidden beneath the fields of artichokes cultivated by the local villagers. Sporadic excavations conducted since 1964 have revealed a theater, dating to the 3rd century B.C. and destroyed in an earthquake in A.D. 100. There are some visible signs of a city plan, including the 6th-century-B.C. Temple of Heracles (unexcavated), a 5th-century-B.C. sacrificial altar, and 2nd-century-B.C. luxury villas and mosaic stone pavement. A climb to the top of the theater and up to the summit of the hill will reveal an old basilica-style church, as well as some of the loveliest views in the region.

About a half-hour's drive (17km/11 miles) on the coastal road north from Ilica. No phone. Admission free. Daily 8am–5pm.

SURF, SUN & SPORTING FUN

Day boats lining Çeşme's harbor tout excursions in the Aegean for swimming, snorkeling, or simply relaxing. A day usually includes stops at **Donkey Island** (there really are donkeys there), the **Blue Lagoon,** and **Black Island.** The cost is 30TL with lunch included (20TL on weekdays). Stroll along the harbor the night before to inspect the boats, and ask if the music will be blaring and what's on the menu. For a quieter (and less crowded) day spent on a boat, snorkeling or just sunning on deck, check with one of the dive outfitters to see if they take stowaways, as these boat trips generally provide a more relaxing atmosphere.

If exploring the shipwrecks offshore is more your speed, or you just want to brush up on some rusty diving skills, contact **Dolphin Land** (✆ **0232/435-7069;** fax 0232/486-2309; www.divecesme.com) for information on their day trips around Çeşme. They also offer PADI certification with English instruction.

You'll need a car to get to **Alaçatı Bay ★★★**, a wind-swept expanse of water surrounded by scruffy sun-scorched hills. Thanks to year-round high winds, shallow waveless water, and wide-open space, the bay is one of the top three **windsurfing** destinations in the world and of late a popular destination for a growing number of windsurf groupies. Windsurfers from the four corners come here to participate in the Windsurf Turkey Cup, in which thrill-seekers compete in a stunt-filled challenge of wits and skill. The rest of the year, neophytes like me get out there and entertain the pros from the on-site windsurfing schools with my ineptitude. (Note to self: Next time go early in the day, when the winds are at their gentlest.) **Alaçatı Surf Paradise Club** (✆ **0232/716-6611;** www.alacati.de; closed Nov–Mar) makes it all possible by renting various models by the hour or by the day, with or without instruction. To keep with the times, they've also added stand-p paddling. To get there, just follow the signs; you can't miss it. If you've just come to Alaçatı for the beach, stake out a lounge chair and umbrella at Makkah Beach Club attached to the school.

A strip of sand over 1.5km (a mile) long, **Ilica Beach ★★★** is the longest beach on the peninsula and also the most popular. A new marina and breakwater provide direct access (no beach), and a series of semi-immersed iron ladders beckon to those wishing to dive right in. The steamy Ilica spring bubbles up right in the middle of a rock-sheltered corner of the marina, which attracts locals and visitors alike with the (free) opportunity to partake in the healing properties of the water.

Southwest of Çeşme are two of the best public beaches the peninsula has to offer. **Pırlanta Beach (Diamond Beach) ★★**, a pristine stretch of lily-white sand, is oriented north toward the rocky coastline. It's a bit windy here, due to the compressed winds that travel through the channel between Chios and Pırlanta Bay. The resulting foamy waves and high winds make this a perfect spot for what has become an area sports craze: **kitesurfing.** Lessons are available in English; contact www.kitesurfbeach.com.

Altınkum Beach ★★★, named "golden" for the color of its sand, is a long stretch of beach wide open to the sea and facing south, making the waters slightly, refreshingly cooler than the other beaches on the peninsula. At these public beaches, the entrance is free and chairs and umbrellas rent for a small fee. A minibus from the yacht harbor will take you to both beaches, a distance just under 8km (5 miles). If you're driving yourself, follow the directions for the "Ionia Hotel" at the multisigned fork in the road heading toward Altınkum/Pirlanta. (**Note:** Don't confuse Altınkum with the disappointing stretch at Tursite; follow the small black sign for PLAJ.) There's also a restaurant shack on the beach at Altınkum that includes a cafeteria/bar/restaurant.

North of Çeşme, hidden amid the olive and orange groves, is **Ayayorgı Beach ★★★**, an intimate and secluded bay with no actual beach—just cement piers (no sand!) and crystalline waters. The very popular Istanbul entertainment venue Babylon staked a corner of the bay with **Babylon Beach Club** (© 0232/712-6339; www.babylon.com.tr); offering a restaurant, cafe, bar, beach club, and concert venue all rolled into one. (Open June–Sept). A 40TL day pass applies for Saturday and Sunday (70TL if you come both days), 30TL weekdays. Rent some jet skis, go wake-boarding or water-skiing, or jump on a banana ride. Hang around long enough and one or both become host to major and popular headliners or some of the area's hottest DJs. You'll need a car (or fairly expensive taxi) for the 3.5km (2¼-mile) ride from Çeşme to this beach; take the road for Dalyan and follow the signs.

A day spent roaming in and out of the leather, carpet, and silver shops of downtown Çeşme doesn't have to mean you've blown your day at the beach. **Tekke Beach,** just north of the port (and past a dizzying array of appealing waterfront fish restaurants), is the perfect escape for a quick cool-down and limited time.

AREA THERMALS

Çeşme owes its current rebirth to its thermal sources, considered sacred by the ancients. Turkish tourism officials are likewise bowing down to the venerable thermal resources, with a strategy to exploit this natural resource to its full tourism potential. Stay tuned, as the places listed here are far from the last word in Çeşme's thermal spa experience. For now, though, you can be sure that any hotel in Çeşme or Ilica worth its salt is tapping into the local liquid gold mine. (See "Where to Stay" for thermal facilities beyond those listed below).

Of note are the on-site spas at the Sheraton Çeşme and the Radisson Blu. The **Botanica Thermal Spa ★★★** at the Sheraton in Ilica (Şifne Cad. 35; © 0232/723-1240), was re-created (it was redesigned a few years after opening) with nothing but sheer bliss in mind. The Oriental fusion concept mixes up a luxurious stew of Buddhist, Chinese, Thai, and Balinese influences, welcoming guests to a full-service facility with four thermal pools, one saltwater and three highly sulfuric (of which one is a Jacuzzi and another is outdoor). The center also has a *hamam,* a steam room, a dry sauna, a solarium, and soothing treatment rooms surrounding the outdoor thermal pool. Spa treatments include 14 types of massage, aromatherapies, and various skin treatments, from the Energy Lift L'Elixir facial, to the Indocéane "works" (body scrub, milk bath, massage, body wrap, and relaxing tea service). Combined use of the thermal pools costs 25TL for hotel guests, 50TL for outside guests. At the **Radisson Blu ★★★** (Altınyunus Mah. 3435 Sok. 25, Ilica; © 0232/455-4500), you can get lost in the 3,500-sq.-m (37,674-sq.-ft.) **Dulcis Thermal Spa** facility, as you make your way past the 21 treatment rooms and the three, count 'em, three *hamams.* Along with a large indoor pool, there's an outdoor thermal pool and another, 1,000-sq.-m (10,764-sq.-ft.) colossus that can only be described as vast.

West of Ilica town center is the tiny **Yıldız Peninsula;** near the point is an oddity of geology: thermal water as hot as 122° to 140°F (50°–60°C) springing forth from beneath the surface of the water. This natural phenomenon doesn't have a price tag, as there's no charge to step off the rocky point into the semi-enclosed rocky pool. (Many who have led sheltered lives come here only to eyeball the bare flesh of women in bathing suits.) It's not uncommon, either, to see women submerged yet covered head to toe in full traditional dress.

North of Ilica on the tip of a small peninsula is a number of small coves, hidden in pine trees and rarely visited. The campground at **Paşa Limanı ★★** does triple duty as a beach, a thermal, and a campsite. The long rectangular thermal pool, located at the back of the property, is partially shaded in pine, and the waters averaging 104°F (40°C) cascade down a small slide onto the pebble beach just steps below.

Where to Eat
ÇEŞME TOWN

A number of stylish restaurants vie for your business at the lovely town marina. There are also plenty of eateries along the happening main drag of Inkilap Cad., but because ownership (and names) change, its best to scope these places out once you're there.

Imren TURKISH   Opened by two immigrants from Yugoslavia in 1960, Imren which is the oldest restaurant in town, serves what looks to the untrained eye as Turkish food, only it's got their hometown Rumelian roots. Their specialties include the eggplant casserole with yellow cheese, stuffed marrow flowers and a variety of grilled meats. And of course they have mastic pudding. Imren also owns the patisserie across the street, and a cafe in Alacatı.

Inkilap Cad. 6, Çeşme ℃ **0232/716-6156** or 0232/712-7620. Appetizers and main courses 7TL–14TL. Daily noon–9pm.

Kale Lokantası HOME COOKING   This unassuming tea garden next to the castle packs up around mealtime, serving good, basic fast food at rock-bottom prices. It's much worse in the winter, when everybody has to fit into the sparsely furnished dining room. There's no menu, just steam pots full of fresh chickpea stew, vegetables with meatballs, and rice and beans. Naturally, they serve *döner kebap* (lamb roasted on a spit), but whatever you choose, a simple hearty meal couldn't be more satisfying.

Çarşı Cad. Kervansaray Yanı 11, Çeşme. ℃ **0232/712-0519.** Main courses 7TL–14TL. MC, V. Daily 9am–midnight.

DALYAN
Dalyan Restaurant "Cevat'ın Yeri" ★★ FISH   This quayside restaurant was the first to open in Dalyan, when the cove was still an unmarred paradise. The three brothers, Cevat, Celal, and Mehmet, plus Arif, their brother-in-law and manager, are still at it, serving fish so fresh that its gills are still moving. It's also the only establishment on this increasingly populated waterfront that clearly identifies the price per kilo of the fish. The meze case presents a great variety, with items I've not seen at other restaurants, such as grilled cheese, stuffed calamari, and potato croquettes. The catch of the day is fished from local waters, some of it even coming from the edge of the harbor wall where you could catch a glimpse of this evening's appetizer.

Liman Cad. 161 (at the far end of Dalyan harbor road), Dalyan, Çeşme. ℃ **0232/724-7045.** www.dalyanrestaurant.com. Reservations suggested. Appetizers 6TL–18TL; fish by weight. MC, V. Daily noon–1 or 2am.

ALAÇATI
Agrilia Café ITALIAN   High ceilings, wooden tables, and city folk relaxing over the Sunday paper set the scene at this former tobacco warehouse. The cafe serves optimal Italian food without the tourist fuss as well as ample breakfasts that include local olives and an area specialty, the fresh olive bread. The full on Turkish breakfast is a favorite of weekenders, and costs 22TL.

Kemal Pasa Cad. 75. ℃ **0232/716-8594.** Appetizers and main courses 9TL–41TL. MC, V. Daily 9:30am–11pm (later on Fri–Sun).

Çeşme After Dark

People come from as far as Istanbul for a night out at one of the beachfront restaurant/ dance clubs of Çeşme. The main event usually takes place in **Ayayorgı cove** where you'll find a handful of clubs with popular DJs. Many of the hotels also have clubs; expect to pay a cover of 40TL or so. For information and tickets for summertime concerts, log onto Biletix (www.biletix.com). Meanwhile, Istanbul's very popular Babylon venue brings the jazz to the coast in summertime. The box office is open Monday to Sunday 10am to 2pm. Babylon runs a free minibus service for ticket holders to events on Fridays and Saturday nights (see website for pickup times and locations).

For a more mellow evening out, perhaps dinner waterside in Dalylanköy, a drink at the stylish Sisus Hotel, or a stroll along Çeşme's Inkilap Caddesi (where you'll find back-to-back, more human-sized bars and cafes) is more your speed.

Where to Stay

ÇEŞME TOWN

Kanuni Kervansaray ★★ ◙   If architecture and history move you, then this recently renovated 500-year-old inn is the place for you. The 16th-century caravansary was at the end of a branch of the road for the merchant caravans trekking across Anatolia to unload their goods here in Çeşme for export to Europe. In typical caravansary style, all rooms encircle a large central stone courtyard which doubles as a restaurant when the swimming pool is not in use. Most of the rooms are sparse yet stylish, offering cool travertine floors and either wrought iron or solid wooden bedsteads. If you can go all out, book the Sultan's Flat or Sultan's Suit (sic), both opulent in their use of faux gilding, velvet textiles, and soaring ceilings. Note that the upper rooms are accessible via the standard overly steep stone stairs, so for those with physical limitations, ask for a room on the ground floor.

Çarşı Mevkii Kale Yanı 5, 35940 Çeşme. Across from the Tourist Information office. www.cesmeker-vansaray.com.tr. ℂ **0232/712-0630.** Fax 0232/712-3011. 29 units. 300TL double July–Aug. See website for off season rates. MC, V. Free parking. Closed Nov–May 1. **Amenities:** Restaurant; bar; babysitting; concierge; *hamam;* room service; smoke-free rooms; free Wi-Fi in lobby. *In room:* A/C, satellite TV, hair dryer, minibar.

DALYAN

Sisus Hotel ★★   Locals call this "the love hotel." This is probably because of the romantic details: white pillows wrapped up in red ribbons, tea candles in the bathroom, and colored stones accenting tabletops and consoles. Public areas are a cross between 2001: A Space Odyssey and SoHo chic; rather than ask questions, I decided to concede that the formula works. All rooms enjoy a balcony, and design-wise, the architects thought to optimize the views by partitioning the bathrooms from the main room via glass walls. Sitting right on the charming cove that is Dalyanköy's Yat Limanı, rooms get either a sea or mountain view, while the 95-sq.-m (1,023-sq.-ft.) party "king suite" enjoys the entire rooftop deck and a downstairs foosball table. The hotel also provides a long list of amenities, not least of which is the luxurious wellness center. The hotel provides a free shuttle to area beaches in summer, and free entrance to the nearby Shayna Beach.

Yat Limani (at the marina), Dalyanköy. www.sisushotel.com. ℂ **232/724-0330.** Fax 0232/724-9656. 51 units. 550TL double; rates less than half that in low season. AE, MC, V. **Amenities:** Restaurant; 3 bars; babysitting; concierge; exercise room and spa; *hamam;* heated outdoor pool; room service; tennis court. *In room:* A/C, satellite TV, CD player, hair dryer, minibar, free Wi-Fi.

ILICA & BOYALIK

My Stone Home ★★ 📷 This family-run inn is all about character and local hospitality. Mehmet, the owner, literally makes you feel right at home with his mom's homemade jams at breakfast and a full five o'clock tea. Tulle-draped, carved four-poster beds and hand-embroidered lace bed linens set the tone for crisp yet romantic rooms. Mehmet himself was a student of hospitality management, and this little hotel turned out to be his unofficial post-graduate thesis.

5082 Sok. 54, Ilica. www.mystonehomehotel.com. ℭ **0232/723-0979.** Fax 0232/723-0138. 6 units. 79€–149€ double. MC, V. Free parking. **Amenities:** Bar; outdoor pool. *In room:* A/C, hair dryer, no phone, free Wi-Fi.

Nars Ilica ★★ 📷 Enchanted (and treated) by the local thermal waters, 19th-century military commander Ahmet Tosun Paşa built himself a seaside retreat that was in 2008 transformed (without making any changes to the original architectural features) into a boutique hotel. The Nars hotel encourages self-indulgence by providing guests with spotless service that would spoil even the most difficult to impress. In fact, the name of the hotel itself is an abbreviation of the word *narcissism*. As a traditional seaside *yalı*, the hotel sits right on the water, and guests can oil themselves up on one of the teak lounges on the expansive stone patio. The pool is filled with local thermal water, and one of the special treatments offered is an aromatherapy massage.

Tosun Paşa Yalısı 5066 Sok. 12, Ilica. ℭ **0232/729-0001.** Fax 0232/723-0881. 8 units. 160€–570€ double. AE, MC, V. Valet parking. **Amenities:** Restaurant; bar; concierge; Jacuzzi (thermal); room service. *In room:* A/C, satellite TV, hair dryer, MP3 docking station, free Wi-Fi.

Radisson Blu ★★ The fourth Radisson to show up in Turkey literally makes a splash thanks to its colossal, 1,000-sq.-m (10,764-sq.-ft.) outdoor swimming pool. But that's not the only record the Radisson hopes to break with this property; here, they're aiming to break the glass ceiling of guest service quality. The luxury hotel has staked out a delicious spot on the pristine waterfront just west of Ilica and is surrounded on the three non-sea-facing sides by verdant, manicured gardens. The hotel is very light and airy, although the beige modernism of the guest rooms leaves me a bit cold. No matter, because the holiday feast is outside the room, partaking of the many really cool diversions on and off the hotel grounds. Plus, it's walking distance to Ilica center, or to the main road where you can hop on a *dolmuş* to your destination of choice. One of the pools is filled with sea water, while another is all local thermal waters.

Altınyunus Mah. 3435 Sok. 25, Ilica. www.radissonblu.com/resort-cesme. ℭ **0232/455-4500.** Fax 0232/455-4501. 312 units. 230€ double in August, half-board. Rates as low as 80€ in winter. AE, MC, V. Free parking. **Amenities:** Restaurant; 3 bars; babysitting; children's center & programs; concierge; elevator; executive-level rooms; golf course; 3 *hamams*; health club and spa; 1 indoor and 2 outdoor pools; room service; smoke-free rooms; tennis courts; watersports equipment/rental. *In room:* A/C, TV, hair dryer, minibar, free Wi-Fi.

Sheraton ★★ ☺ Visually impressive, über-luxurious, and on the beach, this five-star facility boasts a prime spot on the peninsula's most famous beach. The hotel recently added its very own pier, with a cabana and bungalows jutting out into Ilica Bay. The top-flight Botanica thermal spa (drawing on the sources of the local Şifne Hot Spring) aims at nothing less than total immersion in a soothing awe. The full-service, separate on-site convention center, boasting state-of-the-art everything, makes this a fab destination hotel for business meetings.

Şifne Cad. 35, 35940 Ilica. www.sheratoncesme.com. © **800/325-3535** toll free in the U.S., Canada, and Europe, or 0232/723-1240 in Turkey. Fax 0232/723-1856. 373 units. From 210TL–345TL double in August. See website for rates. AE, MC, V. Valet parking. **Amenities:** 10 restaurants; 3 bars; babysitting; children's center and programs; concierge; elevator; executive-level rooms; golf course; hamam; health club and spa; 3 indoor and 2 outdoor pools; room service; smoke-free rooms; tennis courts; watersports equipment/rental. In room: A/C, TV, hair dryer, minibar, free Wi-Fi.

ALAÇATI

Taş Hotel ★★ 📷 This is the pioneer that has set the bar for all of the town's other guesthouses. When I say "this" I mean both the home and the homeowner, Zeynep Öziş, whose dream came true with the completion of this retreat. One feels an aura of warmth walking through this 150-year-old Greek manor, restored to accommodate the demands of today's overnight guests. Ceilings are high, the garden and salon are cozy and private, and even the smallest of the rooms are ample. Homemade pies and cakes are baked daily, furnishing goodies for the daily afternoon tea event, and even better, the large breakfast (with a variety of fresh-made preserves) is served until noon. Zeynep organizes olive harvest weekends in the fall, honoring the fact that the original owner of the house, an olive merchant, stored his oil in terracotta containers in what is now the lobby.

Kemalpaşa Cad. 132, Alaçatı. www.tasotel.com. © **0232/716-7722.** Fax 232/716-8517. 8 units. Summer 120€–140€ double. Rates as low as 70€ in winter. MC, V. No children 11 and under. **Amenities:** Outdoor pool. In room: A/C, hair dryer, no phone.

SELÇUK & EPHESUS ★★

81km (50 miles) south of Izmir; 20km (12 miles) northeast of Kuşadası

Nobody comes to Turkey to visit poor overlooked Selçuk, relegated since ancient times to a secondary position in the shadow of Ephesus, its more illustrious neighbor. But the histories of the two cities are forever intertwined; Selçuk predates Ephesus, and indeed, Selçuk *was* Ephesus.

The rise and fall of Selçuk/Ephesus, which for the purposes of this chapter refers to the combined area between and including present-day Selçuk and Mount Koressos (Bülbül Dağı, where the remains of the original city wall still stand), was directly related to the ebbs and flows of the sea. In the 7th century B.C., Cimmerian invasions relegated the Ephesians to the area around the Artemesian, at the base of Ayasoluk Hill. (Selçuk's castle occupies this hill.) Because the neighborhood of the Artemesian lies below sea level, archaeologists have been unable as of yet to excavate beyond the temple's remains. When, with the death of Alexander the Great, General Lysimachos took control of the whole of Ionia, the city of Ephesus was reestablished adjacent to the harbor. The expansion of Christianity in the 4th century A.D. saw the construction of many important religious and state buildings in Ephesus, including the castle on Ayasoluk Hill and St. John's Basilica. The silting up of the harbor resulted in the gradual decline of Ephesus as a major commercial port, leaving it vulnerable to subsequent invasions, namely the arrival of the Selçuks in the 10th century.

Today a visit to Selçuk seems only to be a necessary sidebar to the main attraction at Ephesus, just 3km (1¾ miles) away. Nevertheless, the presence of a number of noteworthy ruins—including the representative remains of one of the Seven Wonders of the World; the nearby winemaking village of Şirince, the whole of which has been declared a historic preservation site; and the beaches around Kuşadası (only 18 km/11 miles away)—make Selçuk a perfect base for a well-rounded holiday.

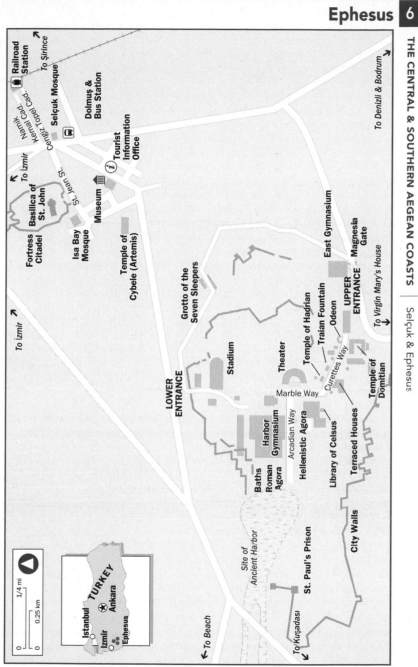

Railroad Station

To Şirince

Selçuk Mosque

Dolmuş & Bus Station

Namlık Cad.

Kemal Topel Cad.

Cengiz Topel Cad.

To İzmir

Tourist Information Office

To Denizli & Bodrum

Basilica of St. John

St. Jean St.

Museum

Fortress Citadel

Isa Bay Mosque

Temple of Cybele (Artemis)

East Gymnasium

Magnesia Gate

To Virgin Mary's House

Grotto of the Seven Sleepers

Trajan Fountain

Odeon

Temple of Hadrian

UPPER ENTRANCE

To İzmir

Stadium

Theater

Curettes Way

Temple of Domitian

LOWER ENTRANCE

Marble Way

Harbor Gymnasium

Baths

Roman Agora

Hellenistic Agora

Arcadian Way

Library of Celsus

Terraced Houses

Site of Ancient Harbor

City Walls

To Beach

St. Paul's Prison

To Kuşadası

TURKEY

Istanbul

Ankara

İzmir

Ephesus

0   1/4 mi

0   0.25 km

233

A Look at the Past

Numerous legends have been attached to the founding of Ephesus, some saying the Amazons, the Lelegians, or the Carians got here first. A favorite myth attributed to the Ionians—who had arrived here by the 10th century B.C.—says that Androclus, guided by the prophesies of an oracle regarding some fish and a wild boar, founded the city.

There must be some truth behind the legend of Croesus, king of Lydia, who upon hearing of the prosperity of the trading capital decided it had to be his. The city fell under the sovereignty of Lydia in the 6th century B.C. and the Ephesians were displaced to the area around the Artemesian.

A century later, the city was once again the target of an empire, with the invasion of the Persians. For the most part absentee administrators, the Persians were subsequently thrown out by an Ionian uprising in the 5th century B.C., remaining in power until Alexander the Great's arrival. After his death, one of his generals, Lysimachos, reestablished the city between the slopes of Mount Koressos (Bülbüldağ) and Mount Pion (Panayır Dağı), and constructed the city's first fortifications, a defensive wall with a perimeter of 9km (5½ miles). The ruins of the archaeological site of Ephesus date to the city established at this time.

In the 2nd century B.C., the city reached its height as the most important port in Anatolia, and subsequent kings of Pergamum ruled here until the city was absorbed by Rome. The city opened up lucrative commercial opportunities with the exotic Middle East and it wasn't long before Ephesus was designated the capital of the Asian Provinces, attracting the likes of Brutus, Cassius, Antony, and Cicero. Under Julius Caesar, Ephesus was forced to submit to heavy taxation, but under Augustus's reign, the city of Ephesus once again became the most important commercial center on the Mediterranean. The final episode in the ebb and flow of Ephesus's prosperity came during the remarkable proliferation of Christianity, continuing through the rule of Justinian (6th c. A.D.). Many buildings of importance, including the castle on Aya-soluk Hill, date to this period.

Nevertheless, during as far back as Roman times, the port had begun to show signs of silting up, and any attempts at halting the process had proved unsuccessful. After centuries of sand and dirt depositing in the harbor, the port was little more than a marsh, and the citizens of Ephesus, by now an insignificant village under Selçuk control, moved farther inland. The swamp at the end of the Arcadian Way (Harbour Rd.) was once at the water's edge; it's now 5km (3 miles) inland.

Essentials
GETTING THERE
BY PLANE   For flight information, see "Getting There," under the Izmir heading, earlier in this chapter. From the Izmir airport, there's a newly restored and refurbished train line making its way the 78km (48 miles) to Selçuk, that *theoretically* departs five times a day (trains may be delayed or cancelled without prior notice). The main number for the Selçuk train station is © 0232/892-6006. The fare is 4TL one way; 7TL round-trip.

BY BUS   Long-distance buses arrive at Selçuk's *otogar* opposite the park to the east side of Atatürk Caddesi. A simple inquisitive *"Selçuk otogar?"* directed at your bus *muavin* (driver's assistant) when you board will help you to know when you've arrived. (**Note:** If you're staying at the Kalehan, ask the driver to let you off at the entrance to the hotel, which is also on the main road.) Several companies provide service from Istanbul, including Metro (© **444-3455;** www.metroturizm.com.tr) and Varan (© **0232/712-0493;** www.varan.com.tr). The ride takes 10 hours; the fare is 65TL and 70TL respectively. From Pamukkale, (on Pamukkale), it's about 5 hours and 20TL. You can get a minibus from Izmir, only 45 minutes away for around 8TL.

BY CAR From Izmir center or airport, follow the green signs for Aydın/Çevreyolu, which will take you onto the toll road. Exit at Selçuk, and then follow the local road for around 12km (7½ miles).

VISITOR INFORMATION

The tourist information office (© **0232/892-6328**), located on the park across from the Ephesus Museum, provides free maps (and a better one for sale), as well as books on topics of local interest. The municipality also runs a helpful website (also in English) at www.selcuk.bel.tr.

ORIENTATION

Bisecting the city of Selçuk is **Atatürk Caddesi,** which runs roughly north to south, and which doubles as the highway to Izmir once you leave the center of town. The tourist attractions are all within walking distance to the west of Atatürk Caddesi, with the castle crowning the summit of **Ayasoluk Hill.** Midway down the hill to the south are the Isabey Mosque and St. John's Basilica, both accessible via **St. Jean's Sokağı.** The train station, good for excursions to Izmir, Aphrodisias, and Denizli, near Pamukkale, is located on the eastern side of town near the end of **Cengiz Topel Caddesi** (the eastern continuation of St. Jean's Sok. to the west). This end of town acts as the hub of Selçuk's shopping and business center, with a good concentration of banks, Internet cafes, kebap houses, and tea gardens.

A green park in the center of town on the west side of Atatürk Caddesi hosts the tourist information office; on the west side of the park is the Ephesus Museum. The road to Kuşadası heads west from the *otogar,* passing the Gendarmerie and the Artemesion on the way past the turnoff for Ephesus.

The ancient city of Ephesus extends beyond the confines of the museum gates, and heartier (and well-watered) types can be seen walking single-file along the road between the Main Gate and the Cave of the Seven Sleepers. Meryemana is about 7km (4⅓ miles) up the hill from the Upper Gate, and therefore (at least for me) too far to walk.

GETTING AROUND

BY DOLMUŞ *Dolmuşes* leave the *otogar* for Ephesus (signs on the minibuses read EFES) every half-hour (3.50TL). Get off at the upper gate so that you can walk through the site heading downhill. At the exit of the site, you can either walk back into town or grab a returning *dolmuş.* You can also catch a *dolmuş* to Kuşadası (4.50TL; 30 min.), Izmir's *otogar* (8TL; 1 hr.), or up in the hills to Şirince (2.50TL; 15 min.). There is no *dolmuş* to the House of the Virgin Mary.

BY TAXI Taxis are available for quick hops from one end of town to the other. For rides to the entrance to Ephesus or the Church of the Virgin Mary, either insist on a metered rate or haggle, haggle, haggle.

What to See & Do

Ephesus Museum (Efes Müzesi) ★★★ MUSEUM The wealth of archaeological findings from the ancient city of Ephesus makes this museum one of the most important in Turkey. As in the case of many other groundbreaking sites, the first excavations were the result of a British railway engineer moonlighting as a scientist and gold digger. The British Museum became the beneficiary of the earliest artifacts, while a later Austrian expedition provided a good amount of fodder for the Kunsthistorisches Museum of Vienna. Some of the treasures actually found their way to the archaeology museums in Istanbul and Izmir, until after World War I when Turkish sovereignty was established and the municipality retained the artifacts in a newly constructed warehouse in the center of Selçuk. By the 1970s the warehouse was bursting at the seams with a startling collection of recovered items, and an expanded and renovated warehouse morphed into the reputable institution that you see today. The museum rooms are stocked full of treasures excavated at Ephesus, so no visit to the ancient city would be complete without a walk through here. Plan on about 90 minutes for the museum, a visit that will be made that much more rewarding *after* you've gained a point of reference over at Ephesus.

The exhibit opens with the Roman Period House Finds Room, displaying items recovered during excavations of the terraced houses of Ephesus's entitled class. Here you'll find examples of household items, including the bronze statue **Eros with the Dolphin ★★** from a 2nd-century fountain, a 3rd-century fresco of Socrates, and finally the inspiration for all of those cheesy souvenir-shop models, the original statue of **Bes ★★** attached to his exaggerated uncircumcised erect penis. Contrary to popular thought, Bes, actually of Egyptian origin, was not the god of the brothel, but the protector of everything associated with motherhood and childbearing. A faded fresco of Socrates recovered from one of the homes indicates the importance of philosophy in the daily life of the citizens.

During the Roman Empire, Ephesus housed an important school of medicine; here you'll also find a collection of medical and cosmetic tools (two inseparable sciences at the time) along with a wall of portraits of several famous Ephesian physicians.

Recovered from several monumental fountains are a beautiful representation of a headless **Aphrodite ★** and a bodiless head of **Zeus ★** dating to the 1st century A.D. Nearby is a narration of **Polyphemus's ★★** mythological attempt on Odysseus's life. From the Fountain of Trajan are a statue of a youthful **Dionysus with a satyr ★**, and additional statues of **Dionysus with members of the imperial family ★**. The list goes on and on. Among the mind-boggling treasures displayed in the museum, keep an eye out for the **Ivory Frieze ★★★**, discovered in an upper story of one of the Terraced Houses, which depicts the emperor Trajan and his Roman soldiers in battle against "the barbarians."

Many monumental artifacts are displayed in the **courtyards ★★**, including the **pediment ★★★** from the Temple of Augustus (Isis Temple), reassembled with statues that had been moved to the pool of the Fountain of Pollio after the destruction of the temple; the **Sarcophagus with Muses ★**, dating to the 3rd century A.D.; and the **Ephesus Monument ★**, inscribed with the Customs regulations as issued by Emperor Nero in A.D. 62 and detailing the process of tax collection, typically undertaken by a third party, rather than as a state activity.

One of the most impressive and illuminating sections in the museum is dedicated to the mother goddess and dominated by two **colossal statues of Artemis ★★★**. Both statues are represented with rows of bull testicles, previously thought to be breasts or eggs, but all symbolically related to the idea of fertility.

"We had two love affairs, one with each other and one with Turkey." These are the words of Janet Crisler, speaking about her late husband, B. Cobbey Crisler, author, academic, and lecturer on biblical archaeology. Motivated by a desire to keep Crisler's legacy of academic inquisitiveness and Turcophilia alive, Janet has established the Crisler Library at Ephesos, a foundation whose mission is to support the exchange of information and ideas related to scholarship on Ephesus, and by force of the inherent influence of religion on these ancient civilizations, on biblical studies.

The foundation maintains a growing library of volumes related to both areas. The Crisler Foundation is fulfilling another one of the late Crisler's goals with a collaborative excavation project with the Austrian Institute of Archaeology to unearth the Early Roman Harbor at Ephesus. After three seasons of geophysical surveys, spades went to ground on this project in the summer of 2007. The library is able to offer group lectures on the latest findings at the site ((€ **0252/892-8317;** www.crislerlibrary ephesos.com).

The final exhibit contains numerous sculptures from Roman times, mostly overshadowed by a **frieze ★★★** recovered from the Temple of Hadrian (sections of which are in Vienna). The frieze narrates the founding of Ephesus, the birth of the cult of Artemis, and the flight of the Amazons.

Atatürk Mah. Uğur Mumcu Sevgi Yolu, opposite the tourist information office. (€ **0232/892-6010.** Admission 5TL. Daily 8:30am–6:30pm.

The Archaeological Site of Ephesus (Efes) ★★★ RUINS

Second only to Pompeii, a visit to Ephesus is as good an introduction as one can get to ancient Roman civilization. Almost as astonishing as the site itself is that only 20% of the ancient city has been excavated so far. Allot at least a half-day for just an overview of the archaeological site and a full day for a comprehensive visit. In the heat of the summer, it's best to avoid the midday sun when the reflection off the stones becomes unbearable.

The visit begins inside the Upper Entrance and basically follows a straight trajectory through the ancient city. You can get a fairly decent overview of the site by following the main street, but with so much interest located in toppled buildings lining the route, you will definitely want to scramble around a bit to get a closer look. Plan on at least 2 hours for the basic overview, and double that if you're planning to really absorb all of the main sites. Add another 30 to 45 minutes in the Terraced Houses, and still more time if you're dedicated enough to trample through every last weed to the "secondary" sites off the main street. If you're visiting during the heat of the summer, begin as early as the ticket gates will allow, and bring bottled water and perhaps a snack. There are no public toilets inside the museum, so avail yourself before entering, preferably in one of the on-site restaurants, rather than in one of the overpriced and underserviced public restrooms outside the site.

Inside the entrance immediately off to the right is the **East Gymnasium** and what's left of the **Magnesia Gate,** built by Emperor Vespasian. Rather than tap into your reserves this early in the game, head straight to the **Upper Agora ★★**, specifically to the **Odeon.** To provide some context for your visit, the Upper Agora, also known as the State Agora, was the administrative center of the city and was constructed between the reigns of Augustus and Claudius. The foundations of an early temple dedicated to the goddess Isis indicate that the site was also used for religious ceremonies. Clustered around the State Agora were the **Various Baths,** attributed to Flavius Damianus. To the south of the Agora is a monumental **Fountain,** which was fed by the River Marnas (now, Dervent) via an aqueduct about 5km (3 miles) east of Ephesus.

The **Odeon ★★**, also known as the Small Theatre, functioned as a *bouleuterion* (place for meetings of the *boule,* or council), although it's reasonable to believe that it served as a venue for concerts and theatrical performances as well. The structure was built in the 2nd century A.D. by Publius Vedius Antoninus, according to an inscription, and was probably covered. To the north are the remains of a covered arcade, converted, according to an inscription found on an architrave, into a **Basilica ★** during the reign of Augustus. Excavations beneath the Basilica have revealed a single-aisle colonnade. The juxtaposition of the Basilica next to the Prytaneum and Odeon lead historians to believe that even the Basilica, in addition to religious purposes, held some state function. Next to the Odeon are the ruins of the **Prytaneum ★**, or Town Hall, constructed by Lysimachos along with the **Altar of Hestia Boulaia ★**, upon which burned an eternal sacred flame. The two famous statues of Artemis now on exhibit in the Ephesus Museum (in Selçuk) were found in this building. Part of the Prytaneum was scavenged in the 3rd century A.D. by a woman named Scholastikia, for building materials for her baths (see below).

At the corner of **Domitian Square ★★** is an edifice referred to by archaeologists as the **Socle Structure,** and whose function is unknown. Just to the right of this is the **Pollio Fountain ★**. The original structure was built in honor of C. Sextilius Pollio, architect of the Marnas Aqueduct; however, the fountain was actually added to the monument at a later date. Built in 97 B.C., the monument was ornamented with statues of the head of Zeus and the torso of Aphrodite, as well as the Polyphemos group of statues, narrating the story of Odysseus, now in the Ephesus Museum. At the far end of Domitian Street (below the southwest corner of the State Agora) is another **fountain,** built in A.D. 80 by Laecanius Bassus.

The **Temple of Domitian ★**, the first temple of Ephesus built in honor of an emperor (A.D. 81–96), is located next to the Domitian Square. Not much remains of the temple, and what little information is available comes from the ruins of the foundation. A colossal statue of Domitian, 5m (16 ft.) high in a seated position, 7m (23 ft.) if you include the base, was the altar centerpiece in a cella only 9m×21m (30 ft.×69 ft.). Remains of this statue can be seen in the Ephesus Museum, while the head is on display in the Izmir Archaeological Museum (p. 215).

The **Museum of Inscriptions** takes up the underground substructure of the temple and contains a collection of stone and marble tablets that provides a rich historical record of the official decrees, state rulings, bureaucratic matters, and civil punishments. The museum is closed more often than not, providing visitors with a good excuse to skip it altogether.

At the junction to the right stand the remains of the **Monument of Memmius ★**, built in the 1st century B.C. in honor of the grandson of the dictator Cornelius Sulla. The figures are those of Memmius, his father, Caicus, and Sulla. Next to and opposite the Monument of Memmius are two fountains: One is semicircular with a long, narrow rectangular pool; the one opposite was brought here from another part of the city in the 4th century. It is decorated with garlands and a **winged Nike ★**.

Leading away from the Upper Agora down a gently sloping street pockmarked by thousands of pounding hoofs is the famous **Curettes Way ★★★**. In mythology, Curettes were demigods, a name later used by the Ephesians to designate a class of priests at first dedicated to the cult of Artemis. In Roman times, the Curettes held a place in the Prytaneum. The main thoroughfare is paved with stone and marble remnants recycled from other parts of the city, added after a 4th-century earthquake; valuable architectural elements like Doric columns and ornamental capitals are now part of the city's foundations.

About halfway down Curettes Way and blocking access to the aristocratic reaches of the Upper Agora is the **Gate of Hercules ★★**. Two of the columns show Hercules wrapped in lion skin.

Immediately on the right is the two-story **Trajan's Fountain ★★**, the point at which the star-studded section of the tour begins. Many visitors peter out because they've already spent a good portion of their time and energy before arriving at this point, so if you're resigned to the fact that you can't see everything, this is where you should begin the serious part of your tour, after having had a peek at the Odeon. Trajan's Fountain was built in the emperor's honor at the beginning of the 2nd century. The ruins have been partially restored, although only the base and a fragment of Trajan's foot have been recovered. The fountain was decorated with statues of Dionysus, a satyr, Aphrodite, and others, now on exhibit in the Ephesus Museum.

Located after the Trajan Fountain and running perpendicular to Curettes Way past the Baths of Scholastikia is another street, paved in some places with marble slabs. The portion leading above the theater has been excavated.

The second sacred building dedicated to a ruling emperor was the **Temple of Hadrian ★★★**, one of the main attractions at Ephesus, marketed in tourist brochures almost as much as the Celsus Library. The Corinthian temple consists of a main chamber and a monumental porch; an inscription on the architrave of the porch facade indicates that the temple was dedicated to the emperor by somebody named P. Quintilius. Ornamenting the semicircular arch that rests on the two inner columns of the porch facade is a bust of the goddess **Tych,** protectress of the city. In the **entablature ★★** over the main portal is a carving of a woman; some interpretations identify the figure as Medusa, symbolically keeping the evil spirits away. The temple was partially destroyed in A.D. 400, and it was during the course of restorations that the four **decorative reliefs ★★** were added to the lintels of the interior of the porch. (The ones in place today are plaster casts of originals now on exhibit in the Ephesus Museum.) The first three panels from the left depict the mythological foundation of Ephesus, and show representations of Androklos chasing a boar, gods with Amazons, and Amazons in a procession. The fourth panel is unrelated and shows Athena, Apollo, Androklos, Heracles, Emperor Theodosius, Artemis Ephesia, and several other historical and mythological figures.

The bases in front of the porch facade are inscribed with the names of Galerius, Maximianus, Diocletianus, and Constantius Chlorus, indicating that at one time, the bases supported statues of these emperors.

Behind the Temple of Hadrian via a stone staircase are the remains of the **Baths of Scholastikia ★★★**, constructed at the end of the 1st century and named after a rich Ephesian woman who enlarged them in the 4th. There were two entrances to the baths leading into a large main hall with niches; in one of these niches is the restored **statue of Scholastikia ★**, in its original position. During the 4th-century renovations, the original **mosaic floor** was covered over with marble slabs; some of these can be seen beneath the level of the current floor.

The original building phase of the baths included the construction of the adjacent **brothel** and the public toilets, which allowed a bit of discreet philandering.

Bizarre in its utility, the **Public Latrine** ★ provides more of a mental image into our humbler functions than one really needs. Men would sit side by side on these narrow stone benches above open troughs hidden under their robes and discuss current events as their waste washed away beneath them. A fountain occupies the center of the atrium, where running water would drown out the, well, sounds.

On the opposite side of Curettes Way is a colonnaded street flanked by a row of 12 shops and covered in a **mosaic floor** ★★★ decorated with geometric patterns. The colonnade dates to the 1st century A.D.; however, the mosaics only date to the 5th century A.D. Staircases in several of the shops indicate the existence of an upper floor, probably used as sleeping quarters for employees.

However you prioritize your time at the site, don't miss the **Terraced Houses** ★★★. Set on the hillside of Bülbül Dağı above the shops are five multichambered peristyle houses that have been uncovered in ongoing excavations. Access is not guaranteed, so try to coax the caretaker to walk you through, and remember to tip. A separate ticket for entry is required (15TL). (**Note to visitors with physical limitations:** As terraced housing, access is via large exterior or interior stairways, making a visit to this exhibit somewhat challenging.)

The houses were inhabited from the 1st to the 7th centuries by the richest members of society and frequently remodeled. All of the houses had running water, sophisticated heating systems, large colonnaded inner courtyards, and rich decor. One had a private basilica. Overwhelmingly they reveal the best craftsmanship the city had to offer, in monumental arched colonnades, well-preserved mosaics, and layer upon layer of frescoes. The course of tourist visits is sure to change in the coming months; but on your way through the marked passage, keep an eye out for the spectacular collection of *in situ* 2nd-century **frescoes and mosaics** ★★★.

As the poster child for Ephesus, the **Library of Celsus** ★★★, whose two-tiered facade reaches us in a remarkable state of preservation, is immediately recognizable. The library was built between A.D. 110 and 135 by the Consul Julius Aquila as a mausoleum for his father, Julius Celsus Polemaeanus, governor of the Asian Provinces, whose remains remain surprisingly intact under the apsidal wall.

Three levels of niches indicate that the building had three stories, the upper two levels accessible via a horseshoe-shaped gallery. Scrolls or books were stored in the rows of niches, and reading materials were dispensed by a librarian.

In the lower niches of the facade are copies of four statues personifying wisdom, knowledge, destiny, and intelligence, the originals having been taken to Vienna. The library was abandoned after a fire of unspecified date destroyed the reading room, and around A.D. 400 the courtyard below the exterior steps was converted into a pool. The facade collapsed in an earthquake in the 10th century, but was restored and re-erected by F. Hueber of the Austrian Archaeological Institute between 1970 and 1978.

Back at the top of the steps above the library begins the **Marble Way** ★★★, a 5th-century street paved entirely with—you guessed it—marble. Chariot traffic on the road was high, calling for a raised lateral platform to be built for pedestrians. Carved into the marble at about halfway down the road is the **imprint** of a footprint, a heart, and a portrait of a woman, accepted by historians as an advertisement for the brothel next door. According to the rumor mill, there was a large underground sewage system running beneath the street—an example of how advanced city engineering was in those days—that doubled as a secret passage between the library and the brothel.

The imperial arched **Gate of Mazaeus and Mithridates ★★** to the right of the library was built in 4 or 3 B.C. by two emancipated slaves of Agrippa who, according to an inscription in both Latin and Greek, had the monument erected in honor of Emperor Augustus, his wife Livia, Agrippa, and Agrippa's daughter Julia. The gate, unsuccessfully named the Gate of Augustus, was designed to provide southeastern access to the Lower or **Commercial Agora ★★**, a space of almost 120 sq. m (1,292 sq. ft.) of shops and colonnaded galleries on prime waterfront real estate that is lamentably off-limits indefinitely. The Agora dates to the 3rd century B.C., was expanded and altered by Augustus and Nero, and attained its final form during the reign of Caracalla. In ongoing excavations, the original foundation of the Agora was discovered about 6m (20 ft.) below current ground level. The middle of the Agora was studded with statues of Ephesian notables, and at the center, a *horologion,* or sundial.

The **Temple of Serapis,** located at the southwestern end of the Agora, is also closed off due to ongoing excavations. The temple was probably built by Egyptian traders and used as a church during Christian times.

For thespians and laypeople alike, the **Great Theatre ★★★** is a dramatic spectacle to behold. Built into the slopes of Panayır Dağı (Mount Pion), the 30m-high (98-ft.) theater (actually, 30m/98 ft. above the level of the orchestra) required 60 years of digging to clear out a space large enough to accommodate 25,000 people, estimated at only one-tenth of the city's population. The theater was begun during the Hellenistic times (some say during the reign of Lysimachos) and was later altered and enlarged by emperors Claudius, Nero, and Trajan. Even more monumentally, St. Paul delivered his sermon condemning pagan worship from the proscenium. Even if you think it'll take an additional 60 years to hoist yourself up the steps to the upper cavea, do so, or you will be missing one of the most stunning views around.

The **Arcadian Way ★★** (or Harbor Rd., also closed for excavation) is the name for the triumphal marble road leading from the harbor to the base of the Great Theatre. At 600m (1,969 ft.), the promenade was flanked by two colonnaded streets paved with mosaics and lined with elegant shops that reflected the prestige of a city of the stature of Ephesus. In fact, in the ancient world, only the wealthiest cities were lit at night, a privilege enjoyed by Ephesus, as well as Rome and Antioch. The **Theatre Gymnasium** is opposite the Great Theatre, at the junction of the Arcadian Way and the Marble Road. Complete with a bathhouse, *palestra* (gymnasium), and classrooms, the Theatre Gymnasium is the largest of its type in Ephesus. You can cut through here to rejoin the path out of the site (this leads to the Lower Entrance); just before reaching the path, turn around to face the theater, and take advantage of one of the best photo ops in the region. If you've still got any blood sugar left in you (and if this portion of the site is open to visitors, which currently it is not), you can wander around the **Verulanus Sports Arena,** the Harbor Gymnasium and Baths, and the Church of the Virgin Mary, located between the path heading out of the site and the old harbor. The arena was built during the reign of Hadrian and extends all the way to the Harbor Gymnasium, also built at this time.

The **Harbor Gymnasium and Baths** sits at the port end of the Arcadian Way and is the largest building complex in Ephesus. The building of the gymnasium is thought to have taken place during the reign of Domitian while the baths date to Constantine II. The complex has yet to be excavated.

Before exiting the Lower Entrance, follow a path and signs for the **Church of the Virgin Mary (Meryem Kilisesi)** ★ to the left. Originally, the building was used as a Roman mercantile center, but was converted to a basilica in the 4th century. The church played an important role in the evolution of Christianity, as the first one to take Mary's name, and as the site of two important ecumenical councils in 431 and 449, in which the natures of Christ and of Mary were hotly disputed. It's a little out of the way, especially at this stage in the game, but worth the energy it'll take to trek over here (again, assuming it's not cordoned off).

A well-paved road heading east of the Vedius Gymnasium leads to **The Cave of the Seven Sleepers** ★, about .8km (½ mile) away. According to the legend, seven young local boys (and a dog, according to one interpretation), refusing to submit to the persecutions of Emperor Decius (A.D. 249–51), fled to these caves with a group of Roman guards in hot pursuit. In characteristic Roman fashion, the guards mercilessly sealed up the cave, putting an end to yet another heretical episode. When the boys were awakened by an earthquake that also broke the cave's seals, they wandered back into town to buy some bread only to find themselves in the 5th century and 200 years older. Evidently, times had changed and Christianity was now the state religion. After their deaths, the "sleepers" were re-interred in the cave, and it wasn't long before the site became a sacred destination for pilgrimages.

This site, one of the many caves used by Seven Sleepers throughout Anatolia (there are others, located in Akhisar, Manisa, Sardes, Tarsus, and Antakya, to name a few), is actually a grouping of small churches dating to the time of the persecutions, superimposed in the rock and containing crypts carved into the walls. The actual cave site has been fenced off, but remains a draw to die-hard pilgrims. (At the time of this writing, a hole in the fence provided access.)

(C) **0232/892-6010.** Admission to archaeological site 20TL; admission to Terraced Houses 15TL. Nov–Mar 8am–5pm; Apr–Oct daily 8:30am–7pm. Follow the road from Selçuk to Kuşadası, turn left following signs for the archaeological site; the official entrance (Lower Entrance) is immediately to the right; follow signs to the Cave of the Seven Sleepers and Meryemana for the Upper Entrance.

The House of the Virgin Mary (Meryemana) ★★★ TEMPLE According to the oral tradition of local villagers of Şirince, Mary finished out her days in this house after migrating to Asia Minor with John. The location was "discovered" in the 19th century by Sister Anna Catherina Emmerich, a German invalid who had never left home. The discovery was in the form of a dream, from which the nun awoke with a stigmata. The site was later found as described and was visited by popes Paul VI and John Paul II, who both verified its authenticity. The validity of the site is also supported by the oral tradition of the villagers who inhabited the village in the 19th century, as they were descendants of the early Christian inhabitants.

The house is a church nowadays, with the main altar where the kitchen was situated; the right wing was the bedroom. The site, now a national park, is a requisite stop on the itineraries of Christians, Jews, and Muslims alike, and therefore always crowded. In fact, in their religious fervor, pilgrims won't think anything of elbowing you out of the way. If you get there early on Sundays you can participate in the morning Mass (7:30 and 10:30am); and every year on August 15 there is a Mass celebrating the Assumption. (**Note:** The admission fee goes to the Selçuk municipality, so donations to the church are welcome. There is no entrance fee when Mass is in progress.)

Orman Yolu (7km/4⅓ miles southwest of Selçuk). Admission to park and house 13TL. Dawn–dusk. From both the Upper and Lower entrances to Ephesus, follow the signs to Meryemana, which is in a park and nature preserve.

Isabey Mosque MOSQUE   Built in 1375 at the direction of the Emir of Aydın and using columns and stones recycled from the ruins of Ephesus and Artemesion, the Isabey Mosque is a classic example of Selçuk architecture. It is also the oldest known example of a Turkish mosque with a courtyard. It is fitting that Isabey translates into "Jesus," as the structure owes its existence to the temples of other religions, and possibly testifies to the religious tolerance exhibited by the Selçuk Turks.

Exit the basilica entrance and turn right. Free admission. Dawn–dusk.

St. John's Basilica ★★★ RUINS   After the death of Christ, St. John came with Mary to Ephesus, living most of his life in and around Ayasoluk Hill and spreading the word of Christianity as St. Paul did before him. John's grave was marked by a memorial, which was enclosed by a church of modest proportions in the 4th century. During the reign of Justinian, the emperor had a magnificent domed basilica constructed on the site. The tomb of St. John located under the main central dome elevated the site to one of the most sacred destinations in the Middle Ages. With the decline in importance of Ephesus and after repeated Arab raids, the basilica fell into ruins until the Selçuk Aydınoğlu clan converted it into a mosque in 1330. The building was completely destroyed in 1402 by Tamerlane's Mongol army.

The current entrance leads into the basilica through (or near) the southern transept. Originally, entry was through the oversize exterior courtyard atrium to the west of the nave, which led worshippers through the narthex and finally into the far end of the nave. The basilica had six domes.

The brick foundations and marble walls have been partially reconstructed; if they were fully restored, the cathedral would be the seventh largest in the world. More recent excavations east of the apse have revealed a baptistery and central pool, along with an attached chapel covered in frescoes depicting the saints.

İsa Bey Mah. St. Jean Cad. (Follow signs from Atatürk Cad.; the ruins are visible from the main road). (℃ **0232/892-6010.** Admission 5TL. Nov–Mar daily 8am–5pm; Apr–Oct 8am–6:30pm.

The Temple of Artemis` (Artemesion) ★ RUINS   In a marshy basin just on the outskirts of town is a lone surviving column from the Temple of Artemis, or Artemesion, representing the remains of yet another plundered Wonder of the Ancient World. The column barely suggests the immensity of the structure, four times as large as the Parthenon and the first monumental building to be entirely constructed of marble. As an illustration of its size, consider that the one remaining column stands an incredible 4m (13 ft.) *below* the point of the architrave. This ancient temple, built around 650 B.C. to the cult of Artemis, was constructed on a site considered to be sacred to the Mother Goddess, Kybele.

In 356 B.C. (the year Alexander the Great was born), a psychopathic arsonist intent on immortality set fire to the temple. Twenty-two years later, during his sweep through Asia Minor, Alexander the Great offered to reconstruct the temple. In a famous refusal related by Strabo, the Ephesians thought it unfitting for one god to build a temple to another god. The temple was eventually rebuilt remaining true to the original except for a raised platform, a feature of classical architecture adopted in the construction of later temples. By A.D. 263, the temple had been plundered by Nero and destroyed by the Goths. The temple was reconstructed in the 4th century, but the strengthening of Christianity condemned the structure to that of a marble quarry for St. John's Basilica and the Hagia Sophia in Istanbul.

Entrance off the road to Kuşadası, just past the Jandarma on the right, and a short walk out of town. No phone. Free admission. Daily 8:30am–5:30pm.

Located on a hillside surrounded by apple and grape orchards is the neighboring village of Şirince. Originally settled by Greeks, the village was inhabited by the Ephesian Christians, who, displaced during the Selçuk conquests, moved up into the surrounding hills. In the Greek exchanges of 1924, Muslims from Salonica resettled here, creating a farming community highly adept at winemaking. Several years ago a couple of Turkish journalists and entrepreneurs restored several of the village's houses, which now rent out as guesthouses (see "Where to Stay," below). A few native villagers followed suit. By day, the village attracts tour buses and aggressive lace-peddling fiends. By night, however, the village settles down, the candles get lit, and several restaurants and wine houses open up. It is located 8km (5 miles) east of Selçuk in the hills (*dolmuş* service departs from the train station every 20 min., daily 8am–5pm).

Where to Eat

The hotels mentioned in this section almost all have restaurants promising superior meals to anything you might get in town (except for the Artemis Wine House in Şirince, which I highly recommend; see below). If you get sick of eating at the hotel (or any of the others; they all take "walk-ins"), try one of these recommendations below.

IN SELÇUK

Okumuş Mercan Restaurant TURKISH   Okumuş is the only full-menu restaurant around, with food and ambiance served under a leafy trellised canopy that shades the outdoor dining patio. Popular dishes include the *hamsi zeytinli* (anchovies in olive oil) and the *kağıtta balık,* where your fish (catch of the day or fish of your choice) is cooked in paper. For a vegetarian alternative (and there are plenty here), try the *etsiz sebze yemeği* (peppers and curry).

Karşısı Hal Bina 43, opposite the PTT. ⓒ **0232/892-6196.** Appetizers and main courses 6TL–18TL. MC, V. Daily 9am–midnight.

Selçuk Köftecisi TURKISH 🍴   This meatball-and-kebap house succeeds in doing a brisk and humble business well away from the tourist bull's-eye of hecklers trying to fill empty tables. Meanwhile, filling tables is not a problem that this joint has. The menu lists a variety of meat-based kebaps and grills, plus steam pots that put out the tantalizing odor of somebody's mother's kitchen. The restaurant has an outdoor cafe in summer.

Atatürk Mah., Şehabettin Dede Cad. 10. ⓒ **0232/892-6696.** Appetizers and main courses 4TL–8TL. MC, V. Daily noon–11pm.

IN ŞIRINCE

Artemis Wine House ★ 🖸 TURKISH   Not to be confused with the Artemis winery next door (other than the fact that the wine house and restaurant make their own wine), this restaurant occupies an old schoolhouse converted into a wine house and terrace restaurant. The backdrop to your starters of creamy broccoli soup or tahini *gözleme* are the rolling hills of the valley surrounding the village. Along with the parade of usual suspects, the menu offers main courses that are equally unique. There are a variety of house wines, but apple wine is the local specialty.

On the left as you enter the village, Şirince. www.artemisrestaurant.com. © **0232/898-3240.**
Appetizers and main courses 12TL–46TL. MC, V. Daily 11am–midnight.

Where to Stay

Given that Selçuk makes the perfect base for visits to Ephesus, and given that almost everyone who comes to Turkey passes through Ephesus, it's odd that there aren't more high-quality places to stay. (If you fly in on Atlas Jet, you make use of their free shuttle to the village). One nearby alternative to Selçuk is **Şirince,** a pastoral village in the hills (options listed below). Five miles east of Selçuk is an embarrassing choice of four- and five-star hotels taking full advantage of **Pamucak Beach.** These hotels include the Richmond Ephesus (www.richmondhotels.com.tr) and the Sürmeli Ephesus (www.surmelihotels.com) both all-inclusives and both with rates as low as 50€ off season.

> **Local hoteliers say, "We'll take you there!"**
>
> When competition for clientele gets stiff, consumers benefit. In Selçuk, hotels and pensions are now commonly offering free rides to Ephesus as part of the price of the room.

IN SELÇUK

Hotel Nilya ★ 👜 Book early for a room at this whitewashed guesthouse located down a quiet street steps from Isabey Mosque and St. John's Basilica. Originally a family-owned pension, the Nilya was bought and restored by the owners of the friendly **Hotel Bella** (Atatürk Mah. St. John Sok. 7; © **0232/892-3944;** www. hotelbella.com; double from 110TL; closed Dec–Feb) around the corner. Now, there is richly carved period furniture in every room (and then some), new mattresses and renovated marble baths. An open flagstone courtyard and fountain anchor the property, creating a sense of serenity; if you score one of the upper balcony rooms, the bonus is the view of the sun setting over the plain. Guests of the Nilya are entitled to all of the perks over at the Bella, including the free shuttle to/from Ephesus and the excellent rooftop restaurants.

1051 Sok. 7, 35920 Selçuk. www.nilya.com. © **0232/892-9081.** Fax 0232/892-9080. 12 units. 170TL double; 230TL suite. MC, V. Street parking only. Closed Nov–Mar. *In room:* A/C, free Wi-Fi.

Hotel Kalehan ★ Located just below Selçuk's castle and St. John's Basilica, the Hotel Kalehan consists of two stately stone buildings separated by a narrow trellised lane, with the rear building standing at the back of a lush, carefully tended English-style garden. The gardens enclose a raised pool area and contain wrought-iron settees, wooden lawn chairs, and the odd cartwheel for fun. Owners Ayşe and Hakan, a brother-and-sister team, are avid collectors of antiques and have filled the inn with period furniture. Rooms are modest but lovely, in a monastic sort of way, and what they lack in luxury they certainly make up for in atmosphere. Recent upgrades include new mattresses in most of the rooms; special rooms now sport new bathrooms, minibars, bathrobes, and the odd extra toiletry.

İzmir Cad., 35920 Selçuk (on the main road below the castle next to the Sunoco station). www. kalehan.com. © **0232/892-6154.** Fax 0232/892-2169. 55 units. 180TL double. MC, V. Free parking on-site. **Amenities:** Restaurant; bar; outdoor pool. *In room:* A/C, satellite TV, free Wi-Fi.

IN ŞIRINCE

Nişanyan Evleri ★★ 🏚 These (illegally!) renovated houses at the top of Şirince's hillside offer total immersion into the daily rhythm of the village life. At the upper edge of the hillside is the main Köşk (pavilion), which contains the reception area and five smartly decorated rooms with nouveau Hellenistic frescoes, fresh tub/shower combinations, and antique furniture. Three characteristic restored houses, standing in sharp contrast to their humbler neighbors, are accessed by a stone staircase, terraced below the Köşk, with an additional five more terraced up to almost the top of the valley. Each house sleeps a minimum of two, but can comfortably accommodate four or a maximum of six people. One features a private *hamam*, another has a semi-enclosed stone veranda, and a third contains a raised-platform canopied bed—great for the kids. The spectacular success of these cottages has acted as a magnet for visitors to the village—many of whom are turned off when quoted the room rate. Fear not, the village has plenty of good quality pensions vying for your business.

Şirince (6.5km/4 miles from Selçuk and 11km/6¾ miles from Ephesus; watch for signs on the right before entering the village, leading to a dirt road that stops at the main house). www.nisanyan. com. 🕐 **0232/898-3208.** Fax 0232/898-3209. 8 self-catering houses and 1 house with 5 rooms. 120TL double in hotel; 360TL for a self-catering house. MC, V. **Amenities:** Restaurant; outdoor swimming pool.

KUŞADASI

20km (12 miles) southwest of Selçuk; 95km (59 miles) south of Izmir; 220km (137 miles) west of Pamukkale; 151km (94 miles) north of Bodrum

Only 20km (12 miles) from Selçuk, Kuşadası long ago earned the dubious honor of hosting—of all things—a steady stream of cruise ships filled with masses of tourists making the obligatory pilgrimage to Ephesus. One would never suspect that only 25 years ago, before it was discovered by the yachting set (and then exploited by mass tourism), Kuşadası was a scenic and unspoiled community of fishermen and farmers, with barely a dirt road running through it. Makes you fear for those unspoiled neighboring villages you just came from.

In addition to patronizing the fat-cat cruisers ready to disgorge the contents of their wallets on jewelry and carpets on their way in and out of Ephesus, the town is characterized by three genres of tourism: mass tourism drawn to Ladies' Beach by cheap package prices from Europe, more mass tourism clustered in cement midrise hotels in the town center, and the more selective mass-tourism establishments north of town mushrooming up on the coastline above the yacht marina. Some of the most splendid coastline on the Aegean can still be found in the protected National Park area (see below), while the Kismet Hotel (adjacent to the yacht marina) is still a delightful oasis in a desert of commerce. If your priority is touring the area archaeological sites by day, practicing some retail therapy and partaking of the typically Turkish resort-style nightlife (with a short poolside rest in between), then Kuşadası might actually fit the bill. If rural charm is what you're after, move on.

Essentials

GETTING THERE

BY PLANE The nearest airport is Izmir's Adnan Menderes Airport, about 97km (60 miles) away. There's no convenient public transport from the airport to Kuşadası (see section 1, "Izmir," earlier in this chapter, for information on transportation out of the airport); private transfers arranged with a local company (or your hotel) in advance will run around 60€, for up to three people and luggage, about the same as a private taxi.

BY BUS   Long-distance buses arrive into Kuşadası from all major cities in Turkey. From Istanbul, the bus takes about 9 hours, 10 hours for service from Ankara. Prices vary from 45TL to 65TL.

Kuşadası's main *otogar* is located about .8km (½ mile) out of the town center on the main road. From there, local *dolmuşes* run through the town center on the way up the shoreline, with the names of hotels posted on the windshield. If you don't see your hotel, ask, because not all are listed.

BY FERRY   Ferries from the Greek island of Samos arrive once daily into the main harbor from April through October (35€ one-way, 45€ same-day return, 55€ round-trip with open-return ticket. Port taxes may be extra.

VISITOR INFORMATION

The tourist information office (*©* **0256/614-1103**) is located across from the main harbor at Iskele Meydanı, within handy reach of disembarking cruise-ship passengers.

ORIENTATION

The heart of Kuşadası is found in the streets around the caravansaray, across from the harbor where the shore roads of **Atatürk Bulvarı** to the north and **Liman Caddesi** to the south converge. The town's commercial thoroughfare, **Barbaros Hayrettin Caddesi,** is a pedestrian mall that heads east into the area of the old bazaar. Turn left at the post office to explore the narrow streets of the old city, lined with restaurants, bars, and souvenir shops.

Just south of the main harbor is **Güvercin Ada,** with its Byzantine fortress; farther south the shore road leads to nearby Ladies' Beach and the national park, about 20km (12 miles) away.

GETTING AROUND

If the thought of getting on a *dolmuş* was too intimidating in the big city, in Kuşadası it's going to be your best friend. Minibuses run regularly along the shore road into and out of town, as well as south to Ladies' Beach and northward along the coastal road above the Kismet Hotel and beyond. A ride costs 1.75TL or 2.50TL to the center; if you go from one end of town to the other (say from the Kismet Hotel to Ladies' Beach); you'll have to change *dolmuşes* in the center and pay another fare.

Countless storefronts up and down Atatürk Bulvarı publicize car rentals at very competitive prices. As a backup, you can contact **Europcar,** Atatürk Bulv. 68/B (*©* **0256/ 614-6770**), or book your car through a reputable travel agent.

AREA BEACHES

Although Kuşadası built itself up around the idea of a beach resort, it wasn't until 2001 that the city took it upon itself to create an actual waterfront and beach. There's a pretty stretch of sand that's certainly an improvement to what was there before. It's free, fairly crowded (as all the beaches in Kuşadası are, especially on weekends), and being in the town center, it funnels vacationers from the cement blocks opposite the shoreline. The waterfront promenade does make for a great sunset stroll though.

day-tripping **TO MILETUS, PRIENE & DIDYMA**

The ancient sites of Miletus, Priene, and Didyma are three of the best-preserved Ionian settlements in Anatolia, and worth an entire day of scrambling down steps and over crumbled ruins. By car from Kuşadası, follow signs south to Söke, and then to Priene (38km/24 miles from Kuşadası). From Priene, it's 22km (14 miles) along the old road through miles of cotton fields to Miletus. It's another 22km (14 miles) from Miletus to Didyma, where you can either backtrack along the inland road to Söke, or continue down to Bodrum (from Didyma, 139km/86 miles; follow the more modern road via Muğla). Day tours to all three sites are available from most travel agents in surrounding towns for around 30€ to 40€ per person.

The ancient Greek city of Priene ★★, later inhabited and left relatively unchanged by the Romans, was the first city built on a grid plan. Formerly a port city and now stranded in the middle of acres and acres of cotton fields, Priene was once an important member of the Ionian League, around 300 B.C. The oldest remains here date to this time, and it's worth the short climb up if only for the Temple of Athena, which sits at the highest point of the city atop Mount Mykale, along with a small Greek theater. The temple was built by the architect Pytheos, the same man responsible for the construction of the Mausoleum at Halicarnassus. The theater was used for both performances and as a meeting place for the *ekklesia*—the people's parliament. Notice the first tier of seating, which is furnished with both bench-backed and "armchair" seating designated for spectators of particular importance. Another section of similar seating, called a *prohedria*, was added to the center of the fifth tier at a later date.

One of the best-preserved buildings in Priene is the *bouleuterion* (Senate House), located south of the Greek theater. The *bouleuterion* is roughly square in shape (21m×20m/69 ft.×66 ft.) with three sides of tiered seating capable of seating a mere 640 people. The building contained both a central altar and an eternal flame. Among the many private houses is one occupying a whole city block, and obviously inhabited by one of the city's wealthier citizens. The house referred to as the Alexander the Great house is actually named for a small marble statue of Alexander (now in the Berlin Museum) that was found in another part of the city. Priene is open summer only daily 8:30am to 6:30pm; admission is 3TL.

Time and effort permitting, I recommend that you skip this beach and try the **Papaz Beach Club** to the left of the causeway to Güvercin Ada.

The town's most popular (and notorious) beach has for years been universally known as **Ladies' Beach** for the overabundance of exposed (mostly foreign) boobs. It's actually not a bad beach, it's located about 3.5km (2¼ miles) south of the town center, easily reachable by any *dolmuş*. There are plenty of restaurants and cafes, changing rooms, umbrellas, and lounges.

Acting as a buffer between the Greek island of Samos less than a mile offshore and the Turkish mainland, **Dilek National Park** (**Dilek Milli Parkı;** ✆ **0256/614-1009**), on the Dilek Peninsula, houses a military base as well as a mountainous natural preserve. A day trip to the quiet isolation of the park's beaches, where pine trees

Miletus ★★ (Balat Köyü, Didim; ℗ **0256/875-5562**), still for the most part buried under rubble, is actually larger than Ephesus. In fact, you'll be driving over half of it on the entry road to the Roman Theatre, one of the noteworthy ruins. Having surrendered to the silting up of four harbors, the city's fate was much the same as that of Ephesus. In fact, the hill 6.5km (4 miles) to the west of the theater was actually the island of Lade, destroyed by fire by the Persian fleet in 494 B.C.

Miletus gave the alphabet to the classical world and was also the breeding ground for many philosophers and scientists, including Thales, who calculated precisely the arrival of the solar eclipse. The archaeological site is notable for the great Roman Theatre and the Baths of Faustina, while a surprising quantity of remnants from the city's classical, Hellenistic, and Roman eras remains for the most part buried or overgrown with bone-dry shrubbery. Several maps and archaeological guides are available to help you walk through the ruins, including those sold at the entrance gate. Miletus is open daily 8am to 7pm; admission is 3TL.

The Temple of Apollo, or Didymaion (Yenihisar Köyü, Didim, Söke;

℗ **0242/811-5707**), served as a sacred sanctuary under the custody of priests called Branchids and was connected to Miletus via a marble road, only partially excavated and visible on the opposite side of the modern road. With columns soaring over 20m (66 ft.) high, it was the largest building of its time when it was erected in the 6th century B.C. (Reconstructed in the 3rd c. B.C., the temple was eclipsed in size only by those in Ephesus and Samos.) Present-day archaeologists stumbled upon the "key" to how ancient Greek stonemasons were able to create the entasis curve—an imperceptible curve of each column of the Parthenon in Athens. This key was a "template" with a condensed version of a column with the entasis curve. Using such a template, stonemasons could then carve each drum section of a column to a precise width. The entrance to the temple is open, revealing the site of the much-revered oracle of Apollo. Don't overlook the colossal column behind the temple, which consists of layers and layers of massive stone discs supporting each other like so many felled dominoes. Didyma is open daily from 8am to 7pm; admission is 3TL.

act as natural shelter for picnickers, is definitely a better alternative to the ordinary, albeit lovely, sand or pebble beaches of central Kuşadası.

To do this, you'll really need a car to make it worth your while. Although minibus service leaves from the *otogar* every half-hour to take you the 20km (12 miles) to the park, you'll still have to get to your chosen beach, which will tack on up to an additional 9.5km (6 miles). Naturally, the closest beach, **İçmeler Köyü,** is the most crowded, with its sand and shady stretches located only .8km (½ mile) from the entrance. There are no public facilities at this beach. **Aydınlık Beach** and **Kavaklı Burun** are less frequented (5km/3 miles and 7km/4⅓ miles, respectively, from the entrance), with nothing but pebbles between you and the shoreline. Both of these have toilet and changing facilities, along with basic snack bars. The last beach, a pine-enclosed, pristine pebble stretch opposite the Greek island of Samos, is **Karasu Cove**. Freshwater showers are available, as well as toilets and changing rooms. There are snack bars open at each of the beaches during high season. The park is open daily at 8am and closes *promptly* at 7pm in summer (winter hours: 8am–5pm). Admission is 3TL per person or 9TL per car including passengers. For a convenient dinner spot on your way back from the park, try **Değirmen** (see "Where to Eat," below).

Where to Eat

Ali Baba in the Belediye Tourist Bazaar near the cruise port (no. 5; ✆ **0256/614-1551**) is one of the oldest established restaurants in town, proffering potential diners a tempting eyeful of the day's catch in tables out along the walkway. Below are two of the more special recommendations, located slightly out of the town center.

Değirmen ★★ ⊞ ☺ TURKISH   More than a restaurant, Değirmen is a veritable nature park located outside of Kuşadası, on the way to Dilek Milli Parkı. The restaurant sits at the top of a small hill surrounded by overfed rabbits and peacocks. All the food is organic, some of it grown on-site. Colossal peasant bread accompanies such dishes as *tandır kebap* (lamb cooked in an "in-ground" oven, Anatolian style) or the special *Değirmen kebap* (spareribs, chicken wings, quail, and lamb chops). Try the *erişte* (homemade egg noodles) or the *içli köfte* (meat-filled bulgur balls, either boiled or fried), and finish off with a slice of the house *künefe* (cheese-filled buttery string pastry covered in syrup and served hot).

Outside the restaurant, a cobbled path leads down from the restaurant to a duck-filled pond, over a hanging bridge, past the chickens and sheep, and straight to the riding stables, a marvelous combination for kids.

Davutlar Yolu (12km/7½ miles from Kuşadası on the way to the Dilek Milli Parkı). www.degirmenltd. com. ✆ **0256/681-2148**. Reservations required to waive the park entrance fee. Prix fixe menu 18TL. (a la carte available). MC, V. Daily noon–midnight.

Tarıhı Çinar Balık FISH   From the seafront outdoor terrace, one would never know that the sights and sounds of a hectic city were just a stone's skip away. The Tarıhı Çinar has been in business for decades (first as a meat restaurant over near the national park before it switched to fish); it's been at the current location for only a handful of these years. Still, it's one of maybe two area restaurants that draws guests from beyond Kuşadası's limits. Specialties of the house are the *tuzda balık* (salt-baked fish) preceded by a plate of grilled king prawns.

Kismet Otel Yanı, Akyar, Kuşadası. ✆ **0256/618-1847**. Appetizers 8TL–18TL; fish by weight, from 40TL per kilo and up. AE, MC, V. Daily noon–midnight.

Kuşadasi After Dark

Kuşadasi's nightlife is concentrated in the old town center, in the narrow streets bordered by Barbaros Hayrettin Bulvarı and Sağlik Sokak. Kuşadasi's boisterous **Barlar Sokağı** (walk up Barbaros Hayrettin Bulv., turn right onto Sağlık Sok., and then left under the arch into the confusion) boasts more Irish pubs per square inch than Dublin. The street is swarming with ruddy-faced boys and house touts who think that dancing on the street like Amsterdam hookers might lure somebody in for a drink. A walk-through is great for a hoot, however.

No trip to Turkey would be complete without a Turkish night folklore show, and the **Club Caravanserail,** Atatürk Bulv. 2 (© **0256/614-4115**), is one of the best places to do it. The entire affair is set up like an oversize wedding banquet, with lengthy tables and long lines at the buffet. The show begins at about the time the main course arrives, and much like at a wedding, it's best to fill up on the appetizers. All in all, the mezes are adequate and the performance is fun—filled with folkloric dances from various regions, belly dancing, a spoon drummer, and the requisite lobster-red, tub-o-lard recruit for the audience-participation segment. Admission is 60€ but less than half that for hotel guests.

Where to Stay

Club Caravanserail ★ 🍴 Of all the caravansaries converted into modern hotels, this is one of the most elegant, and a great opportunity to soak up real Turkish culture. The rooms have been faithfully restored, the floors and furnishings glisten with wood polish, and even the alcove fireplaces found in every room are original. It's also on a prime piece of real estate, centrally located just steps from almost everything worth doing in town. The success of a place can also be judged by the tenure of its staff: Many of the employees have been at this inn for 30 years, creating a warm, familial atmosphere.

A traditional Turkish folklore show is performed in the main courtyard Thursday through Saturday (see "Kuşadası After Dark," below), but the show finishes promptly at midnight so as not to blow nonparticipating guests out of their rooms with high decibel levels. For those wishing to attend, the management offers a meal plan that includes the show.

Atatürk Bulv. 2, 09400 Kuşadası. www.kusadasihotelcaravanserail.com. © **0256/614-4115.** Fax 0256/614-2423. 26 units (all with shower). 80€ double, 140€ suite, July and August. See website for off season rates, as low as 45€ for a double. AE, MC, V. Street parking only. **Amenities:** Restaurant; airport transfer (55€). In room: A/C, hair dryer, free Wi-Fi.

Kısmet Hotel ★★ Co-owned by the granddaughter of the last sultan, Mehmet VI, the Kısmet Hotel occupies a small promontory sandwiched between the harbor and cliffs. Recalling its heyday when the Kismet hosted the Queen of England, the hotel exemplifies elegance, simplicity, and nobility. The hotel sits on a small promontory overlooking the marina and bay; behind the hotel, several levels of waterfront lounging are accessible via stairs that work their way down to a cement pier and the rocky water's edge. And an expansive garden overlooking the marina provides a tranquil spot for a sunset cocktail. The swimming pool, sea views, and exclusive atmosphere provide the perfect Rx for an escape from the real world, but the Kismet's easy location allows for easy jaunts to the area attractions.

Akyar Mevkii Türkmen Mah., 09400 Kuşadası. www.kismet.com.tr.© **0256/618-1290.** Fax 0256/618-1295. 108 units. 185€ double. Tax not included in rates. AE, DC, DISC, MC, V. Free on-site parking. Closed Nov 15–Mar 15. **Amenities:** 2 restaurants; 5 bars; concierge; exercise room; Jacuzzi; outdoor pool; room service; tennis court. In room: A/C, satellite TV, hair dryer, minibar, free Wi-Fi.

The Muses House The house is full these days in Şirince, so it's no surprise to find another local village vying for the spillover. Kirazlı, just 14km (8¾ miles) east of Kuşadası, is that up-and-comer. The restored and refurbished Greek villa-turned-hotel opened in 2006 and is hidden behind a tall, whitewashed wall, a luxuriant oasis made more enjoyable because of the authenticity of the village that embraces it. The decor is a mix of modern art and antique pieces, with each of the five rooms named after a mythological Muse. I wonder how long it will take for this secret to get out . . .

Kirazlı Köyü 158, 09400 Kuşadası, Aydın. www.museshouse.com. (℡) **0256/667-1125.** 5 units. 104€–120€ double. MC, V. Closed Nov–Apr. **Amenities:** Outdoor swimming pool. *In room:* A/C, satellite TV/DVD, CD player, minibar, free Wi-Fi.

THE BODRUM PENINSULA

When Turkish people wax lyrical over Bodrum, they are describing the heavenly land and seascapes of the Bodrum Peninsula, crowned by the Medieval ramparts of St. Peter's Castle. Speckled in Greek-style whitewashed houses, surrounded by tranquil bays, garlanded by oleander and bougainvillea and custodian to the crumbled yet enduring remains of the **Mausoleum**— one of the Seven Ancient Wonders of the World—Bodrum is the sine qua non of Mediterranean resorts and the Jewel in the Crown of the Turkish Riviera.

Imagine that in 1925, shortly after the founding of the Republic and at a time when feelings of nationalism were high, Turkish writer (and Oxford-educated) Cevat Şakir Kabaağaçlı was sentenced to 3 years of imprisonment in Bodrum for penning an article for which he was accused of "alienating the public from military service." Okay, so he was sent to the dungeon of St. Peter's Castle, but having made a friend of the local governor, was released after a year and a half and found a house overlooking the sea in which to live out his charmed period of exile. His essays on the beauty and allure of life in what was then a backwater fishing village is what inspired an industry that would turn this tiny fishing port of fewer than 5,000 inhabitants to the most popular seaside destination in Turkey.

Bodrum's popularity seems to have no limits, and as fast as the Turkish jet set can lay its claim to a secluded cove or sandy bay, tourism follows, spurring the entitled class to seek new unspoiled hunting grounds. Examples of this can be seen all along the **Bodrum Peninsula,** in the exclusive boutique hotels and beaches of **Torba** and **Türkbükü;** in the expansive coastlines at **Yalıkavak, Turgutreis, Ortakent,** and **Akyarlar;** and in the poetry of the sunken ruins and waterside fish restaurants of **Gümüşlük.**

Bodrum is perfectly situated for 1-day trips to Ephesus (2.5 hr. by car; tours usually run on Wed and Sat), **Pamukkale** (3.5–4 hr. by car; tours run Mon and Fri), **Dalyan/Kaunos** (Thurs and Sun) and Miletus/Priene/ Didyma (daily). The trips are scheduled to coincide with local market days in the respective destinations. All are easily arranged through local travel agents for around $50 per person each (private tours are more).

If beachgoing is the main event, a tour of the Bodrum Peninsula will offer a glimpse of fantastic bays and slowly gentrifying and modernizing seaside villages.

Bodrum

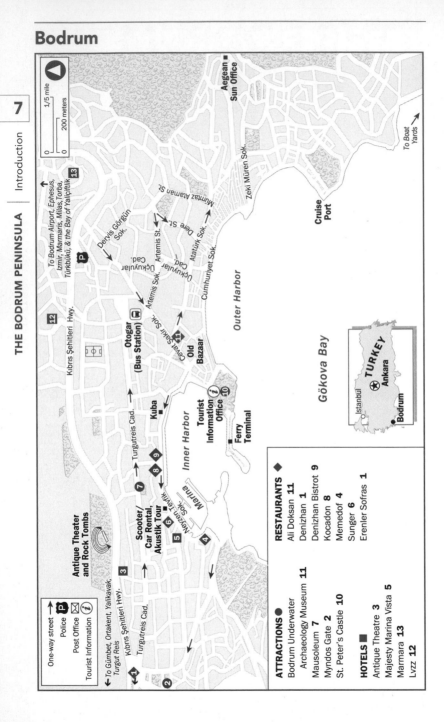

One-way street →
Police 🅿
Post Office ⊠
Tourist Information ⓘ

1/5 mile
200 meters

←To Gümbet, Ortakent, Yalıkavak,
Turgut Reis

To Bodrum Airport, Ephesus,
İzmir, Marmaris, Milas, Torba,
Türkbükü, & the Bay of Yalıçiftlik

Antique Theater
and Rock Tombs

Dervis Görgün Sok.

Kıbrıs Şehitleri Hwy.

Turgutreis Cad.

Scooter/
Car Rental,
Akustik Tour

Neyzen Tevfik Sok.

Marina

Inner Harbor

Kuba

Otogar
(Bus Station)

Old
Bazaar

Cevat Şakir Sok.

Üçkuyular Cad.

Artemis Sok.

Artemis St.

Dere St.

Mumtaz Ataman St.

Atatürk Sok.

Cumhuriyet Sok.

Zeki Müren Sok.

Aegean ■
Sun Office

Cruise
Port

Outer Harbor

Tourist
Information
Office ⓘ

Ferry
Terminal

Gökova Bay

TURKEY
Ankara
İstanbul
Bodrum

To Boat
Yards

ATTRACTIONS ●
Bodrum Underwater
  Archaeology Museum **11**
Mausoleum **7**
Myndos Gate **2**
St. Peter's Castle **10**

HOTELS ■
Antique Theatre **3**
Majesty Marina Vista **5**
Marmara **13**
Lvzz **12**

RESTAURANTS ◆
Ali Doksan **11**
Denizhan **1**
Denizhan Bistrot **9**
Kocadon **8**
Memedof **4**
Sunger **6**
Erenler Sofras **1**

You could also start a coastal adventure in Bodrum and work your way down through Datça and Marmaris, only 1 ½ to 2 hours away by car ferry.

GETTING TO KNOW BODRUM ★★★

In past years, visitors flocking to **Bodrum** sought out a room in one of the whitewashed pensions or hotels in the center of Bodrum, a stone's throw to the castle, Halicarnas night club and the bars and beach clubs along Barlar Sokağı. The first expansion witnessed the rapid and jumbled development of **Gümbet,** spurred by entrepreneurs all too happy to receive the overflow from its historically protected neighbor. Then, the twin bays of **Gölköy and Türkbükü** were discovered by the jet and yachting set, while those seeking luxury and solitude headed for **Torba.** The completion of new marinas at **Yalıkavak** and **Turgut Reis** has helped to raise the fortunes of those two former lands end fishing villages, while the opening several years back of the Kempinski Barbaros Bay put the coastline east of Bodrum on the map. The bays of Bitez, Gundoğan and Akyarlar have almost entirely succumbed to the development of oversized, hillside residential strongholds, so these are only mentioned in the Bodrum Beaches section below (if at all). If you're looking for a more down-to-earth environment, consider **Ortakent,** probably Bodrum's last frontier, offering a delightful Mediterranean landscape just steps from the beachfront crowds.

[FastFACTS] BODRUM

Airlines Turkish Airlines (THY) flies five times daily from Istanbul, and once daily from Ankara. The airline office in Bodrum is located in the Oasis Shopping Center northwest of town off the main road ((ℂ) **0252/317-1203;** and at the airport (ℂ) 0252/523-0101) THY also has a toll-free number: (ℂ) **444-0849.**

Airport The general information line at Bodrum-Milaş Airport is (ℂ) **0252/523-0080.** You can also log on to their website (**www. bodrum-airport.com**).

Car Rentals In Bodrum center, the major car-rental agencies are: **Avis,** Neyzen Tevfik Cad. 92/A ((ℂ) **0252/ 316-2333**), **National Car Rental,** Cevat Şakir Cad. 48 ((ℂ) **0252/313-6110**) and

Europcar (Tepecik Mah. Hamam Sok.; (ℂ) **0252/313-0885**). **Budget** has a location on Caferpaşa Cad. Gül Sitesi 5 (the road leading from the Bodrum marina back up to the main road: (ℂ) **0252/316-9029**), and at the airport ((ℂ) 0252/523-0271). **Sixt** ((ℂ) **0252/559-0340**), **Hertz** ((ℂ) **0252/ 523-0137**), **Avis** ((ℂ) **0252/ 523-0203**) and Europcar (ℂ) **0252/559-0214**) have counters at Bodrum's airport.

Climate Bodrum's climate is Mediterranean, with temperatures rarely falling below freezing.

Embassies & Consulates The United Kingdom has an Honorary Consulate in Bodrum at Cafer Paşa Caddesi 2, Emsan Evleri 7

((ℂ) **0252/313-0017**). The nearest U.S. Consular Agent is in Izmir ((ℂ) **0232/464-8755;** for emergencies, call the embassy switchboard at (ℂ) 0312/455-5555).

Emergencies In an emergency, the **Private Hospital (Özel Hastanesi;** www.ozelbodrumhastanesi. com; (ℂ) **0252/313-6566;** located at Türkkuyusu Mah. Marsmabedi Cad. 33/35) is your best bet. It's open for emergencies 24 hours a day, and most duty doctors speak English. The number for the **ambulance** is also (ℂ) **0252/313-6566.**

Market Day Bodrum's local market is next to the bus station and open on market days from dawn to dusk (watch out for beggars on market day). Thursday and Friday are the days for food, Tuesday for textiles and dry goods. Monday is market day in Türkbükü; Wednesday is market day in Gümüşluk, Gundoğan and Ortakent; Thursday is market day in Yalıkavak, and Saturday is market day in Turgut Reis. There's also a fun flea market in Bitez on Sundays.

Newspapers & Magazines **Bodrum Life** (www.bodrumlife.com; (✆ **0252/348-4602**) has been the go-to source on Bodrum since 1998. On the Web, go to **www.bodrum-museum.com** for online tours of Bodrum's museums.

Parking The most economical place to park in Bodrum town is in the underground lot on Neyzen Tevfik Cad. (the extension of Çevat Şakır Cad., opposite the Post Office) on the left just before you arrive at the waterfront.

Police Dial (✆ **155** for assistance or call the station directly at (✆ **0252/316-8080**.

Post Office The main post office is located on Cevat Şakir Caddesi and is open 24 hours a day for phone calls and other services. The change office operates on business hours, but there are several private change windows nearby.

Travel Agents **Akustik Tour,** Neyzen Tevfik Sok. 200, across from the marina (www.travelshopbodrum.com; (✆ **0252/313-8964**), has grown from a small mom and pop operation to a franchise with bases in Bodrum, Antalya and Izmir. Their professional, friendly, and English-speaking services include day tours to the surrounding sites (including Ephesus), transfers, reservations and ticketing. Yalı Travel (www.yalitravel.com; (✆ **0252/385-3200**) has a corner on the market in Yalıkavak.

GETTING THERE & GETTING AROUND

Getting There

BY PLANE Visitors destined for Bodrum actually fly into Milaş, about 32km (20 miles) away and reachable in under a half-hour by way of the coastal road. **Turkish Airlines** (✆ **444-0849** for call center, or (✆ 0252/23-0129 at the airport), **Atlasjet** ((✆ **0850/222-0000**; www.atlasjet.com), **Onur Air** (www.onurair.com.tr; (✆ **444-6687** for call center), **Fly Air** ((✆ **0212/444-4359**) and **Inter Airlines** all fly from Istanbul's Atatürk Airport while Turkish and **Pegasus Airlines** (www.flypgs.com; (✆ **0850/250-2737**) serve the connection from Istanbul's Sabiha Gökçen Airport. **SunExpress** ((✆ **444-0797**) flies direct from Antalya. There are also several charter companies arriving from Germany, the U.K., France, and the Netherlands; check with your local travel agent for information or log onto the airport's website (www.bodrum-airport.com).

Havaş ((✆ **444-0487 or 0252/523-0040**) provides transfer service by bus into Bodrum's bus station from the domestic terminal; the ride takes about 45 minutes and costs 18TL. Havaş departures for transport to and from the city center are coordinated with Turkish Airlines, Onur Air, Sun Express, Pegasus, Bora Jet, Sky Airlines and Anadolu Jet flights.

Having perfected the challenge of logistics, **Akustik Tourism Center** (Neyzen Tevfik Cad. 146 opposite the marina; (✆ **444-0844** or 0252/313-4523; www.akustik.tc) offers private transfers from the airport to anywhere on the peninsula in comfortable, roomy air-conditioned vehicles. In fact, if you ask your hotel to arrange a pickup for you, chances are pretty solid that someone from Akustik will be there to pick you up. The price of a transfer scheduled directly with Akustik is 80TL- to 90TL, depending on the final destination. Compare that with the taxi fare into Bodrum, which is fixed at 40€ (100TL at the time of this writing).

BY BUS Buses provide the cheapest and most comprehensive service into Bodrum, from pretty much everywhere in Turkey. The major bus companies serving Bodrum are **Pamukkale** (© 0252/316-1369), **Varan** (© 0252/316-7849), **Kamıl Koç** (© 0252/313-0468), and **Metro** (© 444-3455 or 0252/313-2233), but remember that rates vary widely from company to company.

BY FERRY   International Routes   There are currently three companies running ferry and/or hydrofoil service between Turkey and the Greek islands of Koş and Rhodes. All international traffic departs from/arrives into the cruise port (Yolcu Limanı) at Şalvarağa Tepesi, Mantar Brunu Mevkii, just past Halikarnas (© 0252/316-4872; www.bodrumcruiseport.com).

Turkish Seaslines (© 0252/316-1086; www.turkishsealines.com) has the most competitive prices of the three. On one of Turkish Sealines catamarans, you can get from (or to) **Rhodes** in 50 minutes or 2 hours on the slower car ferry. Tickets on the latter cost 28€ for adults; 14€ for children (infants and toddlers to six years travel free on all of the ferry companies).

Bodrum Express Lines (© 0252/316-1087; www.bodrumexpresslines.com) also runs both ferryboat and hydrofoil service between Bodrum and **Koş**. Ferryboats run daily in summer and four times a week in winter. The ride takes 55 minutes and costs 15€ adult one way; 20€ round-trip returning on the same day. The hydrofoil runs from May through October, takes 1 hour and costs 28€ round-trip (2011 prices). **Yeşil Marmaris Lines** (© 0252/412-1033; www.yesilmarmarislines.com) hydrofoils depart four times per week. The ride takes 20 minutes and costs 12€.

From **Rhodes**, Bodrum Express Lines runs fast hydrofoil service June through September departing Monday and Friday. The ride takes 2 hours, 15 minutes and costs 60€ for both a one-way and a same-day round-trip. **Yeşil Marmaris Lines** (© 0252/412-1033; www.yesilmarmarislines.com) plies the same route four times a week from May to October, departing Bodrum at 9am and leaving Rhodes at 2pm (43€ one way; 45€ same day adult round-trip). Turkish Sealines also serves the route between Bodrum and Rhodes.

A fourth company, **Bodrum Ferryboat Association** (© 0252/316-0882; www.bodrumferryboat.com) serves Koş, departing from both Bodrum and from Turgut Reis at the extreme western tip of the peninsula. Service runs once daily in July and August and takes 40 minutes. Service to Koş departs at 10am and returns at 4:30pm. The one way ticket costs 15€; a same day return ticket cost 20€. In all cases, tickets are available through any travel agent or directly through the ferry line operator. Be sure to confirm schedules and to reserve in advance, and if you're heading out of Bodrum, triple-check the place of departure. In general, boats heading to Greece depart from the cruise port, while trips to Datça or Marmaris leave from the wharf on Neyzen Tevfik Caddesi.

From the cruise port, there is a regular, free shuttle for passengers heading in and out of Bodrum six times per day (departure times are posted outside the entrance). You can also take a taxi, but know that the *metered rate* into Bodrum center is around 7TL. You can also rent a bicycle for 5€ per day from Diadem Yachting opposite the entrance to the cruise port.

DOMESTIC ROUTES   If you're arriving from or heading to Marmaris, Bodrum Express Lines runs twice-weekly hydrofoils between Bodrum and **Marmaris** April through September. Hydrofoils arrive in the charming town of Gelibolu (where BEL will complete the journey for you with a bus to Marmaris). Total travel time is 1 hour, 50 minutes (the last 20 min. are on the bus). The one-way ticket costs 25€; a round-trip, same-day excursion costs 30€.

BFA also runs passenger and car-ferry service to **Datça** (2 hr.) for 25TL one-way and 40TL return with a bus transfer from Korman landing to Datça town, and 70€ if you're loading a car (add 10TL per passenger in the vehicle). Children under 6 travel free; 6- to 12-year-olds pay 50%.

ORIENTATION

Working your way clockwise around the peninsula, the first bay over from Bodrum (center) is **Gümbet,** a popular and crowded budget option mostly populated by a steady flood of weekender Brits. Taking advantage of the bays and coves of Bitez and Akyarlar are a series of condominium developments, followed by the town and yacht marina of **Turgutreis.** To the north is the idyllic fishing bay of **Gümüşlük,** protected by the remains of ancient Myndos. **Yalıkavak** finds the perfect balance between local character and a tourist infrastructure, with a town bazaar, waterside restaurants, and stretches of unbroken seafront. **Göltürkbükü** is the merged name of the neighboring coves of Göl (Gölköy) and Türkbükü, two magnificent seaside villages that have morphed into a destination for the international jet set. To the east of Göltürkbükü is **Torba** (which is also directly north of Bodrum), a semi-enclosed and serene bay lined with design hotels and dotted with the odd anchored yacht. At the center of the peninsula is aptly named Ortakent ("middle city"), a pseudo-Tuscan landscape with a pebble and sand beachfront named Ortakent Yahsı on the south shore.

Getting Around

BY DOLMUŞ *Dolmuşes* provide regular service along all of the major thoroughfares through the *otogar* to the city center. From the *otogar,* you're connected to all of the bays and villages of Bodrum's scenic peninsula for a mere 4TL to 4.50TL, while limited service between villages and bays provides connections further out on the peninsula. (See the next section, "Choosing a Base," for specific details on service options.)

BY CAR The narrow and one-way streets of Bodrum discourage the use of a car while the spectacular nooks and crannies of the Bodrum Peninsula encourage it. Within downtown Bodrum, the waterfront spreads out over two harbors, making it easy and scenic to cover with a pair of comfortable shoes and a bit of stamina. A scooter is a good option, because aside from solving the parking problem, you can get away with tooling around aimlessly down side streets or weaving unexpectedly through the pedestrian traffic on the waterfront promenade. See "Fast Facts" above for suggested car rental companies and their contact info.

CHOOSING A BASE

840km (522 miles) south of Istanbul; 240km (149 miles) south of Izmir; 180km (112 miles) west of Marmaris; 25km (16 miles) south of Bodrum Airport

In spite of the hype, Bodrum strikes the perfect balance among whitewashed stucco hillside houses dripping in bougainvillea, magnificent Aegean vistas, historic imprints, and blowout nightlife. **St. Peter's Castle** dominates every corner of Bodrum from its spot at the middle of the resort town's twin harbors. And although it's Turkey's most popular "party destination," by day Bodrum is a delightfully quiet holiday beach resort, with narrow cobbled streets winding up from the harbor all the

---

> ### 📎 The Freshest Fish You Can Find
>
> Meyhaneler Sokağı is Bodrum's version of that tiny little mews crowded by competing fish restaurants. But guess what? You can actually buy your own fish from a market and have it delivered to your meyhane of choice. Yalçin's Balıkçılık (© **0252/316-1148**), located in the market near Meyhaneler Sokağı, is a good, nearby source.

---

way to the **Ancient Theater**. In the summertime the city's twin harbors become densely packed with hundreds of the wooden gulets offering trips to the nearby islands or for the *Mavi Yoluculu* (the "Blue Cruise"), Cevat's romanticized weeklong journey along the glorious coastlines of the Mediterranean. Meanwhile, Bodrum's nightlife—an all-night party organized by club owners each trying to outdo the excesses and spectacle of the others—is infamous throughout Turkey.

Thankfully, the combination of Bodrum's protected status and its minimal, narrow strip beach densely packed with sun beds, keeps the town from becoming just another one of Turkey's overbuilt seaside resorts. For exploring the region, particularly *sans* wheels, it's the perfect place to lay your sun visor.

Essentials

VISITOR INFORMATION

The tourist information office (© **0252/316-1091**), the only official one on the peninsula, is located in the harbor front square just before the entrance to St. Peter's Castle. It's open daily 9am to 6pm. Try to locate a copy of the *Bodrum Guide* as well, for its comprehensive listings of events happening all over Bodrum.

ORIENTATION

The town of Bodrum acts as the southern coastal entry point, an expanded village of white stucco boxes dotting the hillside overlooking twin bays. At the center is a narrow landmass from which the imposing St. Peter's Castle rises almost seemingly from the sea. West of the castle is the **Inner Harbor,** home to the state-of-the-art marina. **Neyzen Tevfik Caddesi** runs the length of the Inner Harbor from the marina to the castle, serving as the nucleus of a neighborhood replete with quality restaurants, upscale boutiques and trendy cocktail lounge catering mostly to the yachting crowd. The **Outer Harbor,** which sits to the east of the castle, is home to the less than stellar town beach. Cumhuriyet Caddesi, aka Barlar Sokağı, follows the curve of the shoreline, itself a narrow fortress pedestrian street lined by boutiques, art galleries, counterfeit purveyors and restaurants with access to the beach. The bustle can be crushing at times, particularly at night, when it seems as if the entire university population of Turkey, plus the human contents of the most recent cruise ship arrival, descend on Cumhuriyet Caddesi to sample the sights, sounds, and smells of summer in Bodrum. It's great fun, if you don't mind crowds.

On the easternmost curve of the Outer Harbor lies the town's brand new **Bodrum Yolcu Limanı** or cruise ship port, a state of the art entry point offering the full range of services (customs, restaurant, currency exchange, hospital, travel agencies, and car/bike rentals. **Cevat Şakir Caddesi** bisects Bodrum, connecting downtown Bodrum with the *otogar,* the weekly market, and the highway, ending up directly at the mouth of the old bazaar.

Where to Eat
BODRUM CENTER

Ali Doksan/Sakallı Restaurant TURKISH   This typical *lokanta* is a down-to-earth, working man's eatery, with food out in large steam trays where you can get a good look at it. Fresh bread fills the plastic canisters on the tables; it's great for wrapping around a kebap or sopping up the tasty stews, rice, and beans. Get there before the local lunch crowd packs both the indoor and outdoor tables.

İncı (across from the post office in outdoor pedestrian mall on the left). ℭ **0232/316-6687.** Vegetable or meat dishes 5TL–12TL. AE, MC, V. Mon–Sat 11am–10pm.

Kocadon ★ TURKISH/MEDITERRANEAN   A stone-cobbled courtyard, quietly nestled between two traditional stone houses, is the setting for one of Bodrum's few restaurants with any longevity. Start with the buffet of cold mezes, stocked with an irresistible variety of salads and fritters—but don't go overboard yet. The kitchen puts out a seasonally rotated menu featuring classic Turkish staples prepared with a twist. A few examples? Grilled octopus in a Bergamot sauce, garlic wild mushrooms, or a pickled tuna with caviar. Prices have unfortunately skyrocketed here, and diners must now pay a "cover" of 10TL per person, justified perhaps by the consistent demand (reservations are highly suggested).

Set back from Neyzen Tevfik Cad. at the corner of Saray Sok. (near the mosque in the Inner Harbor). www.kocadon.com. ℭ **0252/316-3705.** Appetizers and main courses 30TL–60TL. Prix fixe menu 50TL or 140TL. AE, MC, V. Daily 7pm–12:30am. Closed Nov–Apr.

Memedof FISH   For fresh sea bass or sea bream right off the dock, head to the restaurant that has already firmly established itself as Bodrum's de facto fish restaurant (the traditional kind, that is). Prices are the fairest around, and Memedof has become so successful that he opened a branch on the waterfront in Yalıkavak.

Neyzen Tevfik Cad. 176 (opposite the marina at the far end of the street), Bodrum. ℭ **0252/313-4250.** Gerişaltı Mevkii Çökertme Cad. 42, Yalıkavak ℭ **0252/385-4646.** www.memedof.com. Appetizers and main courses 6TL–25TL; fish by weight. MC, V. Daily noon–midnight.

Sunger Pizza PIZZA/SANDWICHES   In my earlier years of visiting Bodrum, I eschewed Sunger Pizza because, from what my friends told me, it sounded so, well, un-Turkish. But after passing by the place and acknowledging that it was consistently full at all hours, I gave in. The pizza turned out to be pretty respectable, coming in four sizes from small to jumbo. Then, on another occasion, I had to try the local favorite, *çökertme,* a sandwich of sliced sirloin on french fries with garlic yogurt (hey, you have to try these things). The rooftop terrace is extremely popular with a local clique of entrepreneurs and expats, and a favorite stop for the boating set docked across the street at the marina.

Neyzen Tevfik Cad. 218, across from the marina. ℭ **0252/316-0854.** Appetizers and main courses 9TL–29TL. MC, V. Daily 9am–2am. Closes earlier off-season.

BODRUM OUTSKIRTS

Denizhan ★★ NOUVELLE TURKISH   This rustic little spot just outside of Bodrum, opened in 1998, is where you'd take a visiting ambassador. The serving style is both elegant and flamboyant, with *şiş kebaps* (skewered lamb cubes) served at the table on skewers the length of yardsticks. The preparation goes on behind a glass-enclosed kitchen in the center of the dining room, where the only thing you won't see is the chef killing the cow. Denizhan is a carnivore's delight; sample an innovative approach to cooking meatballs (fried in a cracked-wheat crust) or try the extraordinary

Choosing a Base

THE BODRUM PENINSULA

Denizhan special (beef baked with cheese, pistachio nuts, and garlic sprinkled with sesame seeds). Find a way to get out to this restaurant. The Denizhan Bistrot in downtown Bodrum (Neyzen Tevfik Cad.), offers a light menu of sandwiches, grills, pastas, and carpaccios.

Turgut Reis Yolu, about 2.5km (1½ miles) outside of town (across from the Tofaş/Fiat service station). www.denizhan.com. Ⓒ **0252/363-7674.** Reservations suggested. Appetizers and main courses 7TL–33TL. Prix fixe menu for two 60TL. AE, MC, V. Daily noon–midnight.

Kismet Lokantası ★ 🍴 It took some coaxing but I finally got it out of 'em. When asked where the locals eat, the response (eventually) was that Kismet was *the* place when people wanted to treat themselves. The large menu relies on the best, freshest local herbs and vegetables that Bodrum has to offer, churning out traditional home cooked delicacies using local recipes. Try the *chicken mantı,* which is simmered and served with yogurt, the *lokum pilav,* or a delectable peapods and pea stew. You can choose among the various kebaps and *köfte,* and Kismet also has its own wood fired oven for made-to-order *pide.*

Atatürk Bulvari 156, Konacık (immediately to your left just after the turnoff to Konacık off the Bodrum road). www.kismetlokantasi.com. Ⓒ **0252/310-0096.** Appetizers and main courses 6TL–12TL. MC, V. Mon–Sat noon–5 or 6pm.

Bodrum After Dark

As the epicenter of Turkish nightlife during the summer months, Bodrum offers an ample selection of top-notch concerts and performances through the year. These events take place in evocative locations such as in St. Peter's Castle, in the restored Antique Theatre and in other historical locations around the peninsula. Major events begin in full force with the **Bodrum Festival,** a roster of music and concert performances lasting from late July through mid-August. The activities peak in August with the **Gümüşluk International Classical Music Festival** (www.gumuslukfestival. org) held in the Byzantine-era church, the Aegean Festival in Yalıkavak's marina (where you'll see folksy music and dance), and the **Bodrum International Ballet Festival** (www.bodrumballetfestival.gov.tr) at St. Peter's Castle in late August. In September 2011, the area Arts and Culture Association (www.bodrumbkst.com) joined with local authorities to launch the first Bodrum Carnival, while in late December, well after the summer party has come to an end, famous musicians and up-and-comers alike come in for **Bodrum Jazz Days** (www.hadigari.com.tr). Tickets are available through **Biletix** (www.biletix.com) or at the castle or ticket booths along Iskele Meydanı in Bodrum.

But somehow, I don't think it was the highbrow concerts that made the nightlife here so legendary, enough to cause people's eyes to glaze over longingly whenever you mention Bodrum (and a different type of glazed the morning after). The more informal choices are endless, from exclusive celebrity-filled lounging, to a more populous trolling of Bar Street, to ear-drum ringing dance clubs to a simple stroll along the twinkling waterfront. Below is a cross-section of the more sophisticated in each category. If you're feeling ambitious, drive to the village of Gümüşlük for a romantic seafood dinner, or head to one of **Göltürkbükü's** Beverly Hills-esque dazzling beach club parties.

Club Catamaran The games begin behind the castle along **Dr. Alim Bey Caddesi,** a narrow health hazard full of crowds working their way past bars, eateries, clothing shops, and booths where you can get an exaggeratedly garish temporary tattoo. This overcrowded stretch reaches full capacity at Cumhuriyet Caddesi, the broad walkway along the Outer Harbor thick with outdoor cafes, bars, loud music, and groups of young party-seekers. Near the entrance to "bar street," (or Barlar Sok), the boat hosts a floating party every night in summer from 10pm (the boat sails at 1am) to 5am, serenaded by Turkish *rakkasse,* and R&B. So as not to trap guests and to allow for latecomers, shuttles run back to shore every 15 minutes. The catamaran is there every year, but every few years the setup changes management (and names). Dr. Alim Bey Calisd. 1025 Sok 44. www.clubcatamaran.com. ✆ **0252/313-3600.** Tickets 30TL weekdays/40TL weekends and include one drink. Daily in summer 10pm–5am.

Bodrum Marina Yacht Club With St. Peter's Castle practically illuminating the entire bay, it's just a matter of choosing your own front seat. The Yacht Club is a favorite of residents, sailors, expats, and Turkish celebrities in both summer and winter, settling in to one of a complex of four bars and three restaurants, among which is **The Jazz Bar** resonating with live bands playing jazz and Latina tunes. The **Roof Bar** offers a sparkling vista of the marina and castle. Live band nightly in summer 9pm to 1am. Bars stay open later. Neyzen Tevfik Cad. 5. www.marinayachtclub.com. ✆ **0252/316-1228.**

Café del Mare With its back up against the waterfront and an entrance on Bar Street, Café del Mare is a beach club, a bar, a narghile cafe, a restaurant, and a musical venue (with DJs) all rolled up into one. You can swim, eat, relax, and imbibe frozen cocktails 24 hours a day. Cumhuriyet Cad. 164–166. ✆ **0252/316-7110.**

Hadigari Nestled at the base of Bodrum Castle, the Hadigari (Turkish for "let's go") occupies 5 square meters of quayside terrace around an old powerhouse-cum-art gallery. An early drink at a candlelit rail-side table with music playing in the background sets the mood for romance. Dinner is served in the restaurant (reservations required) on the upper level from 6pm to midnight. As the night progresses the music adapts, so that by 3am the hammering of an underground beat prevails. Daily 6pm to 4am. Closed November to May. See website or go to www.biletix.com for tickets to concerts and events. Kaledibi (next to the castle). ✆ **0252/316-0048.** 35TL cover after midnight.

Halikarnas Night Club Vegas on the Aegean—and yes, seeing is believing. Touted as the biggest and best open-air disco in the world, it's certainly the most infamous. This is excess at its best (and worst) and a club you love to hate, but everyone is inevitably impressed. The club's three columns tower imposingly above the harbor, a striking backdrop to the laser show later in the evening. Old and new hits from the top of the charts and nightly live shows are interrupted by the occasional appearances of famous pop singers. The nightclub has a capacity of 5,500 people, but it's only the likes of Mick Jagger, Richard Branson, or Pamela Anderson who can score a reservation at a front-seat table (500TL–1,000TL per table). The club opens at 10pm but doesn't attract a soul until midnight. *Note:* The club was closed for the entire 2011 season with no indication whether that would change. Closed November to March. Cumhuriyet Cad. 178. ✆ **0252/316-8000** or 0252/316-1237. Cover in 2010 was 35TL or 40TL depending on the headliner. Free entrance Mon–Wed before midnight, and for ladies on Sun before midnight.

Küba This open-air staple—with its hipster brand of Cuban and Latin music—continues to draw enormous summertime crowds. The whitewashed stone courtyard serves as the bar, enjoying moonlit views of St. Peter's Castle and Marina. Nighttime revelers with an appetite can enjoy a full (and somewhat pricey) alfresco meal. When the temperature dips down below what would require a light sweater, the party heads indoors to share space with the indoor restaurant (reservations required). Daily 9pm to 4am. Closed November to May. Neyzen Tevfik Cad. ⓒ **0252/313-4450.**

Tango This snazzy locale is all about Argentinian spice, both on the menu and off. As an eatery, Tango features Argentina's prized item: meat. There's meat fondu, meaty *köfte*, enormous Texas steak, and pretty decent pasta. Look up from your plate or martini glass and feast your eyes on the oversized wrought iron chandeliers, rich wood decor and warm red cushions. Located opposite the marina, it also has a location at Yalıkavak's marina. Entrees run between 15TL and 85TL. Neyzen Tevfik Cad. 228. opposite the marina. www.mekantango.com. ⓒ **0252/316-0898.**

Zazu Thanks to this bar's pedigree (it's owned by Sinan Özer, ex husband to Turkish phenomenon, Sezen Aksu and a successful entrepreneur in his own right), the Turkish elite flock to Zazu like flies to honey. But don't let that detract you, the bar is popular for a good reason—it's low-key, it's got lots of ambiance, and it's unpretentious. Neyzen Tevfik Cad. 144A. opposite the marina. ⓒ **0252/313-3645.**

Where to Stay

On (or near) the Waterfront

Antique Theatre Hotel This hotel is an unpretentious hillside retreat affording truly stunning views of the castle from every minimalist room. And across the street? The Antique Theatre. All rooms connect to either a shared or private garden lined with trellises overgrown with bougainvillea. Bathrooms are suspiciously like the facilities you'd expect on a yacht, including the ingenious (small!), cylindrically shaped marble showers. (The bathroom setup—you can't quite call it a room—is separated from the bedroom by two louvered doors, making this arrangement possibly too tight for those accustomed to moving around in a bathroom). If you find the accommodations a bit close, the placement of the pool—with views as if you are swimming atop the castle—should compensate enough.

Kıbrıs Şehitleri Cad. 243, 48400 Bodrum (across from the ruins of the antique theater). www.antiquetheatrehotel.com. ⓒ **0252/316-6053.** Fax 0252/316-0825. 20 units (all with shower). 120€–175€ double; 225€–375€ suite. Rates lower Nov–Apr, Christmas excluded. AE, DC, MC, V. Free parking. **Amenities:** Restaurant; bar; outdoor pool. *In room:* A/C.

Lvzz Sleek and fashionable, this outpost opened in 2011, providing visitors to Bodrum something rare for the area: fresh style, parking, *and* proximity. Amply spacious rooms take full advantage of the outside, whether the sliding door to your room opens onto the teak pool deck or takes advantage of views of the castle from the upper panoramic suites. Nautical accents pull together a minimalist yet warm decor, and the spa boasts a salt room in addition to the usual delights. The only iffy thing is that Lvzz sits just above Bodrum's busy main perimeter road, which may make visitors think twice before walking into town. But it's this very feature that allows guests perfect vistas of the castle and bay. And by the time you read this, there may be a shuttle down to the waterfront.

Yokuşgaşı Mah. Akdeniz Caddsi 4, 48400 Bodrum. www.lvzzhotel.com. ⓒ **0252/313-3000.** Fax 0252/313-1099. 17 units. 190€ double; 240€–600€ suite July–Aug. Breakfast 25TL. Rates lower Sept–June. AE, MC, V. Free parking. **Amenities:** 1 restaurant; 2 bars; concierge; elevator; health club and spa; free Internet in lobby; indoor and outdoor pool; room service; smoke-free rooms; free Wi-Fi. *In room:* A/C, satellite TV, hairdryer, minibar, free Wi-Fi.

Majesty Marina Vista ★ ⚑ Although the hotel's address on the main harbor road across from the marina may generate some suspicion as to the tranquillity of its location, the Marina Vista is nothing if not serene. The hotel is far enough from the maddening crowd but within walking distance of practically everything in Bodrum. A recent update (when the Majesty group took over management) gives the hotel a fresh and modern feel, without compromising charm. Only three of the hotel's guest rooms face the marina and street, while the majority of accommodations face a quiet interior courtyard with a pool. In the summertime, there's a persistent layer of flower petals dusting the poolside, a sensory delight that carries over easily to the wellness center. For romance and breathtaking scenery, the rooftop restaurant and Havana Bar offer incredible views of the mountains, harbor, and castle.

Neyzen Tevik Cad. 168 (across from the marina), 48400 Bodrum. www.majesty.com.tr.ⓒ **0252/313-0356.** Fax 0252/316-2347. 93 units. 100€–320€ double. Rate range reflects seasonal fluctuations. AE, MC, V. Street parking only. **Amenities:** 2 bars; babysitting; concierge; exercise room and spa; outdoor pool; room service. *In room:* A/C, satellite TV, hair dryer, minibar.

The Marmara Bodrum ★★★ Skylit hallways, white-on-white themes (including the staff's casual "uniforms"), and an eclectic mix of really cool stuff make this place seem more like an art gallery than a hotel, with a generous dose of warmth and congeniality to remind you that you're in Turkey and not on Madison Avenue. The rooms are simultaneously deluxe and sleek, with aged bamboo closet doors, made-to-order black-on-wood consoles, wrought-iron and wicker chairs, and the finest whiter-than-white bed linens. Every room has a balcony, but the real draw is the bathroom, a glass, marble, and chrome gallery featuring a picture window between the tub and outer room. As if a panorama of Bodrum weren't enough, the landscaping takes advantage of the rocky hilltop, incorporating the stones into the design of the outdoor space. The poolside bar tables are crafted with Iznik tiles, and the poolside lounges, chairs, and barstools are—guess what—white. Don't overlook the top-of-the-line spa facility, where a massage or an hour-long session relaxing in the flotation tank will leave you limp.

Yokuşbaşı Mevkii, PK 199, 48400 Bodrum (on the hilltop above the main road). www.themarmarahotels.com. ⓒ **0252/313-8130.** Fax 0252/313-8131. 95 units (all with tub). 150€–218€ double; 292€–1,441€ suite. Rates lower Oct–May. AE, DC, DISC, MC, V. Free parking on-site. By car from Izmir, Ephesus, Marmaris, and Bodrum airport, entering Bodrum on Kibris Sehitleri Hwy., watch for signs for the hotel entrance on the right. **Amenities:** Restaurant; bar; concierge; *hamam;* health club and spa; 2 outdoor pools (1 Olympic-size); room service; smoke-free rooms; tennis courts (grass) and squash courts. *In room:* A/C, satellite TV, hair dryer, minibar, free Wi-Fi.

GÜMBET & BITEZ

4.6km (3 miles) west of Bodrum.

Located just over the headlands from Bodrum's twin bays and separated at the top by a string of windmills, Gümbet has long been the poor, overlooked stepchild of its polished neighbor. While Bodrum's tourism development evolved under watchful eyes, Gümbet, which began as a quiet outpost of Bodrum, exploded haphazardly and with little to no oversight, creating a monster of inexpensive rates and packages that have attracted the Aegean Coast's fair share of British holiday makers. Granted, the sandy beach, completely blanketed by grass umbrellas and sunbeds, is lovely while the favorable winds of Bitez attract windsurfers and other water sportsmen. And there are plenty of places to eat, drink, and be merry. So although neither Gümbet nor the more residential Bitez would ever be my choice, their proximity to Bodrum's center and affordable options for lodging do have a market, particularly among families on a budget.

Essentials

GETTING THERE/GETTING AROUND It's a 10-minute *dolmuş* ride from Bodrum to Gümbet, or a 20-minute ride to Bitez from Bodrum's *otogar*. By car, from the airport, stay on main Bodrum highway past the Antique Theatre, then follow signs directing you to turn left onto the road into Gümbet or to Bitez.

Both Gümbet and Bitez are compact enough that you won't need much more than a comfy pair of sandals. But if you get tired, *dolmuşes* ply the roads through both regularly; just flag one down. *Dolmuşes* also head out of Gümbet; destinations are clearly marked on the windshield.

Where to Eat

Bitez Mantıçı ☺❢ TURKISH When you've grown tired of eating the same old same old, this clean and glass-enclosed eatery on the main road will hit the spot. True to its name, the specialty is *mantı*, tiny Turkish ravioli stuffed with meat, or nuts or even spinach, either boiled or fried to a crunch. Topped with yogurt and a bit of butter and hot chili pepper, and you'll be lamenting your bikini in no time. The only other items on the menu are light fare: *gözleme* (Turkish crepes), *çiğ börek* and some homemade sweets.

Atatürk Caddesi 60/5, Bitez (right in the middle of town). ✆ **0252/363-0440**. Menu items 7TL–14TL. MC, V. Daily 11am–11pm.

Where to Stay

Bodrium Hotel ❢ Set back near the entrance to Gümbet, the Bodrium offers smaller-scale, boutique-style accommodations at a reasonable price. But what clinched the deal for me were the Tempur-pedic type beds, not just in the suites, but in every room. They also have heated flooring, which admittedly, is less of a perk when the asphalt is melting under the heat of the blazing sun. Still, the idea is to offer that added bit of comfort, a point that is made very clear in the hotel spa. If you're willing to hoof it a bit, it's theoretically possible to walk to both Gümbet and Bodrum centers, both about 15 minutes away on foot.

Buyuk Iskender Cad. No:13, Gümbet. 52 units. 145€ double; 285€ suite July–Aug. Rates lower Sept–June. AE, MC, V. Free parking on-site. **Amenities:** Restaurant; bar; babysitting; concierge; health club and spa; pool; room service; smoke-free rooms; Turkish bath. *In room:* A/C, satellite TV, hair dryer, minibar, free Wi-Fi.

Dorla Hotel Bodrum ⛟ This gem is also located between Gümbet and Bitez, yet although the private beach is located down a steep hill (free hotel shuttle available), it's one of the more delicious waterfronts this close to Bodrum center. The plus? The sunsets from your amply sized, modern sea view room. The rooms are squeaky clean, have comfortable beds, balconies and marble mini-retreats for baths. The hotel is bright and airy, with aquamarine accents and some colorful pieces of art. Another bonus is the silence—no blaring of music throughout the day, and although there are no group activities for kids, chances are they'll stay occupied at one of the three pools or in the blue flag waters.

Gündönümü Mevkii, Bitez, 48400 Bodrum. www.doriahotelbodrum.com. ✆ **0252/311-1020.** 92 units. 195€–280€ double. AE, MC, V. Free parking on-site. **Amenities:** Restaurant; bar; babysitter; concierge; health club and spa; indoor and outdoor pools; room service; smoke-free rooms; Turkish bath. *In room:* A/C, satellite TV, hair dryer, minibar, free Wi-Fi.

TORBA

8km (5 miles) north of Bodrum.

On the northern end of the peninsula and only 8km (5 miles) from Bodrum is the stunning bay **Torba** ★★. Surrounded by land on practically all sides, the waters of Torba Bay are as serene as those in a lake, where fishermen haul in their nets and you can stroll along the beach to the remains of an old Byzantine monastery. It's home to both sand and pebble beaches, and a solid handful of tony boutique resorts shaded by olive trees, reaching into a placed sea.

Essentials

GETTING THERE The road to Torba intersects with the D330 (Milas-Bodrum highway) just before entering Bodrum's commercial heart.

GETTING AROUND Torba is served by the Bodrum-Gundoğan *dolmuş*, which runs every 10 minutes or so in summer and every 30 minutes in winter.

Where to Eat

Gonca Balık ★★ ▮ AEGEAN For more than 20 years, this unassuming little fish restaurant has been the spot where you take whomever you want to impress, and indeed, over the life of Gonca, the likes of Jeremy Irons and Bo Derek sniffed their way over to a table. Now part of the Casa dell'Arte family, the eatery still keeps things simple, allowing the fruits of the sea and sparkling Torba waterfront to take center stage. From your table, you can practically catch your own meal, but leave it to the cooks to transform it into one of their specialties. There are certainly less expensive places to dine, but if you're in Torba, consider yourself worth it.

Kilise Mevkii Mutlu Sok. ✆ **0252/367-1848.** Reservations required. Fish by weight (around 85TL per kilo in 2011). Noon–11pm Sun–Thurs; 7pm–midnight Fri–Sat.

Where to Stay

Amanruya ★★★ The arrival of an Aman property along the Bodrum coastline augers well for a resort that had already become an international phenomenon. So let's be honest with ourselves, most of us can only dream of a week-long respite in our own spacious and secluded stone cottage just a pebbles throw down a windy path to an unspoiled coastline. And although the press materials claim Türkbükü as its home, the Amanruya actually sits on the edge of Torba Bay, just around the bend and engulfed in peaceful (except for the crickets) Mediterranean forest. All 36 cottages come with a private garden and swimming pool, a pergola and an outdoor shower. The cottages were constructed using local stone; furniture was crafted using acajau wood, and Turkish marble clads most surfaces. The hotel also has a 50-meter swimming pool if socializing is your thing, a library stocked with DVDs and books, a wine lounge, an art gallery, two spa suites and dining pavilions for a memorable gastronomic experience.

Bülent Ecevit Cad., Demir Mevkii, 48483 Bodrum. www.amanresorts.com. ✆ **9477/774-3500.** 36 units. 800€–900€ cottages. Rates exclude taxes. AE, MC, V. Free parking. **Amenities:** Restaurant; bar; beach; concierge; fitness room and spa; room service; tennis courts; Turkish bath; limited watersports equipment/rental. *In room:* A/C, satellite TV, hair dryer, minibar, free Wi-Fi.

Casa dell'Arte Residence ★★★ ▣ Each of the Casa dell'Arte's 12 luxury albeit sparsely furnished rooms serves as a canvas for the artwork painted by the house artists. Outside, Mother Nature paints broad strokes of lavender, palm, and ivy on a background of manicured lawns and seductive hazy mountain and sea views. And guests can take part in it all, either proactively (the artists run free workshops for hotel guests in ceramics, painting, and sculpture) or passively (comatose below a thatch pavilion enjoying a massage, or exploring the ruins of the beachfront Byzantine monastery. Because of the risk of damage to the (considerably valuable) artwork, children under 12 are not allowed in the main hotel. They are, however, welcome next door at the adjoining luxury family section (total 27 rooms) at the bargain basement rate of 300€ to 500€, with only slightly less regal service than the residence section.

Kilise Mevkii Mutlu Sok., 48400 Torba. www.casadellartebodrum.com. ℂ **0252/367-1848.** Fax 0252/367-1868. 12 units. 540€–900€ high season. AE, MC, V. Free parking. Closed Nov–Apr. **Amenities:** Restaurant; bar; beach; children's center and programs; concierge; fitness room and spa; outdoor pool; room service; smoke-free rooms; tennis courts (grass) and squash courts; Turkish bath; watersports equipment/rental. *In room:* A/C, satellite TV, hair dryer, minibar, free Wi-Fi.

YALIÇIFTLIK

14 km (8½ miles) east of Bodrum; 38km (24 miles) southwest of the airport

Just a few years back, the Kempinski hotel group planted its flag on an undisturbed tract of land on a cliff above a breathtaking Barbaros Bay. While it wasn't the first hotel in the bay, it was certainly the only one that matters. The down side of Yalıçiftlik is the distance to Bodrum along a singular windy road heading in the *opposite* direction from the main attractions of the peninsula. The Kempinski Barbaros Bay certainly makes it a tough decision.

Essentials

Getting There/Getting Around *Dolmuşes* ply the pine tree-lined road between Bodrum's *otogar* and Yalı from early morning until early evening. The ride takes about 40 minutes.

Where to Stay & Eat

Kempinski Hotel Barbaros Bay ★★★ This five-star property is brought to you by the same people who brought us the opulence of the Çiragan Palace in Istanbul and the new Dome in Belek, along the shoreline of Greater Antalya. Let me start by saying that almost everything about this hotel is postcard-worthy: the "fairy chimneys" emerging out of the meandering mirror pool, the placid waters of Barbaros Bay, the serene Six Senses Spa. I say "almost" because although this resort hotel is pretty close to perfect, it's a bit, well, cold. The rooms are inviting enough, what with plush beds, lazy banquettes, teak-decked terraces (or balconies), an ample dressing area, and a bathroom fit for royalty, while the common areas like the atrium lobby (which sets the tone of the hotel) remain a bit sterile. Sigh. Leave it to Frommer's to find fault in practical perfection. It's a bit of a distance from the center of Bodrum (about a 25-min. drive down a meandering Yalıciftlik road), but if it's pampering and privacy you're looking for, well, you found it.

Kizilagac Koyu, Gerenkuyu Mevkii Yaliciftlik, Bodrum. www.kempinski-bodrum.com. ℂ **0252/311-0303.** Fax 0252/311-0300. 173 units. 294€–585€ double; 540€ and up suite. Rates lower out of high season. AE, DC, DISC, MC, V. Free parking on-site. **Amenities:** 2 restaurants; 4 bars; children's center; concierge; *hamam;* health club and spa; helicopter pad; marina docking; indoor and outdoor pools; room service; smoke-free rooms. *In room:* A/C, satellite TV, CD/DVD player, hair dryer, minibar, free Wi-Fi.

GÖLTÜRKBÜKÜ

16km (10 miles) northwest of Bodrum.

The simple hillside village and serene bay of **Göltürkbükü** ★★★, long a favored hideaway of Turkey's jet set, has, to date, made room for a steady stream of travelers onto this little "secret" destination. The twin villages of Gölköy and Türkbükü have come a long way since they married their fortunes together into one destination for the international glitterati. The villages themselves, centered along the road that follows the curve of the bay, still retain their small-town charm, while down along the waterfront is a parade of exclusive, 10TL-cup-of-coffee beach clubs that offer luxurious cushioned wooden piers draped in sailcloth, fitness areas, grassy lounge areas, and free Wi-Fi. If lazing alongside Michael Douglas and Catherine Zeta-Jones is your idea of a good time, well, then this is the place you and your credit cards should be.

Essentials

GETTING THERE/GETTING AROUND   The twin villages lie on the north shore of the Bodrum Peninsula, just around the coastline to the east of Torba. *Dolmuşes* run regular service from Bodrum, or a taxi ride should take about 10 minutes.

Where to Eat

Miam Restaurant 🍴   One of the quieter spots in this star-struck corner of Bodrum, Miam serves a delicious procession of Aegean delicacies mainly to locals treating themselves to a special celebration. It's located at the head of the entrance into Türkbükü, offering an atmospheric dining experience right on the jetty. Consider the menu an upgraded version of home cooking, with cook Zeynep Hanım preparing special sauces and atypical entrees like the octopus kokoreç or balık pastırma.
Yalı Mevkii 5, Türkbükü. ⓒ **0252/377-5612.** Fish by weight. MC, V. 7pm–midnight daily in summer.

Where to Stay

Ada Hotel ★★★   Fashioned like a stately country villa, this Relais & Châteaux hotel was built from the ground up on a scrubby tract of land at the top of Türkbükü before anybody knew where the bay was. Using the elements of classic Ottoman design, they incorporated such features as hand-carved stonework, outdoor living spaces, and thick stone walls. The rooms are huge and luxuriously rustic, and bathrooms are embellished with plush towels (on warmers), candles, and potpourri. Although the property has no access to the bay, the luxuriant grounds—caressed by the swaying of reed plants in the breeze—along with amenities you never thought you'd need, keep your mind elsewhere. The regal *hamam,* reserved by the hour for private use, enjoys views of the bay via a picture window. Two of the suites share private use of an additional terrace pool. A cinema screening room provides a large selection of films and keeps young ones occupied with a huge video-game station. And the cellar restaurant, with its velours, chandeliers, stone, and ancient wood, could easily set the stage for a scene for *Camelot.* Ultimately, the Ada Hotel is in a class all itself.
Bağarası Mah. Tepecik Cad. 128, 48400 Göltürkbükü, Bodrum. www.adahotel.com. ⓒ **0252/377-5915.** Fax 0252/377-5379. 14 units. Apr–June and Sept–Oct $240–$920 double and suite; July–Aug $280–$1,035 double and suite. AE, DC, MC, V. Closed Nov–Mar. **Amenities:** 2 restaurants; 2 bars; beach club; bikes; exercise room; *hamam;* Jacuzzi; library lounge; outdoor pool; room service; sauna. *In room:* A/C, satellite TV/DVD player, hair dryer, minibar.

Ece Resort If hobnobbing with celebrities is beyond what your wallet allows yet you would still like to see what all the fuss is about, the Ece offers a warm, family-friendly and welcoming option, where owners become fast friends with their guests. Located on the Gölköy side of Göltürbükü, the Ece also predates the arrival of the jet-setting hideaways that have more recently staked their claim to this one-time fishing village. The rooms are small yet adequate, with windows that give out to the exterior gardens and pastures rather than to the common pool area. The smallish bathrooms have quarter-round, glass-enclosed showers, but the Aegean sun will blind you to all but the bougainvillea strewn about and the kitsch, original artwork painted on the pool area's whitewashed walls. The hotel's beach, a mere few hundred meters' walk to the waterfront (or minutes by the free, on-demand shuttle), will serve as your temporary taste of the high life. And acknowledging that their hotel guests are on holiday, Erkan and his wife see that breakfast is served from 9am to 1pm (also served to non-guests).

Hürriyet Caddesi 64, Göltürbükü. www.eceresort.com. © **0252/357-7388.** Fax 0252/357-7389. 33 units. 140€ double June–Aug; 60€ Apr, May, Sept, Oct. Closed in winter. AE, MC, V. **Amenities:** Restaurant; bar; bikes; free Wi-Fi. *In room:* A/C, IV, hair dryer, free Wi-Fi.

Maça Kızı Hotel ★ Stylish, pricey, and waterside, the Maca Kızı features smart, minimalist designed rooms. The designer consciousness spills into the bathrooms, too, which, although equipped with only a shower, sport thick muslin shower curtains and high-end toiletries. Both are recommendable for a day out on the wooden deck "beaches" of Türkbükü, and as stylish alternatives to the extraordinary (and pricier) Ada Hotel (see above). The hotel offers spa treatments in outdoor tents and provides personal training, yoga, and Pilates as part of its fitness center.

Maça Kızı Hotel. Kesireburnu Mevkii, 48483 Türkbükü. www.macakizi.com. © **0252/377-6272.** Fax 0252/377-6287. 46 units. 324€–514€ double; 600€ and up suite. AE, MC, V. Free parking. **Amenities:** Restaurant; bar; beach; concierge; fitness center; outdoor pool; room service; Turkish bath; watersports. *In room:* A/C, satellite TV, hair dryer, minibar, free Wi-Fi.

YALIKAVAK

16km (10 miles) west of Bodrum; 6 km (3¾ miles) north of Gümüşlük

A description of **Yalıkavak** could be entitled a Tale of Two Villages. From its roots as the peninsula's main (sponge) fishing village and rudimentary put-in for the yachting set to the arrival of a number of secluded hilltop hideaways and exclusive beach clubs, Yalıkavak offers simultaneously a seaside respite for the Proletariat as well as pristine coves and beach for those not star-struck by the glitter of Golturkbuku. The village's fortunes may shift now that Yalıkavak has got its own new marina, but in the meantime, it still offers its visitors the simplicity of earlier years. While you're trolling through the weekly market or imbibing tea at the local tea house, plan a short visit inside the cistern turned into an art gallery and admire the remains of the area's typical windmills.

Essentials

GETTING THERE/GETTING AROUND There is a *dolmuş* serving the route from Bodrum (via Gundoğan and Türkbükü or direct) and from Turgut Reis and Yalıkavak. *Dolmuşes* run regularly from around 7am until 11 or 11:30pm (or 1am in summer) A taxi to Bodrum costs around 35€.

> ### Not the Titanic, but Close Enough
>
> Robert Ballard, made famous for his discovery of the Titanic wreck in 1985, bases his boat, the Nautilus, at the Yalıkavak marina for 6 months out of the year.

Where to Eat

4 Reasons Bistro ★★ A very reasonable option even for non-guests, the bistro serves delicious updates to traditional Aegean recipes. Almost all of the produce comes from the local market or Ali and Esra's own garden (except for non-regional staples like helva, which they have shipped from near the Turkish border). Take the arugula salad, for example, combined with grapefruit and homemade grissini, the grilled eggplant and mozzarella or the sublime swordfish carpaccio. The Moroccan tagine offers a choice of lamb (with pear), chicken (with olives and pickled lemon) or fish (with pickled lemon and tomato sauce), resulting in a personalized sensation of flavors. In summer, guests dine on the pool deck under the moonlight; in cooler weather, the festival of flavor moves indoors warmed by the fireplace.

Bakan Cad. 2 Yalıkavak, Bodrum. www.4reasonshotel.com. (*) **0252/385-3212.** Fax 0252/385-3229. Appetizers and main courses 14TL–36TL. Daily 7pm–midnight.

Kavaklı Köftecisi 🛉 For more than 20 years, Kavaklı Köfteçisi has been unceremoniously churning out meatballs and lamb shish to an increasing clientele of local workers and visiting tourists alike. Ask anyone to point you there, or follow your nose to the irresistible fragrance of grilling meats. Be forewarned: There's no menu, just stubby strips of *köfte*, perfectly cooked skewers of lamb, and two salads: mixed or bean. There's also no decor to speak of, just some tables and benches outside under an awning and a handful of institutional tables inside.

Merkez Çarşı İçi (inside the market area). (*) **0252/385-4748.** Appetizers and main courses: 7TL–10TL. Daily 11am–11pm.

Where to Stay

4Reasons ★★ One could easily enumerate many more than four reasons to stay at this hotel beyond the four types of oversize suite rooms dubbed "casual," "passionate," "functional," and the less inspired "junior suite." How about the breathtaking views, the fragrant breezes, the sunsets over the tangerines? 4Reasons is located just 2 miles (uphill) out of the as-of-yet unspoiled seaside resort of Yalıkavak, which for now maintains its salt-of-the-earth roots. Owners Ali and Esra promise a wellness center by 2012 and the possibility of a complete retreat from the world. The 4Reasons, by the way, has already been discovered by *Condé Nast Traveler.*

Bakan Cad. 2 Yalıkavak, Bodrum. www.4reasonshotel.com. (*) **0252/385-3212.** Fax 0252/385-3229. 17 units. July 1–Aug 31 71€–249€ double. Rates fluctuate by season and demand. MC, V. Free valet parking. **Amenities:** Restaurant; bar; bike rental; concierge; outdoor pools; room service; free Wi-Fi. *In room:* A/C, satellite TV, hair dryer, minibar.

Sandima 37★ With its seven warm and minimalist suites overlooking a verdant lawn and mountain and seascapes beyond, Sandıma 37 seems like the Garden of Eden on the Aegean. And while it may not be located on the water, the hotel provides free shuttle service (and as of 2011 free admission) to nearby Dodo Beach. The suites occupy a renovated 70-year-old traditional two-story stone mansion, offering modern and airy decor bordering on the masculine. All suites have separate living rooms, where the Garden Suites also have kitchens, the Junior Suites utilize a slightly smaller space by combining European kitchens with counter seating. There's also a more traditional two-bedroom stone house (with narrow staircase) bedecked in hand-made Anatolian decor that would be good for couples with children. In keeping with the reserved indulgence of the hotel, breakfast is served 24/7 in the garden or on your private balcony.

Atatürk Cad. 37, Yalikavak, Bodrum (on the road heading out of town). www.sandima37suites.com. (C) **0252/385-5337**. 7 units. 180€–360€ July–Aug including breakfast and tax. Rates lower in winter. AE, MC, V. Free parking. **Amenities:** Bar; outdoor pools; room service. *In room:* A/C, satellite TV, hair dryer, minibar, free Wi-Fi.

ORTAKENT

9km (5½ miles) west of Bodrum; 11km (6¾ miles) northeast of Turgut Reis

If you want to avoid the jet-set scene altogether, empty your bottle of sunscreen over at the long stretch of tranquil beach at **Ortakent ★★**. The village, whose name means "middle city," sits at the center of the peninsula, a small town Turkish village with schools and shops serving the local population. The road south through tangerine and olive groves leads to the sand and sea at **Yahşi** (pretty) **Beach,** the longest sandy stretch on the peninsula. The beach is frequented by normal folk, both Turkish and foreign, but unlike most of the rest of Bodrum's beaches, Ortakent retains its small-town, local resort feel.

Essentials

GETTING THERE *Dolmuşes* run regularly between Bodrum's *otogar* (and along the main road—you can flag one down if you're staying at the Lvzz or Antique Theatre) and Ortakent Yahşi (the sign on the minibus will say "Yahşi" or "Bodrum" depending which way you're headed.

Where to Eat

Erenler Sofrası ★ ◨ AEGEAN Taking off where the Yarbasan Stone Houses left off, the restaurant extends the unique wonderfulness of the place to the table. A typical menu might start with local almonds on ice, marinated eggplant "caviar," beets, stuffed peppers and spinach in olive oil and walnut. The cigara böreği would arrive next—hot off the presses (the best I'd ever eaten), followed by a specially created main course. Asli Mütlü, the owner and chef, presides over dinner, and when she's not, she's organizing one-day and week-long cooking courses that begin in the market and end together at the long communal table in Yarbasan's best kitchen. The restaurant is open daily for lunch and dinner except in summer, when it's too hot to think about, let along cook or eat lunch outside.

Muskebi, Ortakent, Bodrum. www.yarbasanholidayhomes.com. (C) **0532/248-2479**. 55TL per person prix fixe (drinks not included). AE, MC, V. Open daily for dinner (usually around sunset).

Vira's TURKISH & INTERNATIONAL Tables on the beach, sunset views over the Greek island of Kos, and a children's playground allowing parents to chew slower than usual is what you'll find here. The quality is pretty consistent, a great feat considering the range of menu options. There are grilled fish and meats, kebaps, steaks and lamb, salads and pizza, vegetarian food, and even fajitas. What's better is that the restaurant bucks the Bodrum's jet-set reputation with reasonable prices.

Yalı Mevkii 74, Ortakent Yahşı. www.ortakentviras.com.(?) **0252/348-3992.** Appetizers and main courses 5TL–29TL. MC, V. Daily noon–midnight, later in July and Aug.

Where to Stay

**Yarbasan Taş Evleri ★★ ** Yarbasan Stone Houses was a long labor of love that after 3 years of planning and 2 of construction, replicates the traditional housing of the area that followed the old Roman style of living. The houses are terraced high up on a hill overlooking Ortakent Bay, connected by decorative stone walkways, banked by high walls hiding courtyards, gardens, and pools. The project created a living village, and indeed, most of the 28 homes are privately owned, leaving a scant yet delightful 8 available to you and me. The homes are tastefully decorated with historically accurate copies of original elements such as handmade tiles, stained glass and whitewashed wooden floors. All have a private garden with swimming pool and fully equipped large American-style kitchens. From your perch atop the hill, it's a short walk down steps (or a very steep stone roadway) through a quiet, residential area, past chickens and the odd cow, to the beach.

Muskebi, Ortakent, Bodrum. www.yarbasanholidayhomes.com. (?) **0532/248-2479.** 8 self-contained houses. 120€ double room in private house. AE, MC, V. Free parking. **Amenities:** Erenler Sofrası Restaurant (see where to dine), bar, free Internet and Wi-Fi. *In room:* A/C, no phone.

What to See & Do

Antique Theatre of Halicarnassus ★ RUIN   Just a gated collection of crumbling stones a decade ago, today, this restored historic amphitheatre takes best advantage of its hilltop position overlooking Bodrum's twin bays with concerts lighting up the marble on summer's eves. The theatre was built by King Mausolus in the 4th century B.C. then enlarged in the 2nd century A.D. under the Romans. Some rock tombs are visible above the theatre, and a little bit of detective work will reveal inscriptions in the seats (believed to be names of those who subsidized the construction of the amphitheatre).

Gümbet Yolu (on the main road just opposite the Antique Theatre Hotel). (?) **0252/316-8061.** Admission 8TL. Tues–Sun 8:30am–5:30pm.

Bodrum Underwater Archaeology Museum ★★★ CASTLE & MUSEUM The museum is housed in **St. Peter's Castle ★★★**, the recognizable town icon. The castle juts out into the center of Bodrum's two harbors on what was once the island of Zefirya, named after Zephyros, the god of the west wind. At the time of Mausolus, there was probably a temple dedicated to Apollo on the site, as well as a palace fortress. The land structure passed to the kingdom of Pergamum and then later to Rome before winding up in the hands of the Turks. Western sources say that the Knights Hospitalers of St. John wrenched the settlement out of Selçuk Turk hands to provide a refuge to Christians and increase their influence over the west coast of Asia during the Crusades. Turkish references say that Sultan Celebi Mehmet granted permission to the Knights Hospitalers to build an outpost. The truth remains that from their base over on the island of Rhodes, the Hospitalers' mission evolved from primarily medical to mostly military. Construction on the castle began in 1402 and became a symbol of the unity of Christian Europe against the Ottoman "infidels." According to the pope, anyone contributing to the construction of the castle would go to heaven; the naming of the five **castle towers** and **seven gates** as well as German and French **coats of arms,** illustrates the involvement of the various European nations, as does the presence of plaques, inscriptions, armor, and other artifacts.

After the earthquake of 1522, the Hospitalers raided the Mausoleum for building stones for repairs (some of which can be seen on the outer wall of the chapel), which apparently was not as effective as the Knights had intended, as the castle was captured by Sultan Süleyman the Magnificent that same year. Under the Ottomans, the church was converted to a mosque, adding a minaret and a public bath.

Although the castle is under the auspices of the Ministry of Culture, the museum exhibitions are overseen by the Institute of Nautical Archaeology, an American non-profit organization with bases both at Texas A&M and in Bodrum. St. Peter's Castle took on double duty in 1963 as Bodrum's **Underwater Archaeology Museum ★★,** where various shipwrecks have been reassembled for display and occupy several buildings in the castle. In the chapel, the **East Roman Ship ★** dates from the 7th century A.D.; the interesting display allows you to walk onto a full-scale reconstruction of part of the ship and the excavation site.

The **Bronze Age Shipwrecks ★** exhibit displays findings recovered from sunken trading vessels discovered by local sponge divers. The artifacts, dating to the 13th and 16th centuries B.C., are indispensable for understanding the late Bronze Age. Also on display is the world's oldest known shipwreck, discovered in 1982 at **Ulu Burun,** which contained a cargo of treasures, including copper ingots, tin, exotic wooden logs, hippopotamus ivory, and precious gems. In addition to Canaanite gold jewelry, one astonishing find was a solid gold scarab attributed in hiero-glyphics to one-time owner Egyptian Queen Nefertiti (scarabs, which were representations of beetles, were often carried by sailors for good luck).

> ### 💬 The Maltese Falcon
>
> After Süleyman the Magnificent's con-quest of Rhodes, Charles V ended the Knights Hospitalers' 8-year exile in 1530, granting them Malta and Tripoli to block Ottoman presence in the west-ern Mediterranean. The annual fee was one falcon, the namesake of a famous American classic, The Maltese Falcon.

Usually, archaeologists can reas-semble an object from broken pieces of glass, because many of the object's pieces are often found in the same place. Not so in the Glass Wreck Hall, which contains piles of recovered glass that defy this theory. Archaeologists deduced that the ship in question was actually transporting broken glass as cargo for recycling. This superb collection of early Islamic glass has proved important in dating similar artifacts from other medieval Islamic sites.

The **Carian Princess exhibit,** also called the Queen Ada Hall, displays the tomb of what is commonly believed to be Queen Ada, a Hellenistic ruler of Halicarnassus, along with a gold crown and a few glass cases of other jewelry. The exhibit is hardly worth the added admission.

While ambling around the extensive castle grounds, home now to families of pea-cocks, doves, geese, and an ostrich, be sure to visit the **dungeon,** a kitschy re-cre-ation of an amusement-park horror exhibit. The castle's two main courtyards provide respite from the relentless sun. Or you can step into medieval England and sip a glass of white wine in one of the stone alcove booths in the castle's **English Tower ★.**

GÜMÜŞLÜK & ancient MYNDOS ★★★

Gümüşlük Bay (30km/19 miles west of Bodrum), site of the ancient city of **Myndos,** is an enchanting and (relatively) unspoiled outpost with a trifecta of charm: it's scenic, historic, and it retains the small, fishing village feel that attracted visitors here in the first place. The remains of ancient harbor walls are scattered at the base of the headlands just to the north and west of the village, remnants of the city to which Brutus and Cassius escaped in 44 B.C. after having murdered Julius Caesar. Guarding the entrance to the cove and harboring its own set of ruins is **Rabbit Island,** connected to the mainland by way of a sunken ancient city wall that allows visitors to wade over from the town center. There's also an inviting beach at the far end of the village.

Gümüşlük increases in magic in the evening, when area residents choose their favorite **waterside fish restaurant ★** (the best is **Gusta;** ✆ **0252/394-4228**) from the many lining the cove. Thanks to its archaeological value, Gümüşlük will (hopefully) hold fast as Bodrum's final frontier. To get there, *dolmuşes* run regular summer service to Bodrum, Turgut Reis, and Yalıkavak (with through service to Türkbükü). The number for the local *dolmuş* is ✆ **0252/394-3253.**

St. Peter's Castle, Bodrum center. ✆ **0252/316-2516.** Admission to castle and museum 20TL. Tues–Sun 9am–6:30pm (last entrance at 6pm; closes earlier in winter). Carian Princess Hall 5TL. Tues–Fri 10am–4pm. Ulu Burun Shipwreck Hall exhibitions 5TL. Tues–Fri 10am–6:30pm.

Mausoleum of Halicarnassus RUIN   Yet another plundered Wonder of the Ancient World, the mausoleum reveals only the foundations of the original masterpiece. King Mausolus of Caria ordered the construction of the 42m (138-ft.) ornate marble monument, and after his death, his wife (also his sister), Artemesia II, saw to the project's continuation. After her death the architects and artisans paid for the project out of their own pockets; it was finally completed in 350 B.C. According to historical accounts, the magnificent tomb featured pillars supporting a pyramid-shaped roof that appeared to "float" above the structure. Atop the summit was a sculpture of the king and queen riding in a chariot. In 1522, after an earthquake caused the monument to collapse, the Hospitalers used the stones from the Mausoleum as building material for the reconstruction of the castle. (Look for the greenish stones on the exterior of the chapel just beyond the entrance to the main portion of the museum.) Because of the damage caused by earthquakes, plundering, and irresponsible excavations, present-day archaeologists can only guess at the building's original appearance.

Turgut Reis Cad. 93, up the hill off Hamam Sok. ✆ **0252/316-1219.** Admission 8TL. Tues–Sun 8am–7pm (8am–5pm Nov–Mar).

Myndos Gate RUIN   After many years of neglect, Ericsson and Turkcell teamed up to restore the ancient walls of Halicarnassus (7km/4⅓ miles' worth), including the remnants of the east-facing monumental Myndos Gate. In 333, the Myndos Gate succumbed to the armies of Alexander the Great, who then sacked the city leaving nothing but the Mausoleum. The gate was a three-towered Trippilion, of which the center tower is gone. According to Arrianus, the Greek historian, the tower was protected by a 15m (49-ft.) wide and 8m-deep (26-ft.) moat.

Myndos Cad. (on the west side of Bodrum near the road leading to Gümbet). No phone. Free admission.

Watersports ADVENTURE TOUR   There's nothing like a walk through the Underwater Archaeology Museum to inspire the diver in you. The waters off Bodrum are full of caverns, caves, and reefs and include two new shipwrecks and one plane wreck. **Aegean Pro Dive Centre** has an office at Kavaklısarniç Sok. Asarlık Sitesi 30, over in Bitez (www.aegeanprodive.com; © **0252/316-0737;** open Apr–Oct), but you can just wander over to talk to them on the boat at the end of the day—the boat is moored in front of Halicarnas Disco every night after 5pm. It's also possible to join one of the scores of diving boats crowding the harbor just past the entrance to the castle, all of which hawk dive tours with certified divers.

If you've thrown caution to the wind ("All About the Blue Voyage," p. 54) and decided to take a last minute Blue Cruise, contact **Aegean Yacht** (© **0252/316-1517;** www.aegeanyacht.com) or **Gino Group** (© **0252/316-2166;** www.gino group.com). As the main yacht agents along the Aegean and Mediterranean, both have multiple locations along the coast, hiring out their own fleet of yachts or booking gulet cabin charters. Tour boats also line the harbor for sun-and-fun day trips to nearby beaches. Day tours cost about 24€, leaving around 11am, and returning by 6pm.

BODRUM'S BEST BEACHES

If Bodrum has earned fame because of its exceptional coastline, startling vistas and luxurious resorts, the truth is it's not because of Bodrum's beaches. Sure, there are lovely strips of sand and pebble in almost every village. But most are narrow and crowded and certainly not what you were looking for when you decided to come to Bodrum. Most of the important people are sequestered poolside at some exclusive resort or in their own private villa. So what's a tourist to do?

Let's get the details out of the way first. Public beaches (look for the signs for "Halk Plaj") are certainly idyllic spots, but know that they are essentially waterfront picnic areas for the local people. No lounge chairs, no watersports, no water, and plenty of kids hollering "*anne!*"—Turkish for "mommy!" Ugh.

The more appealing alternative is to make a lounge chair at a seaside restaurant or beach club yours for the day. In the case of restaurants, there is no charge for the sun bed or umbrella, but the social contract is that you will eventually eat or drink something from the establishment. The more (and more…) expensive option is a beach club, where typically, you pay a certain amount of money for the day, and the cost of the food and drinks you consume is deducted from that amount. Almost all hotels have this latter option, with the most popular being the **Ada Beach** (© 0252/377-5266), **Maki Hotel and Beach** (© 0252/377-6105), **Maça Kızı Beach** (© 0252/377-6272), and **Havana Beach Club** (© 0252/357-8250), all located in Göltürk-bükü. For the honor of lounging around at one of these, possibly surrounded by ambassadors of the international elite, you pony up 125TL.

Yalıkavak is also famous for its pristine beaches, backed by lawns and playgrounds. On the north side of the Yalıkavak peninsula is **Dodo Beach** (under new manage-ment, no phone). A day pass costs around 30TL (children get a discount), which goes towards the cost of food, drink, or watersports. Yalıkavak's other popular beach club is **Xuma Beach** (© **0252/385-4775;** www.xuma.com.tr), but like its counterparts over in Göltürkbükü, the entrance fee is high. There's also a town beach (called the **Belediye Halk Plaj**) at the end of the market street in the center of Yalıkavak, with—contradicting what I said two paragraphs ago—lounges, umbrellas, and all the local charm you could ask for.

A good geographical compromise is the popular **Bianca Beach Club** (© **0252/ 357-7474**), located on an outcropping just over the headlands on the extreme outskirts of Bodrum's twin bays.

In Ortakent, instead of trying to distinguish among the countless spots on the beach, head right over to **Fink Beach** (© **0531/025-0525**). It's free, the food is pretty good, and the prices for food and drinks are reasonable.

If after coming all the way to Bodrum center you insist upon skipping the hot *dolmuş* ride through endless traffic and opt instead for a spot opposite the seriously amazing castle, then head to **Del Mar** (Cumhuriyet Cad. 164–166. © **0252/316-7110**) one of the more reliable destinations on Bodrum's less than wonderful beach.

Other beach destinations are **Akyarlar,** the choice of advanced windsurfers due to the strong winds; and scenic **Bitez Bay,** full of windsurfing traffic and a long sandy beach (see "Watersports," above).

PAMUKKALE ★★, HIERAPOLIS ★★ & LAODICEA ★

75km (47 miles) northeast of Denizli airport; 18km (11 miles) northeast of Denizli; 652km (405 miles) south of Istanbul; 231km (144 miles) southeast of Izmir; 300km (186 miles) northeast of Bodrum

Until a few years ago, the cliffside travertines that had become the poster child of **Pamukkale** were more like a slushy roadside pile of yesterday's snow. The terraces are the result of thousands of years of deposits left by calcium-rich natural springs coursing down the mountain. (In nearby Karahayıt, springs rich in iron and sulfur leave reddish metallic deposits at the point of exit.) But years of irresponsible tourism had turned this wonder of nature into a dismal theme park attraction, until the Turkish authorities finally in desperation called in UNESCO for backup. In an ever-evolving geological environment, it's normal that these natural springs would find new outlets, and part of UNESCO's efforts have been to divert the springs to different sections on a rotating basis to restore much-needed calcium to the upper layers of the travertines. In the 12 years since their efforts began, much of the site has been restored to its original and spectacular blinding whiteness. The travertine terraces, in concert with the plateau housing the ruins of the ancient city of **Hierapolis,** now make up a national park as well as a World Heritage Site, and a visit to one would not be complete without a look at the other.

Problem is, both Pamukkale and especially Karahayıt have become swarmed by package tourists in the market for a cheap stay. Notwithstanding the whopping 20TL entrance fee to the archaeological site (add 3TL if you plan on checking out the museum), they've found it. So there's the dilemma: The only way to enjoy the site is to stay overnight, and an overnight stay necessarily will require you to tolerate mediocre accommodations and brave an unbearable multitude of tourists.

If you must go, do so in the spring or fall and avoid the high-season crush. Once there, save your stroll up the travertines for just before sunset, when you can savor the glow of the setting sun reflected off the faux-icy landscape. Take a dip in the Sacred Pool (assuming you can get near it) and dedicate a couple of hours to bobbing leisurely in your hotel thermal pool.

Essentials

GETTING THERE

All agencies offer day tours into the area from Izmir, Kuşadası, Bodrum, Marmaris, and Antalya (to name just a few). It's an exhausting day, requiring, at minimum, a 4-hour drive each way, plus a quickie visit. The up side? You can sleep on the bus.

BY BUS Buses run regularly into Denizli's *otogar*, about 18km/11 miles from Pamukkale, from all over Turkey. Count on about 3½ to 4 hours from anywhere on the coast with fares under 30TL. From the Denizli *otogar* (✆ **0258/261-1088**), hop on one of the frequently departing *dolmuşes* (every 20 min. 7:30am–10:30 or 11pm; 2.50TL) into the center of Pamukkale.

BY TRAIN Service into Denizli was suspended in 2008 for upgrades.

BY PLANE The nearest airport is the isolated Denizli Çardak Airport (✆ **0258/851-2084**), about 90 minutes by private car over a desert expanse from Pamukkale. Few people, if any, arrive via this route, simply because it's so far. If you insist, **Turkish Airlines** (✆ **444-0849** or 0258/846-1137) has daily evening flights from Istanbul in summer. In winter, there is one weekday early morning flight daily and one evening flight daily over the weekend. To get out of the airport, you can choose to take a taxi (✆ **0258/265-3377**) or arrange an airport transfer in advance with your hotel. If you decide to rent a car, **Avis** has an office in Denizli (✆ **0258/262-2462**).

VISITOR INFORMATION

The tourist information office is located at the top of the travertines (✆/fax **0258/272-2077**).

ORIENTATION

The terraces lie along the base of the Çaldağ Mountains some 200m (656 ft.) above the Curuksu Plain. The upper plateau includes the ancient ruins of **Hierapolis,** a prosperous city in its heyday owing to the natural healing water sources and the local textile industry (cotton grows like weeds in these parts), the same industries that propel the local economy today.

There are two entrances to the historic and natural site, one leading from the village of Pamukkale (the Southern Gate) and the other about 2.5km (1½ miles) past the village up a windy road to the Northern Gate. You can also walk up to the Southern Gate from the edge of the village of Pamukkale, straight uphill alongside the terrace pools of travertine. Admission to the ancient ruins of Hierapolis (top of the travertines, where you'll find the Pamukkale Thermal) is 20TL; admission to the enclosed archaeological museum located in the old Roman Baths is 3TL.

GETTING AROUND

Dolmuşes ply the road from Denizli through Pamukkale up to Karahayıt regularly. You can also hire a scooter or negotiate a driver in either the village of Pamukkale or Karahayıt (good for looking into the roadside textile factories); buses and *dolmuşes* serve the solitary road between the two villages and to Denizli.

What to See & Do

Ancient Hieropolis ★★ RUINS Although you've come all this way to see the white, hillside cascade that is Pamukkale, the reason these extraordinary travertines exist is thanks to the calcium-rich waters that have been bubbling up through the earth for millennia. That a great city-spa grew up around such bubbly was a no-brainer. The city of Hierapolis was founded in 190 B.C. by Eumenes II as part of the great Empire of Pergamum and was probably named after Hiera, the wife of the legendary founder of Pergamum. Considered a sacred site for the magical properties of its waters, Hierapolis reached its peak of development under the Romans at the end of the 2nd and 3rd centuries. During the Byzantine Era, a large church was erected to St. Philip, who was martyred here in A.D. 80.

A swim in the effervescent waters of the **Sacred Pool ★★★** (aka the **Pamukkale Thermal**; ✆ **0258/272-2024**; admission 25TL; 8am–7pm daily or until 5pm in the winter) should be at the top of the list on a visit to the site. Scattered about at the bottom of the crystal-clear pool like so much detritus is an amazing collection of striated columns and capitals, a striking reminder of the pool's pedigree. The Sacred Pool is the main source for the springs feeding the travertines. It lies in the center of a lush garden that, until April 2008, was enclosed within the last remaining commercial-cum-hospitality structure on the plateau (three hotels and 12 cafes were razed when UNESCO stepped in). Try to plan your visit during a fringe season (I showed up recently at 9am and couldn't even get near the place), or at least promptly when the doors open at 8am or after the tour buses have trickled out. Because the thermal water maintains a relatively constant temperature of about 95°F (35°C), a dip in the middle of November is not out of the question. In addition to a high level of natural radioactivity, the water contains calcium bicarbonate, calcium sulfate, magnesium, and carbon dioxide, and after a swim, you should simply dry off and let the minerals do their magic. Don't forget to bring a towel.

Behind the Pamukkale Thermal are the stunning remains of the best-preserved **ancient theater ★★★** in Turkey, and the third-most-impressive theater after Ephesus and Aspendos. The theater was constructed in the middle of the 2nd century by Hadrian and adapted in the 3rd century by Septimius Severus, indicating the importance of the city during both Hellenistic and Roman times. The upper section of 25 rows, added during the restoration, is constructed of stones quarried from the ancient theater to the north of the city rather than of marble, suggesting that the city hit upon financial hardships during this era. The theater comes to life in the late spring for folklore performances during the Festival of Pamukkale.

Just down the hill are the scattered leftovers of the **Temple of Apollo,** patron of the city. If you descend the incline just inside the fence and circle to the other side of the temple's stairs, you can see the **Plutonium,** a niche believed to be sacred for the noxious carbon monoxide vapors that are emitted from a nearby underground stream. Accessible via a (closed) passageway through the temple, the temple priests were the only ones with the power (or lung capacity) to emerge alive, a thesis supported by the deaths of not just a few imprudent tourists.

A pretty good hike up the hill will lead you to the **Martyrium of St. Philip ★**, the remains of an octagonal basilica believed to have been erected on the site where Philip was martyred. From the Martyrium you can cut down the hill toward the **Byzantine Gate** and the **Colonnaded Street.** Crossing the city on a north-south axis for .8km (½ mile), in ancient times the street ran from the Southern Gate and ended at the monumental **Arch of Domitian ★**, a triple arch flanked by two robust cylindrical towers constructed by Julius Frontinus, the proconsul of the Asian Provinces between A.D. 84 and 86. To the right of the gate are the pillars of the latrine, not as graphic as the toilets at Ephesus, but interesting from an architectural point of view nevertheless.

Beyond the Arch of Domitian is the **Necropolis ★★★**, stretching for over 1.5km (1 mile) and ending at the northern entrance to the site. Although people traveled from all over the empire to heal their ills, it's painfully obvious from this extensive burial ground that some diseases just can't be treated by a warm bath. There are various types of sarcophagi, layers of mausoleums designed as houses for the dead, and remarkable examples of the stone cylindrical *drum tumuli* employed during Hellenistic times. Don't pass this up just because it's too hot.

On the paved road heading back to the southern entrance, notice the crumbling but imposing Roman bath, built around the end of the 2nd century and later converted into a **Byzantine basilica ★**. From the looks of several of the archways, one more earthquake and this structure is road dust.

Next to the parking lot of the Pamukkale Thermal are a 6th-century **Christian basilica** and more **Roman baths** (these ones for the rich folk). Now the Hierapolis Archaeology Museum (✆ **0258/241-0866;** separate admission of 3TL), the baths house artifacts from the area, including a fairly impressive marble sarcophagus. The structure dates to the 1st century, constructed in the rebuilding of the city during the reign of Tiberius after a major earthquake severely damaged the city.

Pamukkale, Denizli. ✆ **0258/272-2034**. Admission 20TL. Daily 8am–7pm in summer; Tues–Sun 8am–5pm in winter.

Laodicea ad Lycum RUINS   Usually treated as a second thought to Pamukkale and Aphrodisias, the ancient city of Laodicea is best known as containing one of the Seven Churches of the Revelation. It seems as if Laodicea forever had roots in divinity, as it was known as The City of God (Diospolis, after Zeus) when founded by Antiochus II between 261 and 253 B.C. During the next few hundred very prosperous centuries, the city dubbed itself The Metropolis of Asia, becoming so celebrated as to receive Emperor Hadrian in 129 A.D. This wealth, due in great part to the highly desirable black wool that was a unique feature of the local sheep, supported the construction of great monuments and public works, a few of which survive to today. Of note are the **Gymnasium & Stadium** (built to be complementary and dedicated to Hadrian and his wife), a **small Roman and large Hellenistic theatre**, the latter of which is in an excellent state of preservation, and **Zeus' Temple**. A monumental fountain, or **Nymphaion,** located in the center of the site, was said to have been built during the reign of Caracalla. You can scramble around to enjoy the many sarcophagi on the hill to the north of the site and to the remains of an aqueduct on the south side.

Outside the village of Goncalı, 6km from Eskihisar; 10km from Pamukkale. No phone. Admission 10TL. Daily 8am–7pm in summer; Tues–Sun 8am–5pm in winter.

Where to Eat

A dinner buffet is included in the price of the hotel at all the thermal hotels, a necessary solution to the lack of alternatives in the vicinity. In many of the smaller family-run guesthouses, you'll probably be asked if you're staying for dinner (say yes!). In both villages of Pamukkale and Karahayıt, you can get a basic Turkish meal at one of the little home-style *lokantas*. The most popular is **Mehmet's Heaven** (Atatürk

Caddesi, near the main road; (✆ **0258/272-2643**), a reliable family-run place with views of the travertines.

Where to Stay

All of the better-class accommodations are in Karahayıt close to the Northern Gate into Hierapolis, but age and neglect in some cases may tip the balance in favor of one of the dozens of family-owned pensions in Pamukkale.

Richmond Hotel and Richmond Spa ★ Of the few acceptable thermal hotels in the area, the Richmond is the preferred choice. The hotel, consisting of two buildings sharing a large garden, has the best thermal pool from the sulfur-rich Karahayıt source, boasting the hottest spring water in the entire region. There's both indoor and outdoor swimming and thermal pools, with the temperature of the latter at a steamy 118°F (48°C). The health center smells pleasantly of witch hazel and comes equipped with a fitness room, Jacuzzi, and sauna. Updated rooms are bright but the standards are a bit on the small side. The Richmond has a ballroom, a greenhouse, and two conference rooms, which attract businesspeople and wedding celebrations, so ask for a room away from the festivities.

Karahayıt Köyü, 20027 Karahayıt.(✆ **0258/271-4294.** Fax 0258/271-4078. 315 units. 90€ double; 120€ suite. MC, V. Free parking. **Amenities:** Restaurant; 5 bars; concierge; health club and spa; free Internet; indoor and outdoor thermal pools; room service. *In room:* A/C, satellite TV, hair dryer, minibar.

A Side Trip to Aphrodisias ★★

Just when you think you've been saturated by amazing sights, you round another bend and behold the archaeological ruins of the ancient site of **Aphrodisias** (Geyre Beldesi, Karacasu; (✆ **0256/448-8086;** admission 8TL). The best-preserved example of a Hellenistic civilization in Turkey, Aphrodisias is still undergoing excavations, compliments of New York University. If you've got a car and time for a side trip, this is definitely worth your time.

It is commonly believed that the cult of the mother goddess was central to its origins. As early as the 1st century B.C., Aphrodisias was recognized as a sacred sanctuary and was awarded special privileges that began with Julius Caesar and lasted through the end of the Roman Empire. Popularity in the cult of Aphrodite hung on even as Christianity took hold, but eventually waned. After raids by Selçuk and Turcomen tribes in the 11th and 13th centuries, the city was ultimately abandoned.

The site covers an area of 520 hectares (1,285 acres). Some of the highlights of the site include the **Temple of Aphrodite ★**, built around the 1st century B.C. and converted into a basilica in the 5th century A.D. Excavations, however, have revealed earlier structures, dating to the 7th century B.C. The immense **Stadium of Aphrodisias ★**, an elongated oval of 262m×59m (860 ft.×194 ft.), rivals in grandeur the stadium of Pompeii. Before it was excavated, the truly **Olympic-size pool ★★** was originally thought to be an agora, as it was surrounded by impressive Ionic porticos and covered a vast area. The porticos were simply aimed at creating a fabulous reflection in the pool, which is laid entirely of marble. The pool is best appreciated from the top tiers of the **theater.** Nearby is the **Portico of Tiberius,** and to the west, the **Baths of Hadrian,** who had them built. The archaeological site is open daily 8am to 7pm (8am–5pm Nov–Mar).

GETTING THERE   You can get to Aphrodisias by car from Pamukkale, only 1½ hours away. Also, some day tours from Izmir and Kuşadası include a stopover in

Aphrodisias, on the way to Pamukkale; just comparison-shop along the main drags in Izmir, Kuşadası, Bodrum, or Antalya for a tour to fit your needs. If you're driving from Pamukkale, Karahayıt, or Hierapolis, take the road for Denizli, then follow the Denizli-Muğla road (D585) and then follow the signs for Tavas. At Tavas, take the turnoff for Karacasu and follow signs for the site.

THE TURQUOISE & MEDITERRANEAN COASTS

8

Brochures and photographs do scant justice to Turkey's exquisite southern coastline—a route familiar to saints, sultans, pirates, and one illustrious and infamous Egyptian queen.

The Turquoise Coast, which extends roughly from Antalya to Datça, is a slight misnomer because it ignores the emerald pools reflected at the base of thickets of pine trees and the rich sapphire of the open sea. To the west, the Toros (Taurus) Mountains tumble into the Mediterranean Sea, creating Eden-like pockets of rugged cliffs and shallow coves where land meets sea. Many of these mini-paradises are accessible only to the seafarer. Traveling east to Antalya, rocks give way to small patches of pebble beach, until they cede completely to miles and miles of sandy shoreline. And all along the length of the coastline, a short hop inland reveals long-since-landlocked ancient military and commercial port cities punctuating the fact that the Turkish Riviera is a rich depository of layers of ancient civilizations. Mentioned in Homer's *Iliad* are the **Lycians,** a heroic people that settled the coast from the Fethiye Bay to Antalya, from **Termessos,** where both **Croesus** and **Alexander the Great** came to consult the local priests prior to waging war; **Xanthos,** the capital of Lycia for much of its heyday; the sacred cult site of **Letoon; Patara, Pinara,** and **Tlos,** three of the six principal cities of ancient Lycia; **Antiphellos,** now the modern boating and resort center of Kaş; the mysterious **sunken city of Kekova** and the nearby ruins of **Apollonia** and **Aperla; Myra,** the birthplace of a famous bishop more commonly known as St. Nicholas, or Santa Claus; the spectacularly sited **Arycanda;** the fiery Chimaera of **Olympos;** and the scenic trifecta of harbors of **Phaselis.**

The **Carians,** whose unknown origins invoke contradictory accounts by Herodotus, Thucydides, and others, dominated the southwestern region of Anatolia from the Halicarnassus to the shores of Lake Köyçeğiz. The remains of Caria along the Mediterranean coast, some of which overlap with Lycia, bring us to the strategic harbor of ancient **Knidos** at the western extremity of the Datça Peninsula; and **Kaunos,** with its ancient theater and soaring Lycian rock tombs overlooking the scenic Dalyan River.

THE lycian way & ST. PAUL'S TRAIL

The Lycian Way (Likya Yolu), a 500km (311-mile) footpath between Fethiye and Antalya, is the brainchild of Kate Clow, a British expatriate and advocate of the joys of Lycian Turkey. Over a period of time, she has researched, marked, and signposted a network of rural roads and mountain paths, which cover a variety of terrain through ancient sites and modern-day villages. Most recently, she's established a series of trails that follow (or closely parallel, where conditions require) the route taken by St. Paul on his three missionary journeys to Asia Minor. The latter three trails begin in Perge, Aspendos, and Egirdir, and take in not only Christian history, but also ancient bridges, aqueducts, canyons, lakes, and peaks. Covering the entire distance of a trail on foot could take a month, but the trails are set up for day excursions for independent outdoor enthusiasts, made more colorful with the help of her handbooks, *The Lycian Way* (Upcountry Ltd., 2000) and *St Paul Trail* (Upcountry Ltd., 2004). Kate also conducts 1- or 2-week tours departing from either Fethiye or Antalya. For information on the trail, log on to www. lycianway.com.

The legacy of these peoples can be found in the majestic tombs hewn into lofty cliffs, sarcophagi crowned with Gothic helmets, and ancient cities sunken beneath transparent waters. On a boat excursion into a secluded cove, it's practically inevitable that you will stumble upon an ancient theater, a toppled Roman bath, or the remains of a pagan temple.

Thirty years ago, the destinations in this chapter slowly began to transform from idyllic and unspoiled fishing villages into ports of call for small boats and yachts. These days, you can easily find European amenities and boutique hotels but unlike the polished seaside resorts of the western Mediterranean or the Greek islands, however, the Turkish Mediterranean still comes with a bit of a pleasingly rugged and untamed edge. As tourism continues to gentrify the face of the region, you just may have to drive up into the mountains a bit farther to find it.

A truly satisfying visit to these parts requires a week at minimum, and that doesn't even take into account the irresistible draw of a Blue Voyage (p. 54). For the purposes of this book, I have sectioned out the primary destinations, from where it's reasonable to make a base for day excursions to the surrounding sites (allotted here to the section to which they are most closely located).

For those with the luxury of time, the coast should be tackled by car, minibus, or *dolmuş* (minivan-type public transportation) from end to end, allowing you to sample the diverse local flavors of each individual seaside village resort. This approach is obviously more labor-intensive than lying splayed on a chaise lounge at a beach resort, but if that's all you came all this way for, you may as well have saved the airfare. The more obvious (and convenient, given the availability of transport options) bases for daily activities and excursions are in Antalya center, Kaş, Fethiye, and around Dalyan, while locales a bit more off-the-beaten-track (including just on the outskirts of these major centers) will offer more pristine (and possibly local village) settings. These include the secluded coves around Marmaris (such as those in **Hisarönü, Selimiye, Bozburun, Turunç, Osmaniye,** and **Datça**), the historic and natural attractions in the Dalyan delta, the magnificence of the Gulf of Fethiye (particularly **Kayaköy,**

Faralya, Uzunyurt), and the quieter settings on the outskirts of Antalya (such as **Üçağız, Çiralı, Tekirova, Manavgat,** and **Side**). For those with limited time, I recommend picking a home base and concentrating on the ins and outs of any one of the primary hubs. Here is a hand-picked selection, from my view, of the best the Turkish Mediterranean has to offer.

The Turkish Mediterranean has long been a favorite getaway for British holiday makers, and for this reason, prices in this chapter will have originally been quoted in British pound sterling. Also, because this extended stretch of sunny coastline is no secret, it tends to get a bit overrun in July and August. Best instead to stick to the shoulder months of April, May, early June, late September, October, and if the weather cooperates, early November, when prices are lower as well.

MARMARIS & ENVIRONS ★★★

590km (367 miles) west of Antalya; 165km (103 miles) southeast of Bodrum; 900km (559 miles) south of Istanbul; 185km (115 miles) southwest of Pamukkale; 120km (75 miles) northwest of Dalaman; 98km (61 miles) west of Göcek

When people wax lyrical over Marmaris, they are rightfully describing a stunning landscape of pine-covered peaks, isolated bays and inlets, secluded beaches, and a steady expanse of Mediterranean paradise, some of it accessible only by sea. But this idyllic neo-paradise should not be confused with the city of Marmaris, a sprawling and overdeveloped resort town heavy on fast-food stands advertising baked potatoes to a high concentration of low-budget English tourists lazing about on a bleak public beach.

In past years, the city was a necessary evil for those embarking on a week-long blue cruise. But now, boats routinely depart from Göcek, Fethiye, or even Datça. For those traveling by land, my advice is to head directly out to the dramatic beauty that best characterizes the magical villages of the **Bozburun Peninsula ★★★**, endless rock-strewn mountains that embrace the aquamarine Mediterranean forming tiny, breath-taking coves and fishing villages that have since graduated into adolescence, but still maintain much of their pristine innocence. Highlights include **Selimiye ★★★**, a sleepy hamlet heaven-blessed with geographical poetry such as a tiny crumbled Byzantine chapel rising out of the center of the bay. The village of **Bozburun** sits at the farthest tip of the landmass and in spite of new marina facilities, retains the simplicity of a Turkish port of yore. The bays and beaches of **Hisarönü, Orhaniye** and **Turunç** are popular stopovers for gulets, offering fabulous opportunities for bare-bones swim-ming and snorkeling, while the resort town of İçmeler, nestled into a pristine bay sheltered by some offshore islands, offers a tranquil alternative to staying in Marmaris proper.

GETTING THERE

BY PLANE As of this writing, a record number of airlines were offering direct domestic service into Dalaman: From **Istanbul** you can fly via **Turkish Airlines** (ⓒ444-0849 or 0252/792-5395 at the airport; www.thy.com), **Atlasjet** (ⓒ 0850/222-0000; www.atlasjet.com), **Onur Air** (ⓒ 444-6687; www.onurair.com.tr), **Pegasus Airlines** (ⓒ 0850/250-2737; www.flypgs.com), and **SunExpress** (ⓒ 0232/444-0797; www.sunexpress.com.tr). You can also fly from **Izmir** (Onur, Pegasus, SunEx-press, Thomas Cook), from **Ankara** (Onur Air, Pegasus), from **Bodrum** (Onur, Pegasus, Sun Express, Thomson Airways, and Thomas Cook), from **Kayseri** (Onur, Pegasus), from **Nevşehir** (Onur, Pegasus) and from **Konya** (Pegasus).

Direct international service is provided by British Airways, Onur Air, and SunExpress from a number of cities in the U.K. and elsewhere in Europe. Other European-based discount and charter airlines flying direct into Dalaman include **EasyJet** (www.easyjet.com), **Monarch Airlines** (www.flymonarch.com), **Thomas Cook** (www.fly thomascook.com), **Thomson Airways** (www.thomson.co.uk) and **British Midland** (www.flybmi.com). Log on to the Dalaman Airport website (www.atmairport.com) and click on "flights" for comprehensive service by country.

Havaş (ℂ **444-0487 or 0252/792-5077**) shuttle bus service from the airport is scheduled to coincide with the arrival of *domestic flights*. There are separate shuttles for Marmaris and Fethiye (separate buses for opposite directions). The bus into the Marmaris *otogar* takes 90 minutes (85km/53 miles) via Dalaman center, Ortaca, Köyceğiz, and Gökova. The ride costs 25TL. From the Marmaris *otogar*, it's a 5-minute and 1.50TL *dolmuş* ride to the marina; taxis will also be waiting at the *otogar*. (See "By Bus," below.) There is also an **Avis** at the airport (ℂ **0252/792-5118**), a **Budget** (ℂ **0252/792-5150**) and **Europcar** (ℂ **0252/792-5414**) in the International Terminal of Dalaman Airport. A taxi from the airport costs around 150TL.

BY BUS The *otogar* (station; ℂ **0252/412-3037**) is located close to the junction for the main highway, about 1.6km (1 mile) outside of the town center. If you're coming from Istanbul (14 hr.) or Ankara (10 hr.), buses depart in the evening around 11pm or midnight and arrive the next day. Sample fare on Kamıl Koç is 75TL from Istanbul and 55TL from Ankara. Service from Izmir (4¼ hr.) is more frequent, with fares as low as 27TL (also with **Kamıl Koç**). From some towns like Selçuk or Kuşadası, you may be forced to change buses in Aydın, about halfway to Marmaris. **Marmaris Koop** bus lines (ℂ **0252/413-5543**) runs direct, air-conditioned mini-bus service to and from Ortaca/Dalyan (1½ hr.), Fethiye (3 hr.), Göcek (2½ hr.), and Antalya (7 hr.). **Pamukkale** bus company (ℂ **0252/412-5586**) runs year-round direct daily service through Denizli (change to minibus for the site of Pamukkale: 3½ hr.) on the way to Ankara and Bursa, in addition to Izmir, Bodrum, Fethiye, Antalya, and Kaş (summer only). Bus companies generally provide a free minibus transfer into town.

Dolmuşes (minivan-type public transportation) provide regular shuttle service from the *otogar* into town (1.50TL) and to the villages east and west of Marmaris.

BY FERRY Eight ferries a week (in summer) arrive from (and depart to) the Greek island of Rhodes on Yeşil Marmaris Lines (www.ycsilmarmarislincs.com). A one-way ticket is 43€. At the Datça end of Marmaris, a daily car ferry (in summer; service is reduced in winter) plying the route between Bodrum and Datça leaves both ports simultaneously at 9:30am (Tues, Thurs, Sat, Sun) and 4pm (Mon, Wed, Fri) for the 2-hour crossing. Boats to Datça arrive at Körmen, a lonesome port on the northwestern reaches of the Datça Peninsula. A one-way passenger ticket costs 25TL one-way; cars cost 80TL plus 15TL per person for each additional (non-driver) passenger. Tickets for kids 7 to 12 cost 50% less. Tickets can be purchased at the **Bodrum Ferryboat Association** ticket window at the departure pier in the center of town (ℂ **0252/316-0882** in Bodrum; ℂ **0252/712-2143** in Datça; www.bodrumferry boat.com). From Körmen, a shuttle bus will take you to the town of Datça, about 6.5km (4 miles) away. From Datça (assuming it's not your final destination), you can hop on a *dolmuş* for the mountainous and coastal drive into Marmaris (1 hr., 15 min.).

Bodrum Express Lines (ℂ **0252/316-1087;** www.bodrumexpresslines.com) also runs hydrofoils between Bodrum and Marmaris departing on Thursday and

THE TURQUOISE & MEDITERRANEAN COASTS | Marmaris & Environs

The Turquoise & Mediterranean Coasts

Sunday, March or April through October or November. Hydrofoils from Bodrum depart at 8am and 6pm, arriving in the charming town of Gelibolu (the transfer by bus into Marmaris is included in the price of the ticket). Total travel time is 1 hour, 50 minutes (the last 20 min. are on the bus); the trip costs 25€ one-way.

VISITOR INFORMATION

The **tourist information office** in **Marmaris** is at Iskele Meydanı 2, across from the Atatürk statue (© **0252/412-1035**).

ORIENTATION

As a chief point of departure for the Blue Voyage, the Marmaris harbor is where all of the action takes place. **Ulusal Egemenlik Caddesi** meets the Bay of Marmaris head-on at the main square proudly displaying the statue of Atatürk. The area east of **Ulusal Egemenlik Caddesi** is the older part of town, an appealing cluster of old waterfront houses crowned by the castle and well worth a look. **Kordon Caddesi** is the pedestrian continuation of Atatürk Caddesi to the east of **Iskele Meydanı,** and where the gulets (wooden boats) line the wharf each Saturday night prior to their morning departure. The wharf walk makes a semicircular loop around the base of the castle, arriving at several footbridges leading to the entrance of the marina. Within

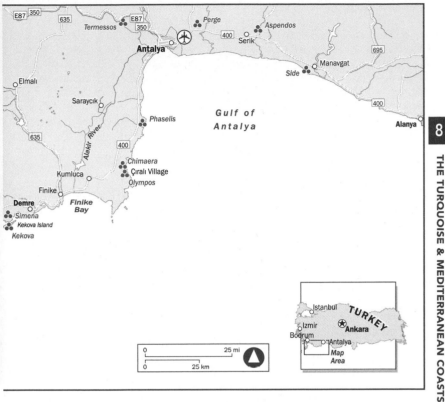

the gates of **Netsel Marina** are a few pubs and restaurants with terraces overlooking the harbor, along with an upscale outdoor shopping mall.

To the west along the shore is **Atatürk Caddesi,** which forks off and changes names several times before it exits Marmaris proper and turns into a hilly country road leading into **İçmeler,** a smaller seaside resort at the base of a beautifully crested, pine-covered mountain range. Beyond İçmeler is the Bozburun Peninsula, with the barest of loop roads leading along the coastal road to Turunç, Osmaniye, Bozburun, Selimiye, Orhaniye, and Hisarönü. The Marmaris–Datça road, meanwhile, is accessed from İçmeler or from above Marmaris center.

GETTING AROUND

Dolmuşes ply the one main road running the length of Datça Peninsula from Marmaris to Datça town (4TL; 90 min.) hourly in high season, reducing to five times a day off-season. Within Marmaris town, *dolmuşes* run frequently from the *otogar* along Marmaris's multinamed main road via the statue of Atatürk to points west. (You can pick one up right outside of the *Tansaş* department store on Uğusal Eğemenlik Cad., just up from the Atatürk Statue at the entrance to the Kordon street that lines the waterfront heading towards the marina.

Transport within the city limits costs 1.75TL; from Marmaris to Içmeler it's 2.50TL. Check the destination on the windshield if you're headed out of town; service runs as far as Datça.

Consider renting a car for forays into the surrounding villages and coves, or get a scooter for ease of transportation in and around the immediate reach of Marmaris town. Ask your hotel concierge if he can help you with a rental, or even ask a bellhop, who will most certainly have a friend in the vehicle-rental business. Cars rent for as little as 35€ per day. Agree on a model and price by phone, and a representative will deliver the vehicle to you at no extra charge.

Several taxi boats provide service between the holiday resorts of Içmeler, Turunç and downtown Marmaris. Service is more frequent when demand is up, so check with your hotel to see how often they are running, if at all, and the time of day they start/finish. The ride costs 8TL each way.

From Marmaris to Içmeler, a taxi should cost around 20TL to 25TL.

Day Trips By Boat

Lining the wharves of most medium- to large-size towns are private captains touting day trips through neighboring waters. A typical excursion tools along the coastline to the south to Turunç, Umlu, Cadirgan, and Çiftlik bays, and to **Cleopatra's (Sedir) Island** (© **0252/241-6948;** admission 10TL; daily 8am–6pm) made famous for the pearly white sands the exotic queen had shipped over from Egypt. Day-boat excursions also leave from **Bozburun** and **Datça,** past scenery more beautiful than the last, where you can swim, snorkel, or just plain snooze, all for about 25TL to 35TL, depending on how well you bargain, lunch included. A second itinerary out of Marmaris heads a little farther out into the Mediterranean to **Dalyan** (later in this chapter), where, at **Iztuzu Beach,** you'll switch from your gulet to a motorized fishing boat for the classic tour up the Dalyan River, including a stop at Kaunos and the mud baths. Prices for this trip are a little higher, at about 35€ per person.

Marmaris is also a convenient jumping-off point for fun and active pursuits. **Alternatif Turizm** (Camlik Sok. 10/1, Marmaris; © **0252/417-2720;** www.alternatif outdoor.com) was the first outfitter to turn the local rivers into water-bound roller coasters. They run day kayaking trips (on demand, Apr–Oct) for a minimum of 4 people to the most scenic spots in the area. Choose from a list of pioneering day paddling trips past the castles of Selimiye, along the idyllic Akyaka Delta, around the bays of Göcek or up the Dalyan River. You may also want to ride the **Dalaman rapids** before the new hydroelectric dam transforms the rumbling river basin into a sleepy reservoir. (Watersports enthusiasts should check with the outfitter to see if the rafting trips are running further upstream.) You'll pay 100TL per person for these tours, including all transfers and professional river guides. Check their website for their other adventure tours such as mountain biking expeditions, ski tours, and canyoning excursions.

Exploring Marmaris

These days, Marmaris is top-heavy with cheap tourism, and it shows. But a short drive out of town reveals the original appeal that drew visitors in the first place. Leaving their mark along the peninsula is a slew of ancient civilizations, some woven into the daily fabric of humble villages, tourist marinas, and magnificent beaches. North of Marmaris on the road to Muğla is **Gökova ★★**, another stop on the yachting trail, dotted with clusters of picturesque wooden houses built in the two-story Ottoman style.

Just outside of Marmaris is the lovely resort of **Içmeler,** magnificently situated in a sheltered cove at the base of rippling pine-covered mountains. The fit and ambitious may want to sample a portion of the **scenic trail ★★** that runs all the way from Içmeler to Değirmenyanı, about 19km (12 miles) west. The village of **Turunç ★**, farther south, sustains the charm of tradition and the comforts of modernity. A popular stop for yachts, it accommodates its visitors with handcrafted products such as honey, garden thyme, and sage tea. The long and winding road southwest to **Selimiye ★★★** is well worth the effort. Frozen in time, this settlement is an ideal spot for enjoying local fish, village wine, and magical sunsets following a day on Sılıman Beach. Or, you could drive all the way down to **Bozburun ★★** and have someone from the **Bozburun Yacht Club** or **Aphrodite** restaurant, pension and beach come pick you up by zodiac for a leisurely lunch and afternoon of swimming. Take your time traveling south from Hisarönü, though: You can walk on water at the beach of **Kızkumu ★** in **Orhaniye,** just beyond Hisarönü, where a lengthy sandbar extends 800m (2,625 ft.) into the bay. In the heat of summer, you may want to stop off at the **waterfall ★** near Turgut village, stroll through the Carpet Weavers Corporation, and relax over *gözleme* (a crepe filled with cheese, spinach, or both) and *ayran* (a Turkish yogurt drink). Any of the hotels and restaurants listed in this section combine sunbathing and sand with their business model. So feel free to grab your swimsuit and towel and just go where the *Meltem* sends you.

Where to Eat

Many of the hotels in this region offer the option of half board (breakfast and dinner) as part of your room rate. This means that meals are cooked daily, usually by a local. In Marmaris town, though, apart from the few exceptions, the best you can hope for is an overpriced plate of fresh caught defrosted fish, an underwhelming plate of chicken schnitzel or a baked potato at a stand along the public beach. The several restaurants and cafes in Netsel Marina (not the ones on the wharf with menus in three languages; keep going until you cross the footbridge) offer the most appealing options.

SELIMIYE

Hidayet'in Yeri ★★★ FISH   Lucky was I when unable to snag a table at the village's most popular restaurant, Sardunya (℘ **0242/446-4003;** www.sardunya. info). Instead, my companion and I strolled over to Hidayet to find outdoor tables atop a narrow wooden T-shaped jetty lit by carriage lights and candles. Our eager and polished young waiter brought us a delectable selection of mezes (stuffed zucchini flower, seaweed salad, octopus salad), then gave us a choice of the daily catch. You can go into the kitchen to have a look at the food—which you should do; because of the distance between the pier and the kitchen, service is slow, forgetful, and utterly delightful. Expect to make it an evening, one that will be well worth it.

On the waterfront next to the Palmetto Yacht Club. ℘ **0252/446-4118**. Reservations suggested. Dinner for two with appetizers, a fish main course, dessert, coffee, and rakı about 100TL for two. AE, MC, V. Dailly in summer, 7pm–midnight.

KUMLUBÜKÜ

Kumlubükü Yacht Club or Hollandali Ahmet'in Yeri. ★★★ TURKISH, MEDITERRANEAN, CHINESE   Chinese, you say? Really? It's true, and it happened when the owner, Ahmet (who worked for years in Holland, thus the name), gave his Chinese chef free rein to experiment with the menu. So besides the typical (yet spicy—the guy's from Sichuan, after all) Turkish mezes and fish entrees, you can also sink your teeth into a mean Peking duck. The yacht club sits in a dramatic spot on the Gulf of Marmaris, and its **beach** is a great place to relax for the day.

25km south of Marmaris via the Içmeler and Turunç road. www.kumlubukuyachtclub.com. 𝒞 0252/476-7242. Appetizers and entrees 12TL–38TL TK. AE, MC, V. Mon 11am–10pm; Tues 11am–4pm and 8–11pm; Wed 10am–2pm and 7–11pm; Thurs & Fri 11am–11pm; Sat 10am–midnight; Sun 11am–7pm..

Marmaris After Dark

The more popular and bustling the town, the more likely it is that the bars will be blaring music in hopes of attracting revelers. But in the quiet villages of the Bozburun Peninsula, watching the sun set and dining on a beachfront jetty by candlelight is (thankfully) about as crazy as it gets. Meanwhile, any of the major hotels provide entertainment options for their guests.

In Marmaris proper, nighttime activities are concentrated around the harbor, with restaurants lining the wharf from Iskele Meydanı all the way into Netsel Marina. Chaos reigns on **Hacı Mustafa Sokağı,** also known as *Barlar Sokağı,* or Bar Street, characterized by an endless lineup of bars indistinguishable from the Barlar Sokağı in countless seaside resort towns along the coast. Marmaris's version is particularly narrow, so in high season it can get claustrophobic.

Where to Stay

IÇMELER

Grand Yazici Mares ☺ With a plethora of activities for adults and children, the all-inclusive Mares is an optimum spot to relax and let other people watch your kids. And while your miniature charges are being plied with free ice cream, splashing in the kids' pool or zooming down the waterslide, you can go diving, kayaking, join in on a beach party, or make a beeline for the spa. Rooms are carpeted and spacious, but only a scant number of them offer sea and mountain views. There are 159 villas dotting the gardens, however, and these will provide you with optimal seclusion. One difficulty independent travelers may encounter is that because these five-star hotels work primarily with groups, they may be booked solid for your dates.

Pamucak Mevkii. www.grandyazicihotels.com 𝒞 **0252/455-2200.** Fax 0252/455-2201. 430 units. 240€ double July–Aug. Rates are all-inclusive. MC, V. Free parking. Closed Nov–Mar. **Amenities:** 3 restaurants; 4 bars; babysitting; beach; children's center and activities; concierge; exercise room; *hamam;* heated indoor and outdoor pools; room service; smoke-free rooms; spa; tennis; extensive watersports equipment/rental. *In room:* A/C, satellite TV, hair dryer, minibar, free Wi-Fi.

Martı Resort Deluxe Hotel ★ ☺ Of the two hotels listed here, the Martı has the more spectacular location, nestled in the cleavage of two pine-covered mountains on a 115m-long (377-ft.) private beach. Built on the site of a 7th-century monastery (some of the ruins are visible out front), the all-inclusive Martı fronts an expansive playground of sand, lawns, and a duplex pool. All rooms have an outdoor entrance and a balcony, although only the deluxe rooms and suites have sea views. Two of the 208 standard rooms are designed for families wanting to spread out a bit into two rooms, rather than one. Villas are composed of one or two bedrooms with mini-kitchens and a balcony or terrace, all with Jacuzzi (two are handicapped-accessible). The adjacent four-star Marti La Perla is slightly less deluxe and shares much of the amenities of its tonier sister, but the room rates are about 50€ cheaper.

Kumlu Örencik Mevkii, Içmeler. www.marti.com.tr. 𝒞 **0252/455-3440.** Fax 0252/455-3448. 272 units. From 220€ double half-board in summer. AE, MC, V. Free parking. **Amenities:** 4 restaurants;

4 bars; babysitting; private beach; children's center and activities; concierge; *hamam*; health club and spa; free Internet in lobby; 1 indoor and 2 outdoor pools and kids' pools; smoke-free rooms. *In room:* A/C, satellite TV, hair dryer, minibar.

HISARÖNÜ

D Hotel Maris   Having completely gutted the property and with an opening slated for spring 2012, the brand-new design-centric D Hotel remains under wraps. What I can guess is that it will most definitely be worth the wait, because it seems as if everything in the hotel was created to ensure breathtaking views, delicious design, and luxuriant behavior.

Datça Yolu Hisarönü Mevkii. www.dhotel.com.tr. ℂ **0252/441-2000.** Fax 0252/436-9228. 200 units. Contact the hotel for rates. MC, V. Free parking. Closed Nov–Mar. **Amenities:** 3 restaurants; 4 bars; babysitting; beach; concierge; heated indoor and outdoor pools; room service; smoke-free rooms; spa; tennis; extensive watersports equipment/rental. *In room:* A/C, satellite TV, hair dryer, minibar, free Wi-Fi.

Golden Key Hisarönü ★★ ☺   Hugging an elevated outcropping, the Golden Key is actually a group of duplex buildings and timber frame bungalows set in a garden paradise right on a sandy stretch of the Gulf of Hisarönü. The setup is great for families, as all of the room types are quite large and all have a balcony or private patio space. The king and deluxe suites are decorated more crisply while the junior suites have a more rustic feel to them. There's also a villa that sleeps up to eight people.

Hisarönü Köyü, 48706 Marmaris (27km/17 miles west of Marmaris center). ℂ **0252/466-6385.** Fax 0252/466-6042. 28 units. Contact the hotel for rates. MC, V. Free parking. Closed Nov–Mar. **Amenities:** Restaurant; bar; beach; children's playground; outdoor pool; room service; limited watersports equipment/rental. *In room:* A/C, satellite TV, hair dryer, minibar, free Wi-Fi.

SELIMIYE

Les Terrasses de Selemiye ★ 📷   Set on the hilltop above the village and bay, this breathtaking spot provides an isolated, intimate, and affordable haven where couples can relax, swim, hike, romance, and dine on French food while dabbling in local scenery and culture. It's really an upscale pension made up of two spare buildings arranged so that each of the 11 rooms enjoys a water view. Rooms are sparse, with little more than tile floors, a few locally made rugs and some organic drapes, and there's not much to do besides soak up the blissful surroundings. Note that it's a steep hike up the drive (car park is down below), one that continues on your meanderings down the hill into the village and to the waterfront.

48483 Selimiye (45km/28 miles southwest of Marmaris). www.selimiyepension.com. ℂ **0252/446-4367.** 11 units. 69€ double, June–Aug. MC, V. Free parking. Closed Nov–Apr. **Amenities:** Restaurant; bar; outdoor pool; massage. *In room:* A/C.

Palmetto ★   As the first hotel in town, the Palmetto clearly had dibs on the best real estate: It sits on a tiny rocky nub jutting out into the bay, taking full advantage of the crystalline waters that beckon vacationers like Sirens. Because of this position, the hotel has no beach, per se, just a small wooden pier and palm-lined garden with lounges from which to laze away entire afternoons. Rooms are small, spare, and somewhat outdated, but all have balconies, and you'll only be sleeping and showering in here anyway. Ask for one of the rooms with a balcony overlooking the pool patio to the cove to make the most of this spot, so that you can get a front-row seat to the waterfront's two harbors, the sheer rocky cliffs rising behind the minaret, and the ruins of an old church or monastery rising out of the center of the harbor. For more upscale conditions, consider a room over at the owner's other property, the Palmetto Yacht Club, located right on the beach near the entrance to the village.

48483 Selimiye. www.palmettoresorthotel.com. © **0252/446-4299.** Fax 0252/446-4301. 18 units (shower only). 90€ double June–Sept. Rates drop up to 50% off-season. MC, V. Free parking in nearby lot. **Amenities:** Restaurant; bar; *hamam*; outdoor pool; room service; limited watersports equipment/rental. *In room:* A/C, satellite TV, hair dryer, minibar, free Wi-Fi.

BOZBURUN

Bozburun Yacht Club ★★ ◲   The only thing yacht clubby about this place—the home of Turkey's late yachting hero Süleyman Dirvana for more than 30 years—is the string of Turkish celebrities that wander in for a drink. Otherwise, don't let the name fool you. Reeking of romance, privacy, and down-to-earth indulgence, home (which is essentially how guests are treated) is now run by Dirvana's widow, Zeynep and their son, Edhem. The property is terraced down a point jutting out into the entrance to the bay opposite *Kiseli Adası*, making for a virgin setting worthy of an extended honeymoon. Zeynep takes pride in the paradise she and her late husband chose, continuing to tend to the gardens herself. She also does much of the food prep, and indeed remains very hands-on. You'll even have to call ahead and discuss your menu with her if you want to arrive for a meal only (and you should, because the food is delectable), so she can then contact the local fishermen to see what's available.

Bozburun. (From the marina, call the property and they will send over a boat to pick you up.) www. Bozburunyatkulubu.com. © **0252/456-2192.** Fax 0252/270-9996. 11 units. 300TL double; 600TL villa. AE, MC, V. **Amenities:** Restaurant; bar; beach; fitness center; massage; room service. *In room:* A/C, satellite TV, hair dryer, minibar, free Wi-Fi.

DATÇA ★★★

72km (45 miles) west of Marmaris; 55 nautical miles south of Bodrum

About 72km (45 miles) west of Marmaris, across a wilderness of forested mountain ranges is the oft-overlooked seaside town of **Datça,** engulfed in a pastoral wonderland of almond, olive, and tangerine groves, of migrating eagles, falcons, and the endangered Mediterranean seal, and of a sea so pristine you can practically see Atlantis.

It's certainly not the case that no one visits these parts. It's just that to get here you have to bypass some of the most seductive destinations in Turkey's southeast coast, namely, Bodrum, Marmaris, and Fethiye. And that's no small feat. With these heavy hitters getting more and more crowded by the minute, the historic, peaceful, and most of all, unspoiled character of Datça makes including this spot on your coastal itinerary a no-brainer.

The relative inaccessibility of the peninsula's westernmost points is probably the main reason why this corner of the Turkish Mediterranean has managed to fend off the scourge of overdevelopment, leaving the landscape still pleasingly rugged and rustic.

The proximity to the Greek islands of Rhodes and Simi can only suggest the richness of the Dorian civilization that was once here, but a visit to the ancient city of **Knidos** ★★★ puts this historic promontory, and Ancient Greece, right here within reach. In Datça proper, you also get to see a more modern representation of a Greek village in **Eski,** or **Old Datça** ★★. Named Reşadiye at the beginning of the 20th century after the reigning Sultan at the time (Reşat or Mehmet V), this maze of narrow, cobbled lanes dripping in bougainvillea gives way to traditional stone houses that have been reclaimed from crumbling piles of rock to be transformed into enchanting settings for hotels, pensions, cafes, and galleries.

The western tip of the peninsula is where the Mediterranean Sea meets the Aegean, and you can swim in both on the same day, or even simultaneously. The stunning coves of **Palmut Bükü, Meşudiye, Domuzçukuru, Akvaryum,** and **Kargı** boast some of the cleanest water in the Mediterranean, and with a 33% presence of oxygen in the air, refreshingly low humidity and a perfect Mediterranean climate, the elements combine to support the legendary longevity of the residents of Datça as well as the proposition that once here, you will be back.

Essentials

GETTING THERE

BY PLANE There's really no easy way to do this. Dalaman Airport is 157 miles to the east. (See "Getting There" in the Marmaris section, above). You could also fly into Bodrum's Milaş Airport (see "Getting There" in the Bodrum chapter), but you will then need to hop on a ferry from Bodrum town (see below).

BY FERRY A car ferry plying the route between Bodrum and Datça leaves both ports simultaneously twice daily (9am and 5pm) for the 2-hour crossing *in summers only* (May–Oct). Boats to Datça arrive at Körmen, a lonesome port on the northwestern reaches of the Datça Peninsula. A one-way ticket costs 20€ one way or 30€ round-trip and can be purchased either at the offices of **Bodrum Ferryboat Association** (© **0252/316-0882** in Bodrum; © **0252/712-2143** in Datça). From Körmen, a shuttle bus will take you to the town of Datça, about 6.5km (4 miles) away.

BY CAR Car ferries from Bodrum arrive into the port of Körmen, about 8km/5 miles from Datça town on the northern coast of the peninsula. From there, (or from Marmaris) just follow the "Marmaris-Datça Yolu" signs towards Datça until you reach the town center. From Marmaris, the ride takes about 1 hour 15 minutes.

BY BUS Long-distance buses serve Datça from Istanbul, Ankara, and Izmir, as well as Marmaris. If you're flying into Dalaman, take the Havaş shuttle to the Marmaris *otogar*, then switch to a bus to Datça.

VISITOR INFORMATION

The tourist information office is located at the marina (© and fax 0252/712-3546 or **0252/712-3163**). You can also plan your visit around the **Almond Festival,** an extravaganza celebrating Datça's production of Turkey's main source of this much-beloved crop, during which the producer of the best almonds is selected. It's held during the last two weeks of August.

ORIENTATION

Datça sits on the Mediterranean Sea at about the halfway mark along the Datça Peninsula. The port of Körmen is about 8km/5 miles to the northwest, on the Gökova Bay section of the Aegean Sea. Heading west, a mountain ridge road passes through the towns of Mesudiye, Sındı, Yakaköy, Cumalı and Yaziköy before continuing on its windy path down the hill to the end of the road at Knidos. From the main road, secondary roads head down towards the Mediterranean coves of Hayıt Bükü, Ova Bükü (both best reached via Mesudiye), and Palamut Bükü (via Yakaköy), and the Aegean coves of Değirmen, Murdala, and Mersincik. Additional coves not mentioned here are reachable by boat only.

GETTING AROUND
What to See & Do

With 52 coves more breathtaking then the next at your fingertips, it's hard to decide where to lay your beach towel. One good option is to take one of the excursion boats that leave daily in season from Datça harbor, making stops in a number of scenic coves on the way to Knidos.

Knidos ★★★ RUINS/BEACH   Rising on a terraced promontory above dueling harbors, Knidos is infinitely more than this Dorian city's toppled ruins, as spectacular as they are. Knidos was once an important member of the Dorian gang of six (which included Halicarnassos, or today's Bodrum), whose power came from the exceptional shelter offered by the headland projecting from the mainland. When the temperamental *Karayel* blew to the east, ships would seek safety in the city's South Harbor; when the winds blew west, the North Harbor provided shelter. Knidos's exceptional beauty also derives from this gift of nature, providing the site with two spectacularly blue lagoons littered by marble architectural detritus and ancient terra cotta shards tumbled down from the ancient city above (bring your swimsuit!). Imagine that Sostratos, the architect who designed the lighthouse at Alexandria, and Eudoxos, one of history's most important astronomers and mathematicians, probably took a dip here. If you bring your bathing suit, you most definitely will too. There's a sole, pretty good **Knidos Restaurant** (✆ 0252/726-1262) on-site and some public restrooms nearby to accommodate the many day picnickers.

Knidos Orenyeri, Yaziköy. www.muze.gov.tr.(✆ **0252/726-1011.** Daily 8:30am–7pm Apr–Oct; 8am–5:30pm; Nov–Mar. Admission 8TL.

Eski, or Old Datça & Reşadiye ★ HISTORIC SITE   Reşadiye, as this entire landlocked village was named in the early 20th century, is straight out of the storybooks, a minuscule cluster of old stone houses, carved doorways, and narrow cobbled lanes dating back to when this was a Greek and Ottoman town. The village, once home to the famed Turkish poet, Can Yucel, has been transformed into a charming enclave of preserved houses now occupied by art galleries, boutiques, teahouses, and eateries. The village exhibits some traditional Turkish architecture and is worth a walk-through.

1.8km/1.1 miles from Datça center. www.olddatca.com. By car from Datça town, turn left at the Petrol Ofisi following signs to/past Hızırşahköyü. Minibuses leave from the Datça Port every hour or so 7:30am–11:45pm; the return minibuses operate 7:45am–midnight. Late-night service is less frequent.

Area Beaches

What make the beaches of Datça so spectacular (as if they need help) is the crystal-clear waters, designated in 2011 by Greenpeace as the cleanest on the Mediterranean. You certainly won't have time to visit all nine public beaches in the vicinity and 52 coves accessible by sea, nor can we list them all here. Below are the main ones to hit during a short visit, and all are relatively easily reached by *dolmuş* from the town center. For the beach at **Knidos**, see "What to See and Do," above.

Hayıt Bükü ★★ BEACH   If sleepy little Palamutbükü is even too much for you, try neighboring Hayıt Bükü, home to a sandy beach and a number of restaurants specializing in local cuisine. Try the rooftop bar and **Ortam Restaurant** (✆ 0252/728-0228; www.ortamdatca.com), located right on the beach and part of the **Ortam Pension.**

From the road to Knidos, take the turnoff at Mesudiye following signs for Hayıt Bükü. *Dolmuşes* depart regularly from the main square near the marina.

Ilıca Göl ★★ BEACH/NATURAL ATTRACTION   Adjacent to Datça's picturesque marina is a wonder of nature—a small lake presiding over the Mediterranean like an eternity pool. The lake is the end point for the warm natural mineral waters fed by the springs at the foot of the mountain.

Up the hill from the marina. (Park your car on the side of the road; there are steps down from the roadway).

Kargı Köyü ★★ BEACH Located just 3km from Datça center, Kargı Beach is a tranquil spot for bathers and boaters alike. There's a small restaurant on the beach, and if you get antsy, there's a small church ruin you can walk to.

Follow the road past Ilıca Lake about 3km (2 miles). Dolmuşes depart regularly from the main square near the marina.

Palamutbükü ★★★ BEACH My Turkish friends with second homes in Palamutbükü have begged me not to write about their quiet little cove, a spectacular stretch of beach lined with an acceptable level of pensions, eateries, and cafes. Most restaurants here offer lounges and even public showers in exchange for your eating and drinking from their menu. The best is the combo hotel, beach, and restaurant of **Mavi Beyaz** ★ ((C) **0252/725-5555**; www.otelmavibeyaz.com). The beach is fabulous, backed by enclosed teak shower stalls for in-between rinses or end-of-the-day cleanups. The beach menu is simple; stay for dinner and partake of some of the best *köfte* around. At the opposite (west) end of the beach you can get some excellent food over at Semra's place, better known as **Le Jardin de Semra** ★ ((C) **0252/725-5296**; www.lejardindesemra.com). Her restaurant, cafe, and bar occupy the sidewalk patio and interior of an old stone customs house, all shaded by an overgrown acorn tree that's been there since well before her great-grandfather's time. As it's opposite the tiny jetty, the nearest beach is on the neighboring property. Snack on grilled octopus, fish wrapped in chard, or a cheese risotto, while sipping an espresso or nibbling from the sugarless, amaretto-laden fig dessert.

From the road to Knidos, take the turnoff at Yakaköy for Palamutbükü. Dolmuşes depart regularly from the main square near the marina.

Where to Stay & Eat
IN AND AROUND DATÇA
Mehmet Ali Ağa Konağı ★★★ 🖻 Known locally as the Koca Ev or "the big house," this old Ottoman mansion was built by an aristocratic landowner around 1881. Sadly, he left no heirs, and the house subsequently found use as a school, a tobacco factory, and then just a sorry ruin. It's the oldest example of civil architecture in Turkey, sporting for the first time what would eventually become standard in all buildings—windows. After a long period of restoration aimed at preserving as much of the original as possible, the building today reveals what can best be described as a living museum. And you can live in it too, if you stay in one of the only two rooms available in the main house. Be forewarned, you'll be stepping back in time, and climbing over the steep lip of the *yukluk*, the enclosed cupboard in which the bathroom facilities were traditionally located. (It's essentially showering and doing your business in a closet). The alternative is to stay in the annex on the opposite side of the gardens—also constructed to stay as true as possible to the original style of building. Bare pine floors, handmade nails, and cross-stitched sheets are the order of the day in the annex, plus the benefit of a "normal" glass-enclosed shower. Even if you don't stay here, the family-style management (it's actually a family-run business) encourages walk-ins for a tour. The **Elaki Restaurant** ((C) **0252/712-9257**; main courses 35TL–50TL), serving delectable Ottoman and Mediterranean creations, is also excellent, and the atmosphere—an outdoor courtyard centered around a bubbling fountain—couldn't get any more romantic.

Reşadiye Mah. Kavak Meydanı, 48900 Datça/Muğla (from the main highway, follow signs for Reşadiye and then for the hotel). www.kocaev.com. (C) **0252/712-9257**. Fax 0252/712-9256. 16 units. 200€ double; 700€ Ottoman suite. AE, MC, V. Free parking on street. Closed Nov–Apr.

Amenities: Restaurant; bar; concierge; *hamam;* outdoor pool; room service; smoke-free rooms; free Wi-Fi. *In room:* A/C, TV, hair dryer, minibar.

Olive Garden Guest House ★ 🎁 Imagine living in your own Mediterranean villa secluded within 400 acres of orange groves and tended gardens. The Olive Farm guest house, associated with the Olive Farm (see "What to Buy") down the road, brings it all into reality. The guest quarters are solid cement and stone structures cozily furnished with whitewashed bedsteads—and in accommodations with sitting areas—comfy chairs and sofas. But this guest house is about what's outside the room: lush, fragrant paths leading to patches of sage, to an airy stained-glass–clad library kiosk, to a refreshing pool lounge or to a hidden hammock. Breakfast is abundant and organic, and the staff treats you like you were home.

Resadiye Mahallesi 30, 48900 Datca/Muğla. www.olivefarm.com.tr (click on "Guesthouse"). ℂ **0252/712-4151.** Fax 0252/712-0158. 10 units. 100€ double; 120€–160€ suite. MC, V. Free parking. Closed in winter. **Amenities:** Restaurant; bar; hamam; outdoor pool; room service; tennis court; free Wi-Fi in common areas. *In room:* A/C, satellite TV, hair dryer.

Villa Aşina ★★ Bulent Sancakdar is a local entrepreneur and real estate guy with a penchant for hospitality. You might say that the Aşina is his hobby, and his love of what he does complements any holiday. Guests are welcomed with an iced glass of geranium tea from the gardens, then led past a great room full of nostalgic antiques to behold a vision of azure beyond an enchanting garden pool terrace. Rooms are spare, with tiled floors, fresh travertine baths, and cool linens on comfortable low beds. Around the pool are some hammock swings, canopied day beds, and lounges, with the lucky one nabbing the spot on the bridge spanning the small pool. The rocky beach is a few steps down a path leading from the hotel, but frankly, I couldn't tear myself away from the hotel's view.

Dinner is another tale of wonder, a menu of creative combinations marrying local produce with a Tarsus flavor—Bulent's hometown. Choose your main course (meat, fish, chicken) then, out comes a parade of flavors that include tahini with parsley, stuffed gourgette, navy beans with cinnamon, wild asparagus, and salmon pastırma. His specialty is fish in dough, preceded by "fish in a jar" —basically a soupy chowder of shrimp, mussels, calamari, and potato simmered in a bell jar. Reservations (for non-guests as well) are essential, and the prix fixe surprise menu costs 60TL for fish (the meat is less).

Iskele Mah. 24, Sok. 10, Saklıköy/Datça/Muğla. (Follow Atatürk Cad through center towards Kargı Köyü; pass Ilica Gol and follow tiny signs left at fork). www.villaasina.com. ℂ **0252/712-0443.** Fax 0252/712-2444. 18 units. 210TL–230TL double. AE, MC, V. Free parking. **Amenities:** Restaurant; bar; beach; outdoor pool; room service. *In room:* A/C, satellite TV, hair dryer; free Wi-Fi.

Zekeriya Sofrasi ★ Ask anyone on the street where they eat and you'll get the same answer. Home cooking in this two-room joint spans the gamut: from chicken stews to delicious vegetables prepared in olive oil, and in fact, the green beans in tomato sauce and the spinach with yogurt were revelations. There's a "condiment station" stocked with sautéed garlic, sumac, oregano, and other spices, that I council you to use generously.

Atatürk Cad. 70, 2 minutes' walk from the marina. www.zekeriyasofrasi.com. ℂ **0252/712-4403.** Appetizers and main courses 6TL–9TL. No credit cards. Open daily 8am–10pm.

What To Buy

Hocaoğlu Balları The fragrance of oregano and sage waft out of this shop on the main road down the hill from the marina. Here you can take home some of the products that grow prolifically throughout the Datça region. You'll find bagfuls of the local culinary mascot, the almond, locally harvested honey from local pine flowers, and a wide selection of dried herbs. Sample prices are 12TL for a kilo of honey, and from 5TL up to 40TL for a 5-kilo container of olive oil.

Iskele Mah. Atatürk Cad, Cumhuriyet Meydani Karşısı. © **0252/712-2977.** MC, V. Daily 9am–9pm.

Olive Farm 🏦 Visitors to Turkey marvel over the superiority of the olive oil. But sheltered from the international craze for quality food products and produced by people yet to compete with an advanced marketing presence coming out of Italy, Turkish olive oil regrettably remains isolated within Turkey's borders. The Olive Farm (also known as Güller Dağı Çiftliği, or the Mountain of Roses Farm, combines top-quality olives, the strictest handling procedures, and savvy marketing techniques to promote an otherwise overlooked national treasure. A tantalizing variety of oils sell on the premises for 5TL for 25ml to 60TL for a 5 liter container. The shop also has flavored vinegars, as well as soaps, creams, and moisturizers (all made from olive oil, of course), and samples are available to try, taste, gift, and keep. And they ship, too. (Important: If you're traveling home to the U.S., your oil will be confiscated unless you pack it in your suitcase).

Reşadiye Mah. 30, Datça. (5 minutes east of Datça town). www.olivefarm.com.tr. © **0252/712-8377.** AE, MC, V. Open daily 9am–9pm.

THE DALYAN DELTA ★★

110km (68 miles) east of Marmaris; 76km (47 miles) northwest of Fethiye

One of the last remaining major breeding sites on the Mediterranean for the sea turtle (loggerhead, or *Caretta caretta*) and the green turtle (*Chelonia mydas*), Dalyan rose from obscurity in 1986 when in protest against the development of a luxury hotel, environmental protectionists rallied to have the nearby beach declared a protected area. The publicity only served as a beacon for the first major wave of tourists, but even if every other street has a pension with the word "turtle" in it, Dalyan still remains, for the most part, a quiet river town.

But even more monumental than the pristine pseudo-sandbar that makes up Iztuzu—better known as Turtle Beach—are the spectacular cliff-top temple-tombs soaring above the tall reeds on the opposite shores of the river. In addition to the ruins of ancient **Kaunos,** the area boasts some natural thermal sources in what has become a local ritual at the nearby mud baths. And as a delightful small village in its own right, Dalyan makes an off-the-beaten-track base for activities such as kayaking, rafting, diving, and snorkeling, exploring village life through treks, jeep tours, and bike rides, or sailing (for days) along some of Turkey's most stunning coastline. Getting around is half the fun: River *dolmuşes* shuttle people up and down the river through an incredible maze of canals enclosed within 3m (9¾-ft.) walls of reeds, past mysterious Lycian cliff tombs. (The mosquitoes come out of the woodwork at sunset in this river town, so bring plenty of repellent for alfresco activities).

What sets Dalyan apart from a coastline of Mediterranean powerhouses is its serene upriver location, its small-town character, the nearby natural treasure that is Iztuzu Beach, and easy access to a collection of some of the most stunning ancient monuments of Turkey's Western Mediterranean. For years, its budget style and convenient location gave visitors access to all of the same activities available to those based in Marmaris, as well as proximity to the Lycian coast west of Fethiye. What's different these days is the arrival of better hotels and restaurants that now allow adults to take advantage of an evening under the Dalyan moonlight.

Essentials

GETTING THERE

BY PLANE Dalaman Airport lies only 26km (16 miles) southeast of Dalyan. (Count on at least 25 min. by car, see "By Plane," under "Getting There," for Marmaris, earlier in this chapter.) It is tediously possible to get in on your own by taking the airport coach to the crossroad in Dalaman (5km/3 miles), changing for a *dolmuş* to Ortaca (9.5km/6 miles), and then changing again for Dalyan (12km/7½ miles), an ordeal that will cost you about an hour (including waiting time) and about 5TL. Better still is to have a trusted driver waiting for you: **Dalaman Transfer Services,** based in Dalaman (**⊘ 0252/692-5684**) provides private transfers for up to four people for 35€. Or you can try **Shuttle Dire**ct (**www.shuttledirect.com**), the Spain-based booking engine which in this case has offers of as little as £6.60 for shared shuttle service from Dalaman Airport.

BY BUS There is no direct bus service to Dalyan. Buses will get you as far as Ortaca, located about 8km (5 miles) west on the Marmaris-to-Fethiye highway, from there you can grab a *dolmuş* (15 min., 3.50TL). There is also limited *dolmuş* service from Fethiye (1 hr., 10 min.) and Marmaris (1 hr., 30 min.).

BY BOAT A wonderful first impression of Dalyan can be had arriving by sea. You can negotiate the cost of transportation from one of the neighboring ports—Marmaris is the closest major one—or book a cheap spot on a day excursion and take it one-way only.

BY CAR The best road into Dalyan is the one from Ortaca along the highway between Göcek and Marmaris.

VISITOR INFORMATION

The **tourist information office** (**⊘**/fax **0252/284-4235**) is located in the town center on Maraş Mahallesi.

ORIENTATION

The little waterfront village of Dalyan is situated halfway up the **Dalyan River** (**Dalyan Cayı**), a river canal connecting Köyceğiz Lake with the Mediterranean. No surprise then that the soul of Dalyan is on the river. Restaurants, waterside cafes, hotels, and pensions line the meandering waterfront, while the business heart of the city (banks and shopping center) is located a few short steps inland. *Dolmuşes* line up near the statue of Atatürk, opposite the riverfront park in the town center. A good number of pensions and hotels dot the landscape, increasingly sprawling out along the flatlands of the river basin, but still within walking distance.

At the mouth of the river is a natural sandbar protecting the canal from the open seas. Known as **Iztuzu Beach,** this beach peninsula divides the rough seas of the Mediterranean from the serene waters of the canal and is one of the last natural breeding grounds for the loggerhead turtle.

Majestic rock-cut temple tombs hover on the cliff face, and farther upriver on the shore opposite Dalyan are the ruins of **Kaunos,** once a thriving Lycian port town and now located slightly inland. Farther north are the open-air mud baths, and continuing upriver the thermal waters flanking the scenic **Köyceğiz Lake.** On the northern bank of the lake is the sleepy village of Köyceğiz, an even more budget alternative jumping-off point for visits to the area attractions.

GETTING AROUND

BY BOAT   Boats are the main mode of transportation in Dalyan. Dalyan's cooperative of river boatmen run river *dolmuşes* daily in summer only (no boats in winter) to
Iztuzu Beach for 7TL round-trip. Since the boatmen are working together, you can
hop on any one of their boats for the return trip. River *dolmuşes* run regularly from
Dalyan to Iztuzu between 9am and 1:30pm, return boats leave Iztuzu beginning at
1pm to the last run at 6pm. Don't wait until late morning to head out, though;
because these are *dolmuşes*, they only leave after they've managed to pick up a reasonable number of passengers, leaving latecomers waiting indefinitely. The cooperative
also runs excursions to the mud baths, the Sultaniye Thermal, and to Köyceğiz Lake
daily, and transport to and from Kaunos, departing at 9am and returning at 3pm daily.
For all of the cooperative's trips, kids to age 6 ride free, 7 to 12 pay half-price. Meanwhile, many hotels have their own boats providing service for free or for a fee.

The more economical option for excursions is to hook up with one of the innumerable agencies around town that offer group tours of the area; this way, the cost of the
private boat rental is shouldered by all participants, and the headache of filling the
boat is borne by the agency. **Kaunos Tours** (✆ **0252/284-2816;** www.kaunostours.
com), also the local representative for Europcar, does guided land and water-based
excursions and adventure trips.

There's an inexpensive and convenient rowboat shuttling those in the know across
the river from Dalyan, at the extreme southern end of the Kordon (not far from the
Dalyan Hotel) to Çandır; at only 4TL, this service is extremely useful for those hearty
and independent enough to brave the heat for the short walk up to the ruins of Kaunos, or the hour it will take to hike up to the mud baths.

BY DOLMUŞ   *Dolmuşes* leave regularly from the town center for Iztuzu Beach
(3.50TL, 20 min.), Ortaca (3.50TL, 15 min.), and Köyceğiz town (3.50TL, 30 min.).
Fares quoted are one-way.

BY BIKE   Getting around on your own juice will give you the freedom to enjoy
Iztuzu Beach, 18 hilly kilometers (11 miles) away, well after the excursion boats have
cleared the docks. Scooters and bicycles are available for rental at Kaunos Moto
(✆ **0252/284-2816**) at reasonable daily rates.

What to See & Do
EXPLORING KAUNOS

The ancient site of Kaunos was a valuable port trading in salt and slaves that, much
like other great cities of its time, eventually suffered the fate of rapidly receding
waters. Lying on the Carian-Lycian border, Kaunos first entered the history books
under Persian rule in the 6th century B.C., passing to Carian rule when the administration of the port was assigned to Carian governor Mausolus of Halicarnassus. From
around 200 B.C., rule of Kaunos was passed around like a hot potato, from Ptolemy
of Egypt to Rhodes, from Rhodes to Rome, from Rome back to Rhodes, and finally
back to Rome in the 3rd century A.D., when Diocletian added Kaunos to the province
of Lycia. The ruins of Kaunos, especially the rock tombs, reflect this cultural jumble,
including Hellenistic city walls, a Roman theater, and typical Lycian tombs.

Excursion boats moor on the river's edge amid the wooden pylons of a fish farm.
The mooring is about 90m (295 ft.) from the entrance to the site, accessible by a
footpath. A concession near the entrance to the ruins is your last chance to buy bottled water; be sure to avail yourself of this, because there's very little shade on the
walk up.

The path that forks to the right will lead you directly up to a **Roman theater** ★, carved into the slope of the acropolis hill. Two of the statue bases that survive are inscribed with the names of Mausolus and Hecatomnos. Farther up the hill are the fairly well-preserved remains of a **defensive sea wall** ★, hard to imagine now that the sea is nowhere in sight. Take care while hiking up to the top, as the terrain is pretty rugged, but evidently not too much of a challenge for the local mountain goats bleating in the distance. If you're not up for a treacherous climb, you can get comparable views of the marshlands (as well as what's left of the Great Harbor) from row 34 of the theater. Now a stagnant marshland, the Great Harbor was the cause of a seriously unhealthy malaria epidemic that stigmatized the locals for centuries.

Northwest of the theater are the **Roman baths** and a **Byzantine basilica** ★; slightly above these are the remains of a **Roman temple,** recently identified as a temple to the cult of Apollo.

Two types of **rock tombs** ★★★ are visible from the river as well as from the summit of the acropolis: those carved in the shapes of ornate Greek temples or simple chambers cut into the lower rock. The tombs were reused during Roman times, and all of the tombs at one time or another have fallen victim to scavengers. Admission to the site is 8TL (© **0252/614-1150**).

A TRIP TO IZTUZU BEACH

One of the last and most important breeding grounds for the near-extinct *Caretta caretta* (loggerhead) turtle on the Mediterranean, **Iztuzu Beach** ★★ came to public consciousness in 1984 when conservationists mobilized against a local developer's plan for construction of a luxury hotel. Some good works backfire, and even though the developer never got around to building his hotel, the publicity only served to put the spot on the map. The Association for the Protection of Wildlife has established strict guidelines to benefit the turtles, among them: no distracting lights at night, no nighttime visitors during the summer months, and a request that sunbathers remain behind the line of wooden stakes so as not to disturb potential nests. Most recently, in 2007, Pamukkale University, under the direction of Professor Yakup Kaska, established the **Sea Turtle Research, Rescue and Rehabilitation Center** (Deniz Kaplumbağaları Araştırma Kurtarma Ve Rehabilitasyon Merkezi) right at ground zero for the *Caretta caretta,* on Iztuzu Beach. Visitors can tour the facility and see firsthand how conservationists are working to save these turtles from the threats caused by ship strikes, loss of habitat, and entanglement in fishing line. There's also a small museum (showing those turtles that didn't make it) on-site.

There are two separate beach areas: the privately run stretch receiving the tide of excursion boats, and the less crowded far end of the beach nearest the road, operated by the Dalyan municipality. With the sea at your feet, the hills over your shoulder, and the calm waters and tall reeds of the river delta at your back, pristine Iztuzu is really one of the loveliest beaches in the region.

A TRIP TO THE MUD BATHS

Most commonly reached by boat, the **Mud Baths** ★, a rough-and-ready outdoor water pool and mud bath fed by the Sultaniye Spring, is a mandatory stop on most guided excursions. Located about 10 minutes upriver and on the bank opposite Dalyan, this idiosyncratic outdoor "spa" was last dubbed "Aqua Mia," after passing through a long line of new management. There's a sign posted with instructions on the suggested procedure, which includes slapping on fistfuls of sulfur-rich mud and embarrassed waiting periods while the mud on your skin dries. Before rinsing under one of the outdoor showers, take a look in the mirror provided, and be sure to bring a camera.

There's a dockside restaurant and snack bar, and the fee for individuals (admission is included in a group price) is 5TL. *A bit of advice:* Leave that white bathing suit at home. A few minutes away by boat farther up the river toward the village of Köyceğiz is Sultaniye and the **Sultaniye Kaplıcaları,** a thermal spring that dates to Hellenistic times with thermal water as hot as 105°F (41°C). There are both hot and cold thermal pools as well as a mud bath, and it's a bit less touristy than the one downriver. You can combine a visit here with an excursion to the Köyceğiz market on Mondays or hire a boat for the 20-minute ride upriver through the lake.

THE ACTIVE TRAVELER

Dalyan's accessibility, relaxed atmosphere, and proximity to the mountains, waterways, and sea make it a good base for activity-filled day excursions. **Kaunos Tours** (*©* **0252/284-2816;** www.kaunostours.com), bills itself as "the Outdoor Specialists," offering daily adventures such as a **jeep safari** (£27; £20 in winter), **canyoning** (£29), mountain biking (£29), and **trekking** to "Turtle Beach" or to the thermal baths (£27), to name the tip of their iceberg. As the first Turkish watersports outfitter to raft and kayak the area rapids, **Alternatif Turizm** (Camlik Sok. 10/1, Marmaris; *©* **0252/417-2720**) has branched out to include **mountain biking** expeditions, **ski tours,** and **canyoning excursions. A day on the rapids,** including all transfers and professional river guides, costs around 100TL. Their kayaking trips are the most pioneering, taking you around the most picturesque bays east of Marmaris, in addition to their kayaking trip up the Dalyan Delta to the hot springs.

Lazier days can be had with the spectacularly beautiful Göcek **12 Island Tour ★★** excursion (See "Glorious Göcek," below; Kaunos Tours will organize it for £40). The day trip, which is run by a number of local agencies including Kaunos Tours and the Dalyan boat cooperative, costs around 80TL per person. Not all tours are offered every day, so plan ahead if you have your heart set on something specific.

Where to Eat

Nothing beats a satisfying meal while seated beneath the spectacular and awe-inspiring cliff tombs across the river. For basic *lokanta* fare, head to the no-frills **Dalyan Dostlar Sofrası** (*©* **0252/284-2156**), right in the town center.

Ceyhan ★ TURKISH   No longer an unpretentious assemblage of shaded tables scattered on the gravel at the water's edge, Ceyhan has matured into an elegant, atmospheric waterfront dining experience. And while Dalyan's other riverside restaurants are homogenous in terms of atmosphere, flavor, and price, this little gem transforms simplicity into grand appeal. There are no surprises on the menu; expect delicious *yaprak dolması* (stuffed grape leaves), a decidedly unusual *fasulye* (green beans) and a flavorful *patlican salatası* (eggplant salad). You'll probably wind up dining here more than once, if not for the food, then for the magical setting under a floodlit rock-cut tomb.

Kordon Boyu (near the rowboat shuttle). *©* **0252/284-5387.** Appetizers and main courses 6TL–22TL. MC, V. Daily 8am–2am.

La Vie ★ TURKISH/INTERNATIONAL   You know when you go out for Chinese and the place is full of Chinese people? You feel good about your choice. La Vie, full-up with Turkish families and honeymooners, gives you that same sense. The restaurant makes the most of its riverfront spot, with tables lining the deck right above the waterline. The menu goes beyond the usual suspects to include appetizers like anchovy fritters and fish croquettes. If you're up for a steak, this is a good place to get it. There's also a kid's menu (chicken nuggets, etc.), and an impressive list of reasonably priced, excellent Turkish wines: you can get an Öküzgüzü for 35TL.

Maraş Mah. Sağlık Ocağı Sok. (From the waterfront promenade, turn left at the municipal tea garden). www.dalyanlavie.com. (C) **0252/284-4142.** Appetizers and main courses 6TL–28TL. MC, V. Daily noon–midnight. Closed in winter.

Dalyan After Dark

Nighttime entertainment can be found all along Maraş Mahallesi, from quiet pubs to smoothie bars, head-banging beer joints, and outdoor cafes. Currently the mellower fare seems to be located farthest away from the town center. If you want to blend, head over to the **Belediye Tea Garden,** which sits at the southern end of Dalyan on a lovely open lawn. At night, locals gather 'round a huge open-air TV to watch the latest football match.

Where to Stay

The village of Dalyan started out as an environmentally conscious little haven that, once discovered, spawned the conversion of many local family houses into guest pensions. Newer hotels and guesthouses are slowly sprouting up on the fringes of the town center, in contrast to the less-than-ambitious pensions that have, to date, rested on the laurels of the riverfront and rock tombs. For those hoping to stay close to the Dalyan Delta but not willing to forgo luxury, the new **Hilton Dalaman Resort and Spa** (Sarıgerme Tourism Center, PO11 Ortaca; (C) **0252/286-8686;** www.hilton. com; closed Nov–Mar) enjoys a sublime beachfront point ending at the mouth of the Dalaman River, just steps from the nearby Osmaniye village and a 10-minute drive to Dalyan.

Dalyan Resort ★ ☺ Both modest and sublime, the Dalyan Resort occupies a prime piece of riverside real estate almost directly under the watchful gaze of ancient rock-cut temples. It's this location that allowed it to coast for years as a tired but lovable pension. But now, the hotel is an expanded and completely renovated resort offering an environment, both in and out, that leaves few rooms unoccupied. The gardens are lush, with secluded little corners that reveal teak cushioned lounges and riverfront deck chairs within view of the rock tombs. Suites and family rooms are actually two adjoining rooms, making up for the fact that standards are rather miniscule. But all are new, clean, and get you access to the best spot in town.

Maraş Mah. Kaunos Sok. 48840 Dalyan. www.dalyanresort.com. (C) **0252/284-5499.** Fax 0252/284-5498. 58 units. 95€ double; 125€ suite June–Sept. Rates lower off-season. AE, MC, V. Free parking. **Amenities:** Restaurant; bar; concierge; exercise room; *hamam;* massage; outdoor pool; room service; sauna; smoke-free rooms; tennis. *In room:* A/C, TV, hair dryer, minibar, free Wi-Fi.

Sultan Palas Hotel ★ When two former employees unexpectedly ran off together leaving this hotel without a chef or receptionist, the manager called her mother, Özdan, to come to the rescue in the kitchen. As fate would have it, Brit Frank Mann was staying at the hotel, having joined his family on vacation at the last minute. Three years later, Frank and Özdan were married and the proud owners of a secluded oasis of gardens and tropical plants resting at the base of a series of rocky outcroppings. The main building resembles a medieval stone tower, from which two two-story buildings radiate. The rooms are showing their age, but most of the needed improvements are cosmetic. The mud baths are an easy 5-minute walk away and a

glorious GÖCEK

The most beautiful—and exclusive—untouched bays and coves along the Turkish Mediterranean converge in the village of **Göcek.** Göcek is recognized by the yachting community as one of the pearls of the Mediterranean, with its postcard-worthy marina, and a village with at least a few years to go before complete gentrification.

The arrival of the **Swissôtel ★** at Göcek Marina made it all happen (www.swissotel.com; toll free in the U.S./Canada ℂ **800/637-9477**; in the U.K. ℂ 0800/6379-4471; in Australia ℂ 800/121043 or 0252/645-2760 local; fax 0252/645-2767). Unlike the typical five-star Swissôtels, this one is a chic and luxurious mini-village, tastefully laid out on a flat plain at the foot of the mountain range. The manicured lawns give the aura of a country club—the only thing that's missing is a golf course. Doubles cost from 225€ in July and August. Rates are lower in shoulder season. The hotel is closed November through May. For a more home-style experience, consider the **Efe Hotel** (ℂ **0252/645-2626;** www.efehotelgocek.com), an inviting and warm hotel-cum-guesthouse set amidst a verdant garden of palm trees and Mediterranean flowers. Rooms cost from 97€ for a double. When you're not promenading down the delightful main street, you can swim and relax in the garden pool or lounge on their private beach deck.

hotel boat shuttles guests to Dalyan center six times a day. Oh, and Özdan's cooking is well enough reason to choose to stay here and never leave.

Horozlar Mevkii, 48840 Dalyan. www.sultanpalasdalyan.co.uk. ℂ **0252/284-2103.** Fax 0252/284-2106. 26 units. £60 double half-board; £33 per person based on double. Add £5 for dinner. (Nonguests pay £12). MC, V. By car via the approach from Marmaris only, from Dalyan center, leave your car in the Denizatı's restaurant lot near the hotel's boat landing for transport to the opposite side of the river. **Amenities:** Restaurant; bar; croquet lawn; children's pool and outdoor pool; room service. *In room:* A/C.

FETHIYE & ÖLÜDENIZ ★★

295km (183 miles) southwest of Antalya; 170km (106 miles) southeast of Marmaris; 290km (180 miles) southeast of Pamukkale; 15km (9½ miles) north of Ölüdeniz

Fethiye is much more than just the Blue Lagoon, that spectacular turquoise poster child of Turkey's Mediterranean coast. Fethiye is rocky cliffs, pine clad mountain ranges, offshore islets that speak of ancient civilizations, and dusty villages where tourism is still a twinkle in the locals' eyes. It's the quiet serenity of a sunset over the ghost village of Kayaköy, set in a valley amidst the piney mountains. And it's the blissful solitude of a swim in one of the innumerable unspoiled crystalline coves, many inaccessible by land. The combination is winning: The ample natural environment inspires physical activity as much as the sun-kissed coastline encourages sloth. Scuba diving, paragliding off a mountain peak, hiking ancient mountain paths, or wading slowly through an ice-cold gorge are just a few of the activities possible in and around Fethiye. From the curvaceous ranges enfolding Göcek to the picturesque coves of Ölüdeniz, the Fethiye Gulf encompasses some of the most sublime scenery in all of the Turkish Riviera. Fethiye is a truly unbeatable holiday destination, offering leisure and sporting activities, ancient history, local culture, and pristine waterways. And of course, there's the Blue Lagoon of Ölüdeniz, one of the most astonishing natural beauties in all of Turkey.

Fethiye is also the perfect jumping off point for excursions to the plentiful Lycian ruins that dot the coastline, as far as Xanthos and Letoon to the east and Kaunos to the west. You can also take advantage of everything the Gulf of Fethiye has to offer from a sublime little perch in Göcek (see above).

Essentials

GETTING THERE

BY PLANE   Most travelers headed to Fethiye fly in to Dalaman Airport, only 40km/25 miles away. For information on flying in to Fethiye, see "Getting There: By Plane," in the Marmaris section, earlier in this chapter. It's also possible to fly into Antalya, but because the drive to Fethiye takes about 3 to 4 hours, choosing Antalya will most likely be a result of fully booked flights into Dalaman, or a desire to explore the coast from east to west. For information on flying into Antalya, see "Getting There," in the Antalya section, later in this chapter.

Havaş (☎ **444-0487 or 0252/792-5077**) shuttle buses from Dalaman Airport into Fethiye are scheduled to coincide with the arrival of *domestic flights*. (A separate shuttle leaves for Marmaris which is in the opposite direction.) The bus into the new bus terminal at the junction of İnönü Bulvarı and Ölüdeniz Caddesi takes about an hour and costs 20TL.

There are also car-rental counters at both airports, sensible if you've arrived here exclusively for an independent land tour. A taxi from the airport will cost around 120TL.

BY BUS   Ulusoy (☎ **444-1888**) buses run once-daily service between Istanbul and Fethiye (11 hr., 42TL). **Pamukkale** (☎ **444-3535**) connects Fethiye daily with Izmir (via Ortaca, 6 hr., 25TL) and Antalya (3½ hr., 22TL). If you're coming to town from one of the other resort towns along the coast, or you simply want to take the (not necessarily scenic) coastal route, you'll need to hop on a comfortable minibus run by **Batı Antalya Tur;** (☎ **0252/612-0499** in Fethiye; ☎ 0242/331-4081 in Antalya; www.batiantalyatur.com.tr). From Antalya, expect to sit for at least 5 hours and pay 28TL. The *otogar* is about a mile east of the town center, at the turnoff for Ölüdeniz at İnönü Bulvarı and Adnan Menderez Bulvarı/Ölüdeniz Caddesi. From the *otogar, dolmuş* service is sketchy: none run to the hotel listings in Fethiye town and it will take some self-propelling from the drop-off point to get to several of the hotels listed here. If you're headed to Ölüdeniz, Uzunyurt, or Kayaköy, theoretically you could manage with the *dolmuş,* but if your destination is central Fethiye, the Hillside Club or the Montana Pine Hotel, I'm afraid you'll have to take a cab.

TOURIST INFORMATION

In Fethiye town, the **tourist information office** is located at Iskele Karşısı 1 (☎ **0252/614-1527**; www.fethiye.gov.tr), across from the harbor nearest the yacht marina. In Ölüdeniz, there's a "Tourism Development Cooperative" at the end of the road before the beach (☎ **0252/617-0438**; www.oludeniztourism.org).

ORIENTATION

The Gulf of Fethiye spans Turkey's Mediterranean from Göcek to the west, through the crowded mass tourism resort of Çalış, to the ancient city of Telmessos, poking its nose above Fethiye's town center, to the famous Blue Lagoon of Ölüdeniz. Unlike other regions of Turkey, where the primary town is also the region's capital, Fethiye

Fethiye & Ölüdeniz

THE TURQUOISE & MEDITERRANEAN COASTS

Fethiye

ATTRACTIONS ●
Antique Theater **4**
Crusader castle tower **7**
Fethiye Archaeological
    Museum **8**
Tomb of King Amyntas **9**

HOTELS ■
Ece Saray **3**
Hillside Beach Club **1**
Villa Daffodil **2**

RESTAURANTS ◆
Meğri **5**
Mozaic Bahçe **6**

ⓘ Information
☒ Post Office

Gulf of Fethiye

Fethiye
Harbor

Marina

ATA PARK

TURKEY
Istanbul
Ankara ✪
Fethiye

Mustafa Kemal Bulvarı
Sadi Pekin Cad.
Muzaffer Dontlu Cad.
Sadi Berkman Cad.
Pürşahbey Cad.
Hastahane Cad.
Hastahane Cad.
Dispanser Cad.
Atatürk Cad.
Atatürk Cad.
Cumhuriyet Cad.
Hükümet Cad.
Belediye Cad.
Okul Cad.
New Bazaar
Old Bazaar
Karagözler Cad.
Feyzi Çakmak Cad.
Çarşı Cad.
Kaya Cad.
Süleyman Demirel Bulvarı
To Ölüdeniz &
New Otogar
Old Otogar
(Bus Station)
To Kayaköy

1/4 m
0.25 km

8

THE TURQUOISE & MEDITERRANEAN COASTS | Fethiye & Ölüdeniz

305

falls under the jurisdiction of the province of Muğla (pronounced MOO-lah). Still, notwithstanding the fact that Marmaris and Bodrum are also located within the boundaries of Muğla, Fethiye is nevertheless one of Turkey's major commercial and tourist heavy-hitters.

Downtown Fethiye, along with its busy harbor and marina, sits at the southern edge of the Gulf of Fethiye, accessible via a turnoff off of the D400, which runs the length of the coast from Datça to Adana. Süleyman Demirel Bulvarı, the main road into downtown Fethiye from the highway, becomes Inönü Bulvarı at Adnan Menderes Bulvarı. This intersection is also where the new, full-service bus station is located. Inönü Bulvarı forks off further into Fethiye central; the central "tyne" is Atatürk Caddesi (until it arrives at the marina and becomes Fevzi Çakmak Cad., which continues along the peninsular coastline to the west).

Also opposite the harbor is **Çarşı Sokağı** (the lower "tyne" where Inönü Bulv. ends), which cuts through the Old Town Bazaar perpendicular to Atatürk Caddesi, forming a triangle of shopping, restaurants, and cafes known as Paspatur. The new bazaar is located on Çarşı Sokağı, which then curves around to continue east until it meets up once again with **Atatürk Caddesi** and turns into **Inönü Bulvarı. Amyntas Tomb** is southeast of the town center amid the barren brush, and farther east are the **Lycian Rock Tombs.** A few **lone sarcophagi** are scattered about town, one in the garden of the municipality building on Atatürk Caddesi, the other on Kaya Caddesi, between the old bus depot and the castle. A pedestrian promenade runs along the marina between the theater and north to Çalış Beach, and is lined with boats of all sizes touting day trips and private charters.

Ölüdeniz, which means "Dead Sea" (but is better known as the "Blue Lagoon"), describes the beach and lagoon bearing its name and the long stretch of Belceğiz Beach. This deservedly ultra-popular seaside resort sits in a small valley at the bottom of a steep hill. Beach bums, daredevil paragliders, and at least one too many partiers base themselves in Ölüdeniz, but with a car or scooter, you can easily make this a day trip. To the left is the public beach, enclosed by the steep slopes of **Babadağ.** The beach is tastefully lined with travel agents offering adventure tours, beach restaurants, Internet cafes, and the Club Belcekız Beach Hotel at the far end. To the right is the overcrowded natural preserve with its lagoon of Mediterranean dreams, pristine and a deep shade of aqua.

GETTING AROUND

BY CAR   To really enjoy Fethiye and the surrounding areas, it's important to have your own wheels and surprisingly enough, it's better to book your vehicle from one of the major international players for the most competitive rates. And if you're going to go with a major brand, you may as well get the car at the airport. Still, local car rental agencies will deliver a car to you at the airport on request, generally at no extra charge. The only major in town is **Avis** (in the marina; ℭ **0252/612-3719**). Lesser-known firms around the yacht marina and in near the Old Town Bazaar are also a decent bet; try **Fethiye Rent-a-Car,** an arm of Oscar Travel (Atatürk Cad. 106; ℭ **0252/612-2281;** www.fethiyerentacar.com), which currently charges from £25 per day for a compact. Because the British pound sterling is the primary quoted currency of the area, the price of renting a car locally might seem a bit high.

BY SCOOTER   This is my mode of choice, but be very careful, as the roads are gravelly and the drivers are no better at the resorts than they are on the highways. Take particular care in rounding steep hilly curves, as oncoming vehicles tend to make wide turns into your lane. Otherwise, riding a scooter through the countryside is a rare joy, a good way to maintain your suntan, and the best way to solve the parking question. Most car-rental agencies have scooters available, and there are several outfitters in downtown Fethiye that will rent you a Honda scooter for about 20€.

BY MINIBUS/DOLMUŞ *Dolmuşes* congregate at the intersection of Atatürk Caddesi and Sedir Sokak (across from the hospital) in downtown Fethiye and provide frequent (about every 15 min.) transport to most of the sites and destinations listed in this section. The most useful routes leave for Ölüdeniz, Kayaköy, Tlos, and Saklıkent.

The Ölüdeniz Minibus Coop runs an hourly shuttle between Fethiye and Kayaköy (4TL); less frequent are the minibuses that run about six times a day between Fethiye and Faralya/Kabak and three times daily between Fethiye and Gemiler Beach.

What to See & Do
ANCIENT HISTORY
Not much remains of ancient **Telmessos,** atop which modern-day Fethiye is built. In spite of centuries of destructive earthquakes, the cliffside Lycian tombs and majestic sarcophagi never fail to draw a gasp.

The city was independent until Alexander the Great's arrival in 334 B.C. Three hundred years later the city came under Roman rule as part of the Lycian union.

The **antique theater** in the center of town dates to Roman times, although its open disposition on the hill indicates Greek influences. The amphitheater was picked apart for the reconstruction of the city after the devastating earthquake of 1957, and in 1994 restorations and further excavations to the site were begun. To the east of the municipal building is a two-story **sarcophagus ★** topped with a Gothic-style lid and decorated with war scenes. Remains of this type of tomb are scattered about the city and hidden in private gardens.

On the hillside east of town stands the ruined **Crusader castle tower,** constructed by the Knights of St. John out of the Hellenistic and Roman stonework of an earlier acropolis.

Rock-cut tombs spot the cliff side, the most notable of which is the **Tomb of King Amyntas ★★★** in the form of a Greek temple dating to 350 B.C. The steps of the facade get a bit crowded around sunset, the favored time for a visit because of the tomb's position on the hill. Price of admission is 8TL or free from afar.

The nearby **Fethiye Archaeological Museum,** Kesikkapi Mah. Okul Sokak in the Fethiye Müze Müdürlüğü Building (**☎ 0252/614-1150**), is small and regrettably unimportant; exhibits consist of stones and columns from the acropolis that should have been left in place. Interesting, however, is the **stele ★** uncovered at Letoon, with inscriptions in Lycian, Aramaic, and Greek. It proved indispensable in cracking the code of the ancient Lycian language. The museum is open Tuesday through Sunday from 8:30am to 5pm, admission is 3TL.

Karmylassos/Kayaköy ★★★ RUINS This haunting and magical place is the result of the population exchange between Turkey and Greece in 1924—in which the Turkish and Greek minorities in each country were repatriated to their "home countries," despite the incalculable suffering such a drastic uprooting caused. The Turkish village of Kayaköy sprouted up in the valley at the base of the abandoned hillside.

Originally the Lycian city of Karmylassos, the village was reestablished by Greek settlers as Levissi in either the 11th or 14th century. The houses that blanket the hills date to the 19th century. Today Karmylassos is a ghost town, and the remains of the

Drinks Are on the House

Just some years ago, Kayaköy was little more than a forgotten pile of stones. Now, along with pensions, villas, and cottages, the village once known as Levissi has a wine houses. The Levissi Garden (© 0252/618-0108; www.levissigarden.com) keeps a wine cellar of more than 2,000 bottles from all over Turkey. Both take advantage of centuries-old stone buildings, the latter occupying a 400-year-old stone house that in 1859 housed the mayor. You can wander through the wine cellar (Levissi's is in the old stables), enjoy wine tastings, or have a multiple-course meal (with wine, of course). Wine costs from around 45TL for a bottle or 8TL for a glass.

3,500 identical square stone houses, each positioned to afford the best views of the countryside, take on a haunting pinkish glow at sunset, the best time to visit. Although the churches and chapels have been scavenged in the search for buried sacred treasure, there's still enough of the original structures and ceramic mosaic flooring to make an impression.

The turnoff from the Fethiye/Ölüdeniz road travels through **Hisarönü,** an untidy enclave of mass British tourism affectionately called Hiroshima by the locals who remember its age of innocence. If you follow this road for about 5 or 6.5km (3–4 miles) through the piney woods, the hollow stone houses will alert you to your arrival. A more inspiring entrance can be made by following the signs up and around Fethiye Castle for Kaya Village/Karmylassos. This winding back way leads through the upper edges of picturesque Kaya Valley, and if you're lucky, you'll get a glimpse of the nomad camp.

Kayaköy. *Dolmuşes* make the 30-min. journey from Fethiye to Kayaköy daily for about 3TL. © **0252/614-1150.** Admission 5TL. Daily 8:30am–6:30pm Apr–Oct; daily 8:30am–5pm Nov–Mar.

Tlos ★★ RUINS Tlos is one of the oldest and most important cites in ancient Lycia, and its position atop a rocky outpost dominates the Xanthos Valley. Hittite artifacts found here indicate the city was founded as early as 2000 B.C. After the decline of the Hittite Empire, Tlos became a Lycian city, and then was later absorbed by the Roman Empire. The city was an important bishopric during the Byzantine Era and was finally conquered by the Turks.

The most immediately impressive feature is the severe slope of the city on the rock, carved into majestic temple-like tombs, and the stone sarcophagi dotting the hillside below. A lone sarcophagus sits dramatically in the middle of a farmer's field best spotted from the stadium, located a few hundred feet up the road of the ruins near a roadside cafe graced with ice-cold springs. Take a look at the stadium first, because after the climb to the summit, it will be too much of a struggle against the heat to tack this on to the end of your tour. On the summit lie the ruins of a castle dating to the Turkish settlement, offering panoramic views of the Xanthos Valley. Excavations conducted by Antalya University have uncovered a tunnel, which seems to have provided a quick escape during times of invasion, leading to the city from the nearby village.

Admission 5TL. Daily 8am–5pm. Follow the Fethiye/Antalya rd., cross the bridge over the Esen Çay and look for indications to turn right onto the Saklıkent rd. The turnoff for Tlos is before Saklıkent on the left.

Yaka Park ★★ ☺ PARK/GARDEN   This trout farm is a wonderful place to take the kids, because after ordering your food, you can try to pet one of the finger-biting swans on the upper terrace. Yaka Park takes up several outdoor terraces on a gently sloping hill, and you can choose to sit at one of the picnic tables or under a tree in an enclosed seating area on pillows and mats. There's also a bar, whose counter has been carved out and filled up with baby trout swimming along its meandering length. The trout come right out of the central pond and, once grilled, are crispy and delicious.

Yaka Köyü (about 44km/27 miles from the center of Fethiye). ⓒ **0252/634-0336.** Meal of trout and all-you-can-eat appetizers around 20TL. MC, V. Daily 9am–10pm. Closed Nov–Mar. Follow the Fethiye/Antalya rd. and turn right on the rd. to Saklıkent; turn left again toward Tlos and follow the signs for Yaka Park.

AREA BEACHES

Arguably the most beautiful beach on the eastern Mediterranean, and the smallest bay in Turkey (and probably the reason you came all this way), **Ölüdeniz** ★★★ has become Turkey's poster child due to its extraordinary beauty. But these days, it's hard to overlook the cheap formula tourism that has overtaken this small beach resort. Still, I'd be remiss if I didn't urge you to go, if even for an off-season day on the beach. Ölüdeniz refers to both the long stretch called **Belceğiz Beach** ★★★ at the foot of Babadağ, as well as the still blue waters of the **Blue Lagoon** ★★★, which actually takes its name from the enclosed pool behind the natural sandbar. *Dolmuşes* leave frequently across from the hospital in Fethiye.

The exposed Belceğiz Beach is ideal as a landing site for the paragliding maniacs launching themselves off the top of the mountain, although you may spot a guy flying around with a jet propulsion pack strapped to his back as well. The beach is undeveloped, the locals touting adventure trips are friendly, and the white sands and turquoise waters are hard to beat (until you walk over to the preserve).

The **Blue Lagoon** ★ is tucked inside a natural preserve that requires an admission fee of 4.50TL (though if you drive in it'll be about double with the parking fee). From the parking lot you can either follow the sandy beach around the sandbar or take the more scenic path over the pine needles and through the woods. Families who had arrived early to stake their claims are now nestled in the shade of little pine niches, and you'll pass hundreds of these picnickers as you follow the woodsy path along the shallow section of the lagoon. Keep walking, because you'll know by the color of the water when you've arrived. If you're not sure, keep going. You might want to get here early (actually, you'll want to go off-season, because in summer, the crowd is crushing), because by midday the lounge chairs are all spoken for, and you may wind up piling your belongings in a heap on the pebbles and diving right in.

Make no mistake, however, the Blue Lagoon has attracted half the population of Lycia, and they've all brought their kids, so a serene afternoon of swimming and solitude is definitely out. But however overcrowded it is, this little corner of Turkey is irresistible.

With your own car, preferably a four-wheel-drive, you can combine a visit to Kayaköy with a day spent tooling around **Gemiler Beach** ★★★, an undeveloped cove opposite the historic ruins of Gemiler Island and some postcard views of the mountains in the distance. From the beachfront, you can swim over to the 7th-century Byzantine monastery of St. Nikola on **Gemiler Island** ★★ (site entrance an extractive 8TL, a rate certainly not commensurate with the site), or hire a speedboat for a group ringo or banana boat ride.

Daily excursion boats offer the "12-island tour" ★★ (actually closer to six) around the Gulf of Fethiye, a popular diversion that can be booked directly at the dock, or through most any travel agent. In Ölüdeniz, contact **Activities Unlimited** (© 0252/616-6316; www.activities-unlimited-turkey.com). The beauty is impossible to describe, but for about 40TL or 50TL, the trip provides an abbreviated taste of what a weeklong Blue Voyage would be like. Highlights of the cruise include stopovers at Hamam Bay, where you can swim above sunken Byzantine baths (erroneously called Cleopatra's Bath), and at Gemiler Island. There's room for a mild adrenaline rush in Turunç Bükü, where you can scale the rocks to a hanging rope and swing into the turquoise waters like Tarzan. Swimming and snorkeling around the tiny coves and bays is a high priority, and the captain is usually flexible about schedules if you decide to swim ashore to explore some medieval ruins up close.

If you haven't booked your Blue Voyage yet and would like a taste of the Lycian Coast by sea, many agencies and boat captains offer what has now become a widely marketed 4-day, 3-night **mini blue-cruise to Olympos** (if you have time, inspect the cabins of several boats before you commit), available April to mid-October. The cruise takes in some of the most stunning scenery along the coast, past Butterfly Valley, Ölüdeniz, Gemiler Island, and the beach of Patara, the final leg of the trip heads by bus overland from Demre/Myra to ancient Olympos (p. 351). Prices at the time of this writing for a cruise from July 15 to September 15 are 175€ per person, including tax and three meals, but excluding drinks. Prices go down slightly off-season. (There are no cruises Nov–Mar.) Most boats provide some type of snorkeling and fishing equipment. **V-GO Tourism Travel Agency,** Fevzi Çakmak Caddesi (btw. the marina and the Yacht Club; © 0252/612-2113; www.boatcruiseturkey.com), invented this trip, but my advice is to shop around and have a look at all of the boats/cabins available.

SPORTS & OUTDOOR ACTIVITIES

EXPLORING BUTTERFLY VALLEY   NATURAL ATTRACTION   A nature lover's paradise is located at **Butterfly Valley** ★★, an untouched beachfront parcel named for the rare Tiger Butterfly which breaks from its cocoon in April and May and turns the skies bright red. The colorful creatures are drawn to the smells of mint, jasmine, laurel, eucalyptus, and thyme emanating from the rich vegetation. A 45-minute hike away from the beach leads to a refreshing waterfall. Happily, the valley is a First Degree Preservation Site, a designation intended to prevent the arrival of mass tourism into this isolated and pristine ecosystem.

Taxi boats from Belceğiz Beach abound, but while all advertise round-trip fares, only the official **Kelebekler Vadisi** and **Kelebekler Vadisi 1** boats will actually transport you back to Oludeniz at the end of the day (the others have been known to collect your 15TL round-trip fare, drop you off at Butterfly Valley to never be seen again). Check their website (© 0555/632-0236; www.kelebeklervadisi.org) for the boat taxi schedule, as there are only a few shuttles each day making the 30-minute trip.

An alternative for the adventurous and well-shod hiker is to follow the *very* steep and rocky slope down from the upper rim of the valley, following the footpath from in front of "George House" pension, on the road to Faralya/Kabak (gauge about 30 min.). For those who miss the last boat out, or for "The Beach" wannabes looking for the best campsite this side of the Himalayas (says me), the spare bungalows, platform huts, and dingalows of the on-site Butterfly Valley "pension" (© 0555/632-0236;

www.kelebeklervadisi.org) are your only alternatives. One night in a bungalow with breakfast and dinner ranges from 60TL to 70TL in summer, less in winter. Bathrooms and shower blocks are communal, and hot water is "available." For day-trippers, there's a basic snack bar offering the usual sparse selection of cold drinks, meatballs, and tea.

HIKING (OR WADING) SAKLIKENT GORGE NATURAL ATTRAC-TION   Also known as the Canyon of the Hidden Valley, **Saklıkent Gorge ★★** is a wonder of nature carved 480m (1,575 ft.) down into the canyon by the constant force of the waters flowing down from Akdağ (Ak Mt.). The water still flows, and boy, is it cold. The entrance to the gorge is down an incline off the main road, surrounded by a parking lot, ticket booth, merchant stalls, and enough tour buses to make you want to turn back.

A sturdy catwalk attached to the cliff wall leads you upstream for about 150m (492 ft.) to landfall, where the gushing waters of the **Gökçesu** and **Ulupınar** springs flow down from Babadağ into the gorge. The air is unexpectedly cold at this juncture thanks to the constant roar of the icy waters, and some clever businessman knew just how to take advantage. The **Saklıkent Gorge River Restaurant ★★★** (② **0252/659-0074;** www.saklikentgorge.net) is a series of cozy wooden platforms constructed over the torrents for optimal enjoyment of a meal prepared in the stone ovens and a respite from the relentless heat. The same establishment also has a River Bar and a handful of newly constructed treehouses (30€ B&B) that could give reluctant traveling kids an experience to remember.

A hike up the gorge through the sometimes thigh-high waters is the highlight of the trip. Enter the gorge above where the springs gush into the creek, but be prepared for the shock of water so cold you just might have gone skiing that day. Your legs will be so numb that you won't even notice that the temperature of the water stabilizes the farther away from the spring source you get. The rock face has been sanded to a silky smoothness, creating slippery slides for kids of all ages. River shoes are advisable, especially if you plan on going the full distance of 18km (11 miles).

Small group tours by minibus or jeep safari leave for Saklıkent Gorge daily in season for around £25 to £30, including a stop at the ancient city of Tlos and lunch at Yaka Park or at the Saklıkent Gorge Restaurant. You can also get to the gorge, located about 40km (25 miles) southeast of Fethiye (about 1 hr.), by picking up a *dolmuş* at the main terminal or flagging one down on the Fethiye/Antalya road out of town. By

Take a Hike

The best of Fethiye's goat paths, dirt tracks, and roadways winding their way through the forests, Mediterranean brush, and along the seacoast comprise a section of the Lycian Way (see the beginning of this chapter), a hiking trail that maximizes the magnificence of this corner of Turkey. At the end of the road from Ölüdeniz to Faralya is The Olive Garden (② 0252/642-1083; www.olive gardenkabak.com), a rural paradise that combines a campground, a restaurant, bungalows (140TL double in summer), and a bar with cushioned, canopied Oriental-style casual "beds" for sitting—all from a spectacular site above a stunning bay. It's a steep stone path down to the Olive Garden from the road, and another 15-minute trek straight down the steep mountainside to the pristine beach (more to get back up, if you actually don't have a heart attack trying).

car, follow the Fethiye/Antalya road and turn left at the road for Kemer, turn left again past Tlos and follow signs for Saklıkent. Entrance to the gorge is 4.50TL.

HORSEBACK RIDING ADVENTURE TOUR   Enjoy the scenic pine forests, ride along the shorefront, or follow a mountain stream on horseback. You can also arrange your own outing by going directly to the **Desperado Ranch** (✆/fax **0252/633-6363;** www.desperado-ranch.com; closed Sun), located over in Yanıklar. They offer a 2-hour beginner's beach tour, a half-day adventure tour and a 5- to 7-hour mountain trek. If you've never ridden before, they even offer single lessons; for experienced riders, they run full overnight, week-long tours. (Note that a couple of local travel agencies run horseback riding day excursions, but over in Patara instead of in the Fethiye area.)

PARAGLIDING ADVENTURE TOUR   Thanks to the 1,950m (6,398-ft.) drop-off of Babadağ over an open body of water, and to the gentle sea breezes and stable winds, Ölüdeniz is one of the foremost sites in the world for paragliding. Professionals come from all over to prepare for international flying competitions, an experience that is now available to the daring—and strong-stomached, as there's really nothing like puking in midair. (If you're the type to get seasick, you may want to take a pill before-hand, or carry a Ziploc bag, just in case; take it from one who thought she had a sturdy stomach.) Flying tandem with an experienced pilot, all of whom are certified profes-sionals, provides a safe and easy introduction to an otherwise extreme sport.

  Skysports Paragliding, located on the beach in Ölüdeniz (✆ **0252/617-0511;** www.skysports-turkey.com), is the most reputable of the dozen or so outfitters touting their flights (although I'm told that pilots rotate among the companies regularly). They run five daily departures in high season, leaving by jeep at 9 and 11:30am, and 2, 4, and 6pm for the hour climb up to the summit. A 2-hour flight excursion costs 185TL a head; because of limited space, book at least 1 day in advance. Other reputable organiz-ers of paragliding jumps are **Airborne-Ikarus** (✆ **0252/617-0500;** www.ikarus.com. tr), located in the Fethiye market at Çarşı Cad. 2/d, and **Easy Riders** (✆ **0252/617-0114;** www.easyriderstravel.8m.com). Prices are fixed among the various companies, so don't bother trying to negotiate. Be forewarned, however, human error has been known to result in fatalities, but then again, the same is true of driving a car.

SCUBA DIVING ADVENTURE TOUR   Spontaneous discovery of sunken ruins awaits you in the clear blue waters of the Gulf of Fethiye, one of the best dive sites for exploring underwater caves. The best outfitter in the area, with branches in Anta-lya, Bodrum, Kaş, Marmaris, and Dalyan, is the professionally run **European Diving Centre,** Fevzi Cakmak Cad. 53 (✆ **0252/614-9771;** www.europeandivingcentre. com), offering single or multiday "dive packs" for up to £55 per day (prices go down the more days you dive). Day packs include three dives, lunch, guide, tanks, weights, and weight belt. The dive center also offers an advanced open water course and other PADI recognized courses.

WHITE-WATER RAFTING & KAYAKING ADVENTURE TOUR   Outdoor enthusiasts may have already zeroed in on the Dalaman River rapids (see "The Active Traveler" in the section on Dalyan, above). But if you've chosen Fethiye as your base, it would be terribly remiss to ignore the paddling opportunities of this pristine and rugged coastline. From their new perch up in Kayaköy, **7 Capes** (Kinali Mah. 140, Kayaköy; ✆ **0252/618-0390;** www.sevencapes.com) launches **daytime and moonlight kayaking trips ★★★** that take advantage of the area's most scenic points. Tours cost from 35€ to 50€, depending on the length and location of the trip.

Where to Eat

Fethiye has its abundance of *pide* (flatbread) joints and kebap houses, and you certainly don't need me to point them out. Below is a small selection of the most memorable and atmospheric places in and around the three main centers. For a splurge, dine in the restaurant of the **Oyster Residences** (see Where to Stay, below) overlooking the bay.

FETHIYE TOWN

Meğri TURKISH   Meğri is hard to miss with its monopoly on dining in town. Its empire includes two neighboring locations in the center of Fethiye's Old Town, an unornamented *lokanta* a few steps away, and a corner cafe. The main restaurant is actually two separate spaces set around the Old Town square—in summertime, tables spill out of the two stone dining rooms (one was an old converted warehouse) monopolizing the public square. The *lokanta*, Çarşı Cad. 26 (✆ **0252/614-4047**), attracts those looking for typical food without the added price, and the location across from the old one provides plenty of pleasant outdoor seating.

Paspatur Eskı Cami Gecidi Likya Sok. 8–9 (in the center of Old Town). ✆ **0252/614-4046.** Appetizers and main courses 7TL–24TL and up for fish. AE, DC, DISC, MC, V. Daily 9am–midnight.

Mozaic Bahçe 🍴 REGIONAL TURKISH   Mozaic Bahçe was opened in May 2009 by Hatay native Doğan and his wife Nichola, with Doğan's cousin Münir heading up the kitchen. Hatay cuisine mirrors the cultural mix of the southeastern region bordering Syria, with spices adding a bit of a kick to seemingly familiar themes: hummus, eggplant salad, thyme salad, and a spicy couscous are just a few examples. Fresh, delicious breads emerge from the kitchen daily, and all of the kebaps (including the classic *tepsi*, Antioch and *kağıt kebaps*) are prepared in the outdoor BBQ. Luckily, the menu is visual so guessing is kept to a minimum.

Cumhuriyet Mah. 90 Sok. 2/A, Kaymakamlık Karşısı (behind Domino's Pizza), Fethiye. ✆ **0252/614-4653.** Appetizers and main courses 4TL–18TL. MC, V. Daily 9am–midnight.

KAYAKÖY

Cin Bal ★★★ 🍴☺ GRILLED MEAT   Originally a butchery, this village garden-style eatery is a well-kept secret, serving up rustic ambience and incredible food at spectacularly low prices. You can sit at one of the few tables in the slightly overgrown valley yard or on rudimentary platforms with plump pillows while a herd of goats nibble at the nearby daffodils. After choosing from a selection of meat, fish, and wild boar, all of it fresh and succulent and in abundant portions, you grill your own food on a small, tableside barbecue. The mezes are almost unnecessary with all the food that arrives, including the essential combination of onions, tomatoes, and peppers to grill alongside the meat. The local crowd of regulars tends to make an evening of it, egged on by the roving minstrels and singing increasingly off-key as the night progresses.

Kaya Köyü. www.cinbal.com. ✆ **0252/618-0066.** Appetizers 6TL; meat courses by weight, about 20TL per kilo. MC, V. Daily 8am–2am.

ÖLÜDENIZ

Buzz Grill INTERNATIONAL   Buzz is very popular with visitors, during the daytime for the outdoor cafe along the promenade and at night for the outdoor Buzz Beach Bar and lounge upstairs. Lunchtime fare trends to standard (wraps, *döner kebaps,* salads, and sandwiches) but dinnertime turns the heat up in the kitchen for grilled fresh fish, steaks, pizzas, and pasta. You can check your e-mail with a coffee in hand, as they also have an Internet corner.

Belceğiz Beach on the promenade, Ölüdeniz. www.buzzbeachbar.com. (✆) **0252/617-0045.** Dinner menu 13TL–23TL. MC, V. Daily 8am–3am. Closed in winter.

Oba ◢TURKISH/PIDES   In a sea change of restaurants that pass from owner to owner, this is the one reliable and consistent dining spot (excluding Beyaz Yunus, which is in a class all its own) in Ölüdeniz. Located 1 long block away from the beach, Oba makes for a quiet lunch or a lively dinner. The menu is traditional Turkish, but the food quality is excellent, and you get to choose between traditional Turkish platform seating or a table in the cool garden. *Pide* and pizza are only served in the evening hours.

225 Sok. From the Belceğiz Beach promenade, take 224 Sok. www.obamotel.com.tr. (✆) **0252/617-0470.** Appetizers and main courses 5L–17TL. No credit cards. Daily 8am–1am.

Fethiye After Dark

Personally, I prefer nothing more than a midsummer eve's stroll through Old Fethiye or a shared bottle of wine at a wine house up in the mountains of Kayaköy. Otherwise, nightlife is centered around three main resort areas. The Old Town Bazaar in downtown **Fethiye** has a good number of bars, restaurants, and shops lining the ancient streets, and shops are open until as late as the money flows in. The promenade along Belceğiz Beach down at **Ölüdeniz,** with its handful of nightspots and frat-boy mentality, is absent of any real sophistication, and utterly avoidable unless you're staying on or near the Blue Lagoon without any transport of your own.

Hisarönü, the enclave located on the road to **Kayaköy,** turns into a fun-house festival and pedestrian market on summer evenings. The streets are lined with restaurants and boisterous bars too numerous to mention (a huge draw for the local British expats), and shops selling beach souvenirs that catch your eye under fluorescent lighting. If you're looking for something of a more organized nature, hotels and resorts organize presentations of live music or some contrived line-dance activity. Look for postings around the properties for options.

Where to Stay

Fethiye is the perfect base for a well-rounded holiday with plenty of forays into exploring all of the wonders the area has to offer. But with so many natural and man-made attractions, it's hard to know in which corner of Fethiye (region) to base yourself. Here are your choices: **Fethiye town** is the commercial center of the region, offering visitors travelers' convenience, shopping, nightlife, and sustenance all in a fairly tight cluster. The two properties listed here also add the option of a sea-view room, along with reasonable walkability to the town center about a kilometer (⅔ mile) down the cobbled waterfront road. **Çalış Beach** is to the north of the center of Fethiye, a strip of beachfront pastel cement blocks standing opposite an expanse of narrow beach. Çalış Beach could be anywhere in the world, with its cheap rates, cheap towels, and cheap blow-up rafts dangling from the rafters of ground-floor shops. The hotels of **Ölüdeniz,** a resort doubling as the poster child for the Turkish Mediterranean, unfortunately cater to backpackers and families on a budget, although this is slowly changing as pensions add villas to their stock and small inns establish themselves along the coastal mountain road to the east. **Kayaköy** sits in a verdant valley located up in the hills, where village life and the tourist influence have struck a tolerant balance. The choices for guesthouses and self-catering cottages have grown, and the quality of the more affordable options in lodging is gaining ground.

Hisarönü and Ovaçık are two locations on the road up from Fethiye to Kayaköy where it seems as if dozens and dozens of lesser expensive hotels just sprouted like mushrooms. And we all know where mushrooms like to grow. Not that the scenery is bad, although it was certainly better before the arrival of massive numbers of tourists from northern England and elsewhere on package trips. Other than the Montana Pine, I have nothing to say about either of these little hamlets, although a walk around Hisarönü can be a hoot in the evenings, as the carnival atmosphere starts cranking.

FETHIYE TOWN

Ece Saray Marina & Resort ★★   Owned by the same company that operates the marina, the palatial Ece Saray occupies an aristocratic waterfront property near the western end of central Fethiye. Parisian-style wrought-iron balconies perch above the stunning scenery from every room. Rooms are trimmed with rosewood and embellished with the finest Vakko textiles, while bathrooms are swathed in Italian marble and come loaded with amenities such as designer soaps and plush bathrobes. The pool is surrounded by teak lounges and stunning views of the Toros Mountains. Guests can while away an hour or so in the spa and wellness center (offering hydrotherapy treatments, stone therapy, and facial treatments, along with the basics), while men congregate in the terribly manly cigar room with high-backed leather chairs.

1 Karagözler Mevkii (in the Marina), 48300 Fethiye. www.ecesaray.net. (✆ **0252/612-5005.** Fax 0252/614-7205. 48 units. Sept–June 220€ double. Rates lower off-season. AE, DISC, MC, V. **Amenities:** Restaurant; 3 bars; children's playground; concierge; exercise room; *hamam;* outdoor pool; room service; spa. *In room:* A/C, satellite TV, hair dryer, minibar, free Wi-Fi.

Hillside Beach Club ★★★ ☺   Occupying one of the more sublimely isolated coves in the Fethiye area, the Hillside Beach Club promises a family-friendly structure that doesn't forget to dote on the adults. In fact, the hotel has a private cove that they blissfully dub the "Silent Beach." Room styles are broken up into five categories of rooms, from singles, small and regular-size doubles, and two types of triples, one of which can accommodate four. And they're not the kind that make you cringe, either: These rooms were designed as eye candy, including the sea view, which is found in all rooms. (All have balconies or terraces of varying sizes.) The hotel, which operates on an all-inclusive formula, has activities galore: aerobics, archery, windsurfing, and water polo; you can even go sailing or take out a catamaran—in fact, I can't think of anything you can't do here. The hotel has a sort of "cruise director" mentality: Expect things like symphony orchestra or opera performances, movie galas, water-skiing competitions, and special activities for children such as workshops and disco parties.

Kalemya Koyu, P.O. Box 123, 48300 Fethiye (4km/2½ miles from the city center). www.hillsidebeach club.com.tr. (✆ **0252/614-8360.** Fax 0252/614-1470. 330 units. 212€ per person per night based on double occupancy. Check website for special offers. AE, MC, V. **Amenities:** 3 restaurants; 8 bars; babysitting; children's programs; concierge; *hamam;* health club and spa; indoor and outdoor pools; room service; smoke-free rooms; squash; 5 tennis courts (3 sand and 2 asphalt); extensive watersports equipment/rental. *In room:* A/C, satellite TV, hair dryer, free Internet, minibar.

Villa Daffodil ★   This charming little guesthouse perched on the road across from the Gulf of Fethiye is a real attention grabber, owing to its traditional Ottoman design and wooden *cumbas* (enclosed ornamented balconies), typical of summer houses of the time. Inside, newly redecorated rooms have new mattresses, plasma TVs, and completely renovated bathrooms. The courtyard of the hotel doubles as a breakfast and bar area, with a functioning lemon tree for a refreshing vodka tonic, and an old 19th-century horseless carriage from which you can admire the bay over the garden wall or literally hand-feed the sparrows.

The disposition of the rooms makes each type slightly different: Side rooms (small) include a small balcony, others share a small inner courtyard, and rear upper-floor rooms have lots of wood and (low, slanted) garret-style ceilings. The owner also manages 3 self-catering apartments in a villa just up the road from the marina ($80–$120), as well as a six-cabin gulet moored in the inlet across the street for easy guest hire.

Fevzi Çakmak Cad. 115, 48300 Fethiye. www.villadaffodil.com. ☏ **0252/614-9595** or 0252/612-5211. Fax 0252/612-2223. 27 units. $30–$45 per person double. AE, MC, V. Free parking on street. **Amenities:** Restaurant; bar; outdoor pool; sauna; free Wi-Fi. *In room:* A/C, satellite TV, hair dryer.

KAYAKÖY

Mısafır Evi ✦ This local hotel and restaurant offers budget accommodations right smack in the middle of paradise. The rooms are simple, with twin beds under wooden roofs (on the top floor, obviously), surrounded by practical and unadorned furniture and whitewashed stone walls. The bathrooms, however, are of the type you would hope to find anywhere: floor-to-ceiling tile, a modern Roman shower separated by a glass partition, and modern fixtures. But more authentic you could not get: shoes are not permitted in the room (nor is smoking)! The lush garden bursts with flowers, and when not lazing drowsily in a hammock, you can be lounging poolside.

Keçiler/Kaya Köyü, 48304 Fethiye. ☏ **0252/618-0162.** www.kayamisafirevi.com. 9 units. 140TL double (add 20TL per person for half-board). No credit cards. **Amenities:** Restaurant; outdoor swimming pool. *In room:* A/C, no phone.

Sakli Vadi ★★ 📷 Jon Carter, who arrived in Kayaköy in 1992, is the helmsman behind the earliest restoration projects in the valley. With the four cottages that make up Sakli Vadi, the trend of preserving buildings' original utility continues. Here it is a "granary," a "byre," a "forge," and a *"küçük ev"* each comprising a rustic retreat with its own private terraced garden. The best thing about the units is that each provides an optimum level of isolation and privacy, embraced in lavender, bougainvillea, and sagebrush. A small freshwater plunge pool is shared by the three cottages, a great amenity for when the summer sun heats up the country mountain air. Ask the manager to borrow one of the bikes on hand (they're not in the cottages), and pedal through the wildflowers of the valley.

Kaya Köyü, 48304 Fethiye. www.sakli-vadi.com. ☏ **0252/675-6225.** 4 self-catering cottages. £350 per cottage per week in summer; £250 winter. Advance payment required. See website for details. No credit cards. *In room:* A/C, kitchen.

ÖLÜDENIZ

Club Belcekız Beach ★ Located at the very end of Ölüdeniz Beach with Babadağ as a backdrop, Club Belcekız Beach sets the stage for a perfect seaside vacation without the fuss. Rooms are in two sections: the main garden complex and an equally nice rear garden annex. All rooms are essentially the same, with updated bathrooms and balconies or patios. The pool overlooks the beach, enjoying views of the cliffs and paragliders descending from the summit of the mountain, and the entire hotel grounds sprout with flowers and lush greenery. The property is usually booked well in advance, and usually for full-week periods, but give them a try anyway. The price to stay here includes all meals, all snacks, and all local drinks, so bring a cover-up: You're going to get fat.

48300 Ölüdeniz. www.belcekiz.com. ℰ **0252/617-0077.** Fax 0252/617-0372. 213 units (some with tub, some with shower). 175€ double all-inclusive. AE, MC, V. Closed mid-Nov to Mar. **Amenities:** 4 restaurants; 3 bars; babysitting; children's facilities; concierge; exercise room; hamam; outdoor pool; room service; sauna; tennis courts; free Wi-Fi in lobby. *In room:* A/C.

Montana Pine Resort ★ This small boutique resort sits amid a pine forest about 1.6km (1 mile) above Ölüdeniz. The resort is a complex of mini-country lodges best described as "modern rustic." Accommodations are divided between valley rooms and the newer mountain rooms. Every comfort has been addressed in the latter rooms, which sport verandas, picture windows, and spacious bathrooms. In comparison, rooms in the original valley section are disappointingly beige in character, and disturbingly close to the evening festivities. All bets are off for the superior valley rooms, which were upgraded in the latest renovation. The two main pools are terraced and connected by a waterfall; there's also an enchanting and cozy şark (Oriental seating) room, with *kilims* and pillows in a private little area for pre- or post-sun relaxing. The hotel provides a free shuttle service to Ölüdeniz Beach.

Ovacık Mah., 48300 Ölüdeniz, Fethiye. www.montanapine.com. ℰ **0252/616-7108.** Fax 0252/616-6451. 159 units. 120€ double. Rates include breakfast and dinner but no drinks. Rates lower for stays longer than a week. MC, V. Closed Nov–Mar. **Amenities:** 2 restaurants; 3 bars; free airport transfer from Dalaman for stays of 7 nights or more; exercise room; Jacuzzi; miniature golf; 3 outdoor pools; room service; sauna; tennis courts; free Wi-Fi. *In room:* A/C, satellite TV, hair dryer, minibar.

Oba Motel ☺ Don't let the down-market name fool you; these relatively new wooden chalet-style "villas" in what used to be the Oba Hostel offer the best indication that the tides are turning for this scrappy beach resort. Located just a half a block from the beach, the cabins are arranged around a well-tended garden, and provide plenty of indoor and outdoor space for those off-beach hours. The restaurant is one of the more reliable in Ölüdeniz.

Ölüdeniz. www.obahostel.com. ℰ **0252/617-0158.** Fax 0252/617-0522. 7 units. £85 double in a villa May–Oct. Rates lower early May and Oct. Closed in winter. MC, V. **Amenities:** Restaurant; bar; Internet cafe. *In room:* A/C, hair dryer, minibar.

Oyster Residences ★★★ 📖 This is just the cure that Ölüdeniz needed to detract from the overwhelming presence of partiers and daredevil paragliders (although the latter are fun to watch from the Oyster's pool garden). It's centrally located along Belceğiz Beach, just steps from the lapping sea. The hotel was the long-time dream of Mehmet Bey and his wife Günsenin, former hosts of the eminent and now defunct Beyaz Yunus restaurant. At the helm of the Oyster Residences they have created the first-quality hotel in Ölüdeniz, a retreat draped in billowing linens, clean design, and oozing hospitality.

Belcekız Mevkii, 1 Sok. www.oysterresidences.com. ℰ **0252/617-0765.** Fax 0252/617-0764. 22 units. 150€–160€ double July–Sept. Rates lower in May, June, and Oct. Closed in winter. **Amenities:** Restaurant; bar; massage; outdoor pool. *In room:* A/C, satellite TV, hair dryer, free Wi-Fi.

KALKAN ★★

81km (50 miles) southeast of Fethiye; 25km (16 miles) west of Kaş; 19km (12 miles) south of Xanthos; 18km (11 miles) east of Patara; 25km (16 miles) southeast of Letoon

At first glance, Kalkan, terraced down a steep slope from the main road to the harbor, presents itself as the quintessential Mediterranean fishing village that made good. Dilapidated Ottoman- and Greek-era houses have been restored to their characteristic yet simple splendor of shuttered windows and timber balconies. The scenery is

FETHIYE'S secluded INNS

The continued development of the towns and villages along Fethiye's coastline means that travelers looking to balance a desire for authenticity with creature comforts must be willing to literally go the extra mile, and in this case, that mile may not be paved. The tradeoff for convenient access to the center of activities, and even transport, is a blissful level of isolation and interaction with other guests, and villagers, some of whom staff the hotels in their villages. If the warmth of a fireplace on a late summer's eve sounds cozy, or the idea of stretching your legs on a trail over goat paths to arrive at a Cliffside tea garden fills your fantasies of vacationing, then the "trouble" will definitely be worth it.

One such inn is the **Villa Mandarin** (www.villamandarin.com; 195€–295€ double), a friendly, hospitable and well-appointed retreat about 9km (5⅔ miles) along the windy road from Ölüdeniz to Faralya. Hosts Ghislain (born in Turkey of a British mother and French father) and his lovely manager Ayşegül treat guests like weekend visitors to their private villette. The nearby Su Değirmeni (The Watermill) in Faralya (www.natur-reisen. de; 55€ –71€ per person half board) is a pension owned by a German ex-pat, who has created a perfectly wonderful (and eco-friendly) inn on the Faralya road just above the Butterfly Valley. Finally, families with children may want to look into the Pastoral Vadı ☺ up in the mountains of Yanıklar (www.pastoralvadi. com; 39€ per person half board), a working farm where guests are encouraged to play farm hand (or not) or join in a whole host of activities, from kilim weaving or wood-carving workshops, to pressing olives or grapes, or simply venturing off to explore the surrounding mine trails and canyons.

stunning: undulating mountains rising above tranquil waters, with nothing but the odd minaret or mast to obstruct it.

But it is this very good fortune that threatens to be Kalkan's undoing. A decade ago, locals reassured me that because the surrounding Mediterranean brushlands were protected, the village was safe from overdevelopment. But economic interests once again prevailed, and building (mostly hotels) has sprawled almost all the way to equally stunning Kalamar Bay. Today, the town's population of around 1,000 swells to 8,000 in summer, a density that Kalkan handles with difficulty during the high-season months of July and August. This is when the English presence in Kalkan becomes overwhelming, as Brit-based tour operators prebook most of the town's better B&Bs and hotels, thus creating a shortage of rooms for the independent traveler during the main tourist season.

Nevertheless, Kalkan retains its small-town feel. The warren of streets leading down to the picturesque harbor are colorfully adorned with the bright colors of vacation memorabilia, handcrafted silver jewelry, locally made carpets, and terra cotta, baking under the hot sun and sharing the ambiance with the pleasant odors of grilling produce.

Like its equally splendid neighbor Kaş, Kalkan's location is convenient to many historical sites, making either a perfect base of operations for sightseeing, shopping, dining, and spending lazy days on the beach. Indeed for those who struggle with the decision on which town to use as a base, keep in mind that Kaş is more laid back and townlike, while Kalkan has a more villagelike feel, plus better restaurants.

Essentials

GETTING THERE

Halfway between Dalaman and Antalya airports, Kalkan lies along the southwestern coast of the Mediterranean. If you're arriving by long-distance bus, direct service is available year round from Istanbul with **Pamukkale** (© **444-3535**; 12 hr., 75TL) leaving at 9pm nightly (on its way through to Kaş), and from Izmir (8 hr., 43TL), leaving twice daily for Kalkan. The luxury **Kamıl Koç** (© **444-0562** or 0242/844-1212 in Kalkan) also serves the long-distance routes to Istanbul, Ankara, and locally, to Ortaca and Dalaman. From Kaş (via minibus) it's about a half-hour (5TL), and to/from Antalya it's about 3½ hours (22TL).

Independent travelers from Dalaman Airport are up against a series of transfers, including the one from the airport to the Dalaman bus station, which must be done by taxi. From the bus station, you can either catch a through-bus headed to Izmir (double-check that it stops in Kalkan) or take a minibus. Or, you could hop on the Havaş shuttle to Fethiye (1 hr., 20TL) and then transfer at the Fethiye *otogar* for a minibus into Kalkan. **Adda Tours** (© **0242/844-3610**; www.addatours.com) offers private transfer from Dalaman Airport for around £55 for up to three people (1 hr., 45 min.) and from Antalya Airport for £85 (4 hr.).

Perhaps most convenient is to visit Kalkan as a port of call on a Blue Voyage. (If you're taking a Blue Voyage, it's worth trying to coax your captain into stopping in Kalkan for an overnight visit.)

VISITOR INFORMATION

There is no tourist information office in Kalkan. A good source of information before you go is **Enjoy Kalkan** (www.enjoykalkan.com). Thursday is market day.

There are a number of banks in Kalkan, all located on Şehitler Caddesi: **Akbank** (no. 26; © **0242/844-1440**), **Deniz Bank** (no. 19; © **0242/844-1380**), **Garanti** (no. 6; © **0242/844-1499**), **Yapı Kredi** (no. 43; © **0242/844-3892**), and **Ziraat Bankası** (no. 18; © **0242/844-1601**).

At the **marina,** you can take care of the basics, such as the use of coin-operated public toilets, showers, or laundry facilities, or hire a local boat and captain for the day.

ORIENTATION

The historically preserved village of Kalkan is built on a steep hillside that tumbles steeply into Kalkan bay, enclosed by rocky and rugged mountains. Although years ago I was told that because of this rocky topography, the village could not succumb to sprawl, economic interests have obviously overturned any reticence on the part of the municipality to welcome further development. Building (mostly of hotels and private villas) persists along the scenic road into Kalkan and out to lovely Kalamar Bay, yet thankfully, the center of Kalkan remains as compact, chaotic, and preserved as it ever was. The main square sits at the top of the village, serving as a parking lot as well as the town's miniscule commercial center. There are two or three bus company offices, some travel agencies, a barber, a PTT, and a handful of bodegas for essential refills of water. The crisscross of narrow streets packed with restaurants, pensions, and shops from the main square down to the marina is known as the catchall **Yalıboyu** neighborhood. This absence of definitive street addresses may at first seem odd, but even though nobody uses a street address, it's unlikely you'll get lost. All of the charming little roads and stairpaths lead to the harbor and marina, and you will find yourself trekking up and down countless times a day.

Also, all of the activities listed in this section are accessible to those based over in Kaş and vice versa, and travel companies routinely provide pickups at both for day tours.

GETTING AROUND

Kalkan center is primarily a deeply sloping pedestrian village of limited size. Some of the hotels lining the road out of the village are still within walking distance, but anything beyond that may require wheels. If you're entering the village by car, be aware that the harbor road closes to traffic at 7pm, so you'll need to be settled in (or plan to leave your car at the top of the village) by then. If you have trouble walking up and down steep inclines, Kalkan is not for you.

BY DOLMUŞ   *Dolmuşes* leave from the main square regularly (as soon as they fill up), heading east toward Kaş or west to Patara and points beyond. There are also *dolmuşes* that depart to specific destinations; these run on a timetable (and you'll have to buy your ticket at the ticket window in advance). In general, *dolmuş* service back into Kalkan ends as early as 6pm, so if you pop out of town for the day, make sure you have a ride home.

BY BUS   There is a limited number of major bus companies in Kalkan, generally servicing only the longer hauls. Destinations and schedules are posted on placards outside the few minuscule ticket offices located on the main square. It's usually okay to buy your ticket at the office just prior to boarding.

If you're headed to or from any of the towns along the coast up to Antalya, catch one of **Batı Antalya Tur's** (℡ 0242/844-2777) air-conditioned buses and head out early in the morning—the lack of traffic can shorten your trip by up to an hour; from Antalya, it'll cost around 22TL.

BY CAR/SCOOTER   It's almost impossible not to trip over a sign touting the rental of a scooter, car, or jeep. You'll find the scooters up in the main square across from the post office and car rentals through most travel agencies for around £22 per day and up, depending on the model and the length of the rental.

What to See & Do

The distinctive features of the coastline around Kalkan and the nearby Xanthos River allow for innumerable options for day trips on or near the water. Here the jagged edges of mountains meet the sea, forming a breathtaking network of islands and coves that present endless possibilities for a day of dive bombing off the roof of a boat and swimming into eerie caves. High up on your list should be a boat trip around the island of **Kekova** and the sunken city, accessible from a number of port towns along the coast (see "Kaş," later in this chapter, for further information).

AREA BEACHES

Usually, a sign reading YACHT CLUB means members only, or more accurately, not you, thank you very much. Not so here at the Kalkan Marina, where a traveler, no matter whether the arrival was by land or by sea, can venture up and over to the other side of the breakwater, to the town "beach," a lovely terrace jutting out into the harbor where you can rent lounges and umbrellas. There is also food service at the club.

Meanwhile, the actual **Kalkan Beach** is a man-made pebble beach, at the eastern end of town. Fed by the icy spring waters channeling down from the mountain, you might want to save this for a bracing sunrise dip or a refreshing cool-off at the end of a hot and dusty day.

Kaputaş Beach ★★★ is a tiny little sandy cove at the mouth of a dramatic gorge only 10 minutes from Kalkan. The *dolmuş* crosses a bridge between the two sides of the formation and drops you off at the highway railing, at the top of a lofty (around 300 steps) narrow stairway down to the beach. **Mavi Mağara (Blue Cave,** named for the hue of the boulders inside) is a short swim from Kaputaş out and to the left, but as the beach is not guarded, only strong swimmers in pairs should do this. Bring plenty of water; there are no facilities (no food, no drink, no umbrellas) on this beach.

To the west of Kalkan, just over the hilly headland is the **Kalamar Beach Club ★★ (© 0242/844-3061)** a secluded grouping of cement patio terraces with beach lounges, backed by a restaurant and snack bar. The guys that run the concession provide free transfers from Kalkan and make up the difference with food prices that are the highest in the area. Day rental of a lounge and umbrella is around 8TL and there are also showers. Boredom is kept at bay thanks to **The Kalkan Dive Center (© 0242/844-2361;** www.kalkandiving.com), the on-site provider of watersports rentals and Kalkan Dive Centre (www.kalkandiving.com; see the info on Kalkan Dive Centre, under "Staying Active," below); they rent jet skis and water skis and also give lessons for water-skiing. Banana boat rides and ringos are also available.

Only 20 minutes away by *dolmuş* is **Patara ★★★**, the longest and certainly one of the most beautiful stretches of sand in Turkey. The beach goes on for 18km (11 miles), which makes for a pretty long surfside stroll, especially when the fierce winds are at their peak. Entrance to the beach is through the **ruins** (see "Exploring Lycian Ruins in the Xanthos Valley" in the next section) of the ancient city, so if you've come by car, you'll have to pay the entrance fee of 5TL to the site, which includes repeat visits to the beach (keep your ticket). The site is open daily April to October 9am to 7pm and November to March 8am to 5pm (© 0242/843-5018). If you've arrived on a *dolmuş*, the beach is free, but you may want to rent an umbrella. Patara Beach is also a lesser-known nesting ground for the *Caretta caretta* turtle, so it is closed after dark.

EXPLORING LYCIAN RUINS IN THE XANTHOS VALLEY

Kalkan is a great base for day excursions to the ancient Lycian cities along the coast. You'll get your biggest bang for your buck/quid visiting the headliners of the Xanthos Valley, including Xanthos, Letoon, Patara, and yes, Tlos (see the Fethiye section earlier in this chapter). But you can also head off the beaten track and visit the "lesser" (read: still blissfully untouched by the hands of archaeologists or tourists) sites of **Pinara ★** and **Sidyma** (accessible via an unpaved dirt road). There are yet others; for more information on antique cities in the area, see "What to See and Do," in the Kaş section, later.

All of the sites are easily accessible by car with a short detour off the main road or by *dolmuşes* that run regularly from the main square. Several travel agencies in town offer excursions to one or more of the sites as part of a day tour, contact **Adda Tours,** Yalıboyu Mahallesi (© **0242/844-3610;** www.addatours.com). You can also get great guidance on local subjects by logging on to Enjoy Kalkan's website and forum (www.enjoykalkan.com).

The oldest and most important antique city of the region is **Xanthos ★★**, the ancient capital of Lycia. Homer mentions this center in the *Iliad:* It was from here that Arpedonte led his troops. More tragic is the actual history of the city: On two separate and unrelated occasions, the inhabitants of Xanthos chose collective suicide rather than submission to invading armies.

The ancient city was uncovered by Sir Charles Fellows in 1838, who had much of the city dismantled and transported to the British Museum, where ruins still reside. Nevertheless, reproductions successfully evoke the originals. On your travels through Kaş/Kalkan, pick up a free map of the site, or, you can buy a book on Lycian sites at the refreshment counter. Two unforgettable monuments are on the road from the village of Kınık—the **City Gate** ★★, dating to the Hellenistic era, and **Vespasian's Arch** ★★, erected in honor of the Roman emperor. The **acropolis** ★★★ is dominated by the remains of the **Roman Theatre** ★★, flanked by the ancient city's three most memorable sites: **Harpies' Tomb** ★★★, named for the Persian General Harpagus through a controversial interpretation by Fellows of the tomb's reliefs, the **Lycian Tomb** ★★★ (one of several), and the **Roman Columned Tomb.** Farther back into the brush is a pillar tomb called the **Obelisk,** whose monumental contribution was lengthy inscriptions in both Lycian and Greek, which proved indispensable to deciphering and classifying the Lycian language (another inscription, found at Letoon and written in Aramaic, Greek, and Lycian, was also important).

The New Acropolis is located on the opposite side of the road and is home to the **Byzantine Church** ★, famed for the well-preserved **mosaic** ★ flooring uncovered beneath layers of sand. Tour groups generally circle these major sites, overlooking entirely the overgrown path that leads along an ancient wall through to the **Necropolis** ★★, a visit that is well worth your time. Sarcophagi are scattered or overturned, keep an eye out for the **Belly Dancer Sarcophagus** ★, named for a relief that more resembles water-bearers, the **Lion's Tomb** ★, a sarcophagus with carvings of lions and a bull in battle, and a 4th-century-B.C. **tower tomb** ★★ rising above a stone-cut Roman acropolis. Admission to the site is 3TL.

Patara ★★★ was Lycia's chief port city until the harbor silted up to form what is today an inland reed-filled marsh. Excavations have been ongoing since 1988 by archaeologists at Akdeniz University, and slowly, as the sand and silt is cleared, a rich, historical, and thoroughly enchanting remnant of ancient Lycia is revealed. If you climb to the hilltop above the **Roman Theatre** ★, the fierce winds and unrelenting lashes of sand will give you a clue why much of this ancient city remained buried under sand for so long—a consequence that served to keep the city in such an outstanding state of preservation. Founded according to legend by Patarus, son of Apollo and the nymph Lycia in the 5th century B.C., the site served during the winter months as one of the two most important oracles of the god, his winter months being spent at the temple at Delphi. Today the city gains its fame as the birthplace of the bishop of Myra, better known in northern and Western circles as Santa Claus. Little by little, ongoing excavations reveal details above and beyond the **Gate of Modestus** ★★, the Roman Triumphal Arch that rose defiantly above the meters of earth for centuries. Near the arch is the **Hurmalık (aka Port) Bath** ★★, one of the more architecturally impressive buildings on the site, where you can still see the original swimming pool in the now-collapsed Palestra. **Hadrian's Granary** sits at the west end of the ancient harbor, a warehouse dedicated in A.D. 131 to Emperor Hadrian and his wife Sabina upon their visit to the city. Patara's **main avenue** ★★★, paved with marble stone and lined by a columned arcade, is clearly visible (albeit sometimes a bit waterlogged). Fleeting features of the **Basilica** ★ poke through the ground, but perimeter excavations provide a cross-section of the city's entombment. The **lighthouse,** albeit in ruins, is one of the oldest in the world. One of the chief findings at the site is the **Parliamentary Building** ★★★ or bouleuterion, the governmental seat of ancient Lycia. When Alexander Hamilton and James Madison were considering the future structure of the new American Republic, they looked to Lycia'a parliamentary model of popular, strong, and representative government for inspiration.

The ruins can be easily explored in combination with a trip to Patara Beach; the road from the turnoff passes a saturated level of home-style pensions with varying degrees of charm and leads to the entrance of the archaeological site (admission 5TL). The beach is at the end of the road.

Letoon ★, located less than 5km (3 miles) south of Xanthos, was the primary religious center of ancient Lycia. And while the buses are circling around Xanthos, you can escape here, smack in the middle of the Turkey you envisioned, along a pastoral village road, admiring the wind in the trees and the goats grazing in the archaeological site. Aren't you clever?

The ruins of **three temples** ★★ rise above an uneven plateau and were dedicated to the gods Apollo, Artemis, and their mother, Leto, the mythical lover of Zeus for which the sanctuary was named. The foundations of the three temples are laid out parallel to each other. The **theater** ★★ is in better shape, and it served for meetings of the Lycian Federation, religious ceremonies, and even sports events. Admission to the site is 5TL.

STAYING ACTIVE

The waters off Kalkan provide some of the best venues for **scuba diving** along the Mediterranean. It was off nearby Uluburun that sponge divers discovered a 14th-century-B.C. shipwreck. Several outfitters organize single or multiple days of diving, as well as a "discover scuba" day for beginners. The main reliables are **Kalkan Dive Centre** over at Kalamar Bay (**ℂ 0242/844-2456;** www.kalkandiving.com), run by a couple of experienced local divers and **Bougainville Travel** (**ℂ 0242/836-3737;** www.bougainville-turkey.com) located over in nearby Kaş (see above). A day of diving for beginners and pros starts at 43€ (two dives). Kalkan Diving also runs a selection of ever-more-dazzling **sea kayaking** tours paddling the waters around Kalamar Bay with stops to **swim and snorkel** (from 27€).

Canoeing along the Xanthos River is an exhilarating way to spend the day. You don't need to be a pro—the excursion organizers design tours geared toward fun rather than physical fitness. **Patara Canoeing** (www.pataracanoeing.com) runs a day tour that includes a stopover at a mud bath and a few hours of relaxation on Patara Beach. A day on the rapids runs from around £26 per person, lunch and transfers to and from your hotel included. These and other activities are generally planned on fixed days of the week. If you don't see a tour package that suits your needs, check around the main square or down by the harbor for tours organized by other outfitters.

Where to Eat

The problem of choice will be a tourist's major complaint when staying in Kalkan, as this village easily has the highest ratio of quality restaurants per capita on Turkey's Mediterranean coast. And the turnover is high, so in recommending the tried and true, I may be missing out on some newer gems. Don't hesitate to ask around to nab a table at your own little "find." The trend also is that all this great "international" food (catering to a wallet full of British pounds sterling) comes with a hefty price tag. Unpretentious, family-friendly *lokanta* fare can be had at **Ali Baba** (**ℂ 0242/844-3627**), up on the main square near the post office with a rooftop terrace restaurant serving more substantial fare in the evenings.

Many of the pensions and hotels have rooftop restaurants and often serve some of the best meals using ingredients bought at market the same day. Whenever possible, I always opt for these. These are even open to nonguests, but in this case it's a good idea to reserve ahead for dinner (even by midmorning), to allow the cook to stock up on an adequate amount of food.

Aubergine Restaurant ★★ TURKISH FUSION *Harika* ("great" in Turkish) best describes a dining experience at this restaurant on the harborfront. Luxuriant rattan armchairs and dining tables line both sides of the stone walkway that follows the waterfront, making for an exceptionally romantic Mediterranean dining or lounging experience. The menu is an easy fusion of Turkish and Italian, featuring typical Turkish and Ottoman dishes alongside duck, rabbit, and pasta. Lighter fare is served at lunchtime, and breakfast is available in the morning. Best to make reservations for dinner, as this place is in-demand.

Patlican: Harborside, Kalkan. Daphne: above the Old Mosque. www.kalkanaubergine.com. 𝄞**0242/844-3332.** Reservations suggested. Appetizers and main courses 8TL–22TL. AE, MC, V. Daily 11:30am–1am.

Belgin's Kitchen ☺TRADITIONAL TURKISH Belgin's Kitchen, presided over by Belgin Hanım herself, is a longtime favorite of locals and tourists alike. Making use of a former olive factory, it's a cozy spot for a casual meal, where you can enjoy crispy fried triangular *börek* or painstakingly stuffed *mantı* while comfortably slouched on mats or a traditional-style floor cushion. It's not one of the town's gourmet offerings, but you came here for a traditional Turkish experience and here it is. And the bonus is that you're guaranteed a delicious bite to eat without emptying the entire contents of your wallet. Belgin's Kitchen has local Turkish musical groups in the evening; get there early to nab the table inside the large boiled-wool traditional tent upstairs (on the roof).

Yalıboyu. 𝄞**0242/844-3614.** Appetizers and main courses 9TL–36TL. MC, V. Daily 7:30am to 1 or 2am. Closed Nov–Mar.

Korsan Meze & Korsan Fish Terrace ★★ ☺NOUVELLE TURKISH The Korsan empire (which also includes apartments; see "Where to Stay") is run by Uluç Bilgutay and his wife Claire. Korsan Meze, opened in 1979, was the family's first foray, dazzling holiday goers and the local community of British expatriates with mouthwatering, Asian-inspired mezes like chicken *şiş* with peanut sauce, fish cakes with pine nuts and berries, and hummus with melted chili butter. **Korsan Fish Terrace** was added a decade ago on the rooftop of the owner's small hotel, Patara Stone House, located just above the harbor with unobstructed views of the seascape and some of the best grills in town. The restaurants are both quite pricey, but if you can splurge, you'll be glad you did.

Korsan Meze: At the Marina. 𝄞**0242/844-3622;** Korsan Fish Terrace: 𝄞**0242/844-3076.** www.korsankalkan.com The fish terrace is in the Patara Stone House and the kebap restaurant is opposite. Reservations suggested. Dress smart. Appetizers and main courses at 2 locations 12TL–46TL and up for fish. MC, V. Daily noon–midnight. Closed Nov–Apr.

Kalkan After Dark

Kalkan's rooftops are a special feature of its Greek houses, camouflaged behind small triangular lintels, yet open to night sea breezes. They're the setting for dinner, drinks, and romance for residents and guests alike. Nightlife is also booming on the harborfront, fragrant and alive with handholding vacationers choosing from an appealing

About a 20-minute drive into the mountains from Kalkan is the minuscule village of Islamlar, built on the Islamlar Spring, a freshwater source that coursed down the mountain. About 10 years ago, Mahmut of Mahmut'un Yeri (the first one on the right as you enter the village of Islamlar; ℂ **0242/838-6344**) had the bright idea to harness the water in a cement pool and stock it with trout, and in no time, his neighbors were standing by in disbelief as the customers began to roll into their wild and unspoiled landscape. Today it has not only grown into a country-style restaurant with a roof terrace with views as far as the sea, but it also has spurred a parade of neighborhood imitations, all essentially identical (which means that in a small village like this one, some friends or family members are no longer on speaking terms). Little ones will love watching the trout leaping up out of the water, sometimes upstream through the mesh barrier to freedom and sometimes out of the pool to their death. The price of a meal (trout, salad, and ayran) is about 45TL. (Ten years ago, I paid 7TL. Sigh.).

array of pubs, restaurants, and shops, while the odd narghile cafe or even sports bar will be located in the warren of streets weaving their way uphill. The most ambience can be found in the **Yacht Club** (ℂ **0242/844-1131**) where candlelight and music reverberate off of the water during the nighttime hours.

Where to Stay

Listed here is a very short list of accommodations that take best advantage of the small-village charm that attracted you to Kalkan in the first place. Almost all are located in the village proper, but there is also an endless string of small and medium-size hotels overlooking Kalkan Bay on the connector road to and in Kalamar Bay. British tour companies pre-book blocks of the best rooms in and around Kalkan, leaving us with the slim pickings (the small room without the view, for example) or the rare property unwilling to be confined to this type of arrangement. The properties listed here operate, for the most part, independently.

Keep in mind that while a pension or special-category hotel in the center of town will at least afford some architectural integrity, don't expect a pool. But thanks to the proximity and accessibility of nearby beaches, this should by no means be a deterrent to staying in town. If your holiday style leans more toward the plush and all-inclusive, choose one of the resorts across the bay; they are connected to the village by a water shuttle.

KALKAN

Korsan Apartments and Patara Stone House ★ Enveloped in bougainvillea, the Patara Stone House is a simple B&B in an authentic Kalkan house at the eastern edge of the village above the lighthouse. The two simple rooms, a double and a family room with unobstructed views to the bay, share the stone building with the Fish Terrace restaurant (roof level). The nine apartments are one-bedroom units that, with the help of two single daybeds in the sitting room, sleep four. All apartments have a balcony or terrace overlooking the two small pools, where you can order from the pool cafe. These are located at the entrance to the village, just before the road heads out to Kalamar Bay.

Kalkan Center/Yalıbolu. Patara Stone House. www.korsankalkan.com. ℂ **0242/844-3076;** Kalkan Korsan Apartments ℂ **0242/844-1020.** Fax 0242/844-3274. £46 double Patara Stone House July–Sept; £52 double Korsan Apartments. AE, MC, V. *In room:* Hair dryer.

Patara Prince ★★   The Patara Prince, set on white stone cliffs against a backdrop of verdant gardens, is a mini seaside paradise. It's constructed on the steep hillside opposite Kalkan, with facilities positioned at various altitudes connected by pure-white, local stone stairways. The extremely terraced landscaping need not be a deterrent; the hotel provides a shuttle service down past the various lodging types via a service road to the waterfront.

The complex consists of traditional hotel rooms, blocks of suites of varying types, smartly decorated with features like Jacuzzis, fireplaces, and bamboo-shuttered windows. The villas (large enough for up to six people and some loosely associated with its timeshare operation) are charming and rustic self-catering houses complete with kitchens, living rooms, multiple bedrooms, and scenic terraces.

There are three outdoor pools, one of which is a circulating seawater pool exclusively for adult use. Terraces for sunbathing step down the cliff side to waterfront platforms, where the watersports activities (including a dive school) are organized. The hotel provides a free shuttle service to Kalkan. Note that out of high season, various hotel services go on hiatus.

P.K. 10, Kalkan. www.pataraprince.com. ℂ**0242/844-3920.** Fax 0242/844-3930. 60 units. £49–£100 double and suites in hotel July and Aug; £560–£1,083 self-catering villa. Rates reflect seasonal differences and include breakfast. AE, DC, MC, V. Parking lot on-site. **Amenities:** 4 restaurants; nightclub, 4 bars; babysitting; children's center; concierge; *hamam;* health club and spa; free Internet in lobby; 3 outdoor and 1 indoor pool; room service; 2 night-lit tennis courts; extensive watersports equipment/rental. *In room:* A/C, satellite TV, hair dryer, minibar.

Rhapsody ★★ 🎁   Lazing amid cushions strewn on your own trellised sun deck is not a bad start to a Mediterranean holiday. This is your entryway into one of Kalkan's rare boutique experiences, one that replaces overused Mediterranean pastels with warm tones of lavender, sage, and powder blue, in a modern seaside interpretation of good taste. Double rooms have beech platform beds and sleek oversize headboards, but you may want to splurge for that terrace suite, which also comes with an outdoor Jacuzzi. The loft-style mezzanine suite comes in a close second, with two twin beds downstairs, separate living rooms, and Jacuzzis in the bedroom for when the kids fall asleep. The room rate includes breakfast, of course, as well as use of the Turkish bath and transfer to and from Dalaman Airport. Now that's entertainment.

Cumhuriyet Cad., Nilüfer Sok. 48, 07960 Kalkan. www.rhapsodyhotel.com. ℂ**0242/844-1444.** Fax 0242/844-2575. 30 units. £65 double; £45–£120 suite. MC, V. **Amenities:** Restaurant; bar; *hamam;* Jacuzzi; outdoor pool; sauna. *In room:* AC, TV, minibar, free Wi-Fi.

Türk Evi ★ 🎁   The owners of this warm and inviting guesthouse, a Turkish and Norwegian team, have created a homey atmosphere, down to the fresh farmer's butter and homemade jams. The open, farmhouse-style living room, dining room, and kitchen area provide an inviting place for guests to come together for meals, and an outdoor patio is used for family-style meals made with the freshest ingredients prepared on the outdoor barbecue (meals are for guests only). Each simple but charmingly decorated room is named after its color (the pink rooms are the ones with bathtubs), and the adjacent blue rooms provide a connecting balcony for families or friends traveling together. Nestled at the top of town in a woodsy setting, it's a bit of a steep climb up, so you may arrive back up from the waterfront a bit winded. Make sure you're in one of the five rooms with air-conditioning in summer, to cool you off.

07960 Kalkan (behind the post office near the town center). www.kalkanturkevi.com. ℭ **0242/844-3129.** Fax 0242/844-3492. 9 units (2 with tub, 7 with shower). 30€–40€ double full board. No credit cards. Parking near main road. Turn off the Kaş road into town, the entrance to the guesthouse is on the road into Kalkan immediately on the left. **Amenities:** Restaurant (for guests). *In room:* No phone.

Villa Mahal ★★ 🄾 Having already been recognized by international style magazines, the Villa Mahal could easily be called the Jewel of the Mediterranean. The large property sits in the middle of an olive grove on a steep bluff overlooking Kalkan Bay and is secluded enough that nothing man-made tarnishes the view. The actual building area takes up very little of the grounds, so the brush along the cliff side provides a good level of privacy. Hotel rooms are at the top of the bluff overlooking the sea, but at 202 steps, it's a long walk down to the waterside and much longer on the way up under the fierce heat. Waterside platforms form the "beach" where there is an array of watersports and an airy and stylish seaside cafe. Villa Mahal has a very special "honeymoon suite," a chillingly romantic secluded circular building with glass walls and its very own private terrace pool overlooking the bay. A complementary water shuttle runs from the platform to Kalkan's marina every 15 minutes in high season or on request.

P.K. 4, 07960 Kalkan. www.villamahal.com. ℭ **0242/844-3268.** Fax 0242/844-2122. 14 units. From £150 double in August. Rates lower Apr–May and Oct. MC, V. Closed Nov–Mar. Take the turn off the main road for Patara Club and follow signs for Villa Mahal. **Amenities:** Restaurant; 2 bars; concierge; free Internet; room service. *In room:* A/C, hair dryer, minibar.

KAŞ ★★

108km (67 miles) southeast of Fethiye; 198km (123 miles) southwest of Antalya; 25km (16 miles) east of Kalkan; 156km (97 miles) southeast of Dalaman Airport

With only 25km (16 miles) separating Kaş from Kalkan, these neighboring towns share the same stunning and broken rocky coastline, so whether you base yourself in one or the other depends on your individual character and travel style. (Keep in mind that tours run by an outfitter based in one routinely involve pickups in the other, so be sure to check out the offerings in the previous section.) Kaş established itself as the more popular of the two in the 1960s and 1970s, first as a hippie hangout, and later as a stopping point for yachts and gulets on the Blue Voyage. Over the decades, the towns-proper of Kalkan and Kaş have developed their own individual character. Whereas Kalkan is contained and insular, Kaş unravels itself into the surrounding landscape. If you choose Kalkan, you'll want to stay in the village center whereas in Kaş, you'll probably opt for a secluded outpost along the peninsula. What both share are narrow cobbled streets shadowed by the protruding balconies of the typical Ottoman houses, the DNA of antiquity, proximity to ancient and traditional places, and a front-row seat to Turkey's most breathtaking mountain and Mediterranean scenery.

In spite of its success as Turkey's second Mediterranean city, Kaş still retains a certain small-town charm. The town is built around the sparse remains of ancient **Antiphellos,** which left behind a few scattered rock tombs, a Greek theater, and an unanticipated **monumental sarcophagus** featuring four lions' heads at the upper end of one of Kaş's narrow shopping streets.

As the definition of a beach resort goes, Kaş falls somewhat short in that it lacks a proper beach. But it makes up for this with rocky terraces over crystal-clear Mediterranean waters both in town and along the peninsula. Kaş (as is Kalkan) is also an optimal jumping-off point for trips to Kekova, Myra, and some of the regions' best undiscovered mountain villages. The abundance of outdoorsy activities around Kaş has also helped to maintain its reputation as a relaxed, satisfying, and generally inexpensive holiday destination, and in the past few years, it's also developed into quite the family destination.

Essentials

GETTING THERE

Because of the proximity between Kaş and Kalkan, a selection of long-distance buses serves one, the other, or both. **Pamukkale** (𝄞 **444-3535;** 12 hr., 75TL) leaves from Izmir (8 hr., 43TL) twice daily at 12:30 and at 11pm. **Kamıl Koç** (𝄞 **444-0562**) serves the long-distance routes from Istanbul, Ankara, and locally, from Ortaca and Dalaman.

Batı Antalya Tur (www.batiantalyatur.com.tr) minibuses leave regularly from Fethiye through Kalkan and on to Kaş on its way through to Antalya (1½ hr., 13TL). The ride by minibus from Antalya takes as little as 3¼ hours (20TL) if you leave early in the morning, longer during the day or when traffic is heavier. Kalkan is about a half-hour away via local *dolmuş* (5TL).

All the hotels and travel agents offer the service of airport transfers. Expect to pay £55 from Dalaman airport and slightly more for Antalya.

VISITOR INFORMATION

The **tourist information office** is located on Cumhuriyet Meydanı 5 (𝄞 **0242/836-1238**). The number for the *otogar* is 𝄞 **0242/836-1020.** Friday is market day. For online information, go to the town's site at **www.kas.gov.tr**.

ORIENTATION

The *otogar* is at the north end of town. If you were arriving by way of the Fethiye road, then you will have passed the new marina, protected within the bosom of the *Çukurbağ Yarımadası* or "half island," meaning peninsula. The marina is the third largest on the Turkish Mediterranean, a veritable playground featuring a restaurant, boutique hotel, shops, and a yacht club with a swimming pool and beach.

From the *otogar*, the sloping street down to the town center, the harbor, and the old marina is called **Atatürk Caddesi.** West of the marina (turn right before the marina at the minuscule roundabout) are the ruins of Antiphellos and the well-preserved antique theater. This road makes the circuit of the Çukurbağ Peninsula and then dumps you back onto the road into town.

In the opposite direction, up the hill past the marina to the east is **Hükümet Caddesi,** which leads to Küçükçakıl and Büyükçakı beaches.

From **Cumhuriyet Meydanı** at the harbor, the street that heads north, **Ibrahim Serin Caddesi,** is lined with shops, cafes, and bars. There are several travel agencies along this street, and the post office and banks are at the end of the commercial stretch. East of **Ibrahim Serin Caddesi** are beautiful craft and jewelry boutiques in converted traditional old wooden houses. A lone **Lycian sarcophagus** towers above the end of Uzun Çarşı Caddesi. Rock tombs are located high above town, obscured by the increased building at the top of the hill.

GETTING AROUND

Few places in Kaş are more than a 10-minute walk away, but if your accommodations are on the peninsula, you'll have to rely on a hotel transfer to get you there, because there is no minibus service, and taxi fares are uncommonly high. To get out of town to the sites mentioned in this section (or even to the new marina), you'll need to use one of the following modes of transport.

BY BUS & DOLMUŞ   Minibuses make the peninsula loop regularly in summer. There is also service that runs regularly between Kaş to Kalkan (5TL, daily service 8:30am–8:30 or 9pm), which you can take for day trips to Kaputaş Beach, as well as to many of the surrounding sights.

BY TAXI   There are three taxi stands in town: Liman Taksi (*©* **0242/836-1489**), Kaş Taksi (next to the central mosque; *©* **0242/836-1933**), and Çakıl Taksi (*© **0242/836-2448***). If you're thinking of hiring one for day excursions, fares are posted outside the taxi stands, but in many cases, local travel agencies will provide more comfortable, air-conditioned cars or vans for lower prices than the taxi fare.

BY BOAT   Occasionally there is water-taxi service from Kaş to Üçağız (3 hr. by boat), from there you can then hire a boat to explore Kekova. Check with the tourist information office to find out if it's in operation when you get there, but you may prefer to drive to Üçağız for the freedom to stop along the way. If you prefer to get around independently and you know how to haggle effectively, head down to the harbor at any port village and see whether you can hire a boat yourself for a reasonable fee.

BY CAR   With everything within walking distance, you'll need a car only to go exploring out of town. You're out of luck if you expected to earn points with Avis, Hertz, National, or Europcar; only local companies rent cars in Kaş. As a consolation for lost frequent-flier miles, the rates will be lower.

What to See & Do

From Kaş to Demre, archaeologists have discovered the remains of no fewer than 17 ancient Lycian sites, some of which remain interred and unidentified. These include **Teimiussa** (at the village port of Üçağız), **Simena,** and the nearby and less visited **Apollonia** and **Aperlai, Andriake,** and **Myra**. If you want to venture up where the air is a bit cooler, the site of **Arykanda,** up in the mountains, will offer you a glimpse of how the heady, pre-mortgage-crisis days of antiquity may have looked to a society with very, very extravagant tastes. You could just as easily backtrack to the archaeological sites of the **Xanthos Valley** (see "Kalkan," earlier in this chapter for details), to the west of Kalkan.

The surrounding protected bays, islands, and bleached coral cliffs provide some of the best opportunities for sun-and-fun boat trips to the sunken city of **Kekova Bay,** or simple days lolling around the deck of a fishing boat or gulet. Travel agencies hoping to grab a piece of the tourist pie line the marina and tout day excursions to the area attractions at very competitive rates. **Bougainville Travel,** at Çukurbağlı Caddesi, the continuation of Ibrahim Serin Caddesi (*© **0242/836-3737;*** www.bougainville-turkey.com), a local English-speaking, British/Turkish/Dutch partnership, is a full-service travel agency and the most well-equipped outfitter for adventure travel and outdoor pursuits on the Mediterranean. Sea-kayaking trips to Kekova cost around 30€. Bougainville recently added mountain-biking tours, diving, and canyoning excursions into the Saklıkent or Kibris canyons to their regular offerings of sea kayaking, white-water rafting, hiking, and jeep safari trips as well as the full suite of travel services such as airport transfers, hotel reservations, and other basics.

BOAT TRIPS TO THE SUNKEN CITY

The region of and around **Kekova** ★★★ offers a view into an unspoiled world of picturesque fishing villages and mysterious archaeological sites that long ago succumbed to burial at sea. The most visible examples of a long-gone sunken civilization lie along the northern coast of Kekova island, submerged beneath the transparent waters of **Kekova Bay.** Glass-bottom boats allow you to see fleeting details of buried amphorae or other artifacts, but the most impressive relics are the city walls and private homes visible just beneath the waterline. Swimming and snorkeling here are prohibited to preserve the location against random disappearances of archaeological findings, and it is still a mystery as to what all these walls, terraces, and pottery shards represent.

In their haste to get on a boat, many people overlook **Üçağız** ★, a perfect example of a sleepy fishing town, with a cluster of truly remarkable **Lycian tombs** ★★ woven into the fabric of life at the far end of the village (some visible by sea). For now, Üçağız is only home to a couple of well-worn pensions, but the village has already begun to show signs of metamorphosis with the completion of the new mooring jetty, so if you want a taste of the Turkey that will eventually be lost forever, you may want to consider bedding down here.

Visits also tend to ignore the ancient sites of **Aperlai and Apollonia,** located west of Üçağız on the mainland and accessible by boat from the sea via the Akar Pass, the effort required to get there has ensured the preservation of another "sunken city," and you can plan some time on land to explore the ruins on foot.

If you're traveling independently, you may want to arrive in Üçağız by 9 or 10am, in order to negotiate the best deals with the local fishermen for a day out on their private boat. In high season and no longer pegging their rates to a sagging dollar, boatmen are now asking for—and getting—hefty amounts of cash for a day out. Plan to arrive in either Kaleköy (ancient Simena) or Aperlai by lunchtime for a scenic, relaxing, and simply marvelous meal of fresh fish practically with your feet in the water. Late sleepers have the option of arriving in Üçağız around lunchtime, grabbing a bite at one of the waterfront restaurants, then hopping on a boat for the latter part of the day. Excursions around Kekova Bay (including to Kaleköy and Aperlai) must be negotiated with the local boatmen, based on a half-day rental. If you're planning on staying overnight, enlist your pension owner in getting transport.

Check to see if the day boat out of the marina is operating (see "Getting Around," above). Otherwise, every travel agent in town offers trips to Kekova, lunch and transfers to Üçağız included. Boats depart out of Üçağız for Kekova Island in the morning, touring the bays and islands with stops for swimming and snorkeling and exploration of some area caves. Tours usually include a stopover at the untouched village of Kaleköy for a hike up the hill to the medieval Byzantine fortress of the Knights of St. John (entrance 8TL; open daily Apr–Oct 9am–7pm and Nov–Mar 8am–5pm) and a close-up of a row of sarcophagi, as well as idyllic views of the islands and bays. Sadly, these tours don't allow time for much more than that, making an all-too-hasty exit off this seaside village.

AREA BEACHES

At the end of the day in Kaş, you can collapse on a lounge at one of the cliff-side "beaches" to the southeast of town, where you're only a coral stone's throw away from a dip in some of the bluest and unspoiled waters this close to a major town. Küçükçakıl Beach ("small pebble beach") sits to the east of the marina, protected by an outcropping of rocks upon which a number of private establishments (mostly the hotels that front the coastline) provide beach lounges and umbrellas. The rocky coast forms a small inlet, into which crazy local kids dive off the low craggy rocks. Farther out about 800m (½ mile) is Büyükçakıl, or "large pebble," Beach, a small but amazing stretch of waterfront embraced and protected on three sides by low hills covered in

It's almost impossible for a fishing village to retain its innocence, but the first time I visited, time seemed to have come to a complete standstill in Simena ★. Recently, though, and in spite of its limited access, this pastoral spot has succumbed to the onward march of commercialism. Still, there's nothing like a stroll through someone's chickens and a waterside meal of grilled fish caught hours earlier to wash away those capitalist blues. Although as an independent side trip it will take a little effort on your part to get to Simena (car to Üçağız, boat to Simena [the modern village name is Kale]), the reward will be a magical setting far removed from the modern world. There are no roads, only worn dirt paths amid the cluster of modest houses that dot the hillside. Several fish restaurants line the jetties, with comparatively excellent feasts of the freshest fish and the best location from which to stare transfixed at the one solitary stone sarcophagus poking its Gothic cap out of the bay.

Mediterranean brush. The beach is free and informal, but there are one or two basic facilities for showering and such, as well as lounge chairs for rent and a snack bar.

There's also the bay of **Limangazı** located on the other side of the bay and accessible only by boat. Ask a local fisherman or boat captain how much he's asking to take you there (and hopefully, back).

STAYING ACTIVE

SCUBA DIVING ADVENTURE TOUR Rated among the top 50 dive sites in the world, the waters off Kaş have some of the best visibility in the Mediterranean and a wide variety of sea life. Sponge divers have been navigating these reefs for decades, and it was along the coast of Ulu Burun that a 14th-century-B.C. merchant shipwreck was discovered, now displayed in the Bodrum Underwater Archaeology Museum (p. 272). There are also several underwater caverns, of which the Mavi, near Kaputaş Beach, is most famous. Several dive outfitters with certified dive masters provide a gateway to the reefs, caves, and shipwrecks (there's even a plane wreck) for around 40€. **Bougainville Travel** (see "What to See & Do," above) and **Barakuda Diving Center,** Iskele Caddesi Liman Sok, (📞 **0242/836-2996;** www.barakuda-kas.de), are two of the more established agencies, while the combined team of Hakan and Ilico at **Sirena Diving Center** at Doğruyol Cad. 35 (📞 **0242/836-3995;** www.sirenadive.com) has logged a combined 13,000 dives. All three offer much the same choices, while Barakuda also does wreck, deep-sea, technical, and nitrox dives. All can accommodate nondivers on their boats.

SEA KAYAKING ADVENTURE TOUR Sea kayaking offers a low-impact opportunity to experience the magical waters of the Gulf of Kekova, past partially submerged sarcophagi and over the sunken cities. The prohibition of swimming in the waters over these archaeological sites makes this sport a superb way to enjoy unhurried close-ups of the mysterious city walls, although admittedly, you'll need some imagination to visualize those vague underwater shadows. A kayak also allows you to navigate where large craft dare not go. The day trip (30€) is low-impact in either single or tandem kayaks, and sets off (after transferring from Kalkan and Kaş) from the docks at Üçağız. For information, contact **Bougainville Travel** (see "What to See & Do," above).

Where to Eat

At last count, Kaş was host to 75 restaurants, cafes, bars, and patisseries—but with the competition so steep, it's difficult to predict which ones will make it to next year. Below is a short list. Meanwhile, some of the best meals in Kaş are prepared at your little hotel. Hotels and pensions that accept dinner reservations from nonguests are **Otel Çapa,** Çukurbağ Yarımadası (✆ **0242/836-3190**), offering a four- or five-course meal with table service, and the **Diva Residence Hotel,** Çukurbağ Yarımadası (✆ **0242/836-4255**). Expect to pay 25TL to 50TL per person, particularly if you are ordering fish and drinking wine.

Bahçe and Bahçe Fish ★★ TURKISH These two lovely gardens serve an abundant and traditional array of seafood and kebaps. The original Bahçe is famous for its mezes, while the newly opened annex across the road serves seriously good fish (and mezes, of course). Ask your waiter what's in season. The meze cases overflow with cold appetizers, such as stuffed mushrooms, vegetable pancakes, fish cakes, and *dolmalar*—flavorful stuffed grape leaves and stuffed peppers worthy of a meal in themselves, making either of these dining options a welcome alternative for vegetarians.

Anıt Mezar Karşısı 31 and Ilkokul Sok. Across from the monumental Lycian Tomb. ✆ **0242/836-2370.** Reservations suggested. Appetizers and main courses 6TL–24TL and up for fish. MC, V. Daily noon–midnight. Closed Nov–Mar.

Bi Lokma/Mama's Kitchen ◆ HOMESTYLE TURKISH The Turkish fare prepared at this little eatery is a popular draw for local diving instructors, hungry for the taste of Mama Banu's (and daughter) cooking. Particularly great are the *börek,* available in both meat and vegetarian versions. The *mantı* also comes in a meat and veggie version, and oh, the moussaka. The kitchen is open all day, but in high season at dinnertime, people are turned away at the door, so best to call ahead.

Hükümet Cad. 2 (on the road above the marina). www.bilokma.com.tr. ✆ **0242/836-3942.** Dinner reservations suggested. Appetizers and main courses 5TL–27TL for fish. MC, V. Daily 8:30am–10pm.

Mercan TURKISH This friendly and popular waterside restaurant also happens to be the oldest show in town; it dates back to 1956, when the owner's father did the cooking. Fish and meat dishes are staples on the traditional Turkish menu, but Mustafa (the son) has added his own special touch, creating fragrant dishes using local herbs. The Mercan Special—a split roast lamb marinated in wine and spices—is a tender and rare treat. Try the grilled swordfish kebap for a lighter, but no less filling or fulfilling, meal.

Cumhuriyet Meydanı on the marina. ✆ **0242/836-1209.** Reservations suggested. Appetizers and main courses 6TL–32TL and up for fish. MC, V. Daily 9am–1am.

Kaş After Dark

Kaş takes on the glow of numerous golden lights strung throughout numerous gardens and candlelight flickering from many of the town's nooks and crannies. Keep in mind that the bars and cafes listed below are mostly closed in winter.

Café Merhaba Catering to an international crowd, Café Merhaba is an atmospheric and cozy spot that would be inconspicuous in, say, SoHo. In Kaş, it stands out like a sore thumb, with its collection of international newspapers and magazines, in addition to the new and used paperbacks on sale. Their apple cake gets raves. Daily 8am to 1am. Closed in winter. Ibrahim Serin Cad. ✆ **0242/836-1883.**

Echo Bar 📷 For a real, and pleasant disconnect, Echo has brought the soothing sounds of jazz all the way from the Bayou to a centuries-old caravansaray on the Mediterranean coast. The venue has caught on and attracts some of the best names in Turkish jazz through a set, summer calendar. May through October, daily 5pm to 3am. Zümrüt Sok. 3 (the street next to Bougainville Travel). ℂ **0242/836-2047.**

Sun Café Located across from Mercan near the marina, Sun Café is a must-do if only to toss back a drink or have a full meal next to the Lycian rock tomb at the back. The restaurant/bar is in a pavilion-type building close to the entrance, where the team of dashing, long-haired owners keep the drinks poured and the music subtle with on-and-off jazz nights. Daily 11am to 2am; closed in winter. Hükümet Cad. 3. ℂ **0242/836-1053.**

Where to Stay

True escapists of civilization have the option of lodging out on the Çukurbağ Peninsula (by car, enter Kaş's main road and turn right at the small roundabout right before the marina; all destinations on the loop road are under 5km/3 miles away), a sparsely populated collection of steep cliffs and terraced access to unspoiled waters. (Most of these hotels have been snapped up and blocked out by British-based tour operators, leaving but a handful of options for the independent traveler.) The other option is to hole up at the brand-spanking-new, and stunning and yet-to-be advertised hotel over at the marina (www.kasmarina.com.tr). (But without a car, it's undeniably more convenient to be located in the town center.

IN TOWN

Gardenia Hotel Rooms are unusually large at the Gardenia compared to other hotels in Kaş and enjoy the added benefit of stunning views of the Greek island of Meis. All have glass-front balconies so as to optimize the view. Actually, glass seems to be a running theme here; a chunky glass bathroom sink and console keep the bathroom both fresh-looking and designer cool. Opt for the slight added cost of a front room with a view, or splurge for the suite, as it comes with its very own Jacuzzi. Breakfast and dinner are available to guests on the dining terrace.

Hükümet Cad. 47, Küçükçakıl Mevkii, 07580 Kaş. www.gardeniahotel-kas.com. ℂ **0242/836-2368.** Fax 0242/836-2891. 11 units. 95€–123€ double; 161€ suite. MC, V. Closed Dec–Apr. *In room:* A/C, satellite TV, hair dryer, minibar, free Wi-Fi.

Medusa Hotel From the outside, this hotel is almost indistinguishable from the other cliff-top pensions lined up above Küçükçakıl Beach. But even though this was the first hotel to set up shop on this stretch of the beach it stays current with regular yearly renovations, in contrast to its neighbors. Like all of the hotels lining the shoreline at this end of Kaş's center, the reception is located up a long stone stairway, up past the level of the pool and restaurant. This positioning provides each of the rooms with a balcony and at least a partial sea view; reserve early and get a full view. Suites get the addition of a minibar and satellite TV. There's an on-site restaurant, and the hotel offers the option of half-board from a buffet.

Küçükçakıl Mevkii, 07580 Kaş. www.medusahotels.com. ℂ **0242/836-1440.** Fax 0242/836-1441. 40 units. July–Sept 70€ double, 115€ suite. Rates are for July–Sept. MC, V. Street parking. Closed Nov–Mar. **Amenities:** Restaurant; 2 bars; outdoor pool. *In room:* A/C.

ÇUKURBAĞ PENINSULA

Barbarossa ★★ 🏨 Add to the paradise of the Çukurbağ Peninsula this stunningly sited little Mediterranean hideaway. The large rooms are both sparsely

ANCIENT MYRA AND (JOLLY, OLD) st. nicholas

The town of Demre plays modern-day host to the ancient city of Myra, once home to a 4th-century bishop making his rounds in 105°F (41°C) weather with not a mammal with antlers in sight. But somewhere during the 1,650 years that followed, several national folklores got mixed up, and legends merged that would elevate old St. Nicholas, the bishop of Myra, to the jolly international hero he is today. As bishop of Myra, St. Nicholas earned himself a reputation of benevolence and good deeds by saving poor village girls from the fate of prostitution by dropping their dowries down the chimney. According to legend, he also rescued several village boys from the clutches of a serial killer disposed to pickling his victims in brine—but that shocking piece of history ruins the feel-good vibe altogether. The legends accumulate, and the tour groups and pilgrims alike flock here to visit the ancient site and the Church of St. Nicholas, renamed by the Turkish authorities as **Noel Baba Museum** ★ (Müze Cad., 🕿 **0242/871-6820;** www.antalyamuzesi.gov.tr; admission 10TL; daily Apr–Oct 9am–7pm; Nov–Mar 8:30am–5:30pm).

The name change was controversial, and seen by followers of Orthodox Christianity as a way for the Turkish authorities to circumvent the celebration of the Mass at the church on St. Nicholas Day, December 6, which is currently not allowed. Another issue under the radar is the evolution of the statue welcoming visitors into Demre: The original bronze sculpture (now in the garden) was replaced in 2000 by a new bronze statue atop a colorful globe. Then in 2005, a preposterous Bakelite form of Santa Claus was installed on the site and was then replaced in 2008 by the present-day fiberglass and iron image that doesn't look like St. Nicholas OR Santa Claus. Sigh.

Also interesting is the fact that Old St. Nick isn't even buried here. In 1087, hoping to redirect the flow of pilgrims back to their home, Italian merchants from Bari raided St. Nicholas's sarcophagus and transported the remains back to Italy. In their haste to get out with the goods, apparently the Barians left a few bones behind, and in 1925 the Turkish authorities were presented with a reliquary containing what was claimed to be the missing parts. Although carbon dating of the remains has proven that the bones date to the correct century, nobody knows if these are actually the

furnished and cozy, with homey yet elegant decorative touches throughout. And each room gets a front-row seat of the deep, and crystal clear, aquamarine sea, backed by the Toros Mountains. Families can also be accommodated in the villa, which rents by the week.

Çukurbağ Yarımadası on the Çukurbağ Peninsula, Ibrahim Cingay Sok., 07580 Kaş. www.hotelbar barossa.com. 🕿 **0242/836-4071.** Fax 0242/836-4084. 26 units. July–Aug 85€–150€ doubles and suites. Rates are for half board; add 15€ for full board. Rates lower off-season. MC, V. Free parking. **Amenities:** Restaurant; bars; rock terrace beach; free Internet; outdoor pool. *In room:* A/C, satellite TV, hair dryer, minibar, free Wi-Fi.

Diva Residence Hotel ★★ ☺ Big stone fireplaces, unobstructed views of the Greek island of Meis, fresh, home-cooked meals. That's what you'll find at the Diva, an all-suite hotel owned and operated by a husband-and-wife team transplanted from Istanbul. Nine of the suites are spacious one-bedrooms, and the two-bedroom units can accommodate a family of four. Both types have living rooms and balconies, while most (but not all) look out over an uncannily stunning view of the sea. Meals in the bones of St. Nicholas, or where the poor guy is buried for sure. The Russians claim to have a piece of him, as does the Antalya Museum.

Unexpected is the **necropolis of Myra** ★★★ (2.4km/1½ miles north of Müze Cad., off Alakent Cad., ℂ **0242/871-6821;** www.antalyamuzesi. gov.tr; admission 10TL; daily Apr–Oct 9am–7pm; Nov–Mar 8:30am–5pm), located above the ancient site and hewn into the rock like a high-rise apartment complex for the dead. This collection of rock-cut Lycian tombs is one of the best-preserved and finest examples of its kind, as pale shades of fading pigment can still be made out against the fine details of the bas-reliefs. The Roman theater, carved into the face of the mountain Greek-style, dates to 141 when it was rebuilt following an earthquake. The two vaults may have been added at this time for additional support against future tremors.

About 4km (2½ miles) to the west of the center is the ancient harbor port of Andriake straddled by the sleepy fishing port and working boatyard of Çayağzı Beach. The main historical structure is Hadrian's Granary, built on the orders of the emperor as storage for grain prior to its delivery to Rome. The site includes a Roman bath supplied by a freshwater spring, and the remains of what was probably a basilica. In 2009, archaeologists uncovered a Jewish temple (identifiable by an inscription of a menorah), the first such finding on Lycian soil indicating that Jews were an integral part of Lycian culture. There are a few fish stands and one restaurant from which you can enjoy wonderful sea and river views, or watch the local fishermen repair their boats.

Demre lies on the road that passes by the Gulf of Finike on its way around the coastline from Antalya. Batı Antalya Tur (in Demre, ℂ **0242/871-2159;** www. batiantalyatur.com.tr) minibuses and *dolmuşes* connect with Demre from Fethiye (3 hr., 18TL), Kaş (40 min., 4TL), and Finike (20–30 min., 4TL) several times a day. There's also a daily connection to Üçağız, if you're headed to or from Kekova Island. Daily bus service is frequent in summer months, allowing for the spontaneity of simply showing up at the *dolmuş* stand (usually in the town center) when you're ready to go. If you're going by car, be aware that Demre also goes by the name of Kale, so keep your eyes peeled for either road sign.

restaurant are served buffet style, but the kitchen will prepare special meals, including vegetarian ones, to complement the selection on the a la carte menu.

Çukurbağ Yarımadası on the Çukurbağ Peninsula, Ibrahim Cingay Sok., 07580 Kaş. www.divakas. com. ℂ **0242/836-4255.** Fax 0242/836-2509. 11 units. July–Aug 110€ double, 170€ family of 4. Rates lower off-season. MC, V. Free parking. Closed Nov–Apr. **Amenities:** Restaurant; 3 bars; rock terrace beach; free Internet; outdoor pool. *In room:* A/C, hair dryer, minibar.

Otel Çapa ★★ 🎁 This hotel overlooks the Mediterranean from the rocky coast on the north side of the peninsula, in a serene and relaxing seafront setting enclosed in jasmine, bougainvillea, and olive and lemon trees. The grounds are terraced down toward the seafront patio, past a shaded hammock, a postcard-perfect saltwater free-form pool, a snack bar, and a fragrant thicket of low Mediterranean brush. The painted pink main building, swimming pool, rooms, and cozy open-air bar salon sit at the top.

Each room enjoys its very own balcony or terrace overlooking the pool area to the sea, keeping it breezy, light, and airy. Rooms, and bathrooms especially, are a bit on the smallish side, but the staff makes you feel like the entire property is all yours, and the result is anything but cramped. If you ever decide to leave the property, the hotel offers a choice of activities, from boat trips to Kekova, watersports, and fishing trips. Çukurbağ Yarımadası on the Çukurbağ Peninsula, 07580 Kaş. www.clubcapa.com. © **0242/836-3190.** Fax 0242/836-3192. 22 units. $150–$200 double. MC, V. Closed Nov–Mar. **Amenities:** Restaurant; 4 bars; rock terrace beach; bikes; 2 pools (1 saltwater); room service; watersports equipment/rental. *In room:* A/C.

ANTALYA ★★

725km (450 miles) south of Istanbul; 467km (290 miles) southeast of Izmir; 298km (185 miles) northeast of Fethiye; 435km (270 miles) east of Marmaris; 634km (394 miles) southwest of Nevşehir

The sun-kissed Gulf of Antalya, with its outstretched arms that embrace an extended string of resorts, is home to seaside towns well outside of the region's capital of Antalya, as far as the rocky shoreline of Kaş to the west (earlier in this chapter) and the sandy stretches of Alanya to the east. The city itself is built on a rocky travertine plateau, formed by natural springs running down the Toros Mountains and surging off the cliffs, with the constant breathtaking silhouette of peaks and snowcaps in the distance. The city's **Archaeological Museum** is custodian to an incredible collection of *richesse* of antiquity collected in excavations at the nearby open-air museums of **Termessos, Aspendos,** and **Perge,** the latter two among the cities on the Anatolian Mediterranean that witnessed the arrival of St. Paul. As for **action:** Antalya has rocky mountains, gushing waterfalls, soaring canyons, and lush gardens, perfect for biking, hiking, cycling, canyoning, rafting, wreck diving, golfing, and even skiing—all just a stone's throw away from your poolside perch. At the city's center is the historic quarter of **Kaleiçi,** a cobbled quarter backed by Roman and pre-Roman ruins and Byzantine ramparts guarding the harbor, a living museum of the area's former Ottoman grandeur. The neighborhood began to undergo a transformation from its former, dusty and neglected self and is now bejeweled with its original, restored timber-framed manses embracing fragrant garden courtyards. A renaissance has also taken root to the west of the historic city center over at **Konyaaltı,** an expansive pebbly strip of prime beachfront backed by a meandering, grassy promenade and "Beach Park," stocked full of diversions such as an aquarium, a children's playground, a paintball area, restaurants, cafes, and shops. It's this winning combination of sun, fun, cultural richness, and a conveniently located state-of-the-art international airport that has made Antalya the focal point of the Turkish Mediterranean.

Essentials

GETTING THERE

BY PLANE As the gateway to the "Turkish Riviera," Antalya's international airport is a destination for visitors on both direct and connecting flights from dozens and dozens of cities worldwide. In 2007, the city completed a second international terminal to accommodate the continued tourist growth of the region as a whole. **Turkish Airlines** (© **444-0849** or 0242/320-6363 at the airport; www.thy.com) flies direct from London (Gatwick) to Antalya. **Pegasus Airlines** (www.flypgs.com) and **Sun-Express** (© **0232/444-0797** in Turkey; www.sunexpress.com.tr) soon followed suit, flying from London's Stansted Airport (summers only). The U.K.-based charter airlines **Thomas Cook** (www.thomascookairlines.co.uk) and **Thomson Airways** (www.thomson.co.uk) fly year round from London Gatwick direct to Antalya, as does **EasyJet** (www.easyjet.com). Check with your travel agent to see about other charter

Antalya

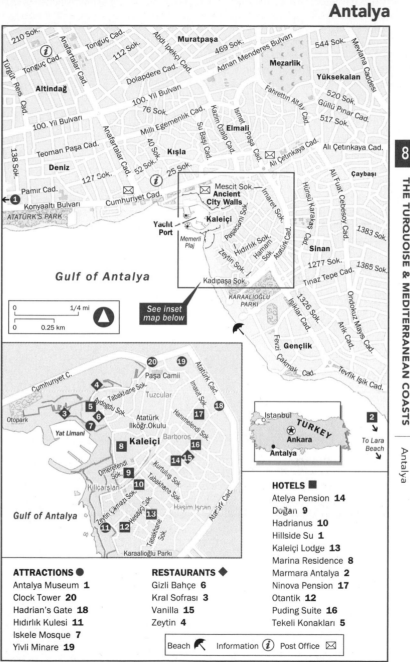

ATTRACTIONS ●
Antalya Museum **1**
Clock Tower **20**
Hadrian's Gate **18**
Hıdırlık Kulesi **11**
Iskele Mosque **7**
Yivli Minare **19**

RESTAURANTS ◆
Gizli Bahçe **6**
Kral Sofrası **3**
Vanilla **15**
Zeytin **4**

HOTELS ■
Atelya Pension **14**
Doğan **9**
Hadrianus **10**
Hillside Su **1**
Kaleiçi Lodge **13**
Marina Residence **8**
Marmara Antalya **2**
Ninova Pension **17**
Otantik **12**
Puding Suite **16**
Tekeli Konakları **5**

Beach 🏖 Information ⓘ Post Office ✉

flights on offer during the summer months or log onto the airport website for information on airlines flying into the region (www.aytairport.com).

Direct domestic service into Antalya from Istanbul's Atatürk Airport is provided by **Turkish Airlines** (© **444-0849**), **Onur Air** (© **0242/330-3432** in Antalya, or 0212/663-9176 in Istanbul), and **Atlasjet** (© **0216/444-3387;** www.atlasjet.com). **Pegasus, AnadoluJet** and **SunExpress** fly from Istanbul's Sabiha Gökçen Airport, while SunExpress connects Antalya with Izmir and Bodrum. AnadoluJet also flies from Ankara.

The airport is about 11km (6¾ miles) to the east of the city center on the main Antalya road/D400. If you're staying on Lara Beach, a taxi will be your best bet from the airport. If you're staying on Konyaaltı Beach, take the **Havaş** airport shuttle (© **444-0487** or 0242/330-3800; 10TL), which stops at the Falez Hotel (adjacent to the Rixos Hotel and near the museum) on its way to the *otogar*. From the drop-off point, you can get a taxi to your final destination. For those (with very little luggage) whose final destination is Kaleiçi, get off the Havaş bus at the Devlet Hastanesi (State Hospital). From there, it's but a few steps through the open-air plaza to Cumhuriyhet Caddesi and the Clock Tower at the edge of the maze of streets that make up the Old City. Havaş shuttle departures are scheduled to coincide with the arrival of domestic flights.

A taxi directly to/from the airport to the center of town costs around 40TL, more if your hotel is farther afield. Nighttime rates are about 50% higher (many cities in Turkey are abolishing this nighttime rate to address the unfortunate fleecing of tourists who can't read the gündüz-day and gece-night indicators on the meter). Hotels in Kaleiçi generally offer an airport transfer as an add-on to your reservation, charging around 15€ to 20€.

BY BUS   Antalya is a major transport hub, with 145 bus companies and 633 minibuses serving a total of 57 routes. The major bus lines serving Antalya with frequent service are Varan, Ulusöy, Kamıl Koç, Pamukkale, Uludağ, and Boss. Sample fares are: from Istanbul (12 hr., 60TL), Izmir (7–8 hr., 35TL), and Denizli (3–4½ hr., 20TL). For transport from the smaller towns along the coastline, you can hop on one of the frequent minibuses, Batı Antalya Tur is a good bet, arriving from Fethiye (21TL), Kalkan (15TL), Kaş (13TL), and Demre (11TL), to name just a few.

The dual-terminal **bus station** (© **0242/331-1250**) lies 4km (2½ miles) northwest of the town center on the highway to Burdur and is easily as user-friendly as the airport. A new light rail system can now transport you from the bus station to the center of town, a three-ride pass card will cost you 5TL. A taxi from the *otogar* to Kaleiçi will cost around 20TL to 25TL.

VISITOR INFORMATION

The **tourist information office** (© **0242/241-1747**) is about a 10-minute walk west of Kaleiçi down Cumhuriyet Caddesi, at Anafartalar Cad. 31. It's worth a visit for fliers and brochures on upcoming events. The online website of the Antalya Promotion Foundation is www.antalyaguide.org. They also operate a Tourism Call Center; simply dial © **179**.

ORIENTATION

The city of Antalya is built upon a limestone travertine formed from the springs that run down from the mountains, so that the city meets the sea by way of breathtaking cliffs. At the center is the cliff-top fortress neighborhood of **Kaleiçi,** full of elegant garden cafes and charming ramshackle eateries, all built atop pre-Roman, Roman, and Byzantine foundations. Kaleiçi, the hassling to get you to empty your wallet notwithstanding, is a charming area of restored Greek houses, Italian villas, and Ottoman Paşas' residences, some converted into guesthouses and hotels along narrow winding streets. At the base of the cliff is the harbor and marina, built over an ancient Roman harbor and now the center of the city's resort nightlife.

About a mile and a half to the west of Kaleiçi is **Konyaaltı★★**, the pebbly beach beginning just west of the archaeological museum and extending (so far) for about 8km (5 miles). Development will continue up to the port, an extension that will simply put the icing on an already successful and crazily popular city/seaside resort destination. By day, beach umbrellas and lounges backed by cafes and green lawns are filled with sun-seekers; by night, the waterfront park gets strewn with oversize colored cushions and romantic lighting, and restaurant tables spill onto the beach park walkway.

To the east of Antalya center just past the cliffs is **Lara Plajı**, a long stretch of pebbly beach that gives way to a long stretch of coarse sand coastline, and enough all-inclusive themed hotels (a replica of the Titanic, the Kremlin, and Venice, just to name a few) to earn the area the moniker "Las Vegas in Turkey." Only 11km (6¾ miles) from Antalya city center, it's still a bit of a stretch to recommend this beach, that is, unless combined with a jaunt to the Lower Düden Waterfalls.

Beyond the city limits, Antalya spreads out to the mountainous winding roads that meander along the Lycian Coast to the west, and to the all-inclusive resort hotels along the sandy beaches sprawled out to the east, past the haphazard, poured-concrete blocks typical of Turkish towns. Most archaeological sites and natural phenomena are within an hour of town.

GETTING AROUND

The primarily pedestrian area in and around the old town of Kaleiçi (including the harbor) is very compact, and you'll have very little need to venture far from here if this is where you're holing up for the night. The tourist information office is at the Cliffside park just on the western fringes of Kaleiçi, while the archaeological museum is about a 20-minute walk to the west of the city center, also accessible by tramway. From Kaleiçi to Konyaaltı, it's about a 15TL unavoidably meandering taxi ride; it'll be cheaper on the way back because the one-way main avenue is now working in your favor.

While it's theoretically possible to get to the sites of Aspendos, Perge and other area ancient cities, truth is that sometimes *dolmuşes* don't stop where they say they will and it's not worth all the stress and wasting of precious time trying to get it right. Best to join a tour offered by one of the plentiful local travel agencies or if your budget allows, rent a car for the day. (There may or may not be a fee to park at the open-air museums).

BY TRAM An 8km (5-mile) tramway runs parallel to the coastline from the Antalya Museum to the neighborhoods east of Kaleiçi. Running every half-hour, it is particularly convenient as a way to get between Kaleiçi and the museum, Atatürk Parkı, and Konyaaltı Beach. There's a hop-on point on Cumhuriyet Caddesi across from the clock tower in Kaleiçi, and the fare is 1.30TL.

BY CAR You don't really want or need to spend your energy sitting in traffic and making sense of the one-way circuitous route through the center of town, particularly since the old city of Kaleiçi is pedestrian only while the museum and Konyaaltı side of town is reachable by tram (1.20TL), and if you like to walk, by foot. But if you've based yourself in Antalya and want to take advantage of all the area has to offer, by all means, rent a car. All major hotels have either on-site car rental or a concierge to help fix you up. Car rental companies abound in Kaleiçi, so your biggest challenge will be one of choice. Sample rates for a Honda Civic automatic is 60TL per day, including full insurance.

BY TAXI Because Kaleiçi is a walking district, a taxi is mostly useful for getting back and forth between the marina/Kaleiçi and the museum (Konyaaltı Beach and the Hillside Su are near the museum on the west side of town). Hiring a taxi is also an (albeit expensive) option for those unable or unwilling to rent wheels for day-tripping out of the city, but be sure to bargain (you will also pay for gas) because quoted rates are exorbitant. I recommend a tour to your nearby attraction of choice, at least for the professional guidance and the camaraderie of your fellow visitors.

[FastFACTS] ANTALYA

Airlines   The local numbers for the main airlines are **Atlasjet** (© **850/222-0000** or 0242/330-3900), **SunExpress** (© **0232/444-0797** or **0242/310-2727**), **Onur Air** (© **0242/330-3488**), **Pegasus** (© **444-0737** or 0242/330-3548) and **Turkish Airlines** (© **0242/330-3230** or **444-0849**). Contact your airline for terminal location.

Airport   For information on departures and arrivals call your airline direct. For general airport information, the main number is © **0242/444-7423** (www.aytairport.com). For domestic flights, contact the domestic terminal (© **0242/330-3098**).

Ambulance   Call © **112.**

Buses   The main bus companies with a presence at Antalya's *otogar* are: **Antalya Finike Tur** (© 0242/331-1084), **Kamıl Koç** (© 0242/331-1170), **Metro** (© 444-3455 or 0242/331-1050), **Pamukkale** (© 0242/332-1020), **Ulusoy** (© 0242/331-1310), and **Varan** (© 0242/331-1111).

Car Rental   Major car rental companies with counters in the Domestic Terminal 1 are **Avis** (© **0242/330-3073;** also downtown at Fevzi Çakmak Cad. 30, in the Divan Talya Hotel across from the Rixos, © **0242/248-1772**), **Budget** (© **0242/330-3395**), **Europcar** (© **0242/330-3068**), Hertz (© **0242/330-3848**), and **National** (© **0242/330-3557**) and Europcar (© **0242/330-3061**) also have a presence in the International Terminal. If you're interested in booking with a local company, log on to the airport's website for a full list of providers (**www.aytport.com**).

Climate   Antalya has four seasons: fall, winter, spring, and hell, when temperatures soar to digits even the government won't accurately report. If you can at all avoid Antalya in August, do so.

Consulates   The **U.K.** maintains a Vice Consulate in Antalya. For contact details log on to **www.ukinturkey.fco.gov.uk**.

Hospitals   The Antalya Anatolia Private Hospital (www.anatoliahospital.com; © **0242/249-3300**) is at Çaybaşı Mah. Burhanettin Onat Cad. 1352 Sok. You will also encounter English-speaking staff at the international Interhospital Antalya at Kızıltoprak Mah., Meydan PTT Arkası (near the post office; © **0242/311-1500**).

Post Office   The main PTT is located at Anafartalar Caddesi, opposite the Turkish Airlines offices. It's open from 9am to 5pm for postal services and 24/7 for phone access.

What to See & Do
A LOOK AT THE PAST
Indigenous tribes were combating the scorching heat on the rocky coastline of Antalya since prehistoric times, until eventually the Hittites migrated off the harsh

Anatolian plains in search of a more gracious climate. The Hittites were succeeded by a number of independent city-states founded in the region, and today's province of Antalya covers Pamphylia and parts of Pisidya to the north, Cicilia to the east, and Lycia to the west.

Antalya officially enters the history books in the 2nd century B.C. when King Attalus II marched in to pick up the pieces of the territorial war that broke out after the death of Alexander the Great. The city was proclaimed Attaleia after the Pergamese king, later morphing into variations of Adalia, Satalia, Adalya, and Antalya by successive cultures. The city was handed over to Rome along with the rest of Pergamum, and one of the more important events in the history of the Roman city was the arrival of Emperor Hadrian, whose visit was honored with a grand monumental gate.

Sovereignty over the region passed from the Byzantines to the Selçuks and back again, and in 1103, the port became a valuable asset to the Crusaders, allowing them to avoid the treacherous overland journey from Palestine. The decline of Byzantine influence allowed the Selçuk Sultanate of Rum to annex the region around 1207 until Antalya was finally incorporated into the Ottoman Empire.

A MONUMENTAL MUSEUM

Antalya Museum (Antalya Müzesi) ★★★   MUSEUM   If you do only one cultural thing in Antalya, make it this. Antalya Province is endowed with one of the richest cultural heritages in Turkey, and much of it can be seen at this museum. More than 5,000 archaeological works are displayed in 13 thought-provoking exhibit halls. The **Prehistory section ★★★** includes an amazing collection of artifacts recovered from the Karain Cave at Burdur—the largest inhabited cave in Turkey, with findings dating back 50,000 years and representing the Paleolithic, Mesolithic, Neolithic, Chalcolithic, and Bronze ages. The **Gallery of the Gods ★★★** gives you the chance to walk among the protagonists of classic mythology, through grand statues of Zeus, Apollo, Athena, **Aphrodite ★**, and the like, followed by statues of the emperor/gods Hadrian and Trajan in the Roman Room. The **Sarcophagus Gallery ★★** is a rich exhibition of intricately carved tombs, one of which was considerately returned by the J. Paul Getty Museum, after having found its way out of the country. There are also small but important exhibitions featuring the **Byzantine period,** which houses a collection of **religious icons,** and the **Selçuk and Ottoman periods,** where you'll find ceramic artifacts, calligraphy, copper, carvings, and carpets. The Antalya Museum devotes an entire room to coins; the chronological display represents 2,500 years of Anatolian history. Considering that this is such a rich collection, it's positively mind-boggling to realize that 25,000 to 30,000 artifacts are buried in storage.

Konyaaltı Cad. No. 1. www.antalyamuzesi.gov.tr. (*℮*0242/238-5688. Admission 15TL. Tues–Sun Apr–Oct 9am–7pm; Nov–Mar 8am–5pm.

ANTALYA ATTRACTIONS

The most outstanding monument in Antalya is **Hadrian's Gate (Hadrian Kapısı) ★★**, halfway between Cumhuriyet Caddesi and 30 Ağustos Cad., built in honor of the emperor's visit to the city in A.D. 130. A classic example of a Roman triumphal arch, Hadrian's Gate is the only remaining entrance gate into the ancient city, and a great introduction to the neighborhood of Kaleiçi.

A few steps north following Imaret Sokağı is the **Yivli Minare ★**, built by the Selçuk Sultan Alaaeddin Keykubat in the 13th century. The fluted brick minaret stands a commanding 38m (125 ft.) high and has come to be the symbol of the city. The adjacent domed mosque (not the original) is an early example of Anatolian multidomed

With more than 2,500 books, Paul's Place (Yenıkapı Sok. 24, Kaleiçi; *(©) 0242/247-6857;* stpaulcc-turkey. com/pauls-place; open Mon–Fri 9am– 6pm), a cafe and reading room, is a cultural exchange adjunct of St. Paul Cultural Center (founded by an expat German pastor and his wife), encouraging cultural (Christian) and language exchange between English and Turkish speakers or those who love them. Grab a tome and detox out in the shady, stone-walled courtyard, or sink into one of the comfy settees and fill up on potent coffee and freshly baked goods.

mosques. A small and charming cluster of souvenir stands has sprouted up in the courtyard and is at least a refreshing break from the relentless touts on the street.

The **Clock Tower (Saat Kulesi)** ★ in nearby Kalekapısı Square rises above the outer reaches of Kaleiçi at Atatürk Caddesi and was once a part of the old city fortifications.

At the opposite end of the quarter of Kaleiçi and dominating the edges of the Karaoğlu Park cliffs, is the 2nd-century **Hıdırlık Kulesi** ★. Also known as the Red Tower, the Hıdırlık Kulesi offers unobstructed panoramas of the sea, suggesting its original use as a lighthouse.

At the bottom of the stone steps leading down from Memerli Sokağı to the harbor is the **Iskele Mosque,** a simple stone structure set on four pillars over a spring. Unfortunately, the description lends more appeal to the site than the actual thing, because careless visitors have been using the small pool as a garbage dump.

COASTAL CITIES OF ANTIQUITY

The Ancient City of Aspendos ★★ RUINS The city of Aspendos, commonly believed to have been settled by colonists from Argos, lies a few miles beyond Perge on the Antalya-Alanya highway. I suggest that you tackle both as a pair.

There's not much left of the ancient city, but the one remaining monument, the **Theatre of Aspendos** ★★★, is enough to warrant a trip. Thanks to the high-quality calcareous stone and the fact that the Selçuks reinforced the structure during its run as a caravansaray, this 2,000-year-old theater is the best-preserved ancient theater in Asia Minor and the best example of a Roman theater in all of Pamphylia. The best way to visit the theater is to see it as it was meant to be, during the national opera and ballet festival in the summer but it's an awesome sight without the show.

Belkıs Beldesi, Serik (Take the Antalya-Alanya hwy. east; watch for the turnoff to Aspendos on the left). www.antalyamuzesi.gov.tr. *(©) 0242/735-7337.* Admission 15TL. Daily Apr–Oct 9am–7pm; Nov–Mar 8am–5pm.

The Ancient City of Perge ★ RUINS Three thousand years away and 18km (11 miles) east of Antalya is the ancient Pamphylian settlement of **Perge.** A clay tablet discovered in the Hittite capital of Hattuşaş shows that Perge was originally settled around 1500 B.C. under the name of "Parha." St. Paul and Barnabas came to Perge on their first missionary journey, but St. Paul preached here only upon his return from Pisidia.

The ancient city's ruins were damaged in the early 1920s when area builders treated it like the local quarry, but the city remains an impressive site. The stadium, one of the best-preserved ones of the ancient world, has a field that extends to almost

7,956 sq. m (1,000 sq. yds.), and an original seating capacity of around 12,000 people. It's now a modest showcase for carvings from around the city. Some finely carved marble reliefs are visible in the Greco-Roman theater, where spectacular views of the plain provide a good overview of the lower city.

Aksu (Take the Antalya-Alanya hwy. east, watch for the turnoff to Perge on the left). www.antaly amuzesi.gov.tr. ✆ **0242/426-2748.** Admission 15TL. Daily Apr–Oct 9am–7pm; Nov–Mar 8am–5:30pm.

The Mountaintop Citadel of Termessos ★★ RUINS   Located on a natural plateau 1,050m (3,445 ft.) above sea level, the impregnable mountaintop city of **Termessos** was the only settlement not conquered by Alexander the Great. Alex likened it to an eagle's nest; you'll think so, too, after the steep climb up. The most impressive of the ruins is the **Greek theater,** cut into the rock with celestial views of Antalya visible through the clouds. The ability of the city's inhabitants to withstand prolonged attacks was in no small part due to the exceptional engineering of its cisterns: five tanks fed by a duct cut into the rock. In addition to the admission to the archaeological site, visitors arriving by car pay the entry fee to the park (don't even think about walking from the ticket gate, a hefty 9km/5½ miles downhill from the plateau parking).

The best approach from the plateau parking area is up the main path to the city and theater for access to the lion's share of the ruins. Rather than backtracking at the end of your visit, follow the sign toward the tombs, which follows a narrow and sometimes rocky footpath past a series of **rock-cut tombs** and free-standing **sarcophagi,** a path that ends about 20 minutes later in the parking lot. The visit on foot takes as little as 2 hours (if you're well hydrated and it's early) to as much as 4 to 5 hours, if you're sluggish and really into seeing every nook and cranny.

The ancient site is located about ½ hr. from Antalya inside the Güllük Dağ Milli Parkı along the Antalya-Burdur Highway. www.antalyamuzesi.gov.tr. ✆ **0242/423-7416.** Admission 5TL. Daily Apr–Oct 9am–7pm; Nov–Mar 8am–5pm.

AREA BEACHES

Located below Mermerli Park at the eastern end of Kaleiçi is **Memerli Plaji** ★ (entrance through the Memerli Restaurant, ✆ **0242/316-5307,** entrance 10TL includes lounges and umbrellas), a miniature beach backed by the ancient sea walls. An icy spring shoots out of the rock at the end of the beach, but the narrow sandy strip tends to get a bit crowded and the service from the cliff-top bar/restaurant is very hands-on.

A favorite beach destination for residents of Antalya is **Konyaaltı** ★★★, a long stretch of pristine pebble beach backed by a meandering promenade chock-full of activities, including playgrounds and the **Dolphinarium–Aqualand–Aquapark** complex (www.antalya-dolphinarium.com), Antalya's largest water park. Kids will particularly enjoy the dolphin show, where for 18€ per person you can smile in wonder along with your little ones, and for 60€ you can swim with the dolphins (combo rates with the Aquapark are available). The whole complex has been dubbed **Antalya Beach Park**; www.beachpark.com.tr, at press time, it featured 7 beach "clubs"— swaths of waterfront brightly equipped with lounges and umbrellas, and serviced by cafes, restaurants, changing cabins, and showers. Beach admission fees vary from about 4TL to 10TL per day and include use of the facilities. Most of the beach establishments have a watersports center, with jet skis for rent by the quarter-hour, parasailing, ringo rides, water-skiing, kayaks, sea bikes, and windsurfing, to name a few. There's also the on-site Yunus Diving School (see below). As the sun sets, beach clubs morph into stylish outdoor nightclubs, providing cushions and lounges for lots of posing and draping, and an atmosphere of high style and frivolity. Main access to the beach is down a switchback road between the archaeological museum and the park; pedestrians can enter via a series of steps and bridges behind the Rixos Hotel or through the Hillside Su.

The sparse and sandy **Lara Beach** stretches along the coast in the opposite direction, a little over 11km (6¾ miles) east of downtown. There are about 11 private beach clubs (named by number) or the public **Lara Halk Plajı,** all with essential services, food, drink, showers, and entertainment. Minibuses (nos. 18, 30, or 77) pass along the beachfront after about a half-hour to 45-minute ride, depending on where you get off. But however lovely the long stretches of sand that extend the length of Lara, it's a bit of a stretch for me to tell you to go there, given the convenience and appeal of Konyaaltı. Unless, of course, your itinerary coincides with Antalya's **Sand Sculpture Exhibition.** A fantasy of artistic caprice, the exhibition lasts from late June through September or October. The theme in 2011 was "Hollywood," and it's the best thing on odd years you can lay your eyes on before the tide comes in.

Freshwater springs gushing off the mountains have found several awe-inspiring outlets in and around Antalya. At the **Lower Düden Waterfalls ★**, on the road to Lara Beach, the waters plunge straight into the sea. Alternately, go an additional 13km (8 miles) to the **Upper Düden Waterfalls ★**, unique because you can walk behind the cascade. Both offer a bracing, high-pressure shower in the midst of some of Mother Nature's best.

Heading west by car, Antalya's sprawl dissipates and small beaches and clusters of resort hotels dot the coastal road. The planned resort village of **Kemer,** 43km (27 miles) later, takes advantage of aquamarine calm waters backed by craggy mountainous cliffs, as waves lap through the pebbles creating a relaxing munching sound. The narrow beach is equipped with lounges and umbrellas, and the overpriced shopping strip stocks enough cash registers to keep you busy after sunning.

Just 14km (8¾ miles) farther west is the ancient port city of **Phaselis ★★★** (daily summer 9am–7pm, winter 8:30am–5pm; ✆ **0242/821-4506**), a nature-lover's delight nestled amid the pine trees on the edge of three pristine and scenic bays. Plan to spend the day (entrance fee 8TL) to wade in the waters and wander through the main streets, agoras, baths, and temples of this enchanting ancient city. Finish the day off with a stroll through the resort of **Tekirova,** a slightly more charming and pleasantly downscale version of Kemer located on the opposite side of Phaselis.

STAYING ACTIVE

A number of hotel-based travel agencies and shopfront outfitters in Kaleiçi offer day trips to the surrounding natural and historic sites, sometimes combining the two into one full-day excursion. You can tackle Perge, Aspendos, and the Kurşunlu Waterfalls (59€); visit the ancient city of Myra, the St. Nicholas (Santa Claus) Museum, and take a boat ride on the spectacular Kekova Bay (59€); or head up to Termessos and the Düden Waterfalls (55€) for the day. If you're stuck for whom to go with, I like **Akustik Travel** (based in Bodrum with offices in Antalya, ✆ **0242/352-0650;** www.akustik. tc) or try **Mithra Travel**, Kılıçarslan Mah. Hesapçı Sok. 70. (✆ **0242/248-7747;** www.mithratravel.com). Resources for independent activities follow.

DIVING ADVENTURE TOUR   In addition to a wide variety of colorful plant and sea life, the Gulf of Antalya is also a graveyard for several unlucky World War II fighter planes and at least one groundbreaking shipwreck. Maybe the *Meltem,* the winds that blow in from the Caucuses, or the rocky coastline have something to do with it, but the results are some of the most fascinating dive sites along the coast. Dive concessions are on-site at all the major hotels and resorts all up and down the region's coastline. You don't have to be a guest to sign up, but a day's notice is generally necessary. **Yunus Diving,** located within the Beach Park near the entrance to Konyaaltı Beach (© **0242/238-4486;** www.yunusdiving.com), offers a 2-hour discovery dive, 2-hour licensed dives, and wreck dives starting from around 40€ (not including equipment rental but including the oxygen tank).

GOLF   SPORTS VENUE   Although a relatively new phenomenon in Turkey, the game of golf has caught on like wildfire, up to 29 courses from only 11 in 2005. Several clubs have created their very own sweet spot along the shores east and west of Antalya, in the secluded hills of Belek and around the tony resort of Kemer. All of the clubs and resorts are clearly signposted along the coastal Antalya road. You can book in advance by contacting the golf clubs individually, or by booking (often at a discount) through **www.bookyourgolf.net.** For a comprehensive listing of courses, log on to **World Golf** (**www.worldgolf.com**) with descriptions of the courses along with contact information for each course.

The most popular of the Antalya courses is the PGA Sultan Course at the **Antalya Golf Club,** in Belek (© **0242/725-5970;** www.antalyagolfclub.com.tr)—a par-71, 450-yard "challenge" designed by European Golf Design and David Jones. The **Gloria Golf Club** (© **0242/715-1520;** www.gloria.com.tr) was the first and only resort to have its very own golf course. Michel Gayon is responsible for the design of two 18-hole championship courses; there's also a 9-hole course. The 27-hole Nick Faldo Course at **Cornelia Golf Club** (© **0242/710-1600;** www.corneliagolfresort.com) opened in 2006. It's got a dune ridge running through the course, and there are three different 18-hole combinations. Turkey's first seaside golf course is **LykiaLinks,** opened in September 2008 (© **0242/754-4343;** www.lykiaworldantalya.com). Stunning scenery and constant breezes coming off of the Mediterranean, the Perry Dye-designed course provides seasoned golfers with the challenges befitting a 285€ greens fee course (check for special packages and rates).

HIKING/CAMPING   WALKING/HIKING TRAIL   Kate Clow, a British woman based in Antalya, turned a labor of love into a hiker's dream. She's mapped and marked a comprehensive network of ancient dirt roads and blissfully solitary footpaths. The first long-distance trail, called the **Lykia Yolu (Lycian Way)** ★★★, connects Antalya and Fethiye; the second network of trails, dubbed **St. Paul's Way,** begins along the coast east of Antalya and heads over the Toros Mountains into the Lakeland around Eğirdir and on up to Antioch in Pisidia, in some cases trodding the ancient Roman roads used by St. Paul on his missionary journeys through Asia Minor. For more on the trails or for information on a DIY trekking trip, log on to **www.lycianway.com** or **www.stpaultrail.com.** If you want the security of trekking in tandem, see p. 283.

ON THE WATER   ADVENTURE TOUR   The amazing caves and waterfalls around Antalya are accessible on 2-, 4-, or 6-hour **boat excursions** ★. Crews begin hawking the next day's tours early in the evening, or you can show up at the last minute for a boat that's about to disembark. Longer tours make trips to nearby beaches and may include a guided tour of the lovely and pine-shaded ancient harbor city of Phaselis, which includes a three-island tour. Not all boats are created equal, though; if it's quiet you're after, ask if the crew will be blasting music all day. Captains offer boat trips at the harbor from around 10TL per person per hour, with a full day (6-hr.) excursion costing up to 50TL, including lunch.

KAYAKING/RAFTING ADVENTURE TOUR The mountainous geography and numerous rivers in the Antalya region create exhilarating white-water rafting appropriate to all levels. The Manavgat River flows through a series of lengthy gorges, but the Grades 4 and 5 rapids are accessible to experienced paddlers only.

The Köprü River, located halfway between Antalya and Side with Grade 1 and Grade 3 rapids, is no less breathtaking but a bit more suitable to beginners. This is an ideal family day out, even if you have no experience whatsoever. **Antalya Rafting,** (℡ **0242/311-4845;** www.antalya-rafting.net), organizes day trips for all levels, as well as 3-day or longer excursions, with top professional and experienced guides, from 19€ per person per day, depending on the tour.

Alpine Rafting Company (www.turkeyrafting.com) runs a full day on the water, with lunch, and with pickups for day tours at the farthest-flung corners of Greater Antalya for similar rates.

Where to Eat

Locals flock to the eateries in the covered walkway at the intersection of Cumhuriyet Caddesi and Atatürk Caddesi, where freshly cooked *lokanta*-style cafes and *döner* stands share the pavement with tiny coffee tables. It's the Turkish equivalent of the food court, and a delicious, friendly, and economical alternative to the more tourist-minded restaurants listed below.

Kral Sofrası TURKISH/MEDITERRANEAN Called the King's Table, Kral Sofrası enjoyed 20 years of success in Ankara before moving to the warmer climes of Antalya, where it was the first restaurant to open on the marina. In the summertime, meals are served on the terrace garden overlooking the rooftops and harbor, but the restaurant seems to take its name from the stately dining room inside this old Ottoman house. The menu offers typical Turkish harbor fare with an occasional standout like the special *kiral güveç* (beef-and-vegetable casserole) or the spicy chili tahini dip. Pay your respects to the Elvis-like Atatürk shrine at the front entrance before you leave. Yacht Harbor 35. (℡ **0242/241-2198.** Reservations recommended. Dress smart for indoor dining. Grilled meat and fish dishes 16TL–28TL and up for fish. MC, V. Daily 11am–1am. Closes earlier in winter.

Vanilla ★ INTERNATIONAL Don't get me wrong: I love Turkish food as much as (actually, more than) anyone. But coming from a world of culinary variety, I just need something different. Apparently so did Brit-born Wayne Hoggart, who lives in Antalya with his Turkish wife, Emel. This cosmopolitan outpost, located in a hugely atmospheric stone building, serves as a bar, a cafe, a lounge, and a restaurant. Grab a newspaper or magazine and dig your fork into the amazing cheesecake, or a plate of local grilled cheeses, or opt for hand-made, wild mushroom and mozzarella pizza or the Thai salad with jumbo prawns. There's a good variety of meat dishes (steak, lamb) sourced from and handpicked by a local butcher. An assortment of curries will keep Hoggart's fellow Brits happy, washed down with a swig of one of the hand-selected Turkish wines. Hesapçı Sok. 33 (diagonally opposite the Alp Paşa Hotel). www.vanillaantalya.com. © **0242/247-6013.** Reservations suggested for dinner. Main courses 16TL–42TL. MC, V. Daily 8am–midnight.

Zeytin ★ GEORGIAN   Unless your palate formed while eating authentic Turkish food, it's unlikely that you'll taste the nuanced flavor in menu items that at first glance, look like all the other stuff you've been eating here. Well, I'll give you a hint: it's in the interesting (exotic?) mix of herbs used to jazz things up. Take the eggplant, for example, prepared with ground walnuts and coriander. The *chaqapuli,* a lamb stew of plum sauce, white wine, tarragon, dill, parsley, mint, and coriander, is practically the mascot dish of Georgia. You can also give Georgian wine a shot (hope it's better than the one I had, not at this restaurant). Iskele Cad. 29, Kaleiçi. © **0242/242-4212.** Call the restaurant from the clock tower and they'll send someone over to get you. Main courses 15TL–22TL. MC, V. Daily 10am–1am.

Antalya After Dark

Visitors to Antalya take to the streets and hidden courtyards of Kaleiçi or along the Yacht Harbor, where an ice cream and a stroll down the jetty are accompanied by sea breezes, waterside cafes, and the lull of folk music emanating from shaded courtyards.

Over at Konyaaltı's **Beach Park** ★★★, cafes illuminated by moonlight line the seaside beach park promenade, sharing the lawns with a decadent array of cushions backed by a handful of *meyhanes.*

Visitors to Antalya should keep their eyes peeled for the numerous concerts and performances on offer throughout the year. In August, the cast and crew show off their talents alfresco in a spectacularly lit Theater of Aspendos. The regular season venue is the Opera Sahnesi (Opera Hall) at Haşim İşcan Kültür Merkezi. For program and ticket information, log onto the website of the Antalya State Opera and Ballet (www.dobgm.gov.tr) or call © **0242/343-3099.**

Ayar   Atmospherically rustic and cozy, this wood-ceilinged and fireplaced *meyhane* kicks off live music in the evenings, spilling downstairs into the indoor nightclub in winter (Nov–Apr). There's a nice menu selection, and the excellent service almost made up for the fact that few of the items on it were available. Hesapçı Sok. 51, Kaleiçi. © **0242/244-5203.**

Gizli Bahçe ★   The presence of two restaurants, four different dining environments, stunning views of the bay via the parapets, and a generally elegant atmosphere are just a few of the things that the Gizli Bahçe/Secret Garden has to offer. A polished and elegant bar area is a great option for a pre- or post-dinner aperitif, while live music is offered Tuesday through Sunday nights. Daily 8am to midnight. Closed

November to mid-April. Selçuk Mah., Dizdar Hasan Bey Sok. 1, Kaleiçi. www.gizlibahce.net. © **0242/244-8010.**

Kale Bar ★ ◙ The Kale Bar, a stylish bar-bistro sitting atop the ramparts of the ancient fortress, has the best views of the harbor from anywhere in town and then some. The bar is attached to the Tütav Türk Evi hotel, ensuring good quality meals and extraordinary prices to match. Daily 11am to 2am. Closed in winter. In the Tütav Türk Evi, Memerli Sok., Kaleiçi. © **0242/248-6591.**

Where to Stay

Antalya is synonymous with sun and fun, and the holiday villages just couldn't resist the sandy beaches and plains ripe for development at the foot of the Toros Mountains. Several luxury four- and five-star playgrounds dot the coastline outward from Antalya's historic Kaleiçi area and marina, while miles and miles farther out, the several become literally *hundreds.* But you didn't come all this way to hide out, did you? Instead, choose one of the four- and five-star hotels perched on the cliffs just outside of the city's nucleus, along Konyaaltı Beach or in Lara Beach.

More attuned to the desires of the independent traveler are the hotels and pensions of Antalya's historic district of Kaleiçi, where hotels are housed in typical restored Ottoman homes of timber or stone. The traditional Ottoman house is built around a front and rear courtyard, so that all of these hotels have at least a pool of cozy dimensions and a serene and fragrant garden. You can also walk down the steep streets and/or steps to Memerli Plajı at the harbor or hop on a day boat.

ANTALYA HOLIDAY RESORTS
In Konyaaltı
Hillside Su ★★★ ◙ The glorious Hillside Su manages to be both futuristic and retro at the same time. Large glass sliding doors open onto an atrium lobby and lounge where four massive disco balls dangle from the ceiling. Get the idea? The Hillside Su is the most fashion-conscious beach club on the strip, offering guests the graciousness of an array of stylish day beds and lounges. Oh, and did I forget to mention that everything is white? Whitewashed floors, whitewashed walls, white linens and towels, white terry-cloth covers for everything. The whiteness of the hotel is offset by little accents of red: red (okay, orange) goldfish, red (or white) bedside tower lamps, and red lava lamps. Rooms are large in size, sporting king-size beds, a sitting area with day bed, and twin ottomans. Every room has a balcony furnished with yet another bed; avoid the scorching heat of August and you just might spend the night alfresco. Bathrooms are industrial/functional, with a blocky half-exposed shower space (also constructed of cement) and bulky designer fixtures. Outside, the Hillside boasts a 53m (174-ft.) uncommonly narrow and exceptionally wonderful teak-decked swimming pool, flanked on two sides by a stylish double row of ground-level beds shaded by bamboo umbrellas. Beyond the second row of beds begin the lawns, which convert to a high-quality and reasonably priced fish restaurant by candlelight. Overall, the wonderful pretentiousness is mitigated by a disarmingly congenial and professional staff, and while the spare minimalism may be disarming to some, I found its clever and kitschy style to be simply enchanting.

Konyaaltı Cad., 07050 Antalya. www.hillsidesu.com. © **0242/249-0700.** Fax 0242/249-0707. 294 units. From 185€ garden-view double. See website for rates and packages. AE, MC, V. Free parking on-site. **Amenities:** 6 restaurants (including sushi bar); 4 bars; babysitting; beach; concierge;

hamam; health club and spa; children's playground w/separate kiddie pool; indoor and outdoor pools; room service; smoke-free rooms; squash court; 2 tennis courts; extensive watersports equipment/rental. *In room:* A/C, satellite TV, hair dryer, minibar, free Wi-Fi.

Lara Plajı

Marmara Antalya ★★★ The newest addition to the Marmara family of deluxe hotels sits atop the Falez Cliffs above the Gulf of Antalya, only 5km (3 miles) from the historic center on the Lara Beach side of the bay. The thing you want to do here is score one of the 24 rooms in the "revolving loft," an ingenious feat of engineering (the building actually floats) providing a constantly changing panorama of city, sea, and mountains. Unless you have an underwater room, that is. And thanks to the placement of furniture in the rooms, you can even enjoy the view while relaxing in the in-room bathtub. Another unique feature (gimmick?) is the "river runs through it" concept to the swimming pool and grounds, a 270m (886-ft.) canal that permits kayaking through the property.

Sirinyalı Mah. Eski Lara Cad. 136, 07160 Antalya. www.themarmarahotels.com. ✆ **0242/249-3600.** Fax 0242/292-3318. 232 units. 99€–129€ double; 159€ suite. See website for packages. AE, MC, V. **Amenities:** Restaurant; 4 cafe-bars; babysitting; beach; bikes; concierge; *hamam;* health club and spa; indoor and outdoor pools; room service; smoke-free rooms; 2 tennis courts; watersports equipment/rental. *In room:* A/C, cable TV, hair dryer, minibar, free Wi-Fi.

KALEIÇI
Expensive

Puding Suite★ This new hotel is an oddly eclectic and strangely appealing all-suite boutique hotel. A pink and gold tea room replete with fluffy pink draperies harkening back to 19th-century Paris serves as the reception and bar. Of the three ground-floor suites, I like the Mediterranean room best, because of the stone walls and inset sconces. Upstairs are the modernish duplex Millennium Suite, and the Anatolian Suite, with its columned archways, decorative ceilings, and polished interpretation of the heartland. Or you can go all-out and book the Ottoman Suite, best described as where Austin Powers meets the House of Osman (think leather sofas, tulip ceramic bowl sinks, and retro white shag rugs).

Barbaros Mah. Mescit Sok. 25. www.pudingsuite.com. ✆ **0242/243-8050.** 6 units. 120€–350€ suite. Free transfers for stays of 3 or more nights and booking via their website. AE, MC, V. Free parking. **Amenities:** Restaurant; bar; free airport transfers; elevator; outdoor pool; room service; smoke-free rooms. *In room:* A/C, satellite TV, hair dryer, Jacuzzi, minibar, free Wi-Fi.

Moderate

Otantik Boutique Hotel ★ This richly restored, 170-year-old mansion is another diamond in a sea of remarkably restored inns. The gleaming wood ceilings and whitewashed faux stucco walls set the backdrop for pristine rooms sparely adorned with mini lanterns, Turkish carpets, and solidly comfy beds. The location is closer to Hadrian's Gate and Atatürk Cad., which has the advantage of being steps from the tram. But if your focal point is the marina, a few meandering (and easily disorienting) minutes away, you may be disappointed. The on-site **Otantik Wine House and Restaurant** is worthy of a stop for lunch or dinner, with an appealing Turkish and Italian menu, friendly and capable service, and competitive prices.

Barbaros Mah., Hesapçı Sok. 14, Kaleiçi, 07100 Antalya. www.otantikbutikotel.com. ✆ **0242/244-8530.** Fax 242/244-8531. 10 units. 60€ double. Rates lower off-season. AE, MC, V. Parking 5€ in public car park. **Amenities:** Restaurant; bar; room service, smoke-free rooms. *In room:* A/C, satellite TV, minibar, free Wi-Fi.

Marina Residence ★ Three Ottoman Paşas' homes of differing styles were restored and redecorated, keeping embellishments such as marble balustrades, wood beams, and polished trim. There's a long marble staircase to the rooms above in the main house, and all rooms are outfitted with bathtubs, comfortable duvets, and feather pillows. The terrace suite has access to its own rooftop sun terrace, offering breathtaking views of the marina (another room gets a Jacuzzi—and twin beds). Afternoons will most certainly be spent in the courtyard, an oasis of peace with a larger-than-life aquarium swimming pool, or in the new fitness room complete with a small sauna. The Marina also has one of the best restaurants in town.

Mermerli Sok. 15, Kaleiçi, 07100 Antalya. www.marinaresidence.net. (© **0242/247-5490.** Fax 0242/241-1765. 41 units. 94€ double (add 20€ for sea view). Rates lower Nov–Mar. AE, MC, V. Free valet parking. **Amenities:** Restaurant; bar; airport transfer (50€); exercise room; outdoor pool; room service; sauna. *In room:* A/C, satellite TV, hair dryer, minibar, free Wi-Fi.

Tekeli Konakları ★ Tekeli Konakları combines six traditional Turkish houses set around a common paved courtyard with several patio levels and a small pool. The rooms—each one slightly different—are elegantly yet sparsely decorated, taking advantage of architectural features such as polished wood floorboards and carved wood ceilings. Those who appreciate attention to detail will be delighted by Kütahya ceramics fashioned into door handles, the odd antique objet d'art—and in some rooms, stained-glass, Ottoman-motif artwork. *Early-to-bedders take note:* The neighboring disco may intrude upon your REM time.

Dizdar Hasan Sok., 07100 Kaleiçi, Antalya. www.tekeli.com.tr. (© **0242/244-5465.** Fax 0242/242-6714. 8 units. Apr–Oct US$100; Nov–Mar US$85 in summer. AE, MC, V. **Amenities:** Restaurant; bar; outdoor pool; room service. *In room:* A/C.

Inexpensive

Atelya Art Hotel ⚔ This family-owned and -operated collection of three Ottoman-era houses offers visitors one of the neighborhood's best values. The three buildings front a large courtyard set around a fountain and decorated in traditional Turkish style. Rooms in the older building are simple, with few amenities besides the original wood plank floors and loads of character; some retain decorative niches and faded original paintings. The newer building has larger rooms, modern details, and comfortable bathrooms.

Civelek Sok. 21, 07100 Kaleiçi, Antalya. www.atelyahotel.com. (© **0242/241-6416.** Fax 0242/241-2848. 30 units. 40€ double in old section; 50€ double. No credit cards. **Amenities:** Bar; meals on request; table tennis; free Wi-Fi. *In room:* No phone.

Doğan Hotel ★ This neighborhood long-timer is made up of four connected, elegantly restored Ottoman houses. The garden takes center stage here, a small swimming pool flanked by orange trees and surrounded by high stone walls. Common spaces, which include a lobby bar and "library," feature marble surfaces and touches of *kilims.* The rooms have wide wooden plank floors and ceilings, while suites are gracious and atmospheric. If you request a *çatı odası,* you'll be happy to step foot into a room up high with a balcony and views of the harbor. Try to avoid the rooms in the rear, formerly known as the "pink building," because bathrooms are smallish.

Mermerli Banyo Sok. 5, 07100 Kaleiçi, Antalya. www.doganhotel.com. (© **0242/241-8842.** Fax 0242/247-4006. 41 units. 48€ double; 75€ suite. MC, V. Limited street parking. **Amenities:** Lobby and garden bars; cozy outdoor swimming pool; room service. *In room:* A/C and ceiling fan, satellite TV, hair dryer, radio, free Wi-Fi.

Hadrianus ★ A few scant years back, the Günbey family restored a modest old building in Kaleiçi maintaining the original attributes while adding lots of eclectic decorative pieces and artistic lighting. The result is a lovely, clean, and tasteful inn with loads of character. The hotel is backed by a large botanical garden, lawn, and living space, where guests can pass a shady afternoon recovering from the dust of the nearby archaeological sights. If you can do without the Jacuzzi (available in two of the rooms), book one of the Paşa rooms, essentially oversized triples (one double bed plus a twin) with plenty of space to spread out. The service here, albeit very friendly, was pretty hands-off when I visited, nor was English widely spoken, although this may change by the time this edition hits the bookshelves.

Kılıçarslan Mah. Zeytin Sok. 4, Kaleiçi. www.hadrianushotel.com. ⓒ **0242/244-0030.** Fax 0242/244-2515. 12 units. 60€ double. Rates lower Nov 1–Apr 9. AE, MC, V. On-street parking. **Amenities:** Bar. *In room:* A/C, TV, hair dryer, minibar, free Wi-Fi.

Kaleiçi Lodge Located right on the main pedestrian drag of the old city, the 2-year-old Kaleiçi Lodge combines simplicity, old-world elegance and the value of a locally owned B&B. Wrought iron lighting fixtures and the odd oversized copper or ceramic urn accent the marble-floored common areas. Try to book one of the rooms on the first floor (above lobby level), or if you don't mind low garret style wooden-beamed ceilings, then opt for the top floor, with its two, two-bedroom setups complete with small balcony and views galore. The peaceful, marbled rear garden patio is an intimate oasis of relaxation, and you can practice your bilingual skills on the mostly Turkish-speaking staff.

Kılıçarslan Mah. Hesapçı Sok. 37. www.kaleicilodge.com. ⓒ **0242/243-2270.** Fax 0242/244-6094. 14 units. 35€–85€ double; 75€–225€. Lower rates reflect "best rate" promotion. MC, V. Free on-street parking. **Amenities:** Bar; room service. *In room:* A/C, satellite TV, hair dryer, free Wi-Fi.

Ninova Pension ◀ This modest but comfortable pension boasts the finest garden in Antalya, pleasantly overgrown with orange trees and an enchanting reflecting pond as a centerpiece. Rooms are basic and small, an additional four units on the upper floors are usually out of commission in the summer because of the oppressive heat. The longtime manager, a sweet woman from Istanbul, creates an atmosphere of warmth, encouraging guests to congregate in the TV room or the sitting area. Nights are bliss-fully silent, even though Hadrian's Gate and Atatürk Caddesi are only steps away.

Hamit Efendi Sok. 9, 07100 Kaleiçi, Antalya. ⓒ **0242/248-6114.** Fax 0242/248-9684. 15 units. 40€–60€ double. AE, MC, V. Closed Jan–Feb. **Amenities:** Smoke-free rooms. *In room:* A/C, TV.

Short Hops From Antalya
THE "MONSTER" AT OLYMPOS

One of the highlights of a visit to the Antalya coast is the **Chimaera** ★★, near the ancient city of **Olympos** ★ and modern-day beachfront **Çıralı** ★★. It's a good idea to combine a visit to both the natural and archaeological sites, keeping in mind that the undisturbed—even unkempt—shoreline of Çıralı is one of the best-kept natural secrets of the Mediterranean coast and a major nesting site for Loggerhead sea turtles (for this reason, the beach closes at dusk).

The Chimaera, or mythical, fire-breathing monster with the head of a lion, the torso of a goat, and the rear of a snake that allegedly roams the hills is actually a series of eternal flames flickering along the rocky slopes above the ancient city of Olympos, which would account for the Lycians' worship of the fire god Hephaestos (Vulcan). But never fear: According to legend, the Chimaera was slain by Bellerophon on his winged horse, Pegasus, from his base over at Tlos. The fires are caused by the combustion of a predominantly methane gas mixture seeping out of the earth and igniting at the point of contact between serpentine and limestone rocks. Although they can be extinguished briefly by covering them, they always reignite. The path up the hill to the site is at the far end of the modern village of Çıralı, about a 6- to 7km (3¾–4⅓-mile) hike from the beach end of the ancient city of Olympos. It's about a 20-minute hike up to the Chimaera, where a fresh pot of tea perks atop one of the flames. Although the flames are no less impressive by daylight, it's best to come at dusk, when the flames are most visible—just don't forget a flashlight.

The ancient site of Olympos hugs both sides of the Ulupınar Stream near the seashore, and dates to Hellenistic times. It's a bit overgrown and spread out on both sides of the stream, so come with a good map of the site. From 100 B.C., Olympos enjoyed the status as one of the six primary members of the Lycian League and was later absorbed as a Roman province. During this period, the area gained renown as a place of worship for the cult of Hephaestos, or Vulcan, the God of Fire.

Admission to the ancient city ruins (ⓒ **0242/892-1325**) is 3TL. The site is open daily from 9am to 7pm April to October and 8am to 5pm November to March. There are two entrances to the site: To combine a visit to Olympos with a climb up to the Chimaera, exit the Antalya highway at the exit marked "Çıralı 7, Yanartaş 11 (Chimaera)" (*Yanartaş* is Turkish for "burning rock".) From here, it's a 10-minute drive along a dry stream bed bursting with oleander, wild orchids, and lavender. You can either cross the bridge and continue straight for about 1.6km (a mile; don't be discouraged by the poor condition of the road during the final mile or so) until you arrive at the "base camp" for the well-marked path up to the Chimaera or turn off onto the rocky road *before* the bridge into Çıralı for access to the beach. (Walk to the right to find the beach entrance to the site of Olympos.) The other main entrance to Olympos can be accessed from the turnoff from the Antalya road marked "Olympos 11, Çavuşköy 15." *Dolmuşes* pass regularly along the Antalya highway, but transportation down to the beachfront via either turnoff is less reliable, which is why I recommend this excursion be approached by car.

WHERE TO STAY & EAT   The road that loops through the village of Çıralı is lined with small, family-run pensions with varying degrees of appeal. But until that fated day when Çıralı becomes polished and unauthentic, the best place to stay is the **Olympos Lodge ★★**, Çıralı, Kemer, P.O. Box 38, Antalya (ⓒ **0242/825-7171;** fax 0242/825-7173; www.olymposlodge.com.tr), just over the bridge into town (take that quick right). With only 12 rooms, this small slice of paradise is like an exclusive country club, the parking lot is consistently full of shiny Mercedes, BMWs, and collectors' Rolls-Royces. The grounds are gorgeous—a Mediterranean garden bursting with color and home to wandering chickens and peacocks abuts the beach. The rooms are rather unadorned and basic, but feature old cedar wood floorboards that reportedly repel mosquitoes. The room rate (from 175€ for two people per night) includes breakfast and dinner. (Rates lower off-season).

When the Olympos Lodge breaks the news that it's full, the **Arcadia** and **Arcadia 2 ★**, Çıralı (ⓒ **0242/825-7340;** www.arcadiaholiday.com), located farther down the beach in a garden of flowers and lemon trees (Arcadia 2 is across the road in a lemon grove), offer a total of 10 spacious and extremely comfortable pine bunga-lows. All were built by Ahmet, the owner, assisted by Canadian-born Ann, a welcome font of local information in English. Together, they've created a cozy, romantic, and rustic environment stocked with all the creature comforts, plus coffee, a tea station, and a wine rack. Arcadia has delicious on-site dining on request, eat under the beach-front pines or relax on the shady platform *köşk*. The room rate for two people is 90€ to 125€ and includes breakfast.

A SIDE TRIP TO SIDE

One of the endearing historical footnotes to this ancient seaside town is that after having been abandoned for centuries, a village of Turks exiled from the Greek islands sprang up atop the ruins. Ancient walls, aqueducts, and temples coexist with low-budget pensions, waterside eateries, and souvenir stands flanked by an endless stretch of beautiful white sand to the east and west of the ancient promontory. Imag-ine the romance of a secret tryst between Antony and Cleopatra, as they came here and surveyed the open seas centuries ago.

If you can withstand the touristy nature of Side center, the ruins of the ancient city, interwoven into the fabric of the modern-day resort town, still exert their charms. Keep it to a simple day trip, where you can stroll around for a few hours and lunch at a harborside cafe, avoid the main shopping street of Liman Caddesi, and get out of Dodge before nightfall, when things really get ugly.

The quickest and easiest way to get here is by car, via the main D400 coastal highway (Side lies around 2km/1¼ south of the turnoff). Buses and *dolmuşes* running along the Antalya/Alanya highway will either take you directly into Side or to Manav-gat, 4km (2½ miles) away, where you can change for service into Side. You can also ask the driver to leave you off at the crossroads to Side, where you can flag down an incoming *dolmuş* into the *otogar*. From there, it's about a 5-minute walk to the ruins and the main pedestrian drag to the beach.

On the road leading to the ancient city walls and the City Gate are the consoled houses strewn with toppled columns. The second gate is the **Monumental Gate,** flanked by the marble **nymphaion,** or city fountain. The fountain, erected in honor of the Emperor Vespasian, was supplied by the Manavgat River 29km (18 miles) away by means of a system of tunnels and aqueducts. Immediately to your left is the **the-atre,** a mammoth structure with a capacity of 15,000. Unlike other Hellenistic the-atres that were traditionally carved into the side of a hill, this theatre was erected on flat land and supported by an infrastructure of vaults and arches—a construction unique to the Eastern Mediterranean. The theatre was altered by the Romans to accommodate gladiators and lions—a high wall was erected to keep the spectators out of reach of the wild beasts. In the 5th century, the theatre was used as an open-air basilica.

From the theatre, the best approach to take is to avoid Liman Caddesi and turn left into the agora. Cut across the agora towards the beach, stopping for a camel ride if the mood strikes you. Cut back in through the city walls and follow the walkway along the harbor until you come across the two **Temples of Apollo and Athena ★★** rising above the sea in all their grandeur. The twin structures were built at the end of the 2nd century to protect the port but didn't do such a hot job, as they were destroyed in an earthquake. The temple ruins were used in the construction of the **Byzantine basilica.**

The harbor walk follows the path of the ancient city walls, and dozens of restaurants have set up tables along the edge. Pick one for lunch or a drink, and then explore the narrow backstreets to discover what else Side has hiding behind those bushes. Much of modern-day Side was constructed without a permit, which accounts for the rickety yet offbeat appearance of the town. The historic baths opposite the agora gate house the **Side Muse**um (© 0242/753-1006). Exhibited are artifacts and sculptures covering the Late Hittite, Hellenistic, Roman, and Byzantine periods, recovered primarily during excavations that took place between 1947 and 1967. The museum is open Tuesday through Sunday from 9am to 7pm in summer, 8am to 5pm winter. The **antique theatre** (© 0242/753-1542) is open daily from 8am to 5pm and the entrance fee is 10TL. There is an additional admission of 10TL for the museum.

CAPPADOCIA & THE INTERIOR

A stark lunar landscape. A mysterious open-air sculpture carved by Mother Nature's chisel. These common descriptions of Cappadocia really just tap-dance around the subject. So let's just get this out of the way: Those fascinating "fairy chimneys" evoke nothing so much as anatomically correct erections—and circumcised ones at that. Imagine what a field day American film censors would have had if George Lucas had succeeded in his original plan to shoot *Star Wars Episode 1: The Phantom Menace* in Cappadocia.

Notwithstanding the inevitable bedroom references, there are few places on earth where you can get a good night's sleep in a cave, and Cappadocia is one of them. The caves, inhabited by rural families (and their cattle) for centuries, having been made over into unexpectedly luxurious quarters fit for kings and queens, are romantic, suggestive and enchanting.

These may be flanked by the traditionally Greek/Anatolian single-vaulted rooms with utilitarian niches and windows (a feature obviously unavailable in interior caves). Because of the multilevel character of the rock, most hotels are terraced around open patios with fantastic views of the valley or of local village life. As a practical point, caves remain pleasantly cool even in the heat of summer.

Nobody knows who the original inhabitants of the region were, or who first hollowed out shelters in the soft rock of these sheltered ravines and odd "chimneys." But as a largely barren area, central Cappadocia was bypassed by most armies, making it a perfect refuge for the early Christians following in the footsteps of St. Paul, who established the first Christian colonies here.

The natural land formations and huge expanses of silence are just a part of the mystery of the region. As an incubator for Christian philosophy, the monasteries, cave dwellings, and feats of underground engineering are a testament to human ingenuity. Cliff walls of the valleys are riddled with cavities that on closer inspection turn out to be centuries-old dwellings or chapels decorated with colorful frescoes and biblical images.

Cappadocian soil is extremely fertile, and a general tour of the region will reveal numerous vineyards. Famous for its local wines, Cappadocia is a major producer; you may want to veer off at a sign for ŞARAP EVI (wine house) for a leisurely tasting. The creatively named Şarap Evi, in Ürgüp, has wine tastings in the evenings, but it's just as fun to drive up to any local producer and fall into the dance of local hospitality.

GETTING TO KNOW CAPPADOCIA

In antiquity, Cappadocia included all of central Anatolia, stretching as far as Ankara in the north and Adana in the south (see the map of Turkey's Ancient Civilizations, on p. 23). Today the region includes the area in and around a small triangle formed by Ürgüp, Avanos, and Nevşehir, where the canyons are the deepest and the paint pigments in the rock-cut churches are the richest. But the fun doesn't stop at the edge of the triangle. There are plenty of potential excursions: to the underground cities of Derinkuyu and Kaymaklı, the Ihlara Valley and surrounding villages, a detour to caravansaries or a thermal bath. With so many options all over the region, an infrequent and inconvenient public transport "system," and the presumed limitations on your time, I highly recommend that you either rent a car when you get there or, barring that, set up base camp at one of the more vibrant (developed) centers mentioned here and buy into a day tour with a local tour operator. This chapter is organized to help the independent traveler choose a base of operations then venture out to explore around the region.

If your time is limited, it's possible to visit the major sites of the area in 2 *full* days with either your own car or the assistance of a local tour operator. Doubtless, you'll wish you had stayed longer. Tours can either be tailor-made—and therefore pricier— or selected from a stable of standard issues. Typical day tours include 1) a visit to the open-air museums of Zelve and Göreme, overviews of the valleys from Paşabağ and Dervent, a climb up to the top of Üçhisar Fortress, and an optional pottery demonstration in Avanos; or 2) visits to the underground cities of Kaymaklı and Derinkuyu and a leisurely 4km (2½-mile) hike through the monastery-rich gorge of Ihlara Valley. Tours may also include horseback riding; more challenging sports such as mountain biking can be easily arranged, but these are generally not advertised.

[FastFACTS] CAPPADOCIA

Airline Information **Turkish Airlines** has an office in Kayseri's Erkilet Airport (☎ **0352/338-3353**), and one at Nevşehir's Kapadokya Airport (☎ **0384/421-4035**). Outside the airports, the official representative for Turkish Airlines is **Argeus,** located at Istiklal Cad. 13, Ürgüp (☎ **0384/341-4688** or 341-5207).

Airport **Kayseri's Erkilet Airport** general number is ☎ **0352/337-5494.** The main number at **Nevşehir Airport** is ☎ **0384/421-4455.**

Bus Companies The main bus companies in the region are: **Nevşehir** (☎ **0212/444-5050**), with local offices in Ürgüp (☎ **0384/0341-4302**), Göreme (☎ 0384/271-2435), Uçhisar (☎ **0384/219-2221**), and at the *otogar* (☎ **0384/213-1171**). **Metro** (☎ **444-3455**) has offices in Göreme (☎ **0384/271-2411**), Ürgüp (☎ **0384/341-5950**), and at the Nevşehir *otogar* (☎ **0384/214-2020**). **Kent** can be reached via their national number (☎ **0212/444-0038** or 0384/271-2627 in Göreme and 0384/213-5537 in Nevşehir).

Car Rental **Europcar,** Istiklal Cad. 10 (☎ **0384/341-8855**), and **Avis** (Istiklal Cad. 19 (☎ **0384/341-2177**), have locations in the center of Ürgüp. **Avis** also has a location in Nevşehir, at Istiklal Cad. Belediye Pasaji 10 (☎ **0384/341-2177**) and at Kayseri's Erkilet Airport (☎ 0352/222-6196).

Festivals Celebrating Cappadocia's optimal weather and soil conditions for viniculture, Ürgüp puts on both a **Grape Harvest Festival** at the beginning of October and an

Cappadocia

The erosion that carves out this fascinating topography began over 60 million years ago and can be seen in various stages even today. As the devastating 1999 earthquakes illustrated, Turkey is caught between the insistent pressure exerted from the Asian and European continental plates. The Erciyes Mountain, Melendiz Mountain, and Hasandag—all dormant or extinct volcanoes—are the result of underground forces that thrust these landmasses above water level eons ago. Recurrent volcanic eruptions blanketed the area with boulders, ash, and lava, over time creating layers of sediment, with the underneath layers more solid than the newer, softer upper levels of sediment.

The formation of the fairy chimneys is just an example of wind and water erosion in an extreme state. The early stages of erosion are visible in the graceful channels and dunes of the valleys. But as the elements carve away at the channels, the mass of tufa splits from its supports and forms pillars or pyramids. And without the protection of those teetering basalt boulders caught in the balance of gravity and time, the pillars slowly whittle down to nothing, and the crowning boulder eventually comes crashing to the ground.

International Wine Festival at the end of October. If you can't make it to Cappadocia in October, free wine tastings are a regular attraction in Cappadocia. There's also a Tourism and Handicrafts Festival in Avanos (Aug 31–Sept), when the red clay of the Kızılırmak comes to life in the local pottery.

Hospitals   The nearest private hospitals are the **Özel Versa Hastanesi** in Nevşehir (43 Ürgüp Cad., Esentepe; ℂ **0384/214-3232**) and the **Özel Kapadokya Hastanesi,** also in Nevşehir (Güzelyurt Mah. Vefa Küçük Cad. 9; ℂ **0384/212-1550**).

Post Office   PTTs are located in Avanos, Göreme, Nevşehir, Ortahisar, Uçhisar, and Ürgüp. The national toll-free number is ℂ **444-1PTT** (1788).

GETTING THERE & GETTING AROUND
Getting There

BY PLANE   The major airport serving Cappadocia is **Kayseri's Erkilet Airport** (ℂ **0352/337-5244**), about 45 minutes by car from anywhere in Cappadocia. The secondary, **Nevşehir Airport** (ℂ **0384/421-4455**), reopened after a number of years out of service, is closer but served by fewer airlines. **Turkish Airlines** (ℂ **0212/444-0849;** www.thy.com) currently has four to five flights daily from Istanbul's Atatürk Airport to Kayseri and one flight daily to Nevşehir. For passengers traveling from the Asian side of Istanbul, Turkish Airlines flights from Istanbul's Sabiha Gökçen Airport are operated by the THY subsidiary, Anadolu Jet. **Pegasus** (ℂ **444-0737;** www.flypgs.com) also flies once daily from the Asian side. One-way fares on all of these airlines (for those who book early enough) begin at 59TL.

SunExpress (ℂ **0232/444-0797;** www.sunexpress.com.tr) flies direct four times daily from Izmir and once daily from Antalya to Kayseri in summer.

Many local tour operators will pick you up at the airport or bus station for much less than it would cost you to take a taxi. Argeus was the first in the region to provide transfers from both airports to anywhere in the Cappadocia region in their private minivans. The fare for the 97km (60-mile) trip (1½ hr.) from Kayseri airport or from Nevşehir Airport to Ürgüp is only 15TL; add 2TL for all other towns (infants ride free; children ages 3–12 ride for half price). There is a minimal number of daily shuttles however, so check their website for times (generally coinciding with Turkish Airlines flight arrivals and departures). Because of the reasonable amount of competition this presents to area taxi drivers, travelers arriving and hoping to "wing it" by jumping on the Argeus bandwagon may get some resistance from the locals. To avoid misunderstandings, travelers are encouraged to *reserve space in advance* with Argeus (**© 0384/341-4688;** fax 0384/341-4888; www.argeus.com.tr). Also be sure to check with your hotel first—they may pick you up for free. There are no other options for transfers in and out of Kayseri. (A taxi from Kayseri will cost around 110TL; from Nevşehir it's about 80TL).

BY BUS All long-distance buses into Cappadocia arrive into Nevşehir's *otogar*. If you've bought a ticket to Göreme, Ürgüp, Üçhisar, or elsewhere in the triangle, the bus company will provide a minibus transfer from the Nevşehir *otogar* to the station of your final destination. Some bus companies simply pass through Cappadocia on the way to points east and south, in which case it is all too common that the driver will simply dump you off on the side of the highway rather than make the detour into the *otogar*. Whether your bus company is ending its journey in Cappadocia or not, if you've paid for a ticket to, say, Göreme, be sure at the time of purchasing your ticket that the terms of transport are understood. For insurance, stick to the more dependable **Nevşehir Seyahat** (**© 0212/444-5050**), **Metro** (**© 0212/444-3455**) and **Süha** (**© 444-1138**) bus lines. Plan B? Carry your cellphone and call your hotel for a roadside pickup.

By bus, expect around 4 to 5 hours from Konya, 2 hours from Kayseri, 5 to 6 hours from Ankara, and 12 hours from Istanbul. If you're headed to the Aegean Coast, you'll have to change buses in either Izmir (13 hr.) or Muğla (14 hr.); for the Mediterranean coast, you'll have to take a bus to either Antalya or Muğla, and then change for minibus service to your final destination. (Certain destinations will require yet another change; for example, to Dalyan, you'll have to change in Ortaca for a *dolmuş* [minivantype public transportation] into the center of town.)

Getting Around

BY DOLMUŞ In most parts of Turkey, *dolmuşes* are practical. In Cappadocia, service is infrequent and at best unreliable. In addition to the *dolmuş* following a circuitous hourly route from the Ürgüp bus station to Zelve, Avanos, Göreme, Üçhisar, and back, it's also possible to go from Ürgüp to Avanos, Mustafapaşa, Ayvalı and Nevşehir (all generally run hourly 9am–5pm except for the *dolmuş* from Ürgüp to Ayvalı, which runs every 2 hr.). There is no direct service between Ürgüp and Üçhisar. The fare is 1.50TL; to Nevşehir it's 2.50TL. If you're headed farther afield to say, Derinkuyu, you'll have to change in Nevşehir. A municipal bus provides service between Nevşehir and Avanos daily on the hour from 8am to 5pm.

Obviously, a day tour will solve the transportation problem (see "Day Tours" below).

BY CAR Several car-rental agencies offering low daily rates of as low as 35€ per day are located in the center of Ürgüp, including **Europcar,** Istiklal Cad. 10

(© **0384/341-8855**), while **Avis** has a location in Nevşehir at Istiklal Cad. Belediye Pasaji 10 (© **0384/341-2177**). You may also save a few dollars by working with one of the neighboring locals. Scooters are also for rent in various shops along the market for around 75TL for an 8 hour day. **Note:** The newest vehicle rental on the scene is the four-wheel all-terrain vehicle (ATV). But penalties are high for riding these in protected areas (read: pretty much everywhere you will want to go). My advice? Steer clear of the ATV. Plus, you want no part in trampling on millennia-old valleys that have weathered the elements, now do you?

DAY TOURS   So many agencies in Cappadocia organize tours that at worst you'll be spoiled for choice. Operating with the most experience and panache is **Argeus,** Istiklal Cad. 47, Ürgüp (© **0384/341-4688;** www.argeus.com.tr) a professional and friendly full-service agency that, in addition to providing expert guidance on Cappadocia and Ankara, treats its clients like royalty. The price to join one of their regular day tours is $110 per person for up to eight people, a good value compared to the lower-end outfitters because with Argeus, there are no shopping detours and all museum fees are included. They also organize private tours for $285 for one person, $160 per person for two, $120 for three, and so on. Argeus is also an official agent of Turkish Airlines.

In addition to full-day "crash course" visits to Cappadocia's must-sees, **Euphrates-Tours** (Istiklal Cad. 59/9, Ürgüp; © **0384/341-7485;** www.euphratestours.com) sends its guests home from Turkey with a deeper attachment to the heartland thanks to a grass-roots approach that moves beyond the museums. In addition to the must-sees of Cappadocia, they also lead visitors to the lesser-visited (if at all) valleys, on safari tours into the mountains, to waterfalls, and to off-the-beaten-track villages and little-explored underground cities. Expect to pay 95€ per person for a private, two-person tour, or 70€ to join one of their group tours, lunch included. (Entrance fees are not included).

For the more budget-minded, consider a day exploring the rock churches and valleys with the help of **Kirkit Voyages** (© **0212/518-2282;** www.kirkit.com); to join one of their group tours, the price is 40€ per person. Private tours start at 140€ per person for two people. **Red Valley Travel** (© **0384/341-0561;** www.redvalley tours.com) also runs a trio of affordable guided tours for around 80TL per person, with discounts if you sign up for 2 or more days. The price includes museum fees (excluding the Dark Church; see Göreme Open Air Museum on p. 374), plus a detour to a carpet production center (speak up if you want to opt out).

The Active Explorer in Cappadocia

HOT AIR BALLOONING   There are few things in this world that warrant a 4:30am wake-up; usually some type of flight is involved. But chasing the sunrise above Cappadocia's spectacular landscape in a wicker basket is altogether different from boarding a 777: It's like riding on the back of a Harley with wings.

Cappadocia's climate is ideally suited to ballooning, with consistently clear summer skies and harmonious breezes. Ballooning day begins *well* before sunrise, when the flame bursts that fill the balloon provide much-needed warmth. Flights last about an hour and a half, offering otherworldly close-ups and stunning panoramas. Your heart will undoubtedly skip a beat several times throughout, including when they hand you the 250€ bill (shorter flights go for 175€; children 6–12 fly for half price). Regular balloon rides run around 1½ hours; the "budget" version lasts about an hour. Reservations are essential for all flights.

It's hard to find a bad hike in Cappadocia, but the journey will be all the more rewarding in this ever-changing landscape of pink, yellow, and sandy-colored "dunes," with nothing but the whisper of the wind for company. Wear good shoes and come prepared with a windbreaker or jacket, because whenever the sun plays coy behind a cloud, the temperature drops momentarily, yet precipitously. The best hikes are in the Red Valley (Kızılçukur Vadisi) from Çavuşin to the entrance of Ortahisar; in Pigeon Valley (Güvercinlik Vadisi) between Üçhisar and Göreme; and in the Uludere Valley from Uludere village to Ayvalı, where you have the option of continuing through Gomede Valley to Mustafapaşa. Also near Mustafapaşa is Kepez Valley, with its impressive cones, plus a number of churches.

A number of outfitters organize hot air balloon rides over Cappadocia. Recently (with the prospects of skyrocketing tourist demand and big money), there have been a number of start-ups on the Cappadocia ballooning scene, resulting in overcrowded conditions in the skies (2009 saw the first in-flight collision in the region, so while safe, be forewarned). Stick with **Kapadokya Balloons** (℗ **0384/271-2442;** www.kapadokyaballoons.com), **Göreme Balloons** (℗ **0384/341-5662;** www.goremeballoons.com), **Royal Balloons** (℗ **0384/271-3300;** www.royalballoon.com) and **Butterfly Balloons** (℗ **0384/271-3010;** www.butterflyballoons.com).

HORSEBACK RIDING Ancient Anatolian lore describes a lovelorn poet on horseback traveling through fields of irises, perpetuating the legend of Cappadocia as a "place of beautiful horses." It's still possible to replicate that equestrian journey through the region's verdant valleys and barren steppes. The **Akhal-Teke Horse Riding Center** (℗ **0384/511-5171;** www.akhal-tekehorsecenter.com) has clean, professionally run stables (and on-site restaurant) on the outskirts of Avanos with horses and guides for all riding levels. The charge is 25€ per hour for a ride along the Kızılirmak River; 50€ for a 2-hour ride into the mountains and natural spring; and 100€ for a 4-hour ride either up the river, through a local fishing village, and up to the Sarıhan caravansaray or through the fairy chimneys at Zelve, Paşabağ, and Çavusin. Daylong and several weeklong excursions are also available, and some of the overnight trips include stays in people's homes and/or overnights in tents. Call ahead and they'll pick you up at your hotel for free.

Kirkit Voyage (℗ **0384/511-3259;** www.kirkit.com), with offices in Istanbul and Avanos, organizes activities in the area, thanks to their own horse farm in the village of Güzelyurt, near the Ihlara Valley. Horseback-riding tours for all levels of experience are available with 2- or 4-hour panoramic rides for 25€ or 35€ respectively. Kirkit also organizes scenic and memorable 1-, 3-, 7-, and 15-day camping treks.

CHOOSING A BASE

Ürgüp

23km (14 miles) east of Nevşehir; 6.5km (4 miles) east of Göreme

More than a decade ago, Ürgüp was gracefully navigating its way between sleepy village and vibrant small town. In the intervening years, as life in a cave became increasingly difficult, as affordable housing became available and as real estate prices soared, villagers cashed out at an ever-increasing rate. These cave dwellings were scooped up by city dwellers or speculators, to be turned into weekend homes or added to the boom in construction of boutique hotels. Crumbled hovels are becoming the exception rather than the rule, but like the transformation of Ürgüp itself, the human odors of food and sweat are being scraped away with the top layers of porous tufa. Of course, one day all of the abandoned terraced houses will have sprouted brand-new facades, a gentrification process that, while polished and attractive, will probably result in overdevelopment, traffic, and crowds.

Thankfully, all is not yet lost. The undeniable plus of staying here is that there are still perfectly charming romantic retreats for an increasingly upscale market, taking advantage of the town's more serene fringes, in close proximity to good restaurants, cafes and wine shops, banks, car rentals, groceries and all of the essentials a tourist might need. So for the time being, Ürgüp remains a convenient corner of Cappadocia that makes an ideal base from which to explore the surrounding valleys, particularly *sans* wheels. The village is also a peaceful retreat for some quiet time, where you can walk around the old deserted section of town or enjoy the view from the lookout point atop windy Temmenı Hill.

ESSENTIALS

VISITOR INFORMATION   The **tourist information office** is in the center of town across from the police station, on Kayseri Cad. 37 (© **0384/341-4059**), and is open daily 8am to 6pm; closed Sunday in winter. You won't need it, though, as all of the hoteliers and agencies have good maps and even better anecdotal information.

ORIENTATION   The village fans out around the bus station and a brand-new cement-block shopping gallery, which is right in the center of town. From the main square outside the bus station running northeast is **Kayseri Caddesi,** Ürgüp's main shopping street, with a wide variety of shopping options, from overstocked antiques stores to jewelry boutiques with the finest selection of lapis lazuli, handcrafted silver, and tribal items. The information office, the police station, and the hospital can be reached down this road as well. Forking east below Kayseri Caddesi is a small street of localized travel agencies, many of which double as bike- or scooter-rental outfits. **Ahmet Refik Caddesi** heads northwest from the center, snaking around the base of the old village of partially collapsed and deserted rock homes to the left and **Temmenı Hill** to the right, on its way up the hill toward Göreme and Nevşehir. Buying a souvenir cluster of fairy chimneys is made all too easy along Ahmet Refik Caddesi, but once you've cleared the souvenir shops, rural life takes over. Near the top of the hill are the **Turasan winery** and the neighborhood of **Esbelli,** where you will find two hotels mentioned below. To re-enter town by car, turn left onto **Istiklal Caddesi,** which leads back into the town center.

GETTING AROUND   Ürgüp is easily walkable, but if you're staying in the neighborhood of Esbelli, you may want to know that the hill up from the center of town is quite steep. During the summer months when the municipality fills the streets with clouds of insect repellent to combat the irritating swarms of bees that hover over your breakfast, it's best to forgo the after-dinner stroll and take a taxi up to your hotel.

WHERE TO EAT
Ürgüp Center
Ocakbaşı ★ 🍴 BARBECUE/SOUTHERN SPECIALTIES   Most people would turn their noses up at the thought of eating a meal in the bus station, but the only

Ürgüp

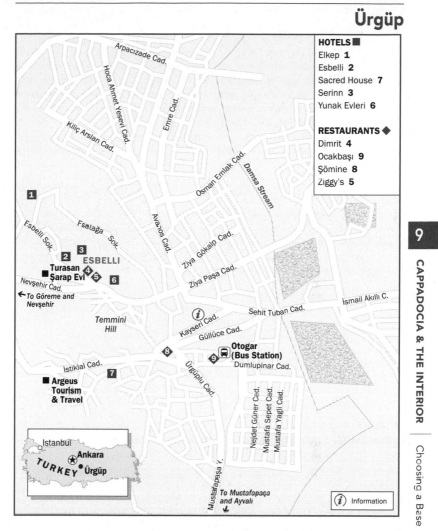

HOTELS ■
Elkep **1**
Esbelli **2**
Sacred House **7**
Serinn **3**
Yunak Evleri **6**

RESTAURANTS ◆
Dimrit **4**
Ocakbaşı **9**
Şömine **8**
Ziggy's **5**

İstanbul
Ankara
TURKEY Ürgüp

ⓘ Information

upturned noses here will be the ones sniffing out the freshly grilled food on the way up the steps to the restaurant's lovely trellised rooftop terrace. Inside and in typical style, a "barbecue bar" circles the hooded area around the charcoal grill; well-dressed tables in the dining room are also located farther away from the hot coals. Whole eggplants get roasted over the flames and then miraculously whipped up into a delectable regional specialty, the *alinazık kebap,* which is topped by chunks of flavorful grilled meat. Don't pass up the hot appetizer, *içli köfte,* mouthwatering hush-puppy-like corn balls stuffed with meat and deep-fried.

In the Ürgüp *otogar.* ⓒ **0384/341-3277.** Appetizers and main courses 5TL–25TL. MC, V. Daily noon–midnight.

Şömine Café and Restaurant ★ REGIONAL TURKISH   In spite of its obvious location, this is the best restaurant in Ürgüp. The marble-paved rooftop terrace overlooks Istiklal Caddesi, while on chillier evenings, you may opt for a spot inside by the cozy, fire-lit open chimney for which the restaurant is named. The menu covers all the bases, but it does each dish with aplomb. The house favorite is the *testi kebap*, a lamb-and-vegetable stew cooked in a type of tandoori oven with peppers and onions. If you're leaning toward this dish, call ahead and reserve a platter or they may be sold out by the time you get there. Another specialty is the *saç tava*, a delectable mixture of eggplant and bite-size chunks of beef.

Ürgüp town center. www.sominerestaurant.com. © **0384/341-8442.** Reservations suggested during high season. Appetizers and main courses 5TL–29TL. MC, V. Daily 9:30am–midnight.

ESBELLI

Dimrit 📷 TURKISH   Just when you thought Cappadocia couldn't get any more romantic, a place like this opens up. It's a restaurant of regal spaces, both indoors and alfresco, each making optimal use of the region's unique cave architecture and truly breathtaking views. The menu is exactly the same as that at Şömine (above), except that it's slightly more limited. But if it's ambiance you're after, this is the ticket.

Yunak Mah. Teyfik Fikret Cad. 40. www.dimrit.com. © **0384/341-8585.** Appetizers and main courses 6TL–29TL. MC, V. Daily 9:30am–midnight.

Ziggy's ★★ TURKISH   Spanning three levels on a perch atop Ürgüp's Esbelli neighborhood, the old stone building that makes up Ziggy's has an atmosphere of barrel vaults, hearths, a roof terrace, and candlelight. Turkish takes on salads and pastas include an irresistible *pastırmalı makarna*—Turkey's version of comfort food—an amazing dish of garlic potatoes, and a good selection of reasonably priced wines and great cocktails for those late summer night sunsets. Ziggy's also has a boutique on the main level stocked full with locally made, high quality handicrafts.

Yunak Mah. Tevfik Fikret Cad. 24, Ürgüp. www.ziggycafe.com. © **0384/341-7107.** Appetizers and main courses 6TL–33TL. MC, V. Daily 11am–11pm.

WHERE TO STAY

Elkep Evi 📷   Three partners have joined forces to cooperatively manage what is essentially three cave houses each with seven rooms. The cave houses rise above and around a garden courtyard while the breakfast lawn—scattered with typically Turkish artifacts—enjoys some of the more fabulous views over Ürgüp. Better yet, most of the rooms have a private terrace with equally outstanding views. The rooms are standard Cappadocia Cave, that is, romantic, spare yet cozy, with carpets, carved wooden headboards and little nooks carved directly into the rock. They've added Jacuzzis in one of the doubles and one suite; another double and suite have Turkish baths.

Eski Turban Oteli Arkası, 50400 Ürgüp. www.elkepevi.com. © **0384/341-6000.** Fax 0384/341-8089. 21 units. 115€–170€ doubles and suites. MC, V. Free parking. **Amenities:** Internet. *In room:* CD player, hair dryer.

Esbelli Evi ★★★ 📷   This is the Cappadocian inn that set the standard for all others, and it's all thanks to Süha, Esbelli's owner, whose genuineness and discreet hospitality are hallmarks of the hotel's warmth and exclusivity. No wonder that every time I pop in, some ambassador is relaxing on the terrace. Nine cave rooms and seven multi-cave suites are chiseled in and around a cluster of contiguous cave dwellings in a breathtaking maze of stone stairways, courtyards, and outdoor terraces. The result is an irresistible collection of rooms that, thanks to polished hardwood floors, ample modern bathrooms, and thick bright white duvets, manage all at once to be prehistoric, modern, and romantic. Cave suites are meandering hideaways with strategic lighting, full kitchens, private terraces, satellite TV, and deliciously oversize bathrooms, where you and that special someone can take rain showers (with two shower heads, nobody gets cold) or soak in the large centerpiece bathtub.

Esbelli Sok. 8, 50400 Ürgüp. www.esbelli.com.tr. ☏ **0384/341-3395.** Fax 0384/341-8848. 13 units. $150 double; $220–$300 suite. MC, V. Free parking. Closed Nov–May and July 15–31. **Amenities:** Bar; smoke-free rooms; free Wi-Fi. *In room:* Hair dryer.

Sacred House ★★★ ◙   Sacred House was originally borne out of a passion for antiques, culminating in a collection of soothing and vital spaces, each infused with a little bit of spirit and soul. Rooms reflect a sort of medieval aristocracy in the richness of the textiles draped over heavy stone walls and invaluable antiques. Rimming an open central courtyard, each room has a slightly different theme; the cleverest (and perhaps creepiest) is the altar room, reflecting the fact that the building used to be a church. The hotel added five super-suite style rooms that defy description, as my jaw is still dangling awkwardly. A roof terrace offers views over town; the restaurant prepares traditional Turkish cuisine with an Armenian twist.

Karahandere Mah., Barbaros Hayrettin, Sok. 25, 50400 Ürgüp. www.sacred-house.com. ☏ **0384/341-7102.** Fax 0384/341-6986. 12 units. $200 double; $300–$500 deluxe and superior. MC, V. Free parking. **Amenities:** Restaurant; rooftop bar; free airport transfer from Kayseri Airport. *In room:* Jacuzzi, free Wi-Fi.

Serinn ★   The scant five rooms that make up the Serinn superimpose a contemporary art feel on top of a prehistoric one. Seeking to carve her niche in an already flooded market, Eren Serpen, a veteran of tourism hospitality from Istanbul, engaged architect Rifat Ergör to come up with a unique and stylish blend of old and new. The result: molded plastic museum pieces and contemporary carpets on stone floors under stone barrel arches or etched cave ceilings. The newest trend in bathrooms in the area—the glass-door step-in rain shower—is featured here in all its deliciousness. And the views are as inspiring as any from the hotel's perch in Esbelli neighborhood.

Esbelli Sok. 36, Ürgüp. www.serinnhouse.com. ☏ **0384/341-6076.** Fax 0384/341-6096. 5 units. $150–$170double. AE, MC, V. Free parking. **Amenities:** Restaurant. *In room:* Hair dryer, free Wi-Fi.

Yunak Evleri ★★ ☺   The Yunak Evleri is a stunning collection of 30 individually sited rooms (renovated from six sprawling cave houses) all set into the base of a dramatic and soaring outcrop, much like an amphitheater around an expansive property. The owner, ex-Istanbul native Yusuf Görürgöz, outfitted his hotel with fine accessories, such as Vakko bed runners, antique furnishings, CD sound systems (deluxe and suites only), and locally made ceramics. He personally designed the bathrooms, installing Swedish multiple-jet and steam showers to create a lavishness even the Four Seasons would be proud of. (The water pressure kicks butt as well!) All rooms enjoy either a private balcony or communal patio, and architectural niches in the main courts of the houses provide wonderful venues for barbecues or bonfires on crisp nights.

Yunak Mah., 50400 Ürgüp. www.yunak.com. ☏ **0384/341-6920.** Fax 0384/341-6924. 30 units. $180 double; $200 deluxe; $250 suite. See website for special offers. MC, V. Free parking. **Amenities:** Restaurant; free Internet; library; music room; smoke-free rooms. *In room:* Hair dryer, minibar.

Ayvalı

23km (14 miles) east of Nevşehir; 6.5km (4 miles) east of Göreme

Ten years ago, this sleepy village of dirt roads and crumbling houses opened up an 8-room hotel. Today, this same hotel has 32 mostly jaw-dropping deluxe cave suites and a pool, with plans for an additional adjacent facility. The village has since sprouted an inn/*tandır* restaurant and another, female-owned B&B. And there's even an Internet cafe attached to the testosterone-heavy village tea house. But if this is your first visit, Ayvalı will still give an impression as a quintessential Anatolian village, a place where life hasn't changed for centuries. A narrow ravine cuts through the bottom of the village with the trickling Içeridere River running the length of the valley all the way to Golgoli Hill, a 6.5km (4-mile) hike away. You can fill up a bottle of sparkling fresh spring water from a source on the edge of the village, while exploring eerie, untouched caves and rock-cut churches.

GETTING THERE

Take the road for Mustafapaşa, and then turn off on the road to Ayvalı. From Ürgüp, take the *dolmuş* which leaves every 2 hours during daytime.

WHERE TO STAY & EAT

Aravan Evi ★ ☑ The Aravan Evi has evolved from its genesis as a family-style restaurant serving Cappadocian dishes prepared in a traditional tandır oven to a welcoming inn that affords visitors an authentic window into life in the village (only much nicer).The inn now has a scant three rooms; two simple yet delightful doubles and a suite/family two-room refuge separated by a carved archway, with a raised cushioned seating area beneath a wood framed window. For the restaurant, the family grows its own fruits and vegetables as the basis for multicourse home-style meals (served for lunch or dinner; daily noon–11pm). The menu revolves around the *tandır*, a small cooking pit and the traditional mode of food preparation for Turks for hundreds, if not thousands, of years. For this reason, you must call ahead (by noon the same day; prix fixe meals cost 30TL per person).

Ayvalı Village. www.aravanevi.com. © **0384/354-5838.** 5 units. $110 double. MC, V. Free parking. **Amenities:** Restaurant (reservations required at least 5 hr. in advance). *In room:* Hair dryer, free Wi-Fi.

Gamirasu Cave Hotel ★★★ ☺ A little more than 10 years ago, a group of German investors fell out of the sky and handed Ibrahim Bey, a then-humble local villager, the funds to turn a group of crumbling caves into a tourist hotel. The inspiration was the dramatic setting: along a wide ravine riddled with abandoned caves on the edge of a still untouched, unspoiled Cappadocian village where bread was (and is) still baked in outdoor ovens and where sun-drying apricots blanket the rooftops. Well, the idea worked, in spades. Gamirasui is a veritable wonderland of fabulous cave suites, each one with elegant and functional decor, creature comforts like TVs and coffeemakers, and spa-like baths with Jacuzzis. Ibrahim's chef d'oevre is the Byzantine King Suite, an over-the-top extravaganza with rock-cut columns, a California king-size bed, a hot tub and a *hamam*. The newly installed swimming pool is a brisk relief after a hot day of trekking through sun-baked valleys, and free bikes and horseback riding are available for guests.

Ayvalı. www.gamirasu.com. © **0384/341-5815.** Fax 0384/341-7487. 30 units. 165€–185€ double; 215€–1,200€ deluxe and suites. Rates lower Nov–Mar. See website for special offers. AE, DC, MC, V. Free parking. **Amenities:** Restaurant; bar; massage; outdoor swimming pool; free Wi-Fi. *In room:* Satellite TV, hair dryer, minibar.

Mustafapaşa

6km (3¾ miles) south of Ürgüp

At first glance, the character of Mustafapaşa (called Sinassos in the past) is defined by its center square, a blink-and-miss-it space for a small cluster of tea houses, locally owned pensions and cafes, and a pleasing cluster of decoratively detailed stone mansions. The village is an enchanting sepia-toned snapshot, illustrating a time when successful Greek merchants created in Cappadocia a vibrant commercial and cultural center. At its center is the esteemed **Church of Sts. Constantine and Helene** (*Konstantin Eleni Kilisesi*), which hosts a lively celebration (perhaps with the Patriarch Bartholomew at the helm), annually at Easter. Just beyond the square are the late 16th-century **Aşağı Mosque,** with two minarets: one dating to Selçuk times and one a more modern addition, and the **Şakır Paşa Medrese,** built in the 1800s to serve the village's Turkish sons. Just outside the center of the village, an ongoing project to rebuild the **Ayos Nikalos,** a philanthropic community center affiliated with the nearby St. Nicholas Monastery. Take some time to enjoy the stately **Greek houses ★,** all of which are now protected. A few (see "Where to Stay & Eat," below) are in use as restaurants or hotels. You should also bring your hiking boots, because the surrounding hills, and particularly the **Gomede Valley,** are riddled with hidden churches and chapels, a few of significance—a sort of mini version of what you'll find in the Ilhara Valley. The bonus of a visit to Mustafapaşa is that the village continues to be a center of winemaking.

GETTING THERE

By car, take the Mustafapaşa road south from Ürgüp. There is also *dolmuş* service from Ürgüp to Mustafapaşa which runs hourly. If you're staying at an inn in town, chances are your hotel owner will provide a transfer or shuttle for a fee, or even for free. Don't be shy to ask.

WHERE TO STAY & EAT

Gül Konakları Upgraded from a humble pension in 2002, this hotel used to be all about the rose gardens. Though the roses remain, the centerpiece now is the combination of distinctive spaces, updated rooms, modern baths, and quality (yet homey) hospitality. The property comprises three Greek homes, two of which serve as guest quarters. You can choose to stay in a stone, barrel-vaulted room, in a cave, or under a rich ceiling of polished wood. A marriage of both Greek and Ottoman antiques and reproductions set the stage throughout, including in the restaurant, where guests will be tempted to pause for a glass of wine. Actually, you'll be pressed to choose where to pause: relax in the windowed and cozy Rose Chalet, brush up on local history in the library, get a tour of the wine room, or unwind in the *hamam*.

Sümer Caddesi, 50420 Mustafapaşa. www.gulkonaklari.dinler.com. ⓒ **0384/353-5486.** 19 units. 130€ double; 160€ suite. AE, MC, V. Free parking. **Amenities:** 2 restaurants; *hamam*; room service; free Wi-Fi; wine room. *In room:* Satellite TV; hair dryer; minibar.

Old Greek House ♨ This old Greek house in the ancient town of Sinassos (now Mustafapaşa), said to be the former mayor's mansion, has been feeding and sheltering guests for years. But it's most known for its meals, a lineup of delicious traditional dishes prepared by the owner Süleyman's wife in the large kitchen off the side of the house (the traditional cave oven she uses for baking is visible from the inner courtyard). The full-course menu for lunch and dinner (there are three choices; 20€, 22€, and 25€) is a tantalizing celebration of Turkish passion for a traditional meal. The

A grape FOR ALL SEASONS: CAPPADOCIA'S WINES

When the winemaking company Kavaklıdere bought 1,600 acres for a new production center in nearby Gülşehir, it was a signal to the rest of Turkish oenophiles that Cappadocian wine had arrived. Families have been making wines in Cappadocia for centuries; a visit to one of these small producers will get you a double dose of traditional Turkish hospitality. Many of them, plus producers from around the world, convene in Ürgüp for the International Wine Festival held annually in October. Two of the majors offer wine tastings in outposts of their vineyards; a number of wine shops around the region also arrange tasting events. Stop by **Turasan Şarap Evi's** new tasting center (just outside of Ürgüp center on the Nevşehir road in the Esbelli section; ℂ **0384/341-4961;** www.turasan.com.tr), May through October daily 8am to 8pm; November through April daily 8am to 6pm. **Kocabağ** (Atatürk Bulv. Göreme Yolu 69, Üçhisar; ℂ **0384/219-2979;** www.kocabag.com) is a slightly smaller operation with award-winning wines that pack a nice punch. Flights start at 10TL in the new, enlarged, and inviting tasting space. There are also a number of small fabricators ("şarapçilik") in Mustafapaşa: check out **Şenol** (ℂ **0384/353-5014**), **Sinasos** (ℂ **0384/353-5354**) or **Kapadokya** (ℂ **0384/353-5003**).

house retains many of its original features, and guests dine either in the main courtyard (daytime), or in one of the two upper-story rooms (dinner and off-season), where some impressive frescoes are still partially visible. There are 13 guest rooms with two-star facilities; contact the hotel/restaurant for rates.

Mustafapaşa. www.oldgreekhouse.com. ℂ **0384/353-5141.** 13 units. 60€ double. AE, MC, V. Free parking. **Amenities:** Restaurant; babysitting; *hamam;* room service; free Wi-Fi.

Perimasalı Hotel ★★ ▢ The cave house that was transformed into this little fairy tale of a hotel dates to 1858, when its original owner staked his claim on this hill just outside of the village. The hotel now conceals a romantic hideaway with rooms and suites each inspired by a different muse. Indeed, you'll feel like you just stepped in to a living version of Aphrodite's chambers. All of the lushly decorated, artistically lit cave rooms, sporting names like Daphne, Lyke, and Galatea, have Jacuzzis and coffee/tea stations.

Davutlu Mah. Sehit Aslan Yakar Sok. 6, Mustafapaşa. www.perimasalihotel.com. ℂ **0384/353-5090.** Fax 0384/353-5066. 24 units. 100€ double; 150€–250€ suite. Rates lower Nov–Mar. AE, MC, V. *In room:* Satellite TV, hair dryer, minibar.

Göreme

15km (9⅓ miles) east of Nevşehir; 6.5km (4 miles) west of Ürgüp

For years, Göreme's name recognition has been high among backpackers, a state of affairs that led to a profusion of charmless, dormitory-style pensions and fly-by-night bars catering to a coed crowd. But as travelers to the region increase, young ambitious entrepreneurs are stepping up to the plate with better-endowed pensions and outright luxury hotels. For the most part, however, the presence of "modern," albeit low-rise, concrete slabs detracts from the magic of the horizon.

Ultimately, I don't usually recommend Göreme as a base, but with the prices of rooms skyrocketing in such places as Ürgüp and even Üçhisar, staying here does have its advantages. The main appeal of Göreme, besides the Open Air Museum located on its fringes, is the village's proximity to some of the most scenic valley walks. Inconspicuous early churches dot the landscape between the town and the Open Air Museum, popping up unexpectedly at the edge of a lonely corner of a valley. In Göreme itself, one of the few villages in which the rock homes and fairy chimneys have been continually inhabited, the attractions share the spotlight with the daily lives of the locals. Gentrification has yet to push out its natives and, with it, the authenticity of the village. In Göreme it's still common to run into a donkey delivery, or stumble upon a devout gaggle of chatty women and chickens, while staying fairly accessible to food, transportation, and Internet cafes.

ESSENTIALS

GETTING THERE   Most bus companies serving Göreme stop a few blocks from the center and provide the quick minibus transfer to the *otogar,* only 2 blocks away. If you planned on taking a taxi from the *otogar* to your hotel, you may as well grab one now. An area *dolmuş* follows a circuit hourly from Ürgüp bus station to Zelve, Avanos, Göreme, Üçhisar, and back. If you're traveling by car out of Ürgüp, you can either take the road to Avanos, turn onto the road past Zelve, and take the northern approach into Göreme; or head out of town on the Nevşehir road and take the steep cobblestone road through the Göreme Open Air Museum on your way into Göreme. The difference in mileage between the two approaches is negligible. So if your purpose is to see the town and museum, then by all means, take one road in and the other out.

GETTING AROUND   Göreme is eminently walkable, especially because much of the center of town is flat. To venture a little farther out, hook up with one of the bicycle or scooter-rental shops at or around the *otogar.*

VISITOR INFORMATION   There's a little **tourist information office** run by the Göreme Tourism Development Cooperative at the *otogar* (Terminal İçi no. 1; ✆ **0384/271-2317**), which mainly caters to visitors looking for accommodations. Inside is a collection of signboards of many of the pensions in town. The office is open Monday through Friday from 8:30am to 7pm, but many of the pensions have signs posted outside as well. Be on the lookout for misunderstandings relating to the cost of extras; sometimes there's a big surprise when the bill arrives. Pop into one of the several travel agencies at the *otogar* for a map of the area.

ORIENTATION   If you blink, you're bound to miss it. The road from the Open Air Museum leads right to the center of town over a dry creek bed; turn left onto Uzundere Caddesi until you get to the *otogar.* Everything you need is located here or just behind the station, including tour operators, car and scooter rentals, taxis, and the tourist information office. The bazaar is located behind the *otogar* around the mosque and Roman tower.

Adnan Menderes Caddesi forks off from Uzundere Caddesi closer to the turnoff from the museum; Kapadokya Balloons is on the right and the Orient Restaurant is on the left.

WHERE TO EAT
Orient Restaurant ★ ☺ TURKISH   The Orient is hands-down the most solidly consistent restaurant in Göreme. Highlights of the menu include a steak rivaling

anything I've had anywhere, and an outstanding lamb rack. Orient also has an exceptional wine list that includes French imports and the best local wines (try the Öküzgözü or the Kalecik Karası). In spite of its location on the edge of town, you could easily feel like you were dining in a country inn. There is both an outdoor patio terrace and a light and airy dining room where you can choose a table or grab one of the many low-to-the-ground tables with reclining-back chairs.

Göreme Center (across from Kapadokya Balloons). www.orientrestaurant.net. ℂ **0384/271-2346.** Appetizers and main courses 8TL–40TL. MC, V. Daily 7am until the last person leaves.

Seten Restaurant ★☆🍴 ANATOLIAN The stars have finally aligned to create in Göreme a range of food more typically found at a celebratory meal rather than on the menu in Göreme or for that matter in Cappadocia. For example, Seten has its own tandır oven, allowing it to slow-cook traditional foods like stuffed grape leaves and a lamb shank served with seasonal vegetables. Other delicacies are the bulgur "wedding soup," the pastırma with onions and tomato, and the Kayseri mantı, which can be served either filled with ground meat or cheese. The restaurant also has its own wine cellar filled with reds and whites made from locally grown grapes using age-old production techniques.

Aydınlı Mah. Aydınlı Sok.42-44, Göreme. www.setenrestaurant.com. ℂ **0384/271-3024.** Appetizers and main courses 8TL–40TL. MC, V. Daily 7am until the last person leaves.

WHERE TO STAY

After reaching a saturation point of cheap accommodations and witnessing the growth in high-end tourism receipts from the neighboring villages, Göreme's hotels and pensions set out to spruce themselves up. Now you can enjoy the romance of a luxury cave suite or a glistening fairy chimney just steps from the heartbeat of town.

Anatolian Houses ★★ The hotel sits inconspicuously up a narrow lane behind an unassuming whitewashed stone wall near Göreme center. Jaws tend to drop upon entering, with its decorative indoor/outdoor dipping pool. Also unexpected is the hotel's stylish glass facade, allowing a peek into the spacious sitting room/lobby. As with almost all Cappadocian cave rooms, rooms are tucked away atop narrow and sometimes steep exterior stone stairways. If vertigo is a problem, ask for one of the rooms in the fairy chimney. Fourteen rooms have Jacuzzis while four have hydromassage showers. Ask for a taste of the house wine on tap *in the wall* of the entry courtyard stocked from the hotel's own wine cellar.

Gaferli Mah., 50180 Göreme. www.anatolianhouses.com.tr. ℂ **0384/271-2463.** Fax 0384/271-2229. 19 units. 280€–800€ suite. AE, DC, MC, V. Free parking. **Amenities:** Restaurant; bar; *hamam;* indoor/outdoor pool; room service; spa; free Wi-Fi. *In room:* Satellite TV, hair dryer, minibar.

Göreme House This humble little guesthouse, converted from a century-old stately Paşa's mansion, is now in the very capable hands of new owner/managers Murat and Pınar, both veterans of Turkey's tourism industry. While before this three-story hotel was a bit sterile, now it's filled with small-town Turkish warmth. A few of the rooms are cut into the rock, but the majority are the typical single-vaulted rooms. Two suites are perked up with the addition of en-suite Jacuzzis. Two upper terraces, one glass-enclosed bar and TV room and the other a spectacular open balcony, offer panoramic views of the neighboring fairy chimneys and rock-cut houses.

Eselli Mah. 47, 50180 Göreme. ℂ **0384/271-2060.** Fax 0384/271-2668. 13 units. 60€ standard; 75€ deluxe; 100€ cave suite. Rates lower Nov–Apr. MC, V. Free parking. **Amenities:** Restaurant; bar; airport transfer (10TL); free Wi-Fi. *In room:* Satellite TV.

Kelebek Pansiyon and Kelebek Boutique Hotel ⚜ A far cry from the scrappy backpacker's pension I first visited in 2000, Kelebek has upgraded, expanded, added a swimming pool and grown into a boutique-style hotel with a majority of suites. The rooms in the pension rate well above pension level, with prices that give those over at the boutique hotels a run for their money. A comparative bargain—double rooms for as low as 50€—can be had in about half of the rooms; the catch is that these units are smaller. Rooms are decked out in Ottoman style and sport bathrooms with marble walls, Jacuzzis, and *hamam* basins. There are also two tiny and basic fairy chimney rooms without bathrooms for 40€.

Aydinli Mah., 50180 Göreme. www.kelebekhotel.com. ℂ **0384/271-2531.** Fax 0384/271-2763. 36 units. 50€–65€; 80€–140€ suites. MC, V. Free parking. **Amenities:** Restaurant; bar; airport transfer (10€ per person); *hamam;* outdoor pool; spa; free Wi-Fi.

Üçhisar

9km (5⅔ miles) east of Nevşehir; 6km (3¾ miles) southwest of Göreme

In the valley surrounding Üçhisar, the advancement of rock formation and erosion can be seen in all of its stages. Cresting above the valley are pink-and-yellow-hued sand dunes that when under closer scrutiny reveal rocky channels. Down below, perforating the rock face of Güvercinlik Vadisi, or Pigeon Valley, are the best examples of pigeon houses, painted white to attract the birds and their valuable guano. The fortress of Üçhisar is the highest peak in the region, drawing tourists to its summit for panoramic views of this fascinating landscape with Mount Erciyes in the distance. Down below, local shops are slowly being transformed into art galleries, and ancient monasteries into atmospheric venues.

The sleepy troglodyte village of Üçhisar, spread out at the base of the fortress, was discovered years back by intrepid French travelers. Word spread, apparently as far as Italy, and quality inns and hotels (as well as English speakers) began the tired pensions of yore. Not surprisingly, the quiet landscape of Üçhisar is increasingly coming at a higher price. Visitors can still get a taste of the elusive and authentic Cappadocian village experience before Üçhisar succeeds in renovating itself beyond recognition. Hurry.

ESSENTIALS

GETTING THERE & GETTING AROUND Regular municipal buses run from Nevşehir to Üçhisar, but the village is close enough to Nevşehir that you could take a cab without breaking the bank. If you're coming from Göreme, you can get on one of the frequent buses running to Nevşehir. Because of its quiet, isolated nature, Üçhisar is more for the independent traveler; staying here is going to require your own wheels.

ORIENTATION The village of Üçhisar is centered around the **fortress,** surrounded by a hillside of oddly shaped house-caves and neatly carved facades. Around Üçhisar is the spectacular scenery of Güvercinlik Valley, dotted with dovecotes and rolling rock dunes. A tea garden and outdoor restaurant occupy the center of town.

WHAT TO SEE & DO

Üçhisar has attracted its fair share of French tourists, drawn by the possibility of utter seclusion in one of the exclusive cave houses of Les Maisons de Cappadoce (p. 372). Life's frenetic pace is all but forgotten in Üçhisar, where tourists rarely venture farther than the towering rock fortress.

WHERE TO EAT

Because of the high turnover rate of moderately priced eateries combined with the arrival of overly expensive (albeit exceptionally atmospheric) restaurants, I've limited the inclusion of restaurants to one. If you're looking for something sophisticated, consider **Seki Restaurant,** in Argos in Cappadocia (see "Where to Stay" below).

Centre Café and Restaurant ✦ Every little town has its own epicenter, and here it's the Centre Café and Restaurant, a tiny dining space attached to the leafy terrace tea garden. Dishes are prepared by Hüseyn, an ex-chef of the Kaya Hotel (when it was a Club Med) down the road. And while eateries in Üçhisar come and go, the Center Café continues to serve consistently good Turkish food plus some embellishments to appeal to the mostly French clientele. Belediye Meydanı. ℂ **0384/219-3117.** Appetizers and main courses 7TL–16TL. AE, MC, V. Apr–Dec noon–midnight.

WHERE TO STAY

Argos in Cappadocia ★★★ More than just another deluxe Cappadocian hotel, this collection of houses, each with a shared expanse of lawn, Arabesque archways, unexpected accents, and spectacular vistas of Güverçinlik Valley, has created a lifestyle experience atop an centuries-old monastery. Rooms are grouped among five houses, terraced down the tufa hillside and connected by stairways and underground tunnels artfully lit as museum showpieces. Most have traditional stone fireplaces and either a private garden, terrace, or balcony, while several of the suites enjoy their own indoor, sublimely sited private pool. No surprise then to see that *Travel + Leisure* has already put its imprimatur on the hotel via the preeminent magazine's 2010 "It List" of the best new hotels.

50240 Üçhisar. www.argosincappadocia.com. ℂ **0384/219-3130.** Fax 0384/219-2055. 42 units. 160€–240€ double; 400€ suite. AE, MC, V. Free parking. **Amenities:** 2 restaurant; bar; concierge; room service; smoke-free rooms. *In room:* Satellite TV, hair dryer; free Wi-Fi.

Kale Konak ★★ 🏕 More like a small, boutique bed-and-breakfast, the Kale Konak takes up three restored cave houses, one of which sits across the street from the other two (and is connected via an underground tunnel). Touches of warmth are everywhere, from the greeting you will receive upon arrival, to the hand-made linens, to the abundant breakfast. Although cave hotels and this hotel reek of romance, families with children have the option of booking the room with a mezzanine level bunk, accessible via a ladder. In fact, most rooms are outsized while all are charming. There's a Turkish bath that's free and open 24/7, and if you're up in the morning for breakfast, you may get a glimpse of hot air balloons on the horizon.

Kale Sok. 9, 50240 Üçhisar (at the base of the fortress). www.kalekonak.com. ℂ **0384/219-2828.** Fax 0384/219-3006. 14 units. 100€–110€ double; 120€ suite. AE, MC, V. Free parking. **Amenities:** Bar; *hamam* (free); room service; smoke-free rooms. *In room:* Satellite TV, hair dryer, free Wi-Fi.

Les Maisons de Cappadoce ★★ ☺ Renovated by Jacques Avizou, an expatriate French architect, these romantic cave houses look as if they stepped right out of a feature in *Maison et Jardin.* Closed gates and unremarkable doorways open to reveal duplex and triplex houses with breathtaking arches, stone terraces, garden courtyards, and huge fully equipped kitchens (except in the studios, which have kitchenettes). A welcome basket full of basic provisions (bread, butter, sugar, salt, eggs, and water) will be waiting for you. Residents are requested to provide access to the gardener or camera crews, who every now and again choose Les Maisons de Cappadoce as a location for a movie or magazine spread. The only problem with this Garden of Eden is that once you've arrived, you never want to leave. The magic of the spot is all the more evident at sunset, when the sky and chimneys turn glorious shades of red and purple.

Semiramis Aş, Belediye Meydanı 24, 50240 Üçhisar. www.cappadoce.com. No phone. Fax 0384/219-2782. 6 studios; 10 houses for 4–7 people. 140€–190€ studio; 240€–980€ house. Breakfast "hamper" included in rate. MC, V. Free parking. *In room:* Hair dryer, kitchen.

Les Terrasses d'Üçhisar ♦ ☺ For those on a budget, this is the best option in town. The hotel consists of seven cave rooms, six Anatolian-style rooms with single-barrel vaults, and one family suite in a group of adjacent stone houses. The setup is typical of the area pensions—accommodations are clean, with floors of stone and tile, and ad-hoc bathroom/shower combos that you eventually do get used to. To sweeten the deal, Les Terrasses includes breakfast and walks in the valley (and maybe a stop at their friend's place?) with the room rate. The suite can accommodate up to five people, making this a good bet for families.

Eski Göreme Yolu, 50240 Üçhisar. © **0384/219-2792.** Fax 0384/219-2762. 14 units. 45€ double; 98€ family suite. MC, V. Free parking. Closed Nov–Mar. **Amenities:** Restaurant; bar. *In room:* no phone.

Ortahisar

4 km (2.5 miles) west of Ürgüp; 3km (1¾ miles) southeast of Göreme

As the region's geological bull's-eye, Ortahisar grew up around the region's central focal point, a massive rock-hewn "chimney" that because of its strategic location, served in ancient times as one of three fortress lookout points (the name of the village means "middle fortress"). The town was, early on, discovered by Spanish nationals who, like the French who descended upon Avanos and Üçhisar, came, liked what they saw, and conquered (by buying real estate). Ortahisar remains suspended in time, no longer a village but not quite yet a town, a mostly unspoiled, residential locale with a tea house, a few eateries and shops, a makeshift wine house, and plenty of satellite dishes and laundry suspended from crumbling balconies. You'll need a private car or plans to join a local tour group if you decide to stay in town, because there is no practical public transport serving Ortahisar (the only direct *dolmuş* comes from Avanos).

WHERE TO STAY & EAT

Hezen This hotel brought the color back to Cappadocia—a sepia-toned landscape traditionally embellished through the use of color applied to wood trim and doors. Hezen has revived the practice, creating a striking contrast to the drop-dead view of Ortahisar Kalesi. Outside is a multi-level terrace dripping in ivy, off of which gives the 10 (and counting) cave rooms. Accommodations vary; #4 has its own banquette nook, the smaller #7 has a private terrace accessible through the window, #8 has an inside sitting cove, and #10 has a stone art feature that divides the room space in two. Rooms are small compared to other hotels in the region, and only the deluxe and suite rooms have TVs and minibars. Breakfast is a revelation, with homemade pastries and cakes supplementing an already abundant traditional spread. Hakan, the owner, also makes his own wine (his dad actually does the work).

Esentepe Mah. Tahir Bey Sok 87, Ortahisar. www. hezenhotel.com. © **0384/343-3005.** Fax 0384/343-2328. 10 units. $150 double; $250 deluxe and suite. AE, MC, V. Free parking. Closed Jan and Feb. **Amenities:** Restaurant; bar. *In room:* Free Wi-Fi.

EXPLORING CAPPADOCIA

Göreme Open Air Museum ★★★ MONASTERY Cappadocia's main attraction and the customary starting point for an overview of what the region has to offer, the Göreme Open Air Museum is a monastic complex composed of churches, rectories, and dwellings, and one of the earliest centers for religious education.

The practice of monasticism was developed by St. Basil the Great, bishop of Caesarea (Kayseri) in the 4th century, as a reaction to his increased disillusionment with the materialism of the Church. St. Basil's definition of monastic life, based on the idea that men should live in small, self-sufficient units with an emphasis on poverty, obedience, labor, and religious devotion, took root in Cappadocia, and later became the basis for the Orthodox monastic system.

St. Basil, his brother St. Gregory of Nyssa, and St. Gregory of Nazianoz (St. Gregorios the Theologian) greatly influenced the course of religious thought through their writings, contributing to the development of Eastern Orthodoxy. In his extensive writings St. Basil describes the nature of the Holy Spirit as a trinity, while St. Gregory of Nyssa wrote of the dogma of the Virgin Mary, and St. Gregory of Nazianoz developed the thesis on Jesus as a representative of the indivisible nature of the human and divine. Because of their contributions, Cappadocia became known as "the land of the three saints," but was soon divided in two in A.D. 371 when Emperor Valens rejected Basil's thesis on Jesus as the son of God.

There are at least 10 churches and chapels in the museum area dating between A.D. 900 and 1200, each one named (after a prominent attribute) by the local villagers who were exploring these caves long before there was an entrance fee. The paintings and decoration represent a flowering of a uniquely Cappadocian artistic style, while the Byzantine architectural features of the churches, like arches, columns, and capitals, are interesting in that not one of them is necessary structurally. The best way to approach the site is to begin in a counterclockwise direction toward a clearly marked path.

During the Iconoclastic period, many of the frescoes and paintings were damaged, while the eyes of the images were scratched out by the local Turkish population superstitious of the "evil eye." Past a small rock tower or **Monks' Convent** ★ is the **Church of St. Basil** ★, whose entrance is hollowed out with niches for small graves. This is a common feature of Cappadocian churches and it's still not uncommon to reach down and come up with a knuckle bone every now and again in the more remote valleys. Another recurring theme in Cappadocian churches is the image of St. George slaying the dragon. St. George was considered a local hero, as local lore equated the dragon with a monster on the summit of Mount Erciyes. The church is decorated with scenes of Christ, with St. Basil and St. Theodore depicted on the north wall.

The **Church with the Apple (Elmalı Kilise)** ★★★ is one of the smaller churches in the area, carved in the sign of a Greek cross with four irregular pillars supporting a central dome. The church was restored in 1991; however, the frescoes continue to chip off, revealing a layer of earlier paintings underneath. Paintings depict scenes of the saints, bishops, and martyrs, and to the right of the altar, a Last Supper with the symbolic fish (the letters of the word *fish* in Greek stand for "Jesus Christ, Son of God, the Savior"). The name of the church is believed to refer to a reddish orb in the left hand of the Archangel Michael in the dome of the main apse, although there's also speculation that there used to be an apple tree at the entrance to the church.

Santa Barbara was an Egyptian saint imprisoned by her father to protect her from the influences of Christianity. When she nevertheless found a way to practice her faith, her father tortured and killed her. The **Church of Santa Barbara ★★★**, probably built as a tribute, is a cross-domed church with three apses, with mostly crudely painted geometrical patterns in red ochre believed to be symbolic in nature. The wall with the large locust probably represents evil, warded off by the protection of two adjacent crosses. The repetitive line of bricks above the rooster in the upper right-hand corner, symbolically warding off the evil influences of the devil, represents the Church.

The **Snake Church ★** is a simple barrel-vaulted church with a low ceiling and long nave. One fresco represents Saints Theodore and George slaying the dragon (looking suspiciously like a snake), with Emperor Constantine the Great and his mother, Helena, depicted holding the "True Cross." Legend has it that she discovered the cross upon which Jesus was crucified after seeing it in a dream, and that a piece of the cross is still buried in the foundations of the Hagia Sophia in Istanbul. Other sections of the cross are in the Church of the Holy Sepulchre and in St. Peter's in Rome. Another interesting portrait is the one of St. Onuphrius on the upper wall to the right of the entrance. The saint, a popular subject in medieval art, lived the life of a hermit in the Egyptian desert near Thebes and is usually depicted with a long gray beard and a fig leaf over his privates.

Until the 1950s the **Dark Church (Karanlık Kilise) ★★★** was used as a pigeon house. After a restoration project that entailed 14 years of scraping pigeon droppings off the walls, these frescoes, depicting scenes from the New Testament, are the best preserved in all of Cappadocia and a fine example of 11th-century Byzantine art. Because light is allowed in through only one small opening, the richness of the pigments has survived the test of time. There is an additional admission of 8TL for entry into the Dark Church.

Cut into the same rock as the Dark Church and accessible via a metal walkway, the **Church with Sandals (Çarıklı Kilise) ★★** takes its name from the two imprints on the floor inside the entrance. In the land of truth-stretching, these footprints have been given some weighty religious significance, but the fact is, they're just footprints and all of those stories are just more creative embellishment. The church is carved into a simple cross plan with intersecting barrel vaults. The frescoes, which date to the 11th century, depict the Nativity, the Baptism, the Adoration of the Magi, and other New Testament themes.

The last thing to see before exiting the museum is the **Nunnery, or Girls' Tower (Kızlar Kalesi) ★★**, a six-story convent cut into the rock with a system of tunnels, stairways, and corridors. The convent housed up to 300 nuns, whose proximity spawned rumors of a tunnel connecting the tower and the Monks' Convent to the right of the museum entrance.

About 5m (16 ft.) outside the exit to the museum site on the right is the **Buckle Church (Tokalı Kilise) ★★★**, the largest rock-cut church and the one with the most sensational collection of frescoes in all of Cappadocia. Of all of the narrations of scenes from the Bible in the region, these are painted with the most detail and use the richest colors.

The Buckle Church is a complex formed of four chambers: the Old Church, the New Church, the Paracclesion, and the Lower Church. The **Old Church** dates to the 10th century, with pale hues of red and green painted in strips to represent scenes from the New Testament. Panels of rich indigo painted with pigments from the lapis

THE CARAVANSARIES OF THE silk ROAD

One of the five pillars of Islam is the Koranic obligation of alms-giving, and in the fulfillment of this obligation, the Selçuks were notorious for their commitment to public works. One of the institutions created by the Selçuks in Anatolia was the *kervansaray,* or "caravan palace." Used as military bases during wartime and as inns in peacetime, these fortresses provided protection to merchants traveling along the trade routes, offering them up to 3 days of free lodging and an unprecedented system of insurance in the event of loss or injury. Caravansaries were spaced out along the trade routes at a distance of about every 49km (30 miles)—1 day's travel—and from sunset to sunrise when the main gate was closed, guests were officially under the protection of the sultan.

With control over the land trade routes and the centralization of power, Anatolia became the center of international trade under the Selçuk Empire. Thus the "Silk Road" became a great source of wealth, as taxes on overland goods continued to fill the coffers of the sultan. Spices, ivory, and fine cloth were brought from the Far East, while surprisingly, much of the trade was in slaves. The Ottoman *devşirme* system was to collect men from the Eastern lands, train them in the art of warfare, and sell them off to neighboring southern states.

Caravansaries also operated as marketplaces, where merchants could unload their goods, have a bath, and move on. It was unusual for anyone to stay beyond the 3-day limit, because a

person's selling power was linked to the availability of new clientele, and that fizzled out after the first day. A typical journey lasted about a month before a merchant headed back home; by the time a shipment of silk brocade found its way to Istanbul, the price had been considerably marked up.

The caravansaray was built according to one of three basic plans: an open courtyard, a covered building, or a combination of the two. The most opulent of the caravansaries were those reflecting the prosperity of the sultan. Called "sultanhans," these caravansaries were built on an essentially identical plan. The main portal opened onto a courtyard with a small raised mosque at the center. To the left was an arcade providing much-needed shade for protection against the scorching summer sun. On the right was a second portal leading into the apartments, which included a kitchen and *hamam.* At the back was an ornamental gate for access into the winter hall, a covered structure that shows a striking resemblance to a medieval church. The vaults in the main nave could be up to 14m (46 ft.) high, while the top of the lantern, a central domed space providing the only light in the hall, could be at a height of up to 20m (66 ft.). The walls were thick enough to provide good insulation, and tiny windows in the lantern kept out the cold. Men and camels sometimes slept in the winter section together, which, combined with the smell of spices and smoke from the oil lamps

stone dominate the **New Church,** carved out of the eastern wall of the Old Church and decorated with Eastern-style arches and a series of arcades. The **Paracclesion** is a chapel with a single apse, and the **Lower Church** has three aisles and a burial space, or *krypto.*

The high plateau behind **Tokalı Church** brings you to Kılıçlar Valley, named "Valley of the Swords" for the jagged formations that seem to slice into the sky. This is a favorite spot for hikers because of its high cliffs, deep ravines, and vineyards, in and water pipes, probably required the use of a *whole* lot of incense.

While the exterior of the fortress structure was plain, the Selçuks had a tradition of richly ornamenting the *pishtaq*, or portal. The *pishtaq*, generally limestone or marble, displayed elaborate geometrical carvings, tracery, rosettes, and inscriptions, and was hollowed out into a stalactite niche much like that of a *mihrab* (a niche that indicates the direction of Mecca).

There were also private caravansaries called *hans*, mostly located in towns that charged a fee for lodging, while the *bedesten* was typically a marketplace and workshop only. These sensational structures dot the Anatolian landscape from Istanbul to Antalya and from Erzurum to Izmir, and are used as hotels, restaurants, or the dreaded discothèque; you'll probably have the opportunity to stay in one in the course of your travels.

The best conserved of all the Selçuk *hans* is the **Sultanhanı** located about 32km (20 miles) outside of Aksaray on the road to Konya. The Sultanhanı, built by Alaeddin Keykubat I in 1229, has a highly ornamented *pishtaq* with a variety of decorative patterns applied in an unrelated, almost spontaneous manner. A fine example of a *sultanhan* is the **Ağzıkarahan,** located 15km (9⅓ miles) outside of Aksaray on the road to Nevşehir. The Ağzıkarahan, the third largest in the area along the Silk Road, has weathered time to remain almost intact and encloses a space of over 6,000 sq. m (64,583 sq. ft.). The open section, now used to display carpets, was built by Alaeddin Keykubat in 1231 and includes the central mosque reachable by steep and cumbersome steps. The winter section is attributed to Sultan Giyaseddin Keyhüsrev and was completed 8 years after the open section. Enormous stone vaults rise above the main aisle of the nave, flanked by raised platforms that were used for meals during the day and as sleep space at night. The camels were kept in the side bays. Unfortunately, the central dome has been lost.

Halfway between Aksaray and Nevşehir is the **Alay Han,** the first *sultanhan* to be built in Central Anatolia. Erected in 1192 by Sultan Kılıçarslan II, the Alay Han is under threat to become another "day facility" by the same investor who "preserved" the **Sarıhan** in Avanos. The Sarıhan (☏ **0384/511-3795;** www.sarihan1249.com) located 5km (3 miles) outside of Avanos, whose name means "yellow han" for the color of its stone, stands on an old trade route between Aksaray and Kayseri. Except for the mosque, the caravansaray follows a traditional *sultanhan* plan. It now serves as a daytime cafe and an evocative setting for a nightly staging of the *sema,* or rite of the **Whirling Dervişes,** which takes place in the winter hall or sleeping quarters. Sarıhan is 5km (3 miles) outside of Avanos center, on the road to Kaysari (reservations required; admission 30€; Apr–Oct nightly at 9:30pm, Nov–Mar at 9pm—show starts promptly, so get there early).

addition to a tunnel that forms part of an old drainage system. The cliff walls are dotted with dovecotes or pigeon houses hollowed out of the rock to harvest valuable fertilizer—pigeon droppings are rich in nitrogen—by area farmers. There are several old churches in this valley, but they are closed to the public. The best way to get to the valley is to enter along an access road from the road between the Göreme Museum and the town.

TURKEY'S TEXAS tea: THE RED CLAY OF AVANOS

With a tradition of pottery making that dates back to Hittite times, Avanos has made its name out of red clay. At one time, the craft so permeated the culture of the city that every household had a pottery wheel or workshop. Now the most prominent feature of the town, besides the unsightly terra-cotta sculpture in the town center, is the word *chez*, as something about this particular corner of Cappadocia acts as a magnet for French nationals. As a base for explorations in Cappadocia, I couldn't recommend Avanos less. For 2 hours of poking in and out of ceramic shops, I have only slightly better things to say, if only regarding the region's distinctive terra-cotta pottery and the admittedly spectacular Ottoman ceramic reproductions.

The city, carved into the rock like so many other ancient Cappadocian towns, sits along the banks of the Kızılırmak (Red River), the longest river in Turkey. The river takes its name from the color of the water, stained by the red clay

exclusive to the region, an abundant source of the raw material necessary in pottery production. Currently there are about 30 pottery shops in town, most of them boasting the same techniques used by the Hittites. But although Avanos has its own homegrown brand of terra-cotta urns, a vast majority of the classic Iznik and Kütahya designs are mass-produced using clay from Kütahya (see "Iznik & Nicaea: A Pilgrimage & Some Plates," under "Side Trips from Istanbul," in chapter 4) and marketed as valuable high-quality "Iznik reproductions." Sure, it's fascinating and fun to participate in a dirty demo on the kick-wheel, but it's all part of the sales pitch, as are the endless fabrications about quality—seems the art of Turkish salesmanship extends beyond the fringes of carpeting to the delicate surfaces of these ceramics. Worse, I have yet to successfully hand-carry a sample home, as many of the plates are much cheaper quality than the price might indicate. Charge it, have it shipped in a

Müze Yolu, outside of Göreme Center, on the road to Üçhisar. www.nevsehirkulturturizm.gov.tr. © **0384/271-2167.** Admission 15TL. Separate ticket for the Karanlık Kilise/Dark Church 8TL. Daily 8am–7pm (8am–5pm Nov–Mar).

Derinkuyu Underground City (Derinkuyu Yeraltı Şehri) HISTORIC SITE The underground city at Derinkuyu, aptly translated as "dark well," is the largest known example of troglodyte living in Cappadocia. Eight of the levels are open to the public, with the lowest level at a depth of 54m (177 ft.). The complex is an organized and functionally advanced public space for galleries, rooms, chapels, access tunnels, water wells, and air shafts for when the communities had to dig in for the long haul. A long raised mound surrounded by trenches is thought to have been used as a school, while the stables occupied the extreme upper floors. The visit can also be strenuous: At 204 steps, the corridor from the lowest level of Derinkuyu to the surface will cause even the most physically fit visitor to catch his or her breath and may require you to hunch over for a good part of the way.

Only about 10% to 15% of the city's total area is available to the public, and it is thought that the city goes much farther down. Like many of the underground cities, the passageways and cavities at Derinkuyu were used as storage by local farmers until 1964, when the complex was opened to the public.

Derinkuyu. www.nevsehirkulturturizm.gov.tr. © **0384/381-3194.** Admission 15TL. Daily 8am–7pm (8am–5pm Nov–Mar). Derinkuyu is 26km (16 miles) south of Nevşehir on the Ürgüp Soğanlı rd.; take the turnoff for Güzelöz. Derinkuyu is 15km (9⅓ miles) south of Kamaklı Underground City.

hard-sided box, and pay the bill only after the piece arrives safely on your doorstep.

Fırca (formerly Sirca; the sons took over from the father and changed the name; Alaeddin Camii Yanı (Fırca *©* **0384/511-3686;** www.Fırcaceramic. com), claims to have the largest collection of ceramics in Turkey, employing more than 100 people. Adding to their traditional and artistic pieces, Fırca also has an original line of Byzantine and religious decorative designs: classical repros of vases and the like decorated with symbols from Hittite mythology or in the Greek style. Fırca has souvenirs from 10TL with the best specimens (several of which are proudly displayed in my own home) in the Top Quality Room costing from 300TL to 20,000TL. Shipping for plates over 16" in diameter is free; otherwise it's around $80.

Another one of my personal favorites is the "special family design" creations at **Güray & Kaya Seramik House and**

Güray Çömlekçilik, Eski Nevşehir Yolu 18 (from Avanos center, ceramic center is just outside of town on the old Nevşehir road on the right; *©* **0384/511-5091;** www.gurayseramik.com.tr). The showroom, stocked chock-full of traditional and one-of-a-kind designs, takes up 12 caves carved into the rock on the road out of town.

Break up your visit with a meal over at **Bizim Ev** (Orta Mah., Baklacı Sok. 1 behind the Sarıhan near the bridge; *©* **0384/511-5525;** www.bizim-ev.com; daily 9am–midnight). It's got four atmospheric dining areas, including an indoor terrace, an outdoor sun patio, and an upstairs "back room" mellowed by stone, arches, and *kilims*. Order the *bostan kebap*, a decadent dish of shredded beef and eggplant covered in cheese and baked in a clay pot, or the uncannily juicy *tavuk şiş* (roasted chicken), all at prices too reasonable to believe.

Güzelyurt HISTORIC SITE Güzelyurt, which means "beautiful homeland," embodies all of the characteristics of Cappadocia: open fields and pastures, troglodyte houses, underground cities, and monastery complexes all within smelling distance of the villagers' freshly baked bread.

The present-day village of Güzelyurt was settled by the early Christians under the name of Gelveri (or Karvali which wound up as Karballa) possibly after the hill of Calvary in Jerusalem. The village grew into an important center of early Christianity during the life of **Gregory of Nazianzus,** who built the church bearing his name (**St. Gregorius Church**) with the support of Emperor Theodosius in the 4th century. The pulpit however, dates to the 18th century, when it was donated by Czar Nicholas I. The spring waters in the courtyard (down about 36 steps) are still believed to be holy. The **Saint Anargiros Church** is a wondrously primitive collection of stairs, columns, arches, and domes all carved into the rock face (tip: head up to the highest point of the church for some spectacular views). The 13th-century St. George Church preserves frescos that include a depiction of the Selçuk Sultan. Just outside of the village is **Monastery Valley** (Manastır Vadısı), a 4.5km (2¾-mile) trek-cum-art history lesson sporting no fewer than 50 rock churches and monasteries.

There are several lookout points and cliffs from which to survey the village and the parade of passing cows, and as Güzelyurt is famous for its hospitality, it's more than likely you'll get stopped to share a pot of tea.

72km (45 miles) southwest of Nevşehir; 11km (6¾ miles) to Belisırma; 14km (8¾ miles) to Ihlara. www.guzelyurt.gov.tr From Ihlara Valley parking entrance, follow the road to Aksaray then signs for Gelveri/Güzelyurt.

The Ihlara Valley and the Churches of the Ihlara Canyon (Peristrema Monastery) MONASTERY A hike through the canyon is an opportunity to see the Cappadocia of more than 1,000 years ago.

Only 49km (30 miles) south of Nevşehir, the austere landscape of the Ihlara Valley splits open to reveal a 15km (9⅓-mile) fissure created by the force of the Melendez River. In contrast with the scenically dusty expanses of the rest of Cappadocia, the bottom of the canyon, nourished by the riverbed, is verdant with vegetation supporting village life much as it did centuries ago. Local women wade along the banks of the river, their traditional baggy trousers trailing in the river's edge as they do the day's washing.

As residents are drawn to Ihlara's canyon fertility, so were the earliest Christians: The canyon is home to over 100 **churches** and an estimated 4,000 **dwellings** sculpted into the soft rock face of the valley.

The canyon descends over 90m (295 ft.) in some places, twisting and turning at the beckoning of the river along wide trails lined with poplars and pistachio trees or narrowly navigable paths. There are a number of official entry and exit points along the canyon, past modest yet viable troglodyte villages. Official entry and exit points at the villages allow for either full-day or abbreviated hikes, but you should leave time for detours to the area churches and to pet the donkeys tied to a tree along the river's edge.

The most common starting point to a hike into the valley is the southern entrance near the village of Ihlara, down an endless man-made serpentine stairway 400 steps to the bottom. About 3.5km (2¼ miles) away, over sometimes-rough terrain, is the village of Belisırma, an ancient center of medicine before Selçuk Sultan Kılıçarslan II transferred the school to Aksaray. The process of mummification was extensively practiced in this part of the valley; a mummy of a woman found here is on display in the Niğde Archaeological Museum.

The churches, some of which are difficult to reach, date from the 8th or 9th century while the decorative frescoes date to a later post-Iconoclastic period, somewhere between the 10th and 13th centuries. The styles of the churches are generally grouped into two categories: those with an Egyptian or Syrian influence mainly found around the main entrance, and those reflecting a typical Byzantine style bunched around Belisırma.

The first church encountered at the bottom of the steps from Ihlara is **Ağaçaltı Kilisesi ★★★**, or the Church Under the Tree, also known as the Church of Daniel or the Church of Pantassa. Designed on a Greek cross plan, the interior, which has succumbed quite a bit to the elements, may appear a bit primitive at first, but a closer inspection reveals a strong Eastern influence, visible through the use of checker patterns, medallions, and rosettes. An interesting detail is in the depiction of the Nativity; notice that the Magi are seen dressed in Phrygian-style caps. The scene of the Dormition of the Virgin recalls the mosaics of St. Savior in Chora in Istanbul, with a depiction of Jesus holding the soul of Mary in the form of an infant.

Other churches in the vicinity of the Ihlara entrance and worthy of note are the **Pürenli Seki Kilisesi (the Church with Terraces) ★★**, and the **Kokar Kilisesi (the Church That Smells!) ★★**; both are to the right of the steps as you descend into the canyon.

Considered the oldest church in the valley, the **Eğritaş Kilisesi (the Church with the Crooked Stone) ★★** was probably a funerary chapel. The vaulted chapel has a single apse and a burial chamber below, much of which has been damaged by erosion and rockslides. The badly decaying frescoes, depicting scenes from the life of Christ, are distinctive for a style that recalls Eastern pre-Iconoclastic art.

On the other side of the river over a wooden footbridge is the **Yılanlı Kilisesi (Church of the Serpents)** ★★. The church is named for the scene on the western wall, showing serpents in the act of punishing four female sinners. "Women as the source of evil" is a common Eastern theme taken up by later monks, and in this case, the representations probably symbolize the sin of adultery, disobedience, and slander. The most graphic of the punishments shows the fourth female sinner with two snakes biting her nipples, probably for her failure to feed her children.

Back on the left bank of the river heading in the direction of Belisırma is the **Süm-büllü Kilisesi (The Hyacinth Church)** ★★, distinctive for its ornate facade of pillars and arched niches carved directly into the rock. A set of steps leads up to the church, passing the wild growths of hyacinths that give the complex its name. The church is actually a monastery complex hollowed out of the cliff; there are spaces for both living and worship. The few surviving frescoes include a well-preserved Annunciation and a Dormition.

Kırk Damaltı Kilisesi (the Church of St. George) ★★★, one of the latest of the region, is interesting from a purely social aspect. A portrait of the donor, a female in

TAKING ON THE ihlara VALLEY

The main entrance to the valley is a little over 1.6km (1 mile) north of the village of Ihlara, allowing entrance to the main gate leading to the long stairway down. The cliff walls are dotted with churches and abodes on both banks of the river, with most of the sites of interest clustered around the wooden footbridge at the base of the main entrance and over near the village of Belisırma. The 3.5km (2¼-mile) hike from the main entrance to the village of Belisırma is a relatively easy one, and many people choose to have lunch at the restaurant near the riverbed and call it a day. It's also possible to begin the hike at the village of Ihlara following the left bank of the river, adding on about 3km (1¾ miles) to the total. The shorter hike takes about 1½ to 2 hours, depending on your level of fitness, while a hike up the entire canyon will take about 5 hours.

If you come by private car, you'll probably have to leave it in the parking lot at the main entrance, which doesn't do you much good way over at the opposite end of the canyon in Belisırma

or Selime. An easier way is to take a guided tour; this will make seeing the valley a whole lot richer, giving you the background information necessary to appreciate the rock churches, rather than taking just a lovely walk through the gorge. Not to be overlooked is the bonus of having someone waiting for you at the end of the canyon, thus saving you the long hike back. (You can also hike up and out to the main road and catch a rare *dolmuş* back to the main entrance.) Guides are expensive, though, so if you've got the stamina, then by all means, go it alone.

It's a 1½-hour drive from central Cappadocia to the Ihlara Valley. From central Cappadocia, follow the road through Nevşehir, to Aksaray, and then to the village of Ihlara. The traditional hike begins at the main entrance about 1.6km (1 mile) outside the village. It is not advisable to take a *dolmuş* (the only choice for public transport), because doing so will require three separate *dolmuşes* plus a taxi from the village of Ihlara to the entrance to the valley.

Byzantine dress, is pictured with her husband, a man in typical Selçuk costume. The inscription reads: "This most venerable church . . . decorated through the assistance of the lady Thamar, here pictured, and of her Emir Basil Giagoupes, under his Majesty the most noble and Great Sultan Masud at the time when Sire Andronikos reigned over the Romans." It is thought to be an expression of Christian gratitude for the religious tolerance of the Selçuk Turks and dates the church to the late 13th century.

Ihlara Canyon, Güzelyurt. ℂ **0382/453-7701.** Admission 5TL; parking extra. Daily 8am–6:30pm (8am–5pm Nov–Mar). Take the Nevşehir-Aksaray rd. and turn off on the rd. south for Ihlara; the rd. leading into the canyon is signposted before the entrance to the village.

Kaymaklı Underground City (Kaymaklı Yeraltı Şehri) HISTORIC SITE   Where the sheer vastness of the underground city at Derinkuyu makes it an impressive example of a troglodyte complex, its functional nature is more easily appreciated at Kaymaklı. On the four levels that have been cleared out since 1964, kitchens, stables, and a winery have been discovered, as well as a chapel with a confessional. The complex, believed to go down 20m (66 ft.), was home to approximately 15,000 people at a time, with air shafts, water wells, and storage spaces capable of supporting the population for several months.

Practical considerations, including protection, survival, and revelry, were given to many facets of living underground. In the face of an attack, keystones were quickly moved into place; these blocked access from the outside and sealed off the various levels. Small holes were carved into the floor and used to communicate with the level above or below, so even when the keystone was pushed back, residents were saved from taking the long way around to pass on messages. The engineering of air shafts that extend beyond the lowest level and exit just below ground level provide an efficient and impressive level of air circulation that even succeeded in emptying the tunnels of the black smoke from the kitchen hearths. Because the same flues were used for communication and for water wells, the shafts did not extend all the way to the surface; this protected the water supply from contamination. Other interesting details are the grape presses that allowed for the grape juice to drain into a stone tank below. Wine was an important consideration in daily life, and probably used in religious rites as well.

Kaymaklı. www.nevsehirkulturturizm.gov.tr. ℂ **0384/278-2500.** Admission 15TL. Daily 8am–7pm (8am–5pm Nov–Mar). Kaymaklı is 18km (11 miles) south of Nevşehir, with another 9km (5⅔ miles) south on the same road to get to Derinkuyu. Both cities can be reached by taking the Ürgüp Soğanlı rd. and taking the turnoff at Güzelöz.

Mazıköy Underground City and Roman Graves HISTORIC SITE   Those with claustrophobic tendencies have mixed reactions to visiting the show-stopping sites of Derinkuyu and Kamalklı: Some find going underground to be a walk in the park, while others don't fare as well. For those concerned with claustrophobia or physical limitations, the more modest Mazıköy is a good alternative to the Derinkuyu and Kaymaklı underground cities. The underground complex is actually built *up* into the rock formation with the entrance at ground level, allowing visitors to avoid descents deep into the earth. Don't get complacent, however, as more adventurous explorers can deploy some rudimentary rock-climbing skills to access the upper levels, a dusty experience described by friends as "epic."

Admission 8TL. Daily 8am–6:30pm.

Paşabağ HISTORIC SITE & NATURAL ATTRACTION   Wherever you see tour buses or souvenir stands, there's bound to be something interesting. Paşabağ, also

EXPLORING THE underground CITIES

While the idea of a prehistoric people seeking shelter in caves is not a foreign one, it's startling to have discovered a system of underground cities as sophisticated as those found in Cappadocia. Over 200 underground cities at least two levels deep have been discovered in the area between Kayseri and Nevşehir, with around 40 of those composed of at least three levels or more. The troglodyte cities at Derinkuyu and Kaymaklı are two of the best examples of underground dwellings, although the lesser-visited sites have the advantage of not having to brave the crowds.

It remains a mystery as to who first started the digging, although Hittite artifacts found around the caves—and the fact that many of the towns' names go back to the Hittite or Sumerian language—suggest they were inhabited as far back as 3,000 to 4,000 years ago. The early Christians probably sought temporary shelter from the persecution of Roman soldiers; and after the 6th century, these dwellings provided protection from raiding Arab tribes. The crude carving of the surface levels of rock gives way to a smoother, more refined face, which indicates that the levels were carved by different people at different times.

Each rock settlement had access to the safe haven of these underground dwellings by way of a secret underground passageway that would provide swift and unseen escape in times of emergency. In fact, an access tunnel can still be found on just about every villager's property. Additionally, the underground cities of Derinkuyu and Kaymaklı, about 9km (5⅔ miles) apart, are believed to be connected by an underground tunnel.

Every crucial entry point into the city was either camouflaged or blocked by a keystone, a large stone wheel that, once fixed in place, was immovable. Keystones were fixed at every level of the city as well. The labyrinth of tunnels and blind passageways hundreds of feet below the ground give shocking testimony to the tenaciousness of a civilization to survive and prosper by sentencing itself to months of existence deep within the earth.

Going underground can present some uncomfortable conditions for those a bit squeamish. Although passageways are well lit and even the lowest levels are ventilated, a few of the access ramps are long and narrow, requiring visitors to ascend or descend in single file, and for even those of average height, hunched over. On a busy day (which is every day June—Aug, it seems), problems can arise for those at the lower levels, as visitors might be stuck waiting for the last of an endless group of arrivals to clear the passageway before exiting.

Arrows mark the direction of the visit (red for in, blue for out). As long as you stick to the route, you should be okay, but don't wander off with a flashlight, because this labyrinth was designed to confuse intruders just like you. It's fine to veer off track in the presence of a guide—incidentally, a great and terrifying way to see how dark absolute darkness can be.

Try to avoid peak visitation hours by getting there early; tours clog the narrow one-way tunnels and cause small galleries to become loud and stuffy. Curious about the possibility of a power outage, I was told that in the event that the lights go out, a backup generator would kick in after 10 seconds.

known as Valley of the Monks, is a forest of cone-shaped fairy chimneys more shocking and lifelike (not life-size) than most. Not surprisingly, it's a popular stop for photo ops.

The chimneys of Paşabağ harbor a number of chapels and dwellings used by Christian hermits, the most prominent of which is a tri-level chapel with depictions of the

life of St. Simeon. St. Simeon the Stylite lived a life of hardship and denial in Antioch around the 4th century, high atop a 15m (49-ft.) pillar. Later hermits were inspired to do the same, initiating a "stylite" movement of isolated living.
On the road to Zelve Valley. 8TL or free with ticket to Zelve Open Air Museum. (*) **0384/411-2525.**

Sarıca Church RELIGIOUS SITE/NATURAL ATTRACTION The Sarıca Church, located in the Kepez Valley, is the perfect example of how a monument can suffer from indifference and neglect, yet be dragged back from the brink of oblivion as a shining example of one person's dedication toward the preservation of national patrimony. Up until October 2002 when work began, this 6th- to 7th-century rock-cut basilica had been reduced to use as an organic factory warehouse for pigeon guano. Local farmers had even cut an aperture into the dome as a porthole for the pigeons. In all fairness, however, much of the deterioration in the condition of the church was due to water erosion. Today, visitors can enter through the (dry) front door—which had to be dug out—and marvel at the carved niches, arched vaults, and capitals decorated under the ochre artwork of the time.
Kepez Valley, near Mustafapaşa. No phone.

Sobesos 🏛 RUIN One day in 1963, Mehmet, a farmer in the village of Şahinefendi, awoke to find that a section of his field had been disturbed—he thought by treasure hunters, a not-uncommon phenomenon in these parts. Upon closer inspection, he spotted something clearly not part of the natural landscape and started clearing away dirt. What he uncovered was a panel of mosaics, a finding he knew to be significant. He reported his discovery to the provincial museum directorate, but was met with silence. Over the years, the buried treasure uncovered in the process of tending his fields included a 1.8m (6-ft.) terra-cotta pot and a 3m (9¾-ft.) high Doric column, all dutifully reported to (and ignored by) the provincial authorities. (He at one point shrugged his shoulders and used the Doric column as a support for the balcony of his home.) It was not until 2002, after decades of attempts to engage the authorities, that the local museum directorate finally stood up and took notice.

Today, a small patch of land on this farmer's property is roped off and reveals a 400-sq.-m (4,306-sq.-ft) **Meeting Hall** whose main draw is the vibrant mosaic flooring throughout. Towards the 6th century, a **Chapel** was constructed atop some of the finer mosaics within the Meeting Hall using materials scavenged from the **Main Room.** A grave was also uncovered, containing the skeletal remains of an adult shrouded male, dating to the same period as the Chapel addition. Further spot tests of the site revealed a **Roman bath complex,** now believed to be the site of Sobesos, a city dating to the late Roman and early Christian period (mid–4th century to 5th century A.D.). The finding of Roman ruins of this sophistication provides historical continuity never before seen in Cappadocia. We know that Christians were for the most part hiding from Roman soldiers, but we've never seen evidence of a full-scale Roman settlement. Sadly, the excavations are at pretty much a standstill because of a lack of funds. The site is still worth a visit, but you'll need permission from the farmer to see it, which means you'll need to get by the guard (he's very friendly, and Mehmet's cousin) hired by the Nevşehir Museum to watch his property.

Şahinefendi. No phone. Daily 8am–sunset. From Ürgüp, follow road past Mustafapaşa and continue towards Cemil. Pass by Taşkinpaşa then take turnoff to Şahinefendi. The sign for Sobesos is at the entrance to the village.

Temmenı Hill CASTLE   Known as The Hill of Wishes, this elevated rock face rises above Ürgüp to form the anchor in the region's three-fortress defenses, the other two being Üçhisar and Ortahisar Castles). A mysterious tunnel (closed; don't bother with those pestering kids) almost .8km (½-mile) long leads from around the 13th-century Kebir Camii to the Selçuk tomb of Nükrettin at the top of the hill; to this day, no one knows who built it or why. The tomb was dedicated to the Selçuk leader Kılıçarslan IV, or the Sworded Lion, and a hilltop cafe allows you to relax and take it all in. If you've got the stamina to reach the top, the reward will be an open-air terrace revealing expansive views of the surrounding area.

Ürgüp Center. Admission 50kr. Daily 8am–sunset.

Üçhisar Castle CASTLE   The highest peak in the region and the most prominent land formation, the Üçhisar Castle is a larger-than-life sculpture. A climb up the 120 steps to the summit of the fortress is a logical introduction to the rocky scapes of Cappadocia. In the 15th and 16th centuries, the Byzantine army took advantage of the natural elevation of three of the area's rock formations and used them as natural fortresses. Üçhisar, together with Ortahisar and a rock castle at Ürgüp (now in ruins), provided the means for an early warning system using mirrors and lights, sending messages among the fortresses and as far afield as Istanbul. Today the outer layers of Üçhisar's rock have been washed away by erosion to reveal a honeycombed structure of tunnels and cavities, rising above the man-made facades of the modern semi-troglodyte village. Recently discovered was a secret tunnel leading to the riverbed, which provided an emergency water supply in the event of an attack.

Üçhisar. © **0384/219-2890.** Admission 3TL. Daily 8am–sunset.

Zelve Open Air Museum ★ MONASTERY   Carved into a uniquely pink tufa, Zelve was once home to one of the largest communities in the region. It was inhabited by a Greek population until the 1922 population exchange, when Greeks and Turks were "repatriated" to their mother countries. When Muslims took over the valley, a mosque was hewn out of the rock and stands near the entrance.

The first known inhabitants of the valley were monks, and although I can say for sure that they carved out the chapels, it's unclear who first began hollowing out the valley. The cave dwellings were used by local villagers up until 1952, when the structures were determined to be unsafe and the villagers were moved en masse over to nearby Aktepe, or New Zelve.

Now a national park, Zelve consists of three consecutive valleys whose walls are riddled with living quarters, blind tunnels, passageways, and traps for protection against attacks. Footholds chiseled into the smooth vertical tufa require an agility once aimed at keeping out unwanted visitors, but now present a fantastic challenge to modern-day rock climbers. Those interested in hiking should set aside plenty of time to explore the area, following a path over the mountain to Red Valley, about 4km (2½ miles) away. Exploring the caves can be exhilarating, challenging, and downright dangerous. Don't attempt anything fancy without a guide; Argeus (see "Getting There

THE road LESS TRAVELED: AKKÖY

While tourists flock to the Cappadocian triangle formed by Avanos, Ürgüp, and Üçhisar, the vast warren of underground cities and troglodyte structures extends for dozens of miles. The village of Akköy sits on a sloping hill about 14km (8¾ miles) down a solitary road southeast of Ürgüp, a tight cluster of cubic stone homes fused to ancient cave structures once inhabited by Hittites and Assyrians. The village sits atop an underground city accessible only to the most courageous spelunkers, and is the caretaker of some above-ground relics—a domed church, a chapel, a wine cellar—hidden behind overgrown brush. Years ago, one village son, Mehmet Güleç, saw the potential, and created the **Akköy Evleri** (✆ **0384/ 352-4704;** www.boutiquecavehotel.com), a collection of five authentically decorated, modestly renovated,

very comfortable cave rooms and one two-story private home. The hotel is a favorite of Turkish weekenders seeking a respite from city life far from the foreign crowds. By day, perhaps with Mehmet's guidance in his well-worn rugged jeep or on foot, guests venture into the surrounding villages to soak up a bit of the simple life. In the evenings, everyone gathers in the living room to watch the large-screen TV, cuddle on the floor cushions, or drink a glass of Mehmet's wine by the bar. If it's a true off-the-beaten-track experience you're looking for, if the language barrier and hands-off management style don't phase you, and you've got your own wheels, Akköy Evleri might very well fit the bill. Rates per night for a double room start at $250. Inquire about the Eco Tours and other available activities.

& Getting Around," at the beginning of the chapter) offers excellent guided tours, but you can also arrange one through one of the many shops in town.

Paşabağları, Aktepe Köyü. www.nevsehirkulturturizm.gov.tr. ✆**0384/411-3535.** Admission 8TL or free with ticket to Pasabağ open air museum. Daily 8am–7pm (8am–5pm Nov–Mar). The road to Zelve Valley is accessible off the Göreme-Avanos or Ürgüp-Avanos rd.

Cappadocia to the Coast: A Visit to Konya

Capital of the Selçuk Empire for only a scarce hundred or so years, Konya, when not described as largely resembling Detroit, exhibits one of the country's richest architectural collections of mosques, baths, caravansaries, and *medreses* (seminaries). Home of one of Islam's greatest mystical movements, the Mevlana, or Sufi sect of "Whirling Dervişes," continues to find spiritual enlightenment through the *sema*, or ritual whirling dance.

Konya is also Turkey's most infamously religious province, so it's a rare hotel or restaurant that serves alcohol, and the mosque entryways turn into traffic jams at prayer time. But like Turkey itself, Konya is a city of contradictions. Although it is the reputed spiritual center of Turkey and one of the most conservative towns in Anatolia, Konya has the highest rate of alcohol consumption of anywhere in the country. Rebellion takes many forms, and in a city with 50,000 students, it's in the lipstick and rouge and in skirts with slits as far up as the knee—probably Konya's version of a pierced nose.

Most travelers come here to make a pilgrimage to the tomb of Mevlana, founder of the venerable Sufi sect of Islam that preaches love, charity, humility, equality, and tolerance, among other elemental principles. Members of the sect seek union with God through a meditative ceremony called the *sema*, a ritual whirling symbolizing the liberation from earthly bonds and a connection with the heavens. Ironically, all Sufi sects were banned by Atatürk in the 1920s in his far-reaching opposition to religious extremism. But Mevlana's ideals are hard to keep down, and in recent years Sufism has gained a popular following not only among Turks, but also internationally.

GETTING THERE

BY PLANE **Turkish Airlines** (℃ **444-0849** or 0332/239-1177 at the airport; www.thy.com), **Atlasjet** (℃ **444-3387;** www.atlasjet.com) and **Onur Air** (℃ **444-6687;** www.onurair.com.tr) provide service from Istanbul's Atatürk Airport to Konya. **Pegasus** (℃ **444-0737;** www.flypgs.com) flies direct from Istanbul's Sabiha Gökçen Airport. Konya Airport is located about 17km (11 miles) outside of the center of town. The general information line at the airport is ℃ **0332/239-1343.**

A **Havaş** (℃ **0212/444-0487,** or in Konya at ℃ 0332/239-0105) airport shuttle provides service from the airport to Konya center (the Iş Bankası at Alaattin Tepesi) with a stop at the *otogar.* Shuttles depart 25 minutes after the arrival of all flights. The ride takes about 30 minutes and costs 9TL. Shuttles to the airport depart daily at 5:30am, 6:40am, 7:25am, 6:20pm, and 8:10pm daily plus 8:10am on Monday, Thursday, Saturday, and Sunday from the THY offices in Anıt Meydanı.

There is also a **Europcar** rental counter in the arrivals terminal, open daily from 8:30am to 7pm. The contact number for the current manager is ℃ **0533/370-3090.**

BY BUS Countless bus companies run hourly service into Konya. These are (in Konya) **Kontur** (℃ **444-4042** or 0332/265-0150), **Kamil Koç** (℃ **0332/265-0118**), **Metro** (℃ **444-3455** or 0332/265-0040), **Ulusoy** (℃ **0332/241-3262**) and **Özkaymak** (℃ **0332/265-1860**). From Antalya, the ride takes about 5 hours, from Istanbul 9 hours, from Ankara 3 hours, from Izmir 8 hours, and from Nevşehir 4 hours.

From the *otogar,* take the tramway (2TL exit the main entrance, walking left along the main road toward the main intersection; the tramway is on the right corner). The ride takes about 45 minutes and is marked ALAADDIN (get off at Alaaddin Hill in the center of town); from there, the Balıkçılar and Rumi are about a 10-minute walk down Alaaddin Caddesi in the direction of the Mevlana Museum, or you can hop on one of the frequent *dolmuşes* plying the length of Mevlana Caddesi. Also from the *otogar,* a *dolmuş* takes half the tramway's amount of time and costs about the same.

BY TRAIN With the ongoing construction of a new, high-speed train infrastructure, the **TCDD** (℃ **0332/332-3670** in Konya; www.tcdd.gov.tr) now offers the fast, appropriately named, **Yüksek Hizli Tren**, departing Ankara four times daily (more to come). The ride takes about 1 hour, 40 minutes and costs 25TL.

BY CAR The Mevlana museum as well as the city's other historical sites are located at the heart of the maze of roadways leading from the periphery to the city center. Just getting in from the highway can take a half-hour, so unless you're planning an overnight, a quick stopover at the tomb of Mevlana on your way down to the coast is not going to be as easy as you might think. From Nevşehir, it's an easy 3 hours through flatlands past Aksaray. It's another easy and scenic 3 hours over the Taurus Mountains via the excellent three-lane highway from Antalya to Konya (via Seydişehir). The road via Beyşehir, passing by Lake Beyşehir, is more scenic, but takes longer.

WHERE TO EAT

Konak Konya Kitchen ◼ REGIONAL TURKISH There's no better place to sample typical dishes from Konya than this mid-19th-century Ottoman mansion-turned-restaurant (formerly known as the Köşk). Among their specialties are the

Patlicanlı Bütün Et (lamb and eggplant casserole), the house special *Konak Kebabı*, a succulently baked casserole of meat topped with slices of tomato and delicious chunks of white cheese. Of course there's Konya's signature dish, the *etli ekmek*, a delectable, pseudo pizza-ish invention that tops flatbread with minced lamb. (It's called *lahmacun* elsewhere). Top it with cubed spiced lamb and it becomes the Konya *boreği*.

Akçeşme Mah. Topraklık Cad. 66. www.konakkonyamutfagi.com. © **0332/352-8547.** Reservations suggested. Appetizers and main courses 5TL–22TL. MC, V. Daily noon–11pm.

Mevlevi Sofrası REGIONAL TURKISH   Adjacent to the Mevlana Museum is the Mevlevi Sofrası, which gives the tourists what they want: Konya specialties, traditional and ambience, several outdoor roof terraces overlooking the Mevlana Museum gardens, two indoor rooms with traditional Oriental seating, and a *sema* show nightly at 9pm. Try Konya's other specialty, *firin kebap*—a slab of slow-cooked mutton stuffed into a roll—a messy affair in all its finger-licking, greasy glory.

Amil Çelebi Sok. 1 (next to the Mevlana Museum). www.mevlevisofrasi.com. © **0332/353-3341.** Appetizers and main courses 5TL–22TL. MC, V. Daily 8am–11pm.

WHAT TO SEE & DO

The history of Konya dates to at least the 8th century B.C.; some of the most important archaeological findings belonging to the earliest stationary civilizations known to man were discovered at nearby **Çatalhöyük,** while Hittite artifacts have been discovered in the regions east of Konya.

Known as Iconium during the Roman and Byzantine eras, the city was the location of one of the earliest church councils. After the Selçuk victory over the Byzantine army at Malazgirt (also called Manzikert) in 1071, the Selçuks migrated west, establishing a capital on Alaeddin Hill, and setting their sights on an empire that would rival Rome—called the Sultanate of Rhum. Some of the foundations of this early Selçuk Empire are still standing on Alaeddin Hill, including the **Selçuk Palace** built for Sultan Kılıç Arslan II between 1156 and 1192, now for the most part a crumbled stone wall sheltered beneath a concrete tripod arch—the unfortunate symbol of the city. The **Alaeddin Mosque,** also built during the reign of Alaeddin Keykubat, dates to 1221; note the *minbar* (pulpit) ★ and the *türbe,* containing the remains of eight of the ruling Selçuk sultans. The Alaeddin Hill is also an attraction in itself, home to five lovely tea gardens.

At the opposite end of Alaeddin Caddesi and about a 10-minute walk is the **Mevlana Müzesi** (Mevlana Mah.; © **0332/351-1215;** daily 9am–6pm, admission 3TL), the original *tekke,* or lodge, of the Mevlevi Dervişes. The complex was built by Beyazit II and Selim I successively at the end of the 15th and beginning of the 16th centuries. The *tekke* includes a *semahane,* where the ritual *sema,* or whirling ceremony, takes place, a *şadırvan* for ritual ablutions, a library, living and teaching quarters, and the mausoleum housing the **tomb of Celaleddin-i Rumi ★★,** founder of the sect and later awarded the honorable title of Mevlana. The mausoleum room is highly ornamented with Islamic script and enameled bas-relief, and contains the tombs of several of the more important figures in the derviş order. The main tomb enclosed behind a silver gate crafted in 1597 is that of Mevlana. The tomb of his father, Bahaeddin Veled, is upright and adjacent to his son's, a position that signifies respect.

The adjoining room, or the *semihane,* is now a museum of Mevlana memorabilia displaying musical instruments and robes belonging to Mevlana, along with Selçuk and Ottoman objects like gold-engraved Korans from the 13th century. Among the fabulous ancient **prayer rugs** ★★ is the most valuable silk carpet in the world.

As in all Muslim holy places, you must remove your shoes to visit the Mevlana Müzesi, but here the floor is bare parquet, so wear socks. Because overnight groups schedule their visits for first thing in the morning, you may want to stagger your visit to Konya by arriving here a little later. (The end of the day is a good time, as most tour buses have already left.)

On an overnight stay, there are several other sites in Konya worth a look. The **Karatay Medrese,** built during the reign of Sultan Keykavus II in 1251 by his Grand Vizier, Celăleddin Karatay, houses the **Ceramic Museum (Alaattin Meydanı; ⓒ 0332/351-1914;** admission 3TL; daily 9am–noon and 1:30–5:30pm). The museum displays a small but noteworthy collection of faience with representations from the most important centers of early ceramic arts in Anatolia. Most impressive are the 13th-century Selçuk tiles, also employed to embellish the interior space. Notice the exterior portal (street side), typical of the restrained ornamentation of Selçuk architecture. The nearby **Ince Minare** is another fine example of the ornamental use of Selçuk tiles. Admission is 3TL; the minaret is open daily 9am to noon and 1:30 to 5:30pm. Next to the Mevlana Museum in the park is the stately **Selimiye Mosque ★**, a classic Ottoman building constructed between 1558 and 1587 when the future sultan Selim II was governor of Konya.

THE "WHIRLING" dervişes

The Mevlevi order of the dervişes arose in Turkey with the spreading of Islam and is based on the philosophies of Mevlana Celaleddin-i Rumi, who was born in Balkh, the first capital of the ancient Turkish territory of Khorasan (Afghanistan) in 1207. An invitation extended by Sultan Keykübad I to his father, a respected spiritual leader, brought Celaleddin to Konya at the age of 21, the " i Rumi" being added upon his migration into the heart of the Selçuk Rum Empire.

The mystical order is based on the principles of universal love and the oneness of creation, which states, "to love man is to love God." While the concepts of the sect were set forth by Celaleddin-i Rumi (the *Mevlana*—Arabic for "lord"—was added to his name as a title of respect), the rites and rituals associated with the order were consolidated by his son, Sultan Veled ("sultan" here used to designate spiritual leadership). The Mevlevi philosophy eventually gained the respect of the Ottoman sultans, and

Selim II, Mahmud II, and Mehmed V were among its members.

The Mevlevi ritual takes the form of the *sema*, a ritual "whirling" dance whose purpose is to create a sphere of divine reality. The Mevlevi believe that purity of heart, peace with self and the universe, and the search for perfection through ritual dance bring them closer to God. Although this and other brotherhoods were officially outlawed by Atatürk's sweeping reforms, the order continues to exist. The Konya order opens the ritual *sema* to a rare public viewing every December 17 in Konya, a celebratory gathering marking the death of Mevlana Celaleddin-i Rumi. The ceremony caps off a 2-week festival (shortened to 10 days in 2009) marked by a rich variety of cultural activities such as Sufi and other mystic music concerts, poetry readings, art exhibitions, and lessons in the *sema*. (For information, go to www.konyakultur.gov.tr.)

WHERE TO STAY

Balıkçılar Perhaps in preparation for the 800th birthday celebration of Rumi (in 2007, which UNESCO declared the Year of Mevlana), the hotel underwent a complete overhaul, upgrading and updating what were essentially tired, mediocre rooms. But it really didn't matter what the rooms were like at this hotel. Who cares, when they overlook the majestic and monumental Selimiye Mosque and Mevlana complex? With such an outstanding location, Turkish bath and sauna, and unexpected ornamental common areas, this hotel should be your first choice.

Mevlana Karşısı 1, 42020 Konya. www.balikcilar.com. © **0332/350-9470.** Fax 0332/351-3259. 51 units. 85€ double. AE, MC, V. Free parking. **Amenities:** Restaurant; 2 bars; babysitting; exercise room; *hamam*; room service; sauna. *In room:* A/C, satellite TV, hair dryer, minibar, free Wi-Fi.

Rumi 🎁 Recently opened, the Rumi is big enough to provide the perfect combination of creature comforts, but small enough so that it doesn't have to sacrifice character. Add in that it's located across the street from the Mevlana Museum and choosing this hotel is a no-brainer. Rooms also strike a balance between simple without going overboard to boring. Expect a bathtub or shower (except in the suites, which have Jacuzzis) and satellite TV. In between visits to the city's monuments, you can even slip in an hour in the hotel *hamam*, or sauna, at no extra charge.

Durakfakı Sok. 5, 42030 Konya (opposite the Mevlana Museum). www.rumihotel.com. © **0332/353-1121.** Fax 0332/353-5366. 33 units. 100€ double; 250€ suite. Tax (8%) not included. Ask for specials. MC, V. Free parking. **Amenities:** Restaurant; bar; babysitting; exercise room; *hamam*; free Internet in lobby; room service; sauna. *In room:* A/C, satellite TV, hair dryer, minibar.

ANKARA

Unlike Istanbul, vulnerable for centuries to neighboring countries with imperialistic motives, Ankara ★ lies deep within the heartland, protected and insulated from uninvited guests. Atatürk deliberately chose Ankara for his new republic; while Istanbul was the seat of an imperial and dissolute empire, he saw Ankara as the clean-slate capital of an entirely new Turkish state. Ankara is almost exclusively geared toward sustaining a wide-ranging population of foreign ambassadors, visiting dignitaries, local politicians, and politically minded business enterprises. It also boasts a number of prestigious universities and technical colleges, as well as the largest library in the country. Ankara is a center for opera, ballet, jazz, and modern dance, and is home of the Presidential Symphony Orchestra, the State Theatre, and the State Opera and Ballet. Ankara's dining scene has also made enormous strides with local branches of some of Istanbul's best restaurants.

10

But while Ankara buzzes with the everyday business of keeping house, you can't compare Ankara to cities like Washington, D.C., or London, even if the brilliant **Museum of Anatolian Civilizations** is worth a special detour. It's not that there's nothing to do here: The short list of worthy monuments and museums includes **Atatürk's mausoleum,** a handful of Roman-era sites, and as mentioned before, the archaeological museum. There's a predictable concentration of statues of Atatürk, a bustling boulevard of Republican-era buildings, and dotting the parks and avenues are monuments to inspire a strong sense of nationalism. The **Victory Monument,** in Ulus Square, honors the heroes of the War of Independence, while the **Monument to a Secure and Confident Future,** in Güvenlik Park, reminds Turks to "be proud, work hard, and have self confidence." The **Hatti Monument ★**, an oversize replica of a bronze solar disc, on Sıhhiye Square stands as a constant reminder of the country's Anatolian roots. If none of this has you clamoring to stop over in the country's capital, I have to admit that to go or not to go is a dilemma borne by many. Most people choose to skip Ankara in favor of a direct transfer to Cappadocia, but as the construction of the fast rail line from Istanbul to Ankara progresses (which will cut travel time down to just 4 hr.), everyone's default excuse for not passing through will disintegrate into thin air.

FATHER OF TURKEY: THE MAN CALLED atatürk

It's impossible to overstate Atatürk's hold on this country—even almost 75 years after his death. His presence is unavoidable; his legacy is everywhere. Children are taught from near birth to revere the heroic, ambitious, revolutionary figure who single-handedly forged a united Turkish state from the tattered remains of the Ottoman Empire.

On May 19, 1919, Mustafa Kemal Paşa landed in the Black Sea port of Samsun, officially launching the War of Independence. Less than a year later, the Grand National Assembly convened, prompting the sultan to condemn Kemal to death. But Kemal's savvy military campaign did not falter, and 2 years later, liberation armies succeeded in clearing the mainland of all foreign presence.

Born Mustafa Kemal in Salonica in 1881, he channeled his energy into a military career at an early age. In 1905, while in the service of the sultan, he co-founded a secret organization to fight the Ottoman ruler's despotism. But unlike some power-hungry despots, Kemal's efforts resulted from a zealous love for his culture, and a refusal to see his country's sovereignty compromised. He gained widespread attention in 1915 for his pivotal role in turning back Allied forces during the long, brutal battle at Gallipoli and emerged from that campaign with the makings of a hero's reputation. At the close of World War I, Allied victors appeared ready to move in and carve up the Ottoman Empire, to the apparent indifference of the sultan. This galvanized Kemal, and he moved to harness nationalist sentiment and recruit an organized resistance.

That military victory was just the beginning, for Kemal intended no less than a societal revolution to follow. "We shall strive to win victories in such fields as culture, scholarship, science, and economics," he declared, adding that "the enduring benefits of victories depend only on the existence of an army of education." With blackboard and chalk in hand, he traveled to every corner of the country, breathing new life into this withering nation.

In his 15-year presidency, Atatürk drew his country into the 20th century through drastic and sweeping changes, not the least of which were the adoption of the Western alphabet and the insistence on a complete separation of church and state. He abolished many of the institutions that lay at the heart of Turkey, thus forcing the country to reject its Ottoman heritage. He created a new national identity, a sense of unity and pride that endures to this day. In 1934, when a law establishing surnames was instituted, the parliament gave him the name *Atatürk*—Father of the Turks. He died in 1938, 18 years after becoming president and utterly transforming his homeland.

Atatürk's influence on modern Turkey has not been without criticism, although much of this must be discreet, because *it has always been illegal to slander the Father of the Republic*. Fundamentalist critics argue that Islam as a way of life provides for all the legal needs of the country; for highly observant Muslims, the separation of mosque and state has gone too far. But Atatürk recognized that a march into the future was inevitable, and his vision lives on in a prosperous and modernizing Turkey. In his words: "Proud is he who calls himself a Turk."

ORIENTATION

454km (282 miles) southeast of Istanbul; 544km (338 miles) northeast of Antalya; 582km (362 miles) east of Izmir; 277km (172 miles) northwest of Nevşehir

Getting There

BY PLANE   Ankara's new and improved **Esenboğa International Airport** is a major hub for domestic flights on Turkish Airlines (℡ **0312/398-0100** at the airport; www.esenbogaairport.com). Direct international flights arrive from Amsterdam, Brussels, Cologne, Dortmund, Düsseldorf, Frankfurt, Kiev, London, and Munich, as well as dozens of other cities, with increased service in the summer.

The Esenboğa International Airport is 32km (20 miles) from the city center. **Havaş** (www.havas.net) provides bus transportation from the airport daily to the Havaş City Center Office in Ulus, with departures tied to the arrival times of domestic and international flights. The ride takes about 35 minutes and costs 10TL. The fare is 25% higher between midnight and 6am.

Half-hourly buses to the airport leave from the Havaş office (located at 19 Mayıs Stadium, Gate B, in Altındağ) daily between 2:30am and 9pm, and then in coordination with flight departures from 9pm to 2:30am. (Havaş buses also leave from the AŞTI bus station, but Ulus is more convenient.) For information on Havaş buses back to the airport, call the national Havaş call center (℡ **444-0487**). There's also a cooperative taxi arrangement at the airport that will get you and three other passengers to Ankara center for around 60TL. The service runs round the clock but reservations must be made at least 24 hours in advance (℡ **0312/398-0897**; www.esenbogataxi.com).

BY BUS   Virtually every city in the country, no matter how small, has at least one bus company with service to Ankara, offering almost as many fare options as buses. For example, **Varan** (℡ **444-8999** or at 0312/224-2010 at the Ankara otogar; www.varan.com.tr) runs about 15 buses daily from Istanbul (travel time 5½–7 hr.; average price 45TL), as does **Metro** (℡ **444-3455** or 312/224-0692; www.metroturizm.com.tr), including two nonstop buses. To get to town from Ankara's **AŞTI Otogar** (℡ **0312/207-1000**) hop a cab or take advantage of the handy metro station just outside the bus entrance (www.ankarametrosu.com.tr). But even from your metro destination of choice (most likely Ulus or Kızılay), you may need to take a taxi to the hotel.

BY TRAIN   The system of railways in Turkey is operated by **Turkish State Railways** (Türkiye Cumhuriyet Devlet Demiryolları; ℡ **444 8233**; www.tcdd.gov.tr). One of the major railway projects under way in Turkey is the laying of tracks for a fast train between Istanbul and Ankara. Upon completion (projected for late 2014), this new fast train will take just 3 hours. Stay tuned to www.tcdd.gov.tr for progress.

Visitor Information

There's a **tourist information office** at the airport (℡ **0312/398-0348**) as well as downtown at Gençlik Parkı 10. 121, ℡ **0312/324-0401**). A third, provincial tourism office is located at Anafartalar Cad. 67, Eski Adliye, Ulus (℡ **0312/310-0446**).

If you're here for an extended stay, why not think about Turkish-language classes? **Tömer** offers courses at two locations: Ziya Gökalp Cad. 18, in the neighborhood of

Ankara

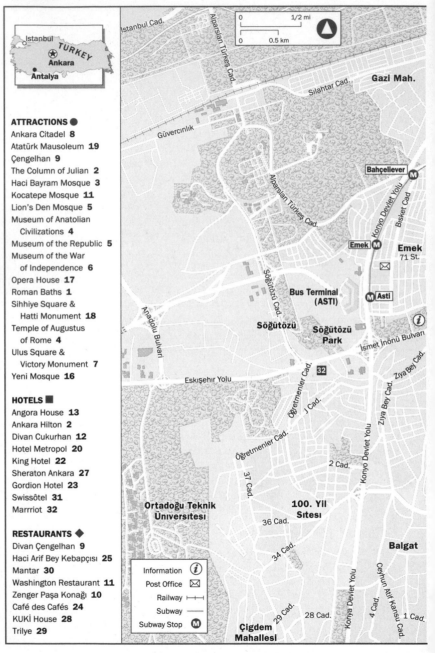

10

ANKARA | Orientation

394

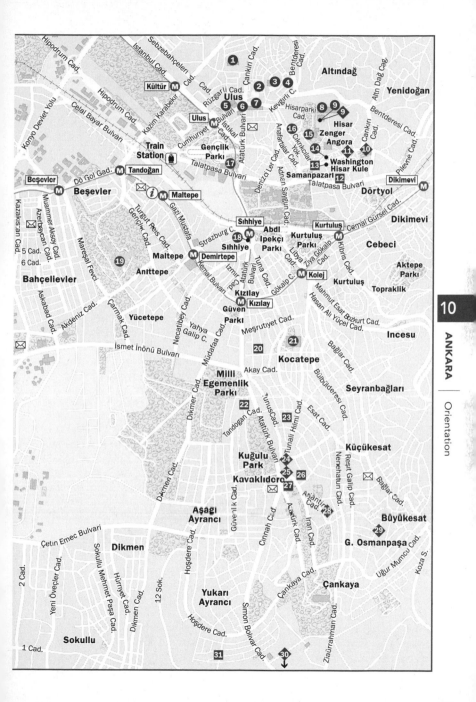

Kızılay (℡ **0312/434-3090**), and Tunalı Hilmi Cad. 97, in Kavaklıdere (℡ **0312/468-7063**), or check out their website at www.tomer.ankara.edu.tr.

City Layout
The city is divided into a number of administrative units, but the ones you will need to be concerned with form the heart of Ankara. They are the districts of **Çankaya**, where you will find embassies, government buildings, shopping, and modern residential neighborhoods, including the **Kızılay**, **Kavaklidere**, and **Gaziosmanpaşa**, and **Altındağ**, most notable for the presence of the Ankara Castle (Kale, or citadel) and some Roman ruins in the neighborhood of **Ulus**. The city's major thoroughfare, suitably named **Atatürk Bulvarı**, runs the length of Ankara from north to south, from the Equestrian Statue of Atatürk at Ulus Meydanı all the way down to the Presidential Mansion in Çankaya, about 5km (3 miles) away.

The area around Ulus Meydanı forms the oldest section of the city. From Ulus Meydanı, located about a 5-minute walk uphill on Hisarparkı Caddesi, east of the Atatürk statue, is where you will find the **Museum of Anatolian Civilizations.** A detour from Hisarparkı Caddesi onto **Çıkrıkçılar Yokuşu** will take you through the market; eventually, all roads uphill lead to the old fortress, a living, breathing mix of modern Turkey and the Turkish heartland. The neighborhood directly opposite the main entrance to the fortress recently got a face-lift thanks to the support of one of Turkey's wealthiest businessmen and a great benefactor of Turkey's patrimony; here you'll find the newly preserved **Çengelhan**, a caravansary dating to 1522 and housing—what else?—but the Rahmi M. Koç Museum, Koç's newest restoration project, the **Çukurhan** (see "Where to Stay" on p. 405), along with a number of newish cafes and teahouses.

To the north of the open-statued square are remnants of ancient Rome. Immediately west of the statue runs **Cumhuriyet Bulvarı,** home to several museums and monuments to Republican Turkey. **AŞTI,** Ankara's *otogar* (bus station), is located southwest of Ulus at the end of the metro line. The **train station** is more centrally located closer to Ulus at the southwestern end of Cumhuriyet Bulvarı. Not surprisingly, the closer you get to the transport hub, the seedier it gets.

South of the starting point at the Atatürk statue along Atatürk Bulvarı is the modern section of **Kızılay,** a bustling zone of modern shopping, outdoor cafes, and bookstores. On the south side of Gazi Kemal Bulvarı is the neighborhood of **Yenişehir,** or "New City," the modern business heart of Ankara; here you'll find airline and bus-ticket offices, restaurants, and a few recommendable three- and four-star hotels.

Still farther south on Atatürk Bulvarı is **Kavaklıdere,** an old vineyard now home to the Sheraton, Hilton, residential housing, and easy living. The cluster of neighborhoods that includes Kavaklıdere, Çankaya, and Gaziosmanpaşa is where you'll find most of the foreign embassies, and a robust infrastructure of modern, middle-class, and business-level shopping, accommodations, and dining.

Getting Around

BY CAR   The Anatolian highway system is uncomplicated enough that a visitor can easily make his or her way to the greater Ankara area. Problem is, once you get there, one-way streets and avenues wind around until you unexpectedly pass your destination in a no-turn lane. And the population boom has resulted in an absence of adequate parking. If you'll be navigating by car, get your hotel to spell out the route in advance—or leave the car at the hotel in lieu of a taxi.

BY TAXI   Taking taxis makes the most sense in Ankara, especially for short stays. The rate is 2.2TL to step in the door plus 1.9TL per kilometer. Rates for day and night are the same.

BY PUBLIC TRANSPORTATION Ankara's rapid transit system is composed of a light metro (called the Ankaray) and the Ankara Metro. There is also a suburban rail system. Currently, construction is under way for the addition of three new metro lines (serving, roughly, areas southwest, west, and north), while five more connections are in the planning stages. The only problem is that the entire system, however efficient and clean, caters to residents of the suburbs and not tourists. So unless you need to get from Kızılay to Ulus (not a great connection, as the stop in Ulus is still a hike from the Roman ruins and the citadel) or to the AŞTI bus station, my recommendation is don't bother. One single ride costs around 1.75TL; multi-ride fare cards are available for 2, 3, 5, 10, and 20 rides. The system runs from 6am to midnight.

Metropolitan buses and *dolmuşes* depart from Güven Park in Kızılay and from Ulus to all points around the city. But if you're trying to catch a bus somewhere along the middle of a route, the system can be perplexing. Unless your stay here is extended, it's not worth wasting the time to decipher the local system.

[FastFACTS] ANKARA

Airline Information
The general number at Esenboğa Airport is (C) **0312/465-5555.** Turkish Airlines has a downtown office at Atatürk Bulv. 211, Kavaklıdere ((C) **0312/465-6363**). They're open weekdays from 8:30am to 7:45pm and Saturdays from 8:30am to 5:15pm.

Ambulance In a medical emergency, dial (C) **112** or take advantage of one of the private ambulance services. **Medline** provides emergency response along with a suite of health care options ((C) **0312/459-4000** in Ankara, (C) **444-1212** from anywhere in Turkey).

Bus Companies The 220 companies serving Ankara include Kamıl Koç ((C) **444-0562**), Kent ((C) **444-0038**), Metro ((C) **444-3455**), Pamukkale ((C) **444-3535**), Ulusoy ((C) **444-1888**), and Varan ((C) **444-8999**).

Car Rental Avis has a location in the domestic terminal ((C) **0312/398-0315**) and at Tunus Cad. 68/2,

Kavaklıdere ((C) **0312/467-2313**); **Alamo,** in the airport ((C) **0312/398-2166**); **Europcar,** in the domestic terminal ((C) **0312/398-0503**) and at Tunus Cad. 79/2, Kavaklıdere ((C) **0312/426-4606**); and **Hertz,** at the airport ((C) **0312/468-6290**) and at Tunus Cad. 71/2, Kavaklidere ((C) **0312/468-6290**).

Courier Services DHL Worldwide ((C) **0312/444-0400**), FedEx ((C) **444-0606**), TNT ((C) **444-0868**), and UPS ((C) **444-0033**) all have locations in Ankara and offer convenient pickup services.

Embassies & Consulates See "Embassies & Consulates," p. 440.

Hospitals Among the private hospitals in town are **Çankaya Hospital,** Bülten Sok. 44, Çankaya (www.cankayahastanesi.com.tr; (C) **0312/426-1450**); **Başkent University Hospital,** Fevzi Çakmak Cad. 10, Sok. 45, Bahçelievler ((C) **0312/212-6868;** www.baskent-ank.edu.

tr); and **Bayındır Hospital,** Atatürk Bulv. 201, Kavaklıdere ((C) **0312/428-0808;** www.bayindir hastanesi.com.tr) and Eskişehir Yolu, Sok. 2, Söğütözü ((C) **0312/287-9000**). The last also has a dental clinic on the premises.

Post Office The main post office is located in Ulus on Atatürk Bulvarı. There is another branch in Kızılay Square and countless others around town, all open from 8:30am to 5:30pm, Monday through Friday. In addition to the regular postal services, the PTT also has competitive currency exchange rates.

Telephone Dial (C) **115** for an international operator (and remember to dial 0 before a city's prefix). For calling cards and collect calls via AT&T, dial (C) **0811/288-0001.**

Turkish Railways Ankara's Gar, or train station, is located at Talatpaşa Bulvarı at the bottom of Cumhuriyet Bulvarı. For

WHAT TO SEE & DO

In spite of Ankara being one of the top three cities in Turkey for work and play, my unofficial subtitle for this section is, "Give Me One Good Reason to Spend the Night in Ankara." Like any capital city, Ankara offers an endless selection of cultural institutions, activities, and events, but let's be realistic—you didn't come all this way to check out the Museum of the Centennial of History of Sports and Education now, did you? But you did come to see the Museum of Anatolian Civilizations, and you won't be disappointed. The question is, then what?

Although the Atatürk Mausoleum (Anıtkabir), set on the western side of the city, deserves a look, most of your free time should be spent in and around the citadel; it's the most picturesque and typical neighborhood of old Ankara, with some of the best views. Then head down to Tunalı Hilmi in the early evening for a walk through Ankara's version of SoHo, and grab a bite and a glass of wine.

The Top Attractions

Ankara Citadel (Hisar or Ankara Kalesi) ★★ CASTLE   The Hisar presides over an outcropping in the oldest settled part of the city. It's believed to have been built by the Galatians, but no one really knows for sure. The fortress has an inner and outer wall, the outer added during the Byzantine occupation of the city. Originally, the citadel was constructed with 20 towers, but only a few have survived to the present day. The castle in its present state was most recently restored by the Ottomans, and dates to the Selçuk period.

Today the citadel retains much of the flavor of a small Anatolian village; from its narrow winding streets, you can catch a fleeting glimpse of the home life within. Many of the traditional wood-beamed houses, complete with large courtyards and gardens, have been restored and converted into marvelously atmospheric restaurants. Gentrification is not yet complete just beyond the main square. As you head down the hill you'll find an eclectic mish-mash of dusty antique shops, stores selling various hardware supplies, and the odd cafe.

Ulus. (Follow Cumhuriyet Bulv. past the statue of Atatürk, and continue along Hisar Parkı Cad.)

Atatürk Mausoleum (Anıtkabir) ★★ MONUMENT/MEMORIAL   The Turkish psychological equivalent of the John F. Kennedy Memorial at Arlington National Cemetery in Washington, D.C., Anıtkabir draws reverent Turks from all over the country to pay their respects to the founder of the republic. Built in 1944 atop a hill overlooking the city, the memorial complex stands starkly unadorned except for the vast mosaic courtyard and the mausoleum itself, the inside of which is covered in gold leaf. Outside, soldiers are present at every corner, and if you time it right, you can witness the severe, imposing Changing of the Guard. The courtyard arcade permits entry into various rooms including the gift shop and the recently installed **Atatürk and War of Independence Museum** ★★. The museum extends the entire circumference of the courtyard (lower level), and honors the founder of Turkey and the republic with sound and light dioramas of the War of

Independence campaigns, portraits, and period artwork, and various exhibits highlighting the history of the republic.

Entrance on Akdeniz Cad., Anıttepe. $\mathcal{C}$ **0312/231-7975.** Free admission. Oct–Nov Tues–Sun 9am–5pm; shorter hours in winter.

Cengelhan ☺ HISTORIC SITE   Standing at the center of what was a major commercial crossroad during the 16th and 17th centuries is this recently restored caravansaray, originally built for the daughter of Süleyman the Magnificent. The restoration, led by the ubiquitous Turkish tycoon, Rahmi Koç, was surely a labor of love. Although a major meeting place for commercial and social goings-on in its heyday, the place was in veritable ruins by the time Koç's father opened up a shop on the ground floor in 1917. The inn now houses thematic exhibits such as engineering, road transport, scientific instrumentation, medicine, and maritime pursuits. Many are interactive and should appeal particularly to fans of *The Way Things Work.*

Sutepe Mah. Depo Sok. 1, Altındağ (opposite the entrance to the citadel). www.rmk-museum.org. tr. $\mathcal{C}$**0312/309-6800.** Admission 6TL. Tues–Fri 10am–5pm; Sat–Sun 10am–6pm.

Museum of Anatolian Civilizations (Anadolu Medeniyetleri Müzesi) ★★★ MUSEUM
This is the finest archaeological collection in all of Turkey and the primary reason Ankara is worth a stopover. Housed in a **15th-century caravansary and covered bazaar ★** constructed under the reign of Mehmet the Conqueror, the museum contains a remarkable record of every civilization that passed through Anatolia as far back as the caveman.

The exhibit begins with artifacts believed to date to the Paleolithic Age and follows the progression of time throughout the museum. The most impressive Neolithic Age findings are an **8,000-year-old wall ★★**, clay and ceramic representations of **bulls' heads ★**, images of a fat and misshapen Mother Goddess called **Kybele ★★★** (later Cybele, forerunner of Artemis and probably the Virgin Mary), and **wall paintings from Çatalhöyük ★**, man's oldest known stationary civilization. The collections illustrate the first time that man tills the soil, builds homes, and takes it upon himself to decorate his surroundings. The Neolithic section gives way to artifacts recovered from Hacılar, the center of the Chalcolithic Era, and includes a large collection of stone and metal tools and decorative jewelry.

The Hatti tribes dominate the Bronze Age display with an abundance of **solar discs ★**, **deer- and bull-shaped statuettes ★★★**, and an evolved (and much thinner) **version of the Mother Goddess ★★**. Loads of **gold jewelry ★** give a rare look into the daily and religious practices of this ancient people.

Findings from the Assyrian trade colonies discovered at Kultepe, near Kayseri, are represented in the southern hall. (The Assyrians are credited with the introduction of the written word into Anatolia, much of which records transactions, receipts, and business agreements.) Over 20,000 **clay tablets ★★★**, inscribed in Assyrian cuneiform, have helped reveal a priceless amount of information on this period.

The highlight of the Great Hittite Empire exhibit is the famous **relief of the God of War ★★★** taken from the King's Gate at Hattuşaş, but the bronze statues of fertility gods, bulls, and deer are not to be overlooked. There are various fruit bowls and vases with animal shapes, and an infamous **vase ★★** that depicts a wedding ceremony along with the popular coital position of the time. Of major significance is the Akkadian-inscribed **tablet ★** (1275–1220 B.C.)—a correspondence between

Egyptian Queen Nefertari (identified here as Naptera), wife of Ramses II, and Hittite Queen Puduhepa, wife of Hattusilis III, written after the treaty of Kadesh. Around 1200 B.C. the Hittite Empire collapsed and left a vacuum in which the foundation of new city kingdoms formed. The Phrygians were one of the more important of these civilizations; most of the artifacts in this section were found in the **royal tumulus at Gordion,** the kingdom's capital. The tumulus measured 300m (984 ft.) in diameter and 50m (164 ft.) in height. A reproduction of the **ancient tumulus ★** (burial mound) in which the tomb of King Midas was believed to have been found is on display here; recent disputes have fueled speculation as to whether the tomb and tumulus are actually those of Gordius. The Phrygian section also includes carved and inlaid wooden furniture, hinged dress pins, ritual vessels in pottery and metal, and depictions of powerful animals such as lions, rams, and eagles.

Displays in the central vaulted building are rotated, but generally contain **monumental statues ★** from the various collections.

On the lower lever (entrance located past the Chalcolithic display; save this for the end of your visit, circling back around to the Neolithic section and taking the stairs down) is a newer section of artifacts dating from the classical period plus a collection of objects recovered from around Ankara. The small exhibition contains some marble statues, jewelry, decorative vessels, and coins.

Gözcü Sokak No:2 06240, Ulus (near the citadel entrance). www.anadolumedeniyetlerimuzesi.gov. tr. © **0312/324-3160.** Admission 15TL. Daily Apr–Oct 8:30am–7pm; Nov–Mar 8:30am–5:30pm.

Other Attractions

10

The Column of Julian (Julianus Sütunu) MONUMENT   The column, popularly known as the Belkıs Minaresi, or Queen of Sheba monument (for reasons unknown), was erected to commemorate a visit by the Emperor Julian in A.D. 362. The Corinthian capital dates to the 6th century; the stork's nest, a permanent crowning feature, is of more recent vintage.

Near Hükümet Meydanı, Ulus. Free admission.

Hacı Bayram Mosque (Hacı Bayram Camii) MOSQUE   Constructed in the 15th century for the founder of the Bayrami derviş sect, a Sufi poet and composer of hymns, the Hacı Bayram Mosque is one of the most important mosques in Ankara. The mosque was built in the Selçuk style and later restored by Sinan. The ceiling is made entirely of ornamental wood, punctuated by a single hexagonal rosette, and floral and plant motifs are found throughout the mosque. The decorative Kütahya tiles were added in the 18th century.

The **Hacı Bayram Mausoleum** attracts the faithful who visit the tomb of the Sufi mystic for prayer and inspiration. The mausoleum, with its marble facade and a sturdy lead dome over an octagonal drum, was completed a year after the mosque and borders the *mihrab's* exterior wall. The tomb's original wooden exterior and interior entrance doors are now part of the collection of the Ankara Ethnography Museum.

Ulus. Free admission. Dawn–dusk. From Ulus Meydanı follow Hisar Parkı Cad., turn left onto Hükümet Cad., and take the right fork.

Lion's Den Mosque (Aslanhane Camii) MOSQUE   Named after the lion statues embedded in the wall of the tomb complex, the Aslanhane Mosque is another fine example of Selçuk architecture, with its polychrome ceramic *mihrab*. The rows of wooden support columns are unusual, all the more because they are topped off with recycled marble Corinthian capitals. The mosque takes its name from the statue of a lion buried under the wall of the tomb of the mosque's founder, Ahi Şerafettin.

Off Kadife Sok. (near the entrance to the citadel), Ulus. Free admission. Dawn–dusk.

Museum of the Republic (Cumhuriyet Müzesi) MUSEUM   This stone building was built from 1923 to 1925 to house the Grand National Assembly, after it was transferred from its original home base just down the road. The building was abandoned from 1961 until 1982, when it was renovated to accommodate the Museum of the Republic.

The center Assembly Hall is surrounded by corridors with access to exterior rooms and constructed entirely of timber. The hall's two stories are decorated in typical Selçuk and Ottoman style, housing a minor display of documents from the early days of the republic. The exhibit is labeled exclusively in Turkish, indicating that this museum is more of a class-trip destination, but if you're in the neighborhood, it's worth a look for the Republican style of the building itself.

Atatürk Bulv., Ulus. ⓒ **0312/310-5361.** Admission 3TL. Tues–Sun 8:30am–5pm.

Museum of the War of Independence (Kurtuluş Savaşı Müzesi) MUSEUM   This modest but dignified two-story building served as the first official seat of the Turkish Grand National Assembly. The exhibition includes documents, pictures, weapons, and objects from the War of Independence up to the founding of the republic, set in the original hall with desks straight out of a classroom scene from *Little House on the Prairie*. Lining the walls are wax figures of all of the presidents, an unusually grotesque custom of veneration repeated in the Atatürk Mausoleum.

Cumhuriyet Cad. 14 (at Ulus Meydanı), Ulus. ⓒ **0312/310-7140.** Admission 3TL. Tues–Sun 9am–5pm.

The Roman Baths (Roma Hamaı) RUINS   The baths were constructed during the time of Emperor Caracalla in honor of the god of medicine, Asklepios. The unusually large complex has three main divisions: a *frigidarium* (cold room), a *caldarium* (hot room), and a *tepidarium* (tepid room). The *frigidarium* had a pool and changing rooms, the *caldarium* contained a washing area and a *sudatorium* (sweating area), and the *tepidarium* was used primarily as a room for relaxing. There are also courtyards, hearths, service areas, and storage in the complex, and a renewal in funding for excavations and restoration projects will be revealing more and more.

Çankırı Cad. (just west of Cumhuriyet Bulv.), Ulus. No phone. Admission 3TL. Daily 8:30am–noon and 1–5:30pm.

The Temple of Augustus and Rome (Augustus Tapınağı) RUINS   The temple was built by the Galatians in A.D. 10 as a tribute to Augustus during the emperor's lifetime, and later reconstructed by the Romans in the 2nd century. In anticipation of his own death, Augustus prepared a total of four documents (a list of his lifetime deeds, a financial and military accounting of the state of the empire, orders for his funeral, and his last will and testament) with instructions that the documents be dispatched and publicly displayed throughout the Roman Empire. Copies of the four documents have been found throughout ancient Rome; this temple displays the best-preserved copy of the *Res Gestae Divi Augusti,* or Deeds of Deified Augustus (written in both Greek and Latin), which represents an invaluable historical resource. Unfortunately, millennia of seismic activity and exposure to the elements have taken their toll on the temple, which is encased in decayed and rusted scaffolding and closed to the public. Inclusion in 2002 on the World Monument Fund's list of most endangered sites has afforded it renewed attention—an ambitious restoration is currently underway via a collaboration between the University of Trieste in Italy and the Middle Eastern Technical University in Ankara. So for now, you can only visit from afar.

Attached to the Hacı Bayram Mosque, Ulus. No phone. Closed for restoration.

Yeni Mosque (Cenab Ahmet Paşa Camii) MOSQUE   This mosque was built in the 16th century by Sinan, the royal architect to Süleyman the Magnificent. It is the largest Ottoman mosque in Ankara and constructed of local red porphyry. The regal-looking *mihrab* and the *minbar* (pulpit) are of white marble.

Ulucanlar Cad. and Çankırı Sok. (just east of the citadel), Ulus. Free admission. Dawn–dusk.

WHERE TO EAT

There are so many great dining options in Ankara, from humble kebap shop, to pleasantly touristy regional (fez and all), to trendy to executive gourmet. If you're only in Ankara overnight, I recommend eating dinner in one of the restaurants converted from an old Ottoman house in or around the citadel. Alternatively, seek out an inexpensive-to-midrange kebap joint around Kızılay or step out in style at one of the see-and-be-seen Ankara branches of Istanbul establishments along Arjantin Caddesi in Kavaklıdere or in Çankaya. Don't forget to grab a midmorning bagel-like snack of *sımıt*, a crispier version than what you'd find in Istanbul, smothered with soft cheese (found at stands everywhere in the mornings). While Turkish food is very vegetarian friendly, non-meat eaters will appreciate the options at **Café des Cafes** on Tunalı Hilmi 83/A, Kavaklıdere (𝄞 **0312/428-0176**) or **Kuki House,** Arjantin Cad. 18, Gaziosmanpaşa (𝄞 **0312/427-1400;** www.kuki.com.tr).

The Old Fortress Neighborhood

Divan Çengelhan Brasserie ★★ TURKISH/INTERNATIONAL   The Divan Brasserie has an extremely atmospheric location, the covered courtyard of a 16th-century caravansaray. As yet another one of Koç's babies (which include the Divan group of hotels, restaurants, and patisserie), the brasserie offers best in quality and creativity with a menu that gained it membership in the prestigious culinary Chaines des Rotisseurs. On weekends the restaurant hosts live music beginning at 10:30pm.

Sutepe Mah. Depo Sok. 1, Altındağ (opposite the entrance to the citadel). 𝄞 **0312/309-6800.** Appetizers and main courses 17TL–36TL. Tues–Sun noon–2am.

Washington Restaurant ★ TURKISH   An institution in Ankara, the Washington Restaurant was established in 1955 with the money the owners raised while working at the Turkish Embassy in Washington, D.C. The restaurant remained in Kızılay until 1992, and then spent the next 14 years in the citadel before heading back to Kızılay. Now installed in a two-story house in Gaziosmanpaşa, Washington remains true to the menu that has drawn politicians, journalists, and artists for more than 50 years.

Doyuran Sok. 5/7 (in the citadel). www.washingtonrestaurant.com.tr. 𝄞 **0312/311-4344.** Appetizers and main courses 8TL–28TL. AE, DC, MC, V. Daily 11:30am–midnight.

Zenger Paşa Konağı ☺ TRADITIONAL TURKISH   If you haven't yet tried *mantı* (Turkish ravioli), do it here. These minuscule dumplings are made on the premises right before your eyes, and served in a warm, spicy, garlicky yogurt sauce (sadly, it's available at lunchtime only). There's a brick oven for crunchy *pide* (flatbread) as well as the ubiquitous *gözleme*, a hearty but light crepelike treat with a selection of fillings. The kebaps arrive on a piping-hot tile. The brick-and-timber house has a back porch for a romantic twilight supper and spectacular views of the hillside below. The top-floor dining room will get you views of Ankara and the serenade of a live guitar player. Before you leave, be sure to have a look at the small collection of Turkish and Ottoman memorabilia.

Doyran Sok. 13, in the citadel. www.zengerpasa.com. © **0312/311-7070.** Appetizers and main courses 6TL–22TL. Prix fixe menu for lunch and dinner from 35TL and 57TL respectively. MC, V. Daily 11am–midnight.

Çankaya

Hacı Arif Bey Kebabçısı KEBAPS As the Turkish Republic's flagship metropolitan city, Ankara these days is more likely to offer up modern, European translations of "World Cuisine." But if you've got a hankering for some mouthwatering *içli köfte*, eggplant salads, and tasty kebaps, then this restaurant comes highly recommended. One of the more established places on Tunalı Hilmi, Hacı Arif Bey Kebabçısı has managed to maintain a loyal clientele by consistently serving perfectly cooked grilled meats and an incredible sticky-sweet baklava every time.

Güniz Sok. 48, Kavaklıdere. © **0312/467-6730.** Appetizers and main courses 6TL–18TL. AE, MC, V. Daily noon–11pm.

Mantar ★★ TURKISH HOME-STYLE A hit with the locals as well as a lunchtime favorite of U.N. employees down the road, Mantar serves grub that is good enough to bring you back again and again. Don't expect tablecloths or even table service, but the dining room is clean (glass-top tables) and there's a few tables outside on the street-side patio. Looking for an outstanding *hunkar begendi* or *yaprak dolması* (stuffed grape leaves)? Try the ones here. They also serve some dishes I've never seen elsewhere. My favorite is the *karamanmaraş köftesi* (delectable balls made of semolina); another is the *irmik* dessert (more semolina) with chocolate sauce.

4 Cad. 4/A, Yıldız. © **0312/440-0978.** Appetizers and main courses 6TL–16TL. MC, V. Daily 11am–midnight.

Trilye While this section has been dedicated to the casual traveler seeking authenticity, it doesn't seem right to exclude the top-rated restaurant in town. Here since 2002, Trilye is unexpectedly outstanding, given that it provides the highest-end seafood dining experience in this landlocked center of the country. The menu includes surprising items such as a sesame fish, paella, or a broccoli walnut salad in pomegranate glaze. The setting is all high society, so dress up and consider this meal a splurge.

Hafta Sok. 11/B, Gaziosmanpaşa. www.trilye.com.tr. © **0312/447-1200.** Appetizers and main courses 5TL–50TL. AE, MC, V. Reservations required. Daily noon–midnight.

SHOPPING

In the street bazaar along **Çıkrıkçılar Yokuşu,** near Ulus Meydanı, the strange sensation of being left alone permeates the air. In all of your travels around Turkey, you can bet that this is the *one* place you will not be accosted, hassled, harassed, or even approached. This might be due to the fact that this bazaar sees few foreign visitors. But even in the face of satin bedcovers, floor-length coats, and plastic shoes, a quiet stroll gazing at the local linens and essential items of daily life in Ankara is a lovely way to spend an afternoon.

At the end of Çıkrıkçılar Yokuşu is **Bakırcılar Çarşısı,** a street of local shops displaying a basic mix of handcrafted copper, kitchen, and hardware items. Heading left up the hill to the citadel gate is a street with a village feel and lined with spices, dried fruits, and nuts, all set out in bulk outside the shop entrances. There's also a good amount of wicker items and copper up this way, until you reach the gate of the citadel, where handicrafts, souvenirs, and carpets are displayed in the most authentic of environments.

Ankara has no shortage of modern shopping centers. Upscale shops like **Burberry's, Beymen, Calvin Klein,** and **Polo** can be found in the **Karum Iş Merkezi,** the shopping mall near the Sheraton and Hilton hotels. For those looking for more ready-to-wear, step outside Karum Iş Merkezi onto **Tunalı Hilmi** Caddesi (the street running north-south between Kocatepe and Kızılay). The nearby Arjantin Caddesi in Gaziosmanpaşa is where you'll find storefronts of the world's poshest labels. Don't bother with the **Atakule Tower** in Çankaya; most of the shops are of low quality or closed altogether.

Even without the slightest intention of buying a sack of potatoes, it's still fun to take a walk through one of the many neighborhood *pazars* **(local markets),** where you're likely to find Polo or Banana Republic overstocks, as well as other necessary and not-so-necessary goods. The largest market is located in the center of Ankara behind the **Abdi Ipekçi Park in Sıhhiye.** The market operates on Wednesdays and Saturdays, and like other local markets, is open from dawn to dusk. Also on Wednesday is the covered bazaar in **Aşağı Arancı,** down the hill off Hoşdere Caddesi near Tomurcuk Sokak. On Mondays the **Maltepe Pazarı** spreads out behind the Maltepe Mosque, and on Fridays, the **Bahçelievler Pazarı** takes over 10 Sokak near Azerbaycan Caddesi in Bahçelievler. The **Ankara Halı** is a chaotic permanent market in Ulus, saturated with stalls of fresh fish, fruit, and vegetables. Farmers gather here in summertime to sell their own produce. The area is also full of butcher shops and charcuteries. Assembling a picnic meal of fresh cheese, meats, olives, and dried fruits is a tempting prospect; if you walk along Hisarparkı Caddesi (Fortress Park Ave.) up the hill toward the citadel, you can picnic on the grass or sit on the wall at the base of the fortress.

ANKARA AFTER DARK

Ankara may be a happening cultural center for the highbrow arts, but because most travelers pass through at a brisk pace, few get to actually take advantage of these events. Many do have time for a drink, though, and can select from a laundry list of pubs, wine bars, and chic cafes catering to the hefty consular population, or, at the other end of the scale, more humble diversions popular with the city's resident students.

The Performing Arts

With Ankara's designation as capital of the new republic, the city had the responsibility of becoming a cultural capital as well. Rising out of the dust of an old village, Ankara has surpassed the other cities in Turkey to become the most active cultural center in the country.

Ankara is home to the prestigious **State Opera and Ballet** (www.dobgm.gov.tr), the **Presidential Symphony Orchestra** (www.cso.gov.tr), and a large number of theaters that feature the work of Turkish artists. The Presidential Symphony Orchestra performs twice weekly on Fridays and Saturdays during the October-to-May season, showcasing classical music by Turkish and foreign composers. Monthly programs for the State Opera and Ballet are listed in the Sunday edition of the English-language *Hurriyet Daily News,* as well as on the venue's Internet site (www.devtiyatro.gov.tr; in Turkish). Tickets can be purchased at the **Opera House** (Atatürk Bulvarı 20, Ulus; ✆ **0312/324-2210**), in Opera Meydanı, Ulus, up to a month in advance of a performance.

FESTIVALS   The capital also nurtures the arts by hosting several festivals throughout the year. Ankara's International Film Days, in March, and the Sevda Cenap International Arts and Music Festival, in April and May, attract the best of Turkish and international musicians. The **Children's Festival** is held in April, with groups of children from all over the world arriving to take part in this colorful, lively event. On August 30, Ankara celebrates Victory Day with pomp and circumstance appropriate for the capital city. Ankara also organizes a series of fairs throughout the year in **Altın Park,** attracting families for an afternoon of cotton candy, piping-hot *gözleme* fresh off the cart, and the occasional kiddie ride. See "Visitor Information," earlier in this chapter, for Ankara tourist offices.

The Club, Cafe & Bar Scene

Much of Ankara's nightlife is geared toward the diplomatic community, with cafes, jazz clubs, and the odd English pub clustered at the south of town. A more youthful crowd, predominantly from the nearby university, congregates in the **outdoor beer gardens** around Sakarya Caddesi in Kızılay. A few restaurants at the citadel offer nightly music, including establishments immediately to the left inside the entrance and next to the Angora Hotel that change management regularly. The **Divan Çengelhan Brasserie** (see "Where to Eat," earlier) features live music on weekends. In the neighborhood of Kavaklıdere, just off Tunalı Hilmi on **Abjantin Caddesi,** is a lineup of smart-looking, candlelit bistros; there's even a Starbucks for those of you feeling homesick. Below are a few additional and popular old reliables.

WHERE TO STAY

The casual visitor (aka tourist) that stops in Ankara is undoubtedly in town for the Museum of Anatolian Civilizations, and while here, hoping to get a taste of modern, Republican Turkey. A low seat on carpeted cushions or an evening spent sipping local wine at a 500-year-old caravansaray are welcome bonuses. If this sounds like you, then the neighborhood of Ulus is where you will want to be. For those of you here for the business of governing the world, or preventing the world from collapsing in on itself, consider staying at the **Hilton** (www.hilton.com) the **Sheraton** (www.sheraton.com), the brand new **J.W. Marriott** (www.marriott.com) or the **Swissôtel** (www.swissotel.com) all conveniently located near the Turkish government buildings. Got your family in tow while you toil away? There are some options for you too, halfway between Ulus and the business center of town.

Ulus

Angora House ★ 🏠   This restored former home of Şakir Paşa, a member of Atatürk's first parliament, provides visitors to Ankara with the only opportunity to live amid the city's early history, smack dab in the historic citadel. Virtually unscarred by tourist overdevelopment, the citadel is literally steps away from the archaeological museum. Each room has the character of a guest room in a private home. Of the scant six rooms, it's hard to say which is best: An antique Assyrian wardrobe stands in no. 18, no. 16 gets a latticed wooden ceiling and the only bathtub in the house, no. 22 (one of the suites) has a spacious bathroom in a hidden niche and a stunning gold-leaf ceiling, and no. 20 (the other suite) enjoys a view of Ankara from the shower. Kalekapısı Sok. 16, 06240 Ankara (in the citadel). angorahouse@gmail.com. $\mathcal{C}$ **0312/309-8380.** Fax 0312/309-8381. 6 units. 65€ double. MC, V. **Amenities:** Bar, free Wi-Fi.

Divan Çukurhan ★★★ 📷 With the restoration of both the Cengelhan (see "Where to Eat," earlier) and the Çukurhan, the Turkish businessman and philanthropist, Rahmi Koç, has almost singlehandedly transformed the neighborhood (a former Horse Market) to a living exhibition of 16th-century Ottoman Ankara. The former *han*, like many of the buildings in the citadel neighborhood is constructed of stone, with timber interlaced in patterns within the stone. The effect is almost Teutonic, with a colossal dose of distinctive Ottoman style. Rooms alternately combine ancient stone with stylish sofas, flatscreen TVs, laptop-sized safes, and marble baths. It's even possible to snag a Jacuzzi in a standard (deluxe) room, while suites have rain showers and more oriental touches. Necatibey Mah..Depo Sok. 3, 06000 Altındağ, Ulus, Ankara (opposite the entrance to the citadel). www.divan.com.tr. $\mathcal{C}$ **0312/306-6400.** Fax 0312/306-6429. 19 units. 170€–210€ double. See website for special rates. AE, MC, V. Free parking. **Amenities:** 2 restaurants; bar; exercise room; massage; smoke-free rooms. *In room:* A/C, satellite TV, hair dryer, minibar, free Wi-Fi.

Çankaya

Gordion Hotel ★★ ☺ For those who prefer the intimacy of a small hotel but can't do without five-star amenities, this is the palace. I mean place. Swathed in Ottoman repro textiles from Vakko and accessorized with lots of leather and brass detailing, the interior clearly has a masculine touch. Still, I'd stay here in a heartbeat, not least of all for the in-house beauty center and spa-like pool setting. The location is also dandy: right off the main shopping/eating district in the heart of Kavaklıdere. All rooms have a small library of books and CDs, and laptops, cellphones, and even PlayStations are available for rental—great for keeping kids busy during Mom or Dad's business meeting. Büklüm Sok. 59 (just off of Tunalı Hilmi), Kavaklıdere. www.gordionhotel.com. $\mathcal{C}$ **0312/427-8080.** Fax 0312/427-8085. 44 units. 120€ double; 160€–200€ suite. Rates include breakfast but exclude tax. MC, V. Free indoor parking. **Amenities:** 2 restaurants; bar; exercise room; indoor pool; room service; sauna; smoke-free rooms. *In room:* A/C, TV/DVD, hair dryer, minibar, free Wi-Fi.

Hotel Metropol Located down a quiet street near the Kocatepe Mosque, this spruced-up cement block is one of the best buys in Ankara. The interior is heavy on marble, wood, and leather details while rooms lack air-conditioning, which might make you think twice before holing up here in the height of summer. The hotel is nestled amid restaurants and coffee shops, making this a very convenient location, but you'll have to take a taxi to visit most of the major sights. Olgunlar Sok. 5, Bakanlıklar (just below Kızılay). www.hotelmetropol.com.tr. $\mathcal{C}$ **0312/417-3060.** Fax 0312/417-6990. 31 units. 60€ double. AE, DC, MC, V. Free parking available. **Amenities:** Restaurant; bar; room service. *In room:* TV (local stations), minibar, free Wi-Fi.

King Hotel Güvenlik ★ 🍴 ☺ The neighborhood west of Kavaklıder is one of the more representative ones that modern, middle-class Ankara has to offer. It's located on a type of local main street and within easy walking distance to the more happening streets over on Tünalı Caddesi. The hotel boasts an on-site restaurant, a pool, a sauna, and a lovely garden. Rooms are tastefully simple without being banal, and some have en-suite kitchens. The bathrooms cover all of the comfort bases, with tub/shower combos and plenty of indigenous marble. The slightly nobler sister hotel (Piyade Sok. 17, Çankaya; ✆ **0312/440-7931**) costs only a few dollars more and is convenient to the U.N. House and to Mantar restaurant (see earlier).

Güvenlik Cad. 13, 06540 Aşagı Ayrancı, Ankara. www.kinghotel.com.tr. ✆ **0312/418-9099.** Fax 0312/417-0382. 36 units. 145TL double. MC, V. Free parking in hotel garage. **Amenities:** Restaurant; 2 bars; exercise room; outdoor swimming pool; room service; sauna. *In room:* A/C, satellite TV, hair dryer, free Internet, minibar.

A SIDE TRIP TO THE HITTITE CAPITAL OF HATTUŞAŞ ★

Religious and political capital of the Hittite Kingdom for almost 500 years, the ancient site of **Hattuşaş** constitutes one of the most important archaeological sites in Turkey. Having imported cuneiform script from Mesopotamia and the Assyrian trade colonies, the Hittites recorded the most minute details of their civilization. Exhaustive archives of public, political, and religious life have been found in several repositories throughout Hattuşaş, and thanks to the work of a Czech linguist who succeeded in deciphering the Hittite alphabet in 1915, a wealth of information on one of the most important ancient civilizations of Anatolia is now available.

GETTING THERE At 210km from Ankara (130 often meandering miles and easily 4½–5 hr. by bus/*dolmuş*), a private car, which will cut the trip down to 2½ hours each way, is an absolute must. To get there, take highway 200-E88 out of Ankara and follow the signs for Samsun. Take the turnoff for Çorum, following past Delice and Süngürlü, and begin looking for signs for Boğazköy and the archaeological site. (The highway winds through a spectacular and desolate landscape—so be sure to fill up the tank before you go, because petrol stations in these parts pump pretty much only diesel.) The site is located at the summit of an imposing and rocky terrain high above the fertile valley of the village of **Boğazköy.**

To get there from Ankara by public transportation (if you insist), take a bus to the *center* of Süngürlü, where you'll be changing to a *dolmuş* for the remaining 22.5km (14-mile) ride into Boğazköy. *Dolmuşes* run from 7:30am to 7pm from Süngürlü and from 7am to 4.30pm from Boğazköy. Taxis from Süngürlü run around 30€; clients of the Hattuşaş Pansiyon, Baykal Hotel, and Aşikoğlu Hotels (see "Where to Stay & Dine," below) can get a pickup for free.

VISITOR INFORMATION A great resource on the excavations and historical site is the German Archaeological Institute (**www.hattuscha.de**). You can also get a rough topographical map on their site, or pick one up at the Hattuşaş Pansiyon (**www.hattusha.com**).

There may be an "employee" at the booth offering his services or, more innocently, asking for a ride through the site, but don't be fooled—this is a local posing as a guide for tips. Although some of the locals can be knowledgeable, you'll have to weigh the fact that you'll be relinquishing your right to silence and self-discovery as you attempt to absorb the enormity of the place. All of the significant sites are signposted, so you don't have to worry about missing them.

Exploring the Hittite Sites of Hattuşaş ★★

A natural stronghold situated atop an impregnable area of steep rocky terrain, Hattuşaş had been inhabited as far back as the 3rd millennium B.C. The Hatti, an Anatolian people of unknown origin, settled here as early as 2500 B.C. Later, around 1800 B.C., King Anitta of Kushara (an ancient kingdom of similarly undetermined origins and whereabouts) invaded and set fire to the city, pronouncing it accursed, before moving on.

King Labarnas, a descendant of Anitta of Kushara, returned several generations later to reconquer and rebuild the city. Labarnas called the city Hattuşaş, or "Land of the Hatti," and changed his name to Hattusilis. Hattusilis I is accepted as the true founder of the Hittite kingdom.

From 1650 to 1200 B.C., the Hittites ruled most of Anatolia, succeeding in spreading out as far as northern Syria—much to the dissatisfaction of the Egyptian pharaohs. Tensions came to a head at the historic Battle of Kadesh, pitting the Hittite king Muwatalli II against Egypt's Ramses II. The battle essentially ended in a stalemate (with both sides claiming victory); nevertheless, for the first time in the history of mankind, a written treaty was drawn up between two warring factions. A copy of this landmark treaty was discovered in the Hattuşaş Palace Archives and is now in the Archaeology Museum in Istanbul.

The Hittites were the undisputed power in western Asia from 1400 to 1200 B.C., but a period of struggle over the ascendancy left the empire weak and vulnerable. Around 1200 B.C. the city was burned and razed by the Phrygians, who sometime between the 9th and 7th centuries B.C. established much of the fortified city that stands today. Minor settlements were later set up by the Galatians, Romans, and Byzantines.

The city was accessible through several monumental stone gates carved with reliefs of lions, sphinxes, and gods, which stand now in various states of erosion. Many of these original reliefs and statues have been moved to the Museum of Anatolian Civilizations (p. 399) in Ankara, and today there is one main entrance to the site. The first set of ruins you pass is the **Büyük Tapinak.** Located at the center of the Lower City and surrounded by a wall, this temple was the most important, consecrated to the Storm God and the Sun Goddess of Arinna, who were identified with their Hurrian equivalents, Teşup and Hepatu. The temple was constructed during the reign of the last great Hittite king, Hattusilis III (1275–1250 B.C.). The ruins of the foundations show an ample presence of storerooms, offices, and workshops; this indicates the temple was an important public building in addition to a sacred one. In some of the corners, you can still find the remains of large pottery receptacles. The actual temple is in the center, isolated from the outer sections; only the king and queen, in their roles as high priest and priestess, could enter it.

From the Büyük Tapinak, follow the road up and take the left fork where you will encounter the **Büyükkale (Great Fortress).** The royal residence occupies the highest point of a naturally rocky crest enclosed by a network of defensive walls. The palace also housed the high guard, with public rooms for the state archives, a large reception hall, and some sacred areas. Not much detail can be discerned from the remaining foundations—invisible from a lower elevation amid the grassy terraces— but a stopover at this point can provide a visual overview of the invincible position of the city.

Farther up the path on the right is **Nişantepe ★**, an artificially smoothed rock outcropping that bears an almost 9m-long (30-ft.) inscription. Badly weathered and only partially deciphered, the inscription is most likely an accounting of the deeds of Şuppiliumus II, last of the Hattuşaş kings. Across the road to the left is a path leading to **Hieroglyphic Chamber no. 1** ★ and the **Southern Fort,** erected several centuries after the collapse of the Hittite Empire. The Hieroglyphic Chamber dates to 1200 B.C. and is built into the side of an artificial dam. (The other end is part of the fortress.) On the back wall is the figure of a man in a long cloak. The figure, probably a god, carries a sign similar to the Egyptian *ankh* ("life") and is possibly representative of an entrance into the underworld. Few remains were found in **Hieroglyphic Chamber no. 2,** which is visible from the road but was inaccessible as this book went to press.

The best-preserved city gate at Hattuşaş is the **Kralkapı ★★★**, or King's Gate, flanked by two towers with both an inner and outer portal. To the left of the inner doorway is a replica of the famous relief of the Hittite God of War. It's a stunning sight to see the relief *in situ,* even if the original is in the Museum of Anatolian Civilizations (p. 399) in Ankara.

On the road up to **Yerkapı,** over 28 temples have been uncovered. Yerkapı, which means "Earth Gate," or "Gate in the Ground," is better known as the **Sphinx Gate ★★** and is the highest elevation in the area. You can either climb the stone steps to the top of the 15m-high (49-ft.) artificial bank or access the exterior of the city via the 69m (226-ft.) alternate access tunnel. The gate was named for four great sphinxes that guarded the inner gate, two of which were reconstructed from fragments and reinstalled on-site. The two remaining great sphinxes are keeping watch over the Museum of the Ancient Orient (part of Istanbul's Archaeological Museum) and a museum in Berlin. The four additional bas-relief sphinxes that were carved into the portal of the outer embankment were unfortunately not spared this end; all that remains of the originals is one badly chipped and almost indistinguishable image on the western wall.

The **Aslanlıkapı (Lion's Gate)** displays one of the best-preserved artifacts remaining on-site at Hattuşaş—symbolically warding off evil spirits. There's a hieroglyphic inscription above the head of the one on the left, but unless the sun stands at high noon, the inscription is invisible.

About 1km (⅔ mile) to the northeast (accessible by backtracking out of the entry/exit road to Hattuşaş and heading right and up the road) is the shrine of **Yazılıkaya ★★**, formed out of the convergence of two natural ravines and the largest known Hittite rock sanctuary. The purpose of the shrine remains a mystery, although we can speculate that it was used for annual cult celebrations or even as a royal funerary site.

In the large rock-enclosed court of **Chamber A ★★★** are some of the most incredible treasures of the Hittite architectural legacy. Hewn from one end of the rock enclosure to the other is a representation of a sacred procession of deities, all of which are of Hurrian origin. Hurrian gods were given prominence by the Hittite Queen Puduhepa, wife of Hattusilis III, who was herself of noble Hurrian or Eastern origin. The cylindrical domed headdress is a symbol of divinity of Mesopotamian influence. The deities are oriented to the main scene on the back wall where the Storm God Teşup and the Sun Goddess Hepatu meet. The Storm God Teşup and Sun Goddess Hepatu, also of Hurrian origin, became the two most important deities in the Hittite pantheon, the accepted counterparts of the Hittite Storm God and the Sun Goddess of Arinna. Towering above the main scene and standing over 3.5m (11 ft.) high is a large relief of King Tudhaliya IV, son of Hattusilis III and Puduhepa.

To the right passing through a narrow rock crevice is **Chamber B ★★**, probably a memorial chapel to King Tudhaliya IV. Because the reliefs in this chamber were buried until the end of the 19th century, they are better preserved than the ones in Chamber A. The largest relief is of King Tudhaliya IV, on the main wall next to a puzzling depiction of a large sword formed by two extended lions with a divine human head for a handle. This possibly represents the God of Swords, or Nergal of the underworld. The relief on the right wall depicts a row of 12 gods bearing sickles similar to the ones in the other chamber. The number 12 as a sacred number is first seen here and repeated many times in subsequent civilizations—there were 12 gods of Olympus, 12 apostles, 12 imams of Islamic mysticism, 12 months in a year, 12 days of Christmas, and 12 to a dozen. The three niches carved into the far end of the chamber are believed to have contained the cremated remains of Hittite royalty.

No phone. Admission 5TL. Tickets good for sites of both Hattuşaş and Yazılıkaya. Daily 8am–sunset.

Where to Stay & Eat

Located 50m (164 ft.) across from the access road to the site is the motel-style **Aşikoğlu Hotel** (Çarşı Mah. 9, Boğazkale; ℮ **0364/452-2004;** fax 0364/452-2171; www.hattusas.com), with its 33 rooms all with balconies, satellite TV, and (weak) hair dryers for 25€. They recently built the **Hittite Houses** (www.hittitehouses.com) a modern rendition of the Hittite fortress with simple, institutional style rooms with modern amenities. The bonus is the great expanse of lawn and gardens on the premises.

The recently restored (2004) **Hattuşaş Restaurant and Pension,** on the main square (℮ **0364/452-2013;** fax 0364/452-2957; www.hattusha.com), offers simple rooms for 12€ including breakfast. The family also owns the **Hotel Baykal** (same address and contact info), with double rooms for 30€. For that matter, any of the campgrounds or "pansiyons" will feed you if you're hungry—and so will the locals, if you hang around long enough.

SOUTHEASTERN ANATOLIA

By Jamie Ehrlich

Archeology and history buffs can't do much better than a visit to Southeastern Anatolia. The region is practically littered with ruins, including the recent archeological discoveries at Zeugma, housed at a new mosaic museum that's the largest in the world (p. 417), and Göbekli Tepe, a hillside sanctuary believed to be the oldest religious structure on earth.

Through the ancient land known as Mesopotamia flow the ancient Tigris and Euphrates rivers. The area around the rivers is extremely fertile, giving the region its name, the Fertile Crescent. Civilizations such as the Sumerians, Assyrians, and Babylonians were established along these rivers. Today, the area remains extremely diverse, with a large Kurdish population. It is bordered to the south by Syria, but has seen none of that country's unrest.

While traveling through the region, you'll encounter beautiful countryside, with steep mountainous roads, arid land, caves dotted with ancient dwellings, wildflowers, and waterfalls. The region is home to Gaziantep, Turkey's sixth largest city, along with the amusingly named Batman; the religious pilgrimage city of Sanliurfa; the predominantly Kurdish city of Diyarbakir (you might enter the region through its airport); and the scenic mountain town of Mardin,

The area has been radically altered in recent years due to the highly controversial Southeastern Anatolia Project (known by its Turkish acronym, GAP). The 22 dams planned throughout the region will cost an estimated $32 billion, and are expected to double the country's irrigable farmland and bring energy to Western Turkey. But it has also displaced many thousands of inhabitants, altered the ecosystem, and flooded major archeological finds. At the time of writing, a major tourist attraction in the area, the ancient city and cave dwellings of Hasankeyf (p. 432), is threatened by a nearby dam that will flood most of the area (though it is currently being fought contentiously by activists).

The towns and attractions here are spread out, and getting around may prove challenging. It's best seen on a tour (see chapter 2 for tour options). Two tour guides we also highly recommend are Taylan Tasibasi (© **532/415-3015;** www.taylantasbasi. blogspot.com), and Umit Isin of Equinox Tours (www.equinox.com.tr), who runs customized private tours and occasional group tours of the region. Both of these guides are archeologists with expert knowledge of the region.

ANTAKYA

560km (348 miles) south of Istanbul; 195km (121 miles) SE of Adana; 214km (133 miles) SW of Gaziantep; 350km (217 miles) SW of Sanliurfa.

Antakya, also known as Antioch, is an ancient center for Christianity. The city was founded in A.D. 323 by the Seluecids, after the death of Alexander, on a site which he was said to have made his camp during his campaigns. It grew to become one of the most important cities in the region. It was later variously threatened or occupied by the Romans, Arabs, Persians, Selchuks, Byzantines, Crusaders, Mameluks, and Ottomans. After Seleucid rule came to an end in 83 B.C., the city was declared capital of the Roman Province of Syria. It grew to become one of the wealthiest cities under the Roman Empire, and was also a long-standing rival of Alexandria. Much later, Antakya was part of a French mandate of nearby Syria, and French rule from 1919 to 1939 left a lasting legacy on the city, seen in its French colonial architecture. The province became a part of the Republic of Turkey in 1939.

The city has great significance for Christians. It is widely believed that followers of Jesus Christ were called "Christians" for the first time at St. Peter's Grotto (p. 413), located outside the city.

Today, Antakya is home to many faiths and denominations, which co-exist peacefully. The city is situated on the Asi (Orrantes) river, one of the few rivers that flows from south to north. You'll also find waterfalls located outside of town. At first glance, Antakya may appear a dusty and lackluster place, but the city's main shopping street is hopping, and it has an alluring old core. Take some time to explore the old part of the city, a warren of quiet alleyways with colorful old homes and decorative doors. It's also worth noting some of the beautiful crumbling structures along the main road. Treat yourself at the end of the day with the local specialty *künefe* (p. 416).

Essentials

GETTING THERE   Small, modern **Hatay Airport** is 25km (16 miles) away from Antakya. Domestic flights arrive at the airport from Istanbul, Ankara, Antalya, and Izmir. This airport sometimes closes due to floods. Flying to Hatay from Istanbul takes about an hour and 45 minutes. *Dolmuş* taxis wait in front of the airport and drop you off wherever you choose in the city, for 10TL per person.

The nearest airport for international flights is Adana Airport, 195km (121 miles) north of Antakya.

Has Turizm (www.hasturizm.com.tr/h_english) operates buses from all major cities in the country. Buses arrive 7km (4½ miles) from the center of Antakya. From there, minibuses can bring you closer to the city center.

VISITOR INFORMATION   Antakya's **tourist office** (Muammer Urgen; © **326/ 216-6098**) is located at a circle at the end of Atatürk Caddesi, a 10-minute walk north from the center of the city. It's open Monday to Friday, 8am to noon, and 1 to 5pm.

Area Attractions

Grotto of Saint Peter RELIGIOUS SITE   This sacred site is located in a hollow in Mount Stauris, about 2km (1¼ miles) from Antakya. To reach the cave, you need to walk a few minutes up a path. This is where St. Peter first celebrated mass, and where Barnabas, St. Peter, and St. Paul did their preaching. The word "Christian" is believed to have first been used here in A.D. 40, and thus many believe that this was the first Christian church. The decorative facade of the cave was built by the Crusaders, during their rule in Antioch from A.D. 1098 to 1268. A nave and two aisles were built in the space. The remains of mosaics can be seen on the floor of the grotto, and upon close view, it is possible to detect traces of frescos on the walls. There was also a tunnel towards the back left of the cave, used as an escape route in the event of an attack.

Further north of the grotto, a face is carved into the mountainside. This is believed by some to be the face of the mythical ferryman Charon, or otherwise to be a woman's face.

In 1963, Pope Paul VI declared the Grotto of Saint Peter a pilgrimage site for Christians. Each year on June 29, the Catholic church holds a St. Peter's festival here.

Reached via Kurtulus Caddesi, northeast for 2km (1¼ miles). Open 9am–noon and 1–6pm Apr–Oct; 8am–noon and 1–5pm Nov–Mar. Admission 8TL.

Museum of Roman Mosaics RELIGIOUS SITE   This large, airy museum dates back to 1948, and is one of the largest mosaic museums in the world. It features a magnificent collection of intricate mosaics from ruins from Antioch and nearby Harbiye (known as Daphne in ancient times), most excavated from the remains of wealthy villas along the Euphrates. The mosaics date from the 1st to 5th centuries A.D. In the first hall, one of the main attractions is the early 2nd century representation of an Evil Eye being attacked by a spear, a trident, a snake, a scorpion, a centipede, and a barking dog. The next room features an enormous mosaic from the 4th century A.D., which is viewed from above. It depicts Titans, Thetys, Okeanos, and personifications of the sea. There is also an open-air sculpture garden. The giant "Antakya sarcophagus," another highlight, was a recent discovery in 1993. You'll also find Roman busts and a large collection of masks and coins.

Cumhuriyet Meydanı, Gündüz Caddesi No. 1, Antakya. © **326/214-6167.** Open Tues–Sun 8:30am–12:30pm and 1:30–5:30pm. Admission 8TL.

Saint Simeon Monastery MONASTERY   This monastery high on a mountain, now in ruins, was built in 521 A.D. Simeon Stylites the Younger, at the mere age of 7 years old and an Antioch native, decided to follow the example of his namesake, Saint Simeon the Elder. Saint Simeon the Elder spent most of his life on a mountaintop near Aleppo, Syria. Simeon Stylites the Younger lived here for 39 years and preached to visitors, and many monks followed in his footsteps after his death, and were called Stylites.

Like the Church of Saint Simeon in Aleppo, this monastery had a design with four points radiating outward. Three of the radiating arms were churches, while the last was likely a living area for monks. In the center was a rock pillar from which Stylites could preach, but today only the base and the staircase leading up to it remain.

15km away from Aknehir, between the Antakya-Samandağ rd. No phone.

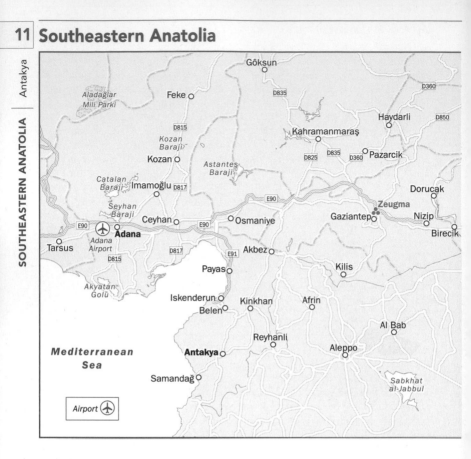

Where to Eat

Antakya boasts fantastic food, which is spicier than the rest of Turkey. Must-tries include kebaps, *içli köfte* (balls of bulgur stuffed with meat), and the walnut, pepper, and pomegranate spread *muhammara,* finished off with *künefe,* a local specialty (see below). The hummus here is also superb.

EXPENSIVE

Haysim Anadolu (Anatolia Restaurant) TURKISH   This popular restaurant is housed in an early-20th-century building that served previously as a coffee shop, public library, and billiard club. It opened as a restaurant in 2004. Service here is very professional. The large second floor has a view overlooking a gorgeous crumbling building across the street. We recommend the thyme salad, *lamacun,* and fresh fish.

Hurriyet Cad. No. 30/A Antakya. www.anadolurestaurant-haysim.com. Ⓒ **326/215-3335.** Main courses 8TL–35TL. V. Mon 2–10pm; Tues 11am–1am; Thurs 1–3pm and 7pm–2am; Fri 2pm–1am; Sat–Sun noon–11pm.

Hatay Sultan Sofrasi TURKISH/KEBAPS   This upscale spot on the main drag of Antakya is considered one of the best dining spots in town. The large space includes a wraparound balcony. Meats abound here, including Adana-style kebobs.

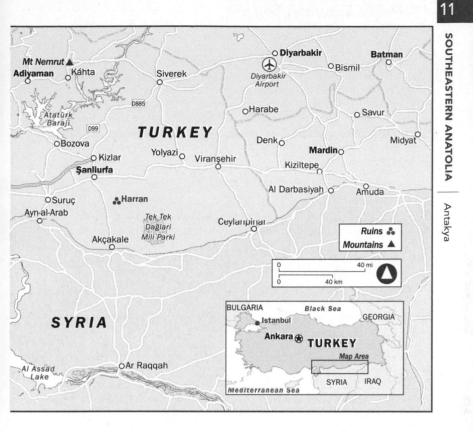

Istikal Cad. No. 20/A, Antakya. www.sultansofrasi.com. © **326/213-8759**. Main courses 8TL–15TL. No credit cards. Mon–Wed 1–3pm and 7–8pm; Thurs–Fri 11am–10pm; Sat 7–8am and 1–9pm; Sun 4–6pm

Antakya Shopping

Antakya Bazaar   Located through a maze of alleys, the covered bazaar has a mix of souvenirs and locally made products. It's a great place to pick up soaps, pomegranate syrup, and red pepper paste, along with spices. Locals frequent the kebap shops found inside the bazaar.

Open Mon–Sat 8:30am–5pm.

EXPENSIVE

Liwan Hotel   This hotel has grand origins: It was built in the 1920s for the President of Syria, who was a Turk. The building's structure features stone vaults and arches. There is also a pretty courtyard, an atmospheric restaurant and bar with stone walls, and a cafe. Crystal chandeliers, carved bed frames, velvet chairs, and a piano in the lobby recreate the atmosphere of Antakya from when it was first built.

KÜNEFE'S sweet TREATS

A treat that's best sampled in Antakya, *künefe* is made with shredded wheat (*kadayıf*) pastry that is stuffed with a mild locally produced cheese and doused in a surprising amount of syrup. If that's not enough sugar for you, you can have it accompanied by ice cream or *kaymak* (clotted cream). The thin strips of pastry are spun on a copper plate, then the cheese is sandwiched between two layers and baked. The best place to watch it being made and sample the sweet results is on Pazar Street, in front of the Ata Bridge at the town center.

Silahlı Kuvvetler Cad. No: 5 Antakya. www.theliwanhotel.com. © **326/215-7777**. Double 98TL–162TL. AC, MC, V. **Amenities:** Restaurant; bar; free Wi-Fi. *In room:* A/C, TV, phone.

Savon Hotel ★   Housed in a building that served as a soap and olive oil factory during the Ottoman period, this is the boutique of choice in Antakya. The long lobby has sloping ceilings and plenty of couches for relaxing. The rooms don't quite live up to the impressive lobby and are a bit stuffy, with a few faults (during my stay the bathroom door was off its hinges and the TV was on the fritz). But these can be easily overlooked due to the hotel's lovely courtyard with high walls covered in colorful flowers, and its large, delicious breakfast. Rooms include tea and a fridge, and there's a gift shop on-site.

Kurtuluş Cad. No. 192, Antakya. www.savonhotel.com.tr/eng. © **326/214-6355**. 43 units. Standard room 184TL–289TL. AE, MC, V. Free parking. **Amenities:** Restaurant; bar; free Wi-Fi. *In room:* A/C, TV, fridge, hair dryer.

GAZIANTEP

1,149km (714 miles) SW of Istanbul; 222km (138 miles) east of Adana; 214km (133 miles) NE of Antakya; 317km (197 miles) west of Diyarbakir; 142km (88 miles) west of Sanliurfa; 332km (206 miles) west of Mardin

A common story about the city of Gaziantep tells of Atatürk once coming to visit the city. After being served a bountiful meal, he was offered a cup of water. His response? "Yes, but make sure it doesn't have pistachios."

While the story is apocryphal, it illustrates how pistachios, called *fistik*, have so thoroughly permeated the cuisine in Gaziantep. The center of pistachio production in the country, Gaziantep's main claim to fame is its magnificent baklava, which is made with pistachios grown outside the city. Fragrant and frequently a bright green hue, the baklava here will convert even those typically averse to sweets. With more than 500 baklava bakeries in the city, a "baklava crawl," especially during the pistachio harvest in September, is a must-do (just be prepared for a serious case of sugar shock).

But there are many more attractions here, including an historic bazaar, a new Mosaic Museum that's the largest in the world, and a long history of this land which has been ruled by 16 different peoples, reaching back to the Bronze Age.

The city is commonly known as Antep—the name Gaziantep translates to Victorious Antep, while Antep derives from Ayintap, probably a later form of the Hittite

Hantap. It's the sixth-largest city in Turkey, and still growing at a rapid pace. The city dates back to the Hittites, and has been ruled by the Assynians, Persians, Babylonians, Greeks, Armenians, Romans, Byzantines, Sassanids, and Arabs, to name a few. Antep was also a stop on the second Silk Road. Today it's a large, cosmopolitan city that has benefited from the GAP dam project. The business center of the region, it has a growing population.

Essentials

GETTING THERE   Flights to **Gaziantep Airport** are available from Istanbul, Ankara, Izmir, and other domestic cities. A flight from Istanbul takes about an hour. The **Gaziantep Bus Station** (© **0342/328-9246**) has regular service to surrounding cities, as well as Istanbul, Ankara, and Izmir.

VISITOR INFORMATION   The Provincial Directorate of Culture and Tourism is located at 100 Yil Atatürk Kultur Park in the center of the city (© **0342/230-9960**; www.gaziantep.gov.tr; Mon–Fri 9am–noon and 1–5pm).

Area Attractions

One of the city's main attractions, the Gaziantep Citadel (kale), was under construction when this guide went to press. In the center of the city, it's impossible to miss. The citadel (not sure of origins), and an Ottoman *hamam* was discovered within the structure. It may be reopened by the time of publication.

Emine Göğüş Cuisine Museum MUSEUM   This quirky two-story museum is housed in a stone house built in 1904 for the city's tourism minister (he bought back the home where he was born and donated it to the town, and the museum is named after his mother). The first museum in Turkey dedicated to food, this homage to local cuisine displays kitchen tools, lists of ingredients found in Gaziantep's traditional dishes, and even a few relevant poems. While the English signage can be sporadic, videos throughout show how the foods are made.

Karagoz Mah. Hasirci Sok., Sahinbey, Gaziantep. No phone. Admission 1TL. Open Mon–Fri 9am–6pm; Sat–Sun 9am–7pm.

Ethnographic Museum MUSEUM   This museum provides a fascinating look into daily life in Gaziantep in the 19th century. The building itself is a traditional house from the early 19th century, located in the Old City. Exhibits include traditional dress, tools, and furniture from this period, and the star attraction is a motorbike once owned by Laurence of Arabia.

Hanifioglu Sokak. No phone. Admission 3TL. Open Tues–Sun 8am–noon and 1–5pm.

Kendirli Church (Kendirli Kiliseri) CHURCH   This impressive tall brick church once served the Armenian Catholic community and is now a local meeting hall. It was built in 1860 by French missionaries and Napoleon III. The structure has interesting details such as a marble checkerboard floor and is surrounded by a garden.

Atatürk Bulvarı, Gaziantep. No phone. Admission 1TL. Open Mon–Fri 9am–6pm; Sat–Sun 9am–7pm. **Note**: The church is currently undergoing renovations.

Zeugma Mosaic Museum ★★ MUSEUM   Opened in September 2011, this massive 30,000-square-meter (about 322,917-sq.-ft.) museum has a striking, modern

THE treasures OF ZEUGMA

Although it's the largest mosaic museum in the world, most of the extensive collection displayed at the Zeugma Museum was discovered only in the past dozen years. The ancient city of Zeugma is located 45 kilometers (28 miles) from Gaziantep. It was founded in 300 B.C. by one of Alexander the Great's commanders, Selecus I Nicator, who first named the city after himself. The city was born due to its strategic location along the Euphrates and the Silk Road, which made it an ideal transit point for trade (the name Zeugma means "bridge of boats"). After being captured by the Romans in 64 B.C., it became the easternmost city in the Roman Empire. The city grew to be extremely wealthy, with villas constructed along the riverbanks with decorative mosaic floors. Zeugma continued to thrive until A.D. 253, the Sassanid Invasion, and was later battered by an earthquake, and never recovered. When the nearby Birecek Dam project in the 1990s uncovered some of the mosaics, an intensive excavation project was undertaken, with archeologists working tirelessly to save what they could before the dam waters rose. So far an area the size of a football field has been excavated.

At the time of writing, though, only about 25% of the site was under water, and there were still many monuments to see in Zeugma. In particular, the Dionysos Danae Houses (protected under a roof) are remarkable monuments to see. To find out more, go to www.zeugma archproject.com.

facade. It was built to hold the ever-increasing discoveries from the ongoing excavation of Zeugma (see box below), which could no longer fit in the city's old mosaic museum. This is indeed the largest mosaic museum in the world, dethroning the Bardo National Museum in Tunisia. It includes a 2,500-square-meter exhibition hall and a children's workshop area. The frescos date back to the 2nd century A.D. The Mona Lisa of this museum is its "Gypsy Girl" mosaic, whose likeness you'll find plastered all over town. Her expression is beguiling and her eyes seem to follow you. A bronze statue of the war god Mars and large floor mosaics extolling Dionysus, Oceanus, Tethys, and the river gods are also must-sees.

Inciliplnar Mah. Sehitkamil Cad. 2, Gaziantep. © **342/324-8809.** Admission 5TL. Open Tues–Sun 8am–5pm.

Where to Eat

Antep is a foodie's delight. While baklava is the main attraction, there are many more local treats to sample in town. The cuisine is influenced by nearby Syria, especially Aleppo, 97km (60 miles) to the south. Kebaps and lahmacun are superb, and eggplant is grown near the Euphrates River nearby.

Aşina TURKISH/GRILLED MEATS/KEBAPS Another local favorite, Aşina serves traditional dishes, including a large variety of kebabs and terrific *lahmacun*. It also is known for its katmar and desserts. Good for large groups, the restaurant is spread over three floors, with an elegant pale-green interior.

Kıbrıs Caddesi No: 46 (Emniyet Müdürlüğü Karşısı), Şehitkamil/Gaziantep. © **342/220-4949.** Fixed price dinner 29TL. AE, DISC, MC, V. Daily 7am–10pm.

Imam Çağdaş Lokantasi ★★ TURKISH/KEBAPS The most famous restaurant in Gaziantep, this Gaziantep institution has been in town since 1887. The large space with high ceilings gets packed with locals. The small menu features kebabs and mixed grills, and the bulgur stuffed with meat is terrific. It's all accompanied by fresh *aryan* served in copper bowls. You'll probably encounter the gregarious owner, who always seems to be smiling. A bakery is located on one side, serving fresh baklava (the baklava to-go keeps very well and makes a great gift to bring home).

Uzun Carsi 49 Sahinbey, Gaziantep. www.imamcagdas.com. ✆ **342/231-2678.** Main courses 10TL–16TL. MC, V. Daily 8am–midnight.

ANTEP'S tastiest BAKLAVA

Baklava is serious business in Gaziantep. While there are more than 500 baklava bakeries in the city, most families are extremely loyal to one place, and will maintain that loyalty throughout their lives. Filiz Hösükoğlu is a food writer and culinary culture correspondent, and one of the driving forces behind the Emine Göğüş Cuisine Museum (p. 417). She's also a lifelong Gaziantep resident. According to her, most baklava in town will probably taste the same to outsiders, since the base ingredients are all derived from the same sources. However, each local has been raised on his or her family's preferred baklava, and can detect small differences between the butter, pistachio, and sugar ratio.

With so many bakeries in town, how do you choose? Here are three of Filiz's favorites:

o **Mahmut Güllü** (Elmaci Pazari No. 4; ✆ **342/231-2105**). Located in the bazaar, this bakery is 150 years old and has had the same ownership through six generations. Their baklava is still served the same way as when the shop first opened. Filiz says, "It's my favorite not only for its baklava, but because I like being in a cozy place in the old quarter, talking with the master baklava chef who has been in this business for almost 50 years and hearing his life stories, and eating from the same copper tins that my grandfather once did."

o **Koçak** (A. Fuat Cebesoy Bulv. Sehit Mehmet Ozdinc Sk. No. 3; ✆ **342/321-0519**). The owner of this bakery started as an apprentice in one of the baklava bakeries in Gaziantep. Gradually he converted his art from apprenticeship to mastership. His baklava bakery is in the new neighborhood with a very elegant interior. He is always in his baklava bakery either checking the baklava production or welcoming his customers.

o **Zeki Inal** (Atatürk Bulv.No:38/B; ✆ **342/231-2069**). This bakery is situated right in the old quarter. It's considered a culinary Mecca for baklava lovers. Pistachios are harvested in August, the best time to enjoy them, as early-harvest pistachios are best. We also recommend you try pistachio coffee—it contains no caffeine, but with the buzz you'll get, you'll never know it. A good place to try it is in the peaceful courtyard of Andolu Evleri Hotel (see below).

Also be sure to try katmar, a pocket of pistachio, sugar, and clarified butter, all enveloped in paper-thin dough and baked. Katmar chefs train for 15 years. Feliz's top choice for katmar? **Orkide Pastanesi** (Gazi Muhtar Pasa Bulv. No. 17; ✆ **342/215-1500**) has perfectly turned out katmar, and serves an immense village-style breakfast.

SOAP stars IN ANTEP

Gaziantep is famous throughout Turkey, Greece, and Bulgaria from the wildly popular soap opera Yabancı Damat, which aired from 2004 to 2007. Translated as "The Foreign Groom," it told the story of the daughter of a Gaziantep baklava baker and the son of a wealthy Greek ship owner. They met in Bodrum, fell in love at first sight, and decided to marry. However, deep-seated anger between the Greeks and Turks led their families to oppose the marriage. The couple moved to Istanbul and started a family, and aptly named their son Ege, for the Aegean Sea that separated them.

Sahan TURKISH   Part of a chain that began in 1970, Sahan specializes in traditional Gaziantep cuisine. This branch has a stunning location in an old Şirehanı, which is where şire candy (with nut and wheat starch) and nuts once were sold. Be sure to try the restaurant's bountiful meze tray.

Ismetpasa Mah, Gaziantep. ✆ **342/232-2719.** Reservations recommended. Main courses 12TL–16TL. AE, MC, V. June–Sept daily 9am–10pm; Oct–May Tues–Sun 9am–10pm.

Gaziantep Shopping

Gaziantep Bazaar   Gaziantep's famous bazaar feels like a step back in time, but isn't too touristy and is frequented by locals. The bazaar is locally known as "black steps bazaar" and has 80 shops and five gates. The Kemikli bazaar dates back to the 19th century, while the coppersmiths' bazaar (*bakırcılar carşısı*) was built in 1781. The coppersmiths' bazaar is filled with the sounds of hammering from coppersmiths at work. There's also an area dedicated to animal husbandry, with products such as saddles on offer. While you're there, look out for locally handcrafted colorful Yemeni slippers, and of course, mountains of pistachios and great spicy nuts. Mahmut Güllü (see above) is also located inside the bazaar if you need a shopping break.

Open Mon–Sat 9am–6pm.

Side Trip to Yesemek Sculpture Workshop

If you are driving from Gaziantep to points west, be sure to stop at the Yesemek statue park and workshop, located on a hill in the countryside 113km (70 miles) away, not far from the border of Syria. The workshop was established in 1300 B.C. during the reign of the Hittites. The workshop produced sculptures that were transported throughout the Hittite kingdom. The blocks of basalt were carved here, and the finishing touches were done at the final destination, to prevent damage during transportation. It was deserted after the Assyrian conquest.

The remaining sculptures were first discovered in 1890 and excavated from 1958 to 1961. The site contains more than 300 statues, including sphinxes, lions, and mountain gods. It's a remarkably peaceful setting, with statues interspersed along the green hillside, surrounded by wildflowers.

The workshop also contains a gift shop, which contains items carved by local children and benefits the community. The site is open from dawn to dusk, and admission for adults costs 2TL. It can only be reached by car; to get there, drive to Kilis, take the road west toward Hassa, and then a sign will indicate a gravel road to Yesemek.

Where to Stay

Antep has a number of newly renovated boutique inns, along with the major chains found all over the country.

Anadolu Evleri (Anatolian Houses) ★★   In the heart of the Old City behind Imam Cagdas (p. 419), this is a stunning boutique hotel. The owners meticulously renovated four historic stone houses which are more than 100 years old. The houses surround a tranquil courtyard, a wonderful place to relax over tea and a book. Each room is unique, with wood paneling, painted ceilings, checkerboard floors, and antique details such as old sewing machines and rotary phones.

Şekeroğlu Mahallesi, Köroğlu Sokak No. 6, Gaziantep. www.anadoluevleri.com/default_eng.php. ✆ **342/220-9525.** Fax 342/220-9528. 13 units. Standard 220TL; suite 278TL; breakfast included. MC, V. Free parking. **Amenities:** Bar/cafe; room service. *In room:* A/C, TV (some), hair dryer, free Wi-Fi.

Novotel   The modern high-rise Novotel (along with the Ibis Hotel next door) is easy to spot in the center of the city. The staff is very helpful. It's also a great value, with Turkish breakfast included.

Yaprak Mah Istasyon Caddesi, No. 80 SehitKamil, 27400 Gaziantep. www.novotel.com/gb/hotel-6914-novotel-gaziantep/index.shtml. ✆ **342/211-0000.** Fax 342/211-0011. 92 units. 196TL–219TL standard room. **Amenities:** Bar; restaurant; fitness center; pool; room service. *In room:* A/C, TV, hair dryer, minibar, free Wi-Fi.

Zeynep Hanim Konagi   This is one of the most charming places to stay in town, and a great deal to boot. The mansion is tucked away in an alley in the Old Town (and it may take a little while to find). The large rooms have stone walls and wood ceilings, with wicker furniture and colorful Turkish rugs. Breakfast is served in their large, cave-like restaurant.

CRUISING ON THE euphrates

On the banks of the Euphrates, the ancient town of Halfeti began as an Assyrian settlement around 855 B.C. The Birecek Dam project in the 1990s flooded the town, and all its inhabitants were relocated a few miles away. Today, the main lure for tourists is the numerous Euphrates cruises that depart from the riverbank, which cost about 100TL. You can easily arrange a cruise, which lasts around an hour and is extremely scenic (though it may be pierced by techno music played by your boat, so choose carefully). Along the way, you'll see a fort that's carved into the mountains, along with numerous cave settlements. The highlight of a cruise: Viewing the remains of a village from the 19th century that's now almost entirely underwater. According to legend, when the town's mosque was submerged, the villagers saw no point in continuing to live there and departed. It can be reached from Gaziantep's *otagar* station, by taking an *otagar* to Birecek, then an hourly minibus to Halfeti.

Bey Mah. Atatürk Bulv Eski Sinema Sok. No. 17, Gaziantep. © **342/232-0207.** Fax 342/232-0204. 14 units. 103TL standard; 138TL suite. MC, V. Free parking. **Amenities:** Room service, smoke-free rooms. *In room:* A/C, free Wi-Fi.

MOUNT NEMRUT

174km (108 miles) from Gaziantep

This UNESCO site, at the summit of a 2,134-meter (7,001-ft.) mountain, was once on many a bucket list. Tourism has waned a bit since the '70s and '80s, when European backpackers came here in droves. Nevertheless, Nemrut's eerily calm statues placed around the assumed tomb of Antiochus I remains a must-see while in the region. A night hike is well worth the payoff of watching the sunrise in this remote, mystical setting.

I recommend getting a very early start in order to view the sunrise, though you could instead choose to watch the sunset from the other side of the site. Sunsets are not as vibrant as they used to be due to the nearby Atatürk Dam, part of the GAP dam project, since the salt burning off from the water during the day causes fog. If you want to see the sunrise, I suggest leaving your hotel in nearby Kâhta about 4am, then driving about an hour to the site entrance (with a 7TL admission fee), and another 10 minutes to the base where the hiking path begins. Be forewarned: This is a very strenuous hike on a dark and uneven gravel path for about 2 miles, and not suitable for seniors. That said, the hike is unquestionably worth the effort. The best time for a visit is in June or July.

Essentials

GETTING THERE   Mount Nemrut is quite remote and best reached with a tour guide. The nearby city of Adiyaman has an airport which has daily flights to Istanbul and twice-weekly flights to Ankara. From there, you can take a taxi to Kâhta. Buses arrive at Harhar Bus Station in the city center of Adiyaman. To get to the site from Kâhta, it's best to arrange a tour through your hotel. If you want to head there yourself, you can reach it by driving on the desolate road D360. Entry to the national park costs 7TL.

VISITOR INFORMATION   There is no formal tourism office in Kâhta, but information on Mount Nemrut and the surrounding area can be picked up from any hotel in town. Due to the difficulty in getting to Mount Nemrut, and to gain an understanding of many historical details of the site, we recommend visiting with a tour guide. Guides can be booked at the Hotel Nemrut or the Zeus Hotel (p. 423).

History and Exploring the Site

The site was built at the height of the Commagene kingdom during the reign of Antiochus I in the 1st century B.C., when the King had a temple built for himself at the summit of the mountain. The East and West terraces of the site contain identical statues, in different order. Each side contains statues of Antioch along with Persian and Roman gods, as Antioch considered himself equal to the gods. The heads of the Gods and Antioch were originally part of larger statues, where each figure was sitting. Only the heads are still intact, and indeed have survived earthquakes at the site. You'll see that parts of the statues are damaged, such as figures with missing noses, which was the work of iconoclasts.

Eagles and lions also adorn the ground, and the east side includes a statue of a lion next to a fire altar. The terraces surround the center, which is believed to have contained a temple-tomb to the king. However, archeologists have never been able to uncover this tomb, despite trying for more than 100 years.

Attractions within Nemrut Dağı National Park

Arsameia RUINS   Once the summer capital and home of the Kings of Commagene, the area is accessed by a rocky path off the main road. It dates back to the 2nd century A.D. There are several stone blocks, one of which is carved with the image of King Mithridaes I clasping the hand of Hercules, carved in A.D. 50. A tunnel (which is dangerously steep and should not be entered) contains Greek inscriptions at its entry, which asserts the political and religious beliefs of the time.

Severan Bridge RUINS   This well-preserved Roman Bridge was built in the 2nd century A.D. It was constructed for the Emperor Septimus Severus, his wife, and two children, with each represented by a column. After Severus died, the column which was built for him was removed, but the other three columns are still intact.

Nearby Restaurants

Neşet'in Yeri TURKISH/KEBAPS/FISH   "Neset's Place" is located about 5 minutes outside of Kâhta, and reached only by car or taxi. Its best asset is a pretty shaded lakeside location, along the Atatürk Dam. Kebaps and fresh fish are excellent. The restaurant is also well known for its excellent grilled trout. Beraj Kenari. ✆ **416/715-7675.** Main courses 7TL–11TL. MC, V. Hours vary; call ahead.

Where to Stay

The best place to base yourself is in Kâhta, a 45km (28 miles) drive from Mount Nemrut's base. While you'll likely be waking up very early in order to see the sunrise on top of the mountain, it's still best to stay at the more upmarket Zeus Hotel, rather than the smoky, dark, and very dingy Hotel Nemrut across the street. Otherwise, you can find a wide range of accommodations options in the lively city of Adiyaman, 14km (23 miles) east of Kâhta.

Zeus Hotel ★   This hotel is the best place to stay in Kâhta (granted, the options are very limited). Rooms are a bit musty but adequate for a night's stay, and the hotel has an Olympic-size pool and relaxing *hamam*. The staff is very helpful, and can help arrange transportation and tours to Mount Nemrut.

M. Kemal Caddesi No. 20, Kâhta. http://zeushotel.com.tr/en. ✆ **416/725-5694.** Fax 416/725 5696. 66 units. Doubles $63–$89. MC, V. Free parking. **Amenities:** Pool; 24-hour room service; free Wi-Fi. *In room:* A/C\, TV, hair dryer, minibar.

SANLIURFA

1,287km (800 miles) SE of Istanbul; 182km (113 miles) SW of Diyarbakir; 192km (119 miles) west of Mardin; 145km (90 miles) east of Gaziantep.

Sanliurfa, a popular religious and pilgrimage site, is decidedly Middle Eastern, much more so than other cities in the region to the west. You'll first notice the women here who don distinctive purple headscarves (which became popular in town about 7 years ago), the separate areas for men and women to relax, along with separate drinking fountains. Modest dress is recommended here, and alcohol is near impossible to find.

The city was called Urfa until 1984, when the prefix was added to its name (which means "Glorious Urfa") to commemorate the city's anniversary from its liberation from the French. It's still commonly referred to as Urfa. Believed to be the Biblical city of Ur, the city is believed to be the birthplace of Abraham, the father of monotheism, and also known as the birthplace of Job. It's also considered to be the site of the throne of Nimrod, the Biblical founder of Babylon, who attempted to burn Abraham when he protested against polytheism. According to the Bible, when Abraham was tossed into flames, God turned the fire into water and the coals into fish. The pond, filled with the sacred carp, resides alongside the caves where Abraham is believed to have been born. From this came the Turkish idiom "Nemrud," to identify a bad person.

The city also served as an important stop on the Silk Road. It was occupied by the French after WWI, until it was liberated in 1920. The sacred area is well laid-out, with pretty, manicured parks and gardens, and separate areas for men to relax and children to play. Residences are set on a hill and topped by the city's ancient citadel. Sanliurfa also has an enormous ancient bazaar that's mostly tourist-free. Two of Sanliurfa's greatest attractions lie outside Urfa: The remains of the ancient city of Harran are about 44km (24 miles) southeast; and the archeological site Göbekli Tepe, now known to be the world's oldest human-made religious monument (see box on p. 427), is 15km (9⅓ miles) northeast. The excavation of Göbekli Tepe is still ongoing, but we predict tourism to the area will explode in popularity upon its completion.

Essentials

GETTING THERE   Sanliurfa Airport (© **414/247-0343**) receives flights from Istanbul and Ankara. It is located 8km (5 miles) from the city, and Havas runs transfers with several stops in the city (10TL)

Buses from most major cities arrive at Sanliurfa Bus Station (© **414/313-1634**), including two buses every day from Istanbul, Ankara, and Izmir. The *otogar* is about a 30-minute bus ride to the main bus station in the city center.

VISITOR INFORMATION   The Provincial Directorate of Culture and Tourism (© **414/312-5332**) is located at 49 Atatürk Bulv., opposite the Valilik Binasi. They also have a very helpful website at www.urfakultur.gov.tr/en.

Area Attractions

Abraham's Birthplace ★★   RELIGIOUS SITE   This sacred cave is where Abraham is believed to have been born and lived for 7 years. There are separate adjacent caves for men and women. Large windows provide views of the holy water, which is believed to heal many ailments, and rugs cover the floor for praying. Modest attire is required.

No phone. Daily 8am–5:30pm. Free admission (donations accepted).

Pool of the Sacred Fish   RELIGIOUS SITE   This pool is believed to have sprung up after Abraham was ordered to be burned to death by King Nimrod for his refutation of idolatry. Abraham then landed safely in a rose garden. The pool is found in the courtyard of the mosque of Halil-ur-Rahman, built by the Ayyubids in 1211 and now surrounded by attractive gardens.

Today, the fish are still considered sacred. A local legend says seeing a white fish will open the door to the heavens, or that anyone who harms a carp will go blind. If the pool needs cleaning, the carp are safely transported and then returned to the pool.

OUTSIDE of town, A TRIP TO HARRAN

Located 1 hour south of Sanliurfa, the ancient town of Harran dates back to Early Bronze Age III (3rd millennium BC). It was a center of pagan worship of the Moon God, Sin. While the temple to the Moon God has never been discovered, written records reveal this cult revering the moon and sun from around the 5th century A.D. Harran was also home to Christians, Syrians, and Hittites. It was inhabited up until the 19th century, though its importance faded after the 1300s. Gates faced towards Baghdad and Aleppo, while only parts the Aleppo Gate have been found. Laurence of Arabia did a first survey of the land.

A Muslim University was founded in the 10th century, and this became the most important intellectual center in the Islamic world. People studied theology and literature, but also astronomy because of the Moon God. Works were also translated here from Arabic to Aramaic. The tower of the university served as an observatory.

While some believe the large tower existing at the site is the observatory, it has actually been found to be the minaret of the Grand Mosque (Ulu Camii). The mosque was built from 744 to 750 by the Ummayad leader Mervan II. It was once the largest mosque in Anatolia, and it remains the oldest example of Islamic architecture in the country.

You'll also be able to take a peek inside old beehive houses, which were made out of mud bricks to keep the interior cooled. The rooms of these houses are traditionally decorated. You'll probably be given a very warm welcome and invited to don a traditional headscarf and robe while exploring the rooms. Afterward, you can enjoy a cup of tea outdoors or buy some of the wares from Bedouins, such as bulgur.

The pool is flanked by the Rizvaniye Madrasa, built in 1736. The nearby pool of Ayn Zeliha is also considered sacred for saving the life of Nimrod's daughter, who was also sentenced to death as a follower of Abraham.

Sanliurfa Bazaar ★★ MARKET   More than just a place to shop, the Sanliurfa Bazaar is one of the most fascinating and varied bazaars in the country. The main section is believed by some to have been built by Suleyman the Magnificent in the 16th century. Coppersmiths work away, and there are large sections dedicated to jewelry, scarves (including Urfa's signature purple scarves), and rugs. Keep an eye out for the "tea guy" here, who fills up plastic bags the size of pillowcases with tea leaves. You can easily take an afternoon taking in the atmosphere and picking up loot to bring home, and pretty much anything you're looking for will be here.

No phone. Open Mon–Sat 8:30am–5pm.

Sanliurfa Citadel (Urfa Kale) and Walls RUINS   The citadel of Urfa, rising from the northern slope of Damlacik Mountain to the south of the city, has great significance both military and religious. It was originally constructed in the 2nd or 3rd century B.C.. It is believed by Christians to have served as the throne of Nimrod and was the site where he threw Abraham down into what was transformed into the Pond of Sacred Fish (see above).

The citadel has 25 watchtowers, and the walls were built in A.D. 812 by the Christians to defend the city against Arab raids. The outer fortress was enlarged and restored by the Crusaders. Two tall Corinthian columns bear inscriptions in Syriac, which has led to the belief that this was part of the Christian church.

Kale Cad. No phone. Admission 3TL. Open daily 8am–8pm.

Grand Mosque (Ulu Cami) MOSQUE   Urfa's Grand Mosque was built in 1170 over the remains of St. Stephen's church, which was known as the "Red Church" for its red columns. Its plan resembles the Great Mosque of Aleppo, and is thought to have been built at around the same time. The congregation area contains a well, which is believed to have been where Jesus Christ sent the Apostle Thaddaeus to bear the holy medallion to King Abgar. He fell with the medallion into the well, and the well is now believed to have healing properties. The outside courtyard is flanked by walls of the old red church, and the northwest section contains an old cemetery.

Divanyolu Cad. No phone. Free admission. Open daily 5am–10pm.

Where to Eat

Sanliurfa is famous for its liver. As with most towns in Southeastern Anatolia, the cuisine is very meat-heavy, and features different varieties of kebaps. Their eggplant kebab is a local specialty. Other local dishes include *yumurtalıköfte* (which has bulgur, onion, peppers, and mashed fried eggs), *bamya* (okra in meat sauce), and *kazan kebabı* (eggplant stuffed with spicy meat, in a spicy tomato sauce).

Due to its sacred significance, the city is completely dry. Instead, try *mirra*, a bitter coffee drink spiced with cardamom.

Cevahir Konukevi Urfa TURKISH   Part of an upscale hotel, this large restaurant contains an outdoor courtyard and terrace. It's a good choice for large groups. Wednesday, Friday, and Saturday nights feature *sira*, Sanliurfa's traditional music (just be patient, as it might be delayed until later in the night to accommodate the evening prayer). Locals say it's best to avoid the kebabs that are churned out in large batches, and instead recommend the *kusbasi* (meat cut in small chunks) or *pirzola* (lamb chops or ribs).

Büyükyol Cad. Selahaddin Eyyübi Camii Karşısı (Eski Devlet), 63200 Şanlıurfa. www.cevahir konukevi.com. ℂ **414/215-9377.** Fixed-price menu 35TL. MC, V. Hours vary, so call ahead.

Gülizar Konuk Evi TURKISH   This old renovated stone house serves as a hotel and also has a refined restaurant with a nice courtyard. All Urfa specialties are served here, including *lahmacun*, eggplant kebab, and after-dinner *mirra*.

Camikebir Divanyolu Cad No. 20, Şanlıurfa. www.gulizarkonukevi.net. ℂ **414/215-0505.** MC, V. Mon 10–11am, 7pm–1am; Tues–Wed 7–8am, 1–2pm, 7–10pm; Thu-Fri 2–11pm; Sat 3pm–1am; Sun 1pm–9pm.

Where to Stay

Sanliurfa has a good range of hotels. Location matters in this sprawling town—be sure to check, as even some of the best hotels can be a far walk from the sacred sites.

Hilton Garden Inn   This modern addition to the Hilton chain was an immediate hit after opening in Sanliurfa last year, and has gotten consistent rave reviews. It's a little farther off from the center, a 15-minute walk from Abraham's birthplace and the bazaar. The clean, sleek rooms all contain 37-inch LCD-screen TVs and large, comfortable beds.

Karakoyunlu Mah. 11 Nisan Fuar Cad., Sanliurfa. http://hilton.com.tr/tr/Hilton-Garden-Inn-Urfa. ℂ **414/318-5000.** Fax 414/215-3165. 8 units. 193TL–237TL standard; 334TL–377TL suite. MC, V. Free parking. **Amenities:** Restaurant; bar; fitness room; pool; room service. *In room:* A/C, TV, free Wi-Fi.

The area around Sanliurfa has gotten much media attention recently due to the ongoing excavation of the site called Göbekli Tepe, 15km(9⅓ miles) northeast of town. Reached from the Urfa-Mardin highway, then down a small winding road, the site, which translates as "Hill with a Potbelly," is located in a mountain ridge in an area that's remarkably green. A newspaper in Germany has gone so far to postulate that area is the location of the Garden of Eden.

The site was discovered in 1964, but at first thought to be a Byzantine Cemetery. In 1994, German archeologist Klaus Schmitt visited the site and immediately realized that previous archeologists had been mistaken, and that it was in fact an ancient Neolithic site. He has led an excavation that continues to this day. Found to be 11,000 years old, the remains at Göbekli Tepe date to the 10th century B.C. It is 1,000 years older than the Walls of Jericho, previously believed to be the world's oldest human-made structure, thus making this monument the most ancient.

Used as a religious sanctuary, the structure was built by hunter-gatherers, changing previously held beliefs about the formation of religion and agriculture. Before the excavation of Göbekli Tepe, it was believed that hunter-gatherers lacked a set of religious beliefs, due to their lack of a symbolic structure; and instead that agriculture led to the creation of religion, due to organization and settlement in one place. The lack of any evidence of habitation at Göbekli Tepe, however, reveals that this is a religious monument that was built by hunter-gatherers. The organization required to build this sanctuary over 9 hectares (22 acres) and the stability brought about by a permanent temple likely brought about agriculture, instead of the other way around.

The more than 60 T-shaped limestone pillars are carved with bas-reliefs of dangerous animals such as scorpions, lions, and snakes. It is hard to not be reminded of Stonehenge when visiting, with its pillars arranged in a large circle. As of now, there isn't much of a structure for tourists in place, but tourists are free to visit. As of now, it's a quiet place filled only with industrious archeologists, but that's certain to change soon.

El Ruha Hotel This large palace-like complex has great views of the city's main attractions. Everything you would need is here, including a hairdresser, *hamam*, and even a "billiard saloon" with ping-pong and air hockey. The building has beautifully carved local stone, and rooms are traditionally furnished with dark wood and large decorative headboards. One common complaint among Western travelers: The pool and *hamam* cost extra and are men-only.

Ballkllgol Yanl Lekeler Cad., Sanliurfa. www.hotelelruha.com/eng.© **414/215-4411**. Fax 414/215-9988 200 units. 114TL-189TL double. No credit cards. **Amenities:** Restaurant; bar; fitness room; pool; room service. *In room:* A/C, TV, hair dryer, minibar.

Manici Hotel ★★ This ultra-romantic and luxe hotel evokes the exotic East. Filled with deep jewel-tones and silk fabrics throughout, the hotel also contains large murals and an all-white courtyard. It's situated right alongside the area which includes Abraham's birthplace and the Pool of Sacred Fish, and it's a very quick walk to the Bazaar. The design may be a bit overpowering to some, and they could use some non-bejeweled pillows, but overall, this hotel evokes a mood like no other. The large buffet breakfast is a delight.

Balikligol Civari, 63000 Sanlıurfa. www.maniciurfa.com. (② **414/215-9911.** 52 units. 106TL single; 142TL double; 166TL triple. MC, V. Free parking. **Amenities:** Restaurant; bar. *In room:* A/C, TV, minibar, free Wi-Fi.

MARDIN

1,477km (918 miles) SE of Istanbul; 193km (120 miles) east of Sanliurfa; 333km (207 miles) east of Gaziantep; 95km (59 miles) south of Diyarbakir.

One of the loveliest cities in Turkey, Mardin is scenically perched on a mountainside, with an expansive view over a sea of green plains that locals call "Our Bosphorus." Located about 30 miles north of the border of Syria, the town is home to Turks, Kurds, Arabs, and Assyrians. It's also the only city in Turkey where Arabic is the predominant language.

The name Mardin comes from the Syriac-Aramaic word "Merdin," or fortress. Excavations indicate human settlement dating all the way back to 4500 B.C. Syrian Orthodox settlement began in Mardin in the 3rd century, Assyrian Christians in the 5th century, and it has since passed through many factions, including Seljuks, Kurdish and Mongol tribes, and Arab occupation from 640 to 1104, until it was conquered by the Ottomans in 1517.

The Deyr-ul Zafaran Monastery, 5 km (3 miles) from town (p. 429), was built in the 4th century. Mardin remains an important center for Syriac Christianity, one of the most ancient Christian denominations.

The buildings in town, with architecture dating from the Artuqid dynasty from the 12th to 15th centuries, have been built using limestone from nearby quarries. Over time, the limestone has changed to a warm tone. The structures are notable for their elaborate stonework and decorative doors, some of which still have separate doorknobs for each sex.

Mardin is far from undiscovered and the town is quite narrow (owing to its mountainside location), so the main street of Cumhuriyet Caddesi can sometimes become clogged with tour buses. But wander through the quiet alleyways, with genuinely friendly locals greeting you, and you'll quickly fall in love with the city. You may well end up taking hundreds of photos of quiet roads, decorative doors, donkeys, tailors, soap-makers, and friendly children around town. Be sure to pop into a few of the many wonderful antique and jewelry shops lining the main drag—Mardin's intricate lacy jewelry, called *telkari,* is famous throughout the country.

Essentials

GETTING THERE   Buses run daily to and from Istanbul, Ankara, and Izmir, where buses leave from the front of the bus company offices in Meydanbasi and Yenisehir.

YOU'RE open WHEN?

The restaurants in and around Mardin, as in many small Turkish towns, tend to keep variable hours, so it's best to call ahead to make sure a place is open.

There are also minibuses that run to the surrounding towns, which leave from the Belediye bus terminal.

Mardin has a small domestic airport that has flights to Istanbul, Ankara, and Izmir. It's located 20km (12 miles) south of town, and can be reached via minibuses to Kiziltepe.

VISITOR INFORMATION The **Mardin Directorate of Culture and Tourism** is located at Valilik Binası, Kat 2, No. 4 Yenişehir/Mardin (**℡ 482/212-3776;** e-mail: iktm47@kulturturizm.gov.tr). It's open 8:30am to 5:30pm.

Area Attractions

Deyr-ul Zafaran Monastery ★★ MONASTERY About a 10 minutes' drive east of Mardin lies this important center of Syriac Christianity. For 650 years, it was the seat of the Syrian Orthodox patriarch (now in Damascus). It's known as the Saffron Monastery due to the color of its stone. It was originally the site of a pagan sun temple in the 4th century B.C., and predates Christianity. This was destroyed by Persians in 607 and rebuilt.

There are 52 Syrian orthodox patriarchs buried in the sarcophagus (cold room). Staff are buried with outfits and cross in hands in sitting position, towards the East, because of the apocalypse Jesus accepted by the east. Wooden doors here, from the 17th century, contain no nails.

Off the courtyard, the first printing press in the Southeast region is displayed, dating from the 1800s from England. The second floor, from the 19th century, is where monks used to stay during theology education, and includes a bell tower from Syria.

A subterranean area, which is definitely not for claustrophobes, was excavated in the 1940s. Here are the remains of the ancient pagan sun temple, which contains big vertical blocks that have survived earthquakes.

The monastery has expansive views, which some call the best view in Mesopotamia. Today, 40 monks live here.

http://deyrulzafaran.org. ℡ **482/219-3082.** Admission 3TL. Open daily 9am–noon and 1–5pm.

Grand Mosque (Ulu Cami) MOSQUE Construction of Mardin's grand mosque began during the reign of the Artukid leader Yavlak Aslan, from 1184 to 1200. It took until the reign of his brother from 1200 to 1239 to complete. This mosque displays early 13th-century Artukid grand mosque architecture. Unlike most of Mardin's buildings, the mosque's vaults are built of brick rather than stone. Of particular note is the mosque's minaret, which at 52 meters (171 feet) rises high above the town. It contains four decorative sections with inscriptions in Kufic, the oldest form of Arabic calligraphy. The bottom level contains a raindrop motif, which was meant to encourage fertility. The circles above contain the name of Allah.

Yenikapı Mh. No phone. Free admission. Open daily 9am–6pm.

Kasimiye Medrese HISTORIC SITE The construction of this old school took two generations to complete. It began during the Artukid reign and was completed in the 15th century. It features two domes, a courtyard, and students' quarters upstairs. In front there is a grand pool, which symbolizes the path of life. The second floor has small lecture rooms and students' quarters. The low, small doors indicated respect for their religious education.

Open daily 8am–5pm. Free admission.

Mardin Museum MUSEUM This three-story museum, housed in a beautiful old building which once served as a military garrison, is well worth a visit. Opened in 1995, the museum holds a varied collection of artifacts from ancient Mesopotamia, from 4000 B.C. all the way to the 7th century B.C., ranging from the Hellenistic, Byzantine, Seljuk, and Ottoman periods, among others. The second story features the Ethnography Hall, which reveals life in ancient Mardin with displays of jewelry, ancient dress, weaponry, and cooper goods. The third story holds the Archeological Hall, with ancient finds including pots, figurines, ceramics, and coins.

Mardin Merkez, Cumhuriyet Meydanı 1. Cad. 2. ℗ **482/212-1664.** Admission 3TL. Open Mon–Sat 8am–5:30pm.

Where to Eat

While in Mardin, be sure to try the ubiquitous kebaps and filled rib (especially at Cercis Mural Konaği, below), followed by saffron-scented *zerde* pudding and a bitter cup of *mirra*.

Cercis Mural Konaği ★★★ TURKISH This is the best place in town for a festive, fun night out. Part of a swanky restored old house, the restaurant has high stone walls and floor-to-ceiling windows. Wine is served in goblets, and colorful mezes in decorative platters are almost too pretty to eat. Be sure to go on a night featuring music, where locals join in an uproarious line dance while waving their napkins. Try the filled rib, a local specialty.

Birinci Cad. No. 517, Mardin. www.cercismurat.com. ℗ **482/213-7517.** Main courses 20TL–25TL. MC, V. Daily noon–11pm.

Kamar Vakfi ★ TURKISH This shoebox-sized, hidden restaurant is well worth seeking out. One of 20 such restaurants throughout the region, it was created by the Moon Foundation, which supports women who are victims of domestic violence. The cafe supplies work for a rotating staff of 10 women who cook the dishes, and proceeds go to local causes. The Mardin specialties here are a delight.

Medrese Mah 255 Sokak. ℗ **482/212-2545.** Main courses 10TL–15TL. No credit cards. Hours vary so call ahead.

Where to Stay

Mardin is a small town and a popular place to visit, especially with religious tour groups coming to see the monastery. Be sure to plan ahead and book a room before your visit.

Artuklu Kervansarayi ★★ Ever stayed in an 800-year-old caravansary dating back to the Artuklu tribe? The 43 restored rooms (with heavy antique keys) vary widely from cave-like to deluxe, many with gorgeous rugs, stone walls and arches, dark wood floors, and antique touches like old radios and rotary phones. If you can afford the splurge, it's worth it to get a suite (we recommend room 315). The Wi-Fi can be temperamental and the hallways a bit dark, but who cares in surroundings like this?

1 Cad. No. 70, 47000 Mardin. www.artuklu.com/ing. ℗ **482/213-7353.** 43 units. 136TL standard. AE, MC, V. **Amenities:** Restaurant. *In room:* A/C, TV, hair dryer, Jacuzzi, minibar, free Wi-Fi.

Erdoba Elegans This large complex may stand in stark contrast to Mardin's quaint charms, but that doesn't mean it's not worth a stay. A recent addition to Mardin's hotels, the Erdoba Elegans (not to be confused with the Erdoba Evleri, a small boutique hotel owned by the same group) has many extras to keep you busy, including a reading area, game salon, cinema, and shopping.

Midyat Yolu 3 Km. Mardin. www.erdobaelegance.com. ✆ **482/212-1500.** Fax 482/212-1510. 220 units. 119TL-249TL standard. **Amenities:** 24-hour room service. *In room:* A/C, TV, minibar, free Wi-Fi.

Side Trip from Mardin
MIDYAT

Midyat is about an hour's drive away from Mardin, on a stunning, mountainous drive. Like Mardin, it is known as a museum city, divided by a modern area that's not worth visiting, and the more appealing old Christian half. This part of town contains structures from every period of history, but also feels a bit dusty and abandoned. Midyat physically has many similarities to Mardin, with structures carved from sandstone with colorful doors. It lacks Mardin's impressive mountainside location, however, and is situated on low, rolling hills.

Midyat is known by the ancient Aramaic name Tur-'Abdin, The city has been invaded many times, from the Assyrians to Mongol and Kurdish tribes. Once an Assyrian-Syriac community, most have now left Midyat after unrest in the 1980s and '90s. Some Syrian Jews still remain here.

Personally, we're partial to Mardin, and while some nice hotels are opening in town, we recommend basing yourself in Mardin and spending a day here as a side trip. While there is much to see, the touts and aggressive children can detract from the experience.

Area Attractions
Deyr Ul Umur (Mor Gabriel Monastery) ★ MONASTERY   Located 18km (11 miles) east of town, this is the oldest Syrian Orthodox monastery in Turkey and one of the oldest in the world. Viewed by Syriacs as a "second Jerusalem," it was constructed in A.D. 397 and restoration was completed in 2002. Saint Gabriel (Mor Gabiel) the 7th century bishop known for miracles and giving life to three people, gave the monastery its name and is buried here. The monastery once housed a library for Syrian scientists. The structure contains the remains of Byzantine mosaics.

The site itself is nestled amongst vineyards that may seem reminiscent of Italy. Adjacent to the complex, there is a cemetery with graves with both orthodox and Catholic crosses. The graves include chambers, which is unlike what you'll find in most of Turkey.

P.K. 4 47510 Midyat – Mardin. http://morgabriel.org. ✆ **482/213-7512.** Fax 482/213-7514. Daily 9:30–11:30am and 1–4pm.

HASANKEYF UNDER threat

At the heart of the battle against Turkey's GAP dam project is the ancient city and cave dwellings of Hasankeyf. Built into the side of a gorge on the Tigris river, Hasankeyf has been ruled by many different factions, including the Romans and the Ayyubids (descendents of Saladin), who turned Hasankeyf into an important Islamic center. The area is filled with cave dwellings that some estimate once comprised 8,000 to 8,500 caves, which remained inhabited up until the 1970s. The area, however, may be largely flooded by the time this guide goes to press. The Ilisu Dam, about 80km (50 miles) away, is likely to flood a large part of Hasankeyf. At press time, the site and the castle were open to visit (open daily 8am–6pm), but the town and most of the archeological site were expected to be under water sometime in 2012, with thousands of residents displaced. If you do make it in time, here are a few highlights not to miss: **Hasankeyf Great Palace,** one of two palaces, was built by the Artuqids. It has a rectangular tower that may have served as a watchtower. **The Old Tigris Bridge,** which spans the Tigris river, was built in 1116 by the Artuqid ruler Fahrettin Karaaslan. This bridge is considered to be the largest of the Medieval period. At the end of the bridge is a house, owned by a family who has deed of ownership from Ottoman times and cannot be forced to move. **The Il Rizk Mosque** has a minaret that dramatically rises above the town. It was built in 1409 by Sultan Suleyman of the Abbuyids. It makes an excellent photo in particular because of the stork which has built a home here (it has lived on top of the minaret for about 10 years). Hasankeyf can be reached by minibus from Mardin. The preservation of the site has gotten worldwide attention and is being fought by activist groups, so there is hope that it will be saved. As Turkish lawyer Murat Cano, who filed a lawsuit to preserve the site, put it in a recent film about Hasankeyf: "Cultural heritage does not belong to anyone; it's the common property of all humanity."

Midyat Guesthouse (Konuk Evi) ★ HISTORIC SITE   This beautiful large mansion was restored in 2000. The three-tiered stone building has expansive terraces (a great photo op) and gorgeous ornamentation. You can explore each level, with some rooms featuring antiques and old-fashioned decor. Today, it's often seen as a backdrop in Turkish soap operas.

Midyat Shopping

If you're looking to pick up a unique gift, try to hunt down 8a, Sefaze Sonat Evi. While you'll find scarves for sale all over the country, we have yet to find ones so gorgeous as these. The scarves are exquisite and made from natural ink, in a range of colors and designs.

Where to Eat

Kerim Ustanin Yeri ★   This restaurant located on a busy road serves delicious and unexpectedly fiery dishes—be ready with a glass of water on hand! The local kebaps are terrific, and you can get a large meal for very good value.

Sıtkı Usta Karşısı Kaplan Apt. Altı, Estel, Midyat. http://kerimusta.mardinport.com. ⓟ 482/464-0200. Meal 20 TL. Daily 6am–midnight.

Where to Stay

Kasr-ı Nehroz ★★   The best accommodation in town, the Kasr-i Nehroz recently opened in the old part of town. It is a meticulously restored residence from 1899, but the building itself dates back 1,600 years. It once was home to six families, with one family per room. Each room is unique, with stone arches, high round tubs with Jacuzzis, and flatscreen TVs. Rooms are centered around a courtyard with a bar and restaurant.

Isiklar Mah, Cad, Sokak 19, No 14, Midyat. www.hotelnehroz.com.ⓒ **482/464-2525.** Fax 482/464-2501. 29 units. Standard rooms 277TL. AE, MC, V. **Amenities:** Restaurant; bar; 24-hr. room service. *In room:* A/C, TV, hair dryer.

PLANNING YOUR TRIP TO TURKEY

12

While planning your trip and consulting this guide, you should know a few things about the nature of travel and tourism in Turkey.

First of all, the very face of Turkey is changing, as the country continues to plow ahead with development and renewal projects that it hasn't experienced in decades, if not centuries. Foreign direct investment, improvements in the tax collection system, an unprecedented commitment to the country's cultural goods, and elevated museum entrance fees are being plowed back into the economy, and Turkey's continued bid for membership in the E.U. have given the entire country a major face-lift. The country is changing at an incredible clip, and unfortunately it's impossible for a biennial guidebook to stay ever-on-top of things.

But there are some time-honored truths. It is no surprise to anyone that hotels, restaurants, and museums raise their prices regularly (and in some cases, annually). However, this natural inflation is compounded by a combination of Turkey's current popularity as a tourist destination and a new thriving (and vacationing) middle class. Some hotels (some of which are now excluding breakfast from the package) nearly triple their rates in August, and restaurants (which shamelessly have begun to charge a "cover" for bread and water) are also taking advantage of the increased level of demand. There is also the unavoidable truth to writing up those rare and secret "finds." Once the secret is out, the floodgates open, and the secret becomes a cliché. The lag time varies, but the process is sadly inevitable. Hotels double their rates, carpet shops double or triple their profits, and restaurants start to cut corners.

What does this mean for you while you plan and fantasize about your trip? In the end, we do our best and expect that you will do yours. In exchange for our experienced and researched advice, we hope that you will be smart travelers, savvy shoppers, selective with your praise and criticism, and that you will continue to let us know what you think.

GETTING THERE
By Plane

With an exponential increase in tourist arrivals, Turkey has also seen historic growth in the number of international airlines flying non-stop into

When arriving from points abroad, if you're flying direct to say, Kayseri, Bodrum, or Dalaman after a change of planes in Istanbul, your domestic flight will arrive into the domestic terminal while your luggage will be sent over to the international terminal for the purposes of clearing customs.

Istanbul's Atatürk International Airport and the newer Sabiha Gökcen Airport, plus direct service to points along the coast and the interior. This chapter will focus on getting in and out of Istanbul from points abroad. For those heading directly to, say, the coastline, please see the relevant destination chapter for specific arrival information.

Istanbul's main airport is Atatürk International Airport (IST; www.ataturkairport.com), located 23km (14 miles) from Taksim and about 19km (12 miles) from the Old City's Blue Mosque. The newer Sabiha Gokcen Airport (SAW; www.sgairport.com) is less conveniently located on the Asian side in Kürtköy, about 44km (27 miles) from Taksim. Both airports are efficient and modern, offering across-the-board services from VIP lounges, on-site airport hotels, and even massages. The advantage of the latter airport is that that's where the majority of low-cost airlines fly.

To see which airlines accommodate your points of arrival and departure, log onto **Skyscanner** (www.skyscanner.com), a great search engine providing near-comprehensive information on airlines and routes, or check out the airport websites listed under "Getting There By Plane" in each chapter.

By Car

With global warming issues and petrol prices in the stratosphere, driving to Turkey makes bad sense. But some people just love a road trip. To enter Turkey in your own vehicle, you will need your passport, an **International Driving Permit (IDP),** an international "green card" (insurance) and the car's registration for proof of ownership. The international documents are available at your country's relevant automobile association (AAA in the U.S. and in Australia; AA in the U.K.; CAA in Canada). The vehicle is permitted for a period of 6 months, with extensions available through the Turkish Touring and Automobile Club (© **0212/282-8140;** fax 0212/282-8042; www.turing.org.tr).

By Train

Turkish State Railways (© **444-8233** or 0216/348-8020 in Istanbul; www.tcdd.gov.tr) operates the **Bosphorus Express** train, departing Bucharest daily for the 32-hour trip. Travelers can also ride the rails from Belgrade and Sophia, in cars hitched onto the Bosphorus Express on the way into Istanbul. The Dostluk/Filia Express serving the Thessaloniki route into Istanbul was suspended in 2011. Fares for the Istanbul Bucharest line are 39TL (58 in first class); from Belgrade the fare is 48TL (73TL first class); from Sofia the fare is 20TL (29 first class). Do yourself a favor and book yourself in a sleeper car; the single supplements for a first class ticket are 35TL, 60TL, and 77TL from Sofia, Belgrade, and Bucharest respectively, with lower prices for two or three people traveling second class sharing the couchette. The Turkish rail system is a member of the InterRail Global Pass ticket. For more information, visit the website of Turkish State Railways. For (sometimes multiple) connections from cities all over Europe, log onto **www.bahn.de**.

By Boat

A number of ferries plying the Mediterranean and Black Sea arrive to ports in Turkey, but regrettably, only ferries from the Ukraine call at Istanbul. Marmara Lines (bought by the German firm, Reca; ℭ **49 07031 866010;** www.marmaralines.com) operates service to Çeşme (1 hr. west of Izmir, along Turkey's Aegean) from Ancona, in Italy, between March and November. Also in summer, ferries provide service between Sochi (ℭ **7 8622 609-603;** www.seaport-sochi.ru) on the Russian coast of the Black Sea, and Trabzon, in Turkey. You can also take puddle jumpers between the Greek Islands and Bodrum, Çeşme, Fethiye, Kaş, Kuşadası and Marmaris, among others. See "Getting There By Ferry" in the individual destination chapters for more information, and check for updates as ferry lines, particularly between Italy and Turkey, come and go. You can also log on to **www.ferrylines.com**, for its comprehensive list of ferries serving Turkey.

GETTING AROUND

By Plane

Domestic airline travel has come a long way since **Turkish Airlines** (ℭ **850/333-0849**) cornered the market. With the arrival of a number of new airlines serving popular routes, along with the opening of Istanbul's Sabiha Gökçen Airport, domestic airline service is plentiful. And with fares as low as 49€, if you book early, the cost actually gives (albeit comfy) long-distance bus travel a run for its money. To keep up with the competition, Turkish Airlines instituted its budget airline subsidiary, **AnadoluJet** (ℭ **444-AJET** [2538]; www.anadolujet.com), primarily operating flights out of Ankara to countless cities in Turkey. The other airlines serving the domestic routes are **Onur Air** (ℭ **444-6687** or 0212/663-9176 in Istanbul; www.onurair.com.tr), **Pegasus Airlines** (ℭ **0850/250-0737;** www.flypgs.com), **Atlas Jet** (ℭ **0850/222-0000;** www.atlasjet.com); BoraJet (ℭ **444-0672;** www.borajet.com.tr) and **SunExpress** (ℭ **444-0797;** www.sunexpress.com.tr). These days, with flights consistently full, it's a good idea to plan ahead, particularly if you plan on traveling during one of the major *bayrams,* or religious holidays. Tickets can be purchased online, at one of the airline offices, or through an officially recognized travel agent.

By Car

Affording you independence and freedom, driving through Turkey is really the best way to connect with the country. This is even more the case now that the road conditions have improved dramatically in recent years. Turkey has been pouring investment into road infrastructure, including the establishment of the multilane toll roads around Istanbul, Ankara, and Izmir and the widening of major provincial thoroughfares. In fact, except for the road signs (which on the toll collection booths are now also in English), you'll almost think you were driving in Europe. Likewise, petrol stations are ubiquitous along highways, usually offering rest facilities, snacks, drinks, and of course tea, while along more humble back roads, you can find wildly typical mom-and-pop roadside stands willing to whip up some *gözleme* (salty crepe filled with your choice of cheese, potato, or spinach) and *ayran.*

But getting to a destination is different than being there. Cities are increasingly implementing one-way traffic systems, and the traffic police are becoming unmistakably enthusiastic over performing their jobs. The shortage of parking makes these one-way roads even more of a challenge; think about arriving, overshooting your destination, stewing in market day traffic and getting ushered all the way back out to the main road into town.

Most major cities are served by the majors in car rental. **Avis** (www.avis.com) has locations in all major cities, at most airports, and at select hotels and resorts. **National Car Rental** (www.nationalcar.com) has outlets pretty much everywhere, too, with rates comparable to those of Avis. Other options are **Budget** (www.budget.com), with limited outlets in Turkey; **Hertz** (www.hertz.com) and the German-based **Sixt** (www.sixt.com), with 20 locations throughout Turkey. See destination chapters for local contact numbers.

But as you plan your road trip across Anatolia, keep in mind that the cost of petrol in Turkey is among the highest in Europe, easily topping 100TL to fill up the tank of a small manual car. (As of June 2011, 1 liter of gasoline sold in Turkey for 3.75TL). Taxes are already included in the printed price. One U.S. gallon equals 3.8 liters or .85 imperial gallons.

By Train

In the years leading up to World War I, Turkey's railroads developed thanks to the "generosity" of German and British government-supported ventures sucking up to an as-yet neutral potential ally. These entrepreneurs recognized the value of old stone, making not-so-convenient detours in the track-laying to valuable archaeological sites. The result was an excruciating and meandering system whose main efficiency was carting away priceless archaeological finds, enriching both foreign museums and the pockets of these "part-time engineers." The Pergamum Altar is now in the Pergamon Museum in Berlin; King Priam's treasures were whisked out of Troy, passing through Berlin's Hermitage Museum and on to Moscow's Pushkin Museum, while many treasures from the Temple of Artemis are now housed in the British Museum. Recognizing this infrastructural Achilles Heel, the Turkish authorities have instituted major railway upgrades, shortening train travel, for example, between Ankara and Konya from 10 hours to just 1½. As part of this railway reorganization and upgrade, which will include the Marmaray Rail, billed as the "backbone of Istanbul's transportation system," the Turkish State Railways suspended all train traffic out of Istanbul's Haydarpaşa Station in January 2012. So for the near future, internal transportation will be confined to air or road travel. For information, log on to **www.tcdd.gov.tr**.

By Bus

Traveling by bus is the primary mode of ground transportation in Turkey, for both long hauls and short hops. It's also a great way to live like the locals. There are several categories of bus travel: municipal buses, the local *dolmuş*, long-distance buses, and short-distance minibuses.

In big cities, such as Istanbul, Ankara, Izmir, and Antalya, **municipal buses** provide a cheap way to get around, if you can actually figure out how. Destinations are posted on the windshield, a handy reference for veterans of a city, but virtually useless for any newcomer. That's why it's always a good idea to ask the driver if he's going your way before getting on. Getting on in the middle of a bus route can also be confusing, but there's always the ubiquitous good Samaritan there to steer you in the right direction.

Another popular and economic way of getting around locally is the **dolmuş**, essentially a minivan with passenger seats. The best description of these little group taxis is in the translation: *dolmuş* in English means "stuffed." The *dolmuş* follows a set route, stopping and starting to pick up passengers until no one else will fit in it. The main stops are posted on the windshield, and you pay according to the distance that you go, anywhere from 1.50TL on up to 8TL for longer trips. This system works well in and around small towns; drivers will politely honk as they drive to see if you want to get on, and routes are direct to the places you want to go. *Dolmuşes* do run on Sunday, so don't let those crafty taxi drivers convince you otherwise.

In major metropolitan areas such as Istanbul, the process is a bit more complicated, even for the locals. The best way to avoid an inner-city trip to nowhere is to board at one of the *dolmuş* stands marked by a blue "D" and take it to the final destination (preferably the same destination as yours). Fares are usually posted and rarely exceed 3.50TL per ride. It's also acceptable to pay the driver just before you get off, so you can enjoy a bit of spontaneity as well. *Dolmuşes* stop running in the early evening, so in the outlying areas, make sure you've got a way back to the hotel.

Long-distance buses are an integral part of the Turkish culture because they're cheap (or at least they used to be) and comfortable, and because service is near-comprehensive. (The one potential downer is that the non-smoking ban that applies to bus travel does not apply to the driver). The major bus companies in Turkey (**Note:** Phone numbers beginning with 444 are national toll-free numbers and can be dialed from anywhere in Turkey) are **Ulusoy** (✆ **444-1888;** www.ulusoy.com.tr), **Varan** (✆ **444-8999;** www.varanturizm.com), **Kamil Koç** (✆ **444-0KOC** [0562]; www.kamilkoc.com.tr), **Uludağ** (✆ **444-2222;** www.uludagturizm.com.tr), **Metro** (✆ **444-3455;** www.metroturizm.com.tr), and **Pamukkale** (✆ **444-3535;** www.pamukkale.com.tr), with the first two costing nearly double the other companies.

All have counters at the local bus station (*otogar*) as well as offices conveniently located around town. The better bus companies offer free shuttle service between the ticket office and your bus at the *otogar*.

If you're on a more relaxed timetable, it's just as easy to show up at the *otogar*; with competition stiff for your business, the bus companies that provide service to your destination will most certainly find you. Take your time and don't be bullied into buying a ticket from the first guy who hooks you in, because his bus may not be the first one to leave for your destination.

If you're like me, you believe it should take approximately 3 hours to cover 322km (200 miles). Gauge at least 40% more time on the bus than what you figure it would take you to get there by car.

Water and soft drinks are served on the bus; if you're lucky, you'll get a little kid-size breakfast cake to tide you over until the next feeding. A sprinkle of cologne is part of the Turkish culture, but better the brand that smells of baby oil and talcum powder than the one with the potent fragrance of Lemon Pledge. Rest stops are made at erratic intervals, but there's usually enough time at one of the pickup and drop-off points for a quick dash to the Turkish toilet. (Let the man onboard know you'll be right back!)

Except on rare occasions, unacquainted men and women do not sit together on the bus. My grievance with this tradition is more practical than unprogressive: Old Turkish ladies tend to be hefty and spill out onto the adjacent seat, while it is common practice for a Turkish mother to save the cost of a bus fare by seating her 6-year-old son on her lap for the 6-hour trip.

[FastFACTS] TURKEY

Area Codes   The three-digit area code for the European side of Istanbul is **212;** for the Asian side, dial **216.** Ankara telephone numbers are preceded by **312.** For additional area codes, refer to the destination chapters.

Business Hours   Banks are open Monday through Friday from 8:30am to noon and 1:30 to 5pm. Government offices are open Monday through Friday 8:30am to 12:30pm and 1:30 to 5:30pm. Official hours of operation for shops are Monday through Saturday 9:30am to 1pm and 2 to 7pm, but I've yet to find a store closed at lunchtime, or a shop outside of the Grand Bazaar or the Egyptian Spice Market closed on Sundays. Museums and palaces are generally open Tuesday through Sunday from 9:30am to 5 or 5:30pm, while the closing day for palaces is Tuesday, Thursday, or both. Museum opening hours are generally extended by an hour or 2 in summer; note that museums generally also stop selling tickets up to an hour prior to the official closing time. Most shops and official offices and museums are closed on January 1, April 23 (National Independence & Children's Day), May 19 (Youth & Sports Day), August 30 (Victory Day) and October 28 and 29 (Republic Day). These same establishments also generally close on the first day of religious holidays. During the 30 days of Ramadan, many shops and businesses close early, while many restaurants either close down completely or offer limited menus at lunchtime.

Car Rental   See "Getting Around by Car," above in this chapter.

Crime   See "Safety," later in this section.

Customs   *What You Can Bring into Turkey:* In addition to personal effects, travelers are permitted luxury items in the form of wine and tobacco et. al. (EU regulations apply); medical items such as drugs for personal treatment; valuables like personal jewelry worth under US$15,000 (although it is recommended that you register these upon entry to avoid problems on exit); and certain sports equipment.

What You Can Take Home from Turkey: For valuables purchased during your stay, be prepared to provide receipts or other proof of purchase—particularly for that 4×6 prize silk Hereke—to avoid problems with Turkish Customs when you leave and to aid in declarations in your home country. Forget about having your carpet salesman lie on the official Certificate of Origin, because the U.S. immigration police are prepared to consult their little carpet blue book if you try to slip through without paying up. Turkey prohibits the export of antiques; in fact, it is illegal to take anything of historical value out of the country (this refers to anything dating to the end of the 19th century). For items dating prior to the 20th century, permission plus a certificate of authenticity from a museum official is needed. It is also illegal to carry out tobacco seeds and plants, or hides, skins, or clothing made from wild animals. Minerals require special documentation obtainable from the General Directorate of Mining Exploration and Research in Ankara (www.mta.gov.tr; ☏ **0312/287-3430**). A more comprehensive list of customs regulations is available on the Go Turkey website (www.goturkey.com).

Disabled Travelers   Turkey's main airports and newer buildings have all been constructed to European standards, which includes handicapped-accessible ramps or lifts. Almost every hotel with an elevator has at least one handicapped-accessible room, although five-star hotels are more apt to cover all bases, such as grip handles and lower sinks. Although ramps have begun to appear at Turkish brick-and-mortar museums, don't expect seamless access. (The crumbling ruins of outdoor archaeological sites are another story altogether; confirm with your travel agent that your needs will be accommodated.) However, Turkish hospitality being what it is, it'll be the odd tour guide or group leader who won't bend over backward to accommodate your individual needs.

Doctors   Any local consulate can provide a list of area doctors who speak English. If you do get sick, you may want to ask the concierge at your hotel to recommend a local doctor, even his or her own. This will probably yield a better recommendation than any information number would. In fact, ask anybody on the street and he/she will likely accompany you to the doctor. Also, local doctors advertise their services through discreet signs near their offices, and most speak English. If you can't find a doctor who can help you right away, try the **emergency room** of one of the private hospitals listed under "hospitals" below.

Drinking Laws   In the years since the religious-leaning Justice and Development (AKP) party came to power, the number of "dry" hotels and restaurants has increased and the legal drinking age has been raised to 24, while punitively high taxes (30%) on alcohol have made imbibing painful to the wallet. Basically, if you want to drink, you'll have to pay. Beer, wine, and Turkey's national drink, raki are widely available in bars and restaurants, while alcohol can be purchased in convenience stores, wine shops, and in grocery aisles.

Driving   See "Getting Around," above in this chapter.

Electricity   The standard is 220 volts, and outlets are compatible with the round European two-prong plug. You may be able to leave your hair dryer at home, as most hotel rooms come equipped with at least a weak one. Visitors from America and Canada with electronics that need to be recharged will need an adapter, a transformer, or both, depending on the appliance.

Embassies & Consulates   **In the U.S.**   The **Turkish Embassy** is located at 2525 Massachusetts Ave. NW, Washington, DC 20008 (℗ **202/612-6700;** fax 202/612-6744; www.washington.emb.mfa.gov.tr). Turkey also maintains consulates in Chicago (℗ **312/263-0644**), Houston (℗ **713/622-5849**), Los Angeles (℗ **323/655-8832**), and New York (℗ **646/430-6560**). For contact information, visit the embassy website.

In Canada   **Turkish Embassy,** 197 Wurtemburg St., Ottawa, ON K1N 8L9 (℗ **613/244-2470;** fax 613/789-3442; www.turkishembassy.com). You can also call the **Consular Call Center** at ℗ 888/566-7656.

In Australia & New Zealand   **Turkish Embassy,** Canberra, 6 Moona Place, Yarralumla, ACT 2600 (℗ **02/6234-0000;** fax 02/6273-4402; www.kanberra.be.mfa.gov.tr) and missions in Melbourne (8/24 Albert Rd., South Melbourne Vic.,3205; ℗ **61 03 9696 6046**) and Sydney (66 Ocean St, Woollahra NSW 2025; ℗ **61 2 9302 4600**).

In the U.K.   The **Turkish Embassy** is at Rutland Lodge, Rutland Gardens, London SW7 1BW (℗ **20 7591 6900;** www.londra.be.mfa.gov.tr).

Emergencies   Local emergency numbers are **fire** ℗ **110, police** ℗ **155,** and **ambulance** ℗ **112.** In addition, see the Istanbul and Ankara chapters for numbers for private ambulances in those cities.

Gasoline   Please see "Getting There By Car," earlier in this chapter.

Health   There are no particular health concerns associated with travel to Turkey and no inoculations are necessary. For information and updates on any epi- or pandemics (such as avian influenza or the H1N1 swine flu), visit the websites of the World Health Organization (www.who.int), the European Centre for Disease Prevention and Control (http://ecdc.europa.eu), or the United States Centers for Disease Control (www.cdc.gov).

Still, any veteran traveler never leaves home without a basic health kit tailored to his or her particular needs. Generally, these should include anti-diarrheal medicine such as Imodium, aspirin, ibuprofen, sunscreen, insect repellent, and sanitary products. While it is imperative to pack prescriptions that you need (insulin, cholesterol-lowering meds, et. al.), many are widely available in pharmacies (called *eczane*) in Turkey, sold by the brand or generic name at prices often lower than at home. If you suffer from a chronic illness, consult your doctor before your departure. Pack **prescription medications** in your carry-on luggage, and carry them in their original containers, with pharmacy labels—otherwise they won't make it through airport security.

Tropical Illnesses Although the persistence and tenaciousness of Turkish **mosquitoes** might cause you to suffer, it is unlikely that malaria will. Keep in mind that you're more likely to catch deadly mosquito-borne diseases in your own backyard than abroad. If you are experiencing symptoms, seek prompt medical attention while traveling as well as for up to 3 years after your return. Don't forget to pack a proven insect repellent (especially for those nights lounging outdoors in a tea garden or spent waterside along the coast).

Dietary Red Flags **Food poisoning and diarrhea** are probably the most prevalent illnesses associated with travel to Turkey. Although water from the tap is chlorinated and generally safe to drink, even the locals drink bottled water. Avoid nonpasteurized dairy products and shellfish during the hot summer months, and maintain a healthy suspicion of street vendors. In the event that you become ill, drink plenty of (bottled) water and remember that diarrhea usually dissipates on its own. Pepto Bismol (bismuth subsalicylate) can often prevent symptoms, but if the problem becomes truly inconvenient, pharmacists are generally sympathetic and bilingual, and will be able to provide an effective remedy. (**Ercefuryl** works wonders.)

Bugs, Bites & Other Wildlife Concerns **Rabies** is endemic in parts of Turkey, and joggers have been known to be bitten by infected strays. But this is extremely rare. Best to stay away from animals altogether—advice that, given the sweet temperaments of the street dogs and cats, I myself am incapable of following. If you're concerned, consult your doctor for pre-exposure immunization.

Internet & Wi-Fi Almost all hotels offer free Internet access via a computer in the lobby, wireless, or an in-room ISDN line. The more deluxe hotel properties may even stock laptops for rent. Internet cafes in Istanbul are generally bunched around Taksim Square, on the upper floors of the side streets perpendicular to Istiklal Caddesi, and more sparsely along Divanyolu in the Old City.

Language English, French, and German are widespread. For the linguistically challenged, it may not be so unusual to encounter some minor language barriers, but the inherent willingness of the Turks to help combined with a little sign language and a lot of laughs will almost always do the trick. See chapter 13 for a glossary of useful Turkish words and phrases or pack a copy of the pocket-friendly edition of Langenscheidt's Turkish Dictionary.

Legal Aid Foreigners and tourists get the benefit of the doubt in most every run-in with the law, but some things you just can't talk your way out of it. For real trouble, contact your embassy or consulate for assistance in understanding the legal process (or if you are arrested, have the Turkish authorities contact them for you, a right afforded to citizens of countries that are signatories of the Vienna Convention on Consular Relations). Consulates also maintain a current list of private law firms catering to English-speaking foreigners. If you are "pulled over" for a minor infraction (such as speeding), never attempt to pay the fine directly to a police officer; this could be construed as attempted bribery, a much more serious crime. Insist on paying the fine directly into the hands of the municipal clerk.

LGBT Travelers In the past few years, gayness has come more and more out of the closet in Turkey; from 2003 to 2011, attendance at the Pride March in Istanbul has burgeoned from 30 participants to more than 10,000. Still although the LGBT community has gained some ground, tell that to those gays who've been beaten, harassed, threatened, or worse. And while homosexuality is technically legal, police have been known to arrest people displaying even minor amounts of PDA, citing offenses against public morality or exhibitionism. Same-sex couples now have many local resources including **www.turkey gay.net** and **www.turkgayclub.org**. The sites provide information such as gay-friendly hotels and links to further resources. **Istanbul Gay** (www.istanbulgay.com) provides Istanbul-specific resources such as gay/lesbian guides, gay bar tours, and gay-friendly hotels. **Kaos GL** (www.kaosgl.com) was the first gay and lesbian magazine in Turkey; their online presence has a substantial section in English, with features addressing issues affecting gays and lesbians in Turkey.

Mail The PTT, hard to miss with its black and yellow signs, offers the usual postal services, in addition to selling tokens (*jetons*) and phone cards for the phone booths located in and around the post office and in most public places. Postcards cost 70kr to Europe and 80kr to all other continents while airmail letters cost 1.50TL and 1.75TL respectively. Rates for an international express mail letter begin at 22TL and go up to 40TL for deliveries farther afield. Delivery however is notoriously slow, so I'd stick with one of the private carriers mentioned such as UPS or DHL. The PTT also has the most competitive rates for currency exchange and traveler's check services.

Medical Requirements There are no severe health risks in travel to western Turkey, nor are vaccinations required. Visitors journeying to southeastern Turkey may want to consider a prophylactic treatment for malaria, particularly prior to travel near the Syrian border and between the months of May and October when transmission rates are highest. Because of globalization and the increasing ease of physical movement across borders, travelers should also ensure that their own and their children's vaccinations are up-to-date, including measles, the incidence of which has been growing in the U.K., as well as parts of Africa. Also, avoid petting the street animals, as while rare, rabies is endemic.

Money & Costs Frommer's lists exact prices in the local currency. The currency conversions provided were correct at press time. However, rates fluctuate, so before departing consult a currency exchange website such as **www.oanda.com/currency/converter** to check up-to-the-minute rates.

Bank notes come in denominations of 1, 5, 10, 20, 50, 100, and 200TL, while coins, called the kuruş (kr), come in 1, 5, 10, 25, and 50 kuruş pieces. There is also a 1TL coin.

In spite of the continued stabilization of the Turkish Lira, local prices for larger-ticket items (hotels, tours, carpets) are still generally quoted in foreign currency, usually the euro. But wishing to accommodate, local salesmen will often quote a price in your home currency. Similarly, prices listed in this book are given in the currency in which they were provided, creating an unavoidable mish-mash of prices in euros, pounds sterling, Turkish Lira, and U.S. dollars. Note that at the time of payment however, prices are converted back to TL *based on that day's rate of exchange*. This may account for minor discrepancies in say, the charge on your credit card bill vs. the amount you thought you were going to pay relevant to the price quoted on a hotel's website.

It's always advisable to bring money in a variety of forms on a vacation: a mix of cash, credit cards, and if you insist, traveler's checks. You should also exchange enough petty cash to cover airport incidentals, tipping, and transportation to your hotel. You can easily withdraw money in local currency upon arrival at an airport ATM located in the arrivals terminal.

ATMs For those of you willing to succumb to the endless, creative bank fees charged by credit card companies, ATMs on the Cirrus (ⓒ **800/424-7787**; www.mastercard.com) and PLUS (ⓒ **800/843-7587**; www.visa.com) networks are widely available in major cities. Among the most reliable of the local banks are **Akbank, Türk İş Bankası, Garanti Bankası, Yapı Kredi Bankası,** and **Ziraat Bankası.** Ask your bank whether you need a new personal identification number (PIN), as most ATMs in Turkey accept numbered passwords only, and some limit their input to four digits. Also, be aware that the ATMs are often fickle

Bait and Switch It's hard to believe, but in the major tourist areas of Turkey, particularly in the streets of Sultanahmet, an entire industry thrives on the acquisition and manipulation of emotions for economic gain. Foreign women, receptive, even eager for new and exotic experiences, are just ripe for the picking. Although less than attractive ones are particularly vulnerable, any single girl with cash in the bank and foreign nationality is a target.

Sultanahmet is filled with professional "gigolos" practiced in the art of courtship and persuasion. Sometimes the goal is simply to gain your trust so that you follow their shopping recommendations (then reap the commissions). Sometimes it's about gaining residency in a foreign country. But in the worst case scenario, it's a nefarious way to seduce you out of large quantities of your hard-earned cash. Some seducers even take this kind of behavior to its limits by pursuing the game as far as the wedding contract. But the most deplorable of the lot have been known to forge the marriage certificate with the assistance of those in the neighborhood even less scrupulous than themselves.

But this kind of behavior doesn't represent all of Turkey, and overall women traveling alone in Turkey are treated with an almost exaggerated courtesy. In some cases, a woman will be in a better position to experience the openness of the Turkish people than if traveling en masse. With all of this warmth and hospitality, it's difficult to know how to temper one's instincts toward friendliness without affirming the general opinion among the more conservative class of Turks that all Western women are prostitutes. Even an innocent greeting or seemingly harmless camaraderie can be misinterpreted, so it's important to find a balance between polite formality and the openness that North American, European, and Australian women find so normal.

Dining Practically speaking, no matter how modern the country may seem on the surface, don't be surprised if you're the only female in a restaurant. Eateries often have an aile salonu (family salon), an unintimidating dining area provided for men, women, couples, and anyone else not wishing to dine among groups of smoking, drinking Turks.

or empty, so always carry around alternatives in the form of cash or traveler's checks for emergencies.

Credit Cards Private bank accounts are not the only method where banks have been creative with mining additional fees. Purchases on credit card accounts are now also subject to a percentage fee, usually around 5%. In an annoying twist, these very same credit cards offer some of the more competitive exchange rates. It's up to you to do the math, though. Nevertheless, it's highly recommended that you travel with at least one major credit card. You must have a credit card to rent a car, and hotels and airlines usually require a credit card imprint as a deposit against expenses. Most establishments accept American Express, MasterCard, and Visa. Debit cards are also a commonly acceptable form of payment in most establishments.

For help with currency conversions, tip calculations, and more, download Frommer's convenient Travel Tools app for your mobile device. Go to http://www.frommers.com/go/mobile/ and click on the Travel Tools icon.

Petrol Please see "Getting Around by Car," earlier in this chapter.

Police To reach the **police,** dial ⓒ **155.**

Safety   Regrettably, terrorism has become a fact of life at home and abroad. While terrorist activity is mostly associated with the provinces of Turkey's Southeast, small- and large-scale bombings have occurred in Istanbul, Ankara and in tourist areas along the coast. While these generally target government buildings, there have been incidents involving areas frequented by foreigners and citizens alike. Turkish authorities have stepped up security around the country, but stay alert, particularly in areas where large numbers of people congregate.

Similarly, avoid public demonstrations, particularly in Taksim Square and in Ankara, as tempers can run hot and even turn violent.

For more information before you go, it might be a good idea to check in with your travel advisories. In the U.S., log onto **http://travel.state.gov/travel**; in the U.K.: **www.fco.gov.uk**; in Canada: **www.voyage.gc.ca**; in Australia: **www.smartraveller.gov.au**; in New Zealand: **www.safetravel.govt.nz**.

For particular concerns for single female travelers, see the box "Important Tips for Single Women Travelers," below.

Smoking   A local saying goes something like this: "Eat like a Turk, smoke like a Turk," which roughly translates to "don't expect anyone to comply with nonsmoking laws." Since the smoking ban went into effect in July 2009 (prohibiting smoking in all public places, including restaurants!), there have been reports of acts of quiet civil disobedience, although all in all, the ban seems to be working.

Taxes   A flat 18% VAT (value-added tax) is incorporated into the price of almost everything you buy. This number is reduced to 8% for tourist services such as hotel tax when not already included in the price of the room rate, although added services such as airport transfers are charged at the 18% rate. There's also the controversial **Special Consumption Tax,** a levy on consumer products including cars and cellphones and targeting such un-Islamic vices as alcoholic beverages and tobacco. As if these consumption taxes weren't high enough already, the rates were increased in October 2011, from 63% to 65% on cigarettes and from a flat tax of 40TL on mobile phones, to 100TL. Meanwhile, the flat tax on beer rose from 44kr to 53kr per liter and from 16TL to a whopping 20TL for a bottle of sparkling wine. (The price of regular table wine will go up by 15% to 20%).

Telephones   To call Istanbul from abroad:

1. Dial the international access code: 011 from the U.S.; 00 from the U.K., Ireland, or New Zealand; or 0011 from Australia.
2. Dial the country code: 90.
3. Dial the city code **212** for the European side and **216** for the Asian side, and then the number. If the number you are trying to dial is a mobile number (beginning instead with 555, 542, or 532 and their derivatives), then use this number instead of the city code.

To make international calls from Istanbul: First dial 00 and then the country code (U.S. or Canada 1, U.K. 44, Ireland 353, Australia 61, New Zealand 64). Next you dial the area code and number. For example, if you wanted to call the British Embassy in Washington, D.C., you would dial 00-1-202-588-7800.

For **reversed-charge or collect calls,** and for person-to-person calls, dial the number 0 then the area code and number; an operator will come on the line, and you should specify whether you are calling collect, person-to-person, or both. If your operator-assisted call is international, ask for the overseas operator. For calling cards and collect calls via AT&T, dial ℂ **0811/288-0001.**

To make local calls while in town: In order to call the Asian side from the European side, you must dial 0216 and then the number. For calls to the same side, dial the city code, but not the 0. To call outside of Istanbul but within Turkey, you must dial the 0 followed by the area code and seven-digit number.

For directory assistance: Dial ℂ **115** (in Turkish) if you're looking for a number inside Istanbul. Unfortunately, there is no international directory.

For operator assistance: If you need operator assistance in making a call, dial ℂ **115** if you're trying to make an international call and ℂ **131** (in Turkish) if you want to call a number in Turkey.

Toll-free numbers: Numbers beginning with 0800 within Turkey are toll free, but calling a 1-800 number in the States from Turkey is not toll free. In fact, it costs the same as an overseas call.

National numbers: More and more prevalent is the local 444 number (no area code). These numbers connect you to service call centers for national businesses for the cost of a local call. (You may have to dial the three-digit local area code, for example, in Izmir, you would dial 0232/444-xxxx).

Time   All of Turkey adheres to **Eastern European Time** (EET), which is Greenwich Mean Time plus 2 hours. To make it easier: When it is noon in New York, it is 7pm in Istanbul. Daylight saving time, when clocks are set 1 hour ahead of standard time, is in effect as **Eastern European Summer Time** (EEST), from 1am on the second Sunday in March to 1am on the first Sunday in November.

Tipping   Gratuities are a way of life in Turkey. Try to keep coins or small notes handy and follow these guidelines: Give the **bellhop** or **skycap** 1TL to 2TL per bag; leave at least an additional 10% of the restaurant bill for your **waiter;** reward your **tour guide** with 10€ to 20€ for a job well done; and give the **attendant** in the Turkish bath 10% to 20%, depending on the quality of the establishment. Shows of appreciation (15% minimum) are also expected from your **barber or hairdresser**. Tip the captain of your Blue Cruise Voyage 50€ for a 3-day cruise and 100€ for a week. It is not customary in Turkey to tip the taxi driver.

Toilets   Turkish toilets have come a long way in the past 10 years. Whereas the toilet seat on the floor setup used to be the standard, today, it is a rare establishment (in Western Turkey, at least) that doesn't have a European thrown. If you should encounter the former, my advice is to lift your skirts high, hang on to the cuffs of your pants, and always carry tissues. Other things you should know about the Turkish toilet: The ridges on the porcelain are your "footrests," the floor-level faucet and bucket are for post business washups and the toilet paper—if there is any—is for drying your freshly washed privates and should be disposed of in the nearby wastebasket. As for the European toilets, most have built-in bidets that send clean water up to your privates when activated. Simply locate the faucet—usually on the wall behind you to the right of the tank—and let her rip.

VAT   See "Taxes" above.

Visas   Because of the seamless ease of obtaining an entry tourist visa on arrival, there is no need to acquire one prior to departure. The visa windows, where functionaries collect payment (in US$, £, €, or Turkish Lira) are prominently located adjacent to the Customs area in every international airport. Be sure to pay up (and get your visa sticker affixed to your passport) before queuing in the Customs line. An entry visa for Turkey is required for citizens of the U.S. ($20/15€), Canada (US$60 or 45€); the U.K. (£10/$20/15€) and Australia (US$20 or 15€). All of these visas are valid for 3 months and multiple entries. A valid passport is sufficient for citizens of New Zealand.

Visitor Information   The Turkish tourism authorities provide a wealth of travel information at your fingertips as well as addresses for the nearest tourism office at www.goturkey.com. In the U.K., go to 29-30 St. James's St., London SW1A 1HB, 4th floor (**℃ 20 7839 7778**); in the U.S., there are offices in Los Angeles (5055 Wilshire Blvd., Ste. 850; **℃ 323/937-8066**), in New York (821 UN Plaza; **℃ 212/687-2194**) and in Washington D.C. (2525 Massachusetts Ave. W. (**℃ 202/612-6800**).

The following sites provide a range of information to help you prepare the most relevant, in-the-know, itinerary:

o **www.goturkey.com** is the official English-language tourism site of the Government of Turkey's Ministry of Culture and Tourism. The site **www.tourismturkey. org** has a more American focus.

o **www.kultur.gov.tr** is another excellent official resource for information and links to the country's museums, archaeological sites, cultural goods, and generalized information.

o **www.mymerhaba.com** and www.expatsturkey.com are for expatriates by expatriates, with essential information on getting settled, restaurant picks, the most up-to-date events, and happenings in the major cities.

o **www.hurriyetdailynews.com**, **www.todayszaman.com**, **www.aa.com.tr** (Anadolu Ajansi, the state-run agency) and **www.turkishpress.com**, the sites for Turkey's English-language dailies, allow you to plug in to real-time issues.

o **http://cat.une.edu.au** is a handy little resource that holds compiled information on all archaeological work being conducted in Turkey.

o **www.turkeytravelplanner.com** is a copious how-to, you might even call it "Traveling to Turkey for Dummies." It's run by Tom Brosnahan, formerly of Frommer's and The Lonely Planet, and author of Bright Sun, Strong Tea.

Water   The water is safe to drink, but will slow you down. Drink bottled water and wash fruits and vegetables thoroughly before eating.

Wi-Fi   See "Internet & Wi-Fi," earlier in this section.

A GLOSSARY OF USEFUL TURKISH PHRASES

PRONUNCIATION GUIDE

VOWELS

a like the "a" in father
â like "ya" (the circumflex adds a diphthong)
e like the "e" in bed
i like the "i" in indigo
ı like the "e" in the
o like the "o" in hope
ö like the German "ö" or like the "u" in the English word further
u like the "u" in super
ü like the French "u" or like the "u" in the English word funeral

CONSONANTS

c like the "j" in jump
ç like the "ch" in church
g like the "g" in gather
ğ is silent and indicates that the preceding vowel should be elongated (*dağ* becomes "daaah," meaning "mountain")
h is **always** aspirated (pronounced without the "h," the proper name Mahmut means "big elephant"!)
j like the "s" in pleasure
s like the "s" in simple
ş like the "sh" in share

BASIC VOCABULARY

NUMBERS

1	bir
2	iki
3	üç
4	dört
5	beş
6	altı
7	yedi
8	sekiz
9	dokuz
10	on
11	onbir
12	oniki
20	yirmi
21	yirmibir
30	otuz
40	kırk
50	elli
60	altmış
70	yetmiş
80	seksen
90	doksan
100	yüz
101	yüzbir
200	ikiyüz
1,000	bin
2,000	ikibin

MONTHS OF THE YEAR

January	**Ocak**
February	**Şubat**
March	**Mart**
April	**Nisan**
May	**Mayıs**
June	**Haziran**
July	**Temmuz**
August	**Ağfustos**
September	**Eylül**
October	**Ekim**
November	**Kasım**
December	**Aralık**

EXPRESSIONS OF TIME

1 hour	Bir saat
Afternoon	Öğleden sonra
Morning	Sabah
Night	Gece
Today	Bugün
Tomorrow	Yarın
What time is it?	Saat kaç? (literally, "how many hours?")
Yesterday	Dün

USEFUL SUFFIXES

ci, cı, çi, çı, cu, cü, çu, çü	indicates the seller of something
i, ı, u, ü	indicates "of something" (an "s" is added after a vowel)
ler, lar	makes a word plural
li, lı, lu, lü	indicates the presence of something; "with"
siz, sız, suz, süz	indicates the absence of something; "without"

USEFUL WORDS & PHRASES

Check, please!	Hesap, lütfen!
Cheers! (drinking)	Şerefe!
Closed	Kapalı
Do you have any dishes without meat?	Etsiz yemek var mı?
Excuse me	Pardon (French pronunciation) or Afadersınız
Gate (travel)	Kapı
Goodbye	Güle güle (said by the one staying); Allahaısmarladık (said by the one leaving)
Goodbye	Hoşça kalın (an all-purpose goodbye)
Good day	İyi günler
Good evening	İyi akşamlar
Good morning	Günaydın
Good night	İyi geceler
Hello	Merhaba
How are you?	Nasılsınız?
How much?	Kaç para? (literally, "how much money?") or Ne kadar?
I'm fine, thank you.	İyiyim, teşekkür ederim.
Is there . . . ?	Var mı . . . ? (question of availability)
Is there any meat stock in this dish?	İçinde et suyu var mı?
No	Hayır (higher)
One ticket, please	Bir tane bilet, lütfen
Open	Açık
Please	Lütfen
Pleased to meet you	Memnun oldun

Thank you (formal)	**Teşekkür ederim** (try to remember: "tea, sugar, a dream")
Thank you (casual)	**Sağol**
Thank you	**Mersi**
There isn't any; no; none	**Yok**
Very beautiful	**Çok güzel** (said also when the food is good)
Welcome!	**Hoş geldiniz!** (response: **Hoş bulduk**)
Well done!	**Bravo!** or **Aferin!**
Where? Where is it?	**Nerede?**
Where's the toilet?	**Tuvalet nerede?**
Yes	**Evet**

GLOSSARY OF TERMS

Acropolis	Highest part of a Greek city reserved for the most important religious monuments
Ada(sı)	Island
Ağa	Arabic title given to commanders in the Ottoman military
Bahçe(sı)	Garden
Bayanlar	Ladies
Baylar	Gentlemen
Bayram	Arabic term meaning "feast" denoting several of the Muslim holidays
Bedesten	Covered inn or marketplace
Bey	Turkish title of courtesy following a man's first name, meaning "Mr.," as in "Mehmet bey"
Bulvarı	Boulevard
Büyük	Big
Caddesi	Avenue
Caldarium	Hottest section of a Roman bath
Cami/camii	Mosque; derived from the Arabic *jama* meaning "place of reunion"
Caravansaray	A fortified inn; Turkish spelling is *kervansaray*
Çarşı(sı)	Market; bazaar
Celebi	Nobleman
Çeşme	Fountain
Cıkış	Exit
Cumhuriyet	Republic
Cuneiform	Linear script inscribed into tablets; used by the ancient Mesopotamians and in Asia Minor
Deniz	Sea
Dervish	A member of a mystical order of Islam
Divan	Word used to refer to the Ottoman governmental administration
Dolmuş	Minibus, minivan, or any car that operates as a group taxi

Döviz	Foreign currency
Eczane	Pharmacy
Efendi	Turkish title of courtesy following a first name, meaning "sir" or "ma'am"
Emir	Arabic title for a military commander or governor of a province
Ev/evi	Home, house
Fatih	Conqueror
Frigidarium	The cold room of a Roman bath
Gar	Station
Gazi	Literally, "warrior"
Giriş	Entrance
Gişe	Ticket window
Hadith	Traditions based on the words or actions of Mohammed
Hamam(ı)	Turkish bath
Han(ı)	Inn or caravansaray
Hanım	Address of respect meaning "lady"
Harem	Women's quarters of a house (literally, "forbidden")
Havaalan(ı) or **hava liman(ı)**	Airport
Hicret	The date in 622 when Mohammad left Mecca for Yathrib (Medina) to escape local hostilities; this event marks the beginning of the Islamic calendar.
Hijab	From the Arabic *hajaba* meaning "to conceal"; used to mean any modest covering worn by a Muslim woman
Hisar	Fortress
Iconoclasm	8th-century Christian movement that opposed all religious icons
Imam	Literally, "leader"; an educated religious guide
Iskele(sı)	Wharf, quay, or dock
Janissaries	The select corps of the Ottoman army
Jihad	Literally, "struggle" or "striving" (Arab; in Turkish: *cihad*)
Ka'aba	Muslim sacred shrine in Mecca
Kale(si)	Castle or fortress
Kat	Floor (of a building)
Kilim	Flat weave rug
Kilise	Church
Konak/konağı	Mansion
Koran	The holy recitations of the Prophet Mohammed; Muslims believe that these revelations are the direct words of God
Küçük	Small
Kule	Tower
Külliye(sı)	Religious and social complex consisting of mosque, school, and buildings for public use
Kümbet	Literally, "cupola" or "dome"; synonym for *türbe*

13

A GLOSSARY OF USEFUL TURKISH PHRASES | Glossary of Terms

Liman(ı)	Port
Mahalle(sı)	Neighborhood
Medrese	Muslim theological school
Mescit	Small prayer space; mini-mosque
Mevlana	Title of respect meaning "Lord" (Arabic)
Meydan(ı)	Public square
Meyhane	Tavern, pub, or rowdy restaurant
Mihrab	The niche in a mosque oriented toward Mecca
Minaret	The towers of a mosque from which the müezzin chants the call to prayer
Minbar	Pulpit
Müezzin	The Muslim "cantor" of the call to prayer
Necropolis	Ancient Greek or Roman cemetery
Oculus	Round "skylight" in the top of a dome
Oda(sı)	Room
Otogar	Bus station
Pansiyon	Pension, guesthouse
Ramadan	Islamic month of ritual fasting; Ramadan (*Ramazan* in Turkish) follows the lunar calendar, so the festival is not confined to one season.
Şadirvan	Literally, "reservoir"; used for ablution fountains
Şarap	Wine
Saray(ı)	Palace
Şarcüteri	Delicatessen
Satrap	Persian governor of a province
Şehzade	Crown prince
Selamlık	In a traditional Turkish house, the part reserved for the men and the reception of guests
Sema	Mystical dance of the Mevlevi order of the dervishes
Seraglio	Sultan's palace
Sokak/sokağı	Street
Stele	Ancient tombstone
Sublime Porte	Originally the main door of the palace where meetings of the divan were held; the term was eventually used to refer to the government, and the entire Ottoman Empire in general
Tepidarium	The tepid room of a Roman bath; used for relaxation
Tuğra	Sultan's imperial seal
Türbe(si)	Turkish monumental funerary tomb
Ulu	Great
Yalı	Traditional wood Ottoman house, usually a secondary residence, built on the sea
Valide Sultan	Turkish title equivalent to Queen Mother
Yol(u)	Road (*karayolu:* highway or autobahn)
Yurt	Nomadic tent, traditionally made of felt

MENU GUIDE

WHAT IS IT?

Alabalık	Trout
Ananas	Pineapple
Ançuez	Anchovy
Balık	Fish
Barbunya	Red mullet
Beyin	Brain
Bezelye	Peas
Biber	Pepper (*kara biber*: black pepper)
Bıldırcın	Quail
Bonfile	Filet of beef
Çam fıstığı	Pine nut
Ciğer	Liver
Çilek	Strawberry
Çorba	Soup
Çupra	Sea bream
Dana	Veal
Domates	Tomato
Domuz	Pork
Dondurma	Ice cream
Ekmek	Bread
Elma	Apple
Enginar	Artichoke
Erik	Plum
Et	Meat
Fasulye	Bean
Havuç	Carrot
Hindi	Turkey
Ispanak	Spinach
Istravrit	Mackerel
Jambon	Ham
Kabak	Squash (zucchini, pumpkin, and the like)
Kalkan	Turbot
Karides	Shrimp
Karnıbahar	Cauliflower
Karpuz	Watermelon
Kavun	Melon
Kayısı	Apricot
Kaz	Goose
Kefal	Gray mullet

Kılıç	Swordfish
Kiraz	Cherry
Köfte	Meatball
Kuzu	Lamb
Lağus	Grouper
Lavaş	Grilled unleavened bread
Levrek	Sea bass
Limon	Lemon
Lüfer	Bluefish
Mantar	Mushroom
Marul	Lettuce
Meyva	Fruit
Meze	Appetizer
Mezgit	Cod
Mısır	Corn
Mürekkep balığı	Squid
Muz	Banana
Ördek	Duck
Patates	Potato
Patlıcan	Eggplant/aubergine
Peynir	Cheese
Pide	Flat bread
Pilaf (pilâf)	Rice
Piliç	Chicken
Portakal	Orange
Salatalik	Cucumber
Sardalya	Sardine
Şeftali	Peach
Şeker	Sugar
Sığır	Beef
Soğan	Onion
Som	Salmon
Sosis	Sausage
Tarak	Scallop
Tatlılar	Sweets
Tavuk	Hen (for stewing)
Tereyağı	Butter
Ton	Tuna
Tuz	Salt
Un	Flour
Üzüm	Grapes
Yumurta	Eggs
Zeytin	Olive
Zeytinyağı	Olive oil

HOW IS IT PREPARED?

Buğulama	Steamed
Çevirme	Meat roasted on a spit
Çiğ	Raw
Doğranmış	Chopped
Dolma	Stuffed
Ezme	Paste
Fırın	Roasted or baked; oven
Füme	Smoked
Guveç	Earthenware dish; casseroles cooked in this pot
Haşlama	Cooked, boiled
Islim	Braised
Izgara	Grilled
Kavurma	Fried or roasted
Kebap	Roasted
Pane	Breaded and fried
Püre	Purée
Rosto	Roast meat
Saç	Iron griddle for cooking over wood fires
Sahanda	Fried
Şiş	Skewer
Sote	Sauté
Tandır	Clay-lined oven
Taşım	Boiled
Tava	Fried

DRINKS

Ayran	Yogurt drink made by the addition of water and salt
Bira	Beer
Çay	Tea
Kayısı suyu	Apricot juice
Kiraz suyu	Cherry juice
Maden suyu or soda	Carbonated mineral water
Meyve suyu	Fruit juice
Portakal suyu	Orange juice
Rak(ı)	Alcoholic drink made of aniseed and diluted with water
Şarap	Wine
Şekerli	With sugar
Şekersiz	Unsweetened
Şişe suyu	Bottled water
Soğuk içecekler	Beverages
Su	Water
Süt	Milk
Suyu	Juice

APPETIZERS

Ara sıcak	Hot appetizers (translated literally, "in the middle hot")
Arnavut ciğeri	Spicy fried liver with onions
Beyin haşlaması	Boiled brain
Beyin kızartması	Fried brain
Börek	Flaky pastry, either baked or fried
Cacık	Salad of yogurt, cucumber, and garlic; often served as a soup
Çiğ köfte	Spicy raw meatballs
Çoban salatası	Salad of tomatoes, peppers, cucumbers, onions, and mint in olive oil and lemon
Fesuliye piyası	White bean with onion salad
Havuç salatası	Carrot salad
Hibeş	Spread of chickpeas, red pepper, onion, and yogurt
Hummus	Chickpea purée
Sigara böreği	Fried phyllo "cigar" pastry filled with cheese
Soğuk mezeler	Cold appetizers
Su böreği	Baked phyllo filled with meat or cheese
Talaş böreği	Puff pastry filled with meat
Yalancı dolması	Stuffed grape leaves (no meat)
Yaprak dolması	Stuffed grape leaves (sometimes with meat)

MEATS & KEBAPS

Adana kebabı	Meatballs of spicy chopped lamb grilled on a skewer
Böbrek	Kidney
Çöp kebabı	Same as çöp şiş
Çöp şiş	Small lamb cubes grilled on a skewer; also called çöp kebabı
Döner kebap	Thin slices of lamb roasted on a vertical revolving spit
İçli köfte	Corn or bulgur balls stuffed with minced lamb (boiled or fried)
Iskender kebabı	Sliced döner kebabı served on pide, tomatoes, and yogurt, and covered with melted butter
Izgara köfte	Grilled meatballs
Kadın budu köfte	"Lady's thigh," meatballs of lamb and rice, deep-fried
Karışık izgara	Mixed grill
Kuzu budu rostosu	Roasted leg of lamb
Kuzu pirzolası	Grilled lamb chops
Şiş kebabı	Marinated lamb cubes grilled on a skewer

DESSERTS

Aşure	Thick sweet pudding of whole wheat, mixed fruits, and nuts
Baklava	Flaky pastries soaked in syrup or honey
Fırın sütlaç	Baked rice pudding
Hanım göbeği	Honey-soaked flour pastry
Helva	National favorite of semolina, sesame paste or flour, sugar, and nuts

Kaymaklı kayısı tatlısı	Poached apricots stuffed with cream
Künefe	Butter-soaked pastry filled with melted cheese, soaked in syrup
Muhallebi	Milk pudding
Revani	Honey-soaked semolina
Sütlaç	Rice pudding
Tatlılar	Sweets or desserts

Index